# Lecture Notes in Computer Science 4700

Commenced Publication in 1973
Founding and Former Series Editors:
Gerhard Goos, Juris Hartmanis, and Jan van L

Cliff B. Jones   Zhiming Liu
Jim Woodcock (Eds.)

# Formal Methods and Hybrid Real-Time Systems

Essays in Honour of Dines Bjørner and Zhou Chaochen
on the Occasion of Their 70th Birthdays

 Springer

Volume Editors

Cliff B. Jones
Newcastle University, School of Computing Science
Newcastle upon Tyne, NE1 7RU, UK
E-mail: cliff.jones@ncl.ac.uk

Zhiming Liu
United Nations University, International Institute for Software Technology
Macao, China
E-mail: z.liu@iist.unu.edu

Jim Woodcock
University of York, Department of Computer Science
Heslington, York YO10 5DD, UK
E-mail: jim@cs.york.ac.uk

The illustration appearing on the cover of this book is the work of Daniel Rozenberg (DADARA).

Library of Congress Control Number: 2007935177

CR Subject Classification (1998): D.2, D.3, C.3, F.3-4, C.2, H.4

LNCS Sublibrary: SL 1 – Theoretical Computer Science and General Issues

ISSN        0302-9743
ISBN-10     3-540-75220-X Springer Berlin Heidelberg New York
ISBN-13     978-3-540-75220-2 Springer Berlin Heidelberg New York

Springer is a part of Springer Science+Business Media

springer.com

© Springer-Verlag Berlin Heidelberg 2007
Printed in Germany

Typesetting: Camera-ready by author, data conversion by Scientific Publishing Services, Chennai, India
Printed on acid-free paper      SPIN: 12164615      06/3180      5 4 3 2 1 0

Dines Bjørner

Zhou Chaochen

# Foreword

Two outstanding computer scientists will soon reach their 70th birthdays: Dines Bjørner was born on October 4, 1937 in Denmark and Zhou Chaochen was born on November 1, in the same year in China. To celebrate their birthdays, we present three LNCS volumes in their honour.

- *Formal Methods and Hybrid Real-Time Systems. Essays in Honour of Dines Bjørner and Zhou Chaochen on the Occasion of Their 70th Birthdays.* Papers presented at a Symposium held in Macao, China, September 24–25, 2007. LNCS volume **4700**. Springer 2007.
- *Domain Modelling and the Duration Calculus.* International Training School, Shanghai, China, September 10–21, 2007. Advanced Lectures. LNCS volume 4710. Springer 2007.
- *Theoretical Aspects of Computing* - ICTAC 2007. 4th International Colloquium, Macao, China, September 26–28, 2007, Proceedings. LNCS volume 4711. Springer 2007.

DINES BJØRNER is known for his many contributions to the theory and practice of formal methods for software engineering. He is particularly associated with two formal methods, although his influence is far wider. He worked with Cliff Jones and others on the *Vienna Development Method (VDM)*, initially at IBM in Vienna. Later, he was involved in producing the *Rigorous Approach to Industrial Software Engineering (RAISE)* formal method with tool support. His three-volume *magnum opus* on software engineering covers *Abstraction and Modelling, Specification of Systems and Languages*, and *Domains, Requirements, and Software Design*. He was a professor at the Technical University of Denmark (DTU) in Lyngby, near Copenhagen. He was the founding director of the United Nations University International Institute for Software Technology (UNU-IIST) in Macao during the 1990s. He was a co-founder of VDM-Europe, which transformed to become Formal Methods Europe, an organisation that promotes the use of formal methods. Its 18 monthly symposia have become the leading academic events in formal methods. Dines Bjørner is a Knight of the Order of the Dannebrog and was awarded the John von Neumann Medal in Budapest in 1994. He received a Doctorate (*honoris causa*) from the Masaryk University in Brno in 2004. He is a Fellow of both the IEEE and the ACM.

ZHOU CHAOCHEN is known for his seminal contributions to the theory and practice of timed and hybrid systems. His distinguished academic career started as an undergraduate in mathematics and mechanics at Peking University (1954–58) and as a postgraduate at the Institute for Computing Technology in the Chinese Academy of Sciences (1963–67). He continued his career at Peking University and the Chinese Academy, until he made an extended visit to Oxford University

Computing Laboratory (1989–92) at the invitation of Sir Tony Hoare FRS. Here he was the prime instigator of *Duration Calculus*, an interval logic for real-time systems, developed as part of a European ESPRIT project on Provably Correct Systems. He made further extended visits during the periods 1990–92 and 1995–96, as a visiting professor at the Technical University of Denmark, Lyngby, at the invitation of Dines Bjørner. He was a Principal Research Fellow at UNU-IIST during the period 1992–97, before becoming its director, an appointment he held from 1997 to 2002. He is a member of the Chinese Academy of Sciences and the Third World Academy of Sciences.

We thank both Dines Bjørner and Zhou Chaochen for their years of generous, wise advice, to us and to their many other colleagues, students, and friends. They have both been unfailingly inspiring, enthusiastic, and encouraging.

July 2007                                                                    J.C.P.W.

# Tabula Gratulatoria

Nazareno Aguirre
Bogdan Aman
Damian Barsotti
Marc Bezem
Nikolaj Bjørner
Javier Blanco
Guillaume Bonfante
Pontus Boström
Aske Wiid Brekling
Jan Bretschneider
Alan Burns
Andrew Butterfield
Zining Cao
Pablo Castro
Haiyan Chen
Huowang Chen
Yinghua Chen
Zhenbang Chen
Gabriel Ciobanu
Robert Colvin
Pascal Coupey
Werner Damm
Dang Van Hung
Rafael del Vado Vírseda
Fredrik Degerlund
Catalin Dima
Wei Dong
Brijesh Dongol
Asger Eir
Estevez Elsa
Ignacio Fábregas
Dirk Fahland
John Fisher
John Fitzgerald
Christophe Fouqueré
Leo Freitas
David Frutos Escrig
Kokichi Futatsugi
Chris George
Michael Reichhardt Hansen

Anne Haxthausen
Ian Hayes
He Jifeng
Michael A. Jackson
Tomasz Janowski
Cliff Jones
Mathai Joseph
Takashi Kitamura
John Knudsen
Maciej Koutny
Padmanabhan Krishnan
Hans Langmaack
Ruggero Lanotte
Alessandro Lapadula
Peter Gorm Larsen
Martin Leucker
Jing Li
Li Xiaoshan
Huimin Lin
Xiang Ling
Daguang Liu
Wanwei Liu
Xinxin Liu
Zhiming Liu
Jean-Vincent Loddo
Niels Lohmann
Roussanka Loukanova
Jan Madsen
Tom Maibaum
Dino Mandrioli
Jean-Yves Marion
Peter Massuthe
Andrea Matta
Alfred Mikschl
Lionel Morel
Peter Mosses
Masaki Nakamura
Virginia Niculescu
Thomas Noll
Jens Oehlerking

Ernst-Rüdiger Olderog
Romain Péchoux
Miguel Palomino
Jun Pang
Jan Peleska
Martin Pěnička
André Platzer
Rosario Pugliese
Brian Randell
Silvio Ranise
Anders Ravn
Wolfgang Reisig
Stefan Rieger
Matteo Rossi
Cesar Sanchez
J.W. Sanders
Christelle Scharff
Marc Segelken
Quirico Semeraro
Kaisa Sere
Arne Skou
Paola Spoletini
Christian Stahl
Volker Stolz
K. Subramani
Francesco Tiezzi
Tullio Tolio
Marina Waldén
Ji Wang
Boris Wirtz
Jim Woodcock
Peng Wu
Zhilin Wu
Bican Xia
Lu Yang
Lu Yang
Naijun Zhan
Huibiao Zhu

# Preface

This volume contains the papers presented at the *Festschrift Symposium* held September 24–25, 2007 in Macao on the occasion of the 70th birthdays of Dines Bjørner and Zhou Chaochen. It consists of 25 papers written by 59 authors. Online conference management was provided by EASYCHAIR.

It is now difficult to remember exactly when it came to us that we should organise a celebration for the 70th birthdays of Dines Bjørner and Zhou Chaochen, which happily coincide this year. But I do know that the idea was a popular one. Zhiming Liu suggested that we should organise the symposium as part of the International Colloquium on Theoretical Aspects of Computing, which seemed perfect given that this series was founded by UNU/IIST. The event quickly took shape as He Jifeng offered to host a Training School in Shanghai with the assistance of Chris George, Geguang Pu, and Yong Zhou, and Cliff Jones agreed to help with the academic organisation of the symposium and the colloquium. Everything then just fell into place, thanks to the excellent help provided by the local organisers in Macao and Shanghai.

The subjects for the lectures for the school were obvious to us all: two topics pioneered by Dines Bjørner and Zhou Chaochen, both currently very active research areas. For the *Festschrift Symposium*, authors were invited to write on an original topic of their choosing. And for the colloquium, a general call-for-papers resulted in a satisfying collection of rigorously reviewed papers in theoretical computer science, including automata theory, case studies, concurrency, real-time systems, semantics and logics, and specification and verification.

So we have ended up with three volumes, one each for the school, symposium, and colloquium, which collectively amount to some 1,300 pages. And still there was not enough room for the many additional distinguished names we would have liked to invite.

To Dines and Chaochen from all of us:

We hope that you enjoy reading these books.

*Happy birthday to both of you!*

June 2007                                                                                   J.C.P.W.

# Organization

## Programme Chairs

Cliff Jones
Zhiming Liu
Jim Woodcock

## Local Organization

Kitty Chan                    Chris George
Wendy Hoi                     Violet Pun

# Table of Contents

Models and Software Model Checking of a Distributed File Replication System . . . . . . . . . . . . . . . . . . . . . . . . . . . . . . . . . . . . . . . . . . . . . . . . . . 1
   *Nikolaj Bjørner*

From "Formal Methods" to System Modeling . . . . . . . . . . . . . . . . . . . . . . . 24
   *Manfred Broy*

A Denotational Semantics for Handel-C . . . . . . . . . . . . . . . . . . . . . . . . . . . . 45
   *Andrew Butterfield*

Generating Polynomial Invariants with DISCOVERER and QEPCAD . . . . . . . . . . . . . . . . . . . . . . . . . . . . . . . . . . . . . . . . . . . . . . . . . . . 67
   *Yinghua Chen, Bican Xia, Lu Yang, and Naijun Zhan*

Harnessing rCOS for Tool Support—The CoCoME Experience . . . . . . . . . 83
   *Zhenbang Chen, Xiaoshan Li, Zhiming Liu, Volker Stolz, and Lu Yang*

Automating Verification of Cooperation, Control, and Design in Traffic Applications . . . . . . . . . . . . . . . . . . . . . . . . . . . . . . . . . . . . . . . . . . . . . . . . . . 115
   *Werner Damm, Alfred Mikschl, Jens Oehlerking,*
   *Ernst-Rüdiger Olderog, Jun Pang, André Platzer,*
   *Marc Segelken, and Boris Wirtz*

Specifying Various Time Models with Temporal Propositional Variables in Duration Calculus . . . . . . . . . . . . . . . . . . . . . . . . . . . . . . . . . . . . . . . . . . . 170
   *Dang Van Hung*

Relating Domain Concepts Intensionally by Ordering Connections . . . . . . 188
   *Asger Eir*

Programmable Messaging for Electronic Government - Building a Foundation . . . . . . . . . . . . . . . . . . . . . . . . . . . . . . . . . . . . . . . . . . . . . . . . . . . . 217
   *Elsa Estevez and Tomasz Janowski*

Balancing Insight and Effort: The Industrial Uptake of Formal Methods . . . . . . . . . . . . . . . . . . . . . . . . . . . . . . . . . . . . . . . . . . . . . . . . . . . . . 237
   *John Fitzgerald and Peter Gorm Larsen*

Proving Theorems About JML Classes . . . . . . . . . . . . . . . . . . . . . . . . . . . . . 255
   *Leo Freitas and Jim Woodcock*

Specification for Testing . . . . . . . . . . . . . . . . . . . . . . . . . . . . . . . . . . . . . . . . . 280
   *Chris George, Padmanabhan Krishnan, P.A.P. Salas, and J.W. Sanders*

Semantics and Verification of a Language for Modelling Hardware
Architectures . . . . . . . . . . . . . . . . . . . . . . . . . . . . . . . . . . . . . . . . . . . . . . . . . . . . .    300
      Michael R. Hansen, Jan Madsen, and Aske Wiid Brekling

A Domain-Oriented, Model-Based Approach for Construction and
Verification of Railway Control Systems . . . . . . . . . . . . . . . . . . . . . . . . . . . . .    320
      Anne E. Haxthausen and Jan Peleska

Compensable Programs . . . . . . . . . . . . . . . . . . . . . . . . . . . . . . . . . . . . . . . . . . . .    349
      He Jifeng

Deriving Specifications for Systems That Are Connected to the Physical
World . . . . . . . . . . . . . . . . . . . . . . . . . . . . . . . . . . . . . . . . . . . . . . . . . . . . . . . . . . . .    364
      Cliff B. Jones, Ian J. Hayes, and Michael A. Jackson

Engineering the Development of Embedded Systems . . . . . . . . . . . . . . . . . .    391
      Mathai Joseph

Design Verification Patterns . . . . . . . . . . . . . . . . . . . . . . . . . . . . . . . . . . . . . . .    399
      John Knudsen, Anders P. Ravn, and Arne Skou

On Revival of Algol-Concepts in Modern Programming and
Specification Languages . . . . . . . . . . . . . . . . . . . . . . . . . . . . . . . . . . . . . . . . . . .    414
      Hans Langmaack

Design in CommUnity with Extension Morphisms . . . . . . . . . . . . . . . . . . . .    435
      Xiang Ling, Tom Maibaum, and Nazareno Aguirre

Symbolic Test Generation Using a Temporal Logic with Constrained
Events . . . . . . . . . . . . . . . . . . . . . . . . . . . . . . . . . . . . . . . . . . . . . . . . . . . . . . . . . . .    467
      Daguang Liu, Peng Wu, and Huimin Lin

Expansive-Bisimulation for Context-Free Processes . . . . . . . . . . . . . . . . . .    472
      Xinxin Liu

VDM Semantics of Programming Languages: Combinators and
Monads . . . . . . . . . . . . . . . . . . . . . . . . . . . . . . . . . . . . . . . . . . . . . . . . . . . . . . . . . .    483
      Peter D. Mosses

Formal Approach to Railway Applications . . . . . . . . . . . . . . . . . . . . . . . . . . .    504
      Martin Pěnička

Services as a Paradigm of Computation . . . . . . . . . . . . . . . . . . . . . . . . . . . . .    521
      Wolfgang Reisig, Jan Bretschneider, Dirk Fahland, Niels Lohmann,
      Peter Massuthe, and Christian Stahl

Author Index . . . . . . . . . . . . . . . . . . . . . . . . . . . . . . . . . . . . . . . . . . . . . . . . . . . . .    539

# Models and Software Model Checking of a Distributed File Replication System

Nikolaj Bjørner

Microsoft Research, One Microsoft Way, Redmond, WA, 98074, USA
nbjorner@microsoft.com

**Abstract.** With the Distributed File System Replication component, DFS-R, as the central theme, we present selected protocol problems and validation methods encountered during design and development. DFS-R is currently deployed in various contexts; in Windows Server 2003-R2, Windows Live Messenger (Sharing Folders), and Windows Vista (Meeting spaces). The journey from an initial design sketch to a shipped product required mainly the dedicated effort of several testers, developers, program managers, and several others; but in some places cute problems related to distributed consensus and software model-checking emerged. This paper presents a few of these, including a distributed garbage collection problem, distributed consensus problems for reconciling tree-like data structures, using model-based test case generation, and the use of software model checking in design and development process.

## 1 Introduction

Designing and building distributed systems is challenging, especially if they need to scale, perform, satisfy customer functionality requirements, and, oh well, work. An example of a particularly challenging distributed system is multi-master, optimistic, file replication. One of the distinguished factors making distributed file replication hard is that file replication comes with a very substantial data component: the protocols need to be sufficiently aware of file system semantics, such as detecting and resolving name conflicting file creates and concurrent updates. Such races are just the tip of the iceberg. In comparison, cache coherence protocols that are known to be challenging to design, have a trivial data component, but to be fair have stronger consistency requirements.

Subtle protocol bugs can go (and have indeed gone) undetected for years due to the large number of interactions that are possible. With a sufficient number of deployments they *will* be encountered in the field, have costly consequences, and be extremely challenging to analyze. Our experience in developing DFS-R from the bottom up, is used to demonstrate several complementary uses of model-based techniques for system design and exploration. This paper provides an experience report on these selected methods. Note that the material presented here reflect only a very partial view of the design and test of DFS-R.

DFS-R was developed to address correctness, scale, and management challenges encountered with a predecessor file replication product. Thus, the original

C.B. Jones, Z. Liu, J. Woodcock (Eds.): Bjørner/Zhou Festschrift, LNCS 4700, pp. 1–23, 2007.

impression was that we had the luxury of tackling a relatively well defined problem; to build a replication system specifically handling features of the file system NTFS, for replicating files between globally dispersed branch offices of corporations. Later on, it would turn out that DFS-R could be embedded within other scenarios, such as, in an instant messenger product. However, we consciously avoided over-loading with features from the onset. It means that DFS-R, for instance does not replicate files synchronously, only asynchronously (as it is meant for wide area networks); does not replicate general directed acyclic graphs, only tree-like structure; and does not maintain fine-grained tracking of operations, only state. While several such problems are interesting in other contexts, they did not fall into the scope of our original goals.

The organization of this paper follows the top-down design flow of DFS-R. The DFS-R system was originally conceived as a strictly state-based file replication protocol. Section 2 elaborates on the differences between state-based and operations-based replication systems. We developed a high-level state machine specification of DFS-R by using a transition system presented as a collection of guarded commands. The guarded commands were subsequently implemented as an applicative program in OCaml. This paved the way for performing efficient state space exploration on top of the design. Section 3 elaborates on the protocol, and Section 4 summarizes prototyping experiences. As the development took place, several assumptions made in the abstract design turned out to be unrealistic, and we redid the high-level design using the AsmL tools that were built at Microsoft for software modeling and test case generation. Section 5 elaborates on the experiences from using AsmL. A number of well-separated distributed protocol problems emerged during the development. Section 6 describes the distributed tree reconciliation problem, and how we used a model checker, Zing, to expose bugs in both protocol proposals and legacy implementations. Section 7 describes the distributed tombstone garbage collection problem and a solution to it. While one cannot expect to get anywhere without a high-level understanding of the protocols involved in DFS-R, it is equally unrealistic to expect developing a production quality system without addressing systems problems. We were thus faced with a potentially large gap between simplified protocol substrates and the production code. Encouraged by the ability of the model-based state space exploration to expose subtle interaction bugs we repeated the state space exploration experiment on top of the production core. The resulting backtracking search tool may best be characterized as a hybrid software model checking, run-time verification tool. It operates directly at the source code level. It uses techniques, such as partial order reduction to prune search and custom allocation routines to enable backtracking search. Section 8 describes the infrastructure we developed and the experiments covering $\frac{1}{2}$ trillion scenarios.

## 2    File Replication

The style of replication systems under which DFS-R falls into is surveyed extensively in [1]. We here summarize a few of the main concepts relevant for

DFS-R. The problem that DFS-R solves is to maintain mirror copies of selected directories across large networks of servers. The directories that are selected for replication are called *replicated folders*. Files and directories within these directories may be created, modified, deleted, moved, or renamed at any of the mirror sites. It is the job of DFS-R to distribute changes, detect and reconcile conflicts automatically when they arise. Distributed replication systems can be categorized according to what problems they solve and how they solve them. Figure 1 summarizes some of the main design choices one has when designing a replication system.

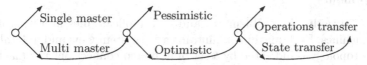

**Fig. 1.** Replication system ontologies

**Multi Master Replication.** DFS-R is a multi-master replication system. Any machine may participate in changing resources, and their updates will have to be reconciled with updates from any other machine. A (selective) single-master system only replicates changes from a set of selected machines. All other machines are expected to maintain a mirror copy of the masters. This would mean that file system changes on non-masters would have to be reverted. If there is a designated master, one can even choose to maintain truth centrally. The challenge there is managing fail-over and network disconnects.

**Optimistic Replication.** To support wide area networks (spanning the globe) DFS-R supports optimistic updates to files. This means that any machine may submit updates to resources without checking first whether the update is in conflict with other updates. Pessimistic replication schemes avoid concurrent update conflicts by serializing read and write operations using locking schemes.

**State and Operation Transfer.** A file system state is the result of the file operations (create, update, delete, move) that are performed on it. This suggests two approaches to realize file replication: intercept and replay the file operations, called operation transfer, or capture the file system state and replicate it as it is, called state transfer. DFS-R implements a state transfer protocol. There are several hard challenges with operations-transfer based systems. One is merging operations into a consistent serialization. Another, is space, as operations are not necessarily amenable to garbage collection.

**Perspective.** There is no single choice of design parameters that handles all customer scenarios. In some configurations, corporations wish to designate machines as read-only, and can manage the additional constraints this leaves on network topologies. In other configurations there are reliable, but slow, wide-area networks and there is a need for file locking. With state transfer only, it is not possible to undo operations with arbitrary fine-grained control.

# 3    A State-Based File Replication System

In this Section we will outline the essence of a file replication system. While highly simplified, it reflects some of the early protocol design maneuvers.

## 3.1    Components

**Network.** Abstractly, the problem at hand is to replicate files in a network of connected machines. Each machine maintains a file system view and a database. The network topology is indicated by a set of in-bound connections per machine. We assume a well-formed network, comprising of a digraph without self-loops, where each node is labeled by a unique machine identifier. A connected network is furthermore desirable for convergence.

$$
\begin{array}{llll}
nw & \in & Network & = MachineId \xmapsto{m} Machine \\
mch & \in & Machine & = FileSystem \times DataBase \times inbound \\
m & \in & MachineId & = \text{Globally unique identifier for a machine} \\
in & \in & inbound & = MachineId\text{-}\mathbf{set}
\end{array}
$$

**File System.** For our purposes, a file system is a collection of files each uniquely identified by an identifier, which is unique per file system. In NTFS, such identifiers are 64 bit numbers, called *file reference numbers*, on Unix-like file systems, these are called *inodes*. Each file has a file name, a parent directory and file data. One would typically expect a file system to be dictated as a tree-like structure comprising of files identified by file paths as strings, but this view turns out to be unsuitable for several reasons. For example, such a view is open to situations where files are moved around, such that the same path gets identified with completely different files. Identifying a file with an identifier makes it easier to support efficient replication of renaming directories with a large number of children, but makes it very hard to support merging contents from different directories. A file system is well-formed when the ancestral relations form a uniquely rooted connected tree (only the root has itself as a parent).

$$
\begin{array}{lll}
fs & \in FileSystem & = FileId \xmapsto{m} FileRecord \\
file & \in FileRecord & = \{name : \mathsf{Name},\ parent : FileId, data : \mathsf{Data}\} \\
fid & \in FileId & = \mathsf{Numeral}
\end{array}
$$

**Database.** The file system only maintains information that is local to the machine where the files reside. In order to realize a file replication system, one needs to maintain information reflecting the shared state between machines. In DFS-R, this state is a database consisting of version vector and a set of records, one per replicated file.

$$(vv, rs) \in DataBase = VersionVector \times (UID \overset{m}{\mapsto} IdRecord)$$
$$vv \in VersionVector = MachineId \overset{m}{\mapsto} \text{Numeral-set}$$
$$r \in IdRecord = \{fid : FileId, gvsn : GVSN, parent : UID,$$
$$clock : \text{Numeral}, name : \text{Name}, live : \text{bool}\}$$
$$gvsn \in GVSN = MachineId \times \text{Numeral Global version sequence number}$$
$$uid \in UID = \text{Globally unique identifier}$$

**Version Vectors.** File replication systems typically use global version sequence numbers, which are pairs (Unique Machine Identifier, Version Sequence Number), to identify a resource and its version globally. The version sequence number is a local time-stamp, which can be assumed monotonically increasing with changes. A version vector is a map from machine identifiers to version sequence numbers. They typically map a machine identifier to a single number, but in the case of DFS-R we found that allowing the vectors to map to a set of numbers (represented compactly as intervals of numerals) allowed handling, for instance, synchronization disruptions. Version vectors are also known as vector clocks. Version vectors are used to record a state of *knowledge*, as the vector indicates a water-mark of versions that have been received from other machines.

We may think of a version vector as a set of $GVSN$ pairs obtained by taking $\{(m, v) \mid [m \mapsto vs] \in vv \land v \in vs\}$. Similarly, one can form a version vector from a set of $GVSN$ pairs. In the future we will switch between the set and map view of version vectors depending on the context. Thus, $vv[m]$ is defined for each $m$. It is the empty set if $m \notin \text{Dom}(vv)$ as a map.

**Database Records.** A file (we will use file to also refer to a directory) is identified globally through a unique identifier $uid$, while the per file system file identifier is the $fid$. The set of database records may be indexed by a $uid$ and a $fid$. Each record stores a global version sequence number $gvsn$ that tracks the version of the file, a file name $name$, a reference to a parent directory $parent$, and an indication whether the resource represents an existing file on the file system. If $live$ is false, we call the resulting record a *tombstone*. The $clock$ field is a Lamport clock [6], it gets incremented with every file update. Lamport clocks are used to enforce causal ordering per record by assuming a total lexicographic ordering on $GVSN$ and define:

$$r < r' \text{ iff } r.clock < r'.clock \lor (r.clock = r'.clock \land r.gvsn < r'.gvsn) \quad (1)$$

We will later establish that property (5), which only uses version vectors, suffices for detecting conflicts (absence of causality) among *all* replicated files. Nevertheless, this property is significant, as the number of replicated files in the context of DFS-R is much larger than the number of replicating machines.

The records in DFS-R contain a number of additional fields, such as file hashes, file creation time and file attributes.

**Local and Global Consistency.** We are now in a position where we can state the main soundness properties that DFS-R aims to achieve:

- Global consistency: Databases of machines connected in a network are equal except for the contents of the *fid* fields.
- Local consistency: On each machine, the database records the content on the file system.

A very substantial part of DFS-R consists in maintaining local consistency. DFS-R uses the NTFS change journal, which for every file operation produces a record, accessible from a special file. The change journal presents an incremental way to obtain file changes. Since DFS-R only tracks files that are replicated, it furthermore needs to scan directories that are moved in and out of the replicated folders. Also, the local consistency algorithms need to take into account that change journals *wrap*, that is, not all consecutive changes are available for DFS-R, and that change journals are deleted, resized and/or re-created by administrators. We will here concentrate only on global consistency as it illustrates the distributed protocol problems later in this paper.

So for the rest of the discussion, we will use simplified definitions of machines and database records. While this approach makes things look much simpler than reality, it allows us to concentrate on the specific topics in this paper.

$$m \quad \in \; Machine \quad = \; VersionVector \times (\, UID \overset{m}{\mapsto} IdRecord) \times inbound$$
$$r \quad \in \; IdRecord \quad = \; \{gvsn : GVSN, parent : UID, clock : \mathsf{Numeral},$$
$$name : \mathsf{Name}, live : \mathsf{bool}\}$$

## 3.2   Operations

The main operations relevant to file replication consist of local file system activity and synchronization.

The file system operations called Create, Update, Rename and file Delete in Fig. 2. cause the local version vector to be updated with a fresh version for the machine that performs the change. The database records are also updated to reflect the new file system state.

We assume an initial state consisting of an arbitrary network of machines all sharing a single replicated root folder and no other files. We use tuples with mutable fields in the guarded commands, and we omit checks for whether elements are in the domain of a map prior to accesses.

A direct way to synchronize two data-bases is by merging version vectors and traversing all records on a sending machine $m_2$; those records whose keys do not exist on the receiving machine $m_1$ are inserted. Records, that dominate existing records on $m_1$ are also inserted. Fig. 3. illustrates the proposed scheme. The scheme implements a *last-writer wins* strategy, as later updates prevail over earlier updates. We will later realize that the check $v \notin vv_1[m]$ is in fact redundant. Another property of this scheme is that each update is processed independently. Notice that this is an implementation choice, which comes with limitations. Conflict resolution that can only perform decisions based on a single record cannot detect that a machine swapped the names of two files. Namely, suppose machine $m_1$ and $m_2$ share two files named $a$ and $b$. Then $m_2$ renames $a$

$$
\begin{array}{l}
\textsf{Create}(nw, m, uid, parent, name) : \\
\quad \textbf{let } (vv, rs, in) = nw[m], \ v = 1 + \max(vv[m]) \\
\quad \textbf{assume } \forall[\_ \mapsto (\_, rs', \_)] \in nw \ . \ uid \notin rs' \ (uid \text{ is fresh in } nw) \\
\qquad rs[parent].live \ \wedge \quad name \text{ is fresh under } parent \\
\quad vv[m] := vv[m] \cup \{v\} \\
\quad rs[uid] := \{gvsn = (m, v), parent, name, clock = v, live = \textbf{true}\}
\end{array}
$$

$$
\begin{array}{l}
\textsf{Update}(nw, m, uid) : \\
\quad \textbf{let } (vv, rs, in) = nw[m], \ v = 1 + \max(vv[m]), \ clock = \max(v, rs[uid].clock + 1) \\
\quad \textbf{assume } rs[uid].live \\
\quad vv[m] := vv[m] \cup \{v\} \\
\quad rs[uid] := rs[uid] \ \textbf{with} \ \{clock, gvsn = (m, v)\}
\end{array}
$$

$$
\begin{array}{l}
\textsf{Rename}(nw, m, uid, parent', name') : \\
\quad \textbf{let } (vv, rs, in) = nw[m], \ v = 1 + \max(vv[m]), \ clock = \max(v, rs[uid].clock + 1) \\
\quad \textbf{assume } rs[uid].live \wedge \ rs[parent'].live \wedge \ name' \text{ is fresh under } parent' \\
\qquad \textbf{Rename} \text{ maintains tree-shape of directory hierarchy} \\
\quad vv[m] := vv[m] \cup \{v\} \\
\quad rs[uid] := rs[uid] \ \textbf{with} \ \{gvsn = (m, v), parent = parent', clock, name = name'\}
\end{array}
$$

$$
\begin{array}{l}
\textsf{Delete}(nw, m, uid) : \\
\quad \textbf{let } (vv, rs, in) = nw[m], \ v = 1 + \max(vv[m]), \ clock = \max(v, rs[uid].clock + 1) \\
\quad \textbf{assume } rs[uid].live \ \wedge \ (\forall uid' \in rs \ . \ rs[uid'].parent \neq uid \ \vee \ \neg rs[uid'].live) \\
\quad vv[m] := vv[m] \cup \{v\} \\
\quad rs[uid] := rs[uid] \ \textbf{with} \ \{gvsn = (m, v), clock, live = \textbf{false}\}
\end{array}
$$

**Fig. 2.** Basic file system operations

to $c$, $b$ to $a$, then $c$ to $b$. The names of the two files are swapped, but each record is name conflicting with the configuration on $m_1$. So when $m_1$ synchronizes with $m_2$, it will be resolving two name conflicts instead of performing the swap.

Our first observation is that the resulting system maintains a basic invariant: the versions of all records are tracked in the version vectors.

$$
\forall[\_ \mapsto (vv, rs, \_)] \in nw, \ [\_ \mapsto \{gvsn = (m, v)\}] \in rs \ . \ v \in vv[m] \tag{2}
$$

Thus, a more network efficient version of BasicSyncJoin proceeds by

1. The receiving machine $m_1$ gets version vector $vv_2$ from the sender $m_2$.
2. It then subtracts $vv_1$ from $vv_2$, forming $vv_\Delta := vv_2 \setminus vv_1$.
3. The sending machine is asked for records whose versions are in $vv_\Delta$.
4. The database of $m_1$ is updated as in BasicSyncJoin.

The more refined version of global consistency we seek can also be formulated in terms of version vectors, namely, that databases coincide on all shared versions:

$$
r_1.gvsn \notin vv_2 \ \vee \ rs_2[u] = r_1 \ \vee \ rs_2[u].gvsn \notin vv_1, \tag{3}
$$

for every $m_1, m_2$, such that $(vv_1, rs_1, \_) = nw[m_1]$, $(vv_2, rs_2, \_) = nw[m_2]$ and $[u \mapsto r_1] \in rs_1$.

```
BasicSyncJoin(nw, m₁, m₂)
    let (vv₁, rs₁, in₁) = nw[m₁]
    let (vv₂, rs₂, in₂) = nw[m₂]
    assume m₂ ∈ in₁
    for each [uid ↦ r] ∈ rs₂:
        let (m, v) = r.gvsn
        if v ∉ vv₁[m] ∧ (uid ∉ rs₁ ∨ rs₁[uid] < r) then
            rs₁[uid] := r
    vv₁ := vv₁ ∪ vv₂
```

**Fig. 3.** Simplified synchronization

So far our transitions ensure that all versions in the version vectors are consecutive,

$$\forall [m \mapsto vs] \in vv \ .vs = \{1, \ldots, \max(vs)\}. \tag{4}$$

The second observation is a basic property of the system: concurrent updates to the same resource may be detected by at least one machine during BasicSyncJoin. Suppose that $m_1$ and $m_2$, and $uid$ are such that $(vv_1, rs_1, \_) = nw[m_1]$, $(vv_2, rs_2, \_) = nw[m_2]$, and $[uid \mapsto r_1] \in rs_1$, $[uid \mapsto r_2] \in rs_2$. When $m_1$ installs $r_2$ we would like to know whether $r_2$ was derived from $r_1$, or if $r_2$ was obtained concurrently with $r_1$. The answer to whether $r_2$ is concurrent with $r_1$ turns out to be simple; $r_2$ is concurrent with $r_1$ iff the version of $r_1$ is not known to $m_2$:

$$r_1.gvsn \notin vv_2 \tag{5}$$

To prove this property, we can add a history variable $rs_{all}$ to each machine. The history variable $rs_{all}$ is a set of all records ever maintained by the machine. If one prefers, one may view this as specifying the cone of causality. Every update to the main set of records $rs$ gets reflected by adding the updated record to $rs_{all}$. In the operation BasicSyncJoin, take the union of $rs^1_{all}$ and $rs^2_{all}$. Now observe that invariant (2) also holds for $rs_{all}$.

Detection of concurrent update conflicts is useful when one wants to perform conflict detection and resolution, either manually or automatically. DFS-R performs the conflict resolution automatically, as replication is a continuous service, but stores conflicting files in a designated folder. Conflict resolution is performed on version vectors, so once a machine has performed conflict resolution and merged version vectors, the conflict is no longer visible to other machines. A different scheme that works for detecting conflicts is by associating a hash-tree [7,8] comprising of hashes of all the previous versions of a file. The size of the unrolled hash-tree is then proportional to the number of changes to the file, while version vectors grow proportionally to the number of machines. If machines are reasonably well synchronized, they do not need to unroll large hash trees from remote peers.

## 3.3   The Real Deal with Join

The use of BasicSyncJoin is insufficient for file replication. There are two fundamental flaws and limitations: First, it allows installing updates that conflict with
file system semantics: it may introduce orphaned files without parent directories,
mark non-empty directories as tombstones, create multiple files in the same directory with the same name, and introduce cyclic directory structures. Second,
BasicSyncJoin processes all updates in one atomic step. This is unrealistic in the
presence of network outages and continuous file system activity. DFS-R realizes
non-atomic joins by committing only versions from the processed records on
disconnects (instead of all of $vv_2$). It also pipe-lines multiple joins should the
sending machine create new updates while (large) files from previous updates
are still being downloaded. A consequence of this relaxation is that condition
(5) is only a necessary, but not sufficient condition for conflict detection. Invariant (4) does not hold either, but this is insignificant, as we introduced sets in
the range of version vectors to deal with partial synchronization. Fig.4. illustrates the additional refinements one needs to add to BasicSyncJoin in order to
address file system semantics. We have limited the iteration of database records
to $vv_2 \setminus vv_1$ to reflect invariant (2), which still holds. We abstain from illustrating
the non-atomic, pipe-lined version.

The refined SyncJoin mentions auxiliary functions *conflict-winner*, *purge-losers*,
and *revert-update*. The definition and analysis of these is the subject of Section 5,
but here, we will summarize some of their requirements.

---

SyncJoin$(nw, m_1, m_2)$
    **let** $(vv_1, rs_1, in_1) = nw[m_1]$
    **let** $(vv_2, rs_2, in_2) = nw[m_2]$
    **assume** $m_2 \in in_1$
    **for each** $[uid \mapsto r] \in rs_2$ **where** $r.gvsn \in vv_2 \setminus vv_1$:
        **if** $uid \notin rs_1 \ \lor \ rs_1[uid] < r$ **then**
            **if** *conflict-winner*$(m_1, r)$ **then**
                *purge-losers*$(m_1, r)$
                $rs_1[uid] := r$
            **else** *revert-update*$(m_1, r)$
      $vv_1 := vv_1 \cup vv_2$

**Fig. 4.** Synchronized join

---

**Non-interference.** It is trivial to realize a convergent, consistent file replication
system that just deletes all files. So, obviously, we would like to ensure that
DFS-R does not touch the file system on its own. Requiring that DFS-R not
delete or move around any files is too restrictive, because a system that must
automatically resolve conflicts will have to handle creation of name conflicting
files and directories.

**Re-animation.** A basic (user) requirement for DFS-R was that directories cannot be deleted if they contain files that have not been processed by the deleting party. Thus, re-animation requires that files and even directories in a transitive way get re-created. They are re-created to preserve content that was created or modified independently of the (remote) deletion.

**Convergence.** A key property of replication is obviously that all replica members should converge to the same mirror image when there are no independent updates to the replica sets. In general one cannot check convergence as an invariant. However, as our experience with Zing (Section 6) illustrates, it is possible to find divergence bugs by checking invariants that imply convergence.

**Feature Interaction.** One of the hard problems with designing a distributed application, like DFS-R, is taking feature interaction into account. Features that are not directly related may interact in unpleasant ways when composed. An illustrative example of two features that interact comprises of re-animation and name-conflict resolution. Name conflict resolution has in DFS-R the side effect of soft deletion. The name conflict loser gets moved to a conflict area, but from the point of view of replication it is deleted. These two features do not compose: a directory may lose a name conflict and be deleted, but a modification to a child file may require the name conflicting directory to be re-animated. Consequently, DFS-R has to take such conflicts into account.

## 4    Prototyping DFS-R with OCaml

Section 3 illustrated a simple file system model and replication protocol. As features and requirements were added, the complexity of the problem rose, and we could see that invariants were easily broken. We therefore found that an informal design would be insufficient in convincing us and our peers to the soundness of any protocol proposal, so we developed a prototype system in OCaml.

Of particular interest was that the OCaml prototype supported both a *simulation* and a *realistic* mode. In simulation mode, the replication system would manipulate in-memory data structures for file systems, and data-bases. In realistic mode, the prototype accessed files on NTFS and updated a persistent store. Neither mode was using a network, so all remote procedure calls would be performed by local procedure calls, and multiple copies of DFS-R ran in the same process. The simulation mode was furthermore applicative in all essential operations. This made implementing a backtracking search over the actions trivial. Operations in simulation mode were several orders of magnitude faster. We also added ad-hoc partial order reduction techniques, and performed massive simulations on top of the synchronization core. Prior to starting the implementation of DFS-R we thus covered some 120 billion scenarios each comprising of 16 file and synchronization actions. Section 8 elaborates on similar methods used for the production core.

# 5    Modeling DFS-R with AsmL

The OCaml prototype soon diverged from the implementation, as constraints, such as database layout changed. It was also inadequate for documenting the protocol at an abstract, yet sufficiently faithful level. We therefore turned to AsmL [9], developed at MSR, for describing the DFS-R protocol. The very readable format of AsmL and the integration with Microsoft Word was particularly useful in our context, as we aimed at a specification which could be read by newcomers to the DFS-R project. Today the AsmL specification serves as the main high-level, executable, overview of DFS-R. We will not repeat the detailed AsmL specification here, as it takes around 100 pages. To give the flavor, Fig.5. summarizes the data types available per replicating machine.

The AsmL description follows the componentization and protocol design in a top-down fashion. At the top-level, the design describes the main modules that comprise synchronizing machines. For the case of DFS-R, this is encapsulated by a Machine class, which contains the main components.

```
class Machine
    machineId as MachineId // Unique identifier to distinguish machine
    var fs as FileSystem      // File system interface
    var db as Database        // Persistent database that DFS-R maintains
    var uc as UsnConsumer // Consuming USN records from the NTFS journal
    var dw as DirWalker     // Walking directories to update the database
    var inbound as Map of MachineId to InConnection
    var outbound as Map of MachineId to OutConnection

class InConnection        // State relevant for an incoming connection
class OutConnection       // State relevant for an outgoing connection
```

Fig. 5. Replicating machine in AsmL

## 5.1    Protocol Description

The AsmL specification elaborates further on fleshing out the contents of the machine components. The main reactive components that are modeled in detail are the (1) consumption of file system events and their effect on the local database, and (2) the main synchronization handshakes.

## 5.2    Test Case Generation

The resulting model is sufficiently detailed to describe the behavior of DFS-R based on local file system events as well as distributed synchronization events. This allows defining virtual networks of machines that can be composed and simulated within AsmL. In particular, we hooked up the FSM generation tool of

AsmL and generated test sequences. Lacking tight .NET integration with DFS-R, we resorted to using the FSM generation tool generate test cases in an XML file and implement a reader that interprets the traces within DFS-R.

# 6  Reconciling Trees

In this Section we illustrate the use of a model-checker Zing [10] for checking conflict resolution strategies for concurrent moves. Recall that one of the requirements for DFS-R was that it replicate and maintain directory hierarchies as tree-like structures. When machines are allowed to move files around on a network, it may however be possible arriving at configurations that cannot be reconciled into a directory tree. Fig.6. illustrates an instance of this problem: two machines share directories $a$, $b$, and $c$. One machine creates the tree $a \to b \to c$, the other $c \to b \to a$. What should $b$'s parent be?

We used Zing to check for convergence of a proposed resolution method for concurrent

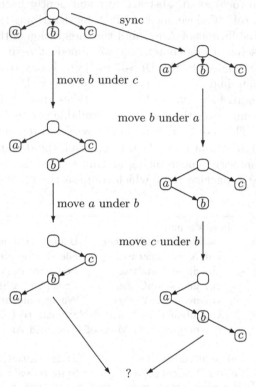

**Fig. 6.** Concurrent conflicting moves

moves. Zing demonstrated that the proposal was open to divergence by producing a counter-example along the lines of Fig.6. The counter-example found by Zing, was subsequently tested against another shipped replication product which failed to converge. This bug had gone undetected for several years.

## 6.1  Zing

Zing is a model checker for multi-process programs. Zing's input language is perhaps easiest compared with Promela [11]. The notion of process and atomic statements are similar, while Zing appeals to an object oriented programming style.

## 6.2  A Zing Encoding

Our Zing encoding of the tree reconciliation problem uses the absolute minimal features necessary to emulate conflict resolution of concurrent moves. Thus, each machine maintains $n(= 3)$ resources, each resource is identified by a number $0, \ldots, n - 1$, and a designated root folder is identified by the number $-1$. A resource has a *parent*, which is a number $-1, 0, \ldots, n - 1$, and a *clock* used to impose a total ordering on resources. Resources can be updated by changing the *parent* and *clock*, but only if the update does not introduce a self-loop. Fig.7. contains the minimal amount of Zing declarations to define two machines each with three resources all residing under a common root.

A model checker is well suited at specifying a set of possible configurations implicitly by using non-deterministic choices. Thus, we arrive at a non-flat configuration by first moving files around randomly on each machine, with each move incrementing globalClock and using its value as the clock on the moved resources.

```
class Node {
    int parent;
    int clock;
};
array Tree[3] Node;

class Machine {
    Tree tree = new Tree{{-1,0},{-1,0},{-1,0}};

    atomic bool cycle(int node, int parent) {
        return (parent != -1) &&
            (parent == node || cycle(node, tree[parent].parent));
    }

    atomic void move(int node, int parent, int clock) {
        assume(!cycle(node, parent));
        tree[node].parent = parent;
        tree[node].clock = clock;
    }
};
array Machines[2] Machine;
static Machines machines;
static int globalClock = 0;
```

**Fig. 7.** Replicating machine in Zing

It remains to define synchronization in Zing. Our model for synchronization is that machines send the state of a random node to a random machine. It requires the recipient to determine the outcome based on the state of a single node. Thus, traces can be identified as sequences of triples

$$\langle node_1, src_1, dst_1 \rangle, \langle node_2, src_2, dst_2 \rangle, \ldots,$$

where node is the index of a node, the content of the node on the source machine is given by src, and dst is a machine that should reconcile the node. The synchronization protocol will need to implement a function, sync, which based on a triple, updates the state of dst. The problem is furthermore narrowed down as we prescribe sync should use the clock numbers to implement a last writer wins-by-default strategy. Unfortunately, the last writer cannot win unconditionally if the update introduces a cycle, and the remaining problem is to find a routine resolve, which applies the update, but does not introduce a cycle. We can check whether an implementation of sync converges by setting a bound on globalClock and systematically examining each possible trace.

```
class Sync {
    static atomic void sync(int node, Node src, Machine dst) {
        if (src.clock > dst.tree[node].clock) {
            if (dst.cycle(node, src.parent)) {
                Sync.resolve(node, src, dst);
            } else {
                dst.move(node, src.parent, src.clock);
            }
        }
    }

    static void synchronize() {
        while (!Sync.allInSync()) {
            assert(globalClock <= maxClock);
            int src, dst = choose(0..1);
            int node = choose(0..2);
            assume(src != dst);
            Sync.sync(node, machines[src].tree[node], machines[dst]);
        }
    }

    atomic bool allInSync(); // true if the trees of all machines are equal
```

**Fig. 8.** Synchronization core in Zing

In the following we will examine a few proposals for resolve. We examined several others, but the ones given here are sufficiently illustrative.

**Priority inversion** is a tempting solution. The clock on the destination machine is increased to dominate the clock of the source node.

```
static atomic void resolve(int node, Node src, Machine dst) {
    dst.tree[node].version = ++globalClock;
}
```

Not only is it not obvious whether this solution is correct, but it is also wrong. Zing found a two-machine counter-example by searching 1.5 million states in 4-5 minutes (on a 2GHz, 512MB Dell Optiplex). The counter example essentially consisted of the configuration from Fig.6. Divergence is exercised when the two machines ping-pong the directory $b$ to each other.

**Intentional grounding** moves conflicting nodes to the root.

```
static atomic void resolve(int node, Node src, Machine dst) {
    dst.move(node, -1, ++globalClock);
}
```

This solution works (and works for Zing too), but it is overly pessimistic, as it may move directories from deeply nested positions directly to the root. Within the context of file systems, where directories have controlled access (using access control lists, ACLs) this furthermore imposes security problems.

**Permutation** does not move conflicting nodes directly to the root, but moves them beneath the immediate parent.

```
static atomic void resolve(int node, Node src, Machine dst) {
    if (dst.tree[node].parent != -1) {
        dst.move(node, dst.tree[dst.tree[node].parent].parent, ++globalClock);
    }
    else {
        dst.tree[node].version = ++globalClock;
    }
}
```

While less pessimistic, it also suffers from security problems with access control: the scheme allows moving directories to places they have never been moved by any replicating machine.

**Parental Demotion.** Another appealing approach is to accept the instruction as is, but if the instruction introduces a directory cycle, then move the new parent under the previous parent of the node.

```
static atomic void resolve(int node, Node src, Machine dst) {
    dst.move(src.parent, dst.tree[node].parent, ++globalClock);
    dst.move(node, src.parent, src.clock);
}
```

Unfortunately, we were able to find a configuration where this scheme diverges. The smallest example we were able to find consists of 6 machines each with 3 directories. It requires a careful coordination between the machines to exercise divergence. This time we had to find the counter-example manually. The state space in this case proved larger than what Zing could handle.

Suppose initially:

$m_1 : a \rightarrow b \rightarrow c$, clocks = $\{a \mapsto 0, b \mapsto 1, c \mapsto 2\}$. That is, $m_1$ has $a$ under the replicated folder root, $b$ under $a$, and $c$ under $b$. The clock of $b$ is set to 1, and $c$'s clock is set to 2.

$m_2 : b \rightarrow c \rightarrow a$, clocks = $\{b \mapsto 0, c \mapsto 11, a \mapsto 3\}$.

$m_3 : c \rightarrow a \rightarrow b$, clocks = $\{c \mapsto 0, a \mapsto 4, b \mapsto 5\}$.

$m_4 : a \rightarrow c \rightarrow b$, clocks = $\{a \mapsto 0, c \mapsto 6, b \mapsto 7\}$.

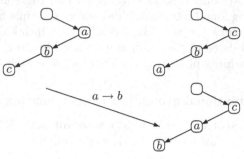

**Fig. 9.** Parental demotion

$m_5 : c \rightarrow b \rightarrow a$, clocks = $\{c \mapsto 0, b \mapsto 12, a \mapsto 8\}$.

$m_6 : b \rightarrow a \rightarrow c$, clocks = $\{b \mapsto 0, a \mapsto 9, c \mapsto 10\}$.

$m_5$ sends $b$ to $m_1$, $m_1' : a \rightarrow c \rightarrow b$, clocks = $\{a \mapsto 0, b \mapsto 12, c \mapsto 13\}$

$m_2$ sends $c$ to $m_4$: $m_4' : a \rightarrow b \rightarrow c$, clocks = $\{a \mapsto 0, b \mapsto 14, c \mapsto 11\}$

$m_1'$ sends $c$ to $m_2$: $m_2' : b \rightarrow a \rightarrow c$, clocks = $\{b \mapsto 0, c \mapsto 13, a \mapsto 15\}$

$m_4'$ sends $b$ to $m_5$: $m_5' : c \rightarrow a \rightarrow b$, clocks = $\{c \mapsto 0, a \mapsto 16, b \mapsto 14\}$

$m_2'$ sends $a$ to $m_3$: $m_3' : c \rightarrow b \rightarrow a$, clocks = $\{c \mapsto 0, b \mapsto 17, a \mapsto 15\}$

$m_5'$ sends $a$ to $m_6$: $m_6' : b \rightarrow c \rightarrow a$, clocks = $\{b \mapsto 0, c \mapsto 18, a \mapsto 16\}$

That state is isomorphic to the starting state using the correspondence:

$$\{m_1 \mapsto m_4', m_2 \mapsto m_6', m_3 \mapsto m_5', m_4 \mapsto m_1', m_5 \mapsto m_3', m_6 \mapsto m_2'\} \quad (6)$$

At this point, $m_6'$ can take the role of $m_2$, and $m_3'$ can take the role of $m_5$ to kick off another round.

### 6.3 A Mountain Too High for Zing?

An attempt was made to extract a more realistic Zing model of DFS-R by using the AsmL specification, and perform comprehensive model checking of the full synchronization core. The resulting 3400 line model was then exercised by Zing, which checked the model for consistency. Unfortunately, the resulting state space was vastly larger than what Zing could reasonably handle. The most effective way we know of performing state space exploration of DFS-R therefore remains the depth-bounded search presented in Section 8.

### 6.4 The Zing Experience

This Section illustrated the concurrent directory move problem in the context of using a state-space exploration tool, Zing, for checking design proposals. The concurrent move problem is interesting in its own right, but the main takeaway here is that state space exploration tools, such as Zing, are valuable for experimenting with design ideas on protocol substrates. Our take-away was to remain using priority inversion as the conflict resolution mechanism in DFS-R. To avoid divergence we imposed stronger restrictions on the order of processing updates.

# 7  Distributed Garbage Collection

Our presentation of DFS-R has so far no mechanism to garbage collect database records for deleted files. We need the database records so that file deletion can be replicated in a timely manner, but when all replicating machines agree that a file has been deleted, it should in principle be possible to remove the tombstone. Prior solutions to detecting when to delete dead resources involve two way commit protocols [12,13,14] to either agree on the when to add machines to a network, or when to safely collect resources marked for deletion. Solutions in replication systems, such as, Clearinghouse [15], NTFRS and other replications systems use a timeout based collection of tombstones: If a record has been marked as tombstone for 30 or 60 days, simply delete it from the database. Fig. 10 contains the corresponding transition that performs the garbage collection non-deterministically.

$$
\begin{array}{l}
\text{GarbageCollect}(nw, m, u): \\
\quad \textbf{let } (vv, rs, in) = nw[m], \quad r = rs[u] \\
\quad \textbf{assume } \neg r.live \\
\quad rs := rs \setminus [u \mapsto r]
\end{array}
$$

**Fig. 10.** Tombstone garbage collection

This solution does not address deleting content on machines that have been disconnected beyond the timeout value of the tombstones. While this situation reflects lack of consensus it also widens the likelihood that this content may reappear in other machines if the offline machine later makes changes to this content or if the machine has to recover from database loss.

It turns out that with synchronous joins we have a necessary and sufficient basis for detecting tombstones. The key is, as in (2), that version vectors maintain a trace of previously observed changes.

Let $m_1, m_2$ be machines, such that $(vv_1, rs_1, \_) = nw[m_1]$, $(vv_2, rs_2, \_) = nw[m_2]$ and $[u \mapsto r_1] \in rs_1$. The resource $r_1$ is subsumed by a tombstone if we have:

$$
r_1.gvsn \in vv_2 \wedge \left[ u \notin rs_2 \vee \left( \begin{array}{l} \wedge\, rs_2[u].gvsn \in vv_1 \\ rs_2[u].gvsn \neq r_1.gvsn \end{array} \right) \right] \tag{7}
$$

The system with SyncJoin, GarbageCollect and the file system operations satisfies the following invariant: Whenever (7) holds, then some time in the past, there is a machine $m_3$, with a tombstone for $u$ that dominates the resource $r_1$; or with notation, if (7), then previously

$$\exists m_3, rs_3 . (\_, rs_3, \_) = nw[m_3] \; \wedge \; \neg rs_3[u].live \; \wedge \; rs_3[u] \geq r_1 \qquad (8)$$

Conversely, if (7) is false, then for $[u \mapsto r_1]$ either $m_2$ does not know about $r_1$, or $m_2$ has a resource that $m_1$ does not know about. Regular synchronization takes care of reconciling the state in these cases.

This property suggests a secondary protocol for asynchronous garbage collection: periodically retrieve the version vector and all records from a partner machine, then garbage collect live records whenever condition (7) holds. DFS-R implements such a secondary protocol, but we observed that condition (7) in the presence of non-atomic joins is no longer necessary and sufficient for detecting missed tombstones. In general, condition (7) is only sufficient for detecting when the standard join does not ensure convergence.

## 8   Implementation Checking

A common theme in the previous sections has been that we could take advantage of somewhat subtle properties of a simple transition system to achieve goals, such as garbage collection, conflict resolution, and reconciling concurrent rename conflicts; but small modifications could break everything, and innocent looking solutions could be broken in complicated ways.

In view of the complexity of the problem and the encouraging results with the OCaml prototype we therefore decided to simulate the production version of the synchronization core of DFS-R using model-checking techniques. This Section describes the components that comprise the simulator. In summary, the simulator works by exercising different combinations of file system operations followed by synchronization steps in alternation, then it backtracks to visit different combinations. Some traces get pruned by partial order reduction techniques. This drastically reduces redundancies in the search tree. Backtracking search requires replacing the memory layer such that old state can easily be retrieved. To relieve the simulator from suspending threads at arbitrary points we ensure that the core makes use of suitable thread abstraction allowing it to single step through large non-blocking atomic units. Finally, certain components are abstracted to gain speed and control.

Thus, the main ingredients in our software model-checking experiment were:

1. Identifying a suitable vocabulary of actions to exercise.
2. Providing a memory layer that supports efficient backtracking.
3. Providing a threading layer that supports context switching and control of which threads run.
4. Virtualize components that change device state.
5. Prune search using partial order reduction techniques.

Ideally, one would like a general framework to be able to handle simulating systems, such as DFS-R. At the time we developed the framework, nothing suitable was available. Since then, efforts have been made to address problems like ours [16] using general frameworks.

## 8.1   Vocabulary

The simulation layer executes tasks in all possible inter-leavings. We will describe tasks in more detail below, as they are used as a thread layer. A task step defines an atomic action. Simulating DFS-R requires providing a handle into the atomic actions that a machine may perform, but of equal importance also provide environment actions, such as file system operations. The actions that are presented to the simulator are summarized as $\mathcal{L}_{action}$. Finally, we can define a simulation trace $\mathcal{S}_{trace}$ as a sequence $d$ of actions. In our experiments we set $d = 16$, with the assumption that most bugs could be exercised with a few number of operations.

$$
\begin{aligned}
\Sigma_{file} &= \{a, b, c, d\} & &\text{vocabulary of files} \\
\Sigma_{dir} &= \{p, q, r\} & &\text{directories} \\
\Sigma_{res} &= \Sigma_{file} \cup \Sigma_{dir} & &\text{resources} \\
\mathcal{L}_{fs} &= \{share/, noshare/\}(\Sigma_{dir}/)^* \Sigma_{res} & &\text{file paths} \\
\Sigma_m &= \{m_1, m_2, m_3, m_4\} & &\text{machines} \\
\mathcal{L}_{action} &= \mathsf{rename}(\Sigma_m, \mathcal{L}_{fs}, \mathcal{L}_{fs}) & &\text{actions} \\
&\cup\ \mathsf{create}(\Sigma_m, \mathcal{L}_{fs}) \\
&\cup\ \mathsf{update}(\Sigma_m, \mathcal{L}_{fs}) \\
&\cup\ \mathsf{delete}(\Sigma_m, \mathcal{L}_{fs}) \\
&\cup\ \mathsf{sync}(\Sigma_m, \Sigma_m) \\
&\cup\ \mathsf{read-journal}(\Sigma_m, N \cup \{\omega\}) \\
\mathcal{S}_{trace} &= \mathcal{L}_{action}^d & &\text{simulation trace}
\end{aligned}
$$

The set of possible file system operations are generated using a finite alphabet of file and directory names. They may take place on one of the machines listed in $\Sigma_m$. The internal actions of DFS-R are split into two sets: (1) reading the USN journal for 1, 2, 3, etc. steps or until reaching a fix-point ($\omega$ steps); (2) synchronizing symmetrically between two machines. Paths starting with *share* are replicated, paths starting with *noshare* are outside the replicated folder.

## 8.2   A Custom Memory Layer

Key to supporting efficient backtracking is to be able to save and restore state. Our simulation does not backtrack over suspensions within stack frames. This limitation allowed us to concentrate on tracking heap allocated memory only. In summary, the simulation environment saves aside a copy of the heap when entering a new backtracking point for the first time. When re-entering the back-tracking point, it can dispense all memory allocated within the branch and restore the previous state. Unfortunately, not all heap-allocated memory can be reclaimed at backtracking points. In particular, memory that is associated with device state cannot just be overwritten on backtracking points. For instance, buffers that are allocated by procedures that print to files cannot be reclaimed using a stack discipline. This led to a dual mode custom memory layer, one for backtracking mode and one for non-backtracking mode.

## 8.3  Thread Layering

It is challenging in itself to model check multi-threaded programs faithfully. A real software model checker would have to allow context switches at arbitrary control locations. The first problem requires infrastructure; the model checker will have to save and restore the stack. This amounts to mirroring thread context switches. A more fundamental problem is the significant increase in the state space as every program counter is potentially a backtracking point.

We bypassed these issues by implementing a thread abstraction that wrapped around thread pools and timer queues. Both facilities are supported by operating system APIs, but require the caller to maintain different context depending on whether a job is spawned directly in a thread pool or delayed in a timer queue.

Our thread layer combines these two concepts into a single *task* entity, which can be set to run immediately, or with a non-zero delay. To support simulation, tasks support dual modes: one for running in a multi-threaded environment, and another for running in a single-threaded simulation environment.

## 8.4  Virtualization

The interfaces to the on-disk database, the file system, and the network layer had to be abstracted and re-coded for speed and control. The abstractions were indispensable in making simulation practical. Creation time of a fresh on-disk JET-blue database takes for instance 2 seconds (it creates several larger files, including logs). Backtracking over such disk operations would slow down simulation to a crawl.

Using abstractions also came with several limitations. Foremost, bugs inside the physical modules were not exposed by simulation, as they were simply not exercised. It was also limited what we found worth to reflect in an abstraction. The database abstraction did thus not implement the ACID properties. This was reasonable as all transactions in DFS-R are short lived, but this prevented us identifying code paths that would lead to conflicting updates. Such errors were only later exposed during stress runs.

## 8.5  Partial Order Reduction

The set of simulation traces introduced in Section 8.1 contain a large number of essentially symmetric traces. For example, the order of creating files $share/p/a$ and $share/p/b$ on the same machine is insignificant.

More precisely, let $\pi, \pi' \in \mathcal{L}_{fs}$ be file paths, then we define $\pi \perp \pi'$ (read as $\pi$ is orthogonal to $\pi'$) as a binary relation on paths if neither path is a prefix of the other. Furthermore, let $m$, $m'$ be machines, $op_1$, $op_2 \in \{\text{create}, \text{delete}, \text{update}\}$, then we define the orthogonality relation $\perp$ on actions by:

$$op_1(m, \pi) \perp op_2(m, \pi') \text{ if } \pi \perp \pi'$$

In general, actions are considered orthogonal if they reside on different machines, thus:

$$op_1(m, \pi) \perp op_2(m', \pi') \text{ if } m \neq m' \wedge op_1, op_2 \in \{\text{create}, \text{delete}, \text{update}, \text{rename}\}$$

We overload the use of $\perp$ to also capture idem-potency of actions. Actions that can be considered idempotent, such as two consecutive updates to the same file, are added to the relation.

Partial order reduction, based on $\perp$, is implemented by representing the vocabulary of actions $\mathcal{L}_{action} = \{a_1, \ldots, a_m\}$ using an mapping $por$ from $\{1, \ldots, m\}$ into $2^{\{1, \ldots m\}}$ such that $a_i \perp a_j$, if and only if $j \in por(i)$. The sets $por(i)$ are implemented as bit-vectors, as $m$ is relatively small and of fixed size. Depth first search then prunes action sequences containing the pair $a_i a_j$ if $a_i \perp a_j$ (that would be $j \in por(i)$) and $j \leq i$.

## 8.6   Experiments

We ran simulation relatively early in the development process. As the product got more stable we ran a two week experiment, distributing the search over a cluster of 200 machines each exploring a different portion of the search space. This helped us covering slightly more than $\frac{1}{2}$ trillion scenarios, for checking main consistency properties.

Early on, simulation caught a large number of bugs that may have been caught later in stress. On the other hand, simulation served as a pretty good regression test as the implementation was evolving at a rapid pace. Some of the bugs found during simulation had the traits of being extremely difficult for a stress test to identify. For instance, the trace below exposed a corner case in the interplay between the components that recycled unique identifiers and those that walked directories.

```
create(m₂, noshare/p)
rename(m₂, noshare/p, share/p)
read−journal(m₂, ω)
sync(m₁, m₂)
rename(m₂, share/p, noshare/p)
rename(m₂, noshare/p, share/p)
read−journal(m₂, ω)
update(m₁, share/p)
sync(m₁, m₂)
```

In comparison, the bugs found in stress were predominantly in the components that are abstracted away during simulation. There were a couple of exceptions, though. Stress exposed a divergence bug that simulation was blind to, it also exposed a protocol error exposed by asynchronous message passing.

# 9   Conclusions

This paper provided an experience report on the design and modeling used for the development of DFS-R. We put emphasis on the use of research tools Zing and AsmL from MSR, taking advantage of applicative features in garbage collected functional languages, and experiences with software model checking. None of these approaches are mainstream in product development, neither can it be said that DFS-R is a mainstream product; but we feel that pieces and variants of the approaches taken for DFS-R are benefitial for developing other distributed systems. The AsmL (now called SpecExplorer) and Zing tools are directly available as general purpose tools. Today, SpecExplorer is mainly directed towards model-based testing, while its use as a design tool is under-emphasized. Our software model checker was built exclusively for DFS-R. I doubt much of our simulation implementation can or should be re-used, as a custom simulation layer is easiest developed by the component owner. There is a ray of hope in future availability of general purpose tools for software model checking concurrent and/or distributed systems, though the task of building these is huge.

It should be noted that modeling, model exploration and software model checking are resource-wise minor activities in the larger picture of developing a product. Far more prolific was stress testing, where multiple instances of DFS-R are run against random file system operations. During development, each developer and tester ran stress sessions with up to 1-2 million file system operations every night. Besides stress runs, BVT regression tests, interoperability testing and bug-bashes each contributed in driving quality.

**Acknowledgments.** DFS-R is the result of several people's hard and diligent work. I am indebted to having had the pleasure to work with Shobana Balakrishnan, Dan Boldo, Richard Chinn, Brian Collins, Scott Colville, Huseyin Dursun, Ben Fathi, David Golds, Huisheng Liu, Ram Natarajan, Joe Porkka, Robert Post, Rafik Robeal, Christophe Robert, Masood Siddiqi, Guhan Suriyanarayanan, Dan Teodosiu; and several others from the Core File Systems group, Windows Live, Windows Networking and MSR. Thanks to Neil Conway for implementing the memory optimizations in the backtracking search, to Rostik Yavorsky for developing large parts of the AsmL specification, proving the garbage collection conditions correct, to Abhay Gupta for taking the AsmL specification and running it through Zing.

# References

1. Saito, Y., Shapiro, M.: Optimistic replication. ACM Comput. Surv. 37(1), 42–81 (2005)
2. Pierce, B.C., Vouillon, J.: Unison: A file synchronizer and its specification. In: Kobayashi, N., Pierce, B.C. (eds.) TACS 2001. LNCS, vol. 2215, p. 560. Springer, Heidelberg (2001)
3. Petersen, K., Spreitzer, M., Terry, D.B., Theimer, M., Demers, A.J.: Flexible update propagation for weakly consistent replication. In: SOSP, pp. 288–301 (1997)

4. Malkhi, D., Terry, D.B.: Concise Version Vectors in WinFS. In: Fraigniaud, P. (ed.) DISC 2005. LNCS, vol. 3724, pp. 339–353. Springer, Heidelberg (2005)
5. Teodosiu, D., Bjørner, N., Gurevich, Y., Manasse, M., Porkka, J.: Optimizing file replication over limited-bandwidth networks using remote differential compression. Technical report, Microsoft Research, MSR-TR-2006-157 (November 2006)
6. Lamport, L.: Time, Clocks, and the Ordering of Events in a Distributed System. Commun. ACM 21(7), 558–565 (1978)
7. Baquero, C., Moura, F.: Improving causality logging in mobile computing networks. ACM Mobile Computing and Communications Review 2(4), 62–66 (1998)
8. Kang, B., Wilensky, R., Kubiatowicz, J.: The hash history approach for reconciling mutual inconsistency. In: ICDCS, pp. 670–677. IEEE Computer Society, Los Alamitos (2003)
9. Barnett, M., Grieskamp, W., Nachmanson, L., Schulte, W., Tillmann, N., Veanes, M.: Towards a Tool Environment for Model-Based Testing with AsmL. In: Petrenko, A., Ulrich, A. (eds.) FATES 2003. LNCS, vol. 2931, pp. 252–266. Springer, Heidelberg (2004)
10. Andrews, T., Qadeer, S., Rajamani, S.K., Rehof, J., Xie, Y.: Zing: A model checker for concurrent software. In: Alur, R., Peled, D.A (eds.) CAV 2004. LNCS, vol. 3114, pp. 484–487. Springer, Heidelberg (2004)
11. Holzmann, G.J.: The Model Checker SPIN. IEEE Trans. Software Eng. 23(5), 279–295 (1997)
12. Jr., T.W.P., Guy, R.G., Heidemann, J.S., Popek, G.J., Mak, W., Rothmeier, D.: Management of Replicated Volume Location Data in the Ficus Replicated File System. In: USENIX Summer, pp. 17–30 (1991)
13. Allchin, J.E.: A Suite of Robust Algorithms For Maintaining Replicated Data Using Weak Consistency Conditions. In: Symposium on Reliability in Distributed Software and Database Systems, pp. 47–56 (1983)
14. Fischer, M.J., Michael, A.: Sacrificing Serializability to Attain High Availability of Data. In: PODS, pp. 70–75 (1982)
15. Oppen, D.C., Dalal, Y.K.: The clearinghouse: A decentralized agent for locating named objects in a distributed environment. ACM Trans. Inf. Syst. 1(3), 230–253 (1983)
16. Lin, S., Pan, A., Guo, R., Zhang, Z.: Simulating Large-Scale P2P Systems with the WiDS Toolkit. In: MASCOTS, pp. 415–424. IEEE Computer Society, Los Alamitos (2005)

# From "Formal Methods" to System Modeling

Manfred Broy

Institut für Informatik, Technische Universität München
D-80290 München Germany
broy@in.tum.de
http://wwwbroy.informatik.tu-muenchen.de

**Abstract.** When engineering software intensive systems the quality of the resulting product depends strictly on the quality of the models used explicitly or implicitly in the engineering process. A rich family of such models has been developed in recent years. We discuss some of these models and describe the requirements for system modeling theories.

## 1  Introduction

There is a long way from early approaches to formal system modeling sometimes called "formal methods" such as denotational semantics, VDM, SADT, algebraic specification to model based system and software engineering as advocated in wide spread approaches such as UML, SysML, or MDA. We discuss this development and properties of the theory and methodology that we require.

System and software development is today one of the most complex and powerful tasks in engineering. Modern software systems typically are embedded in technical or organizational processes, distributed, dynamic, and accessed concurrently by a variety of independent user interfaces. Just by formulating the right programs we obtain engineering artifacts that can calculate results, communicate messages, control systems, and illustrate and animate all kinds of information. Since programs are - implicitly or explicitly - based on models of system behavior and since well-chosen models are a successful way to understand software, modeling is an essential and crucial issue in software construction.

In all scientific and engineering disciplines, models play a prominent role. For physics, mathematics has provided lots of models. The same holds for many engineering disciplines. Economy works with models; biology works more and more with models, chemistry works with models. Constructing, analyzing, and arguing in terms of models is at the heart of science.

In informatics modeling is even more crucial. Developing software is more or less nothing than developing the right models finally represented in the appropriate notation such that they can be executed effectively and efficiently on today's computing devices.

Many different models are needed in the engineering of software intensive systems. To name a few of them:

- Domain models: describing properties of the application domain that are relevant for the system under development (physical, technical, organizational, fiscal, legislation rules and laws),

C.B. Jones, Z. Liu, J. Woodcock (Eds.): Bjørner/Zhou Festschrift, LNCS 4700, pp. 24–44, 2007.

- System models: describing the logical and technical behavior and structure of the system and software under development,
- Quality models: describing quality aspects of the system and software under development or its development process (see [3]),
- Cost models: calculating the cost and required budget for a development project,
- Development process models: describing the structure of the development process (see [5]).

These models are used as the basis for the engineering of software intensive systems. In particular, for the planning of a development project and in requirements engineering such models are indispensable. The formality of these models is only one aspect. Of course, if tool support is requested for the application of these models, formalization is inevitable.

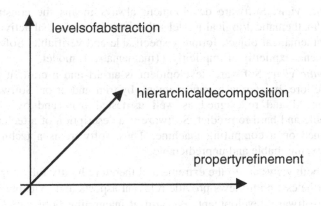

**Fig. 1.** Three Dimensions of Software Development

In the following we concentrate rather on the system modeling aspect. In the development of large complex software system it is simply impossible to provide one comprehensive model for the system in only one step. Rather we

- specify a system or subsystem first in terms of its interface,
- add stepwise details by refinement,
- give several views,
- decompose the hierarchically system into components,
- construct a sequence of models on different levels of abstraction.

Each step in these activities introduces models, refines them, or integrates them. Concentrating on the modeling issues we have to manage the following tasks:

- selection of the appropriate model concept for an aspect,
- identifying and documenting all the properties for a model,
- integrating several views into an overall model,
- decomposing a model hierarchically into components.

Finally software construction is also a modeling activity, which constructs operational models in terms of the canonical execution models of the programming language used.

Fig. 1 shows three dimensions of system modeling in software development which will be explained in detail later on.

## 2 Nature of Software Development

Still we have the ongoing discussion in our scientific community what the essence of software development actually is. Is it an engineering task? Is it an art, a handicraft, or actually science? Of course, there are many views onto program development, more scientific ones or more pragmatic ones. We study and discuss two extreme views in the following:

- *Scientific view*: Software development always means the construction of a formal/mathematical/logical model - therefore it is a formal activity. Software is a mathematical object, formally specifiable and verifiable. Software always implements explicitly or implicitly a (mathematical) model.
- *Pragmatic view*: Software development is an art and a craft; it proceeds by esoteric lore, by stepwise improvement, by trial and error. Software needs to be changed and redesigned as well as tested over and over again. It is unreliable and hard to predict. Software is a description of a technical process performed on a computing machine. Thus, software is a technical artifact, complex, unreliable and unpredictable.

Of course, both views are to the extreme and therefore hardly fully appropriate and correct. Nevertheless, both views provide relevant aspects and valuable insights into the nature of software development. We aim at integrating both views obtaining a realistic and respectable discipline of software engineering. Only if we manage to have a compromise between both these views in a smart way, software development can be improved into a scientifically well-founded, practically relevant engineering discipline.

### 2.1 Models, Their Structures and Views

In this section we define the concept of a model, the structure of models and define what a model view is. In software engineering the word "model" is used in many different ways and contexts with many quite different meanings. Examples are terms like "meta model", "process model", or "system model". In the following we are interested in two variations and meanings of the usage of the word model.

A *model* is and provides first of all an abstraction. Selecting a model for an entity means to focus on specific aspects of that entity. Models are typical chosen in engineering to serve a specific purpose. A model introduces via its abstraction a particular view or perspective onto an entity.

A *thought model* ("Gedankenmodell") is a presentation of particular aspects of an entity, such as a (software) system and its application context. It represents a way to think about a problem, a system, a product, or a process. In essence, it provides an abstraction like any model. To find a good thought model is perhaps the most critical modeling task since the thought model determines the adequacy of the future development approach.

To make a thought model useful we have to find ways to precisely document, communicate the model and to use it in analysis and design. A promising way to do this is to represent a model in terms of well known, well understood concepts and theories. Mathematics and logics is a good choice for that.

A *mathematical model* of a system or some of its aspects is a mathematical structure, in general, an algebra, consisting of sets, functions, graphs, relations, and/or logical predicates. It represents a thought model in mathematical terms. A good mathematical model shows a number of properties such as modularity, flexibility and thus fulfils a number of essential logical and mathematical properties. We come back to this later. A mathematical model is an idealized abstraction that needs syntax to represent it directly. We need techniques to write down, to document, and to communicate mathematical and thought models.

Formalization of models in terms of mathematics and logics is not good per se. However, if we are interested to reason about models in terms of well understood and well established techniques formalization is a promising way to go. In principle, formalization can be done by representing models in classical notation of mathematics and logics. However, for an engineer it might be quite difficult and too demanding to work out a mathematical model from scratch. Using standardized syntax and modeling concepts for the description of models can help.

A *description technique* is a set of syntactic concepts (text, formula, graphs, or tables) for the description of a thought model. Mathematical models provide the semantic theory for description techniques. In essence, we use description techniques (syntax) to represent a mathematical model (semantic) that formalizes the thought model (abstraction and intention) for a particular development aspect. In the following, we are at the same time interested in thought modeling, in mathematical models and description techniques.

## 2.2  Description Techniques, Their Structures and Views

From what we have said about modeling it is obvious that model description techniques are more useful if they address typical modeling needs and patterns, if they provide support for reasoning about models, and if they support the purpose for which the model was selected. If models are deployed in an engineering process for the development, they have to support classical principles such as "divide an conquer", "levels of abstraction", "separation of concerns", "modularity" etc.

The description techniques and also the described models should therefore be *modular* to support the modular decomposition and composition in the design of systems and their description. This requirement induces a requirement on the system model: there we need composition operators to construct such modular systems. In addition, we are interested in an abstraction concept. Given a description of a system building block, we look for an abstraction function that maps the description onto its interface behavior, such that we can calculate the interface behavior of the composed system from the abstractions of its sub-systems. The description techniques and also the described models should therefore be *hierarchical* to support the hierarchical decomposition and a hierarchical top down design of systems and their description.

Often description techniques do not describe a comprehensive model directly, but rather complementary views and properties of it. We speak of a *view-oriented* description. Being interested in software engineering and its foundations we consider all three issues of conceptual and mathematical modeling and description techniques as interesting fields of scientific study.

# 3 Formal Methods and Models in Software Engineering

Our scientific community has invested lots of time and efforts into so called formal methods. In formal methods the idea is that the task of software development including specification, stepwise design, implementation and verification is carried out completely within a formal and thus logical and mathematical theory. This is a striking idea, full of interesting scientific challenges and leading to valuable insights. However, practitioners often consider formal methods inadequate, insufficient, too expensive, too difficult, and "not at all practical".

Indeed the state of the art in pragmatic and practical software development is still far from being satisfactory. Practical software development is to a large extent "ad hoc", "immature", unpredictable, uncontrollable, and "not at all an engineering discipline".

Actually we have to find a good compromise between the rigorous scientific approach to programming and the pragmatic practical approach. One idea is the use of well-chosen, sufficiently formal models and their support by tractable theories, description techniques, methods, and tools. Programming means in any case using models explicitly or implicitly. We claim that it is important to identify the underlying models very explicitly and to exploit them for understanding and analysis. Appropriate formalization is of great practical advantage since finally formal methods provide a rich tool kit of development and validation methods.

## 3.1 Models for Structure and Behavior in Software Engineering

Systematic development of distributed interactive software systems needs basic system models that reduce the complexity and concentrate on particular aspects by simplifying abstractions. Description techniques are to provide specific views and abstractions such as:

- data view,
- interface view,
- architecture, logical structure and distribution view,
- process view,
- interaction view,

- deployment view,
- state transition view.

All these views have to be captured by carefully chosen syntactic description methods leading to helpful thought models. The development of systems concentrates on working out these views leading step by step to an implementation.

We give a mathematical model setting in the following providing abstract views onto a system. A system is based on an algebra A that describes its basic data types and elements as well as its characteristic operations. A system has an *interface view (black box view)* which describes its behavior for the user of a system. Each system has an implementation in terms of a *state machine* or a *composed system*. A system always has a *state space* and can be viewed as a *state machine*. System models can be *refined*. They describe systems at particular *levels of abstraction*. A system has a set of *traces* (processes, system runs) as its histories. Each view defines logical properties in terms of a mathematical model.

# 4  System Model: A Meta Model Theory of Software

In this section we introduce a meta model for software systems. We outline its essential views and how they are related. Later we give a concrete instance of this meta theory.

## 4.1  Criteria for a Theory of Modeling

For a scientifically and practically useful approach to modeling in software engineering we list in the following a number of criteria and essential ingredients.

We need a system model, a mathematical model of a system, powerful enough to incorporate all envisaged views, supporting the concept of levels of abstraction, hierarchical decomposition, and modularity. In the following we identify and define these requirements more precisely.

## 4.2  A System Meta Model

In a system meta model we incorporate all the concepts needed to describe the different parts and views of a system. Formally we define a signature of an algebra, the algebra of system models, and state some algebraic properties.

### 4.2.1  Data Model

Data occur in systems everywhere. Typically today the data view is defined by a family of data types (or sorts) describing sets of data. In most cases, in addition, functions are introduced on the data sets. This leads to heterogeneous algebras. The theory of data algebras is very well understood by now. A data model is an algebra. DM denotes the set of all data models. It defines a signature, being a family of names for types, functions, and operations, together with axioms describing the properties or with an explicit model.

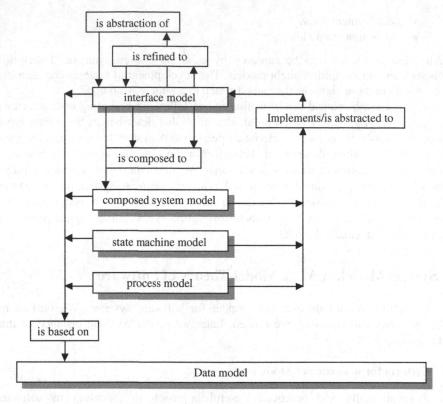

**Fig. 2.** Meta Model of the System Model

Typical description techniques are axiomatic, algebraic specification (abstract data types, see [1]), Entity/Relationship-diagrams or class diagrams.

### 4.2.2  State Model

State machines give a basic view onto interactive systems. A state machine is described by a set of states called a state space, a subset of the state set called initial states, and a state transition function.

Typical we work with state machines with labeled or with unlabelled transitions. As labels we use the elements of a given set of actions. Another class is state machines with input and output. We distinguish this the following classes of state transition functions:

$\Delta$: State $\rightarrow \wp$(State)                       unlabeled state transitions

$\Delta$: Action $\rightarrow$ (State $\rightarrow \wp$(State))           action labeled state transitions

$\Delta$: State $\times$ Input $\rightarrow \wp$(State $\times$ Output)   state transitions with input and output

In the case of a state machine with input and output we may consider pairs of input and output as labels. The description of the state space and the label sets Action, Input and Output is again a data-modeling task. A simple and powerful way to define a state space is the choice of a set of typed attributes such that each valuation of this attributes defines a state.

Given initial states $\Lambda \subseteq$ State and the pair $(\Delta, \Lambda)$ defines a system in terms of a state machine. By SM we denote the set of all state machines.

### 4.2.3 Abstraction: The Interface Model

In general, state machines provide a rather detailed model of a system. Often we are interested in more abstract views. In particular, from a user's point of view we are often not interested in the concrete states of a system. For state machines with input and output or with labeled transitions the abstraction is quite obvious. If the labels describe the effects of the machine to the outside world we are only interested in the labels but not in the states.

For unlabeled state transition systems we may divide the states into local and nonlocal parts. In the cases of state spaces defined by attributes we speak of local and nonlocal attributes. We may furthermore distinguish between attributes that can only be read or written by the machine and those that can only be read or written by the environment.

To begin with, we introduce abstractions between state machines. Mathematically, an abstraction is a mapping of the form

$$\alpha_{SM/SM}: SM \rightarrow SM$$

This is only a syntactic notion so far. Not every mapping between state machines is to be called an abstraction. Particular behavioral similarities are required that we will discuss in detail later. In fact, there are, in general, many abstraction mappings between state machines.

To begin with we are interested in *syntactic interfaces*. A syntactic interface describes syntactic properties of a system that determine if it can be composed with another system (since they syntactically fit together) or if a system A can be replaced another one B in any context without running in any syntactic difficulties. Then B is called *syntactically compatible* for A and we write A $\gg$ B. We assume that the syntactic compatibility relation $\gg$ is partial preorder. If A $\gg$ B and A $\gg$ B then we write A $\approx$ B and say that A and B are *mutually syntactically compatible*.

In the interface model we abstract from all details in the state machine model that are not relevant for working with a system. An interface view provides therefore an abstraction. By **F** we denote the set of all interfaces. We assume that there is a canonical abstraction function called *interface abstraction*:

$$\alpha_{SM/IF}: SM \rightarrow F \qquad\qquad \textit{interface abstraction}$$

We require for all we interface behaviors $F \in \mathbf{F}$

$$F \approx \alpha_{SM/IF} (F))$$

The abstraction function maps a state machine onto its interface. The interface is also called *black box view* or *observable behavior*. In fact, we also define abstractions between interfaces:

$$\alpha_{IF/IF}: F \rightarrow F$$

We require for all we interface behaviors $F \in \mathbf{F}$

$$F \approx \alpha_{IF/IF}(F)) \qquad \text{\textit{syntactic compatibility of interface abstraction}}$$

Clearly not every mapping between interfaces is to be called an abstraction. Particular behavioral properties are required.

State machine abstraction is generally not an injective function: there are several state machines with the same interface abstraction. This shows that there does not exist an inverse function for $\alpha_{SM/IF}$, but we can require a canonical function

$$\rho_{IF/SM}: \mathbf{F} \to \mathbf{SM}$$

such that for all we interface behaviors $F \in \mathbf{F}$ get

$$\alpha_{SM/IF}(\rho_{IF/SM}(F)) = F \qquad \text{\textit{reversibility of representation}}$$

This implies that there is a state machine for each (consistent) interface specification.

### 4.2.4  The Process Model

A run of a system can always be understood as a family of events that are causally connected. Each such run is called a *process*. Every event in a process is the instance of an action. Which actions are considered in a process is again a question of the chosen view and level of abstraction. We can define interface processes or processes that reflect internal actions and internal events. A system behavior then is a set of processes.

By $\mathbf{PRC}(\text{Action})$ we denote the set of system descriptions by sets of processes over the set Action, by $\mathbf{PRC}$ the set of all system descriptions by sets of processes.

Like for state machines and interfaces, we define abstractions between processes by mappings of the form:

$$\alpha_{PRC/PRC}: \mathbf{PRC} \to \mathbf{PRC}$$

Again not every mapping between processes is called an abstraction. Particular behavioral properties are required.

In fact the process view is closely related to the state view. Every state machine defines a set of processes and thus a system behavior in terms of processes. In essence, the process view is a mild abstraction of the state view.

We assume, in particular, the existence of two specific abstraction functions. We assume a process abstraction for state machines:

$$\alpha_{SM/PRC}: \mathbf{SM} \to \mathbf{PRC}$$

and a canonical interface abstraction mapping:

$$\alpha_{PRC/IF}: \mathbf{PRC} \to \mathbf{F}$$

In fact we expect that the composition of these two abstractions yields the state machine interface abstraction. For every state machine M in SM we assume:

$$\alpha_{PRC/IF}(\alpha_{SM/PRC}(M)) = \alpha_{SM/IF}(M)$$

In other words a process abstraction of a state machine followed by an interface abstraction of the process yields the interface abstraction of a state machine.

Any functional composition of abstraction functions should yield an abstraction. In other words, we require that the set of abstractions is closed under functional composition.

Given the canonical function $\rho_{IF/SM}$ we define a canonical

$$\rho_{IF/PRC}: F \rightarrow PRC$$

such that for all we interface behaviors $f \in F$ define

$$\rho_{IF/PRC}(f) = \alpha_{SM/PRC}(\rho_{IF/SM}(f))$$

This is, however, only one option to relate a canonical process to each interface.

### 4.2.5 Composed Systems: Composition

If we compose systems into larger ones out of given components we need an operation of composition. In principle, compositions are useful for all the views and models of systems described so far. To begin with we simply assume a binary composition operator for each system view.

$$\otimes_{IF}: F \times F \rightarrow F$$

$$\otimes_{PRC}: PRC \times PRC \rightarrow PRC$$

$$\otimes_{SM}: SM \times SM \rightarrow SM$$

Ideally $\otimes$ is commutative and associative. It may be a partial function, however. Only certain components can be composed meaningfully. For each of these operators we require:

$$A_1 \gg B_1 \wedge A_2 \gg B_2 \Rightarrow A_1 \otimes A_2 \gg B_1 \otimes B_2 \quad \textit{monotonicity of syntactic compatibility}$$

We furthermore expect that interface abstraction distributes over composition:

$$\alpha_{SM/IF}(M) \otimes_{IF} \alpha_{SM/IF}(M') = \alpha_{SM/IF}(M \otimes_{SM} M') \qquad \textit{compositionality}$$

The same equation can be formulated for the process view. Due to the abstraction function we easily may compose infaces $f$ with state machines $M$ by:

$$\alpha_{SM/IF}(M) \otimes_{IF} f$$

or by

$$M \otimes_{SM} \rho_{IF/SM}(f)$$

It is easy to show due to compositionality that the abstraction of the later is identical to the first:

$$\alpha_{SM/IF}(M) \otimes_{IF} f = \alpha_{SM/IF}(M \otimes_{SM} \rho_{IF/SM}(f))$$

We require, in addition, that the refinement relation that we introduce later is compositional.

### 4.2.6 Composed Systems: Architecture

Assuming associativity and commutativity composition is easily generalized from pairs of systems to sets and families of systems. Then we work with the notion of component identifiers. A component is a system itself also called subsystem. Let $K$ be a set of component identifiers. Then a composed system with components modeled by their interfaces is defined by a mapping

$$v_{IF}: K \rightarrow F$$

that associates an interface with each component identifiers. We speak of *system architectures*.

Often we require additional syntactic properties for the components of a composed system that assure, in particular, that the composition of the components is well defined. The set of all composed system models with subsystems modeled by interfaces is denoted by $CS_{IF}$.

Similar mappings defining composed systems of components modeled by processes or state machines are easily defined by the following functions.

$$v_{PRC}: \mathbb{K} \to PRC$$

$$v_{SM}: \mathbb{K} \to SM$$

This way we get systems structured into components modeled by processes or state machines respectively. The sets of such composed system models with components modeled by processes or state machines are denoted by $CS_{PRC}$ and $CS_{SM}$ respectively. Due to the generalization of composition to we can consider architectures of the form

$$v: \mathbb{K} \to SM \cup F \cup PRC$$

where the components of an architecture are represented by interfaces, state machines or processes.

### 4.2.7   System Hierarchies

So far we have only introduced concepts of flat, composed system models. Now we define inductively the set of hierarchical composed systems. Let $HCS$ denote the set of all *composed hierarchical systems*. We define this set inductively by:

(0)        $HCS_0 = SM \cup F \cup PRC$

(1)        every function $v: \mathbb{K} \to HCS_n$ is in $HCS_{n+1}$

We define

$$HCS = \cup \, HCS_n$$

This allows us to define hierarchical (and by a more sophisticated construction - using ideas from domain theory - even recursive) systems. In most cases and also for our purpose, however, finite hierarchies are sufficient. We define in full generality that a hierarchical system is a mapping:

$$v: \mathbb{K} \to HCS$$

By the notion of component identifiers and hierarchical composed systems we introduce a new concept into our system model namely that of an *instance*. In particular, we include composed systems where one interface or one state machine is used several times by assigning it to different component identifiers.

### 4.2.8   The Use Relation in a System Hierarchy

In a large composed system we have generally many different constituents and components. Typically there is a kind of hierarchy in a system model expressed by the use-relation. We define functions such as

$$\text{is\_used}_{DM/IF}: DM \times F \to \mathbb{B}$$

$$\text{is\_used}_{IF/HCS}: F \times HCS \to \mathbb{B}$$

$$\text{is\_part}_{IF/HCS}: F \times HCS \to \mathbb{B}$$

Taking into account the idea of a component identifier, we can also establish the is_part relation between component identifiers that formalizes the component hierarchy. Note that a hierarchy of composed system defines a tree (an acyclic directed graph where each path is unique). It is called the *component tree* or the *component hierarchy*.

### 4.2.9 Abstractions of Composed Systems

Easily we define abstractions for composed systems:

$$\alpha_{CS/IF}: CS_{IF} \rightarrow F$$

$$\alpha_{CS/PRC}: CS_{PRC} \rightarrow PRC$$

$$\alpha_{CS/SM}: CS_{SM} \rightarrow SM$$

The relationship between composition and composed system and their abstractions is defined as follows. Let $v$ be a composed system with components modeled by interfaces and with component identifiers

$$\mathbb{K} = \{k_1, ..., k_n\}$$

We assume

$$\alpha_{CS/IF}(v) = v(k_1) \otimes_{IF} ... \otimes_{IF} v(k_n) \quad \textit{architectural interface abstraction}$$

This definition essentially assumes that composition is associative and commutative. Composition is the key to hierarchical models. The inverse to composition is decomposition. A decomposition of a system described by an interface model into a family of components yields a composed system the abstraction of which yields the original interface model.

Thus finally we get an interface abstraction for all kinds of systems represented by the mapping

$$\alpha_{IF}: HCS \rightarrow F$$

The idea of an interface abstraction is the basis for the composition and integration of all kinds of systems represented by state machines, processes, or composed systems.

### 4.2.10 Time

Time is a very essential aspect of a system and its behavior. Many systems interact in a time frame. This means that the time and the duration of the execution of actions are essential for the behavior of systems. We denote the set of all timed composed hierarchical systems by TCS and the set of nontimed composed systems by NCS. Again we assume an abstraction function

$$\alpha_T: TCS \rightarrow NCS$$

Time is a concept that is orthogonal to all the concepts introduced so far. We may introduce a notion of time in all the model aspects introduced above. It is in particular interesting to relate system models with explicit time to system models without explicit time.

Forgetting about timing aspects is again an abstraction. We may have timed system models as well as nontimed system models (see [4]).

### 4.3   A System Development Meta Model, Development Relations: Refinement

The system meta model describes the building blocks of all system models. During system development, several system models are constructed that - in an ideal case - are formally related by refinement relations.

We are not only interested in the system modeling elements, the system views, and how they fit together to a complete system description. We are also interested in relating the models as they are successively constructed in the development process. For this purpose we introduce refinement relations between models. We work with three levels of refinement:

- *Horizontal refinement* also called *property refinement*; by property refinement we add properties that restrict the behavior of the system and thus make a system more deterministic.
- *Vertical refinement* also called *design* or *implementation*; by a design or implementation step we replace an interface by a design. A design is given by a decomposition of a system into subsystems or a state machine.
- *Granularity refinement* also called interaction refinement - *levels of abstractions*; by a refinement step changing the level of abstraction we replace system models by a more concrete ones, for instance, by systems with finer grained actions, state transitions, or messages.

These refinements are mathematically relations between modeling elements. These relations form partial orderings. We assume that vertical refinements are special cases of horizontal refinement, which is in turn a special case of granularity refinement.

### 4.3.1  Property Refinement

During development we develop systems step by step adding more and more detail. We work with a refinement relation to relate models to those with more specific properties. Therefore we speak of *property refinement* or *semantic compatibility*. This relation can be introduced for all described system views:

$$\Rrightarrow \; : \; \text{HCS} \times \text{HCS} \to \mathbb{B}$$

If $M \Rrightarrow M'$ holds we say M refines to M' or M is refined by M'. Moreover we assume that refinement implies syntactic compatibility

$$A \Rrightarrow B \Rightarrow A \gg B$$

Each refinement relation is assumed to be a partial ordering. Of course this form of refinement should be compatible with the introduced notions of composition and abstraction.

$$M \Rrightarrow M' \Rightarrow \alpha_{\mathbb{F}}(M) \Rrightarrow_{\mathbb{F}} \alpha_{\mathbb{F}}(M') \qquad \textit{compatibility of refinement}$$

In mathematical terms, abstraction is monotonic for refinement (for $X \in \{\mathbf{F}, \; \text{SM}, \; \text{PRC}\}$).

$$M \Rrightarrow M' \wedge N \Rrightarrow N' \Rightarrow M \otimes N \Rrightarrow M' \otimes N' \quad \textit{compositionality of refinement}$$

In mathematical terms, composition is monotonic for refinement. By refinement we can relate models and parts of models.

### 4.3.2  Implementation as Refinement

Complex systems are modeled during development at different levels of abstraction and granularity. We work with a refinement relation to relate models at different levels of abstraction. One refinement direction in development is steps towards an implementation. Then we speak of an implementation relation. This relation can be introduced for all system views:

$$\Rrightarrow_{IF/SM}: F \times SM \to \mathbb{B}$$

We write

$$F \Rrightarrow_{IF/SM} M$$

to express that the state machine M implements the interface. In particular, we assume

$$\alpha_{SM/IF}(M) \Rrightarrow_{IF/SM} M \qquad\qquad\qquad \textit{correctness of refinement}$$

for each state machine M.

The implementation relation can also be introduced for the other system views such as the process and the state machine view:

$$\Rrightarrow_{IF/PRC}: F \times PRC \to \mathbb{B}$$

$$\Rrightarrow_{PRC/SM}: PRC \times SM \to \mathbb{B}$$

In addition, we may introduce such an implementation refinement relation also for state machines or composed systems.

Of course this form of refinement should be compatible with property refinement composition, and also abstraction.

$$F \Rrightarrow_{IF/SM} M' \Rightarrow F \approx \alpha(M')$$

$$F \Rrightarrow_{IF/SM} M \wedge F' \Rrightarrow_{IF/SM} M' \Rightarrow F \otimes_{IF} F' \Rrightarrow_{IF} M \otimes_{SM} M'$$

In principle, we could work with only one refinement relation, which is a general implementation refinement relation on system models

$$\Rrightarrow : HCS \times HCS \to \mathbb{B}$$

It formalizes the idea of implementation refinement for the set of all systems. Implementation refinement should be a special case of property refinement

$$M \Rrightarrow M' \Rightarrow M \approx M'$$

In implementation refinement the internal structure of a system is maintained.

### 4.3.3 Granularity Refinement: Levels of Abstractions

To study systems at different levels of abstraction and granularity we work with a specific refinement relation. This relation can be introduced for all system views:

$$\sim\!>_{IF}: F \times F \to \mathbb{B}$$

$$\sim\!>_{PRC}: PRC \times PRC \to \mathbb{B}$$

$$\sim\!>_{SM}: SM \times SM \to \mathbb{B}$$

In granularity refinement we do not assume that from $A \approx B$ we may conclude that $A \gg B$.

We assume granularity abstraction functions $\alpha$ and representation functions $\rho$. These are assumed to be partial functions. The abstraction function maps a concrete behavior onto its abstraction:

$$\alpha, \rho: \mathbb{F} \to \mathbb{F}$$

We require for all we interface behaviors $F \in \mathbb{F}$ for which $\rho(F)$ is defined

$$F = \alpha(\rho(F))$$

Clearly not every mapping between interfaces is to be called an abstraction. Particular behavioral properties are required. We require for all we interface behaviors $F \in \mathbb{F}$

$$\alpha(F) \sim_{\mathbb{F}} F$$

and that

$$F \sim_{\mathbb{F}} F'$$

only holds if there is an granularity abstraction $\alpha$ with

$$F = \alpha(F')$$

Nevertheless, this form of refinement should be compatible with composition and abstraction, too.

$$M \sim_{SM} M' \Rightarrow \alpha_{\mathbb{F}}(M) \sim_{\mathbb{F}} \alpha_{\mathbb{F}}(M')$$

The following property can expected only for abstraction functions $\alpha_1$ and $\alpha_2$ that fit together:

$$\alpha_1(F_1) \otimes_{\mathbb{F}} \alpha_2(F_2) \sim_{\mathbb{F}} F_1 \otimes_{\mathbb{F}} F_2$$

Property refinement should be a special case of granularity refinement

$$M \approx_{SM} M' \Rightarrow M \sim_{SM} M'$$

Note that implementation refinement is a special case of property refinement while granularity refinement is a generalization. In principle, we could work with only one refinement relation that is a generalization of all of the refinement relations introduced above. However, the individual refinement relations are more appropriate to reflect the role of these relations in the development process. This allows us to characterize refinement steps.

We assume a general granularity refinement relation on systems

$$\sim : \text{HCS} \times \text{HCS} \to \mathbb{B}$$

It formalizes the idea of granularity refinement for the set of all systems. It is based on the idea of interface abstraction and granularity of interface abstraction:

$$M \sim M' \equiv \alpha_{\mathbb{F}}(M) \sim_{\mathbb{F}} \alpha_{\mathbb{F}}(M')$$

For interfaces we assume that the mapping $\alpha$ is the identity. This way granularity interface refinement is used as a reference relation for granularity refinement for all kinds of systems.

### 4.3.4 Deployment

Typically composed software systems are distributed over a network of hardware units on which they are executed. Each software component is located on one particular hardware unit. We speak of deployment. It is one of the decisive steps in software development to determine the deployment of a system especially for distributed and embedded systems.

Deployment needs a more complex system model in which it can be expressed what it means that a software system is executed on a particular piece of hardware. However, our notion of a composed system and system hierarchy is already a concept that helps to express such a structure. We only have to characterize certain composed systems as hardware structures. Then we can express in our model that a number of subsystems is placed onto one (abstract) hardware unit.

## 4.4 Observation and Degrees of Abstraction

The critical parts of a system model are the interface abstraction functions. They determine the degree of abstraction that is provided by the concept of an interface. The better the abstraction is, the more helpful the method is. It is easy to introduce a partial ordering on abstractions. This allows us to speak about a greatest element and a least element in the family of abstractions.

Without any restriction on the abstractions we are allowed to abstract away everything. But then all state machines are considered to be the same. It is more appropriate to fix a notion of interface *observation,* which is then the basis of an interface abstraction. In a simple case the observation abstraction provides an interface abstraction that is compositional. But this is not true, in general. In the ideal case the interface abstraction is identical to the interface observation. But, in general, the interface abstraction is too abstract to guarantee compositionality. Then additional information has to be added to achieve compositionality.

Therefore given an observation abstraction we may look for an interface abstraction that contains all the information of the observation abstraction, but is compositional. The best (most radical) abstraction with this property is also called *fully abstract.*

## 4.5 Software Development as Modeling Tasks

From the very beginning, when analyzing and understanding a problem domain we start to work towards finding useful models. This goes on and on when we analyze use cases and their specifications, the software architecture, the modularization of the system and its implementation. Software development includes the modeling and description of various aspects, such as:

- application domains, their data structures, laws, and processes,
- software requirements, based on data models, functions, and processes,
- software architectures, their structure and principles,
- software components, their roles, interfaces, states, and behaviors,
- programs and modules, their internal structure, their runs and their implementation,
- test cases, their generality and usefulness.

If models are so important in software and systems engineering, a central question of course is, what is a model in software engineering?

- An annotated graph or diagram?
- A collection of class names, attributes, and method names?

In engineering, a model is always represented and described by a collection of formulas, diagrams, and tables as well as text expressed in some notation with a well-understood mathematical theory! In analogy, software engineering asks for mathematical modeling theories of digital systems – algebra, logic, model theory! Logic provides a unifying frame for that!

### 4.6  Scientific Foundations of Modeling in Software Development

As explained above in software development we perform the modeling (abstractions) by describing *views* in terms of *description techniques* at different *levels of abstractions*. In this activity we have to answer the following question:

- What aspects and properties of a system does a view address exactly?
- What is the meaning of a description technique?
- Which views are helpful for what?
- In which order should the views be worked out?
- How are views related?
- When are several views complimentary, redundant, or consistent?
- How can we combine several views into one comprehensive model?
- What are useful levels of abstraction?
- How are different levels of abstraction related?

These questions touch deep methodological and foundational issues. We concentrate in the sequel on more foundational topics. Our main concern in the following is a comprehensive setting of mathematical models and their integration, their relationships, and theory.

## 5  The Role of Description Techniques

In software development we could, in principle, use a plain mathematical notation. This is sometimes appropriate but often not very convenient, however, since notational conventions and fixed patterns of descriptions are helpful to keep model descriptions short and readable. Therefore description techniques are of major interest to the software engineer. In our case, where we depart from a system meta model, description techniques are a tuned notation for logical predicates that identify properties of a particular system in the class of all system models fixed by the meta model.

Practical software engineers often prefer the use of diagrams to textual notation such as in formulas and programming languages. The reason is quite evident. Engineers believe that diagrams are more telling, easier to understand and better to grasp. Whether this holds actually true is not so obvious and leads into a long, controversial discussion.

Nevertheless in some applications diagrams are certainly helpful. However, on the long run diagrams are only helpful if they are well based on a proper theory of understanding. Well-chosen models and their theories can provide such an understanding. Then the question whether to work with text, formula, tables, or diagram boils down to the mere question of syntactic presentation.

## 5.1 Practice Today: Diagrams

In practice, today we find many diagrammatic methods and description techniques for modeling and specification (SA, SADT, SSADM, JSD, SDL, OMT, UML, ROOM, ..., see [21], [11], [16], [2], [17]) in software and systems engineering. Especially UML has gained much attention.

The idea of universal modeling languages is certainly a great one - a closer look shows, however, how ad hoc most of these "methods" are especially those found in UML. At best, they reflect essential insights into the engineering of software applications. Never have these practical diagrammatic modeling techniques been justified on the basis of a comprehensive mathematical foundation. In contrast, only after the languages where published scientists work hard to define and explain the ad hoc constructs of modeling languages such as UML post mortem.

As a result the description techniques remain vague and imprecise. A basis and theory for the integration of the different views is missing.

## 5.2 Limitations of Diagrams

By a look at the state of the art we see that a lot of diagrams are used without a proper theory and without good support for understanding. To underline this remark we mention three weak examples (see also [22]):

1.  UML and its statecharts dialect with its endless discussions about its semantics.
2.  Behavior specification of interfaces of classes and components in object oriented modeling techniques in the presence of callbacks.
3.  Concurrency and co-operation: Most of the practical methods especially in object orientation seem to live in the good old days of sequential programming and do not properly address the needs of highly distributed, mobile, asynchronously co-operating software systems.

We need proper theories and methodological insights (see [18]) to overcome these shortcomings. And there is an inherent difficulty when dealing with diagrams. Theories can hardly be expressed solely by diagrams.

## 5.3 From Logic to Modeling Languages and Back to Logic

It is a disaster for academic informatics that it did not manage to design a modeling language that is used as widely as UML. The vision, however, remains – an academic, scientific view on modeling! How can we achieve that? We start from foundations: A tractable scientific basis, understanding, and theory for modeling, specifying, and refinement in programs, software and systems. On that basis we identify powerful models supporting levels of abstractions, multi-view modeling, and domain modeling. This leads to comprehensive description techniques properly based on scientific foundations. Thus we gain a family of justified engineering methods based on these foundations and finally a flexible development process model combining these methods.

All these are the necessary prerequisites for a comprehensive tool support in software development including specification refinement, validation, consistency checks, verification, and code generation by algorithms and methods justified by the theories. Finally we arrive at modeling and its theory as an integral part of software construction as an engineering discipline.

## 5.4  Formal Description Techniques

As said before in our approach each of the description techniques defines logical properties for the system under development. These may be a syntactical or a behavioral properties.

### 5.4.1  Logic Based Description

A straightforward way to write system descriptions is a direct use of a tuned logic. Examples are algebraic specifications (abstract data types), VDM, Z, or RAISE. Other examples are the many logic system models that work with structured operational semantics or with temporal logics.

### 5.4.2  From Diagrams to Logic

If diagrams fit well to a system model there is a straightforward translation of them into logic. This is useful for many reasons such as checking consistency and integration of description techniques. A simple and powerful approach is obtained by translating diagrammatic system descriptions schematically into logical formulas in terms of a system model. For that a system model is needed that is well chosen with respect to the spirit of the description technique.

A second option is the introduction of a logical theory that supports the deduction of logical propositions. Then an axiomatisation of this theory is needed.

## 6  Summary and Outlook

Why did we present this setting of mathematical models and relations between them? First of all, we want to show how rich and flexible the tool kit of mathematical model is and how far we are in integrating and relating them. Perhaps, it should be emphasized that the we get first of all an integrated system model very close to practical approaches by SDL or UML where a system is a set or hierarchy of components. In this tree of components the leaves are state machines. In our case the usage of streams and stream processing function is the reason for the remarkable flexibility of our model toolkit and the simplicity of the integration.

Software development is a difficult and complex engineering task. It would be very surprising if such a task could be carried out properly without a proper theoretical framework. It would at the same time be quite surprising if a purely scientifically theoretical framework would be the right approach for the practical engineer. The result has to be a compromise as we have argued between formal techniques and theory on one side and intuitive notations based on diagrams. Work is needed along those lines including experiments and feedback from practical applications. But as our example and experiment already show a lot is to be gained that way.

Theory and practical understanding are the key to mature software development. To achieve that we need a much deeper and more intensive interaction between researchers working on the foundations, the designers of practical engineering methods and tools, the programmers and engineers in charge of practical solutions, and application experts modeling application domains. Successful work and progress along the lines described above does not only require the interaction between these types of people - it also needs *hybrid* people that have a deep understanding in all three of these areas.

# References

[1] Baeten, J.C.M., Bergstra, J.: Process Algebras with Signals and Conditions. In: Broy, M. (ed.) Programming and Mathematical Method. Springer NATO ASI Series, Series F: Computer and System Sciences, vol. 88, pp. 273–324. Springer, Heidelberg (1992)

[2] Booch, G.: Object Oriented Design with Applications. Benjamin Cummings, Redwood City, CA (1991)

[3] Broy, M., Deißenböck, F., Pizka, M.: A Holistic Approach to Software Quality at Work. In: 3rd World Congress for Software Quality (3WCSQ)

[4] Broy, M.: Refinement of Time. In: Bertran, M., Rus, T. (eds.) AMAST-ARTS 1997, ARTS 1997, and AMAST-WS 1997. LNCS, vol. 1231, pp. 44–63. Springer, Heidelberg (1997) Also in TCS

[5] Broy, M., Rausch, A.: Das Neue V-Modell XT, Informatik Spektrum, Band 28, Heft 3, Juni (2005)

[6] Broy, M., Stølen, K.: Specification and Development of Interactive Systems: Focus on Streams, Interfaces, and Refinement. Springer, Heidelberg (2001)

[7] Berry, G., Gonthier, G.: The Esterel Synchronous Programming Language: Design, Semantics, Implementation. INRIA, Research Report 842 (1988)

[8] Harel, D.: Statecharts: A Visual Formalism for Complex Systems. Science of Computer Programming 8, 231–274 (1987)

[9] Hettler, R.: Zur Übersetzung von E/R-Schemata nach Spectrum. Technischer Bericht TUM-I9409, TU München (1994)

[10] Hoare, C.A.R.: Communicating Sequential Processes. Prentice Hall, Englewood Cliffs (1985)

[11] Jacobsen, I.: Object-Oriented Software Engineering. Addison-Wesley, ACM Press, Reading (1992)

[12] Kahn, G.: The Semantics of a Simple Language for Parallel Processing. In: Rosenfeld, J.L. (ed.) Information Processing 74. Proc. of the IFIP Congress 74, pp. 471–475. North Holland, Amsterdam (1974)

[13] Milner, R. (ed.) A Calculus of Communication Systems. LNCS, vol. 92. Springer, Heidelberg (1980)

[14] ITU-T (previously CCITT) Criteria for the Use and Applicability of Formal Description Techniques. Recommendation Z. 120, Message Sequence Chart (MSC), p. 35 (March 1993)

[15] ITU-T. Recommendation Z.120, Annex B: Algebraic Semantics of Message Sequence Charts. ITU-Telecommunication Standardization Sector, Geneva, Switzerland (1995)

[16] Selic, B., Gullekson, G., Ward, P.T.: Real-time Objectoriented Modeling. Wiley, New York (1994)

[17] Rumbaugh, J.: Object-Oriented Modelling and Design. Prentice Hall, Englewood Cliffs: New Jersey (1991)

[18]  Rumpe, B.: Formale Methodik des Entwurfs verteilter objektorientierter Systeme. Ph.D. Thesis Technische Universität München, Fakultät für Informatik. Published by Herbert Utz Verlag (1996)

[19]  Specification and Description Language (SDL), Recommendation Z.100. Technical Report, CCITT (1988)

[20]  Broy, M., Facchi, C., Hettler, R., Hußmann, H., Nazareth, D., Regensburger, F., Slotosch, O., Stølen, K.: The Requirement and Design Specification Language Spectrum. An Informal Introduction. Version 1.0. Part I/II Technische Universität München, Institut für Informatik, TUM-I9311 / TUM-I9312 (May 1993)

[21]  Booch, G., Rumbaugh, J., Jacobson, I.: The Unified Modeling Language for Object-Oriented Development, Version 1.0, RATIONAL Software Cooperation

[22]  Zave, P., Jackson, M.: Four dark corners of requirements engineering. ACM Transactions on Software Engineering and Methodology (1997)

# A Denotational Semantics for Handel-C

Andrew Butterfield

Trinity College Dublin
Andrew.Butterfield@cs.tcd.ie

**Abstract.** We present a denotational semantics for a fully functional subset of the Handel-C hardware compilation language [1], based on the concept of typed assertion traces. We motivate the choice of semantic domains by illustrating the complexities of the behaviour of the language, paying particular attention to the `prialt` (priority-alternation) construct of Handel-C. We then define the typed assertion traces over an abstract notion of actions, which we then instantiate as state-transformers. The denotational semantics is then given and some examples are discussed. As is fitting given those honoured at the Festschrift of which this paper is a part, we show how the work of both Dines Björner and Zhou Chaochen act as inspiration, from the past, into the future for this research work.

## 1 Introduction

This paper describes a denotational semantics for Handel-C which gives a program a meaning as a set of "Typed Assertion Traces".

Handel-C[1][1] is a language originally developed by the Hardware Compilation Group at Oxford University Computing Laboratory, and now marketed by Celoxica Ltd. It is a hybrid of CSP [2] and C, designed to target hardware implementations, specifically field-programmable gate arrays (FPGAs) [3]. The language has sequential and parallel constructs and global variable assignment and channel communication. The language targets synchronous hardware with multiple clock domains. All assignments and channel communication events take one clock cycle. All expression and conditional evaluations, as well as priority resolutions are deemed to be instantaneous, effectively being completed before the current clock-cycle ends.

We see the final semantics of Handel-C as having four components: types; priorities; synchronous cores; and the asynchronous environment. A detailed description of these and their motivation is given in [4]. Here we simply stress that this paper is primarily concerned with the semantics of the synchronous cores, incorporating priorities. The topics of typing and the external asynchronous interface are beyond the scope of this paper.

We first introduce the language, then describe prior and related work in this area, before motivating and describing the domains used for our denotational semantics.

---

[1] Handel-C is the registered trademark of Celoxica Ltd (www.celoxica.com).

C.B. Jones, Z. Liu, J. Woodcock (Eds.): Bjørner/Zhou Festschrift, LNCS 4700, pp. 45–66, 2007.

## 2   The Language

We introduce here the "mathematical" version of a stripped-down Handel-C, which albeit simpler, has all the essential features of the full language.

### 2.1   Syntax

We have variables ($x \in Var$), and we assume the existence of an expression syntax ($e \in Exp$) whose details need not concern us here. We also have identifiers for channels ($c \in Ch$), and we consider all the above as having either boolean or integer type, and occasionally use $b$ to denote a boolean-valued expression. We also have the notion of guards ($g \in Grd$), which denote the offering and accepting of communication actions. Guards either denote a desire to perform output of an expression's value along a channel ($c!e$), to receive input via a channel into a variable ($c?x$), or a skip/default guard which always succeeds ($!?$).

$$g \in G ::= c?v \mid c!e \mid !?$$

A syntax of a process $p : Proc$ is as follows:

$$
\begin{aligned}
p ::= &\ \mathbf{0} \mid \mathbf{1} \mid x := e \\
&\mid p_1 \,;\, p_2 \mid p_1 \parallel p_2 \mid p_1 \vartriangleleft b \vartriangleright p_2 \mid b * p \\
&\mid \langle g_i \to p_i \rangle_{i \in 1 \ldots n}
\end{aligned}
$$

The last clause is shorthand for a list of guard-process pairs.

### 2.2   Behaviour

We can briefly summarise the behaviour of a Handel-C process as follows: $\mathbf{0}$ does nothing, in zero time; $\mathbf{1}$ does nothing, but takes one clock cycle to do it; $x := e$ assigns the value of $e$ into $x$, taking one clock cycle; ($p_1 \,;\, p_2$) first executes $p_1$, and once it has terminated immediately starts $p_2$; ($p_1 \parallel p_2$) runs both $p_1$ and $p_2$ in lock-step parallel, terminating when they have both finished; ($p_1 \vartriangleleft b \vartriangleright p_2$) evaluates $b$ and executes $p_1$ immediately if $b$ is *True*, otherwise it runs $p_2$; and $b * P$ tests $b$ and if *True* it runs $P$ and then repeats, otherwise it terminates.

The $\langle g_i \to p_i \rangle$ construct ("prialt") is an ordered sequence of guard-process pairs. Guards are either communication actions or a default guard to be activated if no communication guard is active. The default guard, if present, must be last. The sequence of guards in a `prialt` denotes that `prialt`'s priority preference, considered as *relative priority* — i.e. it prefers its first guard to its second, its second to its third, and so on.

Each guard is checked against the process environment to see if it is able to execute. If no guards are so enabled, then the prialt blocks until the next clock cycle when it tries again. If one or more guards are enabled, then the first such in the list is executed, and then the corresponding process is executed. An input guard ($c?x$) is enabled if there is a corresponding output guard ($c!e$) in some other prialt executing at the same time, and *vice versa*. The default guard (!?) is always enabled. The input (*c*?*x*) and output (*c*!*e*) guards perform their actions taking one clock-cycle, while the default guard (!?) acts in "zero-time", so the subsequent process starts execution immediately. It is this "instant" execution of !? guards that so complicates the formal semantics of Handel-C, as discussed extensively in [5].

## 2.3 Restrictions

We have a mix of parallel processes and global shared variables, so Handel-C has a restriction which states that no variable should ever be assigned to by two different processes during one clock cycle. It is allowable to have different processes write to the same variable on different clock cycles. The Handel-C language reference manual [1] states that different parallel processes generally should not write to the same variable, but that if they do, the programmer has a proof obligation to show that these writes never occur during the same clock cycle.

This extends to disallowing the simultaneous writing of two different values to the same channel — however having multiple readers of a channel at any one time is permitted.

Another key restriction imposed by Handel-C is that during any clock-cycle, all the relative priorities of all **prialts** executing during that cycle must be consistent with one another in that no priority cycles are introduced when all their preferences are merged.

## 3   Previous and Related Work

Early work on the formal semantics of Handel-C concentrated on a subset of the language that did not contain the **prialt** construct [6,7]. The approach adopted was in the style of the "Irish School" of the VDM [8] which drew its inspiration from the pioneering work in VDM of Dines Björner and his colleagues [9].

However it soon became clear that **prialt** would have to be included. It cannot be simulated using ordinary communication and switch statements, and it has a number of effects on the overall semantics. Also, we viewed the task of developing a formal semantics for Handel-C as being an true exercise in domain modelling [10,11], as our intention was to model an existing artefact, warts and all, rather than construct a nice simple well-behaved hardware process algebra.

A formal description of **prialt** resolution without consideration of default clauses was presented in [12]. An initial denotational semantics was developed [13] which incorporated this **prialt** resolution semantics. Then the **prialt** model of [12] was then extended to handle default clauses properly and an operational semantics for Handel-C incorporating this was developed [4,5]. The operational semantics had to introduce a notion of prioritised transitions in order to correctly capture the behaviour of default guards. This additional notion of priority was completely different and orthogonal to the priorities expressed by the **prialt** construct.

Priority in concurrent processes is difficult to treat formally but many examples abound, in both the CSP setting [14,15,16,17]. and in the more general process algebra areas [18,19,20]. The CSP treatment either fails to handle recursion, or is too complex and general, while the more general process algebra work is closer to what is required. Unfortunately, priority in Handel-C does not fit neatly into the priority schemes that have been considered, as described in [20]

Other work involving formal techniques and Handel-C has been reported, and includes the use of the Ponder policy specification language [21] as a basis for implementing firewalls [22], as well as techniques for performing behavioural transformations from Haskell programs into Handel-C implementations [23]. Beyond the scope of Handel-C, there is considerable work on using formal techniques to develop safety-critical embedded systems, of which the languages Esterel [24,25,26] and Lustre [27,28] are two key examples.

## 4   Overview of `prialt` Semantics

We present here a brief overview of the `prialt` semantics presented in [5], with an explanation of how it can be interfaced with the denotational semantics described later on in this paper.

In any given clock cycle, there will be zero or more `prialts` commencing execution. A guard is deemed to be potentially active if elsewhere there is a complementary guard in some other `prialt` active during the same clock cycle. The process of determining which guards, if any, become active, is called *Resolution*.

In [12] resolution is viewed formally as a function *Resolve* that takes a set of *Prialt Requests* (*PriSet*), and returns a pair called a *Resolution* (*Resltn*), consisting of an *Channel-Prialt Map* (*CPMap*) and the set of `prialts` that have remained blocked.

$$PriSet = \mathcal{P}\,Prialt$$
$$CPMap = Ch \rightarrow PriSet$$
$$Resltn = CPMap \times PriSet$$
$$Resolve \; : \; PriSet \rightarrow Resltn$$

A Prialt Request is simply modelled as a sequence of guards, i.e simply as the corresponding `prialt`-statement with the continuation processes stripped out. The Channel-Prialt Map identifies which channels are going to be active and maps them to those `prialts` which will participate in communication over that channel.

In order to model the semantics of `prialt`, we view a clock-cycle as being composed of four phases: selection (*sel*); request (*req*); resolve (*res*); and action (*act*). During the selection phase, flow of control decisions are taken by evaluating conditions for if-statements and while-loops. During the request phase, any `prialts` which have been selected lodge their prioritised communication requests in a central location. Once all this has occurred, the resolve phase determines which communication requests are going to be granted. In the action phase, all the assignment statements selected earlier, and all the communication actions just resolved, are carried out simultaneously. The clock tick signals the end of the action phase.

The set of `prialts` that are input to *Resolve* are those lodged centrally during the request phase. Conceptually, resolution occurs at the transition between the request and resolution phases and results in the two outputs as mentioned above. During the resolution phase, the resulting channel-map and blocked `prialt`-sets are examined to determine what activities will occur.

Let us consider an example involving default clauses in that manner that causes most semantic difficulty. This example has two `prialts` in parallel, with the second having a default clause which itself contains a statement that subsequently invokes a `prialt`:

$$\langle\, c!66 \rightarrow \mathbf{0}\,\rangle \,\|\, \langle\, d!99 \rightarrow \mathbf{0},\ !? \rightarrow (\, b * P;\ \langle c?x \rightarrow \mathbf{0}\rangle\,)\,\rangle$$

Let us consider the case where $b$ happens to be false. Initially we have a situation where there are no potentially active guards, so the first `prialt` blocks, while the second immediately activates its default clause. The while-loop has a false condition, so immediately terminates, and this introduces another `prialt` to the mix. At this point the program has evolved to look like this:

$$\langle\, c!66 \rightarrow \mathbf{0}\,\rangle \,\|\, \langle\, c?x \rightarrow \mathbf{0}\,\rangle$$

This requires us to lodge a new request, with the existing ones still in place, and to re-perform the resolution step. As a result, channel $c$ becomes active, transferring value 66 across to variable $x$.

Prialts nested inside default clauses of other prialts may become active in the same clock cycle as those enclosing prialts, which requires us to iterate the *sel–req–res* loop several times, in any given clock cycle. Managing this micro-cycle activity severely complicates the semantics[2].

# 5  Semantic Framework

The "prialt-free" denotational semantics in [13], inspired by [29], was based on the notion of "branching sequences" or trees, where non-branching sequences denoted deterministic sequences of actions, and branching was used to model a choice point, such as the conditions of a while-loop or if-statement.

However, this model becomes far too complex when faced with the need to handle multiple choice points per clock-cycle, so the full semantics described here is given in terms of sets of "typed assertion traces". These are sets of sequences of actions (state-transformers), each action typed according to the phase in which

---

[2] Interestingly, the underlying hardware doesn't iterate, as it computes what is to be active in any given clock cycle using combinatorial logic.

it occurs $(sel,req,res,act)$, with an assertion that indicates the conditions under which that action (and all subsequent) may proceed.

This switch also brings the semantics more in line with that of Circus [30] and its slotted variants [31], fitting in with plans to give a complete account of Handel-C and hardware compilation in the UTP framework [32].

## 5.1 Abstraction of Action, States and Predicates

We shall now present an abstract view of typed assertion traces, where actions $(a : Act)$ with an action merge operator $\Diamond$ form a commutative monoid, with the "null" action nop as identity.

$$\mathbf{Mon}(Act, \Diamond, \mathsf{nop})$$

We the introduce an abstract notion of a state $(s \in St)$ as something which can change as a result of actions, and denote the effect of action $a$ on state $s$ by $\triangle[a](s)$. The null action, not unexpectedly, brings about no change of state:

$$\triangle : Act \to St \to St \qquad \triangle[\mathsf{nop}](s) = s$$

We need predicates over states (assertions), with *true* and *false* denoting the everywhere true and false predicates respectively:

$$p \in Pred = St \to \mathbb{B}$$

We are going to capture the linkage between assertions and actions by the concept of a "guarded-action" $(g)$, which is a predicate-action pair $(p, e)$:

$$g, (p, a) \in GA = Pred \times Act$$

We will frequently deal with cases where either the guard is *true* or the action is nop, so we adopt the shorthands where $a$ denotes $(true, a)$ and $\underline{p}$ denotes $(p, \mathsf{nop})$. In particular we often refer to *true* as a null or void action.

We can extend the notion of action-merging to guarded actions in the obvious way by merging the actions and taking the conjunction of the predicates:

$$(p_1, a_1) \Diamond (p_2, a_2) \;\widehat{=}\; (p_1 \wedge p_2, a_1 \Diamond a_2)$$

These guarded actions are the basic building blocks for "assertion traces", so the next step is to describe the typing aspects.

## 5.2 Typed Assertion Traces

We shall view a trace as being a non-empty sequence of slots, were each slot denotes the activity during one complete clock cycle. We allow traces to be either finite or infinite, as this is required for the semantics of any of the loop constructs.

$$\tau \in Trc = Slot^* \cup Slot^\omega$$

The semantics of a Handel-C program is mapped to a set of these traces, which conform to a set of healthiness conditions to be mentioned later.

Slots have internal structure, and are divided into two components: the decision actions which occur early in the clock cycle to determine the course of action to take; and the permanent state-change actions which all occur simultaneously at the end of the clock cycle. The former are modelled as sequences of "microslots" (*MS*), whilst the latter can simply be represented as a single (merged) guarded action. We shall refer to the second component as the "final action" of the slot

$$s, (\mu, a) \in Slot = MS^* \times GA$$

A microslot ($m$) captures the actions in one cycle of selection-request-response and hence is is a triple of guarded actions $(s, q, r)$, where the first ($s$) are of type *sel*, the second ($q$) are of type *req*, and the last ($r$) are of type *res*:

$$m, (s, q, r) \in MS = GA^3$$

We expect that any microslot has at least one non-null action present.

We need to be careful how traces and slots are interpreted: In essence, a slot where the final action is null denotes the case were the clock-tick which ends the slot has yet to happen. As a consequence of this interpretation, only the last slot in a trace can be "tick-free" in this manner. T

We need to be able to identify a null slot, as one with no microslots, and a null final-action:

$$\text{nils} \ : \ Slot$$
$$\text{nils} \ \widehat{=} \ (\langle\rangle, \underline{true})$$

A trace in which no actions, not even a clock-tick, have occurred, is denoted by a singleton sequence consisting of one null slot. The reason for not admitting empty trace sequences is that it introduces ambiguity over interpreting null traces, and complicates the definition of various concatenation operators.

We also need to identify a slot whose only action is an final-action which denotes a clock-tick — we overload the notation $\ddagger$ to denote both such a clock-tick action, and the corresponding slot. We also expect that merging this action with any non-null action will result in that non-null action:

$$\ddagger : Act \qquad \ddagger \Diamond a = a, \qquad a \neq \text{nop}$$
$$\ddagger : Slot \qquad \ddagger \ \widehat{=} \ (\langle\rangle, \ddagger)$$

**Typing.** The typing of actions in slots and microslots is implicitly given by the actions' position. We can extend the notion of typing to cover both microslots and slots themselves.

Transition types fall into four categories, with an ordering as indicated:

$$t \in TType \ \widehat{=} \ \{ sel, req, res, act \}$$
$$sel < req < res < act$$

We define the type of a microslot as the type of the least non-empty action present:

$$ttype_{MS} \; : \; MS \to TType$$
$$ttype_{MS}(\underline{true}, \underline{true}, \_) \; \widehat{=} \; res$$
$$ttype_{MS}(\underline{true}, \_, \_) \; \widehat{=} \; req$$
$$ttype_{MS}(\_, \_, \_) \; \widehat{=} \; sel$$

We define the type of a *Slot* as the type of the first of the microslots, if present, otherwise it is *act*.

$$ttype_S \; : \; Slot \to TType$$
$$ttype_S(\langle\rangle, (p, \_)) \; \widehat{=} \; act$$
$$ttype_S((m : \_), \_) \; \widehat{=} \; ttype_{MS}(m)$$

## 5.3   Trace Operators

We now describe a series of operators which can be used to build and join traces and their building blocks.

**Building with Single Actions.** The first are a series of constructors that construct slots of the various types from a single guarded action and accompanying transition type. We shall refer to the combination of a transition type and guarded action as a *typed action*.

Given a non-*act*, non-void action, we wish to build the corresponding microslot:

$$mkm \; : \; TType \to GA \to MS$$
$$mkm_{sel}(g) \; \widehat{=} \; (g, \underline{true}, \underline{true})$$
$$mkm_{req}(g) \; \widehat{=} \; (\underline{true}, g, \underline{true})$$
$$mkm_{res}(g) \; \widehat{=} \; (\underline{true}, \underline{true}, g)$$

Given a typed action we wish to build the corresponding slot, where the action can be null only if of type *act*:

$$mks \; : \; TType \to GA \to Slot$$
$$mks_{act}(g) \; \widehat{=} \; (\langle\rangle, g)$$
$$mks_t(g) \; \widehat{=} \; (\langle mkm_t(g)\rangle, \underline{true})$$

**Lifting Action Merging.** We want to lift the action merge operators to work with microslots.

We will want to merge a single guarded non-*act* action into a pre-existing microslot:

$$-\Diamond_{-\,-} \quad : \quad GA \times TType \times MS \to MS$$

$$g \, \Diamond_{sel} \, (s, q, r) \; \hat{=} \; (g \, \Diamond \, s, q, r)$$
$$g \, \Diamond_{req} \, (s, q, r) \; \hat{=} \; (s, g \, \Diamond \, q, r)$$
$$g \, \Diamond_{res} \, (s, q, r) \; \hat{=} \; (s, q, g \, \Diamond \, r)$$

We describe the merging of two microslots later when the parallel construct is discussed.

**Typed Cons-ing.** By "typed cons-ing" (:: or $::_t$) we mean the process of placing a typed action at the start of an existing list of actions, at the microslot, slot or trace level. We first consider cons-ing a non-*act*, non-null action into a microslot or slots. If the action has a type greater than that of the microslot, then we have to create a new microslot immediately prior to the given one, containing the action. This is because "consing" means pre-pending an earlier action, so if an action of type *res* (say) is being placed in front of a microslot containing *sel* or *req* actions, then it must have occurred in an earlier microslot. This is why the signature of the function indicates that merging a typed action with a microslot may result in more than one microslot as a result.

$$-\,::_{-\,-} \quad : \quad GA \to TType \to MS \to MS^+$$
$$g \, ::_t \, m \; \hat{=} \; \textbf{if} \; t > ttype_{MS}(m)$$
$$\textbf{then} \; \langle mkm_t(g), m \rangle \; \textbf{else} \; \langle g \, \Diamond_t \, m \rangle$$

We can extend this to work with microslot sequences in the obvious way:

$$-\,::_{-\,-} \quad : \quad GA \to TType \to MS^* \to MS^*$$
$$g \, ::_t \, \langle \rangle \; \hat{=} \; \langle mkm_t(g) \rangle$$
$$g \, ::_t \, (m : \mu) \; \hat{=} \; (g \, ::_t \, m) \,^\frown \mu$$

We can now extend type-consing to slots and traces, in which case we can now handle *act*-actions. Consing an *act*-action always creates a new slot at the front:

$$-\,::_{-\,-} \quad : \quad GA \to TType \to Slot \to Slot^+$$
$$g \, ::_{act} \, s \; \hat{=} \; \langle mk_{act}(g), s \rangle$$
$$g \, ::_t \, (\mu, a) \; \hat{=} \; \langle (g \, ::_t \, \mu, a) \rangle$$
$$-\,::_{-\,-} \quad : \quad GA \to TType \to Trc \to Trc$$
$$g \, ::_t \, (s : \tau) \; \hat{=} \; (g \, ::_t \, s) \,^\frown \tau$$

**Concatenation for Microslots.** We can now define a form of concatenation for microslots ($\frac{\circ}{9}$) which merges the last microslot of the first sequence (*ante-slot*) with the first microslot of the second (*post-slot*), if possible. This is possible when no action in the ante-slot has a type greater than that of an action in the post-slot. We first define an operator ($\boxplus$) taking a pair of micro-slots to a sequence of same:

$$\_ \boxplus \_ \; : \; MS^2 \to MS^*$$
$$(s_1, \underline{true}, \underline{true}) \boxplus (s_2, q_2, r_2) \; \widehat{=} \; \langle (s_1 \lozenge s_2, q_2, r_2) \rangle$$
$$(s_1, q_1, \underline{true}) \boxplus (\underline{true}, q_2, r_2) \; \widehat{=} \; \langle (s_1, q_1 \lozenge q_2, r_2) \rangle$$
$$(s_1, q_1, r_1) \boxplus (\underline{true}, \underline{true}, r_2) \; \widehat{=} \; \langle (s_1, q_1, r_1 \lozenge r_2) \rangle$$
$$m_1 \boxplus m_2 \; \widehat{=} \; \langle m_1, m_2 \rangle$$

We then define microslot-sequence catenation using the binary merge-slot operator:

$$\_ \overset{\circ}{\circ} \_ \; : \; MS^* \times MS^* \to MS^*$$
$$\langle \rangle \overset{\circ}{\circ} \mu_2 \; \widehat{=} \; \mu_2$$
$$\mu_1 \overset{\circ}{\circ} \langle \rangle \; \widehat{=} \; \mu_1$$
$$\langle m_1 \rangle \overset{\circ}{\circ} (m_2 : \mu_2) \; \widehat{=} \; (m_1 \boxplus m_2) \frown \mu_2$$
$$(m_1 : \mu_1) \overset{\circ}{\circ} \mu_2 \; \widehat{=} \; m_1 : (\mu_1 \overset{\circ}{\circ} \mu_2)$$

**Consing Slots onto Traces.** We now consider the task of cons-ing a *Slot* onto the start of a *Trc* in order to extend the *Trc*. Here, no type is specified, but instead is inferred from the slot contents.

The only time this differs from ordinary list cons is when the trailing trace is a singleton null slot or the slot is null or has no *act* action:

$$\_ :: \_ \; : \; Slot \times Trc \to Trc$$
$$s :: \langle \text{nils} \rangle \; \widehat{=} \; \langle s \rangle$$
$$\text{nils} :: \tau \; \widehat{=} \; \tau$$
$$(\mu, \underline{true}) :: ((\nu, a') : \tau) \; \widehat{=} \; ((\mu \overset{\circ}{\circ} \nu), a') : \tau$$
$$s :: \tau \; \widehat{=} \; s : \tau$$

**Catenation of Traces.** We can now define trace catenation in terms of slot-consing:

$$\_ \overset{\circ}{\circ} \_ \; : \; Trc \times Trc \to Trc$$
$$\langle \rangle \overset{\circ}{\circ} \tau_2 \; \widehat{=} \; \tau_2$$
$$\langle s \rangle \overset{\circ}{\circ} \tau_2 \; \widehat{=} \; s :: \tau_2$$
$$(s_1 : \tau_1) \overset{\circ}{\circ} \tau_2 \; \widehat{=} \; s_1 : (\tau_1 \overset{\circ}{\circ} \tau_2)$$

Traces are non-empty, but the first clause is needed simply to handle a base case properly for the definition of the operator. We want the null trace to be an identity for trace catenation, and trace catenation to be associative.

## 5.4   Merging Traces in Parallel

Merging traces in parallel is straightforward — they are merged on a slot by slot basis, with slots merged on a micro-slot by micro-slot basis. We overload the notation $\|$ for all these forms of parallel merging, except trace parallel merge which we denote by $[\![]\!]$.

All these operators are associative and commutative, and the null-trace is the identity for $[\![]\!]$. It is in order to get these properties that we require action merging itself to be both associative and commutative.

Merging two microslots in parallel simply involves merging the corresponding components:

$$ \_\,\|\,\_ \; : \; MS \times MS \to MS $$
$$ (s_1, q_1, r_1) \,\|\, (s_2, q_2, r_2) \;\widehat{=}\; (s_1 \lozenge s_2, q_1 \lozenge q_2, r_1 \lozenge r_2) $$

Merging microslot-sequences in parallel ($\|$) is done on a microslot by microslot basis, but not by merging matching pairs starting at the front of both lists, but rather by matching the ends of the lists together with the front of the longer list simply being copied to the result:

$$ \_\,\|\,\_ \; : \; MS^* \times MS^* \to MS^* $$
$$ \mu_1 \,\|\, \mu_2 \;\widehat{=}\; \mathtt{rev}((\mathtt{rev}\,\mu_1)\ \mathsf{mssaux}\ (\mathtt{rev}\,\mu_2)) $$
$$ \langle\rangle\ \mathsf{mssaux}\ \mu_2 \;\widehat{=}\; \mu_2 $$
$$ \mu_1\ \mathsf{mssaux}\ \langle\rangle \;\widehat{=}\; \mu_1 $$
$$ (m_1 : \mu_1)\ \mathsf{mssaux}\ (m_2 : \mu_2) \;\widehat{=}\; (m_1 \,\|\, m_2) : (\mu_1\ \mathsf{mssaux}\ \mu_2) $$

This counterintuitive notion of parallel merge ("merge from the back") was discovered as part of work animating these semantics[33] by encoding them in Haskell [34]. The reason for merging in this way is to ensure that all decisions are made as late as they possibly can be made, in particular to ensure that all the prialts involved in generating microcycles are complete before final communication resolution is done. Intuitively, this reflects how, in the real hardware implementations of Handel-C, we are waiting for combinatorial logic to settle before the clock edge marking the end of the cycle, and the occurrence of the *act*-actions.

To parallel merge slots, we simply parallel-merge the microslots and action-merge the actions:

$$ \_\,\|\,\_ \; : \; Slot \times Slot \to Slot $$
$$ (\mu_1, a_1) \,\|\, (\mu_2, a_2) \;\widehat{=}\; (\mu_1 \,\|\, \mu_2, a_1 \lozenge a_2) $$

To merge a pair of traces we proceed on a slot-by-slot basis, and copy the longer tail over if the traces are of different length.

$$ \_\,[\![]\!]\,\_ \; : \; Trc \times Trc \to Trc $$
$$ \langle\rangle\ [\![]\!]\ \tau_2 \;\widehat{=}\; \tau_2 $$
$$ \tau_1\ [\![]\!]\ \langle\rangle \;\widehat{=}\; \tau_1 $$
$$ (s_1 : \tau_1)\ [\![]\!]\ (s_2 : \tau_2) \;\widehat{=}\; (s_1 \,\|\, s_2) : (\tau_1\ [\![]\!]\ \tau_2) $$

Unlike the microslot-sequence case, here we do merge slot-sequences from the front.

## 5.5  Framework Summary

We have defined a notion of guarded actions, and microslots capturing sequences of *sel*, *req* and *res* actions, as well as slots which put these before a clock-cycle terminating action action. We have defined traces as non-empty lists of such slots, with all but the last slot obliged to have an action action, and defined trace concatenation ($\S$) and parallel merge ($[\![]\!]$) operators. Both have monoid properties, with the null trace as identity, and $[\![]\!]$ also being commutative.

# 6  Execution State

We now turn our attention to the actions of the previous section, and elaborate how these are in fact state-transformers. To this end, we first need to understand what is meant by the state of a Handel-C program.

## 6.1  Environments

We follow the classical approach for imperative languages in that the state is an "environment": a mapping from identifiers to values. We differ in that while some identifiers denote program variables, others have special meaning and correspond to internal processing carried out during a clock-cycle, largely to do with processing `prialt` communication requests.

We define identifiers (*Id*) to be either variable names (*Var*) or one of four special identifiers $\tau, \Re, \gamma$ or $B$, not present in *Var*. We define a value space (*Val*) to contain integers, booleans and an error value (?), and then define a datum type as being either a value, a function *Fun*, or one of the three types associated with `prialt` resolution, namely *Resltn*, *CPMap* and *PriSet*:

$$i \in Id \ \hat{=} \ Var + \{\, \tau, \Re, \gamma, B \,\}$$
$$Val \ \hat{=} \ \mathbb{Z} + \mathbb{B} + \{\, ? \,\}$$
$$f \in Fun \ \hat{=} \ Var \to Val$$
$$d \in Datum \ \hat{=} \ Val + Fun + Resltn + CPMap + PriSet$$

Although we have used disjoint union or sum above, in the sequel we do not explicitly show the relevant injections, so that we interpret a value $x : \mathbb{Z}$ as also being a value $x : Val$, or even $x : Datum$, rather than writing the more pedantic but verbose forms of $inj_1(x) : Val$ and $inj_1(inj_1(x)) : Datum$.

We define an environment $\rho$ as a mapping from identifiers to data, subject to the proviso that variables map only to values, $\Re$ maps only to *Resltns*, and $\gamma$ and $B$ map respectively to the *CPMap* and *PriGrp* components of $\rho(\Re)$:

$$\rho \in Env \ \hat{=} \ Id \to Datum$$

We denote the updating of a map $\rho$ so that $i$ now maps to $d$ by $\rho \dagger \{i \mapsto d\}$

The identifer $\tau$ is used to denote the clock-tick or clock-cycle count, so it is best viewed as mapping to an integer—however the associated value and its type is simply immaterial, as will become apparent later on.

Data items of type *Fun* do not form part of the state, but are used as a technical device to capture the fact that expressions in channel output guards are evaluated when that guard goes "live", if ever.

Expression evaluation w.r.t an environment is defined in the normal way, and returns a result of type *Datum* that is not itself of type *Fun*:

$$\mathcal{E} \; : \; Exp \rightarrow Env \rightarrow Datum$$

$$\mathcal{E}[\![e]\!]\rho \; \hat{=} \; \text{"standard" expression evaluation...}$$

Note however, that the partial application $\mathcal{E}[\![e]\!]$, where $e$ denotes a value of type *Val*, can be interpreted as a *Datum* value result of (sub-)type *Fun*.

## 6.2  Static State

The "static state" of a Handel-C program is that part of the state which persists across clock-cycle boundaries, and its evolution over those time-slots is what constitutes the observable behaviour of a Handel-C program.

For any Handel-C program, we simply identify all the variables used, in assignments, expressions, and channel inputs. We then tailor the environment so that its domain contains precisely those variables.

## 6.3  Dynamic State

The dynamic state is that which only exists within one clock cycle, and is effectively "zeroed" at every clock tick. It contains information about communication requests and is that part of the environment accessed by the identifiers $\Re, \gamma$ and $B$.

At the start of each clock cycle, these are initialised to be empty:

$$\rho(\gamma) = \theta \qquad \rho(B) = \emptyset \qquad \rho(\Re) = (\theta, \emptyset)$$

## 6.4  Actions for Handel-C

We want our actions to be state-transformers, that is functions from state to state, and we need to define the null action (nop), as well as explaining how actions merge ($\Diamond$).

**Actions.** Formally our actions are functions mapping environments into environments, and the null action is simply the identity function on environments. However, we want to capture the notion of actions that change part of the state, and to be able to merge these, and detect if they are both trying to modify the same variable. With the action model as just described, this is hard to do, so we adopt an alternative model, were we view an action as simply being a partial environment which records the part that changes. The null action is simply the null map ($\theta$), and two actions are merged by simply merging the maps together. Any variable conflict is recognised because the variable occurs in the domain of both maps — in this case we map the value to ? to denote the (runtime) error.

$$Evt \ \hat{=} \ Env$$
$$\mathrm{nop} \ \hat{=} \ \theta$$
$$e_1 \lozenge e_2 \ \hat{=} \ e_1 \cup e_2,$$
$$\textbf{if} \ \mathrm{dom} \ e_1 \cap \mathrm{dom} \ e_1 = \emptyset$$
$$\{v \mapsto e_1\} \lozenge \{v \mapsto e_2\} = \{v \mapsto ?\}$$

The one exception to map conflicts has to do with the way the communication parts are treated ($\Re, \gamma, B$). Here we find that the basic action involves lodging a `prialt` as a request, into the $B$ component, which is a set of such `prialt`s. Multiple references to $B$ are resolved by applying set union (remember that $P_1$ and $P_2$ are of type $PriSet$):

$$\{B \mapsto P_1\} \lozenge \{B \mapsto P_2\} = \{B \mapsto P_1 \cup P_2\}$$

The clock-tick action is simply represented by an environment where the sole identifer in its domain is $\tau$, and the datum to which it maps is immaterial:

$$\ddagger \ : \ Evt$$
$$\ddagger \ \hat{=} \ \{\tau \mapsto ?\}$$

**State Change.** We use such partial maps to change the state by simply overriding the state with a mapping in which any expressions (as $Fun$ in $Datum$) have been first evaluated w.r.t that state:

$$St \ \hat{=} \ Env$$
$$\triangle(e_1)\rho \ \hat{=} \ \rho \dagger \mathcal{E}'_\rho(e_1)$$
$$\mathcal{E}'_\rho\{v \mapsto f\} \ \hat{=} \ \{v \mapsto f(\rho)\}$$

It is this model of actions which motivated the particular form of the abstract action model used when typed assertion traces where described previously, and why in that model we used $\triangle$, rather than simply viewing actions there directly as state-transformers themselves.

**State Predicates.** Any boolean-valued expression in Handel-C provides us with a predicate, simply by evaluating that expression against the state environment in the usual way.

$$Pred \; \hat{=} \; Exp, \qquad \text{boolean-valued}$$
$$e(\rho) \; \hat{=} \; \mathcal{E}[\![e]\!]_\rho$$

## 6.5   Fixpoints

We define an ordering $\preceq$ on traces, with $\tau_1 \preceq \tau_2$ if $\tau_1$ is a prefix of $\tau_2$. We note that $\langle \text{nils} \rangle \preceq \tau$ for any $\tau$. A set of traces has a least upper bound w.r.t $\preceq$ if all the traces are prefixes of some single (longest) trace, which is the shortest possible such trace. For typed assertion traces we say that $\tau_1 \preceq \tau_2$ if there exists $\tau_3$ such that $\tau_1 \, \mathring{9} \, \tau_3 = \tau_2$.

We extend this to an ordering $\sqsubseteq$ over sets of traces by saying that $S_1 \sqsubseteq S_2$ if for every $\tau_1$ in $S_1$ there is a $\tau_2$ in $S_2$ such that $\tau_1 \preceq \tau_2$. The least element in this ordering is the set $\{\,\langle \text{nils} \rangle\,\}$. Again a notion of least upper bound $(\bigsqcup)$ can be defined w.r.t $\sqsubseteq$.

Our semantic domain is therefore one of trace-sets, ordered by $\sqsubseteq$, and our semantic definitions produce directed sets. We therefore handle recursion by taking the least fixed point w.r.t $\sqsubseteq$, and we can compute this as

$$\text{fix} \, L \bullet F(L) = \bigsqcup_{i \in \mathbb{N}} \{\, F^i \{\,\langle \text{nils} \rangle\,\}\,\}$$

# 7   Handel-C Denotational Semantics

We are now in a position to give the denotational semantics of Handel-C. First we need to introduce some shorthands to manage the complexity of the resulting expressions. Given a binary operator $*$ over values $s$ and $t$ of some type we assume the obvious extensions to act between sets $S$ and $T$ over the type, or between elements and sets as follows:

$$S * T \; \hat{=} \; \{\, s * t \mid s \in S \wedge t \in T \,\}$$
$$s * T \; \hat{=} \; \{\, s * t \mid t \in T \,\}$$

The semantics of a Handel-C process is given as a set of typed assertion traces, subject to the following healthiness conditions: (1) *Traces are maximal:* if a trace is present, then none of its proper prefixes are; (2) *Mutual Exclusivity:* if two traces differ, then the pair of guarded actions which first distinguish them must have mutually exclusive predicates, i.e ones that are never true in the same environment (3) *Exhaustivness:* given all traces in the set with a common prefix, then all the guard predicates of the distinguishing actions must exhaust all possibilities, ie. for any environment, at least one (and only one) will return true. Conditions (2) and (3) are weakened slightly when we consider the semantics of prialt later on.

We can now describe the semantics of all constructs except `prialt` in a straightforward manner as follows,

$$
\begin{aligned}
[\![\_]\!] \quad &: \quad Prog \to \mathcal{P}\,Trc \\
[\![0]\!] \quad &\widehat{=} \quad \{\,\langle \mathsf{nils}\rangle\,\} \\
[\![1]\!] \quad &\widehat{=} \quad \{\,\langle \ddagger\rangle\,\} \\
[\![x := e]\!] \quad &\widehat{=} \quad \{\,\langle(\langle\rangle, \{x \mapsto e\})\rangle\,\} \\
[\![p;\ q]\!] \quad &\widehat{=} \quad [\![p]\!] \mathbin{\raise1pt\hbox{$\mathchar"9$}} [\![q]\!] \\
[\![p \parallel q]\!] \quad &\widehat{=} \quad [\![p]\!]\ [\![\![]\!]\ [\![q]\!] \\
[\![p \vartriangleleft b \vartriangleright q]\!] \quad &\widehat{=} \quad (\underline{b} ::_{sel} [\![p]\!]) \ \cup\ (\neg\,\underline{b} ::_{sel} [\![q]\!]) \\
[\![b * p]\!] \quad &\widehat{=} \quad \mathsf{fix}\, L \bullet \{\,\langle mk_{sel}(\neg\underline{b})\rangle\,\}\ \cup\ (\underline{b} ::_{sel} ([\![p]\!] \mathbin{\raise1pt\hbox{$\mathchar"9$}} L))
\end{aligned}
$$

**0**, **1** and assignment have a single singleton trace as semantics, being respectively the empty, clock-tick and single-variable update slots. Sequential and parallel composition simply combine all their traces with the appropriate trace operator. The conditional construct prefixes the traces of the "then" outcome with the condition as a guard predicate, while the traces of the "else" outcome have the negation of that predicate prefixed instead. It is with this construct that multiple traces are introduced, and were we ensure that the exclusivity and exhaustiveness healthiness conditions are met. The while-loop is given a fixpoint semantics, as is standard for such constructs. In effect it either immediately terminates, if the guard is false, or else the guard is true, and it then behaves like the loop-body sequentially composed with the loop itself. Just like the conditional construct, it also ensures the exclusivity and exhaustiveness criteria are met.

## 7.1   Extending the Language

The semantics of `prialt` is best given by breaking the construct down into simpler components, which mainly correspond to the various phases in which `prialt` is active,namely *req*, *res* and *act*. We now introduce some extension to the language to facilitate this —note that these extensions exists solely in order to elucidate the semantics, and are not available for general use by the Handel-C programmer.

We extend the expression syntax to include three special forms — a `prialt`-waiting predicate $(w\langle g_i\rangle)$, an active guard expression $(a\langle g_i\rangle)$, and a channel data expression $(\delta(c))$:

$$
e \in Exp = \ldots \mid w\langle g_i\rangle \mid a\langle g_i\rangle \mid \delta(c)
$$

The waiting predicate takes a `prialt`-request (guard-list) as argument, and returns true if resolution has determined that that `prialt` is blocked. It is evaluated, after the *req* phase, by looking at the $B$ component of the state:

$$
\mathcal{E}[\![w\langle g_i\rangle]\!]\rho \ \widehat{=} \ \langle g_i\rangle \in \rho(B)
$$

The active guard expression takes a **prialt**-request as argument, and returns the index ($i \in 1 \ldots n$) of the guard which is going to be active in this clock-cycle. It is only defined when $w\langle g_i \rangle$ is false, and looks up the channel-prialt map

$$\mathcal{E}[\![a\langle g_i \rangle]\!]\rho \;\hat{=}\; \min j$$
$$\textbf{where } \exists\, c \;\bullet\; \langle g_i \rangle \in \rho(\gamma)(c)$$
$$\wedge \; channel(g_j) = c$$

Here *channel* returns the channel associated with a guard.

The channel data expression $\delta(c)$ returns the data expression associated with an active channel — this information can be extracted from the channel-**prialt** map component, as detailed in [5].

We extend the program syntax to include three new statements — a **prialt**-request statement ($rq\langle g_i \rangle$), a **prialt**-wait statement ($wait\langle g_i \rangle$), and a multi-way conditional branch (or case-statement):

$$p \in Prog ::= \ldots \mid rq\langle g_i \rangle \mid wait\langle g_i \rangle \mid e \blacktriangleright [p_i]$$

The **prialt**-request statement simply lodges its guard-list argument into the input *PriSet* for resolution. In the semantics we use the $B$ component of the state to hold both the prialts input to resolution (during the *req* phase) and the blocked-**prialt** result of resolution (available during the *res* and *act* phases).

The **prialt**-wait statement asks if its **prialt** argument is blocked. If it is, it then waits one clock cycle, then re-submits the corresponding **prialt**-request, before repeating itself. If the **prialt** is not blocked, it terminates immediately.

The case-statement $e \blacktriangleright [p_i]$ evaluates expression $e$, whose value must lie in the range $1 \ldots n$. This value is used to select the process to execute.

We also define a function on guards which gives the underlying action as an equivalent statement:

$$\text{act}() \;:\; Grd \to Prog$$
$$\text{act}(c!e) \;\hat{=}\; \mathbf{1}$$
$$\text{act}(c?v) \;\hat{=}\; v := \delta(c)$$
$$\text{act}(!?) \;\hat{=}\; \mathbf{0}$$

We give **prialt** $\langle g_i \to p_i \rangle$ a semantics by translating it to:

$$rq\langle g_i \rangle; \; wait\langle g_i \rangle; \; a\langle g_i \rangle \blacktriangleright [\text{act}(g_i); \; p_i]$$

This captures the notion that a **prialt** acts in three stages: (i) it submits a request ($rq\langle g_i \rangle$); (ii) it waits until it becomes active, re-submitting the request on every clock cycle ($wait\langle g_i \rangle$); and (iii) once waiting is over, selects and executes the active guard and corresponding process ($a\langle g_i \rangle \blacktriangleright [\text{act}(g_i) \; ; \; p_i]$).

We can now give the semantics of the additional constructs:

$$[\![rq\langle g_i\rangle]\!] \ \hat{=}\ \{\,\langle mk_{req}(\{B \mapsto \{\langle g_i\rangle\}\})\rangle\,\}$$
$$[\![wait\langle g_i\rangle]\!] \ \hat{=}\ \text{fix } W \bullet \{\,\langle mk_{res}(\neg\, w\langle g_i\rangle)\rangle\,\}$$
$$\cup$$
$$(\underline{w\langle g_i\rangle} ::_{act} ([\![rq\langle g_i\rangle]\!] \, \mathbin{\raise2pt\hbox{\tiny$\circ$}\kern-1pt\lower2pt\hbox{\tiny$\circ$}} \, W))$$
$$[\![a\langle g_i\rangle \blacktriangleright [p_i]]\!] \ \hat{=}\ \bigcup_i \{\,\underline{(a\langle g_i\rangle = i)} ::_{res} [\![p_i]\!]\,\}$$

The request statement is simply an update of the state's "$B$' component, tagged as occurring during the $req$ phase. The case-statement simply prepends a guarded action asserting that $e = i$ to the traces associated with process $p_i$, such a choice being made during the $res$ phase.

The $wait\langle g_i\rangle$ statement is a looping construct, so it has a fixpoint definition as expected. It would seem obvious that $wait\langle g_i\rangle$ should be the same as $w\langle g_i\rangle * (\mathbf{1};\ rq\langle g_i\rangle)$, but it is necessary to keep it separate, because not only do the true and false branches of the $wait$ statement not occur in the $sel$ phase, but in fact they occur in different phases: the terminating guarded action $(\neg\, w\langle g_i\rangle)$ occurs during the $res$ phase; while the continuation guarded action $(\underline{w\langle g_i\rangle})$ occurs during the $act$ phase.

The reason for this is the same as that encountered in the operational semantics, namely that the decision to end waiting can be made as soon as a `prialt` becomes unblocked (during some some $res$ phase), but the decision to wait until the next clock cycle to try again needs to be deferred until no more $sel$-$req$-$res$ micro-cycles can occur, i.e. once the $act$ phase has been reached. This is because a subsequent round of request and resolution, caused by a `prialt` in some default guard, may cause a blocked `prialt` to become unblocked. The converse never happens: once a `prialt` is unblocked in one microcycle, it can never become blocked again subsequently.

This means that the Exhaustiveness and Exclusivity healthiness conditions aren't quite adhered to at this point, as the conditions $\neg\, w\langle g_i\rangle$ and $\underline{w\langle g_i\rangle}$ do not occur at the same point in the traces. In fact the latter is delayed until the $act$ phase. The weakening that we allow is that this works because while the $act$ condition occurs later in the trace, no events of any significance occur in that trace from the point in the $res$ phase where $w\langle g_i\rangle$ could return $false$, up to the $act$ point where the predicate can return $true$.

## 7.2   Examples

We now present a few small examples simply to show the semantics at work.

In order to keep expressions readable and manageable, we introduce the following shorthand: (i) for $(\langle\rangle, x \mapsto e)$ we simply write $\{x \mapsto e\}$; (ii) and for $mks_{req}(\{B \mapsto \{\langle g_i\rangle\}\})$ we use $req\langle g_i\rangle$. Rather than showing the slot and microcycle structure explicitly, we simply list the actions separated by commas, and use $\ddagger$ to to mark the slot boundaries (i.e clock ticks). So

$$\langle\ (\langle\rangle, y \mapsto f),\ (\langle\langle(\underline{b}), \mathit{true}, \mathit{true}\rangle\rangle, x \mapsto e)\ \rangle$$

becomes $\langle \{y \mapsto f\} \ddagger \underline{b}, \{x \mapsto e\}\rangle$

**Assignment, Conditional and Sequential Composition.** If we follow an assignment by a conditional as follows:

$$x := y + z;\ y := z \triangleleft (x > 0) \triangleright z := y$$

then calculating this through with the semantics gives:

$$\llbracket x := y + z;\ y := z \triangleleft (x > 0) \triangleright z := y \rrbracket$$
$$= \{\ \langle\{x \mapsto y + z\} \ddagger \underline{x > 0}, \{y \mapsto z\}\rangle,$$
$$\langle\{x \mapsto y + z\} \ddagger \underline{x \leq 0}, \{z \mapsto y\}\rangle\ \}$$

We see clearly the same starting action in both traces, and then a choice based on the sign of $x$ guarding the subsequent behaviour, each covered by one of the two traces.

**Parallel Assignment.** We can swap two variables in one clock cycle:

$$\llbracket x := y \parallel y := x \rrbracket = \{\ \{x \mapsto y, y \mapsto x\}\ \}$$

This works because the expressions are evaluated first during the clock cycle, and the variables are updated simultaneously as the clock ticks. However, if we attempt to simultaneously assign two different values to one variable, the semantics flags this as an error

$$\llbracket x := e_1 \parallel x := e_2 \rrbracket = \{\ \{x \mapsto ?\}\ \}$$

**While Loop.** If we consider a simply busy waiting loop ($b$ will hopefully eventually be set by some other process), then we calculate the semantics as:

$$\llbracket b * 1 \rrbracket = \bigsqcup \{\ F^i \{\,\mathsf{nils}\,\} \mid i \in \mathbb{N}\ \}$$
$$\textbf{where} \qquad F(L) = \{\ \langle \underline{\neg\,b}\rangle\ \} \cup (\ (\underline{b}, \ddagger) :: L\ )$$

Evaluating this leads to the result that the set of traces are of the form:

$$\llbracket b * 1 \rrbracket = \{\ \langle \underline{\neg\,b}\rangle,$$
$$\langle \underline{b}, \ddagger;\ \underline{\neg\,b}\rangle,$$
$$\langle \underline{b}, \ddagger;\ \underline{b}, \ddagger;\ \underline{\neg\,b}\rangle,$$

$$\vdots$$

$$\underbrace{\langle \underline{b}, \ddagger;\ \ldots;\ \underline{b}, \ddagger;}_{i-1 \text{ times}}\ \underline{\neg\,b}\rangle,$$

$$\vdots$$

$$\underbrace{\langle \underline{b}, \ddagger;\ \ldots;\ \underline{b}, \ddagger \ldots\rangle}_{\infty \text{ times}}\ \}$$

We have finite traces which correspond to zero or more iterations before the condition becomes true, and one infinite trace which captures the situation were $b$ is always false —this is why we need to admit infinite traces in our semantic model.

# 8    Conclusions and Future Work

We have presented a denotational semantics for Handel-C as sets of typed assertion traces, which captures all the key behaviour of the language, with particular emphasis on the proper treatment of default clauses in `prialt` statements. We need to show that all this semantics describes the same language as does the operational semantics. The real goal is to use the denotational semantics to verify a series of algebraic laws for Handel-C, which would form the basis for a practical system for formal reasoning about such programs. We also intended to extend this to cover the notion of refinement in a Handel-C setting, linking the language to specification notations such as CSP [35] or Circus [30].

Recently we have also published a "hardware semantics" for Handel-C [36], which will allow us to explore transformations that investigate the trade-off between the number of clock-cycles required to complete a task, and the length of each cycle, which depends on the complexity of the combinatorial logic that is generated. It is here that the well-known work of Zhou Chaochen on duration calculus [37] and his work on modelling synchronous circuits at switch level [38] will provide useful tools and insight for this work.

Finally, we hope to explore the embedding of these results into the UTP framework [32], as a variant of Circus [30]. This work is being funded as a three-year project by Science Foundation Ireland.

# References

1. Celoxica Ltd.: Handel-C Language Reference Manual, v3.0. (2002), www.celoxica.com
2. Hoare, C.A.R.: Communicating Sequential Processes. Intl. Series in Computer Science. Prentice Hall, Englewood Cliffs (1985)
3. Page, I., Luk, W.: Compiling Occam into field-programmable gate arrays. In: Moore, W., Luk, W. (eds.) FPGAs, Oxford Workshop on Field Programmable Logic and Applications. Abingdon EE&CS Books, 15 Harcourt Way, Abingdon OX14 1NV, UK, pp. 271–283 (1991)
4. Butterfield, A., Woodcock, J.: An operational semantics for handel-c. In: Arts, T., Fokkink, W. (eds.) Electronic Notes in Theoretical Computer Science, vol. 80, Elsevier, Amsterdam (2003)
5. Butterfield, A., Woodcock, J.: prialt in Handel-C: an operational semantics. International Journal on Software Tool for Technology Transfer (STTT) (2005)
6. Butterfield, A.: Denotational semantics for prialt-free Handel-C. Technical Report TCD-CS-2001-53, Dept. of Computer Science, Trinity College, Dublin University (2001)

7. Butterfield, A.: Interpretative semantics for prialt-free Handel-C. Technical Report TCD-CS-2001-54, Dept. of Computer Science, Trinity College, Dublin University (2001)
8. Mac an Airchinnigh, M.: The irish school of vdm. In: Prehn, S., Toetenel, H. (eds.) VDM 1991. LNCS, vol. 552, Springer, Heidelberg (1991)
9. Björner, D., Jones, C.B.: Formal Specification & Software Development. Prentice-Hall, Englewood Cliffs (1982)
10. Bjørner, D.: TRain: The railway domain - A "grand challenge" for computing science & transportation engineering. In: Jacquart, R. (ed.) IFIP Congress Topical Sessions, pp. 607–612. Kluwer, Dordrecht (2004)
11. Bjørner, D.: Software Engineering. In: Bjørner, D. (ed.) Domains, Requirements and Software Design. Texts in Theoretical Computer Science, vol. 3, Springer, Heidelberg (2006)
12. Butterfield, A., Woodcock, J.: Semantics of prialt in Handel-C. In: Pasco, J., Welch, P., Loader, R., Sunderam, V. (eds.) Communicating Process Architectures – 2002. Concurrent Systems Engineering, pp. 1–16. IOS Press, Amsterdam (2002)
13. Butterfield, A., Woodcock, J.: Semantic Domains for Handel-C. In: Madden, N., Seda, A. (eds.) Mathematical Foundations for Computer Science and Information Technology (MFCSIT 2003). Electronic Notes in Theoretical Computer Science, vol. 74, http://www.elsevier.nl/locate/entcs
14. Fidge, C.J.: A formal definition of priority in CSP. ACM Transactions on Programming Languages and Systems 15, 681–705 (1993)
15. Lawrence, A.E.: Cspp and event priority. In: Alan Chalmers, M.M., Muller, H. (eds.) Communicating Process Architectures 2001, Amsterdam, sep 2001. Concurrent Systems Engineering, IOS Press, Amsterdam (2001)
16. Lawrence, A.E.: Acceptances, Behaviours and infinite activity in CSPP. In: Communicating Process Architectures - 2002. Concurrent Systems Engineering, IOS Press, Amsterdam (2002)
17. Lawrence, A.E.: HCSP and true concurrency. In: Communicating Process Architectures - 2002. Concurrent Systems Engineering, IOS Press, Amsterdam (2002)
18. Cleaveland, R., Hennessy, M.: Priorities in process algebra. In: Proceedings 3rd Annual Symposium on Logic in Computer Science, Edinburgh, pp. 193–202. IEEE Computer Society Press, Los Alamitos (1988)
19. Cleaveland, R., Luettgen, G., Natarajan, V., Sims, S.: Modeling and Verifying Distributed Systems Using Priorities: A Case Study. In: Margaria, T., Steffen, B. (eds.) TACAS 1996. LNCS, vol. 1055, pp. 287–297. Springer, Heidelberg (1996)
20. Cleaveland, R., Luettgen, G., Natarajan, V.: Priority in process algebra. In: Bergstra, J.A., Ponse, A., Smolka, S.A. (eds.) Handbook of Process Algebra, pp. 711–765. Elsevier, Amsterdam (2001)
21. Damianou, N., Dulay, N., Lupu, E., Sloman, M.: The ponder policy specification language. In: Sloman, M., Lobo, J., Lupu, E.C. (eds.) POLICY 2001. LNCS, vol. 1995, p. 18. Springer, Heidelberg (2001)
22. Lee, T., Yusuf, S., Luk, W., Sloman, M., Lupu, E., Dulay, N.: Development framework for firewall processors ( in Academic Papers section), www.celoxica.com
23. Abdallah, A.E., Hawkins, J.: Formal Behavioural Synthesis of Handel-C Parallel Hardware Implementations from Functional Specifications. In: 36th Annual Hawaii International Conference on System Sciences (HICSS'03), IEEE, Los Alamitos (2003)
24. Boussinot, F., Simone, R.D.: The ESTEREL language. Technical Report RR-1487, (Inria, Institut National de Recherche en Informatique et en Automatique)

25. Bouali, A.: Xeve: An Esterel verification environment. In: Vardi, M.Y. (ed.) CAV 1998. LNCS, vol. 1427, p. 500. Springer, Heidelberg (1998)
26. Tini: An axiomatic semantics for esterel. TCS: Theoretical Computer Science 269 (2001)
27. Holenderski, L.: LUSTRE. In: Lewerentz, C., Lindner, T. (eds.) Formal Development of Reactive Systems, Case Study Production Cell. LNCS, pp. 101–112. Springer, Heidelberg (1995)
28. Andriessens, C., Lindner, T.: AL: Using FOCUS, LUSTRE, and probability theory for the design of a reliable control program. In: Abrial, J.-R., Börger, E., Langmaack, H. (eds.) Formal Methods for Industrial Applications. LNCS, vol. 1165, pp. 35–51. Springer, Heidelberg (1996)
29. Brookes, S.D.: On the axiomatic treatment of concurrency. In: Brookes, S.D., Winskel, G., Roscoe, A.W. (eds.) Seminar on Concurrency. LNCS, vol. 197, pp. 1–34. Springer, Heidelberg (1985)
30. Woodcock, J., Cavalcanti, A.: The Semantics of Circus. In: Bert, D., Bowen, J.P., Henson, M.C., Robinson, K. (eds.) B 2002 and ZB 2002. LNCS, vol. 2272, Springer, Heidelberg (2002)
31. Butterfield, A., Sherif, A., Woodcock, J.: Slotted-Circus-A UTP-Family of Reactive Theories. In: Davies, J., Gibbons, J. (eds.) IFM 2007. LNCS, vol. 4591, Springer, Heidelberg (2007)
32. Hoare, C.A.R., Jifeng, H.: Unifying Theories of Programming. Series in Computer Science. Prentice Hall, Englewood Cliffs (1998)
33. Corcoran, B.J.: Testing Formal Semantics: Handel-C. M.Sc. in Computer Science, University of Dublin, Trinity College presented in partial fullfillment of the M.Sc. requirements (2005)
34. Jones, S.P., et al.: Report on the Programming Language Haskell 98 (1999), http://www.haskell.org/
35. Schneider, S.: Concurrent and Real-time Systems - The CSP Approach. Wiley, Chichester (2000)
36. Butterfield, A., Woodcock, J.: A "hardware compiler" semantics for handel-c. Electr. Notes Theor. Comput. Sci. 161, 73–90 (2006)
37. Zhou, C.: Duration calculus, a logical approach to real-time systems. In: Haeberer, A.M. (ed.) AMAST 1998. LNCS, vol. 1548, pp. 1–7. Springer, Heidelberg (1998)
38. Chaochen, Z., Hoare, C.A.R.: A model for synchronous switching circuits and its theory of correctness. Formal Methods in System Design 1, 7–28 (1992)

# Generating Polynomial Invariants with DISCOVERER and QEPCAD*

Yinghua Chen[1], Bican Xia[1], Lu Yang[2], and Naijun Zhan[3,**]

[1] LMAM & School of Mathematical Sciences, Peking University
[2] Institute of Theoretical Computing, East China Normal University
[3] Lab. of Computer Science, Institute of Software, Chinese Academy of Sciences
South Fourth Street, No. 4, Zhong Guan Cun, Beijing, 100080, P.R. China
znj@ios.ac.cn

Dedicated to Prof. Chaochen Zhou on his 70th Birthday

**Abstract.** This paper investigates how to apply the techniques on solving semi-algebraic systems to invariant generation of polynomial programs. By our approach, the generated invariants represented as a semi-algebraic system are more expressive than those generated with the well-established approaches in the literature, which are normally represented as a conjunction of polynomial equations. We implement this approach with the computer algebra tools DISCOVERER and QEPCAD[1]. We also explain, through the complexity analysis, why our approach is more efficient and practical than the one of [17] which directly applies first-order quantifier elimination.

**Keywords:** Program Verification, Invariant Generation, Polynomial Programs, Semi-Algebraic Systems; Quantifier Elimination, DISCOVERER, QEPCAD.

## 1 Introduction

Loop invariant generation together with loop termination analysis of programs plays a central role in program verification. Since the late sixties (or early seventies) of the 20th century when the so-called Floyd-Hoare-Dijkstra inductive assertion method, the dominant method on automatic verification of programs, [11,14,9] was invented, there have been lots of attempts to handle the loop problems, e.g. [25,13,16,15], but only with a limited success.

Recently, due to the advance of computer algebra, several methods based on symbolic computation have been applied successfully to invariant generation, for example the techniques based on abstract interpretation [7,1,21,6], quantifier elimination [5,17] and polynomial algebra [19,20,22,23,24].

The basic idea behind the abstract interpretation approaches is to perform an approximate symbolic execution of a program until an assertion is reached

---

* This work is supported in part by NKBRPC-2002cb312200, NKBRPC-2004CB318003, NSFC-60493200, NSFC-60421001, NSFC-60573007, and NKBRPC-2005CB321902.
** Corresponding author.
[1] http://www.cs.usna.edu/~qepcad/B/QEPCAD.html

that remain unchanged by further executions of the program. However, in order to guarantee termination, the method introduces imprecision by use of an extrapolation operator called *widening/narrowing*. This operator often causes the technique to produce weak invariants. Moreover, proposing widening/narrowing operators with certain concerns of completeness is not easy and becomes a key challenge for abstract interpretation based techniques [7,1].

In contrast, [19,20,22,23,24] exploited the theory of polynomial algebra to discover invariants of polynomial programs. [19] applied the technique of linear algebra to generate polynomial equations of bounded degree as invariants of programs with affine assignments. [22,23] first proved that the set of polynomials serving as loop invariants has the algebraic structure of an ideal, then proposed an invariant generation algorithm by using fixpoint computation, and finally implemented the algorithm by the Gröbner bases and the elimination theory. The approach is theoretically sound and complete in the sense that if there is an invariant of the loop that can be expressed as a conjunction of polynomial equations, applying the approach can indeed generate it. [24] presented a similar approach to finding polynomial equation invariants whose form is priori determined (called templates) by using an extended Gröbner basis algorithm over templates.

Compared with the polynomial algebraic approaches that can only generate invariants represented as polynomial equations, [5] proposed an approach to generate linear inequalities as invariants for linear programs, based on *Farkas' Lemma* and non-linear constraint solving. In addition, [17] proposed a very general approach for automatic generation of more expressive invariants by exploiting the technique of quantifier elimination, and applied the approach to Presburger Arithmetic and quantifier-free theory of conjunctively closed polynomial equations. Theoretically speaking, the approach can also be applied to the theory of real closed fields, but [17] pointed out that this is impractical in reality because of the high complexity of quantifier elimination, which is double exponential [8]. To handle the problem, [6] exploited the techniques of parametric abstraction, Lagrangian relaxation and semidefinite programming to generate invariants as well as ranking functions of polynomial programs. Compared with the approach of [17], [6]'s is more efficient, as first-order quantifier elimination is not directly applied there. However, [6]'s approach is incomplete in the sense that, for some program that may have ranking functions and invariants of the predefined form, applying the approach may not be able to find them, as Lagrangian relaxation and over-approximation of the positive semi-definiteness of a polynomial are used.

In this paper, we attack the problem raised in [17] on how to efficiently generate polynomial invariants of programs over real closed fields and present a more practical and efficient approach to it by exploiting our results on solving semi-algebraic systems (SASs). The outline of our approach is as follows: we first reduce polynomial invariant generation problem to solving semi-algebraic systems; then apply our theories and tools on solving SASs, in particular, on root classification of parametric SASs [30,31,32] and real root isolation of constant

SASs [28,29], to produce some necessary and sufficient conditions; and finally utilize the technique of quantifier elimination to handle the derived conditions and obtain invariants with the predefined form.

Suppose an SAS $S$ has $s$ ($> 0$) polynomial equations and $m$ inequations and inequalities. All polynomials are in $n = t + (n - t)$ indeterminates (i.e., $u_1, \ldots, u_t$, $x_1, \ldots, x_{n-t}$) and of degree at most $d$ where $t$ is the dimension of the ideal generated by the $s$ equations. According to [3,8], directly applying the technique of quantifier elimination of real closed fields, the cost for solving $S$ is doubly exponential w.r.t. $n$. But using our approach, the cost for the first step is almost nothing, and the second step to apply root classification and isolation costs singly exponential w.r.t. $n$ plus doubly exponential w.r.t. $t$. The cost for the last step is also doubly exponential w.r.t. $t$. Therefore, as $t < n$, our approach is more efficient than the approaches directly based on the techniques of quantifier elimination and Gröbner basis, such as [17,24], in particular, when $t$ is much less than $n$. Moreover, our approach is still complete in the sense that whenever there exist invariants of the predefined form, applying our approach can indeed synthesize them, while [6]'s [2] is incomplete. On the other hand, similarly to [17,6], invariants generated by our approach are more expressive, while applying the approaches based on polynomial algebra can only produce conjunction of polynomial equations as invariants.

The rest of this paper is organized as: Section 2 provides a brief review of the theories and tools on solving SASs; Section 3 defines some basic notions, including semi-algebraic transition systems, polynomial programs, invariants, inductive properties and so on; Section 4 is devoted to illustrating our approach in detail with a running example; We provide the complexity analysis of our approach in Section 5; In Section 6, we compare the application of this approach to invariant generating with the one to ranking function discovering; and Section 7 concludes the paper and discusses the future work in this direction.

## 2   Preliminaries: Theories on Semi-algebraic Systems

In this section, we introduce the cornerstone of our technique, i.e. theories and tools on solving SASs, mainly the theories on root classification of parametric SASs and the tool DISCOVERER.

### 2.1   Basic Notions

Let $\mathcal{K}[x_1, ..., x_n]$ be the ring of polynomials in $n$ indeterminates, $X = \{x_1, \cdots, x_n\}$, with coefficients in the field $\mathcal{K}$. Let the variables be ordered as $x_1 \prec x_2 \prec \cdots \prec x_n$. Then, the *leading variable* (or *main variable*) of a polynomial $p$ is the variable with the biggest index which indeed occurs in $p$. If the leading variable of a polynomial $p$ is $x_k$, $p$ can be collected w.r.t. its leading variable as $p = c_m x_k^m + \cdots + c_0$

---

[2] As far as efficiency is concerned, we believe that our approach could be at least as good as [6]'s, as the complexity of the semi-definite programming adopted in [6] is also very high.

where $m$ is the *degree* of $p$ w.r.t. $x_k$ and $c_i$s are polynomials in $\mathcal{K}[x_1, ..., x_{k-1}]$. We call $c_m x_k^m$ the *leading term* of $p$ w.r.t. $x_k$ and $c_m$ the *leading coefficient*. For example, let $p(x_1, ..., x_5) = x_2^5 + x_3^4 x_4^2 + (2x_2 + x_1)x_4^3$, so, its leading variable, term and coefficient are $x_4$, $(2x_2 + x_1)x_4^3$ and $2x_2 + x_1$, respectively.

An *atomic polynomial formula* over $\mathcal{K}[x_1, ..., x_n]$ is of the form $p(x_1, ..., x_n) \rhd 0$, where $\rhd \in \{=, >, \geq, \neq\}$, while a *polynomial formula* over $\mathcal{K}[x_1, ..., x_n]$ is constructed from atomic polynomial formulae by applying the logical connectives. Conjunctive polynomial formulae are those that are built from atomic polynomial formulae with the logical operator $\wedge$. We will denote by $PF(\{x_1, ..., x_n\})$ the set of polynomial formulae and by $CPF(\{x_1, ..., x_n\})$ the set of conjunctive polynomial formulae, respectively.

In what follows, we will use $\mathbb{Q}$ to stand for rationales and $\mathbb{R}$ for reals, and fix $\mathcal{K}$ to be $\mathbb{Q}$. In fact, all results discussed below can be applied to $\mathbb{R}$.

In the following, the $n$ indeterminates are divided into two groups: $\mathbf{u} = (u_1, ..., u_t)$ and $\mathbf{x} = (x_1, ..., x_s)$, which are called parameters and variables, respectively, and we sometimes use "," to denote the conjunction of atomic formulae for simplicity.

**Definition 1.** *A semi-algebraic system is a conjunctive polynomial formula of the following form:*

$$\begin{cases} p_1(\mathbf{u}, \mathbf{x}) = 0, ..., p_r(\mathbf{u}, \mathbf{x}) = 0, \\ g_1(\mathbf{u}, \mathbf{x}) \geq 0, ..., g_k(\mathbf{u}, \mathbf{x}) \geq 0, \\ g_{k+1}(\mathbf{u}, \mathbf{x}) > 0, ..., g_l(\mathbf{u}, \mathbf{x}) > 0, \\ h_1(\mathbf{u}, \mathbf{x}) \neq 0, ..., h_m(\mathbf{u}, \mathbf{x}) \neq 0, \end{cases} \quad (1)$$

*where $r > 1, l \geq k \geq 0, m \geq 0$ and all $p_i$'s, $g_i$'s and $h_i$'s are in $\mathbb{Q}[\mathbf{u}, \mathbf{x}] \setminus \mathbb{Q}$. An SAS of the form (1) is called* parametric *if $t \neq 0$, otherwise* constant.

An SAS of the form (1) is usually denoted by a quadruple $[\mathbb{P}, \mathbb{G}_1, \mathbb{G}_2, \mathbb{H}]$, where $\mathbb{P} = [p_1, ..., p_r]$, $\mathbb{G}_1 = [g_1, ..., g_k]$, $\mathbb{G}_2 = [g_{k+1}, ..., g_l]$ and $\mathbb{H} = [h_1, ..., h_m]$.

For a constant SAS $S$, interesting questions are how to compute the number of real solutions of $S$, and if the number is finite, how to compute these real solutions. For a parametric SAS, the interesting problem is so-called *real solution classification*, that is to determine the condition on the parameters such that the system has the prescribed number of distinct real solutions, possibly infinite.

## 2.2   Theories on Real Solution Classification

In this subsection, we outline the theories for real root classification of parametric SASs. For details, please be referred to [31,27].

For an SAS $S$ of the form (1), the algorithm for real root classification consists of three main steps. Firstly, transform the equations of $S$ into some sets of equations in triangular form. A set of equations $\mathbb{T} : [T_1, ..., T_k]$ is said to be in triangular form (or a *triangular set*) if the main variable of $T_i$ is less in the order than that of $T_j$ if $i < j$. Roughly speaking, if we rename the variables, a triangular set looks like

$$T_1 = T_1(\mathbf{v}, y_1),$$
$$T_2 = T_2(\mathbf{v}, y_1, y_2),$$
$$\cdots \cdots$$
$$T_k = T_k(\mathbf{v}, y_1, \cdots, y_k),$$

where $\mathbf{v}$ are the indeterminates other than $y_i$. It is obvious that we now only need to consider triangular systems in the following form

$$
\begin{cases}
f_1(\mathbf{u}, x_1) = 0, \\
\quad \vdots \\
f_s(\mathbf{u}, x_1, ..., x_s) = 0, \\
\mathbb{G}_1, \ \mathbb{G}_2, \ \mathbb{H}.
\end{cases}
\tag{2}
$$

Certainly, it can be proven that there exists a correspondence between the solutions of these triangular sets and $S$'s so that we only need to consider the solutions of these triangular sets in order to deal with $S$'s.

*Example 1.* Consider an SAS $S : [\mathbb{P}, \mathbb{G}_1, \mathbb{G}_2, \mathbb{H}]$ in $\mathbb{Q}[b, x, y, z]$ with $\mathbb{P} = [p_1, p_2, p_3]$, $\mathbb{G}_1 = \emptyset, \mathbb{G}_2 = [x, y, z, b, 2 - b], \mathbb{H} = \emptyset$, where

$$p_1 = x^2 + y^2 - z^2, \ p_2 = (1 - x)^2 - z^2 + 1, \ p_3 = (1 - y)^2 - b^2 z^2 + 1.$$

The equations $\mathbb{P}$ can be decomposed into two triangular sets in $\mathbb{Q}(b)[x, y, z]$

$\mathbb{T}_1 : [b^4 x^2 - 2b^2(b^2 - 2)x + 2b^4 - 8b^2 + 4, -b^2 y + b^2 x + 2 - 2b^2, b^4 z^2 + 4b^2 x - 8b^2 + 4],$
$\mathbb{T}_2 : [x^2 - 2x + 2, y + x - 2, z],$

with the relation

$$\text{Zero}(\mathbb{P}) = \text{Zero}(\mathbb{T}_1/b) \bigcup \text{Zero}(\mathbb{T}_2)$$

where Zero() means the set of zeros and $\text{Zero}(\mathbb{T}_1/b) = \text{Zero}(\mathbb{T}_1) \setminus \text{Zero}(b)$.

Second, compute a so-called *border polynomial* from the resulting triangular systems, say $[\mathbb{T}_i, \mathbb{G}_1, \mathbb{G}_2, \mathbb{H}]$. We need to introduce some concepts. Suppose $F$ and $G$ are polynomials in $x$ with degrees $m$ and $l$, respectively. Thus, they can be written in the following forms

$$F = a_0 x^m + a_1 x^{m-1} + \cdots + a_{m-1} x + a_m, \ G = b_0 x^l + b_1 x^{l-1} + \cdots + b_{l-1} x + b_l.$$

The following $(m + l) \times (m + l)$ matrix (those entries except $a_i, b_j$ are all zero)

$$
\left.
\left(
\begin{array}{ccccccc}
a_0 & a_1 & \cdots & a_m & & & \\
& a_0 & a_1 & \cdots & a_m & & \\
& & \ddots & \ddots & & \ddots & \\
& & & a_0 & a_1 & \cdots & a_m \\
b_0 & b_1 & \cdots & b_l & & & \\
& b_0 & b_1 & \cdots & b_l & & \\
& & \ddots & \ddots & & \ddots & \\
& & & b_0 & b_1 & \cdots & b_l
\end{array}
\right)
\right\}
\begin{array}{l} \\ l \\ \\ \\ \\ m \\ \\ \end{array}
$$

is called the *Sylvester matrix* of $F$ and $G$ w.r.t. $x$. The determinant of the matrix is called the *Sylvester resultant* or *resultant* of $F$ and $G$ w.r.t. $x$ and is denoted by $\mathrm{res}(F, G, x)$.

For system (2), we compute the resultant of $f_s$ and $f'_s$ w.r.t. $x_s$ and denote it by $\mathrm{dis}(f_s)$ (it has the leading coefficient and discriminant of $f_s$ as factors). Then we compute the *successive resultant* of $\mathrm{dis}(f_s)$ and the triangular set $\{f_{s-1}, ..., f_1\}$. That is, we compute $\mathrm{res}(\mathrm{res}(\cdots\mathrm{res}(\mathrm{res}(\mathrm{dis}(f_s), f_{s-1}, x_{s-1}), f_{s-2}, x_{s-2})\cdots), f_1, x_1)$ and denote it by $\mathrm{res}(\mathrm{dis}(f_s); f_{s-1}, ..., f_1)$ or simply $R_s$. Similarly, for each $i$ $(1 < i \leq s)$, we compute $R_i = \mathrm{res}(\mathrm{dis}(f_i); f_{i-1}, ..., f_1)$ and $R_1 = \mathrm{dis}(f_1)$.

For each of those inequalities and inequations, we compute the successive resultant of $g_j$ (or $h_j$) w.r.t. the triangular set $[f_1, ..., f_s]$ and denote it by $Q_j$ (resp. $Q_{l+j}$).

**Definition 2.** *For an SAS $T$ as defined by (2), the* border polynomial *of $T$ is*

$$BP = \prod_{i=1}^{s} R_i \prod_{j=1}^{l+m} Q_j.$$

*Sometimes, for brevity, we also abuse $BP$ to denote the square-free part or the set of square-free factors of $BP$.*

*Example 2.* For the system $S$ in Example 1, the border polynomial is

$$BP = b(b - 2)(b + 2)(b^2 - 2)(b^4 - 4b^2 + 2)(2b^4 - 2b^2 + 1).$$

From the result in [31,27], we may assume $BP \neq 0$. In fact, if any factor of $BP$ is a zero polynomial, we can further decompose the system into new systems with such a property. For a parametric SAS, its border polynomial is a polynomial in the parameters with the following property.

**Theorem 1.** *Suppose $S$ is a parametric SAS as defined by (2) and $BP$ its border polynomial. Then, in each connected component of the complement of $BP = 0$ in parametric space $\mathbb{R}^d$, the number of distinct real solutions of $S$ is constant.*

Third, $BP = 0$ decomposes the parametric space into a finite number of connected region. We then choose sample points in each connected component of the complement of $BP = 0$ and compute the number of distinct real solutions of $S$ at each sample point. Note that sample points can be obtained by the partial cylindrical algebra decomposition (PCAD) algorithm [4].

*Example 3.* For the system $S$ in Example 1, $BP = 0$ gives

$$b = 0, \ \pm 2, \ \pm\sqrt{2}, \ \pm\sqrt{2 \pm \sqrt{2}}.$$

The reals are divided into ten open intervals by these points. Because $0 < b < 2$, we only need to choose one point, for example, $\frac{1}{2}, 1, \frac{3}{2}, \frac{15}{8}$, from each of the four intervals contained in $(0, 2)$, respectively. Then, we substitute each of the four values for $b$ in the system, and compute the number of distinct real solutions of the system, consequently obtain the system has respectively $0, 1, 0$ and $0$ distinct real solutions.

The above three steps constitute the main part of the algorithm in [31,34,27], which, for any input SAS $S$, outputs the so-called border polynomial $BP$ and a quantifier-free formula $\Psi$ in terms of polynomials in parameters $\mathbf{u}$ (and possible some variables) such that, provided $BP \neq 0$, $\Psi$ is the necessary and sufficient condition for $S$ to have the given number (possibly infinite) of real solutions. Since $BP$ is a polynomial in parameters, $BP = 0$ can be viewed as a degenerated condition. Therefore, the outputs of the above three steps can be read as "if $BP \neq 0$, the necessary and sufficient condition for $S$ to have the given number (possibly infinite) of real solutions is $\Psi$."

*Remark 1.* If we want to discuss the case when parameters degenerate, i.e., $BP = 0$, we put $BP = 0$ (or some of its factors) into the system and apply a similar procedure to handle the new SAS.

*Example 4.* By the steps described above, we obtain the necessary and sufficient condition for $S$ to have one distinct real solution is $b^2 - 2 < 0 \ \wedge \ b^4 - 4b^2 + 2 < 0$ provided $BP \neq 0$. Now, if $b^2 - 2 = 0$, adding the equation into the system, we obtain a new SAS: $[\ [b^2 - 2, p_1, p_2, p_3], [\ ], G_2, [\ ]\ ]$. By the algorithm in [28,29], we know the system has no real solutions.

## 2.3   A Computer Algebra Tool: DISCOVERER

We have implemented the above algorithm and some other algorithms in Maple as a computer algebra tool, named DISCOVERER. The reader can download the tool for free via "`http://www.is.pku.edu.cn/~xbc/discoverer.html`". The prerequisite to run the package is Maple 7.0 or a later version of it.

The main features of DISCOVERER include

### *Real Solution Classification of Parametric Semi-algebraic Systems*

For a parametric SAS $T$ of the form (1) and an argument $N$, where $N$ is one of the following three forms:
 – a non-negative integer $b$;
 – a range $b..c$, where $b, c$ are non-negative integers and $b < c$;
 – a range $b..w$, where $b$ is a non-negative integer and $w$ is a name without value, standing for $+\infty$,
DISCOVERER can determine the conditions on $\mathbf{u}$ such that the number of the distinct real solutions of $T$ equals to $N$ if $N$ is an integer, otherwise falls in the scope $N$. This is by calling

$$\mathbf{tofind}([\mathbb{P}], [\mathbb{G}_1], [\mathbb{G}_2], [\mathbb{H}], [x_1, ..., x_s], [u_1, ..., u_t], N),$$

and results in the necessary and sufficient condition as well as the *border polynomial BP* of $T$ in $u$ such that the number of the distinct real solutions of $T$ exactly equals to $N$ or belongs to $N$ provided $BP \neq 0$. If $T$ has infinite real solutions for generic value of parameters, $BP$ may have some variables. Then, for the "boundaries" produced by "**tofind**", i.e. $BP = 0$, we can call

$$\mathbf{Tofind}([\mathbb{P}, BP], [\mathbb{G}_1], [\mathbb{G}_2], [\mathbb{H}], [x_1, ..., x_s], [u_1, ..., u_t], N)$$

to obtain some further conditions on the parameters.

**Real Solution Isolation of Constant Semi-algebraic Systems**
For a constant SAS $T$ ( i.e., $t = 0$) of the form (1), if $T$ has only a finite number of real solutions, DISCOVERER can determine the number of distinct real solutions of $T$, say $n$, and moreover, can find out $n$ disjoint cubes with rational vertices in each of which there is only one solution. In addition, the width of the cubes can be less than any given positive real. The two functions are realized through calling

$$\mathbf{nearsolve}([\mathbb{P}], [\mathbb{G}_1], [\mathbb{G}_2], [\mathbb{H}], [x_1, ..., x_s]) \text{ and}$$
$$\mathbf{realzeros}([\mathbb{P}], [\mathbb{G}_1], [\mathbb{G}_2], [\mathbb{H}], [x_1, ..., x_s], w),$$

respectively, where $w$ is optional and used to indicate the maximum size of the output cubes.

# 3    Semi-algebraic Transition Systems and Invariants

In this section, we extend the notion of algebraic transition systems in [24] to semi-algebraic transition systems (SATSs) to represent polynomial programs. An Algebraic Transition System (ATS) is a special case of standard transition system, in which the initial condition and all transitions are specified in terms of polynomial equations; while in an SATS, each transition is equipped with a conjunctive polynomial formula as guard, and its initial and loop conditions possibly contain polynomial inequations and inequalities. It is easy to see that ATS is a special case of SATS. Formally,

**Definition 3.** *A semi-algebraic transition system is a quintuple $\langle V, L, T, \ell_0, \Theta \rangle$, where $V$ is a set of program variables, $L$ is a set of locations, and $T$ is a set of transitions. Each transition $\tau \in T$ is a quadruple $\langle \ell_1, \ell_2, \rho_\tau, \theta_\tau \rangle$, where $\ell_1$ and $\ell_2$ are the pre- and post- locations of the transition, $\rho_\tau \in CPF(V, V')$ is the transition relation, and $\theta_\tau \in CPF(V)$ is the guard of the transition. Only if $\theta_\tau$ holds, the transition can take place. Here, we use $V'$ (variables with prime) to denote the next-state variables. The location $\ell_0$ is the initial location, and $\Theta \in CPF(V)$ is the initial condition.*

If a transition $\tau$ changes nothing, i.e. $\rho_\tau \equiv \bigwedge_{v \in V} v' = v$, we denote by $skip$ $\rho_\tau$. Meanwhile, a transition $\tau = \langle l_1, l_2, \rho_\tau, \theta_\tau \rangle$ is abbreviated as $\langle l_1, l_2, \rho_\tau \rangle$, if $\theta_\tau$ is *true*.

Note that in the above definition, for simplicity, we require that each guard should be a conjunctive polynomial formula. In fact, we can drop such a restriction, as for any transition with a disjunctive guard we can split it into multiple transitions with the same pre- and post- locations and transition relation, but each of which takes a disjunct of the original guard as its guard.

A state is an evaluation of the variables in $V$ and all states are denoted by $Val(V)$. Without confusion we will use $V$ to denote both the variable set and an arbitrary state, and use $F(V)$ to mean the (truth) value of function (formula) $F$ under the state $V$. The semantics of SATSs can be explained through state transitions as usual.

A transition is called *separable* if its transition relation is a conjunctive formula of equations which define variables in $V'$ equal to polynomial expressions over variables in $V$. It is easy to see that the composition of two separable transitions is equivalent to a single separable one. An SATS is called *separable* if each transition of the system is separable. In a separable system, the composition of transitions along a path of the system is also equivalent to a single separable transition. We will only concentrate on separable SATSs as any polynomial program can easily be represented by a separable SATS (see [18]). Any SATS in the rest of the paper is always assumed separable, unless otherwise stated.

Informally, an *invariant* of a program at a location is an assertion that is *true* under any program state reaching the location. An invariant of a program can be seen as a mapping to map each location to an assertion which has inductive property, that is, *initial* and *consecutive*. *Initial* means that the image of the mapping at the initial location holds on the loop entry, i.e. the invariant of the initial location holds on the loop entry; whereas *consecutive* means that for any transition the invariant at the pre-location together with the transition relation and its guard implies the invariant at the post-location. In many cases, people only consider an invariant at the initial location and do not care about invariants at other locations. In this case, we can assume the invariants at other locations are all *true* and therefore *initial* and *consecutive* mean that the invariant holds on the entry, and is preserved under every cycle back to the initial location.

**Definition 4 (Invariant at a Location).** *Let $P = \langle V, L, T, l_0, \Theta \rangle$ be an SATS. An invariant at a location $l \in L$ is a conjunctive polynomial formula $\phi \in PF(V)$, such that $\phi$ holds on all states that can be reached at location $l$.*

**Definition 5 (Invariant of a Program).** *An assertion map for an SATS $P = \langle V, L, T, l_0, \Theta \rangle$ is a map $\eta : L \mapsto PF(V)$ that associates each location of $P$ with a formula of $PF(V)$. An assertion map of $P$ is said to be an invariant of $P$ iff the following conditions hold:*

**Initial:** $\Theta(V_0) \models \eta(l_0)$.
**Consecutive:** *For each transition $\tau = \langle l_i, l_j, \rho_\tau, \theta_\tau \rangle$,*

$$\eta(l_i)(V) \wedge \rho_\tau(V, V') \wedge \theta_\tau(V) \models \eta(l_j)(V').$$

## 4 Polynomial Invariants Generation

Similarly to [24], given an SATS $S$, we predetermine an invariant as a parametric SAS (PSAS for short) at each of the underlining locations (if no invariant is predefined for a location, it is assumed that the mapping takes *true* as value at the location) and therefore all these predefined PSASs form a parametric invariant of $S$ by the Definitions. Subsequently, according to the initial and consecutive conditions of the mapping, we can obtain a set of PSASs such that the mapping is an invariant of the program iff each element the resulted set has no real solution. Afterwards, we apply the algorithm on root classification of PSASs to each of them and obtain a corresponding necessary and sufficient condition on the parameters of the PSAS such that the PSAS has no real solution. Finally, applying quantifier elimination technique, we can get the instantiations of these parameters and therefore get an invariant for each underlining location by replacing with the resulted instantiations the parameters of the predetermined parametric PSAS. The above procedure are supported by the computer algebra tools DISCOVERER and QEPCAD.

We will use the following example to demonstrate our approach in details.

*Example 5.* Consider a program shown in Fig.1 (a).

$$P = \{$$

**Integer** $(x, y) := (0, 0);$     $V = \{x, y\}$

$l_0$ : **while** $x \geq 0 \wedge y \geq 0$ **do**     $L = \{l_0\}$
        $T = \{\tau\}$ $\}$

    $(x, y) := (x + y^2, y + 1);$     where

**end while**     $\tau = \langle l_0, l_0, x' - x - y^2 = 0 \wedge y' - y - 1 = 0,$
        $x \geq 0 \wedge y \geq 0 \rangle$

(a)     (b)

**Fig. 1.**

Thus, the corresponding SATS can be represented as in Fig.1 (b).

In the following, we concretize the above idea and demonstrate with the toy example.

**Predefining Invariant.** Predetermine a template of invariants at each of the underlining location, which is a PSAS, i.e. the conjunction of a set of atomic polynomial formula. All of these predefined PSASs form a parametric invariant of the program. For example, we can assume a template of invariants of $P$ at $l_0$ in Example 5 as

$$eq(x, y) = a_1 y^3 + a_2 y^2 + a_3 x - a_4 y = 0 \tag{3}$$
$$ineq(x, y) = b_1 x + b_2 y^2 + b_3 y + b_4 > 0, \tag{4}$$

where $a_1, a_2, a_3, a_4, b_1, b_2, b_3, b_4$ are parameters. Therefore, $\eta(l_0) = (3) \wedge (4)$.

Note that theoretically speaking we can predefine a PSAS as an invariant at each location like in the above example, but this will raise the complexity dramatically as thus the number of parameters is so large (the reader will see this point from the complexity analysis in the later). In practice, alternatively, we will split a complicated invariant to several simple invariants such that the image of every of these simple invariants at each location is just one of the atomic subformulae of the image of the complicated invariant at the location. For example, in the above example, we can split $\eta$ to $\eta_1$ and $\eta_2$ by letting $\eta_1(l_0) = (3)$ and $\eta_2(l_0) = (4)$. It is easy to prove that a program has a complicated invariant iff the corresponding simple invariant exist, for instance, $\eta$ exists iff $\eta_1$ and $\eta_2$ exist. This is because every invariant of a program is determined by the program itself.

**Deriving PSASs from Initial Condition and Solving.** According to the initial condition in Definition 5, we have $\Theta \models \eta(l_0)$ which means that each real solution of $\Theta$ must satisfy $\eta(l_0)$. In other words, $\Theta \wedge \neg\eta(l_0)$ has no real solution. This implies that for each atomic polynomial formula $\phi$ in $\eta(l_0)$, $\Theta \wedge \neg\phi$ has no real solution. Note that $\eta(l_0)$ is the conjunction of a set of atomic polynomials and $\Theta \wedge \neg\phi$ is a PSAS according to the definition. Thus, applying the tool DISCOVERER to the resulted PSAS $\Theta \wedge \neg\phi$, we get a necessary and sufficient condition of the derived PSAS having no real solution. The condition may contain the occurrences of some program variables. In this case, the condition should hold for any instantiations of these variables. Thus, by introducing universal quantifications of these variables (we usually add a scope to each of these variables according to different situations) and then applying QEPCAD, we can get a necessary and sufficient condition only on the presumed parameters.

Repeatedly apply the procedure to each atomic polynomial formula of the predefined invariant at $l_0$ and then collect all the resulted conditions.

*Example 6.* In Example 5, $\Theta \models \eta_1(l_0)$ is equivalent to

$$x = 0, y = 0, eq(x, y) \neq 0 \tag{5}$$

has no real solution. By calling

$$\textbf{tofind}(([x, y], [], [], [eq(x, y)], [x, y], [a_1, a_2, a_3, a_4], 0)$$

we get that (5) has no real solution iff *true*.
Similarly, $\Theta \models \eta_2(l_0)$ is equivalent to

$$x = 0, y = 0, ineq(x, y) \leq 0 \tag{6}$$

has no real solution. Calling

$$\textbf{tofind}([x, y], [-ineq(x, y)], [], [], [x, y], [b_1, b_2, b_3, b_4], 0)$$

we get that (6) has no real solution iff

$$b_4 > 0. \tag{7}$$

**Deriving PSASs from Consecutive Condition and Solving.** From Definition 5, for each transition $\tau = \langle l_i, l_j, \rho_\tau, \theta_\tau \rangle$,

$$\eta(l_i) \wedge \rho_\tau \wedge \theta_\tau \models \eta(l_j)$$

so $\eta(l_i) \wedge \rho_\tau \wedge \theta_\tau \wedge \neg\eta(l_j)$ has no real solution. This implies that for each atomic polynomial formula $\phi$

$$\eta(l_i) \wedge \rho_\tau \wedge \theta_\tau \wedge \neg\phi \tag{8}$$

has no real solution. It is easy to see that (8) is a PSAS according to Definition 1, so applying the tool DISCOVERER, we obtain a necessary and sufficient condition on the parameters such that (8) has no real solution. Subsequently, similarly to Step 2, we may need to exploit the quantifier elimination tool QEPCAD to reduce the resulted condition in order to get a necessary and sufficient condition only on the presumed parameters.

*Example 7.* In Example 5, for the invariant $\eta_1$, we have

$$eq(x,y) = 0 \wedge x' - x - y^2 = 0 \wedge y' - y - 1 = 0 \models eq(x',y') = 0. \tag{9}$$

This is equivalent to

$$eq(x,y) = 0 \wedge x' - x - y^2 = 0 \wedge y' - y - 1 = 0 \wedge eq(x',y') \neq 0 \tag{10}$$

has no real solution. Calling

$$\mathbf{tofind}([x' - x - y^2, y' - y - 1, eq(x,y)], [\,], [\,], [eq(x',y')\,],$$
$$[x',y',x], [y,a_1,a_2,a_3,a_4], 0),$$

it follows that (10) has no real solution iff

$$a_3 y^2 + 3a_1 y^2 + 2ya_2 + 3a_1 y - a_4 + a_2 + a_1 = 0 \wedge \tag{11}$$
$$a_3(a_1 y^2 + ya_2 - a_4) \leq 0. \tag{12}$$

Further by Basic Algebraic Theorem and simplifying by QEPCAD, $(11) \wedge (12)$ holds for all $y$ iff

$$- a_4 + a_2 + a_1 = 0 \wedge 3a_1 + 2a_2 = 0 \wedge a_3 + 3a_1 = 0. \tag{13}$$

Regarding the invariant $\eta_2$, we have

$$ineq(x,y) > 0 \wedge x' - x - y^2 = 0 \wedge y' - y - 1 = 0 \models ineq(x',y') > 0. \tag{14}$$

This is equivalent to

$$ineq(x,y) > 0 \wedge x' - x - y^2 = 0 \wedge y' - y - 1 = 0 \wedge ineq(x',y') \leq 0 \tag{15}$$

has no real solution. Calling

$$\mathbf{tofind}([x' - x - y^2, y' - y - 1], [-ineq(x',y')], [ineq(x,y)], [\,],$$
$$[x',y'], [x,y,b_1,b_2,b_3,b_4], 0),$$

it follows that (15) has no real solution iff

$$b_4 + b_3 + b_2 + 2b_2 y + b_3 y + b_2 y^2 + b_1 x + b_1 y^2 > 0. \tag{16}$$

It is easy to see that (16) should hold for all $y \geq 0$, and thus, by applying QEP-CAD to eliminate the quantifiers $\forall y \geq 0$ over (16), we get

$$b_1 + b_2 \geq 0 \wedge b_1 \geq 0 \wedge b_2 + b_3 + b_4 > 0 \wedge$$
$$(b_3 + 2b_2 \geq 0 \vee (b_1 b_2 + b_2^2 \geq 0 \wedge 4b_2 b_4 + 4b_1 b_4 + 4b_1 b_3 + 4b_1 b_2 - b_3^2 > 0)) \tag{17}$$

**Generating Invariant.** According to the results obtained from Steps 1, 2 and 3, we can get the final necessary and sufficient condition only on the parameters of each of the invariant templates. If the condition is too complicated, we can utilize the function of PCAD of DISCOVERER or QEPCAD to prove if or not the condition is satisfied. If yes, the tool can produce the instantiations of these parameters. Thus, we can get an invariant of the predetermined form by replacing the parameters with the instantiations, respectively.

*Example 8.* From Examples 6 & 7, it follows the necessary and sufficient condition on the parameters of $\eta_1$ is (13). By using DISCOVERER, we get an instantiation

$$(a_1, a_2, a_3, a_4) = (-2, 3, 6, 1).$$

Thus, $\eta_1(l_0) = -2y^3 + 3y^2 + 6x - y = 0$. Also, the necessary and sufficient condition on the parameters of $\eta_2$ is (7) $\wedge$ (17). By PCAD of DISCOVERER, it results the following instantiation

$$(b_1, b_2, b_3, b_4) = (1, -1, 2, 1)$$

that is, $\eta_2(l_0) = x - y^2 + 2y + 1 > 0$. Totally, we get the following invariant for the program $P$:

$$\begin{cases} -2y^3 + 3y^2 + 6x - y = 0, \\ x - y^2 + 2y + 1 > 0 \end{cases}$$

Note that the above procedure is *complete* in the sense that for any given predefined parametric invariant, the procedure can always give you an answer, yes or no. Therefore, we can conclude that our approach is also *complete* in the sense that once the given polynomial program has a polynomial invariant, our approach can indeed find it theoretically. This is because we can assume parametric invariants in program variables of different degrees, and repeatedly apply the above procedure until we obtain a polynomial invariant.

## 5  Complexity Analysis

Assume given an SATS $P = \langle V, L, T, l_0, \Theta \rangle$, applying the above procedure, we obtain $k$ distinct PSASs so that the predefined parametric invariants form an invariant of the program iff none of these $k$ PSASs has any real solution. W.l.o.g., suppose each of these $k$ PSASs has at most $s$ polynomial equations, and $m$ inequations and inequalities. All polynomials are in $n$ indeterminates (i.e., variables and parameters) and of degrees at most $d$.

For a PSAS $S$, by [3], CAD (*cylindrical algebraic decomposition*) based quantifier elimination on $S$ has complexity $\mathcal{O}((2d)^{2^{2n+8}}(s+m)^{2^{n+6}})$, which is double exponential w.r.t. $n$. Thus, the total cost is $\mathcal{O}(k(2d)^{2^{2n+8}}(s+m)^{2^{n+6}})$ for directly applying the technique of quantifier elimination to generate an invariant of a program as advocated by Kapur [17].

In contrast, the cost of our approach includes two parts: one is for applying real solution classification to generate condition on the parameters possibly together with some program variables; the other is for applying first-order quantifier elimination to produce condition only on the parameters (if necessary) and further exploiting PCAD to obtain the instantiations of these parameters.

The first part consists of three main steps. Firstly, we transform the equations in $S$ into triangular sets (i.e., equations in triangular form) by Ritt-Wu's method. By [12], the complexity of computing the first characteristic set is $\mathcal{O}(s^{\mathcal{O}(n)}(d+1)^{\mathcal{O}(n^3)})$. Thus, the complexity of this step is $\mathcal{O}(s^{n^{\mathcal{O}(1)}}(d+1)^{n^{\mathcal{O}(1)}})$, which is usually called a singly exponential complexity w.r.t. $n$. Secondly, we compute a *border polynomial* (BP) from the triangularized systems through re-sultant computation. Because the polynomials in the first computed characteris-tic sets are of degree $\mathcal{O}(s(d+1)^{\mathcal{O}(n^2)})$ by [12], the polynomials in the computed triangular sets are of degree $\mathcal{O}(s^{n^{\mathcal{O}(1)}}(d+1)^{n^{\mathcal{O}(1)}})$. Thus, the complexity of com-puting BP is at most $(s+m)\mathcal{O}(s^{3s+sn^{\mathcal{O}(1)}}(d+1)^{sn^{\mathcal{O}(1)}})$ because the complexity of computing the resultant of two polynomials with degree $d$ is at most $\mathcal{O}(d^3)$. Moreover, the degree of BP is at most $D = \mathcal{O}(s^{\mathcal{O}(s^2+s^2n^{\mathcal{O}(1)})}(d+1)^{\mathcal{O}(s^2n^{\mathcal{O}(1)})})$. Finally, we use a partial CAD algorithm with BP to obtain real solution clas-sification. The complexity of this step is at most the complexity of performing quantifier elimination on BP using CAD. Suppose the dimension of the ideal generated by the $s$ polynomial equations is $t$, then BP has at most $t$ indetermi-nates. Thus, by [3], the complexity of this step is at most $\mathcal{O}(2D^{2^{2t+8}})$, which is double exponential with respect to $t$. In a word, the cost for this part is singly exponential in $n$ and doubly exponential in $t$.

As the biggest degree of polynomials in the generated necessary and sufficient condition from the above is at most $D$, the cost for the second part is $\mathcal{O}(2D^{2^{2t+8}})$ as well, which is doubly exponential in $t$, according to [3].

So, compared to directly applying quantifier elimination, our approach can dramatically reduce the complexity, in particular when $t$ is much less than $n$.

## 6    Generating Invariants vs. Discovering Ranking Functions

In [2], we showed how to apply the approach to discovering non-linear ranking functions. Although invariants and ranking functions both have inductive prop-erties, the former is inductive w.r.t. a small step, i.e. each of single transitions of the given program in contrast that the latter is inductive w.r.t. a big step, that is each of circle transition at the initial location of the program. The difference results that as far as invariant generation is concerned, our approach can be simply applied to single loop programs as well as nested loop programs, without any change; but regarding the discovery of ranking functions, we have to develop the approach in order to handle nested loop programs, although it works well for single loop programs.

## 7    Conclusions and Future Work

In this paper, we reduced the polynomial invariant generation of polynomial programs to solving semi-algebraic systems, and theoretically analyzed why our approach is more efficient and practical than that of [17] directly applying the technique of first-order quantifier elimination. Compared to the well-established approaches in this field, the invariants generated with our approach are more expressive.

How to further improve the efficiency of our approach is still a big challenge as well as our main future work, as the complexity is still single exponential w.r.t. the number of program variables and parameters, and doubly exponential w.r.t. the number of parameters (at least). The high complexity restricts to scale up our approach yet. Moreover, it deserves to investigate how to combine our approach with other program verification techniques such as abstract interpretation and Floyd-Hoare-Dijkstra's inductive assertion method in order to resolve complicated verification problems. In addition, implementing our approach in a verification tool also makes so much senses in practice.

## Acknowledgements

The work of this paper is a continuation of the one in [2], we are therefore so grateful to Prof. Chaochen Zhou for his contribution to the previous joint work as well as lots of fruitful discussions on this work and valuable comments on the draft of this paper. Naijun Zhan's work owes much to Prof. Chaochen Zhou, who taught him formal methods and many other things.

## References

1. Besson, F., Jensen, T., Talpin, J.-P.: Polyhedral analysis of synchronous languages. In: Cortesi, A., Filé, G. (eds.) SAS 1999. LNCS, vol. 1694, pp. 51–69. Springer, Heidelberg (1999)
2. Chen, Y., Xia, B., Yang, L., Zhan, N., Zhou, C.: Discovering non-linear ranking functions by solving semi-algebraic systems. In: ICTAC 2007. LNCS, Springer, Heidelberg (2007) (Invited paper)
3. Collins, G.E.: Quantifier elimination for real closed fields by cylindrical algebraic decomposition. In: Brakhage, H. (ed.) Automata Theory and Formal Languages. LNCS, vol. 33, pp. 134–183. Springer, Heidelberg (1975)
4. Collins, G.E., Hong, H.: Partial cylindrical algebraic decomposition for quantifier elimination. J. of Symbolic Computation 12, 299–328 (1991)
5. colón, M., Sankaranarayanan, S., Sipma, H.B.: Linear invariant generation using non-linear constraint solving. In: Hunt Jr., W.A., Somenzi, F. (eds.) CAV 2003. LNCS, vol. 2725, pp. 420–432. Springer, Heidelberg (2003)
6. Cousot, P.: Proving program invariance and termination by parametric abstraction, Langrangian Relaxation and semidefinite programming. In: Cousot, R. (ed.) VMCAI 2005. LNCS, vol. 3385, pp. 1–24. Springer, Heidelberg (2005)
7. Cousot, P., Halbwachs, N.: Automatic discovery of linear restraints among the variables of a program. In: ACM POPL'78, pp. 84–97 (1978)
8. Davenport, J.H., Heintz, J.: Real Elimination is Doubly Exponential. J. of Symbolic Computation 5, 29–37 (1988)
9. Dijkstra, E.W.: A Discipline of Programming. Prentice-Hall, Englewood Cliffs (1976)
10. Dolzman, A., Sturm, T.: REDLOG: Computer algebra meets computer logic. ACM SIGSAM Bulletin 31(2), 2–9
11. Floyd, R.W.: Assigning meanings to programs. Proc. Symphosia in Applied Mathematics 19, 19–37 (1967)
12. Gallo, G., Mishra, B.: Efficient Algorithms and Bounds for Wu-Ritt Characteristic Sets. In: Mora, T., Traverso, C. (eds.) Effective methods in algebraic geometry, Birkhäuser, Bosten. Progress in Mathematics, pp. 119–142 (1994)

13. German, S., Wegbreit, B.: A synthesizer of inductive assertions. IEEE Transactions on Software Engineering 1(1), 68–75 (1975)
14. Hoare, C.A.R.: An axiomatic basis for computer programming. Comm. ACM 12(10), 576–580 (1969)
15. Karr, M.: Affine relationships among variables of a program. Acta Informatica 6, 133–151 (1976)
16. Katz, S., Manna, Z.: Logical analysis of programms. Communications of the ACM 19(4), 188–206 (1976)
17. Kapur, D.: Automatically generating loop invariants using quantifier llimination. In: Proc. IMACS Intl. Conf. on Applications of Computer Algebra ( ACA'04), Beaumont, Texas (July 2004)
18. Manna, Z., Pnueli, A.: Temporal Verification of Reactive Systems: Safety. Springer, Heidelberg (1995)
19. Múller-Olm, M., Seidl, H.: Polynomial constants are decidable. In: Hermenegildo, M.V., Puebla, G. (eds.) SAS 2002. LNCS, vol. 2477, pp. 4–19. Springer, Heidelberg (2002)
20. Múller-Olm, M., Seidl, H.: Precise interprocedural analysis through linear algebra. In: ACM SIGPLAN Principles of Programming Languages, POPL 2004, pp. 330–341 (2004)
21. Rodriguez-Carbonell, E., Kapur, D.: An abstract interpretation approach for automatic generation of polynomial invariants. In: Giacobazzi, R. (ed.) SAS 2004. LNCS, vol. 3148, pp. 280–295. Springer, Heidelberg (2004)
22. Rodriguez-Carbonell, E., Kapur, D.: Automatic generation of polynomial loop invariants: algebraic foundations. In: Proc. Intl. Symp on Symbolic and Algebraic Computation (ISSAC'04) (July 2004)
23. Rodriguez-Carbonell, E., Kapur, D.: Generating all polynomial invariants in simple loops. Journal of Symbolic Computation 42, 443–476 (2007)
24. Sankaranarayanan, S., Sipma, H.B., Manna, Z.: Non-linear loop invariant generation using Gröbner bases. In: ACM POPL'04, pp. 318–329 (2004)
25. Wegbreit, B.: The synthesis of loop predicates. Communications of the ACM 17(2), 102–112 (1974)
26. Wu, W.-T.: Basic principles of mechanical theorem proving in elementary geometries. J. Syst. Sci. Math. 4, 207–235 (1984)
27. Xia, B., Xiao, R., Yang, L.: Solving parametric semi-algebraic systems. In: Pae, S.-l, Park, H. (eds.) Proc. the 7th Asian Symposium on Computer Mathematics (ASCM 2005), Seoul, December 8-10, pp. 153–156 (2005)
28. Xia, B., Yang, L.: An algorithm for isolating the real solutions of semi-algebraic systems. J. Symbolic Computation 34, 461–477 (2002)
29. Xia, B., Zhang, T.: Real Solution Isolation Using Interval Arithmetic. Comput. Math. Appl. 52, 853–860 (2006)
30. Yang, L.: Recent advances on determining the number of real roots of parametric polynomials. J. Symbolic Computation 28, 225–242 (1999)
31. Yang, L., Hou, X., Xia, B.: A complete algorithm for automated discovering of a class of inequality-type theorems. Sci. in China (Ser. F) 44, 33–49 (2001)
32. Yang, L., Hou, X., Zeng, Z.: A complete discrimination system for polynomials. Science in China (Ser. E) 39, 628–646 (1996)
33. Yang, L., Xia, B.: Automated Deduction in Real Geometry. In: Chen, F., Wang, D. (eds.) Geometric Computation, pp. 248–298. World Scientific, Singapore (2004)
34. Yang, L., Xia, B.: Real solution classifications of a class of parametric semi-algebraic systems. In: Proc. of Int'l Conf. on Algorithmic Algebra and Logic, pp. 281–289 (2005)

# Harnessing rCOS for Tool Support
# —The CoCoME Experience*

Zhenbang Chen[1], Xiaoshan Li[2], Zhiming Liu[1,**], Volker Stolz[1], and Lu Yang[1]

[1] United Nations University
Institute for Software Technology (UNU-IIST)
[2] Faculty of Science and Technology, The University of Macau

**Abstract.** Complexity of software development has to be dealt with by dividing the different aspects and different views of the system and separating different concerns in the design. This implies the need of different modelling notations and tools to support more and more phases of the entire development process. To ensure the correctness of the models produced, the tools therefore need to integrate sophisticated checkers, generators and transformations. A feasible approach to ensure high quality of such add-ins is to base them on sound formal foundations. This paper reports our experience in the work on the Common Component Modelling Example (CoCoME) and shows where such add-ins will fit. In particular, we show how the formal techniques developed in rCOS can be integrated into a component-based development process, and where it can be integrated in and provide extension to an existing successful commercial tool for adding formally supported checking, transformation and generation modules.

**Keywords:** Software development tool, software process, formal methods, tool design.

## 1 Introduction

Software engineering is now facing two major challenges on

1. how to handle the huge complexity of system development, and
2. how to ensure the correctness and quality of the software

The complexity of software development is inherent due to many different aspects of the system, including those of static structure, flow of control, interactions and functionality, and different concerns of functionality correctness, concurrency, distribution, mobility, security, timing, and so on. Large software development

---

* This work is partially supported by the projects HighQSoftD and HTTS funded by Macao Science and Technology Development Fund, NSFC-60673114 and 863 of China 2006AA01Z165.
** I started working on separation and integration of models of different aspects and concerns of systems when I started my study for my Master Degree [24] under the supervision of Professor Zhou Chaochen.

C.B. Jones, Z. Liu, J. Woodcock (Eds.): Bjørner/Zhou Festschrift, LNCS 4700, pp. 83–114, 2007.

requires a large team of people playing different roles and carrying out different activities of design, construction, analysis, verification and validation. The management of the development process is complex, too.

In *practical software engineering* nowadays, complexity is dealt with by a component-based and model-driven development process [7,9] where

1. the different aspects and views of the system are described in a UML-like multi-view and multi-notational language, and
2. separation of design and validation of different concerns is supported by design patterns, object-oriented and component-based designs.

However, there are no rigorous unified theories and tools which support specification, verification and validation of the models produced in such a process.

Rigorous verification and validation of a software system requires the application of formal methods. This needs a formal version of the requirements specification, and the establishment of a property to imply that the specified requirement holds as long as the assumptions hold. The assumptions are specifications for or constraints on the behavior of environment and system elements. In the past half a century, semantic foundations, formal notations and techniques and tools of verification and validation have been developed, including *testing, static analysis, model checking, formal proof and theorem proving*, and *runtime checking*. They can be classified into the following frameworks:

- event-based models [29,15] are widely used for specification and verification of interactions, and are supported by model checking and simulation tools [30,2].
- pre-post conditions and Hoare logic are applied to specifications of functionality and static analysis. These are supported by tools of theorem proving, runtime checking and testing [22,11,28].
- state transition systems and temporal logics are popular for specification and verification of dynamic control behaviours. They are supported by model checking tools [17,21].

However, each framework is researched mostly by a separate community, and most of the research in verification has largely ignored the impact of design methods on feasibility of formal verification. Therefore, the formal techniques and tools are not good with regard to scalability and they are not easy to be integrated into practical design and development processes. The notion of *program refinement* [4] has obvious links to the practical design of programs with the consideration of abstraction and correctness, but the existing refinement calculi are shown to be effective only for small imperative programs. There is a lack of a formal foundation for object-oriented and component-based *model refinement* until the recent work on formal methods of component and object systems [10,25,14,6].

The formalism, rCOS [14,6], that we have recently developed, is a rather rich and mature formalism that models static and dynamic features for component based systems. It is based on the UTP framework [16], and its accompanying methodology of *separation of concerns* [7], have been applied in a case study of a Point Of Sale terminal within the CoCoME (Common Component Modelling Example) challenge [8]. In this paper, we discuss our experience on how the construction of formal models and their verification and validation can be integrated in a use case driven and component-based development process. In particular, we will show with examples from the CoCoME case studies

1. what the models of the different aspects of the systems are at each stage of the development, including the *requirement elicitation, logic design, detailed design, code generation,*
2. how these models are constructed and derived by application of design patterns that are proved to be a refinement in rCOS, and
3. how verification and validation tasks are identified for the models and what are the effective tools for these tasks.

With regard to model construction and derivation, we focus on the aspects of interactions, dynamic behaviour, and static functionality of the system and show how the design and refinement of constraints on these aspects can be separated, and how they can consistently form a whole model of the system. For verification and validation, we look at consistency between interactions and dynamic behaviour, component interaction protocols, static analysis and testing of functionality. We discuss how the activities of model construction, transformations, model verification and validation can be embedded into an existing commercial software development tool, MasterCraft [31]. We have selected this tool, because it has extensive coverage of the whole software development life-cycle, from requirements gathering and analysis, through early design stages to implementation and testing, with support for deployment and maintenance. Finally, it plays a major role that the producer of MasterCraft, Tata Research Development and Design Centre (TRDDC), generously had permitted us to inspect the tool in detail.

**Overview.** The following Section 2 gives an overview on the main ideas and theme of our research on the rCOS methodology, and provides the formulation of the main concepts of model-driven development. In Section 3, we demonstrate, with our recent experience in the work on CoCoME case study, how the formalization of the concepts, models and techniques developed in rCOS can be integrated in a model-driven development process. The integration unifies the different formal techniques of verification and validation with correctness by design. We then discuss in Section 4 how we can enhance the industrial model-driven tool, MasterCraft, for the support of the integration of formal design, verification and validation into a practical engineering development process. Finally Section 5 summarizes our experience and discusses the plan for our future work.

## 2   The Basic Ideas Behind rCOS

The motivation of the research on rCOS is to provide a semantic foundation for *model driven development* in the combined framework of object-oriented and component-based software development. Practical software engineering shows that this is a promising approach to heighten productivity in software development while maintaining a high quality. It lets developers design systems at a higher level of abstraction using models or specifications of components which will be produced and integrated at a later implementation, assembly and deployment stage.

### 2.1   rCOS Formulation of Software Concepts

A project using model driven development starts with a set of component specifications which may be given for previously developed components or be newly introduced for components that are to be developed later. The designers then proceed to

- build new components by applying component operators (connectors) to the given ones,
- build new components by programming glue processes,
- define application work-flows as processes that use services from components,
- verification and validation are performed on components before and after composition.

To provide formal support to such a development process, we formulate in rCOS the key notions as mathematical structures and study the rules for manipulation of these mathematical entities. These notions include *interfaces, contracts of interfaces, components, processes, compositions* and *refinement relations* on contracts, components and processes. In the next subsection, we give a brief introduction to formulations.

**Interfaces and Contracts.** An interface $I$ provides the syntactic type information of an interaction point of a component. It consists of two parts, the *data declaration section* denoted by $I.FDec$, that declares a set of variables with their types, and the *method declaration section*, denoted by $I.MDec$, that defines a set of method signatures each with the form $m(T_1\ in;\ T_2\ out)$. Interfaces are used for syntactic type checking. The current practical component technologies only provide syntactical aspects of interfaces and leave the semantics of interfaces to informal naming schemes. This is obviously not enough for rigorous verification and validation. For example, a component with only syntactic interfaces shown in Fig. 1 has no information about its functionality or behavior.

A *contract* is a specification of the semantic details for the interface. However, different usages of the component in different applications under different environments may contain different details, and have different properties:

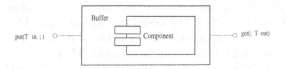

**Fig. 1.** A component with syntactic interface only

- An interface for a component in a sequential system is obviously different from one in a communicating concurrent system. A contract for the former only needs to specify the functionality of the methods, e.g. in terms of their pre- and post-conditions. A contract for the later should include a description of the communicating protocol, for example in terms of interaction traces. The protocol specifies the order in which the interaction events happen.
- An interface for a component in a real-time application will need to provide the real-time constraints of services, but an untimed application does not.
- Components in distributed, mobile or internet-based systems require their interfaces to include information about their locations or addresses.
- An interface (component) should be stateless when the component is required to be used dynamically and independently from other components.
- A service component has different features from a middleware component.

*It is the contract of the interface that determines the external behavior and features of the component and allows the component to be used as a black box.*

Based on the above discussion, rCOS defines the notion of an interface contract for a component as a description of what is needed for the component to be *used* in building and maintaining software systems. The description of an interface must contain information about all the viewpoints among, e.g., functionality, behavior, protocols, safety, reliability, real-time, power, bandwidth, memory consumption and communication mechanisms, that are needed for composing the component in the given architecture for the application of the system. However, this description can be incremental in the sense that newly required properties or view points can be added when needed according to the application. Also, the consistency of these viewpoints should be formalizable and checkable. For this, rCOS is built on Hoare and He's Unifying Theories of Programming [16].

**The Minimal Use of UTP.** In UTP, a *sequential program* (but possibly non-deterministic) is represented by a *design* $D = (\alpha, P)$, where

- $\alpha$ denotes the set of state variables (called observables) of the program
- $P$ is a predicate $p(x) \vdash R(x, x') \stackrel{def}{=} (ok \land p(x)) \Rightarrow (ok' \land R(x, x'))$, meaning that if the program is activated $ok$ in a state where the *precondition* $p(x)$ holds the execution will terminate $ok$ in a state where the postcondition holds that post-state $x'$ and the initial state $x$ are related by relation $R$.

It is proven in UTP that the set of designs is closed under the classical programming constructs of *sequential composition, conditional choice, nondeterministic choice*, and fixed point of iterations. Refinement between designs is defined as logical implications, and all the above operations on designs are monotonic with regard to refinements (i.e. the order of implication). These fundamental mathematical properties ensure that the domain of designs is a proper semantic domain for sequential programming languages. There is a nice link from the theory of designs to the theory of predicate transformers with the following definition:

$$\mathbf{wp}(p \vdash R, q) \stackrel{def}{=} p \wedge \neg(R; \neg q)$$

that defines the *weakest precondition* of a design for a post condition $q$.

Concurrent and reactive programs, such as those specified by Back's action systems [4] or Lamport's Temporal Logic of Actions (TLA) [19], can be defined by the notion of *guarded designs*, written as $g \& D$ and defined by

$$(\alpha, \mathbf{if}\ g\ \mathbf{then}\ P\ \mathbf{else}\ (true \vdash wait' \wedge v' = v))$$

The domain of guarded designs enjoys the same closure properties as that domain. And refinement is defined as logical implication, too.

The basic UTP has no notions of objects, classes, inheritance, polymorphism, and dynamic binding. For a combination of OO and component-based modelling, we have extended UTP to object-oriented programming [14].

**Contracts of Interfaces.** In the current version of rCOS, we only consider components in the application of concurrent and distributed systems, and a *contract Ctr = (I, Init, MSpec, Prot)* specifies

- the allowable initial states by the initial condition *Init*,
- the synchronization condition $g$ on each declared method and the functionality of the method by the specification function *MSpec* that assigns each method to a guarded design $g \& D$.
- *Prot* is called the *protocol* and is a set of sequences of call events; each is of the form $?op_1(x_1), \ldots, ?op_k(x_k)$. Notice a protocol can be specified by a temporal logic or a trace logic.

For example, the component interface in Fig. 1 does not say the buffer is a one-place buffer. A specification of a one-place buffer can be given by a contract $B$ for which

- The interface: $B_1.I = \langle q : Seq(int), put(item : int; ), get(; res : int) \rangle$
- The initial condition: $B_1.Init = q = <>$
- The specification:

$$B_1.MSpec(put) = q = <> \& true \vdash q' = < item >$$
$$B_1.MSpec(get) = q \neq <> \& true \vdash res' = head(q) \wedge q' = <>$$

- The protocol: $B_1.Prot$ is a set of traces that is a subset of

$$\{e_1, \ldots, e_k \mid e_i\ is\ ?put()\ if\ i\ is\ odd\ and\ ?get()\ otherwise\}.$$

The formulation of contracts supports separation of views, but the different views have to be consistent. A contract $Ctr$ is *consistent*, indicated through a predicate $Cons(Ctr)$, if it will never enter a deadlock state if its environment interacts with it according to its protocol, that is, for all $\langle ?op_1(x_1), \ldots, ?op_k(x_k) \rangle \in Ctr.Prot$,

$$\mathbf{wp} \left( \begin{array}{c} Init; g_1 \& D_1[x_1/in_1]; \ldots; g_k \& D_k[x_k/in_k], \\ \neg wait \land \exists op \in MDec \bullet g(op) \end{array} \right) = true$$

Note that this formalization takes both synchronization conditions and functionalities into account, as an execution of a method with its precondition falsified will diverge and a divergent state can cause deadlock too.

We have proven the following *theorem of separation of concerns*:

**Theorem 1 (Separation of Concerns)**

1. *If* $Cons(I, Init, MSpec, Prot_i)$, *then* $Cons(I, Init, MSpec, Prot_1 \cup Prot_2)$, $i \in \{1, 2\}$
2. *If* $Cons(I, Init, MSpec, Prot_1)$ *and* $Prot_2 \subseteq Prot_1$, *then* $Cons(I, Init, MSpec, Prot_2)$
3. *If* $Cons(I, Init, MSpec, Prot)$ *and* $MSpec \sqsubseteq MSpec_1$, *then* $Cons(I, Init, MSpec_1, Prot)$

This allows us to refine the specification and the protocol separately.

We are now current working on an extension to the model of contracts for specification of the timing information of a component. An interesting and important point that we would like to make is that the notation for timing aspect at the contract level should be different from that used for the model of the design of components. At the contract level, we propose the use of interval based notation to describe the minimal time and maximal time $[t_e, T_e]$ that the environment has to wait when calling an interface method (that is the worst case execution time of the interface methods), and the minimal time and maximal time $[t_w, T_w]$ that the component is willing to wait for a method to be invoked. Zhou Chaochen's Duration Calculus [32] is an obvious choice for reasoning about these interval based timing properties. However, for the design and verification of the implementation of a component, clocks or timers in the timed automata model are more feasible. This indicates the use of different notations at different levels of abstraction in system development. A challenge is to link the clock time model for the design of components to the interval-based time model of its contract. Initial results on this work can be found [26].

**Contract Refinement.** A contract $Ctr$ has a denotational semantics in terms of its *failure set* $\mathcal{F}(Ctr)$ and divergence set $\mathcal{F}(Ctr_1)$, that is same as the failure-divergence semantics for CSP (but we do not use the CSP language) [6]. $Ctr_1$ is *refined* by contract $Ctr_2$, denoted by $Ctr_1 \sqsubseteq Ctr_2$, if the later offers the same provided methods, $Ctr_1.MDec = Ctr_2.MDec$, is not more likely to diverge than the former, $\mathcal{D}(Ctr_1) \supseteq \mathcal{D}(Ctr_2)$, and not more likely to deadlock than the former, $\mathcal{F}(Ctr_1) \supseteq \mathcal{F}(Ctr_2)$. We have established a complete proof techniques of refinement by simulation.

**Theorem 2 (Refinement by Simulation)**
$Ctr_1 \sqsubseteq Ctr_2$ *if there exists a total mapping* $\rho(u, v') : FDec_1 \longrightarrow FDec_2$ *such that*

1. $Init_2 \Rightarrow (Init_1; \rho)$
2. $\rho \Rightarrow (guard_1(op) = guard_2(op))$ *for all* $op \in MDec_1$.
3. *for each* $op \in MDec_1$, $MSpec_1(op); \rho \sqsubseteq \rho; MSpec_2(op)$

Similarly, contract refinement can also be proved by a surjective upward simulation [6].

## Theorem 3 (Completeness of Simulations)
*If* $Ctr_1 \sqsubseteq Ctr_2$, *there exists a* $Ctr$ *such that*

$$Ctr_1 \preceq_{up} Ctr \preceq_{down} Ctr_2 \qquad Ctr_1 \sqsubseteq Ctr \sqsubseteq Ctr_2$$

$\preceq_{up}$ *and* $\preceq_{down}$ *denote upwards and downwards simulations, respectively.*

**Components.** A component is an *implementation* of a contract. Formally speaking, a *component* is tuple $C = (I, Init, MCode, PriMDec, PriMCode, InMDec)$, where

- *MCode* and *PriMCode* map a public method to a private method $m$ to a guarded command $g_m \rightarrow c_m$,
- *InMDec* is the set of required methods in the code, called *required interface*.

The *semantics* $[\![C]\!]$ is a function that calculates a contract for the provided interface for any given contract *InCtr* of the required interface

$$[\![C]\!](InCtr) \stackrel{def}{=} ((I, MSpec), Init, PriMDec, PriMSpec)$$

where the specification is calculated from the semantics of the code, following the calculus established in UTP.

A component $C_1$ is refined by another component $C_2$, denoted by $C_1 \sqsubseteq C_2$ if

1. the later provides the same services as the former, $C_1.MDec = C_2.MDec$
2. the later requires the same services as the former $C_1.InMDec = C_2.InMDec$, and
3. for any given contract of the required interface, the resulting provided contract of the later is a refinement of that of the former, $C_1(InCtr) \sqsubseteq C_2(InCtr)$, holds for all input contracts *InCtr*.

Note that the notion of component refinement is used for both *component correctness by design* and component *substitutability* in maintenance. One of the major objectives of rCOS is to prove *design patterns* as refinement rules, and automate refinement rules as *model transformations*. We hope this will help to reduce the amount of verification required.

**Simple Connectors.** To support the development activity, the semantic framework also needs to define operators for connecting components, resulting in new contracts, constructs for defining glue processes, and constructs for defining processes. In summary, the framework should be *compositional and support both functional and behavioral specification*. In rCOS, simple connectors between components are defined as component compositions. These include *plugging* (or *union*), *service hiding*, *service renaming*, and *feedback*. These compositions are shown in Figs. 2-4.

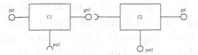

**Fig. 2.** Plug Composition

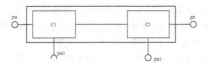

**Fig. 3.** Hiding after Chaining

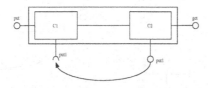

**Fig. 4.** Feedback

## 2.2   Coordination

From an external point of view, components provide a number of methods, but do not themselves activate the functionality specified in the contracts; we need active entities that implement a desired functionality by coordinating the sequences of method calls. In general, these active entities do not share the three features of components [13].

In [6], we introduce *processes* into rCOS. Like a component, a process has an interface declaring its own local state variables and methods, and its behavior is specified by a process contract. Unlike a component that is passively waiting for a client to call its provided services, a process is active and has its own control on when to call out to required services or to wait for a call to its provided services. For such an active process, we cannot have separate contracts for its provided interface and required interface, because we cannot have separate specifications of outgoing calls and incoming calls [13]. So a process only has an interface and its associated contract (or code). For simplicity, but without losing expressiveness, we assume a process like a Java thread does not provide services and only calls methods provided by components. Therefore, processes can only communicate via shared components. Of course, a component can also communicate with another component via processes, but without knowing the component that it is communicating with.

Let $C$ be the parallel composition of a number of disjoint components $C_i$, $i = 1 \ldots k$. A glue program for $C$ is a process $P$ that makes calls to a set of $X$ of provided methods of $C$. The composition $C \| [X] P$ of $C$ and $P$ is defined similarly to the alphabetized parallel composition in CSP [30] with interleaving of events. The gluing composition is defined by hiding the synchronized methods between the component $C$ and the process P. We have proven that $(C \| [X] P) \backslash X$ is a component, and studied the algebraic laws of the composition of processes and components. The glue composition is illustrated in Fig. 5, where in Fig. 5(a) $C1$ and $C2$ are two one-place buffers and $P$ is a process that keeps getting the item from $C1$ and putting it to $C2$. In Fig. 5(b), the *get* of $C1$ and *put* of $C2$ are synchronized into an atomic step by component $M$; and $M$ proves method $move()\{get1(;y); put2(y;)\}$, that process $P$ calls.

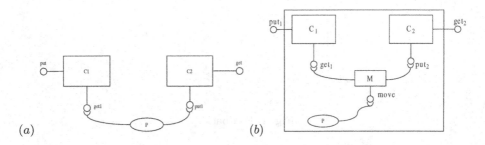

**Fig. 5.** (a) Gluing two one-place buffers forms a three-place Buffer, (b) Gluing two One-place buffers forms a two-place buffer

An *application program* is a set of parallel processes that make use of the services provided by components. As processes only interact with components via the provided interfaces of the components, interoperability is thus supported by the contracts which define the semantics of the common interface description language (IDL), even though components, glue programs and application programs are not implemented in the same language. Analysis and verification of an application program can be performed in the classical formal frameworks, but at the level of contracts of components instead of implementations of components. The analysis and verification can reuse any proved properties about the components, such as divergence freedom and deadlock freedom without the need to reprove them.

## 2.3   Object-Orientation in rCOS

The variables in the field declaration section can be of object types. This allows us to apply OO techniques to the design and implementation of a component. In our earlier work [14], we have extended UTP to formal treatment of OO program and OO refinement. This is summarized as follows.

**Classes.** In rCOS, we write a class specification in the following format:

$$
\begin{aligned}
&\textbf{class} && C \, [\textbf{extends} \; D]\{ \\
&\textbf{attr} && T_1 \, x = d, \dots, T_k \, x = d \\
&\textbf{meth} && m(T \; in; V \; return) \, \{ \\
& && \textbf{pre:} \quad c \vee \dots \vee c \\
& && \textbf{post:} \quad (R; \dots; R) \vee \dots \vee (R; \dots; R) \\
& && \qquad \wedge \dots \dots \\
& && \qquad \wedge \, (R; \dots; R) \vee \dots \vee (R; \dots; R) \, \} \\
& && \dots \dots \\
&\textbf{meth} && m(T \; in; V \; return) \, \{\dots \dots \} \\
& && \dots \dots \\
&\textbf{invariant} && Inv \, \}
\end{aligned}
$$

The initial value of an attribute is optional, and an attribute is assumed to be public unless it is tagged with reserved words *private* and *protected*. If no initial value is declared it will default to *null*.

Each $c$ in the precondition represents a condition to be checked; it is a conjunction of primitive predicates.

A *design* $p \vdash R$ for a method is written as **Pre** $p$ and **Post** $R$. An $R$ in the postcondition is of the form $c \wedge (le' = e)$, where $c$ is a condition, $le$ an *assignable expression* and $e$ an expression. An assignable $le$ is either a primitive variable $x$, or an attribute name $a$ or $le.a$. An expression $e$ can be a logically specified expression such as the greatest common divisor of two given integers.

We allow the use of *indexed conjunction* $\forall i \in I : R(i)$ and *indexed disjunctions* $\exists i \in I : R(i)$ for a finite set $I$. These would be the quantifications if the index set is infinite. The reader can see the influence of TLA$^+$ [19], UNITY [5] and Java on the above format.

**OO Refinement.** Doing an OO design is to design object interactions so that objects interact with each other to realize the functionality specified in the class declarations. In rCOS, we provide three levels of refinement:

1. Refinement of a whole object program. This may involve the change of anything as long as the behavior of the main method with respect to the global variables is preserved. It is an extension to the notion of data refinement in imperative programming, with a semantic model dealing with object references, method invocation, and polymorphism. In such a refinement, all non-public attributes of the objects are treated as local (internal) variables.
2. Refinement of the class declaration section: *Classes₁* is a refinement of *Classes* if *Classes₁* • *main* refines *Classes* • *main* for all *main*. This means that *Classes₁* supports at least as many services as *Classes*.
3. Refinement of a method of a class in *Classes*. Obviously, *Classes₁* refines *Classes* if the public class names in *Classes* are all in *Classes₁* and for each public method of each public class in *Classes* there is a refined method in the corresponding class of *Classes₁*.

Interesting results on completeness of the refinement calculus are available in [23].

In an OO design there are mainly three kinds of refinement: *Delegation of functionality* or *responsibilities, attribute encapsulation,* and *class decomposition.*

**Delegation of Functionality.** Assume that $C$ and $C_1$ are classes in *Classes,* $C_1$ $o$ is an attribute of $C$ and $T\,x$ is an attribute of $C_1$. Let $m()\{c(o.x', o.x)\}$ be a method of $C$ that directly accesses and/or modifies attribute $x$ of $C_1$. Then, if all other variables in the method $c$ are accessible in $C_1$, we have *Classes* $\sqsubseteq$ *Classes*$_1$, where *Classes*$_1$ is obtained from *Classes* by changing $m()\{c(o.x', o.x)\}$ to $m()\{o.n()\}$ in class $C$ and adding a fresh method $n()\{c[x'/o.x', x/o.x]\}$. This is also called the *expert pattern of responsibility assignment.*

This rule and other refinement rules can prove big-step refinement rules, such as the following **expert pattern**, that will be repeatedly used in the design of the system.

**Theorem 4 (Expert Pattern).** *Given a list of class declarations Classes and its navigation paths $r_1.\ldots.r_f.x$ (denoted by le), $\{a_{11}.\ldots.a_{1k_1}.x_1, \ldots, a_{\ell 1}.\ldots.a_{\ell k_\ell}.x_\ell\}$, and $\{b_{11}.\ldots.b_{1j_1}.y_1, \ldots, b_{t1}.\ldots.a_{tj_t}.y_t\}$ starting from class C, let $m()$ be a method of C specified as*

$$C :: m()\{ \quad c(a_{11}.\ldots.a_{1k_1}.x_1, \ldots, a_{\ell 1}.\ldots.a_{\ell k_\ell}.x_\ell)$$
$$\wedge\, le' = e(b_{11}.\ldots.b_{1s_1}.y_1, \ldots, b_{ts1}.\ldots.b_{ts_t}.y_t) \}$$

*Then Classes can be refined by redefining $m()$ in C and defining the following fresh methods in the corresponding classes:*

$$C :: \quad check()\{return' = c(a_{11}.get_{\pi_{a_{11}} x_1}(), \ldots, a_{\ell 1}.get_{\pi_{a_{\ell 1}} x_\ell}())\}$$
$$m()\{\textbf{if } check() \textbf{ then } r_1.do\text{-}m_{\pi_{r_1}}(b_{11}.get_{\pi_{b_{11}} y_1}(), \ldots, b_{s1}.get_{\pi_{b_{s1}} y_s}())\}$$

$$T(a_{ij}) :: \quad get_{\pi_{a_{ij}} x_i}()\{return' = a_{ij+1}.get_{\pi_{a_{ij+1}} x_i}()\} \ (i : 1..\ell, j : 1..k_i - 1)$$

$$T(a_{ik_i}) :: \quad get_{\pi_{a_{ik_i}} x_i}()\{return' = x_i\} \ (i : 1..\ell)$$

$$T(r_i) :: \quad do\text{-}m_{\pi_{r_i}}(d_{11}, \ldots, d_{s1})\{r_{i+1}.do\text{-}m_{\pi_{r_{i+1}}}(d_{11}, \ldots, d_{s1})\} \ i : 1..f - 1$$

$$T(r_f) :: \quad do\text{-}m_{\pi_{r_f}}(d_{11}, \ldots, d_{s1})\{x' = e(d_{11}, \ldots, d_{s1})\}$$

$$T(b_{ij}) :: \quad get_{\pi_{b_{ij}} y_i}()\{return' = b_{ij+1}.get_{\pi_{b_{ij+1}} y_i}()\} \ (i : 1..t, j : 1..s_i - 1)$$

$$T(b_{is_i}) :: \quad get_{\pi_{b_{is_i}} y_i}()\{return' = y_i\} \ (i : 1..t)$$

*where $T(a)$ is the type name of attribute $a$ and $\pi_{v_i}$ denotes the remainder of the corresponding navigation path $v$ starting at position $j$.*

This pattern informally represents the fact that a computation is realized by obtaining the data that distributed in different objects via association links and then delegating the computation tasks to the target object whose state is required to change.

If the paths $\{a_{11}.\ldots.a_{1k_1}.x_1, \ldots, a_{\ell 1}.\ldots.a_{\ell k_\ell}.x_\ell\}$ have a common prefix, say up to $a_{1j}$, then class $C$ can directly delegate the responsibility of getting the $x$-attributes and checking the condition to $T(a_{ij})$ via the path $a_{11}\ldots, a_{ij}$ and then follow the above rule from $T(a_{ij})$. The same rule can be applied to the $b$-navigation paths.

The expert pattern is the most often used refinement rule in OO design. One feature of this rule is that it does not introduce more couplings by associations between classes into the class structure. It also ensures that functional responsibilities are allocated to the appropriate objects that *knows* the data needed for the responsibilities assigned to them.

**Encapsulation.** The *encapsulation rule* says that if an attribute of a class $C$ is only referred directly in the specification (or code) of methods in $C$, this attribute can be made a *private attribute*; and it can be made *protected* if it is only directly referred in specifications of methods of $C$ and its subclasses.

**Class Decomposition.** During an OO design, we often need to decompose a class into a number of classes. For example, consider classes $C_1 :: D a_1$, $C_2 :: D a_2$, and $D :: T_1 x, T_2 y$. If methods of $C_1$ only call a method $D :: m()\{...\}$ that only involves $x$, and methods of $C_2$ only call a method $D :: n()\{...\}$ that only involves $y$, we can decompose $D$ into two $D_1 :: T_1 x; m()\{...\}$ and $D_2 :: T_2 y; n()\{...\}$, and change the type of $a_1$ in $C_1$ to $D_1$ and the type of $a_2$ in $C_2$ to $D_2$. There are other rules for class decomposition in [14].

An important point here is that the expert pattern and the rule of encapsulation can be implemented by automated model transformations. In general, transformations for structure refinement can be aided by transformations in which changes are made on the structure model, such as the class diagram, with a diagram editing tool and then automatic transformation can be derived for the change in the specification of the functionality and object interactions. For details, please see our work in [23].

# 3    Integrating rCOS Support into Model-Driven Development Process

In a realistic project there are more *activities* than just design. These activities are performed by project team members in different *roles*, such as *Administrator, Analysis Modeler, Architecture Modeler, Design Modeler, Construction Manager, Construction Programmer, Model Manager*, and *Version Manager* [31]. The concepts of activities and roles define at which point various models, that are also informally called *artifacts*, are produced by which roles, and what different analysis, manipulation, checking and verification are performed, with different tools. The concept of roles is also useful for the control of the work flow in that different roles are allowed to access and modify certain models in the development environment. These concepts and ideas have been implemented in the industrial tool, MasterCraft, for model transformation [31]. In this section, we use the our experience with the in the recent work on the Common Component Modelling Example (CoCoME) to show how the rCOS methodology can be integrated into a model-driven development processes in supporting the development activities. We first introduce the modelling example, that is followed by a summary of the application of rCOS.

### 3.1   POST—The Common Modelling Example

The point of sale terminal (POST) was originally used as a running example in Larman's book [20] to demonstrate the concepts, modeling and design of object-oriented systems. An extended version is now being used as the case study in the Common Component Modeling Contest (CoCoME) [8].

POST is a computerized system typically used in a retail store. It records sales, handles both cash payments and credit card payments as well as inventory update. Furthermore, the system deals with ordering goods and generates various reports for management purposes. The system can be a small system, containing only one terminal for checking out customers and one terminal for management, or a large system that has a number of terminals for checking out in parallel, or even a network of these large systems to support an enterprise of a chain of retail stores. The whole system includes hardware components such as computers and bar code scanners, card readers, and a software to run the system. To handle credit card payments, orders and delivery of products, we assume a *Bank* and a *Supplier* that a terminal can interact with.

The common modelling exercise requires each team to work on a common informal description of the system, and carry out a component-based modelling and design. Various aspects should be modelled and analysed, including functionalities, interactions, middlewares, and extra-functionalities (also known as non-functional requirements) such as timing. Also, code should be generated for the implementation.

The problem description that we received is largely based on *use case descriptions*. There can be many use cases for this system, depending on what business processes the client of the system want the system to support. One of the main use cases is *processing sales*, that is denoted by the use case **UC1**: *Process sales*. An informal description can be given as follows.

This use case can perform either *express checkout process* for customers with only a few items to purchase, or a *normal checkout process*. The main course of interactions between the actors and the system is described as follows.

1.  The *cashier* sets the checkout mode to express check out or for normal check out. The system then sets the *displaylight* to *green* or *yellow* accordingly.
2.  This use case starts when a *customer* comes to the *checkout point* with their *items* to purchase.
3.  The cashier indicates the system to handle a new sale.
4.  The cashier enters all the items, either by typing or scanning in the *bar code*, if there is more than one of the same item, the cashier can also enter the *quantity*. The system records each item and its quantity and calculates the subtotal.

      In express checkout mode, only a purchase of a limited number of items is allowed.
5.  At the end of entering the items, the *total* of the sale is calculated. The cashier tells the customer the total and asks her to pay.
6.  The customer can pay by cash or a credit card:

(a) If by cash, the cashier enters the amount received from the customer, and the system records the *cash payment* amount and calculates the change. The cashier gives the change to the customer.

(b) If the customer chooses to pay by a credit card, the cashier enters the card information (manually or by the card reader). The system sends the credit payment to the *bank* for *authorization*. The payment can only be made if a positive authorization reply is received.

The inventory of the sold items is updated and the completed sale is logged in the *store*.

7. The customer leaves with the items they purchased at the end of the process.

There are exceptional courses of interactions. For example, the entered bar code is not known in the system, the customer does not have enough money for a cash payment, or the authorization reply is negative. Systems need to provide means of handling these exception cases, such as canceling the sale or changing to another way of paying for the sale. At the requirements level, we capture these exceptional conditions as preconditions.

Other use cases include **UC2**: *Order products*, that orders products from the supplier; **UC3**: *Manage inventory*, that includes changing the amount of an item (after receiving deliveries from the product supplier), changing the price of a product, and adding a new product, and deleting a new product; **UC4**: *Produce monthly reports on sales* that is to show the reports of all sales in the last 30 days and information of profit and loss; and **UC5**: *Produce stock reports*, that produces the reports on stock items.

## 3.2 Development of POST with rCOS

There has been a wide view that object-oriented and component-based design should be bottom up. We in fact take a use-case driven, incremental and iterative Rational Unified Development Process [18].

**The Sketch of the Development Process.** In each iteration, a number of use cases are captured, modeled and analysed at the requirements stage. Each use case is modeled as a contract of a component that provides services to the actors of the use case. The fields of the contract declare the domain objects involved in the realization of the use case. The classes of these objects are organized as a class diagram representing the structural view of the data and objects of the components. The contracts should be analyzed and the consistency of the contracts should be checked.

The contracts of the use case components are then designed and organised into bigger components to form the component-based architecture for the application software components with identified *object-oriented interfaces*. We call this step the *logical design* of the iteration. This involves object-oriented refinement of each use case component, identifies interactions among objects in different components, and composes components (i.e. use cases) by simple connectors. The resulting model is the *logical component model*.

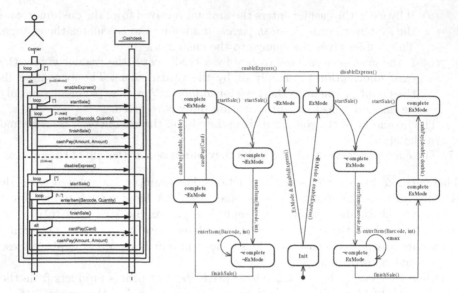

**Fig. 6.** Sequence Diagram          **Fig. 7.** State Diagram

The model of logical design should be further refined by class decomposition, data encapsulation and refactoring. We call this step the *detailed design*. The detailed design also involves replacing the object-oriented interfaces with concrete and appropriate interaction mechanisms (or middlewares) such as RMI, CORBA or shared event channels. Verification and validation, such as runtime checking or testing (unit testing), can be applied to components before and after introducing the concrete middlewares.

Code can be constructed for each component and static analysis, unit testing and runtime checking can be done on the components.

Before or after coding, the design of the GUI, the software controller of the hardware devices and their interactions with the application software components can be modeled and designed. This is done in a purely event-based model following the theory of embedded system design. The business components, GUI components, hardware controllers and middlewares are integrated and deployed.

**Requirements Modelling of POST.** A use case is modelled as a contract of a component, that corresponds the concepts of *use case controller class* in our earlier object-oriented modelling [7]. To help practical software engineers to understand the formal models, the protocol of a use case contract is illustrated by a UML sequence diagram that defines all the possible traces of the interaction between the actors and the system in the use case. The guarded design specification of each interface method is further divided into the guard, the control state transition, and the data functionality. The guards and the control state transitions are shown by a UML state diagram, and the data functionality of a method is specified as unguarded design. For such a style of modelling and their formal integration, we refer to our paper [7]. The protocol of use case process a sale **UC1** is modelled by the sequence diagram in Fig. 6 and its state diagram is given in Fig. 7.

The specification of the functions of the use case and the component invariant are given as follows.

| Use Case | UC 1: Process Sale |
|---|---|
| **Class** | *Cashdesk* |
| **Method** | *enableExpress()* |
| | **pre**: *true* |
| | **post**: *ExMode'* = *true* |
| **Method** | *disableExpress()* |
| | **pre**: *true* |
| | **post**: *ExMode'* = *false* |
| **Method** | *startSale()* |
| | **pre**: *true* |
| | **post**: /* a new *sale* is created, and its *line items* initialized to empty, and the date correctly recorded */ |
| | *sale'* = *Sale.New(false/complete, empty/lines, clock.date()/date)* |
| **Method** | *enterItem(Barcode c, int qty)* |
| | **pre**: /* there exists a product with the input barcode *c* */ |
| | *store.catalog*.find(c) ≠ *null* |
| | **post**: /* a new *line* is created with its *barcode c* and *quantity qty* */ |
| | *line'* = *LineItem.New(c/barcode,qty/quantity)* |
| | ; *line.subtotal'* = *store.catalog*.find(c).*price* × *qty* |
| | ; *sale.lines*.add(*line*) |
| **Method** | *finishSale()* |
| | **pre**: *true* |
| | **post**: *sale.complete'* = *true* |
| | $\wedge$ *sale.total'* = *sum*[[*l.subtotal* | *l* ∈ *sale.lines*]] |
| **Method** | *cashPay(double a; double c)* |
| | **pre**: $a \geq$ *sale.total* |
| | **post**: *sale.pay'* = *CashPayment.New(a/amount, a-sale.total/change)* |
| | /* the completed *sale* is logged in *store*, and */ |
| | ; *store.sales*.add(*sale*); /* the inventory is updated */ |
| | $\forall l \in$ *sale.lines*, $p \in$ *store.catalog* • (**if** *p.barcode* = *l.barcode* **then** *p.amount'* = *p.amount* − *l.quantity*) |
| **Method** | *cardPay(Card c)* |
| | **pre**: *Bank.authorize(c,sale.total)* |
| | **post**: *sale.pay'* = *CardPayment.New(c/card)* |
| | ; *store.sales*.add(*sale*); |
| | $\forall l \in$ *sale.lines*, $p \in$ *store.catalog* • (**if** *p.barcode* = *l.barcode* **then** *p.amount'* = *p.amount* − *l.quantity*) |
| **invariant** | *store* ≠ *null* $\wedge$ *store.catalog* ≠ *null* |
| | $\wedge$ (*exmode* = *true* $\vee$ *exmode* = *false*) |

The structure of the data and classes of the objects are declared as class declarations in rCOS and can be illustrated by a UML class diagram. Then the state

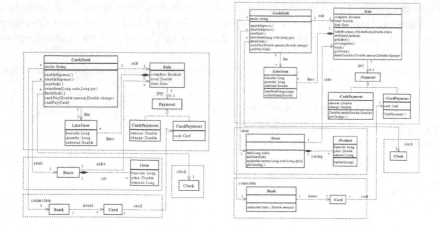

**Fig. 8.** Class Diagram of Process Sale  **Fig. 9.** Object Diagram of Process Sale

space of the component is the set of the object diagrams and the class diagram. Fig. 8 shows the class diagram of use case **UC1** and Fig. 9 is an example of an object diagram.

The execution of an invocation to an interface method changes from one object diagram to another [14,23]. The behaviour of the use case components (the methods used above) will be implemented in an *abstract class*, and the used methods and arguments indicate its abstract interface:

```
public abstract class Cashdesk implements SalesHandlerInterface {
    protected boolean exmode;
    public abstract void enableExpress();
    public abstract void disableExpress()
    public abstract void startSale();
    public abstract void enterItem(Barcode code, int qty);
    public abstract void finishSale();
    public abstract void cardPay(Card c);
    public abstract void cashPay(double a ; double c);
}
```

**Requirements Consistency.** Static consistency between methods in the diagrams and the functional specification, their types, and navigation paths must be consistent. This step is usually done by some tools like a compiler, but is done manually in the case study due to a lack of machine readable specifications.

Dynamic consistency ensures that the separately specified behavior in the sequence diagram, the state diagram and the trace are consistent. Informally, the consistency must ensure that whenever the actors follow the interaction protocol defined by the sequence diagram, the interactions will not be blocked by the system, i.e. no deadlock should occur. Formally speaking, this requires that the traces are accepted by the state machine defined by the state diagram. Also, the sequence diagram should completely define the set of traces that can be accepted by the state diagram. While, the sequence diagrams specifies the traces in a denotational manner, the state diagram describes the flow of control in an operational semantics and

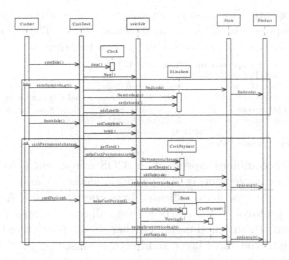

**Fig. 10.** Design Sequence Diagram of Process Sale

thus model checking and simulation can be easily applied. The state diagram allows verification of both safety and liveness properties.

As all three specifications mechanisms are based on *regular* techniques and can be interpreted as defining languages of traces, we translate them manually into CSP specifications and use the FDR model checker to prove *trace equivalence* of the sequence and the state diagram. Likewise, we can generate PROMELA specifications for the SPIN model checker to check additional properties such as certain liveness or application specific properties.

**Logical Design.** The logical design step has two kinds of activities. First each use case contract is refined from its functional specification through application of design patterns, the Expert Pattern [9] in particular. This step delegates the functionality responsibilities to the internal domain objects (i.e. those of the fields). This derives a refinement of the use case sequence diagram into a *design sequence diagram*. For example, applying the expert pattern to the use case operation of **UC1** we can refine it to the design sequence diagram shown in Fig. 10. We can specify the other use cases and refine them in the same way. For the formal refinement of the use cases in rCOS, we refer the reader to the rCOS solution to CoCoME [8].

After the initial object-oriented refinement we can identify further components. For use case **UC1**, we single out the component ≪ *Clock* ≫ and ≪ *Bank* ≫ from the component ≪ *SalesHandler* ≫. We also compose the use cases for "order products", "manage inventory items", "produce sales reports" and "produce stock reports" into one component called ≪ *Inventory* ≫. From the design sequence diagrams of the use cases (and formally the refined design of the use case operations specified in rCOS), we can organize the interaction among objects from the different components into provided and required interfaces of the identified components. This then transforms the model of the use case contracts into a logical component architecture as shown in Fig. 11. The rCOS specification of the refined component ≪ *SalesHandler* ≫ can be given as

**component** SalesHandler **required interface** ClockIf { date() }
**required interface** BankIf { authorize(..) }
**required interface** StoreIf { update(..), find (..), addSale(..) }
**provided interface** SaleIf { startSale, enterItem, finishSale , cashPay, cardPay }
**protocol** { ( [ ?enableExpress ( ?startSale (?enterItem)$^{(max)}$ ?finishSale ?cashPay)$^*$
            | ?disableExpress ( ?startSale (?enterItem)$^*$ ?finishSale
                            [ ?cardPay | ?cashPay ] )$^*$ ] )$^*$ }
**class** *Cashdesk* **implements** SaleIf

This notation thus combines aspects of an rCOS *component* (provided/required interface and class implementing the provided methods) and *contract* (protocol). Call-ins in the protocol are indicated by a question mark. A *process* can be recognized by a protocol which starts with a call-out, denoted by an exclamation mark following the method name. Further decomposition of the component ≪ *Inventory* ≫ into the three layer architecture consisting of ≪ *Application* ≫, data representation component ≪ *Store* ≫ and ≪ *Database* ≫ is shown in Fig. 12.

Notice that in the logical component models, interfaces are object-oriented interfaces, meaning that the interactions are through direct object method invocations.

**Detailed Design.** In the detailed design, refinement translates the specifications in the logical design into an object-based programming language resembling Java. In this step, class decomposition, refactoring [12] and data encapsulation, that proved as refinement rules in the object-oriented rCOS [14], can be applied.

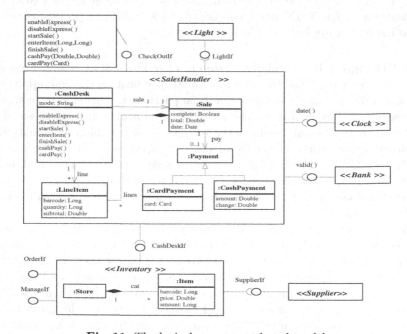

**Fig. 11.** The logical component-based model

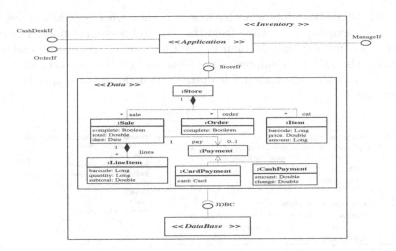

**Fig. 12.** The components of ≪ *Inventory* ≫

Significant algorithms for specifications of methods of classes are designed. Such a method usually does not need to call methods outside its owning class. The specification of such a algorithms often uses quantifications over elements of a multi-object (or a container object). In rCOS, this is resolved through standard patterns like iteration. The correctness of those patterns has been formally proved in previous rCOS literature.

This representation allows almost direct translation into Java. We invite the reader to observe the introduction of the intermediate classes which finally break down the *store.catalog.find()* in class *Cashdesk* down to the *set*-implementation, which is given again as a purely functional specification, under the assumption that a corresponding data structure is available in the target language:

| | |
|---|---|
| **class** *Cashdesk*:: | *enterItem(Barcode code, int qty)* { |
| | **if** *find(code)* ≠ *null* **then** { |
| | *line:=LineItem.New(code, qty)*; |
| | *line.setSubtotal(find(code).price* × *qty)*; |
| | *sale.addLine(line)* } |
| | **else** { **throw** exception e } } |
| | *find(Barcode code; Product r)* {r:=*store.find(code)*} |
| **class** *Store*:: | *find(Barcode code; Product r)* {r:=*catalog.find(code)*} |
| **class** *set(Product)*:: | *find(Barcode code; Product returns)* |
| | **Pre** ∃p : *Product* • *(p.barcode = code ∧ contains(p))* |
| | **Post** *returns.barcode' = code* |
| **class** *Sale*:: | *addLine(LineItem l)* {*lines.add(l)*} |
| **class** *LineItem*:: | *setSubtotal(double a)* {*subtotal:=a* } |

| | | |
|---|---|---|
| **class** *Cashdesk*:: | *finishSale()* | { *sale.setComplete()*; *sale.setTotal()* } |
| **class** *Sale*:: | *setComplete()* { *complete:=true* } |
| | *setTotal()* | { *total:=lines.sum()* } |

Separately, the abstract interfaces have been refined with Java Modelling Languages (JML) annotations derived from the pre- and post-conditions. These can be checked at runtime, and we plan to use them for further static analysis in future work: the JML code snippet of the *enterItem()* design is shown on the left of Fig. 13. Notice that the code in the dotted rectangle gives the specification of the exception.

```
/*@ public normal_behaviour
   @   requires (\exists Object o; theStore.theProductList.contains(o);
   @             ((Product)o).theBarcode.equals(code)); ...
   @   ensures  theLine != \old(theLine) &&
   @            theLine.theBarcode.equals(code) &&...
   @ also
   @ public exceptional_behaviour
   @   requires !(\exists Object o; theStore.theProductList.contains(o);
   @             ((Product)o).theBarcode.equals(code));
   @   signals_only Exception;
   @*/
public void enterItem(Barcode code, int qty) throws Exception;
```

```
public void enterItem(Barcode code, int qty)
                     throws Exception{
   if (find(code) != null) {
      line = new LineItem(code, qty);
      line.setSubtotal(find(code).price * qty);
      sale.addLine(line);
      t = true;
   } else {
      throw new Exception();
   }
}
```

**Fig. 13.** JML Specification and Implementation

In the detailed design, some of the object-oriented interfaces are replaced by appropriate interaction mechanisms and middlewares, for example

- We keep the interface *StoreIf* between the application layer and the data representation layer as an oo interface.
- As all the *SalesHandler* instances share the same inventory, we can introduce a connector by which that the cash desks get product information or request the inventory to update information of a product by passing a product code. This can be implemented asynchronously using an event channel.
- The interaction between the *SalesHandler* instances and *Bank* can be made via RMI or CORBA.
- The interaction between the *Inventory* instance and the *Supplier* can be made via RMI or CORBA.

**Design of GUI and Controllers of Hardware Devices.** In our approach, we keep the design of an application independent from the design of the GUI, so that we do not need to change the application. The GUI design is only concerned about how to link methods of GUI objects to interface methods of the application components to delegate the operation requested and to get the information that are needed to display on the GUI. In general, the application components should not call methods of the GUI objects. Also, no references should be passed between application components and GUI components (the so called service-oriented interfaces should be used). This requires that all information that is displayed on the GUI should be provided by the application components and corresponding interface operations should be provided by the

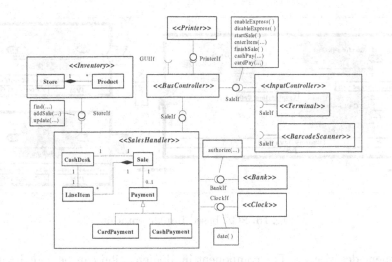

**Fig. 14.** Component diagram of Process Sale

application components to the GUI components. Existing GUI builders can be used for the implementation.

Each *SalesHandler* instance is connected to a bar code scanner, a card reader, a light, a cash box, and a printer. The hardware controllers also communicate with the GUI objects. For example, when the cashier presses the *startSale* button at his cash desk, the corresponding *SalesHandler* instance should react and the printer controller should also react to start to print the header of the receipt. The main communication can be done by using events which are sent through event channels. An obvious solution is that each *SalesHandler* has its own event channel, called *checkOutChannel*. This channel is used by the *CheckOut* instance to enable communication between all device controllers, such as *LightDisplayController*, *CardReaderController* and the GUIs. The component, the device controllers and the GUI components have to register at their *checkOutChannel* and event handlers have to be implemented and a message middleware, such as JMS, is needed to call the event handlers. The channels can be organized as a component called *EventBus*. The component-based model of the system with the hardware components is shown in Fig. 14.

After all the components discussed in the previous subsections are designed and coded, the system is ready for deployment, that we leave out of this paper.

**Service Component Architecture Based Implementation.** Based on the design of classes and components, additionally to the Java implementation of the business log, we implemented the system using Service Component Architecture (SCA) [3] and its supporting platform Tuscany Java SCA [1]. SCA provides a language-independent way to define and compose service components in the system, and it also supports different language-specific ways to implement the components. The SCA component specification can be generated from rCOS

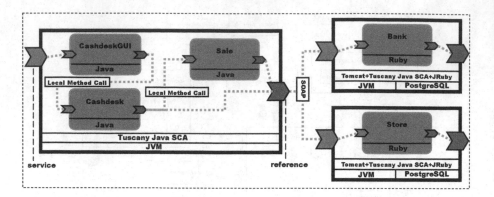

**Fig. 15.** SCA based Implementation

component description. The component implementation can be coded with respect to the component function features and the corresponding rCOS class design. We have implemented a prototype CoCoME system that contains six different distributed applications. The system components and their implementation and running information included in the sale process are shown in Fig. 15. The bold black rectangles represent the independent applications that can be deployed and run on different machines. The *Bank* and *Store* components are published as Web services, whose WSDL method description can be generated from the method definitions in rCOS component description, and the SOAP protocol binding on HTTP is used for the communications between applications. In addition, the *Bank* and *Store* components currently will create a new component instance for handling each client request.

During the development process, from the rCOS design, the most appropriate implementation technology can be used for different components, such as the *Ruby* language for the *Store* component, and we can also build the application based on the generated Java implementation from the rCOS design. The implementation only took two days. This process also corresponds to the spirits of Agile Software Development (Extreme Programming and Adaptive Software Development) [27].

## 4   Enhance Industrial Tool Support: MasterCraft

MasterCraft [31] is developed by TRDCC to support efficient development of software system. In MasterCraft, different activities at different stages of development are performed by project participants in different roles. We see this distinction as very important, as it allows us to define at which point in the development process should various models (or informally called *artifacts*) be *produced*, and different kinds of *manipulation, analysis, checking* and *verification* be performed, with different tools. We make the particular roles responsible for assuring the correctness of the resulting software system.

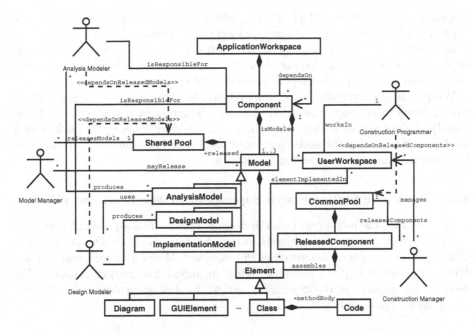

**Fig. 16.** MasterCraft: class diagram of process-oriented concepts

## 4.1   Concepts in MasterCraft

MasterCraft introduces a body of concepts and a hierarchy of artifact repositories, designed to support team collaboration on development of the models and
code. Fig. 16 shows the relations among these concepts as a class diagram. At
the top-level of component repositories is the *application workspace*, representing
the whole modelling and development space of an application. The application
workspace is further partitioned into *components*. Different from conventional
component-based software development (CBSD) focusing on architecture, MasterCraft is oriented towards organizing the development activities in the individual components. Nevertheless, a component is characterized by its interface
(consisting however only of the component's provided operations) and its dependencies on other components.

As analysis and design models are created in the individual components of
the application workspace, stable versions of these models can be released into
the *shared pool*. This allows developers of other components, depending on the
components already released, to use stable versions of the models. In order to
preserve consistency, once the model has been released, it is "frozen" and any
subsequent change starts a new modelling cycle; this is also reflected by a change
in the version identifier of the new model.

The models in MasterCraft are created as instances of a metamodel based
on UML. Besides the modelling constructs already available in UML, Master-
Craft introduces a few technology-oriented concepts, such as database queries
(eventually translated into classes), and also several concepts for modelling the

graphical user interface (GUI) of the application. The GUI interacts with the application by invoking operations provided by a classes.

In parallel with the shared pool, the *common pool* is a repository of code artifacts, where stable implementations of components are released. Such stable releases can be used by developers of dependent components.

While a single programmer (a Construction Programmer, as the role will be named later) works on the assigned tasks for a component (such as classes to be coded), the development takes place in a separate development area called *user workspace*. Only after the tasks are completed (including unit testing), the code is committed into the application workspace.

## 4.2    Developing Software with Support of MasterCraft and rCOS

In MasterCraft, the members of the development team are assigned different *roles* in the development process: *Administrator, Analysis Modeler, Design Modeler, Construction Manager, Construction Programmer, Model Manager,* and *Version Manager.* Each role gives different rights to access the project artifacts. We describe the support of rCOS with respect to the different roles and their tasks and activities in the project.

**Support to Administrator.** At the very beginning of the development, the *Administrator* is responsible for creating user accounts and components, and assigning roles to project participants for acting on the components they are involved in. As the development of the application progresses, if a version control system is in use, the *Version Manager* may store snapshots of the whole application workspace (the models and code it contains) in the version control system repository, and if needed, restore them as a separate application workspace for parallel development.

The administrator starts by creating the components identified as groups of related use cases, such as ≪ *SalesHandler* ≫ for use case **UC1**, ≪ *Inventory* ≫ for use cases **UC2-UC5**, and component ≪ *Enterprise* ≫ for the use cases related to the whole enterprise management. Next, the administrator creates user accounts, let's say *Alice* and *Brian*, and assigns them roles. In this case, Alice may become both Analysis Modeler and Design Modeler for ≪ *SalesHandler* ≫ and ≪ *Inventory* ≫, and Brian may be granted these roles for the ≪ *Enterprise* ≫ component. Furthermore, we have *Martin* who is assigned the global role of Model Manager.

**Support to Analysis Modeler.** An *Analysis Modeler* starts work on a component by studying its textual requirements. Based on the textual requirements, the Analysis Modeler creates a model of the requirements This model consists of conceptual class diagrams, use case diagrams, and behavioral models, i.e. the use case sequence diagrams and state diagrams, of the use cases, the specification of the contracts of the use case handlers. For example, Alice has to create the models in Figs. 6-9 and the rCOS specification of the contract. The Analysis

Modeler may iterate over this model, creating a new refined model based on the original analysis model. The Analysis Modeler can declare a dependency on another component and, if the component depends on other components, the Analysis Modeler first fetches the models of these *supplier components* from the shared pool. Upon completing the model, the Analysis Modeler is responsible for verifying that the model is consistent, and validating that it realizes the requirements. Prototyping can be done and run-time checking can be applied in addition to the analysis of the requirements specification outlined in Section 3.2.

*Note that for formal analysis and its automated tool support, MasterCraft must be extended by adding translators of the UML diagrams into machine readable textual specifications in rCOS. Formal verification and validation tools, such as FDR, SPIN and JML or static checkers must be integrated into MasterCraft so that these tools can be invoked by the analysis modeller. For this, programs for converting rCOS specification to inputs of the tools should be implemented.*

The *Model Manager* can afterwards release the model into the shared pool, making it available for Analysis Modelers working on components depending on this component. The release is not to simply drop the model there. The Model Manager should check on the consistency of the model with the others by removing redundancy and integrating identical modelling elements. After being released into the shared pool, the model in the application workspace is frozen, and any additional changes would start a new modelling cycle. Before releasing the model into the shared pool, the model manager has to ensure that the Analysis Modeler has validated the model.

**Support to Design Modeller.** A *Design Modeler* (e.g. Alice) fetches the released model of requirements of a component (≪ *SalesHandler* ≫ resp.) from the shared pool assigned to her, and refines the analysis model into a logical design model. This involves the application of the expert pattern for refining the use case sequence diagram to a design sequence diagram. The conceptual classes from the analysis model are also refined into design classes.

Then the Design Modeler decomposes a component into composition of internal components, and composes a number of components together to for a component model. For example, the original design of ≪ *SalesHandler* ≫ is designed into the composition of ≪ *SalesHandler* ≫, ≪ *Clock* ≫ and ≪ *Bank* ≫ and mark the latter two as components already implemented. The Design modeller may also decide on which objects should be persistent, and defines database mapping and primary keys for these classes. This is the case for the decomposition of the ≪ *Inventory* ≫ component into the three layer architecture in Fig. 12. Further, the Design Modeler defines the *component interface* in terms of class operations and queries provided, and may declare additional dependencies on other components. This is the case for Alice. She has to declare that component ≪ *SalesHandler* ≫ requires services from ≪ *Inventory* ≫ to get product descriptions and to log a completed sales via interface *CashDeskIf*. It is the same for ≪ *Inventory* ≫ that requires services from ≪ *Supplier* ≫ via interface *SupplierIf*. Note that before commencing the work on the design model, the Design Modeler needs to fetch models of the supplier components from the shared pool.

The design modeller then transforms the logical design to a detailed by further refinement rules and patterns, such as class decomposition, refactoring, data encapsulation and synchronization on access to persistent data, and selection of middlewares to replace the object-oriented interfaces in the logical design.

Just as the Analysis Modeler, the Design Modeler may also iterate over the design model, refining it into a new version. Upon completing the work on the design model, the Design Modeler is responsible for verifying its consistency, and validating it with respect to the analysis model.

*To have formal support from rCOS, MasterCraft should be extended with model transformations that automate the design patterns and other refinement and refactoring rules. Application of refinement rules and design patterns are often constrained by conditions on the models before and after the transformation. Tools for checking these conditions on the models should be integrated into the MasterCraft environment, too. In the current version, MasterCraft has automated transformations to generate code for database queries and for synchronization control on access to shared data. We are now working on QVT implementations of the expert pattern, data encapsulation and transformation of an object-oriented model to a component-based model.*

**Support in Construction Tasks.** The *Construction Manager* is the key role responsible for construction tasks. The Construction Manager starts by exporting the design model of a Component into an external representation, and invokes code generation tools, which generate code templates for all the classes. The code template of a class contains for each attribute of the class its declaration and accessor methods. For persistent classes, the code template also contains database interaction methods for transferring the state of the class between its attributes and a relational database. Further, the code template contains declarations of all the operations declared for the class. However, implementations of the operations defined in the design model are missing. Subsequently, the Construction Manager assigns coding of these operations (as well as coding of Queries) to *Construction Programmers* by *defining* a User Workspace for each selected Construction Programmer. A Construction Programmer starts work by *fetching* the workspace. After coding and unit testing the assigned operations and Queries, the Construction Programmer *builds* the workspace. Finally, the Construction Manager accepts the code by *synchronizing* the workspace, and eventually *dissolves* the workspace. After receiving code for all the tasks assigned to different Construction Programmers, the Construction Manager integrates the code together. After integration testing of the code of the Component, the Construction Manager releases the compiled binary code of the component into the common pool, making it available for development of other, dependent components.

*Therefore, the current version of MasterCraft generates code templates, and the sequence diagrams and state diagrams in the final design model are used as an informal guide to the Construction Programmer to program the bodies of the class methods.*

*With the model of detailed design defined in rCOS, we can enhance the MasterCraft code generator to generate method invocations in the body of a class method with correct flow of control (i.e., the conditional choice and loop statements). Furthermore, the model of the detailed design specifies class invariants and the functionalities of each class method in terms of its precondition and postcondition. This makes it possible for these conditions to be automatically inserted as assertions into the code generated. Therefore, code will have method bodies with method invocations and assertions. We call such a code a probably correct code. Static analysis techniques and tools such as ESCJava [11] can be used for verification of correctness of the code against the design model.*

The Construction Programmer can now work on the generated code with method invocations and assertions, and produce executable code. However, the assertions should not be removed and thus the result should be code with assertions. Testing and static analysis again can be carried out with the aid of tools such as ESCJava and JML. If the assertions are written in Spec# assertion commands and the Construction Programmer code the program in Spec#, the executable code could be a Spec# program. In this case, the Spec# compiler takes care of the static analysis. We think it would be significant for Spec# to be realistically useful as it is not feasible for a programmer to code the assertion commands correctly. The assertions should be derived from the design models.

*An important advantage of our proposed method would be that these assertions would be already included in the code generated by the Construction Manager from the model, and the Construction Programmer would be bound to follow and aim to assure these assertions.*

## 5   Conclusion

We have presented our experience in the application of a formal calculus to the CoCoME case study.

Our experience shows the need of a semantic model that formalises the main concepts and software entities in a model-driven development, and supports multi-view modelling and separation of concerns in a complex software development. rCOS provides these formalisations and support. Model-driven development must also complemented with property-driven analysis techniques. Properties are specified in rCOS as logical formulas and algebraic properties of modelling elements that are formulated as mathematical structures. The algebraic properties form the foundation for model transformations. To ensure consistency and correctness, both static and dynamic consistency of the specification must be checked, and both abstraction and refinement techniques are needed for model transformation and analysis. The work also shows that different models and tools are more effective on the design and analysis of some aspects than the others. Proved correct model transformations should be carried out side by side with verification and validation. Correct model transformations preserve properties, so that it is not required to verify again, and verification and validation are used to check the condition on when the transformations can be applied and extra properties required for the transformed model. rCOS is a methodology that supports a consistent use of different techniques and tools for modelling, design, verification and validation.

We have analyzed the software development process in a commercially successful tool (MasterCraft [31]) and identified where formal methods support can be "plugged" into the tool to make software development more efficient. However, as discussed in Section 4, there is still a lot to implement to make the tool powerful enough to support the proposed rCOS methodology effectively, and this is part of my current and future work. This is challenging. Yet, our discussion shows that this is feasible. For instance:

1. With the QVT engine that is being developed at TRDDC, we can program the expert pattern, the rule for data encapsulation and structural refinement rules that have been proved for rCOS in [23].
2. Automatic generation of executable code is challenging, however, with the semantics of state diagrams, sequence diagrams and textual specifications, it is possible to generate code with control structures, method invocations, assertions, and class invariants.
3. With human interaction, transformations for decomposing components and composing components in the design stage can be automated.

The current version of MasterCraft does not support the design of controllers of hardware devices and their integration with the application software components and GUI components. However, the discussion at the end of Section 3 shows, this is purely event-based and can be done by following the techniques of embedded systems modelling, design and verification.

**Acknowledgements.** This paper is dedicated to the 70th birthdays of Professors Dines Bjørner and Zhou Chaochen who together founded UNU-IIST in 1992. Also under the supervision of professor Zhou Chaochen, Zhiming Liu did his master study and Xiaoshan Li his PhD degree. The work of Dines on domain engineering and the work of Zhou on logics and calculi have great influence on the research presented in this paper. We also thank our colleagues who have made contributions in the development of rCOS and CoCoME, He Jifeng, Chen Xin, Zhao Liang, Liu Xiaojian, Vladimir Mencl, Zhan Naijun, Anders Ravn and Joseph Okika.

# References

1. Apache tuscany project, http://incubator.apache.org/tuscany/
2. The concurrency workbench, http://homepages.inf.ed.ac.uk/perdita/cwb/
3. Service component architecture, http://www.osoa.org/display/Main/Home
4. Back, R.J.R., von Eright, J.: Refinement Calculus: A Systematic Introduction. In: Graduate Texts in Computer Science, Springer, Heidelberg (1998)
5. Chandy, K., Misra, J.: Parallel Program Design: A Foundation. Addison-Wesley, Reading (1988)
6. Chen, X., He, J., Liu, Z., Zhan, N.: A model of component-based programing. In: Biryukov, A. (ed.) FSE 2007. LNCS, vol. 4593, Springer, Heidelberg (2007)

7. Chen, X., Liu, Z., Mencl, V.: Separation of Concerns and Consistent Integration in Requirements Modelling. In: van Leeuwen, J., Italiano, G.F., van der Hoek, W., Meinel, C., Sack, H., Plášil, F. (eds.) SOFSEM 2007. LNCS, vol. 4362, Springer, Heidelberg (2007)

8. Chen, Z., Hannousse, A.H., Hung, D.V., Knoll, I., Li, X., Liu, Y., Liu, Z., Nan, Q., Okika, J., Ravn, A.P., Stolz, V., Yang, L., Zhan, N.: The common component modelling example in rCOS. In: CoCoME—The Common Component Modelling Example. LNCS, Springer, Heidelberg (2007)

9. Chen, Z., Liu, Z., Stolz, V., Yang, L., Ravn, A.P.: A Refinement Driven Component-Based Design. In: Proc. of 12th IEEE Intl. Conf. on Engineering of Complex Computer Systems (ICECCS 07), IEEE Computer Society Press, Los Alamitos (2007)

10. de Boer, F.S., Bonsangue, M.M., Graf, S., de Roever, W.P.: Formal Methods for Components and Objects. In: de Boer, F.S., Bonsangue, M.M., Graf, S., de Roever, W.-P. (eds.) FMCO 2003. LNCS, vol. 3188, Springer, Heidelberg (2004)

11. Flanagan, C., et al.: Extended Static Checking for Java. In: Pro. PLDI' 2002 (2002)

12. Fowler, M., et al.: Refactoring: Improving the Design of Existing Code. Addison-Wesley, Reading (1999)

13. He, J., Li, X., Liu, Z.: Component-Based Software Engineering. In: Van Hung, D., Wirsing, M. (eds.) ICTAC 2005. LNCS, vol. 3722, Springer, Heidelberg (2005)

14. He, J., Li, X., Liu, Z.: rCOS: A refinement calculus for object systems. Theoretical Computer Science 365(1-2), 109–142 (2006)

15. Hoare, C.A.R.: Communicating Sequential Processes. Prentice-Hall, Englewood Cliffs (1985)

16. Hoare, C.A.R., He, J.: Unifying Theories of Programming. Prentice-Hall, Englewood Cliffs (1998)

17. Holzmann, G.J.: The SPIN Model Checker: Primer and Reference Manual. Addison-Wesley Professional, Reading (2003)

18. Kruchten, P.: The Rational Unified Process—An Introduction. Addison-Wesley, Reading (2000)

19. Lamport, L.: The temporal logic of actions. ACM Transactions on Programming Languages and Systems 16(3), 872–923 (1994)

20. Larman, C.: Applying UML and Patterns. Prentice-Hall, Englewood Cliffs (2001)

21. Larsen, K.G., Pettersson, P., Yi, W.: UPPAAL in a nutshell. STTT 1(1-2), 134–152 (1997)

22. Leavens, J.L.: JML's rich, inherited specification for behavioural subtypes. In: Liu, Z., He, J. (eds.) ICFEM 2006. LNCS, vol. 4260, Springer, Heidelberg (2006)

23. Liu, X., Liu, Z., Zhao, L.: Object-oriented structure refinement—a graph transformational approach (Extended version submitted for journal publication). In: Intl. Workshop on Refinement (REFINE'06). ENTCS (2006)

24. Liu, Z.: A continuous algebraic semantics of CSP. Journal of Computer Science and Technology 4(4), 304–314 (1989)

25. Liu, Z., He, J. (eds.): Mathematical Frameworks for Component software: Models for Analysis and Synthesis. In: Liu, Z., He, J. (eds.) Series on Component-Based Software Development, vol. 2, World Scientific, Singapore (2006)

26. Liu, Z., Ravn, A., Li, X.: Unifying proof methodologies of duration calculus and timed linear temporal logic. Formal Aspects of Computing 16(2), 140–154 (2004)

27. Martin, R.C.: Agile Software Development: Principles, Patterns, and Practices. Prentice-Hall, Englewood Cliffs (2003)

28. Meyer, B.: Eiffel: The Language. Prentice-Hall, Englewood Cliffs (1992)
29. Milner, R.: A Calculus of Communicating Systems. Springer, Heidelberg (1980)
30. Roscoe, A.W.: The Theory and Practice of Concurrency. Prentice-Hall, Englewood Cliffs (1997)
31. Tata Consultancy Services. MasterCraft, http://www.tata-mastercraft.com/
32. Zhou, C.C., Hoare, C.A.R., Ravn, A.P.: A calculus of durations. Information Processing Letters 40(5), 269–276 (1991)

# Automating Verification of Cooperation, Control, and Design in Traffic Applications*

Werner Damm[1,2], Alfred Mikschl[1], Jens Oehlerking[1], Ernst-Rüdiger Olderog[1],
Jun Pang[1], André Platzer[1], Marc Segelken[2], and Boris Wirtz[1]

[1] Carl von Ossietzky Universität Oldenburg, Ammerländer Heerstraße 114-118, 26111
Oldenburg, Germany
[2] OFFIS, Escherweg 2, 26121 Oldenburg, Germany

**Abstract.** We present a verification methodology for cooperating traffic
agents covering analysis of cooperation strategies, realization of strategies through control, and implementation of control. For each layer, we
provide dedicated approaches to formal verification of safety and stability
properties of the design. The range of employed verification techniques
invoked to span this verification space includes application of pre-verified
design patterns, automatic synthesis of Lyapunov functions, constraint
generation for parameterized designs, model-checking in rich theories,
and abstraction refinement. We illustrate this approach with a variant
of the European Train Control System (ETCS), employing layer specific
verification techniques to layer specific views of an ETCS design.

## 1 Introduction

Our society at large depends on the transportation sector to meet the increased
demands on mobility required for achieving sustained economic growth. Major
initiatives such as ERTRAC[1], eSAFETY[2] and the car2car consortium in automotive, ACARE[3] in avionics, and ERRAC[4], ETCS/ERMTS[5] in rail drive standards for inter-vehicle and vehicle to infra-structure cooperation, are thriving to
push safety by enforcing cooperation principles between traffic agents.

Automatic collision avoidance systems form an integral part of such systems,
with domain specific variants ranging from fully automatic protection to partial
automation combined with warning/alerting, to warning combined with directives. For example, in the automotive domain, based on pre-crash sensing, close

---

* This work was partly supported by the German Research Council (DFG) as part of
the Transregional Collaborative Research Center "Automatic Verification and Analysis of Complex Systems" (SFB/TR 14 AVACS, http://www.avacs.org/).
[1] European Road Transport Research Advisory Council (www.ertrac.org)
[2] http://ec.europa.eu/information_society/activities/esafety/
[3] Advisory Council for Aeronautics Research in Europe (www.acare4europe.com/)
[4] European Rail Research Advisory Council (www.errac.com/)
[5] European Rail Traffic Management System (www.ertms.com)

C.B. Jones, Z. Liu, J. Woodcock (Eds.): Bjørner/Zhou Festschrift, LNCS 4700, pp. 115–169, 2007.
© Springer-Verlag Berlin Heidelberg 2007

distance warnings are automatically displayed, and hydraulic pressure for the braking system is built up, reducing the response time to a driver's reaction to such warnings. Full automation using brake-by-wire/steer-by-wire technology is technically feasible, and has been demonstrated early in research vehicles, e.g., within the California Path project. Anticipated future traffic scenarios include communication between cars and cars, and roadside infrastructure to guide co-ordinated maneuvers for collision avoidance. We use as running example in this paper a variant of the European Train Control System standard, which provides collision avoidance through a fully automated coordinated movement of trains, based on information obtained from track-side infrastructure called Radio Block Centers (RBC). An RBC is responsible for monitoring the position of all trains in its track segment, and provides authorities for trains to freely move ahead until so-called End-of-Authority points (EoA) are reached. As soon as the on-board Automatic Train Protection system ATP detects that a train risks to move beyond the current EoA, the ATP system takes control of the train's speed and enforces a braking curve leading to a complete stop of the train ahead of the EoA. Under ETCS level 3, EoAs are moved ahead by the RBCs, as soon as it has gained safe knowledge of the fact that the train ahead has reached a safe distance to the successor train. This "moving block principle", where each train is protected by an envelope surrounding and moving with the train, contrasts to classical interlocking principles, where tracks are partitioned statically into blocks, and trains are guaranteed exclusive access to blocks by interlocking protocols. Our running application is an extension of the moving block principle to include rail-road crossings, see Section 2 for more details.

In the avionics domain, the Traffic Alert and Collision Avoidance System (TCAS) provides directives to pilots how to avoid a near-collision situation using combined ascend/descent maneuvers, or through recently investigated "go-around" maneuvers, see [22].

This paper provides a formal verification methodology addressing such application classes. Specifically, we provide dedicated verification methods for establishing safety and stability requirements for three key design layers:

1. The *cooperation layer* addresses inter-vehicle (and infrastructure) cooperation, where traffic-agents and infrastructure elements negotiate and agree on maneuvers executed jointly to enforce safety while optimizing throughput.
2. The *control layer* focuses on the design of control-laws implementing the suit of maneuvers supported by a traffic agent.
3. The *design layer* focuses on the implementation of control-laws through digital controllers.

Jointly, the techniques presented here combine to a holistic system verification approach, ensuring that system-level requirements are guaranteed by the implementation of control-laws supporting the maneuver capabilities of cooperating traffic agents.

Technically, the verification methodology rests on techniques for the verification of hybrid systems developed by the large-scale foundational research project AVACS (www.avacs.org) on automatic verification and analysis of complex systems. The range of employed verification techniques invoked to span this verification space includes application of pre-verified design patterns, automatic synthesis of Lyapunov functions, constraint generation for parameterized designs, model-checking in rich theories, and abstraction refinement.

The verification of the correctness of collision avoidance system has been studied extensively, e. g., within the PATH project [36], by Leveson [31], Sastry *et al.* [53], Lynch *et al.* [32], Clarke [47], and Damm *et al.* [14] for various versions of the TCAS system, or by Peleska *et al.* [24] and Damm *et al.* [6] for train system applications. Sastry *et al.* presents in [53] a general approach of developing such distributed hybrid systems. More recently, R-Charon [30], a semi-conservative extension of Charon [1,2] has been proposed for modular specification and dynamic reconfiguration of large distributed hybrid system based on hybrid automata.

This paper is structured as follows. We give a sufficiently detailed presentation of the variant of the ETCS level 3 protocol used as running example in Section 2. As unifying underlying formal model we use communicating hybrid automata presented in Appendix 8. Section 3 describes the overall verification methodology as well as the underlying assumptions for each modelling layer. Section 4 shows how a pre-verified design pattern for collision avoidance protocols can be instantiated for our ETCS application. The focus of Section 5 is on generating constraints on design parameters for collision avoidance protocols ensuring collision freedom. Sections 6 and 7 discuss automatic verification methods for proving stability and safety, respectively, using as running example the drive train controller for maintaining the operator selected speed. Both sections discuss the local control as well as the design layer. We finally wrap by pointing out directions for further work in Section 8.

## 2    Extending ETCS Level 3 for Rail-Road Crossings

In this section we describe the model of a train system running under a variant of the ETCS level 3 protocol. We have extended the protocol to deal with the protection of track segments before a train gets access to enter this segment. As an example of an unsafe element inside a track segment we have chosen a rail road crossing. To be able to evaluate the different aspects of an embedded system we have developed a dynamic system model extended with different control levels. The system dynamics are modelled in Matlab-Simulink and the control parts of the ETCS protocol are modelled in Stateflow. The model of the dynamics consists of three parts. The first is the mechanical transmission, which converts the input torque into the angular velocities of the wheels. The second part consists of the outer conditions, used to produce the present train velocity. This velocity depends on the angular velocity of the wheels, the present adhesion between wheel and track, and other losses such as air resistance, rolling resistance etc. The third part of the model contains the control part of the ETCS protocol and communicates to the crossing station and to the radio control block.

## 2.1  Mechanical Transmission

The mechanical transmission consists of the engine which is coupled directly on the driven wheel where the dynamics of the shaft are neglected. The train dynamic contains the engine dynamics, the brake dynamics and the block which calculates the present velocity of the train as a function of the friction force and the angular momentum between the wheel-track system. The block produces the values of the present torque on a driven wheel $T_w$, the angular velocity of the wheel $\omega_w$ and the present velocity of the train $v$.

The angular momentum of the engine is modelled as a function of the drive current ($I$) as the controlled variable, and the present angular velocity of the engine ($\omega$). The $i_s$ and $w_s$ are constants and the $t_n$ and $\omega_{max}$ are parameters.

$$T_w = min(i_s \cdot \omega + t_n \cdot I,\ w_s \cdot \omega + w_s \cdot \omega_{max} \cdot I) \tag{1}$$

The drive current is driven by a PI controller with the desired velocity and the present velocity as input.

$$I(v, v_d) = P_d \cdot (v_d - v) + T_d \cdot \int (v_d - v) dt \tag{2}$$

To limit the maximum acceleration additional parts have been added. If the current acceleration ($a$) exceeds the max_acceleration ($max\_acc$) the difference of them is multiplied by a scaling factor and then subtracted from the drive current. Equation 2 can then be rewritten to:

$$I(v, v_d) = \begin{cases} P_d \cdot (v_d - v) + T_d \cdot \int (v_d - v) dt & : \quad a \le a_{max} \\ P_d \cdot (v_d - v) + T_d \cdot \int (v_d - v) dt - (a - a_{max}) \cdot a_{limit} & : \quad a > a_{max} \end{cases} \tag{3}$$

The dependency of the angular velocity $\omega$ and the toque is given by the formula

$$\omega = \int_0^t \frac{T_\omega - R_w \cdot (F_e + F_b)}{I} dt \tag{4}$$

where $I$ is the moment of inertia of the rotating mass of the engine and the driven wheel, $F_e$ is the resistance force of the environment, $R_w$ denotes the radius of the wheel and $F_b$ describes the braking force. The present velocity is calculated in the same way

$$v = \int_0^t \frac{F_t - F_e - F_b}{m} dt \tag{5}$$

where $m$ is the mass of the train and $F_t$ the traction force induced from the wheel into the track. The traction force is calculated by

$$F_t = \frac{T_w}{R_w} \cdot \mu_a \tag{6}$$

where $\mu_a$ denotes the adhesion coefficient between wheel and track.

## 2.2    Outer Losses

The outer losses are summarized in the resistance force $F_e$ based on air resistance and roll resistance.

$$F_e = F_{air} + F_r + m \cdot g \cdot \sin \phi \tag{7}$$

The term $m \cdot g \cdot \sin \phi$ is the loss due to the lateral slope angle $\phi$ of the rail. The roll resistance is described by the formula

$$F_r = m \cdot c_r \tag{8}$$

where $m$ is the total mass of the train and $c_r$ the velocity independent roll resistance coefficient. The air resistance is described by

$$F_{air} = c_1^{air} \cdot v^2 + c_2^{air} \cdot v \tag{9}$$

The coefficient $c_1^{air}$ depends on the density of air, the cross section of the train and such things, the coefficient $c_2^{air}$ describes aerodynamic phenomenon which cannot be described as functions of $v^2$.

## 2.3    Brake

The main goal of this brake model is to bring up the train model in a non-moving state and not to study the brake behaviour in detail. For this reason the brake model is very simple. The brake model consists of two kinds of brake systems: an eddy current brake and an emergency brake. An eddy current brake consists of an electromagnetic shoe where the electromagnetic force is controlled by the brake current. The change of the magnetic field caused by the speed difference between the brake and the adjacent rail induces an eddy current in the rail. This eddy current leads to a resistance force which depends on the current and the speed difference. In high speed region ($v \geq 20 \ m/s$) the resistance force is nearly linear to the speed difference. The resistance force tends to zero if the speed difference becomes zero. Therefore we need an additional brake mechanism for the low speed region. These two brake systems work as the service brake for the train model. For the emergency case there exists an additional brake called emergency brake. This brake is typically an electromagnetic rail brake. Both brake types, the eddy current brake and the electromagnetic rail brake, work directly between the train and the rail and do not depend on friction between the wheels and the train. This simplifies the brake model. The brake force $F_b$ is modelled by

$$F_b = (I_b \cdot v + (v_{offset} - v)) \cdot sb_{sc} + eb_c \tag{10}$$

where $I_b$ is the brake current to control the service brake, $v$ is the present velocity of the train and $v_{offset}$ is a constant to ensure brake force if the present velocity is close to zero. The constant $sb_{sc}$ is a scaling factor for sufficient brake force. The emergency brake is modelled as a constant and denoted by $eb_c$. Deceleration is controlled through setting a proper brake current using a PI controller. The

input of this controller is the present deceleration of the train and the coefficient
for a comfortable deceleration of the service brake.

$$I_b = P_b \cdot (\frac{d\,v}{dt} - a_{sb}^d) + T_b \int_0^t \frac{d\,v}{dt} - a_{sb}^d \, dt \tag{11}$$

We have presented here a sufficient precise description of the dynamical system. The equations are kept simple to get a linear system. The model can be
extended mostly and a more detailed description can be found in [54].

## 2.4   ETCS Control Part

We consider a train system which is under the control of a variant of the ETCS
level 3 protocol. The ETCS level 3 provides collision avoidance through a fully
automated, decentralized interlocking scheme where the trains are moving in
safe blocks. These blocks are controlled track-side by radio block centers (RBC)
which are control centers to supervise and control train movements in a terri-
tory with radio based train control. One RBC is responsible for a fixed number
of track segments and the trains currently on these track segments. The RBC
grants movement authorities for trains to freely move ahead until so called *end
of movement authority* (EoA) points. At each time there exist a certain EoA
for each train, which is typically the end of a track segment, the position of a
possibly unsafe point (e.g., a rail-road crossing), or the end of a train driving
ahead. The granted movement authority defines a safety block surrounding the
train. It is a moving block system which means that the signaling system will
clear the track behind a train continuously.

This protocol is completely modelled in Stateflow and consists mainly of four
states running in parallel. The *rbc_req* state shown in detail in Fig. 1 is responsible for the communication to the RBC. The *rbc_req* state is entered in the *init*

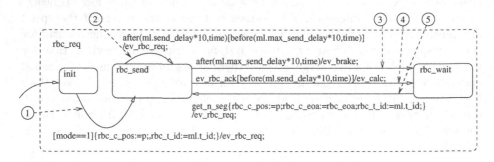

**Fig. 1.** RBC communication control part

state. This state will be left by taking the transition ① only if the variable *mode*
is equal to 1 which means that this train is under the supervision of the *ETCS*.
After enabling this transition and before entering the destination state *rbc_send*,

the variables $rbc\_c\_pos$ and $rbc\_t\_id$ will be set to the current position $p$ of the train and to the specific $id$ of the requesting train. By taking this transition a request for a new EoA will be sent to the RBC and a timer will be started by entering the $rbc\_send$ state. After the time interval of a normal transmit action but before the upper bound of transmit actions has been reached, the request will be transmitted again. This behaviour is modelled in the transition on top ② of the $rbc\_send$ state. If no message arrived before the maximum send delay period is reached the service brake will be initialized by taking the transition ③ and generating a brake event $ev\_brake$ which will be consumed in the $moved$ state in Fig. 6. If an acknowledge arrived before the max send delay the transition ④ will be enabled and an $ev\_calc$ event is generated, leading to the destination $rbc\_wait$ state. This state will be left after consuming a $get\_n\_seg$ event and enabling the transition ⑤ to the $rbc\_send$ state. This transition is a model of a request for travelling to a new track segment after the current EoA which will be sent to the RBC. The parameters of this request are the current train position $rbc\_c\_pos$, the current EoA $rbc\_eoa$ of the train and the train id $t\_id$. The RBC will then calculate the new EoA with respect to the current train position of train $t\_id$, the current EoA of this train and the current positions of possible other trains moving ahead.

The second state is the $com\_cross$ state (Fig. 2) containing the communication model between the train and a rail-road crossing. If an $ev\_com\_cross$ event is

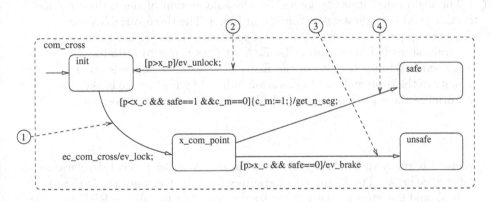

**Fig. 2.** Level crossing communication control part

consumed the transition ① will be taken and a lock request will be sent to the rail-road crossing. If the level crossing has transmitted the safe state message before the train has reached the start-of-communication-point-to-rbc $x\_c$, the transition ④ is taken, generating a request for a new EoA to the RBC. The variable $c\_m$ will be set to 1 which means that this train has already sent a lock message to the rail-road crossing. The new state is the $safe$ state. If the train is behind the start-of-communication-to-rbc point and receives an unsafe message from the rail-road crossing the transition ④ is enabled and the service brake will be initiated by an $ev\_brake$ event. The $unsafe$ state will only be left by switching off the automatic mode of this train. The *safe* state will be left if the train position is behind the position of the rail-road crossing and an unlock message is sent to the rail-road crossing ②. The new state is the *init* state and this train is ready to initiate a new request to a rail-road crossing.

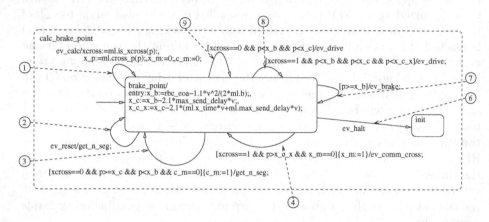

**Fig. 3.** Monitoring of safe motion

The main calculations to guarantee the safe motion of the train are done in the third state *calc_brake_point* shown in Fig. 3. The three variables $x\_b$, $x\_c$ and $x\_c\_x$ are updated every time the *brake_point* state is entered. To guarantee that the train stops before reaching the EoA, the train has to initialize the service brake some distance in front of the EoA. This distance depends on the current velocity of the train and the deceleration induced by the service brake. The point to initialize the service brake ($x\_b$) is dynamically calculated every time step by

$$x\_b = EoA - \frac{1.1 \cdot v^2}{2 \cdot b} \qquad (12)$$

where $v$ is the actual velocity of the train and $b$ is the typical deceleration of the service brake. The factor 1.1 guarantees a 10% safety margin. Typically, the train should not stop at every EoA, so the train has to ask the RBC for a new EoA before reaching the actual EoA. For comfort reason the new EoA should be received before the train has switched to the braking mode so the request has to be sent early enough in time before reaching the service brake initialization point $x\_b$. The train will travel the distance $p = v \cdot t$ in time $t$ with the velocity $v$. The delay for the request of the new *EoA* is two times the maximal send delay to the RBC plus the response time to serve this request. The point to initialize the request for the new *EoA* can then be calculated by

$$x\_c = x\_b - 2.1 \cdot max\_send\_delay \cdot v \qquad (13)$$

In case that the EoA is a rail-road crossing the train has to lock the rail-road crossing before the train will reach this point. The train has to initiate a lock request to the rail-road crossing and the rail-road crossing has to lock the crossing and acknowledge the lock request. After receiving a *safe* message the train can send a request for a new EoA to the RBC. The point to initialize a lock request to a level crossing is calculated by

$$x\_c\_x = x\_c - 2.1 \cdot (x\_time + max\_send\_delay) \cdot v \qquad (14)$$

The time to set up the rail-road crossing in a safe state is stored in the $x\_time$ variable. These three points ($x\_b$, $x\_c$ and $x\_c\_x$) are updated every time the *brake_point* state is entered. A spatial view of this scenario is shown in Fig. 4, and

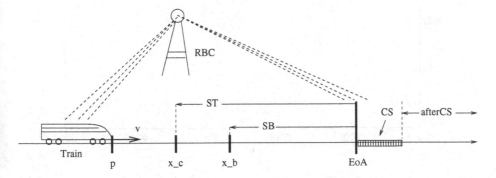

**Fig. 4.** Radio-based train control

a snapshot of the dynamical behaviour can be seen in Fig. 5. After explaining the main ideas to guarantee a safe motion, we continue to discuss Fig. 3. The transition ① is enabled after receiving an end-of-authority message from the RBC. By taking this transition the two variables which count the messages to the RBC and to the rail-road crossing are initialized to 0. The variable *xcross* picks up the information if a rail-road crossing is just in front of the current position $p$ of the train. The position of the rail-road crossing itself is stored in the $x\_p$ variable. The information of the rail-road crossing is read out of the track data dictionary. If there is no rail-road crossing ahead and the current position of the train is before the point to initialize the service brake and before the point to initialize an EoA-request the transition ⑨ will be taken and an *ev_drive* event is generated to switch into the driving mode of the train. In case there is a rail-road crossing ahead the transition ⑧ will be enabled. If the train has passed the point to send an EoA-request to the RBC but in front of the $x\_b$ point the transition ③ will be taken and a *get_n_seg* event is generated to initialize the request of a new EoA. If there is a rail-road crossing ahead and the train has passed the $x\_c\_x$ point a lock request is generated by the *ev_com_cross* event released by the transition ④. If the train has passed the $x\_b$ point the transition ⑦ is enabled which leads to the service brake mode by the *ev_brake* event. In case of an emergency halt indicated by the *ev_halt* event the *brake_point* state will be left by enabling the transition ⑥ to the *halt* state.

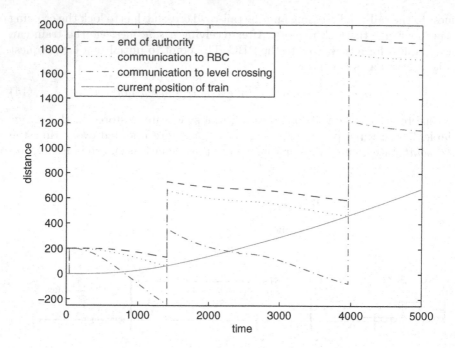

**Fig. 5.** Snapshot of dynamic calculations

The supervision of the velocity of the train is modelled in the fourth state labelled *move* (Fig. 6). The previous value of the desired speed is set to 0 on entering the default *init* state and stored in the $o\_v\_d$ variable. The drive mode is switched on by receiving the *ev_drive* event enabling the transition ① and the variable $d\_c$ (for drive control) is set, the desired speed at the current position of the train is read out of the track data dictionary and stored in $v\_d$ and the slope of the current track segment is stored in the variable *slope*. The destination state is *change*.

- If the current desired speed is different from the previous value the transition ② is enabled and this change is signalled through a reset on the $c\_v\_d$ variable, state *switch* and the transition ③. The new value of the current desired speed is stored in the *move* state.
- If there is no change in the desired speed, the transition ④ is enabled and the *move* state is entered.
- If a brake event (*ev_brake*) occurs in the *change* state, the transition ⑫ is enabled, the drive mode is switched off ($d\_c = 0$), the service brake mode is switched on ($sb\_c = 1$) and finally the *init_brake* state is entered.

After reading the desired speed the current speed of the train is supervised in the *move* state.

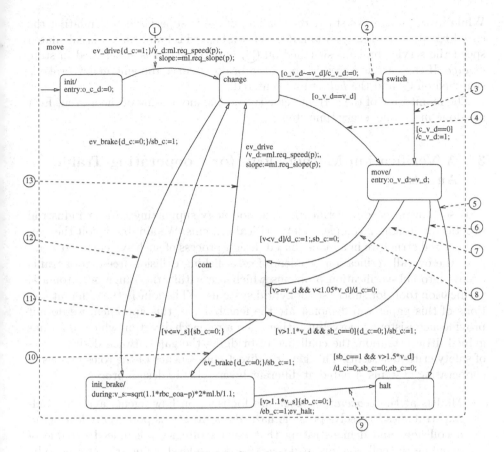

**Fig. 6.** Speed control

- If the current velocity of the train is below the desired value the transition ⑧ is enabled, the drive mode is set, and the service brake mode is switched off.
- If the current velocity is equal or greater than the desired velocity but not greater than 5% of the desired velocity the transition ⑦ is taken and the drive mode is switched off.
- If the speed is greater than 10% of the desired speed and the service brake mode is not active, the mode is switched from driving mode to the the service brake mode by activating the transition ⑥.
  The destination state in all three cases is the *cont* state. This state is left either by receiving an *ev_drive* event taking the transition ⑬ to the *change* state and updating the slope and the desired speed variable or receiving an *ev_brake* event ⑩ and switching to the *init_brake* state.
- If in the *move* state the service break mode is active and the current speed is greater than 50% of the desired speed, then the emergency brake mode is switched on by taking the transition ⑤ to the *halt* state.

While in the *init_brake* state, the braking curve is supervised by updating the speed $v\_s$ at the current position. If the current speed is lower than this calculated speed the service brake is switched off ⑪ and the speed is supervised in state *change*. If the current speed is above the braking curve the emergency brake is switched on ⑨ and the *halt* state is entered.

The monitoring of the current velocity and the monitoring of the current EoA are done in parallel every time step.

## 3    A Verification Methodology for Cooperating Traffic Agents

This section proposes a verification methodology supporting current industrial practice in designing complex safety critical systems. We aim to exploit the typical layered structure in a model based design process of such systems to decompose the overall verification problem of establishing collision freedom of traffic agents into sub-verification problems which are within the range of automatic verification tools for subclasses of hybrid systems. While jointly the different sections of this paper will demonstrate the feasibility of this approach, we do not provide a consistent theory, but rather open a research direction which so far has gained little attention: the challenge of bridging the gap between design layers of safety critical systems. This gap is a direct consequence of the roles models of cooperating systems situated at different layers play in design processes:

- Models at the *cooperation layer* are focusing on how agents agree in finding strategies to resolve possible hazardous situations potentially leading to a collision, and demonstrating that such strategies are indeed capable of avoiding the collision. Strategies at this design level define trajectories to be followed by traffic agents, such as circular go-around, changing lanes, decelerating until a safe distance is achieved. The realization of such strategies is delegated to subsequent design steps – strategies are described directly in terms of dynamic models assuming direct control of speed and acceleration, and undisturbed immediate knowledge of location, speed, and acceleration.
- Models at the *control layer* provide a first step towards realization of strategies, in separating between control and plant, identifying sensors and actuators, and developing control laws ensuring stability and safety of such strategies. The focus at this stage is on getting the control laws right – typically assuming an ideal execution engine, which provides immediate visibility of sensor changes and impact of actuator settings, in a dense time model.
- Models at the *design layer* must deal with the inherent limitations of digital implementations of controllers. This includes the limited observability of the planned at defined sampling points, discretization errors, delayed impact of actuator settings, physical distribution of sensors, controllers, and actuators, as well as addressing diagnostic and fault-tolerance. Idealized control laws must be made robust, in the sense that stability and safety must be guaranteed in spite of such impurities.

While such a layered approach is highly beneficial for a separation of concerns in design processes, the inherent differences between models situated at different layers make it a challenge to provide semantic bridges between these, as would be required for a complete verification methodology spanning all three levels.

Indeed, models at the control layer would hardly be able to exactly realize the trajectories prescribed by strategies at the cooperation layer. While highly elaborated plant models are available, e.g., capturing car dynamics, control designers typically work with simplified models which have been proven to be practically sufficient for validating stability and safety. Such simplified models ignore higher-order effects and use linear approximations whenever reasonably possible, trading exactness for simulation speed. Similarly, the induced limitations of digital control (cf. [3]) make it impossible for digital controllers to enforce the plant dynamics of control models; rather, robustness is designed into digital controllers to "sufficiently" approximate such dynamics.

Industrial design processes cater for these gaps, e.g., by enforcing design for robustness, re-validating stability and safety at each layer, in particular ensuring complete traceability of safety requirements throughout all design steps, and by rapid prototyping. Extensions to Matlab-Simulink such as the Jitterbug [10] allow for an early assessment of the impact of design level impurities on control-strategies.

However, as argued in Section 8, theoretical approaches to cover multi-layered designs, such as refinement and compositional reasoning, fail to provide semantic bridges across this design space, due to their inability to support the degree of deviations between models tolerated by industrial design processes. We thus leave the development of a theoretical approach building on compositional extensions of robust refinement to future research, and focus in this paper on a verification methodology which adds mathematical rigor to industrial approaches to bridge the gap between design layers. Specifically, we enhance established practices of providing full traceability for safety requirements in offering techniques of assigning responsibility of derived safety requirements jointly guaranteeing collision freedom to subsystems, and provide formal verification techniques tailored to the particularities of model classes at each level, to formally verify such delegated safety requirements. Regarding stability of local control, as well as stability of design models, we provide automated formal techniques establishing various notions of stability. The remainder of this section outlines the overall approach, which is then refined in individual sections.

Our verification methodology addresses the cooperation layer by formalizing design patterns for collision avoidance as a proof rule reducing collision freedom to locally dischargeable safety requirements on individual subsystems of the involved traffic agents. The design patterns builds on the following central concepts (see Section 4):

- Each agents is seen enclosed in a safety envelope, which must not be entered by other agents;

- A *criticality function* measures for each configuration of the (physical) state of involved agents its closeness to collisions;
- Thresholds of this function are chosen taking into account the dynamics of traffic agents to initiate negotiations on agreeing on strategies, as well as on their initiation;
- Strategies are reducing criticality of the agents state.

These design patterns have been proven to be expressive enough to cover rail, automotive, as well as avionics applications. A key feature of our approach to the verification of the coordination level is the capability to automate the generation of candidate criticality functions for linear strategies, by using linear matrix inequality (LMI) solvers to instantiate parameters in a suitably chosen quadratric generic form for candidate criticality functions taking into account the dynamics of the strategies. Moreover, the application of the design pattern generates safety requirements for the subsystem of the traffic agents responsible for inter-agent communication as well as strategy realization.

Such safety requirements are discharged at the control-level using symbolic reachability analysis (see Section 7). We have tuned the verification algorithms to cater for control models with non-trivial discrete control (e.g., resulting from the interaction between inter-agent coordination and control). This calls for a fully symbolic representation of the hybrid system state space in reachability analysis – in contrast to the explicit representation of discrete states used in hybrid system verification tools such as PHAVer [21], Checkmate [49], HyperTech [27]. The key to achieve this are recent results to lift techniques for compact discrete state space representations based on And-Inverter Graphs to the theory of linear arithmetic (Lin-AIGs) required to deal with hybrid system verification. The current prototype of our verification engine [11] uses substitution in backward image computation along jumps, providing for linear guards and linear expressions in assignments, and Loos-Weispfennig quantifier elimination for backward image computations at flows, and redundancy elimination for sets of linear-constraints, assuming linear hybrid automata. Future work will lift this extension to include plant models supporting linear differential equations. To cater for the transition to design models, we re-verify the safety requirements allocated to this subsystem, now using an abstraction refinement approach addressing discrete time reachability analysis for models with linear dynamics [48].

Stability of control models is demonstrated using LMI based candidate generation for Lyapunov functions for hybrid systems with linear differential equations, developed in [41]. As discussed in Section 6, we also show that stability can be re-proven after discretizing the system model with a given sampling rate, resulting in a discrete-time hybrid system with linear difference equations. This allows for the identification of safe sampling rates maintaining stability, which can in turn be used for discrete-time reachability analysis.

Jointly, these techniques allow a formal verification of stability and safety properties, with traceability of requirements from the coordination layer to design models.

# 4   Verification of the Cooperation Layer

In [13] we proposed a rule that decomposes the proof of the global property of collision avoidance of two traffic agents into simpler properties with the aim that they can be automatically verified. In this section we give a summary of this proof rule and show that an important ingredient of this rule, the criticality function, can indeed be found automatically. This is illustrated with the train case study.

## 4.1   A Design Pattern for Collision Avoidance

Proving the global safety property of collision freedom for a collection of traffic agent is extremely difficult because each traffic agent is (modelled by) a hybrid system with a number of (discrete) modes and a different continuous dynamics in each mode. To break down the complexity of this verification task we exploit that traffic agents typically cooperate using a certain pattern of operation modes that can be described as a generic *phase-transition diagram* shown in Fig. 7.

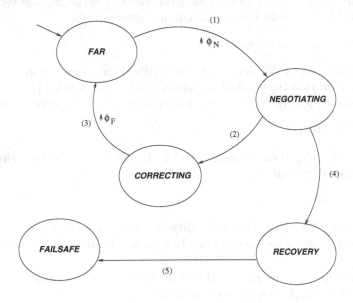

**Fig. 7.** Phase-transition diagram for proof rule

The phase *FAR* collects all controller modes that are not pertinent to collision avoidance. The protocol may only be in phase *FAR* if it is known to the controller that the two agents are "far apart". Determining conditions for entering and leaving phase *FAR* is thus safety critical. The *NEGOTIATION* phase is initiated as soon as the agents might evolve into a potentially hazardous situation. Within the negotiation phase the two agents determine the set of maneuvers to be performed. The *CORRECTING* phase is entered when matching correcting modes have been identified. During this phase, maneuvers associated with the correcting modes will cause the distance between traffic agents to increase, eventually allowing them to reenter the *FAR* phase. For instance, TCAS distinguishes maneuvers like "descent", "maintain level", and "climb" for aircrafts.

The cycle of transitions numbered (1) to (3) in the diagram thus characterizes successful collision avoidance maneuvers. Other phases and transitions shown in Fig. 7 increase the robustness of the protocol, by providing recovery actions in case of failures (e.g., disturbed communication channels) in the *NEGOTIATION* phase, and can only be offered by agents with fail-safe states (like trains). For instance, in its *RECOVERY* phase a train may initiate a braking maneuver to avoid a collision with a preceding train.

Stipulating the pattern in Fig. 7, we proposed a generic proof rule that decomposes the global safety proof of collision freedom (for the case of two traffic agents) into a number of simpler properties that involve only parts or limited aspects of the agent system. The proof rules employs two key concepts: a *safety envelope* surrounding each traffic agent and a *criticality function* providing an abstract measure of the distance between the traffic agents. The rule states that for all traffic agents $A$ and all criticality functions $cr$ satisfying the verification conditions VC of the rule, collision freedom is guaranteed:

$$A \models \text{VC} \quad \Rightarrow \quad A \models \neg \, collision$$

where $cr$ may occur in VC but not in the *collision* predicate. In an application we have to show that the verification conditions VC are satisfied by the concrete traffic agents $A_0$ and the concrete criticality function $cr_0$ substituted for $cr$:

$$A_0 \models \text{VC}[cr_0/cr]$$

Thus the proof rule, when instantiated with $A_0$ and $cr_0$, yields the desired property of collision freedom:

$$A_0 \models \neg \, collision.$$

In Subsection 4.3 we show that criticality is a *Lyapunov-like function* and that (for certain dynamics) the concrete function $cr_0$ can be discovered automatically.

**Formalization.** Now we outline the formalisation of the approach as given in [13]. A traffic agent $A$ is represented as the parallel composition of a plant $P$ and a controller $C$, in symbols $A = P \parallel C$. Each of these components is modelled by a hybrid automaton $H = (\mathbb{M}, Var, R^d, R^c, m_0, \Theta)$ defining trajectories

$$\pi = ( \, \hat{M}, \, (\hat{X})_{X \in Var} \, )$$

where $\hat{M} : Time \rightarrow \mathbb{M}$ and $\hat{X} : Time \rightarrow \mathbb{R}$ for $X \in Var$. For details see Appendix A and for an example see Fig. 9.

To specify behavioural properties over time of hybrid automata and state the verification conditions of our proof rule for collision freedom, we use the State

Transition Calculus [56], an extension of the Duration Calculus (DC) [57]. In DC, real-time interval properties of system observables $obs$, which are interpreted as functions $obs_{\mathcal{I}} : Time \rightarrow Data$, can be expressed and proven. For example,

$$\Box(\lceil M = NEG \rceil \Rightarrow \lceil acc = 0 \rceil)$$

expresses that in every interval ($\Box$) if the mode observable $M$ has the value $NEG$ (for *negotiating*) throughout this interval ($\lceil M = NEG \rceil$) then the observable $acc$ (for *acceleration*) is zero throughout this interval ($\lceil acc = 0 \rceil$).

The State Transition Calculus can additionally express properties of instantaneous transitions. For example, $\uparrow M = NEG$ is true at $t \in Time$ if then the truth value of the assertion $M = NEG$ switches from false to true. In DC, this can be expressed as $\lceil \neg(M = NEG) \rceil$; $\lceil M = NEG \rceil$ which is to hold in an interval surrounding $t$. The chop operator ; is applied at time $t$ and expresses the concatenation of two intervals where $\lceil \neg(M = NEG) \rceil$ holds in the first one and $\lceil M = NEG \rceil$ in the second one.

It can be defined that a hybrid automaton $H$ is a *model* of a formula $F$, abbreviated as $H \models F$.

**Correcting Modes.** For each controller $C_i$ we stipulate a set $COR(C_i)$ of *correcting maneuvers*. Then we assume a relation

$$\text{MATCH} \subseteq COR(C_1) \times COR(C_2)$$

of *matching modes* characterizing which pairs of maneuver are claimed to resolve hazardous states. For each pair $(m_1, m_2) \in \text{MATCH}$ there is an *activation condition* characterized by a state assertion $\Phi(m_1, m_2)$. Activation conditions of maneuvers must observe the following constraints:

- *timely activation*: the activation of the maneuvers occurs early enough to guide the traffic agents to a safe state using the associated control laws.
- *completeness*: for each possible approach to a hazardous state there is at least one matching pair of correcting modes whose activation condition is enabled in time.

For ground-based traffic agents like trains there is a special class of corrective modes, enforcing a complete stop of the traffic agent, thus reaching a *fail-safe state*. We refer to such corrective modes as *recovery modes* and assume that there is a single matching pair $(r_1, r_2)$ of recovery modes.

Let $\Phi_{start}$ be the disjunction of all activation conditions of these modes:

$$\Phi_{start} \Leftrightarrow \Phi(r_1, r_2) \vee \bigvee_{(m_1, m_2) \in \text{MATCH}} \Phi(m_1, m_2).$$

Intuitively, if any of these conditions becomes true, a hazardous state has been reached, which can compensated by the associated matching pair of correcting modes. By completeness of the set of activation conditions, $\Phi_{start}$ thus characterizes all hazardous states.

The flexibility of having multiple matching correcting modes entails the need for a *negotiation phase*, in which agents agree on which pair of maneuvers is to be activated. The design of this phase has to address the following critical issues:

- *limited time window*: the decision must be reached within a certain time $\Delta_N$, catering for latencies occurred by inter-agent communication, as well as local computation times to perform the selection.
- *timely activation*: the activation of the negotiation phase must be early enough to guarantee timely activation of the chosen maneuvers.
- *adequacy of selection*: the negotiation phase may only choose among such matching pairs whose activation condition is known to become activated.

We cater in our generic scheme for the latter two items by the concept of *warnings* "announcing" that the activation condition for a matching pair will become true in $\Delta_C$ time units, with $\Delta_N < \Delta_C$. The warning $\Phi_N$ causing the *initiation of the negotiation phase* should thus be given as soon as it is known that the agent will in $\Delta_C$ time units hit one of these activation conditions. Formally, this is expressed as follows: $\Phi_N \Leftrightarrow pre(\Delta_C, \Phi_{start})$.

**Safety Envelopes.** We define collision freedom as maintaining disjointness of safety envelopes associated with each traffic agent. A safety envelope of an agent is a vicinity. Formally, safety envelopes are convex subspaces of $\mathbb{R}^3$ surrounding the current position, whose extent can depend on the valuation of plant variables.

**Definition 1.** *The* safety envelope *of an agent* $A = P \parallel C$ *is a continuous piecewise differentiable function*

$$SE_A : \mathbb{R}^{Var(P)} \to \mathcal{P}(\mathbb{R}^3),$$

*which is a convex subset of* $\mathbb{R}^3$ *including the current position. Given a run* $\pi$, *and a point in time* $t$, *the* current safety envelope *is given by* $SE(\pi(t))$.

Two traffic agents $A_1$ and $A_2$ are collision free if in all trajectories of the composed traffic system $A_1 \parallel A_2$ the safety envelopes associated with $A_1 = C_1 \parallel P_1$ and $A_2 = C_2 \parallel P_2$ have an empty intersection.

**Definition 2.** *Consider a run* $\pi$ *of* $A_1 \parallel A_2$. *The state assertion* collision *holds in* $\pi$ *at time* $t \in Time$ *if* $SE_{A_1}(\pi(t)) \cap SE_{A_2}(\pi(t)) \neq \varnothing$. *The two-agent system* $A_1 \parallel A_2$ *is* collision free *if* $A_1 \parallel A_2 \models \lceil \neg collision \rceil$, *i.e. if for all runs of* $A_1 \parallel A_2$ *and all intervals* $\neg collision$ *holds.*

**Criticality.** A central notion is that of *criticality* of plant states. Given valuations $\sigma_1$ and $\sigma_2$ of the plant variables of $P_1$ and $P_2$, respectively, the criticality $cr(\sigma_1, \sigma_2)$ measures the "distance" of $(\sigma_1, \sigma_2)$ from unsafe states. A key property of such a criticality function is the separation of safe and unsafe states, in the following sense: whenever the criticality of plant states is below a fixed threshold $c_{safe}$ the plant state is safe.

Formally, a *criticality measure* for given traffic agents $A_1 = P_1 \parallel C_1$ and $A_2 = P_2 \parallel C_2$ is a continuous piecewise differentiable function

$$cr : \mathbb{R}^{Var(P_1)} \times \mathbb{R}^{Var(P_2)} \to \mathbb{R}_{\geq 0}$$

satisfying the implication $cr(\sigma_1, \sigma_2) < c_{safe} \Rightarrow SE_{A_1}(\sigma_1) \cap SE_{A_2}(\sigma_2) = \varnothing$.

**A Proof Rule for Collision Freedom.** For two cooperating traffic agents $A_1 = C_1 \parallel P_1$ and $A_2 = C_2 \parallel P_2$ the proof rule of [13] has the form

$$\frac{(\textbf{VC 1}),\dots,(\textbf{VC 18})}{C_1 \parallel P_1 \parallel C_2 \parallel P_2 \models \lceil \neg collision \rceil}$$

where the verification conditions **(VC 1)** ... **(VC 18)** require only verification tasks of the following types:

(A) off-line analysis of the dynamics of the plant in fixed modes,
(B) mode invariants for $C_1 \parallel C_2$,
(C) real-time properties for $C_j$,
(D) local safety properties, i.e., hybrid verification tasks for $C_j \parallel P_j$.

In the following we give a flavour of these verification conditions.

*Criticality and safety.* Our approach to establishing collision freedom is to reduce this to an analysis of the criticality of the system. The criticality measure separates safe from unsafe states: here a constant $c_{safe}$ of type $\mathbb{R}_{>0}$ represents the level of criticality below which the two travel agents are *safe*, i.e., in no danger of a collision. The following type A verification condition checks this property.

**(VC 1)**    Safety

$$Th(\mathbb{R}) \models cr < c_{safe} \Rightarrow \neg\, collision$$

This yields $P_1 \parallel P_2 \models \lceil cr < c_{safe} \rceil \Rightarrow \lceil \neg\, collision \rceil$.

*Phase-transition diagram.* It is straightforward to generate verification conditions enforcing compliance of the concrete protocol to the phase-transition system of Fig. 7. To this end, the phases *far away, negotiating, correcting, recovery* and *fail-safe* of the controllers $C_i$ are represented as disjoint subsets $FAR(C_i)$, $NEG(C_i)$, $COR(C_i)$, $REC(C_i)$, $FSA(C_i) \subseteq \mathbb{M}_i$ of the set of modes. When specifying the behaviour of the controllers $C_i$ in DC, we use $FAR(C_i)$ as a shorthand for $M(C_i) \in FAR(C_i)$ and analogously for the other phases. Then we check the following simple type B verification condition.

**(VC 2)**    Controllers observe phase-transition diagram. For $i = 1, 2$

$$C_i \models_0 \Phi_{phase}(C_i)$$

Thus the controllers satisfy the above phase constraints from the start. Here $\Phi_{phase}(C_i)$ is a conjunction of formulae of the following type:

| | | |
|---|---|---|
| *Initial phase:* | $\lceil \rceil \vee \lceil FAR(C_i) \rceil;$ true | for $i = 1, 2$ |
| *Phase sequencing:* | $\lceil FAR(C_i) \rceil \longrightarrow \lceil FAR(C_i) \vee NEG(C_i) \rceil$ | for $i = 1, 2$ |
| | $\dots\dots\dots\dots\dots$ etc $\dots\dots\dots\dots$ | |

*Warnings.* The following type A verification condition checks that each trajectory leading from a plant state without warning to a collision must cross an activation condition of one of the correcting modes, i.e., it checks whether the set of provided maneuvers is *complete*.

**(VC 4)**    Completeness of maneuvers.

$$P_1 \parallel P_2 \models (\lceil \neg \phi_N \rceil; \ true) \wedge (\lceil \neg collision \rceil; \ \uparrow collision) \ \Rightarrow \ \Diamond \uparrow \Phi_{start}$$

The activation conditions for maneuvers must be chosen in such a way that criticality is below the critical threshold when maneuvers become enabled, leading to the following type A verification condition.

**(VC 5)**    During warning period criticality is still low.

$$Th(\mathbb{R}) \models \forall \delta \leq \Delta_C : (acc_1 = acc_2 = 0 \wedge \uparrow pre(\delta, \Phi_{start}) \Rightarrow cr < c_{safe})$$

This yields $P_1 \parallel P_2 \models (\lceil acc_1 = acc_2 = 0 \rceil \wedge \ell = \Delta_C; \uparrow \Phi_{start}) \Rightarrow \lceil cr < c_{safe} \rceil$. In particular, this ensures that maneuvers are not activated too late.

*Negotiation phase.* The negotiation phase must be initiated as soon as a first warning occurs. Recall that this event is represented by $\Phi_N$ becoming true. The following type B verification condition checks this.

**(VC 6)**    Initiating negotiating phase. For $i = 1, 2$

$$C_i \parallel P_1 \parallel P_2 \models \lceil FAR(C_i) \rceil \xrightarrow{\uparrow \Phi_N} \lceil NEG(C_i) \rceil$$

Note that both controllers enter their negotiating phase simultaneously when the trigger $\uparrow \phi_N$ occurs.

The following type D verification condition guarantees that $pre(\Delta_C, \Phi_{start})$, the warning to start maneuvers according to $\Phi_{start}$, was raised early enough. If the traffic agents changed their speeds during negotiation and selection (sub-) phase, the calculations of the warning would be wrong.

**(VC 11)**    No acceleration during negotiation and selection. For $i = 1, 2$

$$C_i \parallel P_i \models \lceil NEG(C_i) \vee SEL(C_i) \rceil \Rightarrow \lceil acc_i = 0 \rceil$$

The last type C verification condition for the negotiation phase checks, that indeed negotiation is completed within the given time window of length $\Delta_N$.

**(VC 12)**    Negotiation completes in time.

$$C_1 \parallel C_2 \models \lceil NEG(C_1) \vee NEG(C_2) \rceil \Rightarrow \ell \leq \Delta_N$$

where $\Delta_N < \Delta_C$. Thus *both* controllers have left their negotiating phase after at most $\Delta_N$ time units.

*Adequacy.* The following type A verification condition ensures that the critical-ity does not increase when collision avoidance maneuvers are activated. Note that these are part of the hybrid automata resulting from the restriction of the controller to the selected correcting mode.

**(VC 15)**    Adequacy of matching modes. For all $(m_1, m_2) \in \text{MATCH}$

$$C_1 \upharpoonright m_1 \parallel P_1 \parallel C_2 \upharpoonright m_2 \parallel P_2 \models$$
$$\upharpoonright \varPhi(m_1, m_2); \text{true} \Rightarrow \forall c \in \mathbb{R}_{\leq 0} : \lceil cr \leq c \rceil \longrightarrow \lceil cr \leq c \rceil$$

For the recovery maneuver, a similar verification conditions additionally requires that after a suitable braking time $t$ depending on their speeds at the start of the maneuver, the traffic agents have come to a complete halt.

*Far away phase.* The following type B verification conditions enforces that the correcting phase can be left in favour of the phase *far away* only when there is no warning that new correcting maneuvers have to start in $\Delta_C$ time.

**(VC 17)**    Termination of maneuvers. For $i = 1, 2$ and $\phi_F \Leftrightarrow \neg \phi_N$

$$C_i \parallel P_1 \parallel P_2 \models \lceil COR(C_i) \rceil \xrightarrow{\uparrow \varPhi_F} \lceil FAR(C_i) \rceil$$

*Fail-safe state.* The following type B verification condition ensures that the recovery maneuver is concluded by entering the fail-safe state, when the agent has come to a complete stop. By **(VC 2)**, each traffic agent stays in this state. We require that in this state the traffic agent does not change its position, and that the criticality does not increase.

**(VC 18)**    Fail-safe state. For $i = 1, 2$

$$C_i \parallel P_i \models \lceil REC(C_i) \rceil \xrightarrow{\uparrow(spd_i = 0)} \lceil FSA(C_i) \wedge spd_i = 0 \rceil$$
$$C_i \parallel P_1 \parallel P_2 \models$$
$$\forall c \in \mathbb{R}_{\geq 0} : \lceil FSA(C_i) \wedge spd_i = 0 \wedge cr \leq c \rceil \longrightarrow \lceil spd_i = 0 \wedge cr \leq c \rceil.$$

In [13] the following was shown.

**Theorem 1 (Soundness).** *The verification conditions* **(VC 1)**,...,**(VC 18)** *together imply*

$$C_1 \parallel P_1 \parallel C_2 \parallel P_2 \models \lceil \neg collision \rceil ,$$

*i.e., the proof rule for collision freedom is sound.*

## 4.2   Case Study: Movement Authority

Let us revisit the ETCS train control introduced in Subsection 2.4. However, in-stead of using Matlab-Simulink and Stateflow as modelling techniques, we shall now represent the scenario more abstractly by time-dependent observables and hybrid automata. We consider one train moving along a track and communicating with a radio block center (RBC) that grants movement authorities to the train. At each moment of time there is a certain end of movement authority (EoA) for the train because after the EoA a critical section begins, which may be a rail-road crossing or a track segment occupied by a preceding train (cf. Fig. 4).

We start from domains $Position = \mathbb{R}_{\geq 0}$ with typical element $p$ for the position of the train on the track, $Speed = \mathbb{R}_{\geq 0}$ with typical element $v$ for the speed of the train, and $Acc = \mathbb{R}$ with typical element $a$ for the acceleration of the train. Let $v_{max}$ denote the maximal speed of the train and $-b$ the *braking force* of the train, represented as a negative acceleration, i.e., with $-b < 0$. The current *end of authority* for the train is modelled by an observable

$$EoA : Time \rightarrow Position$$

which is maintained by the RBC. We require

$$\forall\, t_1, t_2 \in Time : t_1 \leq t_2 \Rightarrow EoA(t_1) \leq EoA(t_2).$$

The *critical section CS* behind the *EoA* is represented by an interval of positions

$$[CS.s,\, CS.e] \subseteq Position$$

starting at $CS.s$ and ending at $CS.e$, with a fixed positive length $CS.e - CS.s$. A predicate describing all positions *after the critical section* is

$$afterCS : Position \rightarrow \mathbb{B} \quad \text{with} \quad \forall\, p \in Position : afterCS(p) \Leftrightarrow CS.e \leq p.$$

When the train approaches the current EoA it has to *start talking* to the RBC to get permission to extend the EoA. The distance relative to EoA where start talking has to be initiated is modelled by a function

$$ST : Speed \times Time \rightarrow Position$$

depending on the train's speed, the maximal time delay needed to communicate with the RBC, and implicitly on the fixed braking force $-b$. If the permission is not granted by the RBC the train has to *start braking* with the braking force $-b$. The distance relative to EoA where the braking has to be initiated is modelled by a function

$$SB : Speed \rightarrow Position$$

depending on the train's speed and implicitly on the fixed braking force $-b$. These positions and distances are illustrated in Fig. 4. We require

$$\forall\, v \in Speed, \Delta \in Time : ST(v, \Delta) \geq SB(v).$$

*Safety.* For the train's safety envelope $\mathbf{SE}_{Train}(p)$ we choose an extension around its current front position $p$ which encompasses the length of the train, independent of mode and speed:

$$\mathbf{SE}_{Train}(p) = [p - L_T, p] \subseteq Position$$

where $L_T$ is the length of the train. The critical section's safety envelope depends on the position of the *EoA*:

$$\mathbf{SE}_{CS} = \begin{cases} \varnothing & \text{if } CS.e < EoA \\ [CS.b, CS.e] & \text{otherwise} \end{cases}$$

The choice of $\varnothing$ as the extension of the safety envelope caters for the case that the RBC has granted an extension of the *EoA* beyond the critical section. This permits the train to pass the critical section without safety violation.

We define $inCS(p) \Leftrightarrow CS.s \le p \le CS.e + L_T$. The predicate $inCS$ describes all positions where the safety envelopes of the train and the critical section overlap, i.e.,

$$\mathbf{SE}_{Train}(p) \cap \mathbf{SE}_{CS} \ne \varnothing \; \Leftrightarrow \; inCS(p) \wedge EoA \le CS.e.$$

Thus *collision freedom* is equivalent to $inCS(p) \Rightarrow CS.e < EoA$, i.e., whenever the front position $p$ is in the critical section, the *EoA* has been extended beyond the critical section.

**Traffic Agents.** The scenario movement authority is modeled as a system $MA$ with two traffic agents:

$$MA = \text{Train} \parallel \text{RBC},$$

one train consisting of plant and controller interacting with an RBC consisting of a controller only. Fig. 8 shows how these agents are represented by real-valued variables *pos* (position), *spd* (speed), *acc* (acceleration) and *EoA* (end of authority), and which (other) variables the four components share for communication with each other.

We assume that the *train plant* has knowledge of its position on the track and controls its speed depending on requests from the train controller. It will react to speed control commands from the train controller. Thus we consider the variables below. We do not distinguish between the (syntactic) variables of the automaton and the corresponding trajectories in runs. So we take for the type of a variable the type of its time-dependent trajectory, and we permit variables with discrete ranges without explicitly coding them in reals.

| Variables: | | Train plant |
|---|---|---|
| input | $sc : Time \rightarrow \{Keep, Brake\}$ | (speed control) |
| output | $pos : Time \rightarrow Position$ | (position of the train) |
| | $spd : Time \rightarrow Speed$ | (speed of the train) |
| | $acc : Time \rightarrow Acc$ | (acceleration of the train) |

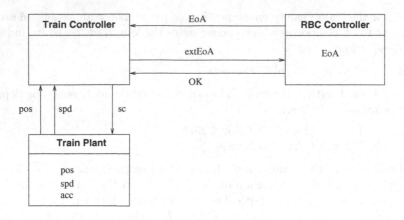

**Fig. 8.** Communication between train and RBC

For the dynamics of the train we assume the continuous transition relations $pos^\bullet = spd$ and $spd^\bullet = acc$ and the invariants $-b \leq acc$ and $spd \leq v_{max}$. Here we are interested only in the change of speed during braking:

$$
acc = \begin{cases} 0 & \text{if } sc = Keep \vee (sc = Brake \wedge spd = 0) \\ -b & \text{if } sc = Brake \wedge spd > 0 \end{cases}
$$

The *train controller* monitors the position and speed of the train. When approaching the current end of authority *EoA* (guarding a critical section) it requests for an extension from the RBC by sending an *extEoA* signal. If the RBC sends a signal *OK* the controller requests the train plant to keep the (desired) speed. If the RBC does not reply in time and instead the train passes the position *SB* the controller forces the train plant to brake. Thus the train controller has the following time dependent variables.

| Variables: | | | Train controller |
|---|---|---|---|
| input | $pos : Time \rightarrow Position$ | | (position of the train) |
| | $spd : Time \rightarrow Speed$ | | (speed of the train) |
| | $EoA : Time \rightarrow Position$ | | (current EoA) |
| | $OK : Time \rightarrow \mathbb{B}$ | | (EoA is extended) |
| local | $CS.s : Time \rightarrow Position$ | | (begin of critical section) |
| output | $extEoA : Time \rightarrow \mathbb{B}$ | | (request to extend EoA) |
| | $sc : Time \rightarrow \{Keep, Brake\}$ | | (speed control) |
| Modes: | **Far, Appr, SafeAppr, Braking, FailSafe** | | |

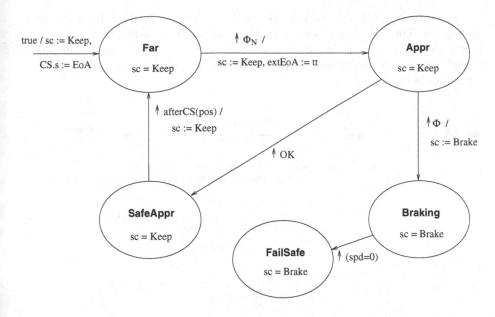

**Fig. 9.** Train controller

The dynamics of the train controller is described by the automaton in Fig. 9. Initially, the controller is in the mode **Far**. When the predicate $\Phi_N$ abbreviating $pos \geq EoA - ST(spd, \Delta_C)$ becomes true the controller switches to the mode **Appr**. On occurrence of a signal $OK$ the controller switches to the mode **SafeAppr** indicating that the train can safely approach the critical section. In this mode the train continues to keep its speed. If the predicate $\Phi$ abbreviating $pos \geq EoA - SB(spd)$ becomes true the controller switches to the mode **Braking** where it forces the train to brake until a complete stop. If the train's speed is zero, the controller enters the mode **FailSafe**. In the terminology of Fig. 7, the mode **Appr** is the phase $NEGOTIATION$, **SafeAppr** is $CORRECTING$, and **Braking** is $RECOVERY$.

The RBC is modelled only as far as the communication concerning the extension of $EoA$ is concerned. It outputs of current $EoA$ to the train and if requested to extend it by an $extEoA$ signal may grant an $OK$ signal. Thus the $RBC$ $controller$ has the following time dependent variables.

| Variables: | | RBC controller |
|---|---|---|
| input | $extEoA : Time \rightarrow \mathbb{B}$ | (request to extend EoA) |
| local | $x : Time \rightarrow Time$ | (clock) |
| output | $EoA : Time \rightarrow Position$ | (current EoA) |
| | $OK : Time \rightarrow \mathbb{B}$ | (EoA is extended) |
| Modes: | **Idle, Check, Unsafe** | |

The dynamics of this simplified RBC controller is described by the automaton in Fig. 10. The expression *update(EoA)* abbreviates an assignment of a new, larger value to the variable *EoA*. The clock $x$ with upper bound $\varepsilon$ in mode **Check** models the maximum delay it takes for the RBC to answer the request for extending the *EoA*.

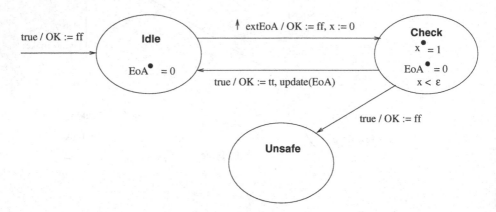

**Fig. 10.** RBC controller

## 4.3    Automatic Discovery of the Criticality Functions

It is critical for a system according to Fig. 7 that a recovery maneuver will always lead into a fail-safe state without violating any safety constraints. To ensure this, recovery needs to be initiated in time, so that potentially hazardous situations can be avoided. For the train example given in the previous sections, we will now demonstrate how to determine states which lead to a safe recovery maneuver. In this particular case we will ensure that the train will always come to a stop before an end-of-authority point associated with a critical section. In particular, we will construct a predicate $\Phi$ guaranteeing that the train system is safe in the sense that no critical section can be passed, unless the RBC sent the signal *OK* to the train passing it. In other words, once the train system enters the **Braking** mode, the safety condition $pos \leq EoA$ will not be violated and the train will come to a stop in the **FailSafe** mode — braking is always initiated in time.

We will now show that the criticality function in the verification conditions from Subsection 4.1 can be seen of an instance from a generic class Lyapunov-like functions. Methods for synthesis of Lyapunov functions can then be adapted to automatically compute a suitable criticality function. Since contour lines of the function can be used to separate reachable and non-reachable states, we call this class *Lyapunov-like boundary functions*.

**Definition 3.** *Let $x(t) \in \mathbb{R}^n$ be a hybrid system's state vector (the vector of the valuations of all variables [6]) at time t. Given a set of initial states vectors*

---

[6] For the ease of mathematical treatment, the state of the system is represented as a *vector* of real numbers, instead of a function $\sigma : Var \to \mathbb{R}$ like in Subsection 4.1.

$S \subseteq \mathbb{R}^n$ *and a set of unsafe state vectors* $U \subseteq \mathbb{R}^n$, *a Lyapunov-like boundary function of the hybrid system is a function* $V : \mathbb{R}^n \to \mathbb{R}$, *such that:*

– *for all runs of the system and all reachable states* $x \in \mathbb{R}^n$:

$$V^\bullet(x) := \frac{dV}{dx}\frac{dx}{dt} \leq 0$$

– $\exists k \in \mathbb{R} : (x \in S \Rightarrow V(x) < k) \wedge (x \in U \Rightarrow V(x) > k)$

The function $V$ has Lyapunov-like properties, as it will never increase throughout the evolution of any trajectory due to the condition $V^\bullet(x) \leq 0$, which forces the function's time derivative to be non-positive. Furthermore, there exists a contour line, given by the points $x$ with $V(x) = k$, such that the possible initial states $S$ lie on one side of this line, while the unsafe states $U$ lie on the other (see Fig. 11). Due to the Lyapunov-like property it is then impossible for a trajectory beginning in the set of initial states to cross into the unsafe region, as this would require an increase of $V(x)$.

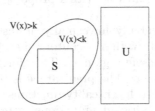

**Fig. 11.** Criticality function contour line with initial set $S$ and unsafe set $U$

Since such a Lyapunov-like criticality function is a variant of a Lyapunov function, computational approaches for Lyapunov function synthesis can be adapted for this case. For instance, linear matrix inequalities can be employed to *automatically* compute a suitable quadratic $V$, and then the maximal $k$ such that $x \in U \Rightarrow V(x) > k$. The computation procedure is very similar to the one that will be described in detail in Section 6.

Such a Lyapunov-like boundary function is a special case of a criticality function as described in Subsection 4.1. The function $V$ can be used as criticality function $cr$ and the contour line value $k$ represents the maximal admissible criticality value $c_{safe}$. Setting $cr = V$ and $c_{safe} = k$, the verification condition **(VC 1)** is fulfilled since $(x \in U \Rightarrow V(x) > k)$ implies $(x \in U \Rightarrow V(x) \geq k)$, which is equivalent to **(VC 1)** by contraposition. For condition **(VC 5)**, in the case of $\delta = 0$, the set $S$ assumes the role of $pre(0, \Phi_{start})$. The condition $x \in S$ means that $x$ is an admissible state vector for initiating the maneuver, which is equivalent to the requirement that the variables at time of initiation fulfill $pre(0, \Phi_{start})$. If $\delta > 0$, a backward reachability computation is needed to show that $V(x) < k$ for the entire negotiation period. Since verification condition **(VC 5)** requires an acceleration of zero during negotiation, this simplifies the computation. Condition (**VC 15**) is implied by the Lyapunov-like condition $V^{\bullet}(x) \leq 0$ stating that $V$ cannot increase over time.

Therefore, a criticality function as needed in (**VC 1**), (**VC 5**) and (**VC 15**) can be computed automatically, using methods for Lyapunov function synthesis. The dynamics for the given tuple of maneuvers is needed as an input, as is the set of unsafe states. Condition (**VC 4**) needs to be checked separately, since a Lyapunov-like function does not guarantee that the set $\{x \mid V(x) < k\}$ is always entered before a trajectory can pass into the unsafe region $U$. It is then possible to synthesize a Lyapunov-like boundary function (serving as the criticality function) and a contour line value $k$ (serving as the maximal admissible criticality level) such that initiating the maneuver with criticality lower than $k$ guarantees safety. Each admissible set of initial state vectors $S$ for the maneuver corresponds to a possible safe condition for the maneuvers.

For the rail-road crossing case study, will now employ Lyapunov-like boundary functions to identify a safe guard $\Phi$, such that $pos \leq EoA$ is always guaranteed. Therefore we put $U = \{pos > EoA\}$. As $\Phi$ is not given, but to be derived, we define $\Phi := V(x) < k$. All states with this property are separated from $U$ by the contour line $V(x) = k$.

Since a system can potentially have many admissible criticality functions, this even holds for any state within a contour line of *any* criticality function with respect to the same unsafe region $U$. Therefore, we are not restricted to one function, but can use many. The predicate $\Phi$ is then the disjunction of the predicates $V_i(x) < k$ for all such criticality functions $V_i$ and associated contour line values $k_i$. Using many criticality functions instead of one can result in a weaker, and therefore less conservative, predicate $\Phi$.

For the case study, it was sufficient to use just one criticality function, as the use of several functions brought no significant improvement. As a result we obtained the following criticality function $cr$ and boundary value $c_{safe}$:

$$cr = 0.0014616 * (pos - EoA + 2000)^2 + spd^2 \tag{15}$$
$$c_{safe} = 5846.445 \tag{16}$$

Figure 12 shows the position of the train in meters before the EoA point on the horizontal axis and its velocity in $m/s$ on the vertical axis. The shaded set of states is safe set $\{x \mid V_i(x) < k_i\}$. Initiating the braking within this set guarantees that the unsafe region to the right of the vertical line cannot be entered. For this particular example, where the speed is decreasing at a fixed rate, this implies an eventual transition to the **FailSafe** phase, without breaching any safety requirements. Furthermore, assuming a maximal speed $v_{max} = 76.46 m/s$, condition (**VC 4**) is also fulfilled, since system trajectories could not enter the unsafe region without first passing through the ellipsoid. Any predicate $\Phi$ which evaluates to false everywhere outside this set is admissible as a guard for the transition between the *Appr* and *Braking* modes.

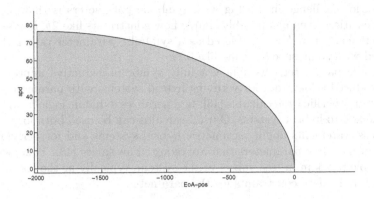

**Fig. 12.** Safe region for initiating the braking

# 5 Parameterized Verification of the Cooperation Layer

In this section, we present results for verifying parameterized instances of traffic protocols. On the one hand, system safety in systems like ETCS crucially depends on the right choice of parameter values. For instance, whether a train can keep its speed safely depends on the relationship of EoA to the current velocity $v$ and maximum braking power $b$. If these values are imbalanced then the train protocol is no longer guaranteed to avoid crashes. Hence, it is utterly important to analyze and discover safety constraints between such parameters or state variables and adjust design parameters in accordance with those parametric constraints.

On the other hand, once those constraints have been discovered, all instances of the traffic scenario that satisfy the parametric safety constraints can be verified at once. Generally, safety statements do not only hold for a particular setting but generalise to a broader range of possibilities. For instance, train control is not only safe for a particular initial speed $v \leq 10$ and a specific braking force $b = 0.1$ with remaining EoA-distance of $5km$. Instead, the system remains safe for *all* choices of parameters that satisfy a corresponding constraint. Using our techniques from [43,45,44,46], all such instances of the system can be verified at once, and the required safety constraints on the free parameters can be discovered.

## 5.1 Parameterized Hybrid Systems

Parameters naturally arise from the degrees of freedom of how a part of the system can be instantiated or how a controller can respond to input. They include both external system parameters like the braking force $b$ of a train, and design parameters of internal choice like $SB$, i.e., when to start braking before approaching EoA in order to ensure that the train cannot possibly run into an open gate or preceeding train.

The major challenge in dealing with symbolic parameters is that they lead to nonlinearities: Even comparably simple flow constraints like $2b(EoA - p)$ become nonlinear when $b$ is considered as a symbolic parameter rather than instantiated with some specific value like 0.1.

To handle parameters, we follow a fully symbolic deductive approach. We have introduced a logic, $d\mathcal{L}$, for verifying hybrid systems with parameters and a corresponding verification calculus [43]. It generalizes dynamic logic from the discrete case [23] to hybrid systems. Our $d\mathcal{L}$ calculus can be used both for verifying correctness statements about parametric hybrid systems and for deriving constraints on their free parameters that are required for safety [43]. Thus, with $d\mathcal{L}$, it is possible to zoom in to a subset of the system, typically at the coordination layer, and find safety constraints for the parameters.

## 5.2   Technical Approach: Differential Logic

To illustrate how our techniques for parameterized hybrid systems work, we provide a short survey of the $d\mathcal{L}$ principles. The full details of the theory behind $d\mathcal{L}$ are reported in [43,45,44,46].

The logic $d\mathcal{L}$ provides modal formulae like $[MA]\phi$, which express that all runs of the parametric hybrid system $MA$ (see Subsection 4.2) lead to states which satisfy some safety constraint $\phi$. Further, such formulae can be combined propositionally, by quantifiers, or modalities $[\beta]$ about other automata $\beta$. With this, safety of parametric hybrid systems can be stated as formulae in the logic $d\mathcal{L}$, for instance:

$$b > 0 \wedge \epsilon \geq 0 \Rightarrow [MA](p \leq EoA) . \tag{17}$$

This $d\mathcal{L}$ formula states that all runs of the hybrid system $MA$ are such that the train position $p$ remains within the movement authority $EoA$, provided that the braking force $b$ is non-zero and the maximum reaction-cycle-time is some $\epsilon \geq 0$. Both symbols, $b$ and $\epsilon$, are train model parameters and given externally. Their values depend on the specific characteristics of the actual train and should be handled symbolically for a thorough analysis of all trains. From the perspective of a single train automaton, $EoA$ can also be considered as an external parameter. In the full system $MA$, which involves trains and RBCs, it can also be considered as a state variable instead.

Using the $d\mathcal{L}$ calculus, such a formula can be analyzed systematically in order to find out if it holds or under which parameter constraints the system is safe. For instance, for the safety constraint (17), the $d\mathcal{L}$ calculus reveals that the system is only safe when the initial velocity does not exceed the braking capabilities and the control parameters are chosen in accordance with the movement authorities, speed, and reaction times.

To make our calculus compositional and simplify its step-wise symbolic processing principle, we use a textual notation of hybrid automata as *hybrid programs* [43]. As hybrid automata [25] can be embedded in hybrid programs by a simple canonical construction [43], we identify hybrid automata and their corresponding program rendition, here. With this embedding, parametric safety statements can be easily expressed using d$\mathcal{L}$ formulae of the form (17) and analyzed in the d$\mathcal{L}$ calculus.

Given a safety statement like (17), the d$\mathcal{L}$ calculus performs a symbolic analysis of the parametric hybrid system and identifies safety constraints on the free parameters. Figure 13 contains a corresponding abbreviated proof outline for a part of the system analysis in the d$\mathcal{L}$ calculus. At this point, we only want to remark that the proof starts at the bottom with the full $MA$ controller and splits into sub-goals that symbolically analyze a part of the ETCS behavior each. For instance, the left branch analyzes the train behavior in the recovery mode, the right branch investigates acceleration cases, see [43] for details. The calculus works by successive symbolic decomposition of the system, which can be understood to follow a symbolic case analysis. As a basis, our implementation uses an integration of the KeY prover [5,4] with quantifier elimination in Mathematica for arithmetic reasoning about the continuous dynamics.

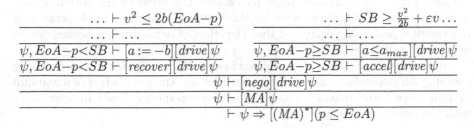

**Fig. 13.** Proof outline for ETCS protocol in d$\mathcal{L}$

## 5.3 Analysis of Parameters in ETCS Protocol Phases

In the d$\mathcal{L}$ calculus, we can derive constraints on the parameters for a safe operation of train control. These parameters are limits in the ideal-world model of the coordination level, hence, general engineering principles advise using additional safety margins to compensate for inaccuracies and disturbances.

From an analysis of the braking behavior in recovery mode, we can automatically determine a *controllability constraint* for the train, see [43]. If the following constraint is violated, no safe control of the train is possible at all, because its speed exceeds the braking power $b$ for the remaining movement authority $EoA - p$:

$$v^2 \leq 2b(EoA - p) \ . \tag{18}$$

Assuming that condition (18) holds, it remains to show that the particular train control choices maintain safety. Especially, the controllers must maintain (18) invariably during all possible driving behavior.

The two most crucial control parameters for the cooperation protocol $MA$ in ETCS are $ST$ and $SB$. Both are design parameters of internal choice by the controllers and, thus, need an adequate instantiation to ensure safety. The parameter $ST$ determines when the train enters negotiation mode to ensure that it can get an EoA-extension from the RBC before reaching EoA. The control parameter $SB$ is the safety distance at which the speed supervision needs to initiate braking when no positive EoA extension has occurred yet (recovery mode). Both parameters are formulated as points on the track in terms of distances from EoA (see Fig. 4).

The parameter $SB$ is a very important safety parameter that needs to be chosen adequately such that the train can guarantee to remain within its movement authority, regardless of the behavior of other traffic agents like preceeding trains or gates at critical sections as mediated by the RBC agent. Especially, if $SB$ is chosen right, the system remains safe, whatever the outcome of the RBC communication may be.

The safety constraint for parameter $SB$ can be derived from an analysis of the hybrid program rendition of the $MA$-automata using a proof of the form in Fig. 13, see [43] for details. In addition, the underlying RBC and train models bridge the gap from cooperation layer models to design layer models as they take maximum controller response times into account. Similar to the notion of lazy hybrid automata [51], we account for the fact that controller implementations react with a processing delay and that the effect of actuators like brakes can be delayed as well.

An acceleration $a \leq a_{max}$ is permitted in case $EoA - p \geq SB$, when adaptively choosing $SB$ depending on the current speed $v$ and the parameters of maximum braking force $b$ and maximum speed supervision response time $\epsilon$ in accordance with the following constraint:

$$SB \ \geq \ \frac{v^2}{2b} + \left( \frac{a_{max}}{b} + 1 \right) \left( \frac{a_{max}}{2} \varepsilon^2 + \varepsilon v \right) \ . \tag{19}$$

This constraint expresses that it is only safe to keep on driving when the controllability constraint (18) is maintained even after a maximal acceleration of $a_{max}$ during a maximum period of $\epsilon$ time units. In particular, constraint (19) makes the controllability constraint (18) inductive.

Observe that constraint (19) is a refined and parameterized version of the (12) (remember that $x_b$ is the point on the track corresponding to the distance $SB$ from $EoA$). The actual symbolic constraints in (19) identify what needs to be captured by the 10% safety margin in (12). It also clearly identifies under what conditions a 10% safety margin is sufficient. Likewise, constraint (19) explains the shape of the safety region given in Fig. 12 and gives insights about a systematic symbolic generalization of the numerical criticality function in (15). It identifies fully symbolic constraints as opposed to specific real numbers that only hold for a particular scenario.

Parameter $ST$ is a liveness parameter. Depending on the expected maximum RBC communication latency $L$, which again is a parameter for the train analysis, it ensures that the RBC can still respond in time before the train needs to decelerate. That is, when the train enters negotiation at $ST$, it does not need to brake unless an EoA extension cannot be granted by the RBC within $L$ at all. For instance, an RBC may not be able to grant an EoA extension despite an early request because other traffic agents occupy the track segment beyond EoA.

Constraints on the parameter $ST$ can be derived [45] from an analysis of a single negotiation and correction phase. A proof yields the following necessary constraint depending on the expected maximum RBC communication latency $L$:

$$ST \geq Lv + \frac{v^2}{2b} . \tag{20}$$

Again, (20) corresponds to a version of (13) that has been synthesized from the system model deductively.

The constraints (19) and (20) can be used to find out how dense a track can be packed with trains in order to maximize throughput without endangering safety, and how early a train needs to start negotiation in order to minimize the risk of having to reduce speed when the MA is not extendable in time.

## 6  Proving Stability of Local Control and Design Models

Stability is a property of a dynamic system that subsumes its ability to withstand, and eventually compensate for, outside disturbances that affect a system. For a local closed-loop control system, this is a very desirable property, because stability ensures that the controller is actually able to keep the controlled parameter close to the desired value. Furthermore, if one requires asymptotic stability, there cannot be any undamped oscillations or cyclic behavior in the closed-loop system. For instance, one would expect from a speed controller for a train, that it forces the speed to converge toward a desired value, without producing needless cycles of acceleration and deceleration. Very little controller activity should be needed, once the train is close to this desired speed. In this section, we will apply methods based on the concept of *Lyapunov-functions* [35] to the speed controller of the train model from Section 2. Lyapunov functions are functions that map each system state onto a nonnegative real value. For every run of the system, the sequence of values this function attains is required to be decreasing, eventually converging to zero at the desired control point. If a function with these properties is found, then the system is *asymptotically stable*. We will detail how methods for automatic computation of these functions can be applied to a model of a speed controller.

**Definition 4.** *Consider a continuous-time dynamic system with state vector $x \in \mathbb{R}^n$. Let $x(t)$, $t \geq 0$, denote its state at time $t$ during a run of the system. The system is called* globally asymptotically stable *if the following two properties hold for all possible runs:*

*a)* $\forall \epsilon > 0 \quad \exists \delta > 0 \quad \forall t \geq 0 : \| x(0) \| < \delta \Rightarrow \| x(t) \| < \epsilon$ (stability)
*b)* $t \to \infty \Rightarrow x(t) \to 0$ (global attractivity)

*If a) and b) hold only on a bounded set containing 0, the system is called* locally asymptotically stable.

Without loss of generality we assume that the origin of the continuous state space $\mathbb{R}^n$ is the equilibrium point all trajectories converge to. If one wants to show asymptotic stability with respect to a different equilibrium – as is the case in the drive train example – the state space of the hybrid system can simply be "shifted" to move this point into the equilibrium.

Intuitively, the stability property guarantees that there is an upper bound on how far the system can stray from the equilibrium point, depending on its initial state. Moreover, the global attractivity property tells us that the system will eventually converge to the equilibrium point. Together, this implies that there is an upper bound on the temporary change of state a disturbance can cause, relative to the size of the disturbance, and that eventually the system will have compensated for the disturbance.

We will consider hybrid systems with a finite number of discrete modes. With each mode $m$, we associate an affine differential equation $x^\bullet = A_m x + b_m$ with $A_m \in \mathbb{R}^{n \times n}, b_n \in \mathbb{R}^n$ for describing the continuous evolution of the system's state variables. A possible transition between a pair of modes $m_1$ and $m_2$ is given as a quantifier-free first-order predicate over the continuous variables. No discrete updates of continuous variables are allowed. We also allow for an invariant in each mode, given by a quantifier-free first-order predicate[7] on the continuous variables. The system may only stay in a mode while its invariant is satisfied. We assume that the system does not exhibit Zeno or blocking behavior, so that all trajectories are continuous and unbounded in time (cf. Appendix 8).

Since the state space of such a hybrid system is $\mathbb{R}^n \times M$, the cartesian product of the continuous and discrete state (mode) space, one is usually interested in local stability. The invariants specify which continuous states can be active with which modes – combinations violating the invariants need not be considered. Therefore the stability property is local as defined by the invariants. Furthermore, we only expect the continuous variables to converge, but for all permissible initial hybrid states $(x(0), m(0))$.

For systems of this kind, local asymptotic stability can be shown with the help of a *common Lyapunov function*. It is defined as follows (see [29,9]).

**Definition 5.** *Consider a hybrid system with state vector $x \in \mathbb{R}^n$ and mode $m \in M$, where $M$ is the finite set of modes. Assume that the dynamics in mode $m$ are given as $x^\bullet = f_m(x)$ and that the invariant belonging to mode $m$ is the predicate $I_m$. A (common) Lyapunov function for this system is then a function $V : \mathbb{R}^n \to \mathbb{R}$ such that:*

a) $V(x) = 0$ if $x = 0$ and $V(x) > 0$ otherwise
b) for all $m$: $V_m^\bullet(x) := \frac{dV}{dx}(x)f_m(x) < 0$ if $0 \neq x \vDash I_m$
c) $0 \vDash I_m \Rightarrow V_m^\bullet(0) = 0$
d) $V(x) \to \infty$ when $\| x \| \to \infty$

---

[7] In principle, any quantifier-free predicate over the continuous variables is admissible for mode transitions or invariants. If the resulting invariant set is not a convex polyhedron, it will need to be over-approximated for the actual computation, increasing conservativeness.

A Lyapunov function maps each state of the system onto a nonnegative real number, such that the value of the function is decreasing *at all times for all possible trajectories*, eventually converging to zero at the origin of the state space. Condition a) enforces a global minimum of $V$ at 0. Conditions b) and c) imply that $V$ is decreasing over time in every mode, whenever its invariant is true, except at the equilibrium, where $V_m^\bullet(0) = 0$ for all applicable modes. Condition d) is needed to enforce the stability property a) in Definition 4.

**Theorem 2 ([9]).** *Consider a hybrid system as in Definition 5. The existence of a common Lyapunov function for such a system implies local asymptotic stability for all initial hybrid states that are covered by at least one invariant.*

There are also refinements to the common Lyapunov function approach, using piecewise continuous functions instead [9,28,42,16]. This allows the use of different functions for each mode. However, for the train controller application in this paper, this extension was not necessary. Lyapunov functions can be found automatically via numerical optimization [28,42,16]. We will demonstrate this on the following example from the train control context.

## 6.1   The Drive Train Subsystem

The proof techniques outlined above will now be applied to the drive train part of the train model from Section 2. The drive train is generally active in the *Far* phase of the system when no full braking action is imminent. In this part of the system, the actual velocity of the train should be kept in line with the desired velocity, in the presence of outside disturbances. Furthermore, a change of desired velocity should result in an adequate convergence of the actual velocity towards this new value.

This is achieved by closed-loop control of the drive train via a PI-Controller, i.e. a linear controller with proportional and integral part. This controller takes the difference between current and desired velocity as an input and outputs a current that is used to accelerate/decelerate the train.

In Equations 2-8, all constants and parameters have been instantiated with sensible values, to represent a concrete drive train system. Braking force is assumed constant, as is the environment force $F_e$. All these equations have then been collapsed into a set of two differential equations per mode, through elimination of superfluous variables and exploitation of variable dependency. The functions $f$ an $g$ are therefore the representation of Equations 2-8 for these fixed values. The three relevant unknowns that remain in the drive train model given in Fig. 14 are the desired speed $v_0$, the actual speed $v$ and the integral value in Equation 2, denoted as $s$. Since Equation 2 describes dynamics modelled as the minimum of two affine functions (Equation 1), there are two corresponding modes, *Motor_1* and *Motor_2*, in the closed-loop hybrid system, each with affine dynamics. The mode *Max_acceleration* is used to model the cutoff at maximum acceleration in Equation 3. If the current speed is far beyond the desired speed, we activate the brakes, which are assumed to produce constant negative acceleration. This is represented by mode *Brake*.

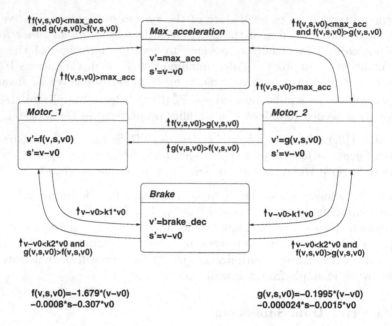

$$f(v,s,v0)=-1.679*(v-v0)$$
$$-0.0008*s-0.307*v0$$

$$g(v,s,v0)=-0.1995*(v-v0)$$
$$-0.000024*s-0.0015*v0$$

**Fig. 14.** Hybrid automaton of drive train subsystem

## 6.2   Synthesizing Lyapunov Functions

To compute a function $V$ that fulfills the conditions in Definition 5, we use a fixed parameterized function template: quadratic functions of the form $V(x) = x^T P x$, $P \in \mathbb{R}^{n \times n}$. In this representation, the parameters are isolated in the symmetric matrix $P$. This means we have to compute matrix entries for $P$, such that conditions a) to d) are satisfied.

As detailed in [28,42], this can be done with the help of *linear matrix inequalities* [8], as long as the differential equations for all modes are affine. Linear matrix inequalities are optimization problems with constraints given as definiteness constraints on matrices. They will be formally defined in the following. Phrasing the problem to find an adequate $P$ as a linear matrix inequality allows the use of convex optimization software like CSDP [7] to identify suitable matrix entries.

**Definition 6.** *A matrix* $P \in \mathbb{R}^{n \times n}$ *is called* positive semidefinite *if* $x^T P x \geq 0$ *for all* $x \in \mathbb{R}^n$. *This is also denoted* $P \succeq 0$. *For given matrices* $M_1, \ldots, M_j \in \mathbb{R}^{n \times n}$, *a* linear matrix inequality *is a problem of the form:*

*Find* $x_1, \ldots, x_j \in \mathbb{R}$ *such that* $x_1 M_1 + \ldots + x_j M_j \succeq 0$.

Define $I$ as the $n \times n$ identity matrix. The problem of finding a Lyapunov function as in Definition 5 corresponds to the following linear matrix inequality [42]. Find $P, \mu_m^i$ such that:

$$P \succeq \alpha * I$$

$$\forall m \in \mathbb{M} : A_m^T P + PA_m - \sum_i \mu_m^i \, Q_m^i + I \preceq 0$$

The matrices $Q_m^i \in \mathbb{R}^n$ are the result of the so-called $\mathcal{S}$-procedure [55]. They are computed a priori from the invariants $I_m$ such that $I_m \Rightarrow x^T Q_m^i x \geq 0$ for all $i$. The details of this computation, which only involves basic algebra in the case of polytopic invariants, can be found in [42].

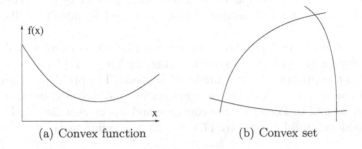

(a) Convex function                    (b) Convex set

**Fig. 15.** Convex set and function

Intuitively, this linear matrix inequality can be visualized as follows. Figure 15(b) shows an illustration of the parameter space of the Lyapunov function candidate. Note that the parameter space will generally be high-dimensional (for example 10 dimensions in case of 4 continuous variables, plus the $\mathcal{S}$-procedure variables $\mu_m^i$), so the parameter space for an actual system can not be represented visually in a meaningful way. Each linear matrix inequality constraint bounds the set of feasible Lyapunov functions with a convex (that is, "curving inward", see Fig. 15(a)) constraint, resulting in a convex solution set. Each point in this solution set corresponds to one admissible Lyapunov function for the system, and identifying one is a *convex feasibility problem*, which can be solved with standard nonlinear optimization software [7]. Additionally, it is possible to identify an optimal feasible point, with respect to a convex constraint. This is for instance used to maximize the volume of the ellipsoid or the value of $k$ in Section 4. One can also use this to obtain an estimate on the convergence rate of an asymptotically stable system [42]. As opposed to linear optimization, the optimum will not generally lie on the edge of the feasible set – therefore interior point algorithms [40] are used. Here the convexity of the solution set can be exploited.

### 6.3   Stability of the Drive Train with Continuous-Time Controller

For the drive train with continuous controller, as described above, the solver CSDP [7] gives the following solution

$$P = \begin{bmatrix} 0.0021 & 0.0021 \\ 0.0021 & 8.4511 \end{bmatrix}$$

leading to a Lyapunov function

$$V(v - v_0, s) = 0.0021 * s^2 + 0.0042 * (v - v_0) * s + 8.4511 * (v - v_0)^2.$$

The contour lines of $V$ are visualized in Fig. 16. These contour lines are only passed "outside-in" by all trajectories, resulting in convergence to the center, which represents $v - v_0 = 0$ and $s = 0$. Therefore, the velocity $v$ will converge to the desired velocity $v_0$ and the integral value $s$ of the PI-controller will converge to 0.

The existence of this Lyapunov function is sufficient to prove global asymptotic stability for the drive train system. Using the YALMIP [33] frontend under Matlab, this computation took around 0.65 seconds. The problem consists of 17 scalar constraints and 6 three-by-three matrix inequality constraints, on a total of 23 scalar variables. Therefore, the convex search space visualized in Fig. 15(b) is 23-dimensional and bounded by $17 + 6 = 23$ constraint surfaces.

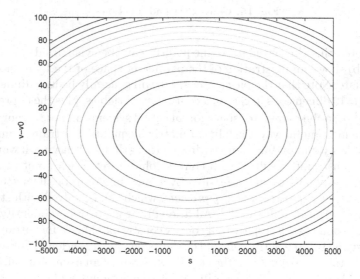

**Fig. 16.** Lyapunov function contour lines

## 6.4   Stability of the Discretized Drive Train

For a time-discretized version of the drive train, stability can be shown in a very similar manner. The discrete-time system is obtained by choosing an appropriate sampling rate. Too slow sampling might destroy stability, while too fast sampling increases the computational cost for proving safety properties (see Section 7). For linear/affine dynamics, the discretized system can then be computed through the matrix exponential $e^{A\tau}$, where $\tau$ is the sampling rate and $A$ the matrix representing the dynamics (i.e., $x^\bullet = Ax$).

For such a discrete-time hybrid system with dynamics given as difference equations, asymptotic stability can be shown using the same methods as for the continuous case [16]. Again a (slightly different) set of LMIs can be obtained and solved through convex optimization. For instance, for a sampling rate of 0.1 seconds, the following Lyapunov function was obtained:

$$V(v - v_0, s) = 0.0105 * s^2 + 0.0172 * (v - v_0) * s + 6.0591 * (v - v_0)^2$$

## 6.5  Stability of the Sampled-Data Drive Train

Stability analysis of discrete-time hybrid systems can also be used to shed light on stability properties of sampled-data systems, that is control loops with continuous plant and discrete controller. In this case sensor measurements are sent to the controller in periodic intervals. The actuators will also periodically receive updates from the controller.

In case of linear plant dynamics, stability analysis can be conducted on a purely discrete-time system which is obtained by also discretizing the plant via zero-order-hold discretization. This procedure is lossless in case of a non-hybrid linear plant because the state of the plant at each sampling instant can be exactly computed from its state at the previous sampling instant and the current controller output. If the plant is hybrid, but with linear dynamics, the dynamics can still be discretized exactly, but the switches are possibly inexact. With the absence of so-called "grazing switches" [15], it is usually possible to approximate the sampled system closely enough.

For the drive train system, we have performed this kind of analysis for a fixed sampling rate (0.1 seconds) and a discrete controller obtained by a textbook discretization method for linear systems (zero-pole matching transformation [17]). The resulting sampled-data system consists of the continuous-time drive train dynamics given in Subsection 2.1 and the discretized controller, and it can still be proven stable by this method.

## 7  Proving Safety of Local Control and Design Models

In this section, we present our approach of model checking safety properties of local control and design models of the example. We first outline our general methods for verification of hybrid systems with non-trivial discrete behaviour (Subsections 7.1 and 7.3); then we build both continuous-time and discrete-time models of the system based on its Matlab-Simulink description and show model checking results of these models (Subsections 7.2 and 7.4).

## 7.1  Model Checking Hybrid Systems with Large Discrete State Spaces

We have proposed an approach for verification of hybrid systems, which contain large discrete state spaces and simple continuous dynamics given as constants [11] (methods dealing with richer dynamics, e.g., given as differential inclusions, are currently under development). Large discrete state space arise naturally in industrial hybrid systems, due to the need to represent discrete inputs, counters, sanity-check bits, possibly multiple concurrent state machines *etc*, which typically jointly with properties of sensor values determine the selection of relevant control laws. Thus this non-trivial discrete behavior cannot be treated by considering discrete states one by one as in tools based on the notion of hybrid automata. We have developed a model checker dealing with ACTL properties for this application class.

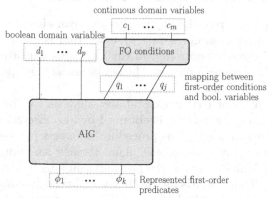

**Fig. 17.** The Lin-AIG structure

*Representation of state-sets.* In our setting, the state-sets of hybrid systems consist of both discrete states, represented by Boolean formulas, and continuous regions, represented by a Boolean combination of linear constraints. We use an extension of And-Inverter-Graphs [39] with linear constraints (Lin-AIGs) as a compact representation format (see Fig. 17). In Lin-AIGs Boolean formulas are represented by Functionally Reduced And-Inverter Graphs (FRAIGs), which are basically Boolean circuits consisting only of AND gates and inverters. In contrast to BDDs, FRAIGs are not a canonical representation for Boolean functions, but they are "semi-canonical" in the sense that every node in the FRAIG represents a unique Boolean function. To be able to use FRAIGs to represent continuous regions, we introduce a set of new (Boolean) *constraint variables* $Q$ as encodings for linear constraints, where each occurring linear constraint is represented by some $q_\ell \in Q$ as illustrated in Fig. 17. Thus we arrive at state-sets encoded by Boolean formulas over Boolean variables and $Q$, together with a mapping of $Q$ into linear constraints.

*Step computation.* Our model checker can handle continuous-time models, which contains both discrete transitions and continuous flows. Discrete transitions are given in the form of *guarded assignments*, while continuous flows are given in the form of *modes*, which define the evolution of continuous variables by constants. For each mode there is a boundary condition, the mode is left as soon as the boundary condition is satisfied.

For checking an *invariance* property, the model checker performs a symbolic backward reachability analysis, to ensure that no state in the complement of the property is reachable from the initial state set. The key achievement lies in the capability of reducing this backward analysis to pure substitution. It can be done easily for discrete transitions as detailed in [12]. The capability of representing as well the effect of continuous flows through substitution rests on our ability to perform pre-image computations for arbitrary Boolean combinations of linear constraints using the Loos-Weispfenning quantifier elimination method [34]. In contrast to other verification methods for hybrid systems, this allows us to handle non-convex polyhedra directly [11]. Note that during each step computation new linear constraints can be introduced, thus the set $Q$ is dynamically updated.

*Example 1 (Discrete transitions).* Assume that we want to check an invariance property $\neg FAIL$, stating that the failure state can never be reached. In the model, one discrete transition can set the Boolean variable $FAIL$ to true:

$$REC \wedge (v \leq 0.0) \wedge (p > EoA) \rightarrow FAIL := true;$$

The transition says that if currently the cooperation protocol is in the $REC$ phase, the train has come to a stop, and the position of the train is beyond the end of authority point (EoA), then the system reports a failure. One backward step computation of such transition leads to the following state-set (after optimizations in Lin-AIGs): $\neg FAIL \wedge \neg(REC \wedge v \leq 0.0 \wedge \neg(p <= EoA))$.

*Example 2 (Continuous flows).* The pre-image of the state-set in the previous example under the mode with continuous evolution $v^{\bullet} = 0.0 \wedge p^{\bullet} = v_d$ and boundary condition $p < EoA - ST$ (start talking) will remain the same.

*Fix-point detection.* We need to perform subsumption checks to detect whether a fixpoint has been reached during model checking. In our approach, since linear constraints enter the state-set descriptions, one has to check implications between two state-set representations. We use HySAT [18] for this purpose.

*Optimizations.* Using efficient methods for keeping the state-set representation as compact as possible is the key point for our approach. This is achieved by integration of different techniques, ranging from purely Boolean methods to (increasingly) exploiting knowledge about linear constraints.

- We use inexpensive methods such as simulation, test-vector generation, detection of implications between linear constraints, and propagation of learned implications to simulation vectors to identify inequivalent Lin-AIG nodes.

- We use HySAT [18] for reducing the size of the Lin-AIG representation by detecting equivalent Lin-AIG nodes, which is applied only to candidates obtained by inexpensive methods.
- We extract "don't cares" from conflicts of calls of HySAT to remove redundant linear constraints in the state set representations. This allows us to restructure Lin-AIGs based on internal node equivalences modulo "don't cares", and to achieve new compact representation as a Boolean combination of a minimal subset of the original set of linear constraints.

We have demonstrated [12,11] that the tuned combination of these deeply integrated methods leading to significant performance improvements.

## 7.2   Continuous-Time Models and Verification Results

The models of the system mainly consists of two parts: (1) a cooperation protocol between the train and the rail-road crossing for collision avoidance, (2) a speed supervision of the train. Compared to its original description in Matlab-Simulink, we have made some simplifications.

*The cooperation protocol.* The protocol distinguishes a number of phases as shown in Fig. 7. Additionally, we add one more transition from the *RECOVERY* phase: If the train stops in front of the crossing, and the position of the train is beyond the end of authority point (EoA), then a *FAILURE* phase is entered. The safety property of collision freedom is equivalent to prove that this *FAILURE* phase of the cooperation protocol can never be entered.

*The speed supervision.* Figure 6 gives an overview of the train speed control. Here, we summarize the modes and the switching conditions between them in our models, as derived from Fig. 6. For each segment of the track, there is a pre-defined desired train speed. The modes for driving the train are decided by the relation of the desired speed $v_d$ and the current speed $v$. In the *NormalMove* mode ($v < v_d \leq 1.05 \cdot v$), the train is driven under a PI controller. Once the condition $1.05 \cdot v_d < v \leq 1.1 \cdot v_d$ holds, the train switches to the mode *MotorOff*, where the drive force for the train becomes zero, and the train decelerates on a constant $-0.05 m/s^2$. From the *MotorOff* mode, the train can re-enter the *NormalMove* mode as soon as $v \leq v_d$. If the difference between $v_d$ and $v$ is large, the mode *EmergencyBraking* (*ServiceBraking*) will be entered if $v \geq 1.5 \cdot v_d$, ($v \geq 1.1 \cdot v_d \wedge v \leq 1.5 \cdot v_d$) from the *NormalMove* mode. In modes *EmergencyBraking* and *ServiceBraking*, the train decelerates on constants $-3.0 m/s^2$ and $-1.0 m/s^2$, respectively. During *ServiceBraking*, the mode *NormalMove* (*MotorOff*) is re-entered if $v \leq v_d$ ($1.05 \cdot v_d < v \leq 1.1 \cdot v_d$). There is one special case when the train enters the *EmergencyBraking* mode. Since the train is desired to stop, it is not possible to re-enter the modes *NormalMove* and *MotorOff*. Constants in the conditions are derived from the Matlab-Simulink model.

*Approximations.* Currently, our model checker only supports models with dynamics given by constants. In the train example, the dynamics $v^\bullet$ in mode *NormalMove* (controlled by a PID controller) relies on the difference between $v_d$ and $v$ (see Fig. 6), and the evolution for the position $p$ is normally defined as $p^\bullet = v$. Therefore, both $v^\bullet$ and $p^\bullet$ are linear if $v$ is a variable. So the train system cannot be described and checked directly by our approach. We need to have an over-approximation of the train's behavior using the method developed in [26]. First, the mode *NormalMove* is split into a set of sub-modes, we define accelerations $v^\bullet$ as constants, depending the relation between $v$ and $v_d$. Second, for each mode defined in the previous section (together with sub-modes for *NormalMove*), we divide the speed into several regions, and use this information to safely over-approximate the evolution of the position $p^\bullet$ by its possible maximal changing rate. Therefore, the number of modes depends on the concrete approximation. The constraints on the speed and the desired speed and the constraints whether the train has reached the positions $EoA - ST$ (start-talking) or $EoA - SB$ (start-braking), are treated as the boundary conditions for each mode. An appropriate mode is selected depending the phase of the cooperation protocol, current velocity $v$ and its relation to $v_d$. For instance, if $v_d \geq 1.5 \cdot v$, $30.0 \leq v \leq 40.0$, and the cooperation protocol is in the *FAR* phase, then the speed controller of the train will choose a mode with $v^\bullet = 2.0$ (a fast acceleration) and $p^\bullet = 40.0$ (the maximal changing rate of $p$). The condition $v_d \geq 1.5 \cdot v$ and $30.0 \leq v \leq 40.0$ will be part of the boundary condition for such mode. The condition whether the crossing is secured is treated as a discrete input. The decisions in the cooperation protocol constitute discrete transitions in the model.

*Experimental results.* The safety property for the models is that the *FAIL* phase can never been entered, i.e., the train comes to a complete stop in front of the crossing if it is not secured. For the continuous-time models, we have successfully proven the given safety invariant for a model with 16 modes in 376 seconds. The final state set representation contained 3906 Lin-AIG nodes with 2358 linear constraints. During model checking, up to 7798 Lin-AIG nodes were used, 36683 HySAT calls occurred and 2582 redundant linear constraints were removed. Experiments are performed on a PC with an AMD Opteron Processor with 2.6 GHz and 16 GB RAM.

## 7.3  Iterative Abstraction Refinement for Step-Discrete Linear Hybrid Systems

Alternatively, an iterative abstraction refinement approach called $\omega$-Cegar [48] is being developed with the focus on open-loop systems, exploiting the characteristics of huge discrete state spaces by ruling out comprehensive classes of spurious counterexamples for subsequent iterations, so that counterexamples with common reasons of invalidity cannot occur again. With the incremental construction of an omega-automaton and its parallel composition with a course abstraction of the model, all runs containing already detected reasons of being invalid are excluded. Since the reasons are fully independent from the discrete behavior, the approach converges fast also for huge discrete state spaces.

The implementation is currently restricted to step-discrete linear hybrid models being represented as a discrete transition graph where the transitions are guarded by linear constraints (*guard expressions*) and extended with linear transformations (*computations*) on the set of continuous variables. This corresponds exactly to the semantics of linear reactive systems being modeled in industrial contexts based on CASE-tools, where executable target code can be generated from. Thanks to an appropriate compiler and the realization of the algorithm on a symbolic representation level, the procedure can be applied to the generated C code of such models even for very large systems.

*Initial abstraction.* To verify a property $\varphi$, the procedure starts by creating an *initial abstraction* $A_0$ of a hybrid automaton $H$ by removing all guard expressions and computations on continuous items, but fully preserving the discrete structure of the model. This entails a translation of $\varphi$ to a new property $\hat{\varphi}$ to hold for some corresponding states in $A_0$.

*Analysis phase.* $A_0$ can be analyzed by any *finite state model checker* being able to generate a *counterexample* $\hat{\pi}$. The counterexample $\hat{\pi}$ consisting of a sequence of discrete states is analyzed by projecting it to the hybrid automaton $H$ to retrieve the corresponding guard expressions and computations (*regulation laws*) that have to be fulfilled or performed in $H$, respectively, for $\hat{\pi}$ to be a valid counterexample. For linear hybrid automata, this analysis consists of solving conjunctions of linear constraints directly derived from the projected regulation laws. The result of this analyzation is either a valid sequence of valuations of continuous state variables or a *generalized conflict* $(\rho_1, \rho_2, \ldots, \rho_k)$ consisting of a minimized sequence of partial regulation laws for which no solution exists in the corresponding conjunctive formula.

Since such conflicts are fully independent of the discrete state sequence they occurred with, there is a high probability that they apply to many other fragments of the discrete transition system as well, especially for huge discrete state spaces combined with only few regulation laws exhibited by the model.

*Construction of $\omega$-automaton.* Thus we follow a strategy of completely ruling out generalized conflicts by constructing an $\omega$-automaton $A_C$ that accepts all runs not containing any known conflict as a subsequence. Considering partial regulation laws as atomic characters and $C$ as the set of all previously detected generalized conflicts, the behavior of $A_C$ can be described by an LTL formula:

$$A_C \models \neg \mathbf{F} \bigvee_{(\rho_1, \rho_2, \ldots, \rho_k) \in C} (\rho_1 \wedge \mathbf{X}(\rho_2 \wedge \mathbf{X}(\ldots \wedge \mathbf{X}\rho_n))) \qquad (21)$$

Instead of using standard algorithms to translate LTL formulae to Büchi-automata, we apply an efficient automaton construction algorithm dedicated to the structure of LTL formulae as presented above, resulting in rather small automata, especially in comparison to general Büchi-automata construction algorithms [50].

*Abstraction refinement.* A parallel composition $A = A_0 \times A_C$ ensures that any (infinite) run not accepted by $A_C$ cannot be exhibited by $A$. With $A_C$ being incrementally extended to not accept conflicts found in subsequent model checking iterations, we get a sequence $A_1, A_2, \ldots, A_n$ of refined abstract transition systems, where the model checker can finally prove that either $A_k \models \hat{\varphi}$ from which can be concluded that $H \models \varphi$ or that a counterexample $\hat{\pi}$ violates $\varphi$ with $\hat{\pi}$ having a valid projection to a path $\pi$ in $H$ as computed in the analysis phase.

*Remarks.* The finite state model checker used to verify the abstract system in each iteration can be freely exchanged even in between iterations. Thus, advantages of different technologies can be combined by

1. starting with (faster) bounded model checking (BMC) while counterexamples within the given bound can be generated and
2. switching to unbounded model checking (e.g., CTL model checker) if no counterexamples within a given bound $k$ are found anymore.

This way computation times of iteration cycles can be kept short while being able to prove if a property $\varphi$ holds for a model (*certification*). However, since the approach is a semi-decision one, affirmation of properties might fail even by using unbounded model checkers.

The restriction to step-discrete linear hybrid models is due to the implementation only and does not follow from the approach. Currently, only safety properties can be verified. An extension to CTL-formulae is possible with the limitation, that valid infinite counterexamples cannot be confirmed as such.

## 7.4 Discrete-Time Modes and Verification Results

Our abstraction-refinement approach deals with step-discrete linear hybrid systems modelled as discrete transition graphs, in which assignments and transition guards may use linear arithmetical expressions, this subsumes the capability to describe the evolvement of plant variables by linear equations. Hence, the approximations in Subsection 7.2 are not necessary. The discrete-time models of our example can be derived from the Matlab-Simulink model with a given sampling rate $\delta$. The discrete transitions for the cooperation protocol and for mode-switchings in the speed supervision are encoded exactly the same as in the continuous-time models (see Subsection 7.2). In this part, we focus on time-discretization of the plant behavior. Our main assumption is that the acceleration of the train during a discrete time step keeps unchanged. If the train is in the modes of *MotorOff*, *EmergencyBraking* and *ServiceBraking*, the velocity and position of the train can be simply updated by $v' = v + \delta \cdot a$ and $p' = p + v \cdot \delta + a \cdot \delta^2/2$, where $a$ is the constant deceleration for those modes. If the train is in the *Normal-Move* mode, the formulas for computing acceleration are given in the form of $f$ and $g$ in Fig. 14. Hence, we can calculate the train's new acceleration using $a' = c_1 \cdot (v - v_d) + c_2 \cdot s + c_3 \cdot v_d$ at each discrete time step ($c_1$, $c_2$, $c_3$ are constants in Fig. 14). Updates of the velocity and position can be done in the same way

**Table 1.** It shows: number of continuous dimensions (*inputs+state-based*), number of exhibited regulation laws/generalized partial regulation laws, number of conflicts, iterations, final path length, size of $A_C$ in terms of statebits, and total runtime.

| Proof | dimensions | regulation laws | conflicts | iterations | $\pi$ | $A_C$ | time |
|---|---|---|---|---|---|---|---|
| $\neg(v = 0 \Rightarrow p \leq EoA)$ | 0+10 | 34 | 31 | 15 | $\nexists$ | 3 | 3 min |

as for other modes. Here, $s$ denotes the integration part of the PI controller (see Equation (2)), and it is accumulated at each step by $s' = s + (v_d - \bar{v}) \cdot \delta$, where $\bar{v} = v + a \cdot \delta$ denotes the average velocity during the time interval $\delta$.

Table 1 shows statistical data of the application of the $\omega$-Cegar approach to a central part of the train system presented in Section 2: to prove that the train always stops before the crossing if it is not secured. The property was certified within 3 minutes and only 15 iterations by first using BMC (Prover-CL V5.0.6) for the iterations and switching to an unbounded model checker (VIS Version 2.0) to finally prove the unreachability on the refined model, which consisted of 16 state bits.

# 8   Conclusion and Future Work

Industrial design processes for cooperating traffic agents exploit a layered design structure to separate concerns in addressing cooperation strategies, control design, and design implementation. We have provided a verification methodology covering these design steps, where safety and stability properties resulting from the overall safety objective of collision freedom are traced to design entities at all levels, and have provided layer specific verification approaches to establish such derived safety and stability requirements at each layer. The feasibility of the approach has been established using a variation of the ETCS level 3 protocol enforcing collision freedom of trains following the moving block principle.

Theoretical approaches to cover multi-layered designs, such as refinement and compositional reasoning, fail to provide semantic bridges across this design space, in particular due to their inability to support the degree of deviations between models tolerated by industrial design processes. Horizontal composition theories provide the semantic foundation for compositional verification, deducing properties of composed systems in terms of their constituents. Vertical composition theories exploit the layered structure of designs, allowing to abstract from design aspects manifest at lower levels when verifying safety properties such as collision freedom for a "higher" level model.[8] Vertical composition theories typically built on refinement relations.

Of particular relevance to our application domain are approaches for refinement and compositional verification of hybrid systems. Compositional verification techniques for hybrid systems have only recently being investigated, e.g.,

---

[8] We assume that the cooperation layer is "higher" than the local control layer, which in turn is "higher" than the design layer.

in [37,38]. Frehse [19] provides an assume-guarantee based approach for hybrid systems which do not share variables. The restriction to event-based communication is reasonable for controller models; however, as soon as closed loop models are considered, plant models will typically share system states; in particular, for collision avoidance protocols, it is exactly the shared physical state space which is subject to the analysis. The extension to shared variables provided in [20] requires unique statically assigned owners of shared variables – only owners are allowed to write on shared variables.

Frehse's approach only addresses refinement of specifications. For hybrid systems with shared variables, the notions of refinements presented do not track continuous evolutions, but only require matching continuous states at end-points of continuous evolutions. Stauner [51,52] studies more general notions of refinement, which in particular aim at bridging the gap between local control and design models. The key concepts of using bounded perturbations to provide room for discretization and inter-sampling errors in the transition to design models are promising. Systematic methods are proposed for constructing a discrete time model refining the relaxed local control model under certain conditions are provided. However, a general notion of refinement, applicable to design models not constructed using Stauner's approach, is not given. Since design models also must cater for additional aspects such as fault-tolerance and diagnosis, a general theory for refinement between design models and local control models is desirable. Additionally, a compositional extension of this framework is needed.

We plan to elaborate our research along multiple dimensions. First, we will extend the model at the cooperation layer emphasizing the dynamic aspect of traffic applications, in which traffic agents enter and leave "interaction areas", and lift the technique of reducing collision freedom to arguments on criticality functions and local control properties to this richer semantic setting. Secondly, while we demonstrated the scalability of our AIG based verification methods to linear hybrid automata with large discrete state spaces (e.g., to a flap controller with $2^{20}$ discrete states [11]), future work will address support for plant dynamics governed by linear differential equations. Thirdly, we plan to research into robust refinement relations and non-standard semantics of hybrid automata to extend compositional refinement techniques to a theory providing semantic bridges across the layered design space of cooperating traffic agents.

# References

1. Alur, R., Grosu, R., Hur, Y., Kumar, V., Lee, I.: Modular specification of hybrid systems in CHARON. In: Lynch, N.A., Krogh, B.H. (eds.) HSCC 2000. LNCS, vol. 1790, pp. 6–19. Springer, Heidelberg (2000)
2. Alur, R., Grosu, R., Lee, I., Sokolsky, O.: Compositional modeling and refinement for hierarchical hybrid systems. Journal of Logic and Algebraic Programming 68(1-2), 105–128 (2006)
3. Balluchi, A., Benvenuti, L., Engell, S., Geyer, T., Johansson, K., Lamnabhi-Lagarrigue, F., Lygeros, J., Morari, M., Papafotiou, G., Sangiovanni-Vincentelli, A., Santucci, F., Stursberg, O.: Hybrid control of networked embedded systems. European Journal on Control, Fundam. Issues in Control 11(4-5), 478–508 (2006)

4. Beckert, B., Giese, M., Hähnle, R., Klebanov, V., Rümmer, P., Schlager, S., Schmitt, P.H.: The KeY System 1.0 (deduction component). In: Pfenning, F. (ed.) CADE 2007. LNCS, vol. 4603, Springer, Heidelberg (2007)

5. Beckert, B., Hähnle, R., Schmitt, P.H. (eds.): Verification of Object-Oriented Software: The KeY Approach. LNCS (LNAI), vol. 4334, Springer, Heidelberg (2007)

6. Bohn, J., Damm, W., Klose, J., Moik, A., Wittke, H.: Modeling and validating train system applications using Statemate and live sequence charts. In: Proc. Conference on Integrated Design and Process Technology. Society for Design and Process Science (2002)

7. Borchers, B.: CSDP, a C library for semidefinite programming. Optimization Methods and Software 10(1), 613–623 (1999)

8. Boyd, S., Ghaoui, L.E., Feron, E., Balakrishnan, V.: Linear Matrix Inequalities in System and Control Theory. In: SIAM (1994)

9. Branicky, M.S.: Multiple Lyapunov functions and other analysis tools for switched and hybrid systems. IEEE Transactions on Automatic Control 43(4) (1998)

10. Cervin, A., Henriksson, D., Lincoln, B., Eker, J., Arzén, K.: How does control timing affect performance? IEEE Control Systems Magazine 23(2), 16–30 (2003)

11. Damm, W., Disch, S., Hungar, H., Jacobs, S., Pang, J., Pigorsch, F., Scholl, C., Waldmann, U., Wirtz, B.: Exact state set representations in the verification of linear hybrid systems with large discrete state space. Technical report, AVACS (2007)

12. Damm, W., Disch, S., Hungar, H., Pang, J., Pigorsch, F., Scholl, C., Waldmann, U., Wirtz, B.: Automatic verification of hybrid systems with large discrete state space. In: Graf, S., Zhang, W. (eds.) ATVA 2006. LNCS, vol. 4218, pp. 276–291. Springer, Heidelberg (2006)

13. Damm, W., Hungar, H., Olderog, E.-R.: Verification of cooperating traffic agents. International Journal of Control 79(5), 395–421 (2006)

14. Damm, W., Pinto, G., Ratschan, S.: Guaranteed termination in the verification of LTL properties of non-linear robust discrete time hybrid systems. International Journal of Foundations of Computer Science 18(1), 63–86 (2007)

15. Donde, V., Hiskens, I.A.: Shooting methods for locating grazing phenomena in hybrid systems. Intern. Journal of Bifurcation and Chaos 16(3), 671–692 (2006)

16. Feng, G.: Stability analysis of piecewise discrete-time linear systems. IEEE Transactions on Automatic Control 47(7), 1108–1112 (2002)

17. Franklin, G.F., Powell, J.D., Workman, M.: Digital Control of Dynamic Systems. Pearson, London (1998)

18. Fränzle, M., Herde, C.: HySAT: An efficient proof engine for bounded model checking of hybrid systems. Formal Methods in System Design 30(3), 179–198 (2007)

19. Frehse, G.: Compositional verification of hybrid systems with discrete interaction using simulation relations. In: Proc. 13th IEEE Conference on Computer Aided Control Systems Design, IEEE Computer Society Press, Los Alamitos (2004)

20. Frehse, G.: Compositional Verification of Hybrid Systems using Simulation Relations. PhD thesis, Radboud Universiteit Nijmegen (2005)

21. Frehse, G.: PHAVer: Algorithmic verification of hybrid systems past HyTech. In: Morari, M., Thiele, L. (eds.) HSCC 2005. LNCS, vol. 3414, pp. 258–273. Springer, Heidelberg (2005)

22. Hager, G.: European ACAS operational evaluation – Final report. Technical Report EEC Report No. 316, Eurocontrol (1997)

23. Harel, D., Kozen, D., Tiuryn, J.: Dynamic Logic. MIT Press, Cambridge (2000)

24. Haxthausen, A.E., Peleska, J.: Formal development and verification of a distributed railway control system. IEEE Transactions on Software Engineering 26(8), 687–701 (2000)

25. Henzinger, T.A.: The theory of hybrid automata. In: Proc. 11th IEEE Symposium on Logic in Computer Science, pp. 278–292. IEEE Computer Society Press, Los Alamitos (1996)

26. Henzinger, T.A., Ho, P.-H., Wong-Toi, H.: Algorithmic analysis of nonlinear hybrid systems. IEEE Transactions on Automatic Control 43(5), 540–554 (1998)

27. Henzinger, T.A., Horowitz, B., Majumdar, R., Wong-Toi, H.: Beyond HyTech: Hybrid systems analysis using interval numerical methods. In: Lynch, N.A., Krogh, B.H. (eds.) HSCC 2000. LNCS, vol. 1790, pp. 130–144. Springer, Heidelberg (2000)

28. Johansson, M., Rantzer, A.: Computation of piecewise quadratic Lyapunov functions for hybrid systems. IEEE Transactions on Automatic Control 43 (1998)

29. Khalil, H.K.: Nonlinear Systems, 2nd edn. Prentice-Hall, Englewood Cliffs (1996)

30. Kratz, F., Sokolsky, O., Pappas, G.J., Lee, I.: R-Charon, a modeling language for reconfigurable hybrid systems. In: Hespanha, J.P., Tiwari, A. (eds.) HSCC 2006. LNCS, vol. 3927, pp. 392–406. Springer, Heidelberg (2006)

31. Leveson, N.G.: Safeware: System Safety and Computers. Addison-Wesley, Reading (1995)

32. Livadas, C., Lygeros, J., Lynch, N.A.: High-level modeling and analysis of TCAS. Proceedings of IEEE – Special Issue on Hybrid Systems: Theory & Applications 88(7), 926–947 (2000)

33. Lofberg, J.: YALMIP: a toolbox for modeling and optimization in Matlab. In: IEEE Intern. Symp. Computer Aided Control Systems Design, pp. 284–289. IEEE Computer Society Press, Los Alamitos (2004)

34. Loos, R., Weispfenning, V.: Applying linear quantifier elimination. The Computer Journal 36(5), 450–462 (1993)

35. Lyapunov, M.A.: Problème général de la stabilité du movement. *Ann. Fac. Sci. Toulouse.* 9, 203–474 (1907) (Translation of a paper published in Comm. Soc. Math. Kharkow, 1893, reprinted Ann. Math. Studies No. 17, Princeton Univ. Press, 1949).

36. Lygeros, J., Godbole, D.N., Sastry, S.S.: Verified hybrid controllers for automated vehicles. IEEE Transactions on Automatic Control 43(4), 522–539 (1998)

37. Lynch, N.A., Segala, R., Vaandrager, F.W.: Hybrid I/O automata revisited. In: Di Benedetto, M.D., Sangiovanni-Vincentelli, A.L. (eds.) HSCC 2001. LNCS, vol. 2034, pp. 403–417. Springer, Heidelberg (2001)

38. Lynch, N.A., Segala, R., Vaandrager, F.W.: Hybrid I/O automata. Information and Computation 185(1), 105–157 (2003)

39. Mishchenko, A., Chatterjee, S., Jiang, R., Brayton, R.K.: FRAIGs: A unifying representation for logic synthesis and verification. Technical report, EECS Dept., UC Berkeley (2005)

40. Nesterov, Y., Nemirovskii, A.: Interior Point Polynomial Algorithms in Convex Programming. In: SIAM (1994)

41. Oehlerking, J., Burchardt, H., Theel, O.: Fully automated stability verification for piecewise affine systems. In: Buttazzo, G., Bemporad, A., Bicchi, A. (eds.) HSCC 2007. LNCS, vol. 4416, pp. 741–745. Springer, Heidelberg (2007)

42. Pettersson, S.: Analysis and Design of Hybrid Systems. PhD thesis, Chalmers University of Technology, Gothenburg (1999)

43. Platzer, A.: Differential dynamic logic for verifying parametric hybrid systems. In: Olivetti, N. (ed.) TABLEAUX 2007. LNCS, vol. 4548, Springer, Heidelberg (2007)

44. Platzer, A.: Differential logic for reasoning about hybrid systems. In: Buttazzo, G., Bemporad, A., Bicchi, A. (eds.) HSCC 2007. LNCS, vol. 4416, pp. 746–749. Springer, Heidelberg (2007)
45. Platzer, A.: A temporal dynamic logic for verifying hybrid system invariants. In: Proc. International Symposium on Logical Foundations of Computer Science. LNCS, vol. 4514, pp. 457–471. Springer, Heidelberg (2007)
46. Platzer, A.: Towards a hybrid dynamic logic for hybrid dynamic systems. In: Blackburn, P., Bolander, T., Braüner, T., de Paiva, V., Villadsen, J. (eds.) Proc. LICS Intern. Workshop on Hybrid Logic. ENTCS (2007)
47. Platzer, A., Clarke, E.M.: The image computation problem in hybrid systems model checking. In: Proc. 10th Workshop on Hybrid Systems: Computation and Control. LNCS, vol. 4416, pp. 473–486. Springer, Heidelberg (2007)
48. Segelken, M.: Abstraction and counterexample-guided construction of omega-automata for model checking of step-discrete linear hybrid models. In: Proc. 19th Conference on Computer Aided Verification. LNCS, Springer, Heidelberg (2007)
49. Silva, B.I., Richeson, K., Krogh, B.H., Chutinan, A.: Modeling and verification of hybrid dynamical system using CheckMate. In: Proc. 4th Conference on Automation of Mixed Processes (2000)
50. Somenzi, F., Bloem, R.: Efficient Büchi Automata from LTL Formulae. In: Emerson, E.A., Sistla, A.P. (eds.) CAV 2000. LNCS, vol. 1855, pp. 248–263. Springer, Heidelberg (2000)
51. Stauner, T.: Systematic Development of Hybrid Systems. PhD thesis, Technische Universität München (2001)
52. Stauner, T.: Discrete-time refinement of hybrid automata. In: Tomlin, C.J., Greenstreet, M.R. (eds.) HSCC 2002. LNCS, vol. 2289, pp. 407–420. Springer, Heidelberg (2002)
53. Tomlin, C., Pappas, G.J., Sastry, S.S.: Conflict resolution for air traffic management: A case study in multi-agent hybrid systems. IEEE Transactions on Automatic Control 43(4), 509–521 (1998)
54. Wende, D.: Fahrdynamik des Schienenverkehrs. Teubner (2003)
55. Yakubovich, V.: S-procedure in nonlinear control theory. Vestnik Leningrad University, pp. 62–71 (1971)
56. Zhou, C., Hansen, M.: Duration Calculus: A Formal Approach to Real-Time Systems. Springer, Heidelberg (2004)
57. Zhou, C., Hoare, C., Ravn, A.P.: A calculus of durations. Information Processing Letters 40(5), 269–276 (1991)

# Appendix

## A Communicating Hybrid Automata

For the sake of completeness, we include from [13] the description of communicating hybrid automata which we use as a model for cooperating traffic agents in this paper. We assume that the signature of the real numbers is given with function and predicate symbols like $0, 1, +, \cdot, <, =$ interpreted on the domain $\mathbb{R}$ in the usual way. (Real-valued) expressions, Boolean expressions, and first-order formulas over this signature are defined as usual. By $Th(\mathbb{R})$ we denote the theory of the real numbers, i.e., the set of all first-order formulas that hold in $\mathbb{R}$.

**Definition 7 (Hybrid Automaton).** *A hybrid automaton is a tuple* $H = (\mathbb{M}, Var, R^d, R^c, m_0, \Theta)$ *where*

1. $\mathbb{M}$ *is a finite set of* modes, *with typical element* $m \in \mathbb{M}$ *and with a distinguished* mode observable $M$ *ranging over* $\mathbb{M}$,
2. *Var is a set of* variables *ranging over the set* $\mathbb{R}$ *of real numbers. Typical elements of Var are* $X, Y$. *Var is partitioned into disjoint sets of* input, local *and* output *variables:* $Var = Var^{in} \cup Var^{loc} \cup Var^{out}$, *where local variables cannot be accessed by other hybrid automata in a parallel composition (see Subsection 8),*
3. $m_0 \in \mathbb{M}$ *is the* initial mode,
4. $\Theta$ *is a mapping that associates with each mode* $m \in \mathbb{M}$ *a* local invariant $\Theta(m)$, *which is a quantifier-free first-order formula over Var,*
5. $R^d$ *is the* discrete transition relation *with elements* $(m, \uparrow \Phi, \mathcal{A}, m')$ *called* transitions, *which are graphically represented as* $m \xrightarrow{\uparrow\Phi/\mathcal{A}} m'$, *where*
   - $m, m' \in \mathbb{M}$,
   - *the* trigger $\uparrow \Phi$ *guarding the transition describes the event that a quantifier-free formula $\Phi$ over Var becomes true,*
   - $\mathcal{A}$ *is a (possibly empty) set of (disjoint) assignments of the form $X := e$ with $X \in Var^{loc} \cup Var^{out}$ and $e$ an expression over Var.*
6. $R^c$ *is the* continuous transition relation, *i.e., a mapping that associates with each mode* $m \in \mathbb{M}$ *and each variable* $X \in Var^{loc} \cup Var^{out}$ *an expression* $R^c(m)(X)$ *over Var, which is taken as the right-hand side of the differential equation $X^\bullet = R^c(m)(X)$ describing the evolution of $X$ over time while $H$ is in mode $m$.*

*Valuations* or *states* of the variables in *Var* are given by functions $\sigma : Var \to \mathbb{R}$. A valuation $\sigma$ assigning to each variable $X$ the value $v_X \in \mathbb{R}$ is denoted by $\sigma = \{X \mapsto v_X \mid X \in Var\}$. For a valuation $\sigma$ and a set of assignments $\mathcal{A}$ let $\mathcal{A}(\sigma) : Var \to \mathbb{R}$ denote the *update* of $\sigma$ according to $\mathcal{A}$ defined by

$$\mathcal{A}(\sigma) = \{X \mapsto \sigma(e) \mid \exists e : X := e \in \mathcal{A}\} \cup \{X \mapsto \sigma(X) \mid \neg \exists e : X := e \in \mathcal{A}\}.$$

For a valuation $\sigma$ and a formula $\Phi$ let $\sigma \models \Phi$ denote that $\sigma$ *satisfies* $\Phi$.

We require of the discrete transition relation that the execution of one transition does not immediately enable a further transition.

**Definition 8 (Transition Separation).** *The discrete transitions in a hybrid automaton H are separated, if for any two transitions* $(m_1, \uparrow \Phi_1, \mathcal{A}_1, m_1')$ *and* $(m_2, \uparrow \Phi_2, \mathcal{A}_2, m_2')$ *in* $R^d$ *of H with* $m_1' = m_2$ *the following condition holds:*

$$\forall \ \sigma : Var \to \mathbb{R} : (\sigma \models \Phi_1 \ \Rightarrow \ \mathcal{A}_1(\sigma) \not\models \Phi_2) \ .$$

Separation implies that at any given point in time during a run, at most one discrete transition fires. Thus our models have dense time but not *superdense* time, where a sequence of discrete transitions is permitted to fire at one instant in time.

Discrete variables may be included into hybrid automata according to our definition via an embedding of their value domain into the reals, and associating a derivative of constantly zero to them (locals and outputs). Timeouts are easily coded via explicit local timer variables with a derivative taken from $\{-1, 0, 1\}$.

Note that this general model subsumes both controller and plant models, by choosing the set of variables appropriately and enforcing certain modeling restrictions. For our plant models, we require the absence of discrete transitions. This entails that plant variables only evolve continuously and cannot be changed by discrete jumps. This is convenient for the formulation of our approach but not essential.

**Definition 9 (Restriction).** *For a hybrid automaton H and a mode* $m \in \mathbb{M}$ *let the restriction* $H \upharpoonright m$ *be defined as H, but with the mode fixed to m. Formally, this is the following hybrid automaton:*

$$H \upharpoonright m = (\{m\}, Var, R^d \upharpoonright m, R^c \upharpoonright m, m, \Theta \upharpoonright m)$$

*where* $R^d \upharpoonright m = \{(m, \uparrow \Phi, \mathcal{A}, m') \in R^d \mid m = m'\}$ *and* $R^c \upharpoonright m$ *and* $\Theta \upharpoonright m$ *are the restrictions of the mappings* $R^c$ *and* $\Theta$ *to the singleton set* $\{m\}$*.*

## A.1 Behaviour

We will in the definition of *runs* of a hybrid automaton interpret all transitions as urgent, i.e., a mode will be left as soon as the triggering event occurs. This can either be the expiration of a time-out or a condition (e.g., on the plant sensors) becoming true. Valid runs also avoid Zeno behavior and time-blocks, i.e., each run provides a valuation for each positive point in time. We did not take provisions to ensure the existence of such a run, nor the property that each initial behavior segment can be extended to a full run. Such might be added via adequate modeling guidelines (e.g., by including the negation of an invariant as trigger condition on some transition leaving the mode). As these properties are not essential to the purpose of this paper we left them out.

We now give the formal definition of runs of a hybrid automaton $H$ capturing the evolution of modes and the real-valued variables over time. To this end, we consider the continuous time domain $Time = \mathbb{R}_{\geq 0}$ of non-negative reals, for the mode observable $M$ a function $\hat{M} : Time \to \mathbb{M}$, and for every variable $X \in Var$ a corresponding function $\hat{X} : Time \to \mathbb{R}$ describing for each time point $t \in Time$

the current mode $\hat{M}(t) \in \mathbb{M}$ and the current value $\hat{X}(t) \in \mathbb{R}$, respectively. Further on, for $\hat{X}$ and $0 < t \in Time$ we define the *previous value* of $\hat{X}$ at $t$ by $prev(\hat{X}, t) = \lim_{u \to t}(\hat{X}(u))$. Satisfaction of a condition containing *prev* entails that the respective limes does exist.[9]

**Definition 10 (Runs of a Hybrid Automaton).** *A run of a hybrid automaton $H = ( \mathbb{M}, Var, R^d, R^c, m_0, \Theta)$ is a tuple of trajectories*

$$\pi = \left( \hat{M}, (\hat{X})_{X \in Var} \right),$$

*with $\hat{M} : Time \to \mathbb{M}$ and $\hat{X} : Time \to \mathbb{R}$ for $X \in Var$, iff*

$$\exists (\tau_i)_{i \in \mathbb{N}} \in Time^{\mathbb{N}} : \tau_0 = 0 \ \wedge \ \forall \ i \in \mathbb{N} : \tau_i < \tau_{i+1},$$

*a strictly increasing sequence of discrete switching times, satisfying the following conditions:*

1. non-Zeno: $\quad \forall \ t \in Time \ \exists \ i \in \mathbb{N} : t \leq \tau_i$
2. mode switching times: $\quad \forall \ i \in \mathbb{N} \ \forall \ t \in [\tau_i, \tau_{i+1}) : \hat{M}(t) = \hat{M}(\tau_i)$
3. continuous evolution:

$$\forall i \in \mathbb{N} \ \forall t' \in [\tau_i, \tau_{i+1}) \ \forall X \in Var^{loc} \cup Var^{out} : \sigma \models X^\bullet = R^c(\hat{M}(\tau_i))(X)$$

*where $\sigma$ is the valuation $\sigma = \{X^\bullet \mapsto \frac{d\hat{X}(t)}{dt}(t')\} \cup \{Y \mapsto \hat{Y}(t') \mid Y \in Var\}$.*
*Thus in $\sigma$ the variable $X^\bullet$ gets the value of the derivative of the function $\hat{X}$ at $t'$ and all other variables $Y \in Var$ get the value of the function $\hat{Y}$ at $t'$.*
4. invariants: $\quad \forall \ t \in Time : \{X \mapsto \hat{X}(t) \mid X \in Var\} \models \Theta(\hat{M}(t))$
5. urgency:

$$\forall i \in \mathbb{N} \ \forall t \in [\tau_i, \tau_{i+1}) \ \forall (m, \uparrow\Phi, \mathcal{A}, m') \in R^d \text{ we have that}$$
$$\hat{M}(t) = m \Rightarrow \{X \mapsto \hat{X}(t) \mid X \in Var\} \not\models \Phi$$

6. discrete transition firing: $\quad \forall \ i \in \mathbb{N}$ *we have that*

$$(\hat{M}(\tau_{i+1}) = \hat{M}(\tau_i) \ \wedge \ \forall \ X \in Var^{loc} \cup Var^{out} : \hat{X}(\tau_{i+1}) = prev(\hat{X}, \tau_{i+1}))$$
$$\vee$$
$$(\exists \ (m, \uparrow\Phi, \mathcal{A}, m') \in R^d : \hat{M}(\tau_i) = m \ \wedge \ \hat{M}(\tau_{i+1}) = m' \ \wedge$$
$$\exists \ \sigma \in Var \to \mathbb{R} : \forall \ X \in Var^{loc} \cup Var^{out} :$$
$$\sigma(X) = prev(\hat{X}, \tau_{i+1}) \ \wedge \ \sigma \models \Phi$$
$$\wedge \ \forall \ X \in Var^{in} : \hat{X}(\tau_{i+1}) = \sigma(X)$$
$$\wedge \ \forall \ X \in Var^{loc} \cup Var^{out} : \hat{X}(\tau_{i+1}) = \mathcal{A}(\sigma)(X))$$

---

[9] In fact, our definition of a run implies that these limits do exist for all local and output variables in any run.

For a run $\pi = \left( \hat{M}, \, (\hat{X})_{X \in Var} \right)$ of $H$ and $t \in Time$ let $\pi(t)$ denote the state

$$\pi(t) = \{M \mapsto \hat{M}(t)\} \cup \{X \mapsto \hat{X}(t) \mid X \in Var\}.$$

assigning to the mode observable $M$ and the all variables $X \in Var$ the values in the run $\pi$ at time $t$.

The time sequence $(\tau_i)_{i \in \mathbb{N}}$ identifies the points in time, at which mode-switches may occur, which is expressed in Clause (2). Only at those points discrete transitions (having a noticeable effect on the state) may be taken. On the other hand, it is not required that any transition fires at some point $\tau_i$, which permits to cover behaviors with a finite number of discrete switches within the framework above. Our simple plant models with only one mode provide examples. As usual, we exclude zeno behavior (in Clause (1)). As a consequence of the requirement of transition separation, after each discrete transition some time must elapse before the next one can fire. Clause (3) forces all local and output variables (whose dynamics is constrained by the set of differential equations associated with this mode) to actually obey their respective equation. Clause (4) requires, for each mode, the valuation of continuous variables to meet the local invariant while staying in this mode. Clause (5) forces a discrete transition to fire when its trigger condition becomes true. The effect of a discrete transition is described by Clause (6). Whenever a discrete transition is taken, local and output variables may be assigned new values, obtained by evaluating the right-hand side of the respective assignment using the previous value of locals and outputs and the current values of the input. If there is no such assignment, the variable maintains its previous value, which is determined by taking the limit of the trajectory of the variable as $t$ converges to the switching time $\tau_{i+1}$. Values of inputs may change arbitrarily. They are not restricted by the clauses, other that they obey mode invariants and contribute to the satisfaction of discrete transitions when those fire.

## A.2 Parallel Composition

The parallel composition of two such hybrid automata $H_1$ and $H_2$ presupposes the typical disjointness criteria for modes, local variables, and output variables. Output variables of $H_1$ which are at the same time input variables of $H_2$, and vice versa, establish communication channels with instantaneous communication. Those variables establishing communication channels become local variables of $H_1 \parallel H_2$ (in addition to the local variables of $H_1$ and $H_2$), for other variable sets we simply take the union of those not involved in communication. Modes of $H_1 \parallel H_2$ are the pairs of modes of the component automata. One may define the set of runs of $H$ as those tuples of trajectories which project to runs of $H_1$ and $H_2$, respectively. It is not always possible to give a hybrid automaton for $H_1 \parallel H_2$, because of problems with cycles of instantaneous communications. Therefore, we impose the following additional condition on the composability of hybrid automata.

**Definition 11 (Composable Hybrid Automata).** *Let two hybrid automata* $H_i$, $i = 1, 2$, *with discrete transition relations* $R_i^d$, $i = 1, 2$, *be given. For a pair of transitions* $s_i = (m_i, \uparrow \Phi_i, \mathcal{A}_i, m_i') \in R_i^d$, $i = 1, 2$, *the transition* $s_1$ *is unaffected by* $s_2$, *if each variable for which there is an assignment in* $\mathcal{A}_2$ *appears neither in* $\Phi_1$ *nor in* $\mathcal{A}_1$ *(on any of the right-hand sides).*

*The two transition relations are* composable, *if for each pair of transitions* $s_i \in R_i^d$, $i = 1, 2$, *either* $s_1$ *is unaffected by* $s_2$ *or vice versa.*

Composability establishes essentially a direction on instantaneous communications – communications may have an immediate effect on the output and thus the partner automaton, but they must not immediately influence the originator of the information. Assuming composability, the rest of the construction of the parallel composition automaton is rather standard.

For a mode $(m_1, m_2)$, the associated invariant condition is the conjunction of the invariance conditions associated with $m_1$ and $m_2$. Similarly, the set of differential equations governing the continuous evolution while in mode $(m_1, m_2)$ is obtained by simply conjoining the set of differential equations attached to $m_1$ and $m_2$, respectively – note that the disjointness conditions on variables assure, that this yields a consistent set of differential equations. Finally, the discrete transition relation consists of the following transitions:

1. $((m_1, m_2), \Phi_1 \wedge \mathcal{A}_1(\Phi_2), \mathcal{A}_1 \cup \mathcal{A}_1(\mathcal{A}_2), (m_1', m_2'))$
   for each pair of transitions $s_i = (m_i, \uparrow \Phi_i, \mathcal{A}_i, m_i') \in R_i^d$, $i = 1, 2$ where $s_1$ is unaffected by $s_2$,
2. $((m_1, m_2), \Phi_1 \wedge \{\neg \mathcal{A}_1(\Phi_2) \mid \Phi_2$ trigger in $R_2^d\}, \mathcal{A}_1, (m_1', m_2))$
   for each $(m_1, \uparrow \Phi_1, \mathcal{A}_1, m_1') \in R_1^d$, and
3. transitions of the forms (1) and (2) with the role of $H_1$ and $H_2$ interchanged,

where $\mathcal{A}(\Phi)$ denotes the substitution into $\Phi$ of $e$ for $v$ for each assignment $X := e \in \mathcal{A}$, and $\mathcal{A}_1(\mathcal{A}_2)$ denotes the substitution of the assignments of $\mathcal{A}_1$ into the right-hand terms of $\mathcal{A}_2$.

Composability ensures that the simultaneous transitions of Clause (1) indeed capture the combined effect of both transitions. The separation of transitions in the resulting automaton is inherited from separation in the component automata by the way single-automata transitions (Clause (2)) are embedded.

# Specifying Various Time Models with Temporal Propositional Variables in Duration Calculus

Dang Van Hung

The United Nations University
International Institute for Software Technology
P.O. Box 3058, Macau
dvh@iist.unu.edu

**Abstract.** Many extensions of Duration Calculus (DC) have been proposed for handling different aspects of real-time systems. For each extension several different semantics are defined for different time structures which are suitable for different applications and achieve low complexity for the decidability of some properties. Hence, different proof systems have to be developed for reasoning in different calculi. We demonstrate that with temporal propositional letters, many useful time structures and operators can be completely described in the original DC with continuous time. Hence, we can use the proof system for original DC and the specification of the specific time structure to reason in that time structure without the need of introducing a new calculus.

## 1 Introduction

Since it was introduced in 1992 by Zhou, Hoare and Ravn [3], Duration Calculus (DC) has attracted a great deal of attentions. Details on DC are presented in Zhou and Hansen's monograph [2]. Many extensions of Duration Calculus have been proposed for handling different aspects of real-time systems [15,5]. For each extension several different semantics are defined for different time structures which are suitable for different applications and have low complexity for the decidability of some properties [13,9]. Among the different time structures, the abstract time domain makes the calculus complete when it is abstracted away from dedicated properties of real numbers or natural numbers [6], and the discrete time domain makes the calculus decidable, able to carry out model checking, and suitable for the specification of digital systems [14,13,8]. When proposing a new time domain, one has to give semantics and develop a proof system for the calculus within the given semantics. This sometimes makes the calculus inconvenient to use. We found that in most cases, the proof system for the calculus on special domains is the original one with some small modification. Therefore, it would be convenient if we can use the original calculus without any modification for different applications which can still capture special aspects of the application domains. From our earlier works on specification and reasoning about real-time systems with Duration Calculus [10,11], we found that it is very convenient to use temporal propositional letters with specific meaning to specify

C.B. Jones, Z. Liu, J. Woodcock (Eds.): Bjørner/Zhou Festschrift, LNCS 4700, pp. 170–187, 2007.

the properties of time intervals. In this paper, we demonstrate that we can use this technique to model different time structures and time models. Then, reasoning in these time structures can be carried out using the original proof system of DC and the specification of the structures in DC with continuous semantics. We show that our technique works well for some case studies.

The paper is organised as follows. In the next section, we give a summary of Duration Calculus. Our main technique for modelling time structures is described in Section 3. Sections 4 demonstrates how our technique can be used for describing data sampling and projection. In Section 5, we show how the technique is used in modeling and reasoning in the development of real-time systems via the well-known case study "Biphase Mark Protocol".

## 2   Summary of Duration Calculus

We give a brief summary of Duration Calculus in this section. Readers are referred to [2] for more details on DC. The version of Duration Calculus we present here has several additional operators that are useful for the specification purposes.

Time in DC is the set $\mathbb{R}^+$ of the non-negative real numbers. For $t, t' \in \mathbb{R}^+ (t \leq t')$, $[t, t']$ denotes the time interval from $t$ to $t'$. Let $intv$ denote the set of all time intervals.

### 2.1   Syntax of Duration Calculus

Assume that $V = \{P, Q, \ldots\}$ is a countable set of state variables, and $T = \{X, R, \ldots\}$ is a set of temporal propositional letters. Let $f^n$ and $A^n$ ($n \geq 0$) denote $n$-ary function and $n$-ary predicate names respectively. The syntax classes *state expressions*, *terms*, and *formulas* will be then defined as follows.

**State expressions:** The set of state expressions is generated by the grammar

$$S \ \hat{=} \ 0 \mid 1 \mid P \mid \neg S \mid S \wedge S,$$

where $P$ stands for state names in the set $V$.

**Terms:** The set of terms is generated by

$$r \ \hat{=} \ \int S \mid \ell \mid f^n(r, \ldots, r),$$

where $S$ stands for state expressions.

**Formulas:** the set of formulas is generated by the grammar:

$$D \ \hat{=} \ A^n(r, \ldots, r) \mid X \mid D^\frown D \mid \neg D \mid D \vee D \mid$$
$$D^* \mid \lceil P \rceil^0 \mid \mid \lceil P \rceil \mid \lceil \lceil P \rceil$$

where $A$ stands for atomic formulas, and $X$ for temporal propositional letters.

## 2.2  Semantics of Duration Calculus

Assume that each $n$-ary function name $f^n$ is associated with a total function from $\mathbb{R}^n$ to $\mathbb{R}$ which is denoted by $f^n$ also, and each $n$-ary predicate name $A^n$ is associated with a total function from $\mathbb{R}^n$ to $\{tt, ff\}$ which is also denoted by $A^n$. In this paper, for simplicity we interpret the functions $f$ as operators on reals, e.g. $+, *$, and the relations $A$ as comparative operators between reals, e.g. $<, \leq, =, >, \geq$.

An interpretation $\mathcal{I}$ is a function $\mathcal{I} \in (V \to (\mathbb{R}^+ \to \{0,1\})) \cup (T \to (intv \to \{0,1\}))$, for which each $\mathcal{I}(P)$, $P \in V$ has at most finitely many discontinuity points in any interval $[a, b]$. We shall use the abbreviation $P_{\mathcal{I}} \;\widehat{=}\; \mathcal{I}(P)$ for $P \in V$ and $X_{\mathcal{I}} \;\widehat{=}\; \mathcal{I}(X)$ for $X \in T$. The semantics of state expression, terms, and formulas in an interpretation $\mathcal{I}$ are then defined as follows.

**Semantics of state expressions:** The semantics of a state expression $P$ in an interpretation $\mathcal{I}$ is a function $\mathcal{I}_P \in Time \to \{0,1\}$ defined inductively on the structure of state expressions by:

$$
\begin{aligned}
\mathcal{I}_0(t) &\;\widehat{=}\; 0, \\
\mathcal{I}_1(t) &\;\widehat{=}\; 1, \\
\mathcal{I}_P(t) &\;\widehat{=}\; P_{\mathcal{I}}(t), \\
\mathcal{I}_{(\neg S)}(t) &\;\widehat{=}\; 1 - \mathcal{I}_S(t), \text{ and} \\
\mathcal{I}_{(S \vee Q)}(t) &\;\widehat{=}\; \begin{cases} 0 \text{ if } \mathcal{I}_S(t) = 0 \text{ and } \mathcal{I}_Q(t) = 0, \\ 1 \text{ otherwise.} \end{cases}
\end{aligned}
$$

**Semantics of terms:** The semantics of a term $r$ in an interpretation $\mathcal{I}$ is a function $\mathcal{I}_r \in intv \to \mathbb{R}$ defined inductively on the structure of terms by:

$$
\begin{aligned}
\mathcal{I}_{\int P}([a,b]) &\;\widehat{=}\; \int_a^b \mathcal{I}_P(t)dt, \\
\mathcal{I}_\ell([a,b]) &\;\widehat{=}\; b - a, \text{ and} \\
\mathcal{I}_{f^n(r_1,\ldots,r_n)}([a,b]) &\;\widehat{=}\; f^n(\mathcal{I}_{r_1}([a,b]), \ldots, \mathcal{I}_{r_n}([a,b])).
\end{aligned}
$$

**Semantics of formulas:** The semantics of a formula $D$ in an interpretation $\mathcal{I}$ is a function $\mathcal{I}_D \in intv \to \{tt, ff\}$ defined inductively on the structure of formulas as follows. Using the following abbreviations:

$$
\begin{aligned}
\mathcal{I}, [a,b] &\models D \;\widehat{=}\; \mathcal{I}_D([a,b]) = tt \text{ and} \\
\mathcal{I}, [a,b] &\not\models D \;\widehat{=}\; \mathcal{I}_D([a,b]) = ff,
\end{aligned}
$$

$\mathcal{I}_D$ is defined by:

$\mathcal{I}, [a,b] \models A^n(r_1, \ldots, r_n)$ iff $A^n(\mathcal{I}_{r_1}([a,b]), \ldots, \mathcal{I}_{r_n}([a,b])) = tt$,

$\mathcal{I}, [a,b] \models X$           iff $X_{\mathcal{I}} = 1$,

$\mathcal{I}, [a,b] \models (\neg D)$     iff $\mathcal{I}, [a,b] \not\models D$

$\mathcal{I}, [a,b] \models (D_1 \vee D_2)$    iff $\mathcal{I}, [a,b] \models D_1$ or $\mathcal{I}, [a,b] \models D_2$

$\mathcal{I}, [a,b] \models (D_1 {}^\frown D_2)$    iff $\mathcal{I}, [a,m] \models D_1$ and $\mathcal{I}, [m,b] \models D_2$ for some $m \in [a,b]$

$\mathcal{I}, [a,b] \models D^*$         iff either $a = b$ or $\mathcal{I}, [m_i, m_{i+1}] \models D$ for some $n \in \mathcal{N}$ and
                         $a = m_0 < m_1 < \ldots < m_n = b$

$\mathcal{I}, [a,b] \models \lceil P \rceil^0$      iff $a = b$ and $P_{\mathcal{I}}(a) = 1$

$\mathcal{I}, [a,b] \models \lceil P \rceil$       iff $a < b$ and $P_{\mathcal{I}}(t) = 1$ for all $a < t < b$

$\mathcal{I}, [a,b] \models \lceil \lceil P \rceil$      iff $a < b$ and $P_{\mathcal{I}}(t) = 1$ for all $a \leq t < b$

A relatively complete proof system for Duration Calculus with no operator $^*$ and $^0$ has been given in [2], and the complete proof system for Duration Calculus with Iteration on the abstract time domain is given in [6].

# 3   Specifying Substructure of Time with Temporal Propositional Letters

In this section we consider how Duration Calculus can specify some classes of time models with temporal propositional letters. We show that different classes of Duration Calculus time models can be expressed by sub-languages of Duration Calculus. Hence, there is no need to have different definitions of Duration Calculus for different classes of time models. Using the original DC with the sub-language of DC for a class of models as the assumption we can reason about the validity in the model class.

## 3.1   Discrete Duration Calculus Models

Discrete models of Duration Calculus use the set of natural numbers $\mathbb{N}$, which is a subset of $\mathbb{R}^+$, for time (we assume that $0 \in \mathbb{N}$). We can embed the discrete time models into continuous time models by considering a state variable in discrete DC models as a state in continuous models that can change its value only at the integer points. For that purpose, we introduce several fresh temporal propositional letters and state variables with specific meaning. Let $int$ be a temporal propositional letter with the meaning that $int$ is interpreted as 1 for an interval if and only if the interval is from an integer to an integer, i.e. for any interpretation $\mathcal{I}$, $int_{\mathcal{I}}([a, b]) = 1$ iff $a, b \in \mathbb{N}$. Let $C$ be a state variable that changes its value at each natural number which represents a tick of the real-time clock, i.e. $C_{\mathcal{I}}(t) = 1$ iff $\lfloor t \rfloor$ is odd. The axioms to characterise the properties of the temporal propositional letter $int$ can be given as follows. First, the integer intervals have integral endpoints, and remain integer intervals when extended by 1 time unit:

$$int \Rightarrow ((int \wedge \ell = 0)^\frown(int \wedge \ell = 1)^*) \wedge$$
$$((int \wedge \ell = 1)^{*\frown}(int \wedge \ell = 0)) \tag{1}$$
$$int^\frown(\ell = 1) \Rightarrow int \tag{2}$$

Second, $int \wedge \ell = 1$ should be a unique partition of the greatest integral subinterval of any interval with length 2 or more, i.e.

$$\ell \geq 2 \Rightarrow \ell < 1^\frown((int \wedge \ell = 1)^* \wedge \tag{3}$$
$$\neg(true^\frown(int \wedge \ell = 1)^\frown\neg(int \wedge \ell = 1)^*) \wedge$$
$$\neg(\neg(int \wedge \ell = 1)^{*\frown}(int \wedge \ell = 1)^\frown true))^\frown$$
$$\ell < 1$$

Similarly to Lemma 3.2 in [4] we can show that the axiom 3 is equivalent to the fact that any interval $[b, e]$ that have the length 2 or longer has the unique set of time points $b \leq \tau_0 < \tau_1 < \ldots < \tau_m \leq e$ such that $\mathcal{I}, [\tau_i, \tau_{i+1}] \models int \wedge \ell = 1$, $\tau_0 - b < 1$ and $e - \tau_m < 1$, and $[\tau_i, \tau_{i+1}]$ are the only subintervals of $[b, e]$ that that satisfy $(int \wedge \ell = 1)$.

Let $\mathcal{ID}$ denote the set of these three axioms 1, 2 and 3. $\mathcal{ID}$ specifies all the properties of integer intervals except that their endpoints are integer.

## Proposition 1

1. *Let $\mathcal{I}$ be an interpretation satisfying that $int_{\mathcal{I}}([b, e]) = true$ iff $[b, e]$ is an integer interval. Then $\mathcal{I}, [b, e] \models D$ for any integer interval $[b.e]$, and for any formula $D \in \mathcal{ID}$.*
2. *Let $\mathcal{I}$ be an interpretation satisfying that $\mathcal{I}, [b, e] \models D$ for any interval $[b.e]$, and for any formula $D \in \mathcal{ID}$. Then, $int_{\mathcal{I}}([0, 0]) = true$ implies that for $int_{\mathcal{I}}([b, e]) = true$ iff $[b, e]$ is an integer interval.*

*Proof.* The item 1 is obvious, and we only give a proof of Item 2 here. Let us consider an interval $[0, n]$ with $n > 100$. From the fact that $\mathcal{I}, [0, n] \models D$ where $D$ is the formula 3, we have that there are points $0 \leq \tau_0 < \tau_1 < \ldots < \tau_m \leq e$ such that $\mathcal{I}, [\tau_i, \tau_{i+i}] \models int \wedge \ell = 1$, $\tau_0 < 1$ and $n - \tau_m < 1$, and

$$\mathcal{I}, [\tau_0, \tau_m] \models (\neg(true^\frown(int \wedge \ell = 1)^\frown \neg(int \wedge \ell = 1)^*) \wedge$$
$$\neg(\neg(int \wedge \ell = 1)^* {}^\frown(int \wedge \ell = 1)^\frown true))$$

If $\tau_0 > 0$, from the axiom 2, it follows that $\mathcal{I}, [0, k] \models int$ for all $k \in \mathbb{N}$ and $k \leq n$ and $k < \tau_k < k + 1$. Applying the axiom 1 for the interval $[0, k]$ implies that $\mathcal{I}, [k, k + 1] \models int \wedge \ell = 1$. Consequently, $\mathcal{I}, [m - 1, \tau_m] \models \neg(int \wedge \ell = 1)^*$ and $\mathcal{I}, [m - 2, m_1] \models (int \wedge \ell = 1)$. This is a contradiction to $\mathcal{I}, [\tau_0, \tau_m] \models \neg(true^\frown(int \wedge \ell = 1)^\frown \neg(int \wedge \ell = 1)^*)$. □

Note that Item 2 of Proposition 1 can be generalised as

Let $\mathcal{I}$ be an interpretation satisfying that $\mathcal{I}, [b, e] \models D$ for any interval $[b.e]$, and for any formula $D \in \mathcal{ID}$. Let $h \in \mathcal{R}^+$, $h < 1$. Then, $int_{\mathcal{I}}([h, h]) = true$ implies that for $int_{\mathcal{I}}([b, e]) = true$ iff $[b, e]$ is of the form $[h + n, h + m]$, $m, n \in \mathbb{N}$ and $n \leq m$.

So, $\mathcal{ID}$ is a set of formulas specifying the set of intervals of a discrete time obtained by shifting $\mathbb{N}$ by $h$ time units ($h < 1$).

The state variable $C$ can also express if an interval is an integer interval. Namely, we have

$$(\lceil C \rceil \vee \lceil \neg C \rceil) \wedge \ell = 1 \Rightarrow int$$
$$int \wedge \ell = 1 \Rightarrow (\lceil C \rceil \vee \lceil \neg C \rceil)$$
$$\lceil C \rceil^\frown \lceil \neg C \rceil \Rightarrow true^\frown int^\frown true$$
$$\lceil \neg C \rceil^\frown \lceil C \rceil \Rightarrow true^\frown int^\frown true$$
$$(int \wedge \ell = 1)^\frown(int \wedge \ell = 1) \Rightarrow$$
$$((\lceil C \rceil \wedge \ell = 1)^\frown(\lceil \neg C \rceil \wedge \ell = 1)) \vee$$
$$((\lceil \neg C \rceil \wedge \ell = 1)^\frown(\lceil C \rceil \wedge \ell = 1))$$

Let $\mathcal{CC}$ denote the set of these formulas. $\mathcal{CC}$ specifies all the properties of the special clock state variable $C$. Any interval satisfying $int \wedge \ell > 0$ can be expressed precisely via a DC formula with state variable $C$ (without $int$). Perhaps $int \wedge \ell = 0$ is the only formula that cannot be expressed by a formula via state variable $C$ without $int$. $CC$ can also be used as a means to define the variable $C$ via $int$ and vice-versa. If we use $CC$ to define $int$, the axioms for $C$ simply are:

$$\lceil C \rceil \vee \lceil \neg C \rceil \Rightarrow \ell \leq 1 \tag{4}$$
$$((\lceil C \rceil \frown \lceil \neg C \rceil \frown \lceil C \rceil) \vee (\lceil \neg C \rceil \frown \lceil C \rceil \frown \lceil \neg C \rceil)) \Rightarrow \ell \geq 1 \tag{5}$$

The relationship between these axioms and the axioms for $int$ presented earlier is formulated as:

**Proposition 2.** *Let interpretation $\mathcal{I}$ be such that the formulas in $CC$ and axioms (1) and (2) are satisfied by all intervals.*

1. *If the axioms (4) and (5) are satisfied by all intervals, the axiom (3) is satisfied by all intervals.*
2. *If the axiom (3) is satisfied by all intervals then the axioms (4) and (5) are satisfied by all intervals, too.*

*Proof.*
*Proof of Item 1.* The axioms (4) and (5) implies that the formula

$$(\lceil \neg P \rceil \frown \lceil P \rceil \frown \lceil \neg P \rceil)) \Rightarrow (\lceil \neg P \rceil \frown (\lceil P \rceil \wedge \ell = 1) \frown \lceil \neg P \rceil))$$

is satisfied for any interval when $P$ is either $C$ or $\neg C$. For any interval $[b, e]$, if $e - b \geq 2$ then there are $b = \tau_0 < \ldots < \tau_n = e$ such that $[\tau_i, \tau_{i+1}]$ satisfies $\lceil C \rceil \vee \lceil \neg C \rceil$, and $\tau_i$, $0 < i < n$ are the points the state $C$ changes its value. Therefore, from (3), (4) and $CC$ the formula $int \wedge \ell = 1$ is satisfied by $[\tau_i, \tau_{i+1}]$ when $0 < i < n - 1$, and $\tau_1 - \tau_0 < 1$ and $\tau_n - \tau_{n-1} < 1$. Furthermore, from $int \wedge \ell = 1 \Rightarrow (\lceil C \rceil \vee \lceil \neg C \rceil)$ it follows that $[\tau_i, \tau_{i+1}]$, $0 < i < n - 1$ are the only intervals satisfying $int \wedge \ell = 1$. Hence, (3) is satisfied by $[b, e]$.

*Proof of Item 2.* Let $h > 0$ be the first time point that state $C$ changes its value. From the axioms (1), (2) and (3) it follows that $h \leq 1$ and $int \wedge \ell = 1$ is satisfied by and only by the intervals of the form $[n + h, n + 1 + h]$, $n \in \mathbb{N}$. Hence, if $CC$ is satisfied by all intervals, the axioms (4) and (5) are also satisfied by all intervals.     $\square$

So, with the assumption that 0 is an integer point, the axioms (4) and (5) are equivalent to the axiom (3).

Let $step$ be a temporal propositional letter that represents two consecutive state changes of the system under consideration. When there are several state changes at a time point $t$, $step$ evaluates to 1 over interval $[t, t]$. When two consecutive state changes are at $t$ and $t'$ such that $t \neq t'$, $step$ is true for the interval $[t, t']$, and for any state variable $P$, either $\lceil P \rceil$ or $\lceil \neg P \rceil$ holds for the interval $[t, t']$. This is represented by:

$$step \wedge \ell > 0 \Rightarrow (\lceil P \rceil \vee \lceil \neg P \rceil) \text{ for any state variable } P$$
$$step \wedge \ell > 0 \Rightarrow \neg((step \wedge \ell > 0) \frown (step \wedge \ell > 0))$$

Let $\mathcal{SC}$ denote this class of formulas.

Now consider two kinds of Duration Calculus semantics which are different from the original one defined earlier for continuous time, and called discrete semantics and discrete step time semantics.

Discrete Duration Calculus semantics are defined in the same way as for continuous time semantics except that all intervals are integer intervals. So, $a$, $b$, $m$ and $m_i$ in the definition should be integers instead of reals, and an interpretation $\mathcal{I}$ should assign to each state variable $P$ a function from $\mathbb{N}$ to $\{0,1\}$, and then expanded to a function from $\mathcal{R}^+$ to $\{0,1\}$ by letting $\mathcal{I}_P(t) = \mathcal{I}_P(\lfloor t \rfloor)$ which is right continuous, and could be discontinuous only at integer time points. Let us use $\models_{DDC}$ to denote the modelling relation in these semantics.

Similarly, discrete step time Duration Calculus semantics are defined by restricting the set of intervals to that of intervals between state change time points. So, $a$, $b$, $m$ and $m_i$ in the definition should be time points where states change, and an interpretation $\mathcal{I}$ should assign to each state variable $P$ a function from $\mathcal{S}$ to $\{0,1\}$, where $\mathcal{S}$ is a countable subset of $\mathcal{R}^+$ intended to be the set of time points for state changes that includes the set $\mathbb{N}$. $\mathcal{I}_P$ is then expanded to a function from $\mathcal{R}^+$ to $\{0,1\}$ by letting $\mathcal{I}_P(t) = \mathcal{I}_P(t_s)$, where $t \in \mathcal{R}^+$ and $t_s = \max\{t' \in \mathcal{S} \mid t' \leq t\}$. Then $\mathcal{I}_P(t)$ is also right continuous, and could be discontinuous only at a point in $\mathcal{S}$. Let us use $\models_{SDC}$ to denote the modelling relation in this semantics.

To express that states are interpreted as right continuous functions, we can use formula called $\mathcal{RC}$

$$\lceil P \rceil \Rightarrow \lceil \lceil P \rceil \text{ for any state variable } P$$

In [14], Paritosh also proposed a semantics using only the intervals of the form $[0,t]$. We can also specify this interval model with a temporal propositional letter $Pre$. $Pre$ is interpreted as true only for the interval of the form $[0,t]$. $Pre$ is specified by the set of formulas $Pref$ defined as

$$Pre^\frown true \Rightarrow Pre$$
$$\neg(\ell > 0^\frown Pre)$$
$$Pre \wedge D \Rightarrow (Pre \wedge \ell = 0)^\frown D$$
$$Pre \wedge (D1^\frown D2) \Rightarrow (Pre \wedge D1)^\frown D2$$

**Proposition 3.** *Let $\mathcal{I}$ be an interpretation that validates the set of formulas $Pref$ and $\mathcal{I}, [0,0] \models Pre$. Then, $\mathcal{I}, \mathcal{V}, [a,b] \models Pre$ iff $a = 0$.*

*Proof.* Straightforward                                                                    $\square$

Then, a formula $D$ is valid in the prefix time interval model if and only if $Pre \Rightarrow D$ is a valid formula in the original model of time interval.

So far, we have introduced special temporal propositional letters $int$, $step$ and $Pre$ together with DC formulas specifying their special features. We are going to show that with these propositional letters we can provide a complete description of many useful time models.

*Integer Time Model* To specify that a state can only change at an integer time point, we can use the formula $\mathcal{IS}$:

$$step \Rightarrow int$$

Let $\mathcal{DL}$ be the union of $\mathcal{SC}$, $\mathcal{IS}$, $\mathcal{ID}$, $\mathcal{RC}$. $\mathcal{DL}$ forms a relative complete specification for the discrete time structure. Let $\varphi$ be a formula which does not have any occurrence of temporal variables $int$ ans $step$. Let $intemb(\varphi)$ be a formula that obtained from $\varphi$ by replacing each proper subformula $\psi$ of $\varphi$ by $\psi \wedge int$. For example $intemb(\phi^\frown\neg\psi) = (\phi \wedge int)^\frown(int \wedge \neg(\psi \wedge int))$.

**Theorem 1.** *Let $\varphi$ be a DC formula with no occurrence of temporal proposition letters. Then, $\mathcal{DL} \vdash int \Rightarrow intemb(\varphi)$ exactly when $\models_{DDC} \varphi$.*

*Proof.* Any discrete time model $\mathcal{I}, [a, b]$ can be extended to a model that satisfies the formulas in $\mathcal{DL}$ in the obvious way, namely with the interpretation for $int$ and $step$ with the intended meanings for them. By induction on the structure of the formula $\varphi$, it is easy to prove that $\mathcal{I}, [a, b] \models_{DDC} \varphi$ if and only $\mathcal{I}, [a, b] \models intemb(\varphi)$.

Then, the "only if" part follows directly from the soundness of the proof of the DC system that $intemb(\varphi)$ is satisfied by any integer model that satisfies $\mathcal{DL}$.

The "if" part is proved as follows. From the above observation, if $\models_{DDC} \varphi$ then $int \Rightarrow intemb(\varphi)$ is a valid formula in DC with the assumption $\mathcal{DL}$. Consequently, from the relative completeness of DC, $intemb(\varphi)$ is provable in DC with the assumption $\mathcal{DL}$. $\qquad\square$

*Discrete Step Time Model.* As it was said earlier, a discrete step time model consists of all time points at which there is a the state change. Since we have assumed that the special state variable $C$ for the clock ticks is present in our system that changes its value at every integer point, this model of time should also include the set of natural numbers. This is the reason that we include $\mathbb{N}$ as a subset of $\mathcal{S}$. This time model was defined and used by Pandya et al in [14]. To represent a time point in this model, we introduce a temporal propositional letter $pt$, $pt$ holds for an interval $[t, t']$ iff $t = t'$ and $t$ is a time point at which there is a state change. $pt$ should satisfy:

$$pt \Rightarrow \ell = 0$$
$$step \Rightarrow pt^\frown true^\frown pt$$
$$int \Rightarrow pt^\frown true^\frown pt$$
$$int \Rightarrow pt^\frown step^*$$

Let $\mathcal{DP}$ denote this set of formulas. The last formula in this set expresses our assumption that no Zeno computation is allowed, i.e. in any time interval, there are only a finite number of state changes. Let us define a DC formula $dis$ as

$$dis \;\widehat{=}\; (pt^\frown true^\frown pt)$$

*dis* represents an interval between two discrete points. When considering the Discrete Step Time Models, the chop point should satisfy *pt*.

The sublanguage $\mathcal{DSL}$, which is the union of $\mathcal{SC}$, $\mathcal{ID}$, $\mathcal{CC}$, $\mathcal{DP}$ $\mathcal{DC}$ and $\mathcal{RC}$, forms a relatively complete specification for the discrete time structure.

Let $disemb(\varphi)$ be a formula that is obtained from $\varphi$ by replacing each proper subformula $\psi$ of $\varphi$ by $\psi \wedge dis$. For example $disemb(\phi^\frown \neg \psi) = (\phi \wedge dis)^\frown(dis \wedge \neg(\psi \wedge dis)$.

**Theorem 2.** *Let $\varphi$ be a DC formula with no occurrence of temporal proposition letters. Then, $\mathcal{DSL} \vdash dis \Rightarrow disemb(\varphi)$ exactly $\models_{SDC} \varphi$.*

*Proof.* The proof works in exactly the same way as the proof of Theorem 1.

Any discrete step time model $\mathcal{I}, [a, b]$ can be extended to a model that satisfies formulas in $\mathcal{DL}$ in the obvious way, namely with the interpretation for *int* and *step* with the intended meanings for them. By induction on the structure of the formula $\varphi$, it is easy to prove that $\mathcal{I}, [a, b] \models_{SDC} \varphi$ if and only $\mathcal{I}, [a, b] \models intemb(\varphi)$.

Then, the "only if" part follows directly from the soundness of the proof of the DC system that $intemb(\varphi)$ is satisfied by any discrete step time model that satisfies $\mathcal{DL}$.

For the "if" part, notice that if $\models_{SDC} \varphi$ then $dis \Rightarrow intemb(\varphi)$ is a valid formula in DC with the assumption $\mathcal{DL}$. Consequently, from the relative completeness of DC, $disemb(\varphi)$ is provable in DC with the assumption $\mathcal{DL}$.    □

*Sampling Time Models.* A sampling time model consists of the time points where we sample the data. Assume that the samplings are frequent enough and that any state change should be at a sampling point. To specify this time model, we can use $\mathcal{DSL}$ and an additional assumption

$$step \Rightarrow \ell = 1/h$$

where $h \in \mathbb{N}$, $h > 0$, i.e. $1/h$ is the sampling time step. Let $\mathcal{SL}_h$ be the language for the sampling time model with the sampling time step $1/h$.

## 4  Specifying Sampling, Periodic Task Systems and Projection to Discrete Time

### 4.1  Sampling

Sampling and specifying periodic task systems are immediate applications of the results presented in the previous section.

We have built a language for sampling time models based on the continuous time DC. Hence, we can use the proof system of DC to reason about validity of a formula in that time and state model. How to relate the validity of a formula $D$ in that time and state model with the validity of a formula $D'$ in the original DC? In our early work [9], we have considered that relation, but had to formulate the results in a natural meta language due to the use of different semantic models. With the help from the time modeling language, we can also formulate the relationship as formulas in DC.

Let $P$ be a state variable. Let $P_h$ be a state in the sampling time model with the sampling time step $1/h$ such that $P_h$ is interpreted the same as $P$ at any sampling time point, i.e. $\Box(pt \Rightarrow (\lceil P \rceil^0 \Leftrightarrow \lceil P_h \rceil^0))$ (denoted by $samp(P, P_h)$), and $\Box(step \wedge \ell > 0 \Rightarrow (\lceil P_h \rceil \vee \lceil \neg P_h \rceil))$ (denoted by $dig(P_h)$). Let $stable(P, d)$ denote the formula $\Box((\lceil \neg P \rceil \frown \lceil P \rceil \frown \lceil \neg P \rceil) \Rightarrow \ell \geq d)$.

**Theorem 3.** *Let $d > 1/h$. The following formulas are valid in DC:*

1. $(stable(P, d) \wedge samp(P, P_h) \wedge dig(P_h)) \Rightarrow$
   $(\int P = m \Rightarrow | \int P_h - m| \leq \min\{\ell, (\ell/d + 1)1/h\}$
2. $(stable(P, d) \wedge samp(P, P_h) \wedge dig(P_h)) \Rightarrow$
   $(\int P = m \wedge dis) \Rightarrow | \int P_h - m| \leq \min\{\ell, 1/h\ell/d\}$
3. $(stable(P, d) \wedge samp(P, P_h) \wedge dig(P_h)) \Rightarrow$
   $\int P_h = m \Rightarrow | \int P - m| \leq (\ell/d + 1)1/h$
4. $(stable(P, d) \wedge samp(P, P_h) \wedge dig(P_h)) \Rightarrow$
   $\int P_h < m \Rightarrow \int P < m + 1/h(\ell/d + 1)$
5. $(stable(P, d) \wedge samp(P, P_h) \wedge dig(P_h)) \Rightarrow$
   $\int P < m \Rightarrow \int P_h < m + 1/h(\ell/d + 1)$
6. $(stable(P, d) \wedge samp(P, P_h) \wedge dig(P_h)) \Rightarrow$
   $\int P_h > m \Rightarrow \int P > m - 1/h(\ell/d + 1)$
7. $(stable(P, d) \wedge samp(P, P_h) \wedge dig(P_h)) \Rightarrow$
   $\int P > m \Rightarrow \int P_h > m - 1/h(\ell/d + 1)$
8. $(stable(P, d) \wedge samp(P, P_h) \wedge dig(P_h)) \Rightarrow$
   $dis \Rightarrow (\lceil P_h \rceil \Leftrightarrow \lceil P \rceil)$

*Proof.* This is just a reformulation of Theorem 1 in [9].                    □

This theorem is useful for deriving a valid formula in the original DC from valid formulas in discrete time model. It can be used in approximate reasoning, especially in model checking: to check if a system $S$ satisfies a DC property $D$, we can check a sampling system $S_h$ of $S$ whether it satisfies a discrete DC property $D_h$. $D_h$ is found such that $S_h \models D_h$ implies $S \models D$. This technique has been used in [14].

## 4.2   Periodic Task System

A periodic task system $T$ consists of $n$ processes $\{1, \ldots, n\}$. Each process $i$ raises its request periodically with period $T_i$, and for each period it requests a constant amount of processor time $C_i$. A specification of system $T$ in DC has been given in many works, see e.g [2], which assume that all the processes raise their request at time 0. We can give a complete specification of the system without this assumption using the same technique that was introduced for temporal variable *int* in the previous section. To specify periodic behaviour of process $i$, we also use temporal variable $dLine\_i$ as in [2] whose behavior is similar to temporal variable $int$, and specified by:

$$dLine\_i \Rightarrow ((dLine\_i \wedge \ell = 0)^\frown(dLine\_i \wedge \ell = T_i)^*) \wedge \qquad (6)$$
$$((dLine\_i \wedge \ell = T_i)^*{}^\frown(dLine\_i \wedge \ell = 0))$$
$$dLine\_i^\frown(\ell = T_i) \Rightarrow dLine_i \qquad (7)$$
$$\ell \geq 2T_i \Rightarrow \ell < T_i{}^\frown((dLine\_i \wedge \ell = T_i)^* \wedge \qquad (8)$$
$$\neg(true^\frown(dLine\_i \wedge \ell = T_i)^\frown\neg(dLine\_i \wedge \ell = T_i)^*) \wedge$$
$$\neg(\neg(dLine\_i \wedge \ell = T_i)^*{}^\frown(dLine\_i \wedge \ell = T_i)^\frown true))^\frown$$
$$\ell < T_i$$

Let $Run_i$ be a state variable saying that process $i$ is running on the processor, i.e. $Run_i(t) = 1$ if process $i$ is running on the processor, and $Run_i(t) = 0$ otherwise. Let $Stand_i$ be a state variable saying that the current request of process $i$ has not been fulfilled. The behaviour of process $i$ is fully specified by:

$$dLine\_i \wedge \ell = T_i \Rightarrow (((\textstyle\int Run_i < C_i \Leftrightarrow \lceil Stand_i\rceil)^\frown true)\wedge$$
$$(\textstyle\int Run_i = C_i{}^\frown\ell > 0 \Rightarrow \textstyle\int Run_i = C_i{}^\frown\lceil\neg Stand_i\rceil))$$

The requirement of system $T$ is simply specified by: for all $i \leq n$,

$$dLine\_i \wedge \ell = T_i \Rightarrow \textstyle\int Run_i = C_i$$

Formulas 6, 7 and 8 form a complete specification of temporal propositional variables $dLine_i$, $i \leq n$, and are useful in proving the correctness of a scheduler for system $T$. A priority-based scheduler $\mathcal{S}$ for system $T$ with single processor is characterised by state variables $HiPri_{ij}$ ($i, j \leq n, i \neq j$) which specify the dynamic priority among the processes defined by $\mathcal{S}$, and the following state formulas characterising its behaviour:

$$\wedge_{i\neq j}((Run_i \wedge Stand_j) => HiPri_{ij})$$
$$\wedge_{i\leq n}(Run_i => Stand_i)$$
$$\wedge_{i\neq j}(HiPri_{ij} \Rightarrow \neg HiPri_{ji})$$
$$\wedge_{i\neq j}\neg(Run_i \wedge Run_j)$$
$$\vee_{i\leq n}Stand_i \Rightarrow \vee_{i\leq n}Run_i$$

A deadline driven scheduler is a priority-based scheduler that considers process $i$ to have a higher prioity than process $j$ (i.e. the value of $HiPri_{ij}$ at the current time point is 1) iff the deadline for process $i$ is nearer than the deadline for process $j$. The deadline driven scheduler can be modelled in a much more convenient way than in [2] with the additional formula specifying the behaviour of state variables $HiPri_{ij}$ ($i, j \leq n$):

$$\wedge_{i\neq j}\lceil HiPri_{ij}\rceil^\frown\ell = T_i \Rightarrow (\neg\Diamond dLine_j)^\frown dLine_i{}^\frown true$$

The interesting thing here is that variables $HiPri_{ij}$ can be defined in DC, without any quantification on rigid variables, via temporal propositional variables

$dLine_i$ $(i \leq n)$ which are completely specified by formulas 6, 7 and 8. With defining $HiPri_{ij}$ in this way, we don't have to assume that all the processes raise their request at time 0. Hence, reasoning about the correctness of the scheduler for the general case can be done with the proof system of DC. We believe that the general model for task scheduling presented in [1] can be clearer and simplified a lot using this technique.

### 4.3  Hybrid States and Projection to Discrete Time

In [12], He Jifeng introduced the projection from continuous time to discrete time to reason about hybrid systems where we have continuous state and temporal variables. In that paper, intervals are either discrete or continuous. Discrete intervals are embedded in continuous intervals. He introduced an operator for projection $\backslash\backslash$ defined as: let $F$ and $G$ be a DC formula, then $F\backslash\backslash G$ is also a formula with the following semantics: $\mathcal{I}, [a, b] \models F\backslash\backslash G$ iff for for some $n \in \mathbb{N}$ and $a = m_1 \leq m_2 \leq \ldots \leq m_n = b$ $\mathcal{I}, [m, m_{i+1}] \models F$ and $\mathcal{I}, < m_1, m_2, \ldots, m_n > \models G$, where $< m_1, m_2, \ldots, m_n >$ is a discrete interval. In [4], Guelev also showed that $F\backslash\backslash G$ can be expressed by a formula in the original DC with a temporal propositional letter. In the framework of this paper, $F\backslash\backslash G$ is described in DC as follows. We assume two kinds of states in the system: continuous states and discrete ones. Instead of forcing $\mathcal{SC}$ to be satisfied by any state, we enforce it to be satisfied by discrete states only. So, $F\backslash\backslash G$ is expressed by

$$((F \wedge step)^* \wedge disemb(G[P_s/P]))$$

where $G[P_s/P]$ is obtained from $G$ by the substitution of discrete state $P_s$ for state $P$ such that $samp(P, P_s)$ for each state $P$ occurred in $G$. Formula $((F \wedge step)^* \wedge disemb(G[P_s/P]))$ says that the reference interval is discrete interval that satisfies formula $disemb(G[P_s/P])$, and each discrete step satisfies continuous formula $F$. So, with using temporal propositional letters $step$, the projection $\backslash\backslash$ can be defined and reasoning in the original DC as well.

## 5  Modelling Communication Protocols with Digitizing in DC

In this section, we show that with discrete time structure formalised, we can model communication protocols using Duration Calculus (DC) in a very convenient way without any extension for digitising. This model has been presented in our earlier work [10,7]. Consider a model for communication at the physical layer (see Fig. 1). A sender and a receiver are connected via a bus. Their clocks are running at different rates. We refer to the clock of the receiver as the time reference. The receiver receives signals by digitising. Since the signals sent by the sender and the signals received by the receiver are functions from the set $\mathbb{R}^+$ to $\{0, 1\}$ (1 represents that the signal is *high*, and 0 represents that the signal is *low*), we can model them as state variables in DC.

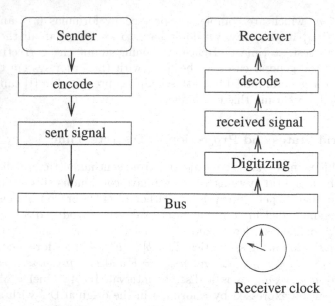

**Fig. 1.** Communication Protocol Model

The communication protocols are modelled in DC as follows. The signal sent by the sender is modelled by a state $X$. The signal received by the receiver by sampling the signal on the bus is modelled by a state $Y$ in the sampling time model with the sampling time step 1. So, $step \Leftrightarrow int \wedge \ell = 1$. However, it is not the case that $samp(X, Y)$ due to the fact that it takes a significant amount of time to change the signal on the bus from high to low or vice-versa, and hence, the signal on the bus cannot be represented by a Boolean function. Without loss of generality, assume that the delay between the sender and the receiver is 0. Assume also that when the signal on the bus is neither high nor low, the receiver will choose an arbitrary value from $\{0, 1\}$ for the value of $Y$. The phenomenon is depicted in Fig. 2. Assume that it takes $r$ ($r$ is a natural number) receiver-clock cycles for the sender to change the signal on the bus from high to low or vice-versa. Then if the sender changes the signal from low to high or from high to low, the receiver's signal will be unreliable for $r$ cycles starting from the last tick of the receiver clock and during this period it can be any value chosen nondeterministically from 0 and 1. Otherwise, the signal received by the receiver is the same as the signal sent by the sender (see Figure 2). This relationship between $X$ and $Y$ is formalised as

$$(\lceil X \rceil \wedge (\ell \geq r + 1)) \Rightarrow (\ell \leq r) \frown (\lceil Y \rceil \wedge int) \frown (\ell < 1),$$
$$(\lceil \neg X \rceil \wedge (\ell \geq r + 1)) \Rightarrow (\ell \leq r) \frown (\lceil \neg Y \rceil \wedge int) \frown (\ell < 1).$$

Since the behaviour of a state can be specified by a DC formula, a communication protocol can be modelled as consisting of a coding function $f$, which maps a sequence of bits to a DC formula expressing the behaviour of $X$, and a

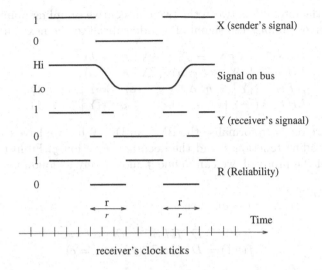

**Fig. 2.** Signal patterns

decoding function $g$, which maps a DC formula expressing the behaviour of $Y$ to a sequence of bits. The protocol is correct iff for any sequence $w$ of bits, if the sender puts the signal represented by $f(w)$ on the bus then by digitising the receiver must receive and receives only the signals represented by a DC formula $D$ for which $g(D) = w$.

### 5.1   Biphase Mark Protocols

In the Biphase Mark Protocols (BMP) the sender encodes a bit as a cell consisting of a mark subcell of length $b$ and a code subcell of length $a$. The sender keeps the signal stable in each subcell (hence either $\lceil X \rceil$ or $\lceil \neg X \rceil$ holds for the interval representing a subcell). For a cell, if the signal in the mark subcell is the same as the signal in the code subcell, the information carried by the cell is 0; otherwise, the information carried by the cell is 1. There is a phase reverse between two consecutive cells. This means that, for a cell, the signal of the mark subcell of the following cell is held as the negation of the signal of the code subcell of the cell. The receiver, on detecting a state change (of $Y$), knows that it is the beginning of a cell, and skips $d$ cycles (called the *sampling distance*) and samples the signal. If the sampled signal is the same as the signal at the beginning of the cell, it decodes the cell as 0; otherwise it decodes the cell as 1. ·

At the beginning of the transmission, the signal is low for $a$ cycles (this means, $\lceil \neg X \rceil$ holds for the interval of length $a$ starting from the beginning). When the sender finishes sending, it keeps the signal stable for $cc$ time units which is longer than the code subcell. We use *HLS, LHS* to denote the formulas representing intervals consisting of the code subcell of a cell and the mark subcell of the next one for the sender, and use $HLR^\frown(\ell = d)$, $LHR^\frown(\ell = d)$ to denote the formulas representing the intervals between the two consecutive sampling points (from the time the receiver samples the signal of a code subcell to the next one. Formally,

$$HLS \triangleq (\lceil X \rceil \wedge \ell = a)^\frown(\lceil \neg X \rceil \wedge \ell = b),$$
$$LHS \triangleq (\lceil \neg X \rceil \wedge \ell = a)^\frown(\lceil X \rceil \wedge \ell = b),$$
$$HLR \triangleq (\lceil Y \rceil \wedge int \wedge 1 \leq \ell \leq \rho)^\frown(\lceil \neg Y \rceil \wedge \ell = 1),$$
$$LHR \triangleq (\lceil \neg Y \rceil \wedge int \wedge 1 \leq \ell \leq \rho)^\frown(\lceil Y \rceil \wedge \ell = 1).$$

Now, we are ready to formalise the BMP in DC. What we have to do is write down the encoding function $f$ and the decoding function $g$. From the informal description of the protocol, we can define $f$ inductively as follows.

1. $f(\epsilon) \triangleq (\lceil \neg X \rceil \wedge \ell = c)$
2. If $f(w) = D^\frown(\lceil X \rceil \wedge \ell = c)$, then

$$f(w0) \triangleq D^\frown HLS^\frown(\lceil \neg X \rceil \wedge \ell = c)$$
$$f(w1) \triangleq D^\frown HLS^\frown(\lceil X \rceil \wedge \ell = c)$$

3. If $f(w) = D^\frown(\lceil \neg X \rceil \wedge \ell = c)$, then

$$f(w0) \triangleq D^\frown LHS^\frown(\lceil X \rceil \wedge \ell = c)$$
$$f(w1) \triangleq D^\frown LHS^\frown(\lceil \neg X \rceil \wedge \ell = c)$$

For example, $f(1) = LHS^\frown(\lceil \neg X \rceil \wedge \ell = c)$, $f(10) = LHS^\frown LHS^\frown(\lceil X \rceil \wedge \ell = c)$, and $f(101) = LHS^\frown LHS^\frown HLS^\frown(\lceil X \rceil \wedge \ell = c)$.

Because the decoding function $g$ is a partial function, we have to describe its domain first, i.e. what kind of DC formulas on the state $Y$ are detected (received) by the receiver. According to the behaviour of the receiver, first it skips $r$ cycles. Then it begins to scan for an edge ($HLR$ or $LHR$). When an edge is detected, it skips $d$ cycles and repeats this procedure until it detects that the transmission has completed ($Y$ is stable for more than $\rho$ cycles). Thus, a DC formula $D$ is received by the receiver iff $D$ is of the form $A_0^\frown A_1^\frown \ldots ^\frown A_n$, $n \geq 1$, where

- $A_0 = (1 \geq \ell \wedge \ell > 0)^\frown(int \wedge (\ell = r - 1)))$
- and either $A_n = (int \wedge \lceil Y \rceil \wedge (\ell > \rho))^\frown(\ell < 1))$,
  or $A_n = (int \wedge \lceil \neg Y \rceil \wedge (\ell > \rho))^\frown(\ell < 1))$
- and for $j = 1, \ldots, n - 1$ either $A_j = LHR^\frown(\ell = d)$ or $A_j = HLR^\frown(\ell = d)$
- and if $n = 1$ then $A_n = (int \wedge \lceil \neg Y \rceil \wedge (\ell > \rho))^\frown(\ell < 1))$ and if $n > 1$ then $A_1 = LHR^\frown(\ell = d)$ (since at the beginning the signal is low).

Now, the decoding function $g$ can be written as follows. Let $D$ be a formula received by the receiver.

- If $D = (\ell \leq 1 \wedge \ell > 0)^\frown(int \wedge \ell = r - 1)^\frown(\lceil \neg Y \rceil \wedge \ell > \rho \wedge int)^\frown \ell < 1$ then $g(D) = \epsilon$.
- Let $g(D)$ be defined.
  - If $D = D'^\frown(\lceil Y \rceil \wedge int \wedge \ell \geq \rho)^\frown \ell < 1$ then
    $g(D'^\frown HLR^\frown(\ell = d)^\frown(\lceil Y \rceil \wedge int \wedge \ell \geq \rho)^\frown \ell < 1) = g(D)1$, and
    $g(D'^\frown HLR^\frown(\ell = d)^\frown(\lceil \neg Y \rceil \wedge int \wedge \ell \geq \rho)^\frown \ell < 1) = g(D)0$.

- If $D = D'^\frown(\lceil\neg Y\rceil \wedge int \wedge \ell \geq \rho)^\frown \ell < 1$, then
  $g(D'^\frown LHR^\frown(\ell = d)^\frown(\lceil Y\rceil \wedge int \wedge \ell \geq \rho)^\frown \ell < 1) = g(D)0$, and
  $g(D'^\frown LHR^\frown(\ell = d)^\frown(\lceil\neg Y\rceil \wedge int \wedge \ell \geq \rho)^\frown \ell < 1) = g(D)1$.

For example, let $D$ be $(\ell \leq 1 \wedge \ell > 0)^\frown(int \wedge \ell = r-1)^\frown LHR^\frown(\ell = d)^\frown LHR^\frown(\ell = d)^\frown HLR^\frown(\ell = d)^\frown(\lceil Y\rceil \wedge \ell > \rho \wedge int)^\frown(\ell < 1))$. Then,

$$\begin{aligned}
g(D) &= g((\ell \leq 1 \wedge \ell > 0)^\frown(int \wedge \ell = r - 1)^\frown LHR^\frown(\ell = d) \\
&\quad ^\frown LHR^\frown(\ell = d)^\frown(\lceil Y\rceil \wedge \ell > \rho \wedge int)^\frown(\ell < 1))1 \\
&= g((\ell \leq 1 \wedge \ell > 0)^\frown(int \wedge \ell = r - 1)^\frown LHR^\frown(\ell = d)^\frown \\
&\quad (\lceil\neg Y\rceil \wedge \ell > \rho \wedge int)^\frown(\ell < 1))01 \\
&= g((\ell \leq 1 \wedge \ell > 0)^\frown(int \wedge \ell = r - 1) \\
&\quad ^\frown(\lceil\neg Y\rceil \wedge \ell > \rho \wedge int)^\frown(\ell < 1))101 \\
&= \epsilon 101 \,.
\end{aligned}$$

## 5.2   Verification of BMP

As said earlier, we have to verify that for any sequence of bits $w$, if the sender puts on the bus the signal represented by DC formula $f(w)$, then the receiver must receive and receives only the signals represented by a DC formula $D$ for which $g(D) = w$. We can only prove this requirement with some condition on the values of the parameter $r, a, b, c, \rho$ and $d$. The requirement is formalised as:
   For all sequence of bits $w$,

- there exists a DC formula $D$ received by the receiver such that $f(w) \Rightarrow D$, and
- for all $D$ receivable by the receiver, if $f(w) \Rightarrow D$ then $g(D) = w$.

   Since in BMP $g$ is a deterministic function, for any sequence of bits $w$ there is no more than one receivable formula $D$ for which $f(w) \Rightarrow D$. Thus we can have a stronger requirement which is formalised as:
   For all sequences of bits $w$ there exists uniquely a receivable formula $D$ such that $f(w) \Rightarrow D$ and $g(D) = w$.
   Our verification is done by proving the following two theorems.

**Theorem 4.** *For any receivable formulas $D$ and $D'$, if $D$ is different from $D'$ syntactically then $\models ((D \wedge D') \Rightarrow ff)$.*

This theorem says that each time at most one receivable formula $D$ is received by the receiver.

**Theorem 5.** *Assume that $r \geq 1$, $b \geq r + 1$, $a \geq r + 1$, $c \geq \rho + a$, $d \geq b + r$, $d \leq a + b - 3 - r$, and $\rho \geq a + 1$. Then for any sequence of bits $w$ there exists a receivable formula $D$ for which $f(w) \Rightarrow D$ and $g(D) = w$.*

In [7] we proved these two theorems, with PVS proof checker, with the encoding of the proof system for Duration Calculus.

# 6    Conclusion

We have presented our approach to the specification and verification of real-time hybrid systems using Duration Calculus. By using temporal propositional letters we can specify many classes of time models that are suitable for our applications. The properties of the introduced temporal propositional letters are then specified by a class of Duration Calculus formulas. Using this class of formulas and the proof system of the original Duration Calculus we can reason about the behaviour of our real-time systems in different time domains without any further efforts for developing a new proof system. We have shown that this technique works well for reasoning about the relationship between real systems and digitised systems. This enables us to use a proof checker of Duration Calculus for different classes of applications.

By embedding discrete DC into the continuous ones, we can use the decidability of the discrete DC to decide the falsifiability of a subclass of formulas in DC. The technique demonstrated in this paper could be considered as an effort for unifying different versions of DC.

# References

1. Chan, P., Van Hung, D.: Duration Calculus Specification of Scheduling for Tasks with Shared Resources. In: Kanchanasut, K., Levy, J.-J. (eds.) Algorithms, Concurrency and Knowledge. LNCS, vol. 1023, pp. 365–380. Springer, Heidelberg (1995)
2. Chaochen, Z., Hansen, M.R.: Duration Calculus. Springer, Heidelberg (2004)
3. Chaochen, Z., Hoare, C.A.R., Ravn, A.P.: A calculus of durations. Information Processing Letters 40(5), 269–276 (1992)
4. Guelev, D.P.: A Complete Proof System for First Order Interval Temporal Logic with Projection. Technical Report 202, UNU-IIST, P.O.Box 3058, Macau, June 2000. A revised version of this report was published in the Journal of Logic and Computation 14(2), 215–249 (2004)
5. Guelev, D.P., Van Hung, D.: Prefix and projection onto state in duration calculus. In: Asarin, O.M.E., Yovine, S. (eds.) Electronic Notes in Theoretical Computer Science, vol. 65, Elsevier Science Publishers, Amsterdam (2002)
6. Guelev, D.P., Van Hung, D.: On the completeness and decidability of duration calculus with iteration. Theor. Comput. Sci. 337(1-3), 278–304 (2005)
7. Van Hung, D.: Modelling and Verification of Biphase Mark Protocols in Duration Calculus Using PVS/DC⁻. In: Research Report 103, UNU-IIST, P.O.Box 3058, Macau, April 1997. Presented at and published in the Proceedings of the 1998 International Conference on Application of Concurrency to System Design (CSD'98), Aizu-wakamatsu, Fukushima, Japan, 23-26 March 1998, pp. 88–98. IEEE Computer Society Press, Los Alamitos (1998)
8. Van Hung, D.: Real-time Systems Development with Duration Calculus: an Overview. In: Aichernig, B.K., Maibaum, T.S.E. (eds.) Formal Methods at the Crossroads. From Panacea to Foundational Support. LNCS, vol. 2757, pp. 81–96. Springer, Heidelberg (2003)
9. Van Hung, D., Giang, P.H.: A sampling semantics of duration calculus. In: Jonsson, B., Parrow, J. (eds.) Formal Techniques in Real-Time and Fault-Tolerant Systems. LNCS, vol. 1135, pp. 188–207. Springer, Heidelberg (1996)

10. Van Hung, D., Ko Kwang Il,: Verification via Digitized Model of Real-Time Systems. In: Research Report 54, UNU-IIST, P.O.Box 3058, Macau, February 1996. Published in the Proceedings of Asia-Pacific Software Engineering Conference 1996 (APSEC'96), pp. 4–15. IEEE Computer Society Press, Los Alamitos (1996)
11. Van Huong, H., Van Hung, D.: Modelling Real-time Database Systems in Duration Calculus. Technical Report 260, UNU-IIST, P.O. Box 3058, Macau, September 2002. Presented at and published in the proceedings of the IASTED International Conference on Databases and Applications (DBA 2004). In: Hamza, M.H. (ed.) Innsbruck, Austria, February 17 – 19, 2004, pp. 37–42. ACTA Press (2004)
12. Jifeng, H.: A behavioural Model for Co-design. In: Woodcock, J.C.P., Davies, J., Wing, J.M. (eds.) FM 1999. LNCS, vol. 1709, pp. 1420–1439. Springer, Heidelberg (1999)
13. Martin, F.: Synthesizing Controllers of Duration Calculus. In: Jonsson, B., Parrow, J. (eds.) Formal Techniques in Real-Time and Fault-Tolerant Systems. LNCS, vol. 1135, pp. 168–187. Springer, Heidelberg (1996)
14. Pandya, P.K., Krishna, S.N., Loya, K.: On Sampling Abstraction of Continuous Time Logic with Duration Calculus. Technical Report TIFR-PKP-GM-2006/1, Tata Institute of Fundamental Research, India (2006)
15. Pandya, P.K., Ramakrishna, Y.: A Recursive Duration Calculus. Technical Report CS-95/3, TIFR, Mumbai (1995)

# Relating Domain Concepts Intensionally by Ordering Connections

Asger Eir

Maconomy Corp.
aei@maconomy.dk

**Abstract.** The present paper suggests a modelling method for relating domain concepts intensionally. The method is based on modelling concepts formally and establishing two ordering connections between objects of the concepts. The former connection, we call the *characteristics connection*. It is a Galois connection and states how objects of the two concepts, describe each other. The latter connection, we call the *information flow connection*. It is a connection between classifications of objects of the two concepts. The connection states how specialization of one kind of objects, cannot imply generalization of objects succeeding in an information flow. We put the method to work by modelling the domain concepts of budgets and project plans, and we establish the two ordering connections between the models of these. In doing so, we reveal interesting domain knowledge. Hence, we believe that our contribution adds clarity and transparency to the methodology of domain engineering and conceptual modelling.

**Keywords:** Conceptual modelling, Domain Engineering, Intension, Abstract Interpretation, Galois Connection, Classification, Formal Methods, The RAISE Specification Language (RSL).

## 1 Introduction

There are many things that can be said about a budget: what the number of figures is, what the total cost estimate is, etc. These are abstract properties of the budget and the results of abstract interpretation. Also more complex properties exist. An example is the property of financially covering the expenses for executing a certain project plan. The formal predicate representing this property, states the condition that project plans must satisfy in order to be executable within the financial restrictions of the budget. In fact, the predicate states a duality. With it, we can check whether a project plan can be executed within the financial restrictions of a budget, and we can check whether a budget designates the necessary expenses for executing a project plan. The reason for this duality is that budgets describe and determine project plans and project plans describe and determine budgets. Going either way can be understood as abstract interpretation defined by either of two interpretation functions: one from budgets to project plans, and one from project plans to budgets. The function pair defines

C.B. Jones, Z. Liu, J. Woodcock (Eds.): Bjørner/Zhou Festschrift, LNCS 4700, pp. 188–216, 2007.
© Springer-Verlag Berlin Heidelberg 2007

a Galois connection similar to the Galois connection between sets of object and sets of their common properties in Formal Concept Analysis [1].

In order to create a realistic project plan, a budget is needed and most often budgeting is a stage preceding project planning because the budget determines the financial scope of the project plan. If changes are made to a budget, corresponding changes need to be made to the project plan in order for it to still fit that scope. A general understanding of budgets is that they follow a so-called *work breakdown structure*. The structure expresses that general budget figures are broken down into more specific budget figures. Such a structure can be used to express the phases, sub-phases, and parallel areas of work, financially. Breaking down budget figures or restricting to a sub-set of general figures, narrows the financial scope of the budget. Hence, we shall say that doing so, specializes the budget. A similar perspective can be applied on project plans. Project plans designate works to be done. Some works may be done in parallel whereas other works need to be done in sequence. Removing parts of the project plan narrows the result of executing it. Hence, we shall say that doing so, specializes the project plan. It appears that specialization of budgets implies specialization of project plans if the Galois connection between is to be maintained.

The above analysis indicates that there are two interesting aspects in a concept relation between domain concepts like budgets and project plans. The former is that budgets describe and determine project plans and vice versa. Generalized, this is a connection between object sets of the two concepts. The latter aspect is that budgets and project plans can be ordered respectively and that specialization in the budget classification implies specialization in the project plan classification, assuming the first aspect to be maintained.

The two aspects define separate dual connections. The former is a Galois connection defined by two dually, monotonously, decreasing functions; one from sets of budgets to sets of project plans, and one from sets of project plans to sets of budgets. The latter connection is an order-preserving connection between two classifications; one of budgets and one of project plans.

The two aspects are interesting from a concept modelling perspective for the following reasons. The Galois connection is the foundation in conceptualizations where characteristics of objects are modelled by designating their abstract properties. In our case, the abstract properties are special in the sense that they are possessed by the objects in virtue of these standing in certain relations to other objects. That is, the properties are *extrinsic* properties. We shall say that these other objects are part of the *intensions* of the objects in question.

The order-preserving connection ensures consistent concretisation from budgets to project plans. This means that the corresponding concept relation — when introduced in a conceptual web of concepts related likewise — maintains the systematics of concretising information from stage to stage in project development. The connection adds intensional knowledge as it describes some of the dynamical characteristics of objects; namely, what effect it has on objects of one kind to change objects of another.

In the cross-disciplinary areas between computer science and application domains, modelling of domain concepts and defining their relations, is an essential process for founding computerized management. Also, it is essential for reaching a clarification of the domain in general. However, there is a lack of methods for defining such relations. Consequently, the domain engineering approach may be quite informal and implicit; or even given up.

In this paper, we outline a method for relating domain concepts based on formalizations of these concepts. The method establishes concept relations on (i) a Galois connection between object sets of the concepts, and (ii) an order-preserving connection between classifications of objects of the concepts. In order to put the method to work, we model the domain concepts of budgets and projects plans formally, and we establish the Galois connection and the order-preserving connection between these concepts[1]. Founding a concept relation on the two ordering connections, we believe makes the concept relation more rigour than a relation simply claimed to hold between two concept names. It is so, as it includes the semantic aspects of characteristics and change effects. Hence, we consider the utilization of the two kinds of ordering connection as a contribution to the current debate on the methodology of domain engineering in computer science. In essence it puts the semantic question of what it means for two domain concepts to relate, on the agenda — a question which is present in almost any development of software and IT systems.

Throughout the paper, we use The RAISE Specification Language (RSL) to express the formal models, relations and conditions [4,5]. However, effort has also been made to informally express the understanding and intuition behind the models.

## 2   Domain Engineering

In the paper, we shall assume the following understandings of concept relations:

**Definition 1 (Concept Relation).** *By a concept relation, we understand a relation between two concept names, implicitly or explicitly stating the criteria for objects of the concepts to relate.*

Hence, when we talk about a concept relation, we also talk about a relation between the objects of the concepts.

**Definition 2 (Implicit Concept Relation).** *By an implicit concept relation, we understand a concept relation for which the criteria are implicitly or informally expressed.*

**Definition 3 (Explicit Concept Relation).** *By an explicit concept relation, we understand a concept relation for which the criteria are explicitly and formally expressed.*

---

[1] Pre-studies have been done in [2] and [3].

Concept relations are an important part of domain and requirements model. Some concept relations define concept specialization and generalization. We shall say that such relations stand between concepts of the same kind as they are *kind-of* relations. Other concept relations hold between what we shall call concepts of *distinct kinds*. That is, concept pairs which are not naturally related by kind-of relations. The distinction has been treated further in [2] and [3].

Several domain and requirements acquisition methods provide notations for expressing both kinds of concept relations. Basically, we can classify concept relation approaches in four levels concerning rigidity and formality. On the first level, we have graphical and other informal notations like UML. Such approaches define *implicit concept relations*. Hence, it is not possible (without further formalization) to check nor justify that two arbitrarily chosen objects satisfy the criteria of the concept relation. On the second level, we have modelling approaches which relate concepts by expressing simple criteria for distinct concept objects to relate. When modelling databases, such criteria are expressed in join structures. However, the criteria are merely that objects (here tuples) have identical values on certain fields. The concept relation is here explicit, but still very simple as the objects are related based on having properties in common. Not all domain concepts have that. Hence, there would be concepts that could not be related this way. On the third level, we have approaches which offer a full mathematical range of expressions for formalizing the criteria. The approaches (as in this paper) may include facilities for implicitly expressing the change effects on objects. Relations on this level are *explicit concept relations*. On the fourth level we have approaches which — in addition to what is on the third level — also facilitate expressing how objects of one kind can be calculated explicitly from objects of other concepts. However, this is certainly not be possible for objects of all kinds of domain concepts. The approach taken in this paper belongs to the third level; including the mentioned facilities.

## 3   Intensional Modelling: A Proposed Method

This section outlines a proposed method for relating domain concepts formally. The method is motivated by the analysis from Sect. 1 and draws on the definitions from Sect. 2; namely (i) a Galois connection between sets of objects of the two concepts considered, and (ii) an order-preserving connection between classifications of objects of the two concepts. We shall refer to these as the *characteristics connection* and the *information flow connection*, defined as follows:

**Definition 4 (Characteristics Connection).** *By a characteristics connection, we understand a relation between objects and their common properties. The connection is founded by a Galois connection. In Formal Concept Analysis, a context relates objects to properties. The Galois connection is then utilized for defining general concepts by clustering objects and properties [1].*

In this paper, we shall consider the *characteristics connection* between objects and the common properties these have in virtue of standing in a certain relation to objects of another concept.

**Definition 5 (Information Flow Connection).** *By an* information flow connection, *we understand a relation between domain concepts appearing in different
stages of an information flow. The connection states how one kind of information
serves as input to the creation and elaboration of other kinds of information.*

In this paper, we shall consider the *information flow connection* between objects
representing the information on different stages of projects. However, the notion
is applicable in many other domains.

In the following, we shall consider the theoretical foundation of these two
kinds of connections.

### 3.1   Galois Connections and Abstract Interpretation

Formulated in RSL, the definition of Galois connections is:

**Definition 6 (Galois Connection).** *A Galois connection is a dual pair of
mappings* $(\mathcal{F}, \mathcal{G})$ *between two ordered sets* $(P, \leq)$ *and* $(Q, \leq)$. *Most often the
ordering is based on set-inclusion* $(\subseteq)$ *and this is also the version we shall use
here. The mappings must be monotonously decreasing[2]:*

**type**
  P, Q

**value**
  $\mathcal{F}$: P-set $\rightarrow$ Q-set
  $\mathcal{G}$: Q-set $\rightarrow$ P-set

**axiom**
  $\forall$ ps$_1$, ps$_2$:P-set, qs$_1$, qs$_2$:Q-set •
    ps$_1$ $\subseteq$ ps$_2$ $\Rightarrow$ $\mathcal{F}$ ps$_2$ $\subseteq$ $\mathcal{F}$ ps$_1$,
    qs$_1$ $\subseteq$ qs$_2$ $\Rightarrow$ $\mathcal{G}$ qs$_2$ $\subseteq$ $\mathcal{G}$ qs$_1$,
    ps$_1$ $\subseteq$ $\mathcal{G}$ $\mathcal{F}$ ps$_1$,
    qs$_1$ $\subseteq$ $\mathcal{F}$ $\mathcal{G}$ qs$_1$

In [1], the following Theorem is given on Galois connections (here omitting the
proof):

**Theorem 1 (Galois Connection[3]).** For every binary relation $R \subseteq M \times N$, a
Galois connection $(\varphi_R, \psi_R)$ between M and N is defined by

$$\varphi_R X := X^R \ (= y \in N | xRy \ for \ all \ x \in X)$$
$$\varphi_R Y := Y^R \ (= x \in M | xRy \ for \ all \ y \in Y).$$

---

[2] Note, that there are in fact two different definitions of Galois connections in the
literature: the *monotone* Galois connection and the *antitone* Galois connection. We
follow Ganter and Wille by assuming the former [1].
[3] In [1] this is named Theorem 2.

The notion of Galois connections is a mathematical concepts which founds a variety of applications. The application we shall consider here is the Galois connection between of objects and their common properties; a central subject in Formal Concept Analysis [1]. Consider the set of physical objects in a living room. For each object — chair, picture, table, candlelight, etc. — we can observe its properties like colour, weight, material, dimensions, length, etc. The notion of properties is here a wide notion; any predication of an object will do. Pick a subset of the objects and list the set of their common properties. That is, the properties that all objects in this set have. If we extend this set with more objects, we will either get a smaller set of common properties or have the same set. Similarly, we may pick a subset of properties and list the set of objects all having these properties. If we extend this set with more properties, we will either get a smaller set of objects or have the same set. Between objects and their common properties there is a Galois connection [1]. This connection is fundamental in all conceptual modelling and classification.

Now, consider another kind of objects and another kind of properties. The objects may be more abstract rather than physical. Examples of such kinds of objects are (from the domain of project planning): Budgets, project plans, resource allocations, plan executions, products, services, collaborations, etc.; basically any kind of thing or phenomena existing or potentially existing in the domain. Similarly, the properties of these objects may be abstract. Just as we can observe the colour and texture of a physical object, we can determine the relations to which an object stand to other kinds of objects; i.e., the extrinsic properties in addition to the intrinsic properties. As an example, we may say that a budget relates to the project plans that are executable within the financial restrictions of the budget; and vice versa.

Defining a Galois connection between two domain concepts can be an important foundation for conceptual domain modelling as it defines the characterisations of domain objects based on their relations to other objects. For this reason we shall say that the concept connection is *intensional*. The connection is a *characteristics connection*. Furthermore, a Galois connection provides a range of theorems that are convenient in context of model checking or other kinds of analysis of a domain model.

## 3.2   The Order of Information Flow

In order to carry out a project, a project plan is needed; and in order to produce a project plan, a budget is needed. This exemplifies that some kinds of information are input knowledge to the process of creating other kinds of information.

Now, consider a collection of domain concepts that are placed in a hierarchy describing the order in which information is created and used through stages of projects. If changes are made to one object (e.g. a budget is changed), it may influence other objects (e.g. put or release restrictions to a project plan). In order to formalize this, we shall consider changes to objects as either specializations or generalizations within classifications of the objects for each domain concept. For a budget, we may increase or decrease a budget figure, introduce a new or remove a figure, and break down figures. To maintain a consistent ordering in the information flow, we require that specialization of one object cannot imply generalization of succeeding objects if the characteristics connection is to be maintained. Note, that we do not require similar for objects preceding the changed object.

Formally, we express the above by defining classifications of the objects of the concepts, and an axiom expressing the above implication. Furthermore, meet and join operations are formalized. Meet takes two objects and gives the combined object which is a specialization of both argument objects. Join takes two objects and gives the combined object which is a generalization of both arguments. Further order-theoretic considerations and arguments are outside the scope of this paper.

In Sect. 10, we shall argue that *characteristics connection* and the *information flow connection* are intimately related.

### 3.3   Steps

The method of relating domain concepts intensionally is a sequence of steps towards concept models and establishing the *characteristics connection* and the *information flow connection*. The method is based on modelling the so-called *intrinsics* of domain concepts:

**Definition 7 (Domain Intrinsics).** *By the* intrinsics[4] *of a domain or a domain concept, we understand the very basics of the domain or domain concept. That is, the characteristics, structure and understanding that cannot be removed or abstracted from without undermining the understanding of the domain or domain concept in question.*

The steps of the method are as follows:

**Formally model the two concepts.** We establish formal models of the concepts, focusing on the intrinsics (i.e. the very basics) of the concepts. See Sect. 4 and 6.

**Define object classification.** For each concept define a classification of object by formally defining a partial order of objects. The partial orders are utilized when defining the *information flow connection*. See Sect. 4 and 6.

**Define object meet.** For each concept define a function *meet* which expresses what it means to combine two objects of the concept in question. The function is utilized in the definitions of the *characteristics connection* and the *information flow connection*. See Sect. 4 and 6.

**Formally model possible mediating ties.** Some concept pairs can be related without considering additional concepts. However, this is not always the case and we may then need to formalize additional domain concepts. We call such additional domain concepts the *mediating ties*. See Sect. 7.

---

[4] The notion of intrinsics and its role in formal domain engineering is also defined and treated in [6].

**Define a Galois predicate.** Quantifying over objects of the formalized domain concepts, we explicitly formalize the predicate stating the criteria that objects of the concepts must satisfy in order to relate to each other. We call this predicate the *Galois predicate* and it has the form:

**value**

$\phi$: $c_1$ × $c_2$ → **Bool**

Assuming the mediating ties $m_1$, ..., $m_n$, the form is:

**value**

$\phi$: $c_1$ × $c_2$ → $m_1$ × ... × $m_n$ → **Bool**

The predicate must be explicitly defined; i.e. the function body must be given. The predicate is utilized in the definition of two dual functions from sets of objects of the one concepts to the sets of objects of the other, and vice versa. The dual function pair defines a Galois connection. Thereby, the *characteristics connection* is defined. See Sect. 8.

**Define an order-preserving connection.** Based on classifications of objects of the two concepts, a connection between the two hierarchies is defined. This connection shows that specialization of objects of the one concept, implies specialization of objects of the other concept, if the characteristics connection is to be maintained. Thereby, the *information flow connection* is defined.

# 4   Budgets

A budget is a financial instrument for structuring the works of a project financially, and for managing and adhering to estimates for the works to be done. By *structuring*, we here understand that a budget may designate figures representing costs of phases, work areas, tasks as well as breaking down of such figures into sub-phases, sub-work areas, sub-tasks, etc. That is, budgets often reflect a so-called *work breakdown structure*.

## 4.1   Intrinsics

The intrinsics of a budget is that it is a hierarchical structure in the sense that each figure can be broken down into a set of sub-figure. Each figure in the structure uniquely identifies a specific subject of expenses. However, figures having sub-figures, are considered to cover the subjects constituted by the subjects of the sub-figures.

We model budgets (b:B) as maps from budget figures (bf:BF) to pairs (cf:CF) of which the first value is the cost (c:C) of the figure and the second is a sub-budget. A sub-budget is a budget as well. A sub-budget may be empty which means that the figure is not broken down. Each figure in a budget (including sub-budgets) uniquely identifies a subject of expenses concerning work, material, man-hour costs, etc. That is, it designates the maximum amount of money allowed or estimated to be spend on certain works. We assume that the same figures may exist in different budgets so budgets can be compared. Costs are modelled as non-negative reals.

From a budget, we can observe the list (obs_BFl_B) as well as the set (obs_BFs_B) of budget figures. Furthermore, we can observe the cost and sub-budget of a given figure (obs_CF_B), we can calculate the total cost of a budget (totalcost), and we assume that we can scale the costs of a budget (scale).

A budget is well-formed (wf_B) if and only if each cost is equal to the sum of costs in the corresponding sub-budget; if such one exists. Furthermore, budget figures must be unique.

We define an ordering on budgets after the following intuition. If a budget ($b_2$:B) only has a subset of figure compared to another budget ($b_1$:B), we consider it a specialization of the other budget; written $b_2 \leq b_1$. If a budget has figures with lower costs compared to another budget with the same figures, the former budget is a specialization of the latter. Furthermore, if a budget has a figure which is broken down and a similar budget does not break down this figure, the former budget is considered a specialization of the latter. Breaking down a budget figure means that the figure having a cost aimed at a certain range of applications, is restricted to a set of sub-figures having costs (in total) aimed at a more narrow range of applications. Thereby, specialization of budgets means narrowing the budget towards more specific applications. Generalization is considered the opposite of specialization.

We define two operations *meet* and *join* for combining budgets. *meet* takes two budgets and gives the combination which is a specialization of both argument budgets. *join* takes two budgets and gives the combination which is a generalization of both argument budgets. We shall not be concerned with whether the two operations satisfy lattice criteria. In the definitions of the operations, we need to consider that *meet* may take budgets without common figures. The result is, however, not the empty map as we need the empty map to represent the most general budget as well as sub-budgets for figures not broken down. Therefore, we make a distinction between the most specialized budget ($\perp_B$:B) and the most generalized budget ($\top_B$:B). Only the latter is modelled as the empty map. The *meet* operation is special in the sense that when combining two budgets with this operation, a figure in the one budget may put restrictions on the same figure in the other budget. In the resulting budget we handle this by possibly scaling the sub-figures proportionally such that the resulting budget is the most general specialization of both argument budgets. The operation *join* is included for completeness on and is not used further in this paper.

## 4.2   Formalization

**type**
    $B' = BF \xrightarrow{\quad} CF$,
    BF,
    CF :: cost:C  subbudget:$B'$,
    $C = \{|c:\textbf{Real} \cdot c \geq 0.0|\}$,

B = {|b:B' • wf_B(b)|}

**value**
　[instanses]
　$\top_B$ : B = [ ],
　$\bot_B$ : B,

　[observer functions]
　obs_BFl_B: B → BF*,
　obs_BFs_B: B → BF-**set**,
　obs_CF_B: B × BF $\overset{\sim}{\rightarrow}$ CF
　　**post** obs_CF_B(b,bf) **as** cf
　　**pre** bf ∈ obs_BFs_B(b),

　totalcost: B $\overset{\sim}{\rightarrow}$ C
　totalcost(b) ≡
　　**if** b = $\top_B$ **then** 0.0
　　**else let** bf:BF • bf ∈ **dom** b **in**
　　　　　cost(b(bf)) + totalcost(b \ {bf})
　　　　**end**
　　**end**
　**pre** b ≠ $\bot_B$,

　[misc]
　scale: B × **Real** → B
　scale(b,r) ≡
　　[ bf ↦ mk_CF(c,bs) | bf:BF, c:C, bs:B •
　　　bf ∈ **dom** b ∧
　　　c = r∗cost(b(bf)) ∧
　　　bs = scale(subbudget(b(bf)),r) ],

　min: C × C → C
　min($c_1$,$c_2$) ≡ **if** $c_1$ ≤ $c_2$ **then** $c_1$ **else** $c_2$ **end**,

　max: C × C → C
　max($c_1$,$c_2$) ≡ **if** $c_1$ ≥ $c_2$ **then** $c_1$ **else** $c_2$ **end**,

　[predicates]
　unique_BF: B → **Bool**
　unique_BF(b) ≡
　　**len** obs_BFl_B(b) = **card** obs_BFs_B(b),

　is_superior_BF: BF × BF × B → **Bool**,
　is_subordinary_BF: BF × BF × B → **Bool**,

is_sumfigure: BF × B → **Bool**
is_sumfigure(bf,b) ≡
   (∃ bf′:BF •
      bf′ ∈ obs_BFs_B(b) ∧ is_superior_BF(bf,bf′,b)),

wf_B: B → **Bool**
wf_B(b) ≡
   unique_BF(b) ∧ checksubcost(b) ∧
   (∀ bf:BF • bf ∈ **dom** b ⇒ wf_B(b)),

checksubcost: B → **Bool**
checksubcost(b) ≡
   b ≠ ⊥$_B$ ∧
   (∀ bf:BF • bf ∈ **dom** b ⇒
     cost(b(bf)) = totalcost(subbudget(b(bf)))),

≤: B × B → **Bool**
$b_1$ ≤ $b_2$ ≡
   $b_2$ = ⊤$_B$ ∨
   $b_1$ = ⊥$_B$ ∨
   (
     $b_1$ ≠ ⊤$_B$ ∧ **dom**($b_1$) ⊆ **dom**($b_2$) ∧
     (∀ bf:BF • bf ∈ **dom**($b_1$) ⇒
       cost($b_1$(bf)) ≤ cost($b_2$(bf)) ∧
       subbudget($b_1$(bf)) ≤ subbudget($b_2$(bf)))
   ),

meet: B × B → B
meet($b_1$,$b_2$) ≡
   **if** $b_1$ = ⊤$_B$ **then**
     $b_2$
   **elsif** $b_2$ = ⊤$_B$ **then**
     $b_1$
   **elsif dom** $b_1$ ∩ **dom** $b_2$ = {} **then**
     ⊥$_B$
   **else**
     [ bf ↦ mk_CF(c,bs)| bf:BF, c:C, bs:B •
       (bf ∈ **dom** $b_1$ ∧ bf ∈ **dom** $b_2$ ∧
       (subbudget($b_1$(bf)) = ⊤$_B$ ∧ subbudget($b_2$(bf)) = ⊤$_B$ ⇒
         bs = ⊤$_B$ ∧
         c = min(cost($b_1$(bf)), cost($b_2$(bf)))) ∧

       (subbudget($b_1$(bf)) = ⊤$_B$ ∧ subbudget($b_2$(bf)) ≠ ⊤$_B$ ∧
        cost($b_1$(bf)) ≤ cost($b_2$(bf)) ⇒
         bs = scale(subbudget($b_2$(bf)), cost($b_1$(bf))/cost($b_2$(bf))) ∧

$$c = \text{totalcost}(\text{bs})) \wedge$$

$$(\text{subbudget}(b_1(\text{bf})) = \top_B \wedge \text{subbudget}(b_2(\text{bf})) \neq \top_B \wedge$$
$$\text{cost}(b_1(\text{bf})) > \text{cost}(b_2(\text{bf})) \Rightarrow$$
$$\quad \text{bs} = \text{subbudget}(b_2(\text{bf})) \wedge$$
$$\quad c = \text{cost}(b_2(\text{bf}))) \wedge$$

$$(\text{subbudget}(b_1(\text{bf})) \neq \top_B \wedge \text{subbudget}(b_2(\text{bf})) = \top_B \wedge$$
$$\text{cost}(b_1(\text{bf})) \leq \text{cost}(b_2(\text{bf})) \Rightarrow$$
$$\quad \text{bs} = \text{subbudget}(b_1(\text{bf})) \wedge$$
$$\quad c = \text{cost}(b_1(\text{bf}))) \wedge$$

$$(\text{subbudget}(b_1(\text{bf})) \neq \top_B \wedge \text{subbudget}(b_2(\text{bf})) = \top_B \wedge$$
$$\text{cost}(b_1(\text{bf})) > \text{cost}(b_2(\text{bf})) \Rightarrow$$
$$\quad \text{bs} = \text{scale}(\text{subbudget}(b_2(\text{bf})), \text{cost}(b_2(\text{bf}))/\text{cost}(b_1(\text{bf}))) \wedge$$
$$\quad c = \text{totalcost}(\text{bs})) \wedge$$

$$(\text{subbudget}(b_1(\text{bf})) \neq \top_B \wedge \text{subbudget}(b_2(\text{bf})) \neq \top_B \wedge$$
$$\quad \text{bs} = \text{meet}(\text{subbudget}(b_1(\text{bf})), \text{subbudget}(b_2(\text{bf}))) \wedge$$
$$\quad c = \text{totalcost}(\text{bs})))\,]$$

**end,**

join: $B \times B \to B$
$\text{join}(b_1, b_2) \equiv$
    **if** $b_1 = \top_B \vee b_2 = \top_B$ **then**
      $\top_B$
    **else**
      $[\, \text{bf} \mapsto \text{mk\_CF}(c, \text{bs})\mid \text{bf:BF, c:C, bs:B} \bullet$
        $(\text{bf} \in \text{\textbf{dom} } b_1 \wedge \text{bf} \in \text{\textbf{dom} } b_2 \Rightarrow$
          $\text{bs} = \text{join}(\text{subbudget}(b_1(\text{bf})), \text{subbudget}(b_2(\text{bf}))) \wedge$
          $c = \text{totalcost}(\text{subbudget}(b_1(\text{bf}))),$
            $+ \text{totalcost}(\text{subbudget}(b_2(\text{bf})))) \wedge$

        $(\text{bf} \in \text{\textbf{dom} } b_1 \wedge \text{bf} \notin \text{\textbf{dom} } b_2 \Rightarrow$
          $\text{bs} = \text{subbudget}(b_1(\text{bf})) \wedge$
          $c = \text{cost}(b_1(\text{bf}))) \wedge$

        $(\text{bf} \notin \text{\textbf{dom} } b_1 \wedge \text{bf} \in \text{\textbf{dom} } b_2 \Rightarrow$
          $\text{bs} = \text{subbudget}(b_2(\text{bf})) \wedge$
          $c = \text{cost}(b_2(\text{bf})))\,]$
  **end**

Let $bf_{ij..k}$ range over values of type BF, and let $c_{ij..k}$ range over values of type C. Budgets then have a sub-structure of the following general form (here in one of many schematic unfoldings):

$$
\begin{bmatrix}
bf_1 \mapsto & & (c_1, \top_B) \\
\vdots & & \\
& & \begin{pmatrix} bf_{m1} \mapsto & (c_{m1}, \top_B) \\ & \ddots & \\ bf_m \mapsto & c_m, & bf_{mn..1} \mapsto (c_{mn..1}, \top_B) \\ & & \vdots \\ & & bf_{mn..r} \mapsto (c_{mn..r}, \top_B) \end{pmatrix}
\end{bmatrix}
$$

An example is the following:

*Example 1.* Consider an overall budget for a software project involving development. Sub-figures are displayed indented according to their general figures; thereby, indicating the hierarchical structure of the budget break down.

| | |
|---|---|
| **Pre-investigation** | **213000** |
| Use cases | 120000 |
| Domain analysis | 35000 |
| Requirements acquisition | 58000 |
| **Design** | **160000** |
| Server enhancements | 30000 |
| GUI | 65000 |
| Web access | 45000 |
| Integration | 20000 |
| **Programming** | **920000** |
| Server enhancements | 230000 |
| GUI | 400000 |
| Web access | 180000 |
| Web services | 50000 |
| Framework | 60000 |
| **Finalizing** | **910000** |
| **Verification** | **230000** |
| Server enhancements | 70000 |
| GUI | 50000 |
| Web & Framework | 110000 |
| **Testing** | **680000** |
| Usability | 340000 |
| Automatic testing | 140000 |
| Internal system testing | 200000 |

◇

Figure 1 displays a few examples of meet and join of budgets. In the diamond structures, the upper node is the *join* of the two nodes in the middle, and the bottom node is the *meet* of these two nodes. In the figure, capital letters denote top-level budget figures and small letters denote budget figures on the level below that.

# 5  Operations, Resources, and Object Aspects

Operations, resources and object aspects are domain concepts concerning the execution of projects. Models of these concepts are prerequisite for modelling the concept of project plans and defining the *characteristics connection* between budgets and project plans.

## 5.1  Intrinsics

The intrinsics of work is a pair of two values. The former value is the type of operation to be performed (on:On). The latter value is the context in which it is applied. When executing a construction work like painting a wall, the painting is a type of operation and the wall is the context. Several works may concern the same context and in various ways. Hence, it is tempting to model work as a function from input resources (e.g. including the wall to paint) to output products (e.g. including the painted wall). However, this approach would obstruct some basic metaphysical/mereological understandings that we shall assume.

One obstruction is as follows. The same wall may be the subject to different works. Each of these works should then take the wall as an input resource and produce a modified version of it. This approach indicates that we can make a distinction between the products at each stage of development — in the extreme, for every single brush stroke that is or may be performed. However, this requires as many resource types as there may be stages for products. Ontologically we then commit to as many concepts as there are objects of these concepts. This is violates the metaphysical principle of *one-over-many* claiming that concepts cover classes of objects. The problem in this ontological commitment is in [7] called *the problem of flux*. This philosophical problem has obstructed many approaches to apply a part–whole theory explicitly in practice [8].

Another obstruction is as follows. The same object may be involved in different works, but in different ways. In work descriptions we may have references to different parts of the object like the *inner* and *outer* side of a wall. If we want to model e.g. physical resources and their compositions into products explicitly, we run into the problem of being able to distinguish which parts that physically overlap and which that do not as this depends on the current context. E.g., the hinges of a door may be part of the door in one context, and of the frame in another as we usually can take off the door. This will provide infinite many part-whole combinations if explicitly expressed.

What prominent extensional mereological theories aim at covering is, however, more far reaching than what is often needed in order for sentences indicating part-whole information to make sense. For this reason, we introduced the notion of *object aspects* in [7]. The definition is as follows[5]:

---

[5] We only state this definition for completeness. Understanding the philosophical terms used is not necessary for a comprehension of this paper.

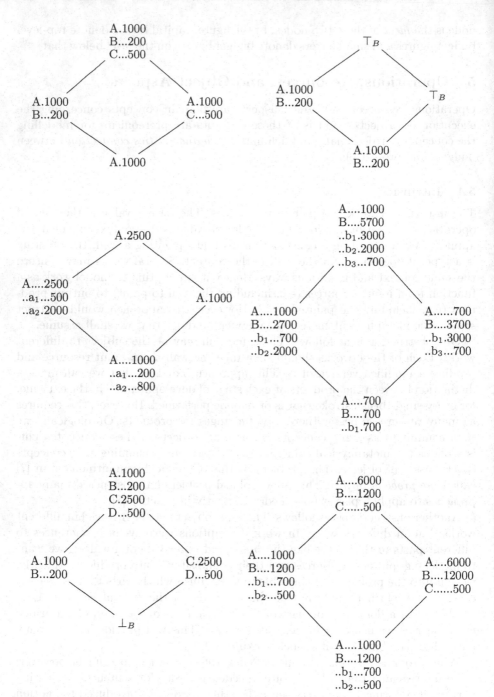

**Fig. 1.** Meet and join of budgets

**Definition 8 (Object Aspect).** *By an* object aspect *(x:X), we understand a proper part of an object existing in a possible world causally reachable from the actual world*[6].

With object aspects we abstract from the actual elaboration of artefacts; elaborations which change the artefacts physically but not change the identity of the artefacts. In the area of building construction, object aspects are the various parts of the building to be build and they are referred to in construction specifications, budgets, project plans, and other documents. In the area of the service and consulting sector, object aspects are the services to be provided and these are likewise referred to in specifications, budgets, project plans, and other documents.

Resource types (rn:Rn) denote the kinds of resources that are consumed by operations in a construction works. In the area of building construction, resources are building components like pre-cast concrete walls, materials like sand, etc. They are also machines and personnel. In the area of the service and consulting sector, resources are usually personnel, but can also be machines. Resources are counted in quantities (q:Q) which may be considered discrete or continuous. Resources constitute the entire input to works and are thus the subject for expense calculation and estimation.

A mapping from resource types to natural numbers defines the quantities of resources for each resource type. We define the operations *meet* and *join* for combining such mappings. The operation *meet* gives the map where all resource type are in both argument maps, and the quantities are the smallest from the argument maps. The operation *join* gives the map where each resource type is in either argument map, and the quantities for common resource types is the sum.

We shall say that a map (rm:(Rn $\overrightarrow{m}$ **Nat**)) is a sub-map of another map if and only if all resource types of the former map is present in the other map and quantities are either equal of less than in the other map.

We assume that resources consumed by operations concerning one object aspect are distinct from those consumed by operations concerning other object aspects. That is, the cost of reusing a tool is distributed on the works in which it is used. The types and quantities of resources may be the same but the physical resources are not[7].

## 5.2 Formalization

**type**
    On,
    X,
    Rn,
    Q = {|q:**Real** • q > 0.0|}

---

[6] Note, that this definition does not commit ontologically to a concept for every object aspect there may be.

[7] Note, that we abstract from the physical resources in this paper.

**value**

    meet: $(Rn \xrightarrow{m} Q) \times (Rn \xrightarrow{m} Q) \to (Rn \xrightarrow{m} Q)$

    $meet(rm,rm') \equiv$

      $[\, rn \mapsto q | rn{:}Rn, q{:}Q \bullet$

        $rn \in \mathbf{dom}\ rm \wedge rn \in \mathbf{dom}\ rm' \wedge$

        $q = min(rm(rn), rm'(rn))\,]$,

    meets: $(Rn \xrightarrow{m} Q)\text{-set} \to (Rn \xrightarrow{m} Q)$

    $meets(rms) \equiv$

      **if** $rms = \{\}$ **then** $[\,]$

      **else**

        **let** $rm{:}(Rn \xrightarrow{m} Q) \bullet rm \in rms$ **in**

          $meet(rm, meets(rms \setminus \{rm\}))$

        **end**

      **end**,

    min: $Q \times Q \to Q$

    $min(q_1,q_2) \equiv$ **if** $q_1 \leq q_2$ **then** $q_1$ **else** $q_2$ **end**,

    join: $(Rn \xrightarrow{m} Q) \times (Rn \xrightarrow{m} Q) \to (Rn \xrightarrow{m} Q)$

    $join(rm,rm') \equiv$

      $[\, rn \mapsto q | rn{:}Rn, q{:}Q \bullet$

        $(rn \in \mathbf{dom}\ rm \wedge rn \in \mathbf{dom}\ rm' \wedge q = rm(rn) + rm'(rn)) \vee$

        $(rn \in \mathbf{dom}\ rm \wedge rn \notin \mathbf{dom}\ rm' \wedge q = rm(rn)) \vee$

        $(rn \notin \mathbf{dom}\ rm \wedge rn \in \mathbf{dom}\ rm' \wedge q = rm'(rn))\,]$,

    joins: $(Rn \xrightarrow{m} Q)\text{-set} \to (Rn \xrightarrow{m} Q)$

    $joins(rms) \equiv$

      **if** $rms = \{\}$ **then** $[\,]$

      **else**

        **let** $rm{:}(Rn \xrightarrow{m} Q) \bullet rm \in rms$ **in**

          $join(rm, joins(rms \setminus \{rm\}))$

        **end**

      **end**,

    $\leq$: $(Rn \xrightarrow{m} Q) \times (Rn \xrightarrow{m} Q) \to \mathbf{Bool}$

    $rm_1 \leq rm_2 \equiv$

      $\mathbf{dom}(rm_1) \subseteq \mathbf{dom}(rm_2) \wedge$

      $(\forall\ rn{:}Rn \bullet rn \in \mathbf{dom}(rm_1) \Rightarrow rm_1(rn) \leq rm_2(rn))$

## 6   Project Plans

A project plan is a planning instrument for structuring a collection of works to be done and for stating the dependencies between and criteria of these works.

## 6.1   Intrinsics

The intrinsics of a project plan is that it is a directed acyclic graph (a $DAG$) of works to be done. The ordering of the DAG specifies that some works can be done in parallel, whereas other works need to be done in sequence due to certain dependencies. Such work dependencies may lie deeply in the nature of the works and may not be possible to formalize explicitly. Certainly, project planning can be much more than this. However, in this paper, we shall abstract from notions like time, deadlines, milestones, follow-up specifications and other administrative aspects. Such notions we consider additional and not intrinsic as we certainly can have project plans without them.

We model a project plan (pp:PP) as a map from nodes (g:$\Gamma$) to sets of nodes. Nodes correspond to works, and the edges define a partial ordering of works. The execution order follows the direction of the graph.

From a node in a project plan, we can observe the work to be performed; i.e. the operation type (obs_On_$\Gamma$) and the object aspects (obs_Xs_$\Gamma$). We can also observe the kinds of resources to be used (obs_Rn_$\Gamma$). Here, we need two definitions.

**Definition 9 (Resource Usage).** *By a resource usage (re:Rn $\xrightarrow{m}$ Q), we understand the resources which are consumed by an operation.*

**Definition 10 (Relevant Resource Usage).** *By a relevant resource usage, we understand a resource usage which concerns a given object aspect.*

From a node in a project plan, we can observe the resource usage of the work to be done (obs_Rm_$\Gamma$). Also, from a node and an object aspect of a project plan, we can observe the relevant resource usage concerning the object aspect (obs_rel_res). The relevant resource usage for a node in a project plan is given by adding together (i.e. applying *join*; see Sect. 5.2) pair-wise on the resource usage for each work concerning each object aspect involved in the operation.

A project plan is well-formed if and only if it satisfies the criteria of being a directed, acyclic graph.

We define a partial ordering of project plans based on the idea that a project plan is a sub-plan of another project plan if and only if its graph is a sub-graph of the other project plan. Furthermore, for nodes existing in both graphs, the resource usage of the sub-graph must be a sub-map (see Sect. 5.1). Thus, specialization of project plans is based on the principle that restricting to a sub-graph implies narrowing the scope of the total work. That is, the products or services being the results of executing the project plan, are limited.

As for budgets, we assume that the same nodes may exist in different project plans so project plans can be compared.

We define two operations *meet* and *join* for combining project plans. *meet* takes two project plans and gives the combination which is a specialization of both argument project plans. *meet* gives the project plan for which each node is in both argument project plans. For each such node, the set of object aspects is the intersection set and the resource usage maps the common resource types to the smallest quantity. *join* gives the project plan for which each node is in either argument project plans. For each such node, the set of object aspects is the union set and the resource usage maps resource types present in either nodes to the largest quantity. *join* is included for completeness only and is not used further in this paper. Due to the abstraction of using observer functions, the two operations are defined implicitly.

## 6.2    Formalization

**type**
$$PP' = \Gamma \underset{m}{\rightarrow} \Gamma\text{-set},$$
$$PP = \{|pp:PP' \bullet wf\_PP(pp)|\}$$
$$\Gamma,$$

**value**
  obs_On_$\Gamma$: $\Gamma \times$ PP $\overset{\sim}{\rightarrow}$ On
    **post** obs_On_$\Gamma$(g,pp) **as** on
    **pre** g $\in$ **dom** pp,
  obs_Xs_$\Gamma$: $\Gamma \times$ PP $\rightarrow$ X-set,
  obs_Rn_$\Gamma$: $\Gamma \times$ PP $\rightarrow$ Rn-set,
  obs_Rm_$\Gamma$: $\Gamma \times$ PP $\rightarrow$ (Rn $\underset{m}{\rightarrow}$ Q),
  obs_rel_res: $\Gamma \times$ X $\times$ PP $\rightarrow$ (Rn $\underset{m}{\rightarrow}$ Q)

**axiom** $\forall$ g:$\Gamma$, pp:PP $\bullet$
  obs_Rn_$\Gamma$(g,pp) $\equiv$ **dom** obs_Rm_$\Gamma$(g,pp),

  obs_Rm_$\Gamma$(g,pp) $\equiv$
    meets({rm|rm:(Rn $\underset{m}{\rightarrow}$ Q) $\bullet$
        ($\exists$ x:X $\bullet$ x $\in$ obs_Xs_$\Gamma$(g,pp) $\Rightarrow$ rm=obs_rel_res(g,x,pp))})

**value**
  wf_PP: PP $\rightarrow$ **Bool**
  wf_PP(pp) $\equiv$
    ($\forall$ gs:$\Gamma$-set $\bullet$ gs $\in$ **rng** pp $\Rightarrow$ gs $\subseteq$ **dom** pp) $\wedge$
    ($\forall$ g:$\Gamma$ $\bullet$ g $\in$ **dom** pp $\Rightarrow$
      g $\notin$ {g_succ|g_succ:$\Gamma$ $\bullet$ is_before(g,g_succ)(pp)}),

  is_before: $\Gamma \times \Gamma \rightarrow$ PP $\rightarrow$ **Bool**
  is_before(g,g')(pp) $\equiv$
    g' $\in$ pp(g) $\vee$
    ($\exists$ g'':$\Gamma$ $\bullet$ g'' $\in$ pp(g) $\wedge$ is_before(g'',g')(pp)),

  meet: PP $\times$ PP $\rightarrow$ PP
  meet(pp$_1$, pp$_2$) **as** pp
    **post** pp = [g$\mapsto$gs|g:$\Gamma$, gs:$\Gamma$-set $\bullet$
              g $\in$ **dom** pp$_1$ $\wedge$ g $\in$ **dom** pp$_2$ $\wedge$

$$\text{obs\_Rm\_}\Gamma(g,pp) = \text{meet}(\text{obs\_Rm\_}\Gamma(g,pp_1),$$
$$\text{obs\_Rm\_}\Gamma(g,pp_2))\,],$$

join: $\text{PP} \times \text{PP} \to \text{PP}$
join($pp_1$, $pp_2$) **as** pp
   **post** $(pp = [\,g{\mapsto}gs|g{:}\Gamma, \ gs{:}\Gamma\text{-set} \ \bullet$
                $(g \in \textbf{dom} \ pp_1 \wedge g \notin \textbf{dom} \ pp_2)\,]$
      $\wedge \ \text{obs\_Rm\_}\Gamma(g,pp) = \text{obs\_Rm\_}\Gamma(g,pp_1)) \ \vee$
      $(pp = [\,g{\mapsto}gs|g{:}\Gamma, \ gs{:}\Gamma\text{-set} \ \bullet$
                $(g \notin \textbf{dom} \ pp_1 \wedge g \in \textbf{dom} \ pp_2)\,]$
      $\wedge \ \text{obs\_Rm\_}\Gamma(g,pp) = \text{obs\_Rm\_}\Gamma(g,pp_2)) \ \vee$
      $(pp = [\,g{\mapsto}gs|g{:}\Gamma, \ gs{:}\Gamma\text{-set} \ \bullet$
                $(g \in \textbf{dom} \ pp_1 \wedge g \in \textbf{dom} \ pp_2)\,]$
      $\wedge \ \text{obs\_Rm\_}\Gamma(g,pp) = \text{meet}(\text{obs\_Rm\_}\Gamma(g,pp_1),$
                        $\text{obs\_Rm\_}\Gamma(g,pp_2))),$

$\leq$: $\text{PP} \times \text{PP} \to \textbf{Bool}$
$pp_1 \leq pp_2 \ \bullet$
   $\textbf{dom}(pp_1) \subseteq \textbf{dom}(pp_2) \ \wedge$
   $(\forall \ g{:}\Gamma \ \bullet \ g \in \textbf{dom} \ pp_1 \Rightarrow$
      $\text{obs\_Rm\_}\Gamma(g,pp_1) \leq \text{obs\_Rm\_}\Gamma(g,pp_2))$

*Example 2.* Figure 2 shows an overall project plan of a software development project involving enhancements of server technology, a graphical user-interface part (GUI) and web development.

In Ex. 2, the sub-plan concerned only with server enhancements, is a specialization of the whole project plan.

## 7 Mediating Ties

The mediating ties are the additional basic concepts necessary for establishing an *explicit concept relation* between two domain concepts. Here, we need to make a distinction between concepts that are necessary for establishing the *characteristics connection* and the concepts considered important because they are part of the context in which objects are understood and managed. E.g., it may be claimed that in the area of building construction, the notion of a building model is essential for talking about construction budgets and construction project plans. It is true that the notion is important as it defines the scope of the budgets and the project plans. Hence, it is prerequisite knowledge for creating budgets and project plans. However, when considering the concept relation between budgets and project plans isolated, it is irrelevant.

For relating the notions of budgets and project plans, we shall include the mediating ties of *work index* and *price index*. A work index states the relation between work to be performed and where the expenses for performing the work,

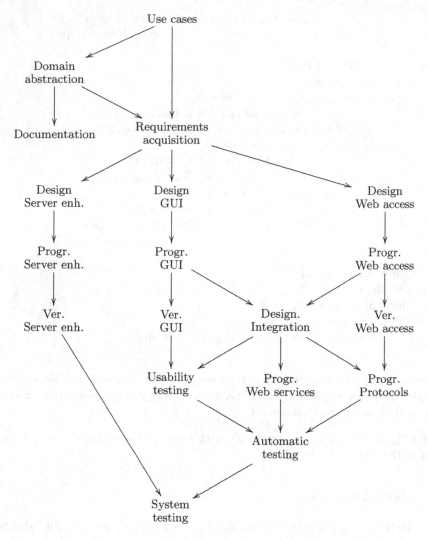

**Fig. 2.** A software project plan

are designated in the budget. A price index states the costs of resources. These two concepts appear to be necessary in order to establish a relation between budgets and project plans.

## 7.1   Intrinsics

The intrinsics of a work index (wrkidx:WrkIdx) is that it is a map from works (an operation type and an object aspect) to the budget figure designating the cost of this work. The intrinsics of a price index (prcidx:PrcIdx) is that it is a map from resource types to a unit cost function (ucm:UCF). A unit cost function maps quantities (q:Q) to their costs (c:C). We assume a distinction between budget figures that have sub-figures and budget figures that do not. A work index only considers budgets figures having no sub-figures.

We cannot, however, directly relate types of resources to budget figures as the cost of the same type of resources may belong to different budget figures; e.g. costs for painting different parts of a building. Neither can we relate operation types directly to budget figures as the same type of operation may consume resources belonging to different budget figures, when concerning different object aspects. E.g. molding may be performed several distinct places for a building, and the costs for these works may belong to different budget figures.

In the domain of project planning of construction projects, service-oriented projects, etc., work indices are background (sometimes almost tacit) knowledge. However, it often becomes explicit in contracts and other kinds of agreement or planning documents. If we cannot express the intrinsics of such information, we have no way of expressing how budgets and project plans relate. Work indices are necessary in order to know what resources cost. Thus, the notion of work index and price index are truly mediating ties required in the definition of a *characteristics connection* between budgets and project plans.

## 7.2   Formalization

**type**
    PrcIdx = Rn $\overrightarrow{m}$ UCF,
    UCF = Q $\overrightarrow{m}$ C,
    WrkIdx = (On × X) $\overrightarrow{m}$ BF

A work index (wrkidx:WrkIdx) can be verified according to a budget (b:B). All budget figures should be defined in the given work index. That is:

**value**
    consistent: B × WrkIdx → **Bool**
    consistent(b,wrkidx) ≡
        (∀ bf:BF • bf ∈ obs_BFs_B(b) ⇒
            is_sumfigures(bf,b) ∧ bf ∈ **rng** wrkidx)

Similar, we can verify a project plan according to a work index. For a project plan, all observable works (an operation type and an object aspect) must be present in the given work index. That is:

**value**
    consistent: PP × WrkIdx → **Bool**
    consistent(pp,wrkidx) ≡
        (∀ g:$\Gamma$, on:On, x:X •
            g ∈ **dom** pp ∧ on=obs_On_$\Gamma$(g) ∧ x ∈ obs_Xs_$\Gamma$(g) ⇒
            (on,x) ∈ **dom** wrkidx)

Price indices concern project plans. Consistency here means that the unit cost function of the price index, is defined for all resource types referred to in the project plan.

**value**
　consistent: PP × PrcIdx → **Bool**
　consistent(pp,prcidx) ≡
　　(∀ rn:Rn •
　　　(∃ g:$\Gamma$ • g ∈ **dom** pp ∧ rn ∈ obs_Rn_$\Gamma$(g,pp)) ⇒ rn ∈ **dom** prcidx)

We shall assume that the unit cost function is complete such that it (some way or another) covers the quantities necessary. Also, we shall assume that any quantity discount is handled by the price index itself.

# 8　The Characteristics Connection

In this section, we shall define the *characteristics connection*; i.e., a Galois connection between budgets and project plans.

## 8.1　Identifying Abstract Properties

As a first step, we need to define the abstract properties of budgets. For doing so, we need the following definition:

**Definition 11 (Relevant Nodes).** *A node in a project plan is relevant with respect to a given budget figure, if and only if there exists an object aspect of the node such that the work given by the operation of the node and the object aspect, is mapped to the budget figure in the work index.*

Formally, we write:

**value**
　rel_nds: PP × BF × WrkIdx → $\Gamma$-**set**
　rel_nds(pp,bf,wrkidx) ≡
　　{g|g:$\Gamma$ •
　　　g ∈ **dom** pp ∧
　　　　(∃ x:X • x ∈ obs_Xs_$\Gamma$(g) ∧ bf=wrkidx(obs_On_$\Gamma$(g),x))}

The mapping from *relevant nodes* to *relevant resource usage* (see Sect. 10) is defined as a variant of rel_nds:

**value**
　rel_map: PP × BF × WrkIdx → ($\Gamma$ $\overrightarrow{m}$ (Rn $\overrightarrow{m}$ Q))
　rel_map(pp,bf,wrkidx) ≡
　　[ g ↦ rm|g:$\Gamma$,rm:(Rn $\overrightarrow{m}$ Q) •
　　　g ∈ rel_nds(pp,bf,wrkidx) ∧
　　　　(∃ x:X • x ∈ obs_Xs_$\Gamma$(g) ∧ bf=wrkidx(obs_On_$\Gamma$(g),x) ∧
　　　　　rm=obs_rel_res(g,x)) ],

## 8.2  Galois Predicate

We now define a predicate stating that a given budget and a given project plan relate to each other. That is, the budget designates (at least) the necessary expenses for executing the project plan; and the project plan is executable within these restrictions. We call this predicate the *Galois predicate*, formally defined as:

**value**
$\quad \phi$: B × PP → (PrcIdx × WrkIdx) $\overset{\sim}{\to}$ **Bool**
$\quad \phi$(b,pp)(prcidx,wrkidx) ≡
$\qquad$ (∀ bf:BF • bf ∈ **dom** b ⇒
$\qquad\qquad$ sumcost(rel_map(pp,bf,wrkidx),prcidx) ≤ cost(b(bf)) ∧
$\qquad\qquad\quad \phi$(subbudget(b(bf)),pp)(prcidx,wrkidx))
$\quad$ **pre** consistent(b,wrkidx) ∧ consistent(pp,wrkidx) ∧ consistent(pp,prcidx)

$\quad$ sumcost: ($\Gamma$ $\overset{}{\underset{m}{\to}}$ (Rn $\overset{}{\underset{m}{\to}}$ **Nat**)) × PrcIdx $\overset{\sim}{\to}$ C
$\quad$ sumcost(gm,prcidx) ≡
$\qquad$ **if** gm = [ ] **then** 0.0
$\qquad$ **else**
$\qquad\quad$ **let** g:$\Gamma$ • g ∈ **dom** gm **in**
$\qquad\qquad$ sumcost'(gm(g),prcidx) + sumcost(gm \ {g},prcidx)
$\qquad\quad$ **end**
$\qquad$ **end**
$\quad$ **pre** (∀ rn ∈ **dom** rm ⇒ rn ∈ **dom** prcidx),

$\quad$ sumcost': (Rn $\overset{}{\underset{m}{\to}}$ **Nat**) × PrcIdx $\overset{\sim}{\to}$ C
$\quad$ sumcost'(rm,prcidx) ≡
$\qquad$ **if** rm = [ ] **then** 0.0
$\qquad$ **else**
$\qquad\quad$ **let** rn:Rn • rn ∈ **dom** rm **in**
$\qquad\qquad$ prcidx(rn)(rm(rn)) + sumcost'(rm \ {rn},prcidx)
$\qquad\quad$ **end**
$\qquad$ **end**
$\quad$ **pre** (∀ rn ∈ **dom** rm ⇒ rn ∈ **dom** prcidx)

The pre-condition is implied by the consistency predicates of $\phi$. Note, that the Galois predicate takes it origin in a quantification over budget figures. The reason is due to the order in which budgets and project plans are created. That is, usually it is the budget which restricts the project plans. Project plans are made in a *constructive* way having budget knowledge in mind.

By means of the predicate $\phi$, we can define the set of *valid* project plans, being the project plans which each can be executed within a given budget; assuming the mediating ties:

**value**
    valid_plans: B × PrcIdx × WrkIdx $\overset{\sim}{\to}$ PP-**infset**
    valid_plans(b,prcidx,wrkidx) ≡
        {pp|pp:PP • $\phi$(b,pp)(prcidx,wrkidx)}
    **pre** consistent(b,wrkidx) ∧ consistent(pp,wrkidx) ∧ consistent(pp,prcidx)

Similarly, we can define the set of *applicable* budgets begin the budgets which apply financially, given a project plan; assuming the mediating ties:

**value**
    appl_budgets: PP × PrcIdx × WrkIdx $\overset{\sim}{\to}$ B-**infset**
    appl_budgets(pp,prcidx,wrkidx) ≡
        {b|b:B • $\phi$(b,pp)(prcidx,wrkidx)}
    **pre** consistent(b,wrkidx) ∧ consistent(pp,wrkidx) ∧ consistent(pp,prcidx)

Generalising these two functions, gives a pair of dual functions $(\mathcal{F},\mathcal{G})$ between the power set of budgets and the power set of project plans; hence, between the two concepts.

**value**
    $\mathcal{F}$: B-**set** → (PrcIdx × WrkIdx) $\overset{\sim}{\to}$ PP-**infset**
    $\mathcal{F}$(bs)(prcidx,wrkidx) ≡
        {pp|pp:PP • (∀ b:B • b ∈ bs ⇒ $\phi$(b,pp)(prcidx,wrkidx))}
    **pre** consistent(b,wrkidx) ∧ consistent(pp,wrkidx) ∧ consistent(pp,prcidx),

    $\mathcal{G}$: PP-**set** → (PrcIdx × WrkIdx) $\overset{\sim}{\to}$ B-**infset**
    $\mathcal{G}$(pps)(prcidx,wrkidx) ≡
        {b|b:B • (∀ pp:PP • pp ∈ pps ⇒ $\phi$(b,pp)(prcidx,wrkidx))}
    **pre** consistent(b,wrkidx) ∧ consistent(pp,wrkidx) ∧ consistent(pp,prcidx)

**Theorem 2.** *The mapping pair $(\mathcal{F},\mathcal{G})$ is a Galois connection.*

*Proof. The proof is by inspection using Theorem 1. The functions $\mathcal{F}$ and $\mathcal{G}$ correspond to $\varphi_R$ and $\psi_R$, respectively. The binary relation $R \subseteq M \times N$ is the binary relation between budget values (b:B) and project plan values (pp:PP). The binary relation is defined by the predicate $\phi_{fp}$; assuming ∀-quantification over the mediating ties (prcidx:PrcIdx) and (wrkidx:WrkIdx). X and Y correspond to finite sets of values having type B and type PP, respectively; x and y are values in these sets.* □

The above shows that any predicate indicating a relation between objects of two concepts, may be utilized in a definition of a Galois connection. What gives substance to the Galois connection in this paper (and in the proposed method), is expressed by the formal models of the two concepts.

# 9   The Information Flow Connection

In this section, we shall define the *information flow connection* between the classifications of budgets and project plans. As we consider budgets to precede project plans in a flow of information, we require that changes done in a budget are likewise reflected in a succeeding project plan.

Consider a budget and a project plan which satisfy the criteria of the *characterization connection*. Changing the budget through specialization (see Sect. 4.2) should imply that the corresponding project plan needs to be specialized likewise. The reason is that when specializing the budget we are decreasing its financial scope, meaning that the set of project plans executable within its restrictions, cannot increase. Hence, the project plan of concern should be specialized in such a way that it is still executable within the specialized version of the budget. The implication is, however, not a *bi-implication* as specializing the project plan does not put restrictions on the preceding budget. However, if the project plan is generalized, it implies that the budget must be generalized likewise. Again, this is not required in the other direction.

The above states that order must be preserved when specializing and generalizing budgets or project plans. This is a property of the definitions of the partial orders and of the Galois predicate. We shall say that the connection is *order-preserving*. If the above implication is satisfied, we shall say that we have an *information flow connection* between the concepts. If this is not the case, it is worth investigating the model as we may then have inconsistency in the way specialization/generalization works together with the *characteristics connection*; hence, inconsistency in the understanding and the model of the concept relation.

**Theorem 3.** *The* information flow connection *between budgets and project plans with respect to the Galois predicate, is* order-preserving:

**axiom**

$\forall\ b_1,\ b_2\ :\ B,\ pp_1,\ pp_2\ :\ PP\ \bullet$
$\quad b_2 \leq b_1 \land \phi(b_1,\ pp_1) \land \phi(b_2,\ pp_2) \Rightarrow pp_2 \leq pp_1$

*Proof. We can specialize a budget in two ways: (i) by reducing costs, and (ii) by breaking down costs figures. We shall consider these cases separately.*
*Reducing costs:*
*Reducing a cost means subtracting this cost from the cost of the budget figure. From the definition of $\phi$, we have:*

sumcost(rel_map(pp,bf,wrkidx),prcidx) $\leq$ cost(b(bf)) $-$ c $\equiv$
sumcost(rel_map(pp,bf,wrkidx),prcidx) $+$ c $\leq$ cost(b(bf))

*Let* $rm_2 =$ sumcost(rel_map($pp_2$,bf,wrkidx),prcidx) $+$ c
*and let* $rm_1 =$ sumcost(rel_map($pp_1$,bf,wrkidx),prcidx). *As we cannot have negative costs, the only way of satisfying the above is for $pp_2$ to designate less resources than $pp_1$. That is, $pp_2$ must be a sub-graph of $pp_1$ and the individual*

*resource usage of nodes in $pp_2$ cannot be larger than the individual resource usage of corresponding nodes in $pp_1$. That is, $pp_2 \leq pp_1$.*
*Breaking down cost figure:*
*This means that we compare a sub-budget $b_{2x}$ in the specialized budget $b_2$ with a corresponding sub-budget which is $\top_B$ in the budget $b_1$. The cost of $\top_B$ is by definition the largest cost. This means that for each budget figure $bf_{2x}$ in $b_{2x}$, we have: $\mathrm{cost}(b_{2x}(bf_{2x})) \leq \top_B$. This corresponds to a cost reduction of each figure $bf_{2x}$. Hence, the axiom holds; given the result of the above case. The cases of generalization budgets, are dual to the above.* $\qquad\qquad\square$

## 10   Relating the Two Connections

Even though the *characteristics connection* is monotonously decreasing and the *information flow connection* is order-preserving, the two connections are intimately connected. We shall argue this by taking origin in the *characteristics connection* and show that this leads to the *information flow connection*.

Consider a set of budgets and a set of project plans. Assume that each project plan is executable within the restrictions of each budget in the set. Thereby, it is also executable within the restrictions of *meet* applied pair-wise on the budgets in the set. This can easily be seen as follows. For budgets having distinct budget figures satisfying all, is impossible. For budgets with overlapping budget figures, satisfying these budgets means that the project plan should comply with only the common budget figures; else it does not satisfy every budget. Hence, satisfying all the budgets in the set, corresponds to satisfying *meet* applied pair-wise on the budgets in the set. Budget *meet* is a specialization of both argument budgets; in the above example, a specialization of each budget in the set.

According to the *characteristics connection*, extending the set of budgets cannot extend the corresponding set of executable project plans. Hence, the specialization due to applying *meet*, cannot extend the corresponding set of executable project plans. That is, *meet* applied pair-wise on a set of budgets is only satisfied by a project plan which is a specialization of every project plan in the set. We can see specialization of budgets as combining budgets and apply *meet*. Hence, specializing a budget means specialization of a corresponding project plan. Thereby, we got from the *characteristics connection* to the *information flow connection*.

## 11   Conclusion

In this paper, we have proposed a modelling method for relating domain concepts intensionally. The method suggests that domain concepts (formally modelled) are related by two ordering connections. The former connection is called the *characteristics connection* and is a Galois connection between objects of one concept and objects of another concept. The connection adds intensional knowledge as it states how objects of one concept are part of the characteristics of objects of another concept. The latter connection is called the *information flow connection* and is an order-preserving connection between classifications of the objects of two concepts. The connection adds intensional knowledge as it describes what effect it has on objects of one kind to change objects of another. We have defined the steps of the method and expressed the axioms of the two connections.

In order to put the method to work, we have formally modelled the notions of budgets and project plans. In addition, we have modelled the necessary mediating ties which (as prescribed by the method) are the additional concepts that are necessary in order to establish a formal relation between the two concepts in question.

Furthermore, the two ordering connections have been defined for the models. The *characteristics connection* between budgets and project plans, has been defined such that project plans relate to budgets if and only if they are executable within the financial restrictions of the budgets; and budgets relate to project plans if and only if they (at least) designate the necessary expenses for executing the project plans. We have shown that the connection is a Galois connection. The *information flow connection* between budgets and project plans, has been defined such that specialization of budgets cannot imply generalization (and vice versa) of succeeding project plans if the *characteristics connection* is to be maintained. Thereby, we have ensured that the concept relation between budgets and project plans maintains the systematics of concretising information from budgeting to project planning.

The axiom of the *information flow connection* — utilizing the *characteristics connection* — shows that we are able to reason (to some extend) about the rationality of how the domain concepts have been modelled. Isolated, neither of the two connection incorporate domain knowledge but are mathematical axioms over domain models. This means that the predicate founding the Galois connection might define other criteria for objects to relate. Similar considerations may apply for the classification of objects. By putting the two connections together, however, we provide the kind of domain reason abilities that are often missed when following an informal modelling approach. Future work is to focus on strengthening the formal foundation on this area.

# References

1. Ganter, B., Wille, R.: Formal Concept Analysis. Springer, Heidelberg (1999)
2. Eir, A.: 3. Models of two civil engineering concepts and their Galois connection. In: Construction Informatics — issues in engineering, computer science and ontology. Ph.D. thesis. Informatics and Mathematical Modelling, Technical University of Denmark, 65–88 (2004)
3. Eir, A.: Relating civil engineering concepts intensionally by Galois connections. In: eWork and eBusiness in Architecture, Engineering, Construction. In: Proceedings of the ECPPM 2006, Swets & Zeitlinger Publishers, pp. 247–254 (2006)
4. The RAISE Language Group.: The RAISE Specification Language. Prentice-Hall, Englewood Cliffs (1992)
5. The RAISE Method Group.: The RAISE Development Method. Prentice-Hall, Englewood Cliffs (1995)

6. Bjøorner, D.: Software Engineering, Domains, Requirements and Software Design. Texts in Theoretical Computer Science, EATCS Series, vol. 3. Springer, Heidelberg (2006)
7. Eir, A.: 8. Object Aspects. In: Construction Informatics — issues in engineering, computer science and ontology. Ph.D. thesis. Informatics and Mathematical Modelling, Technical University of Denmark, 235–254 (2004)
8. Simons, P.: Parts: A Study in Ontology. Clarendon Press, Oxford (1987)

# Programmable Messaging for Electronic Government - Building a Foundation

Elsa Estevez and Tomasz Janowski

Center for Electronic Governance
United Nations University - International Institute for Software Technology
P.O. Box 3058, Macau
{elsa,tj}@iist.unu.edu
http://www.egov.iist.unu.edu

**Abstract.** Electronic Government offers citizens and businesses a single interface to all public services, implemented through cross-agency processes and applications. This paper presents a fragment of a software infrastructure that enables agencies to collaborate in the delivery of public services, responsible for automated, process-driven exchange of messages between applications. In addition to basic message exchange, the infrastructure supports high-level messaging through dynamically-enabled horizontal (process independent) and vertical (process dependent) extensions. In particular, the paper presents a fragment of a semantic model to formalize the process of specifying and implementing messaging extensions, and demonstrates a prototype implementation of this model to underpin a reliable delivery of government services.

**Keywords:** Electronic Government, Asynchronous Messaging, Messaging Middleware, Domain Specific Languages, Software Specification.

## 1 Introduction

Responding to public demands, many governments around the world are engaged in organizational transformation enabled by Electronic Government. Traditionally, the main objective underpinning such efforts has been to publish government information online and to make public services available through agency websites. However, with many initiatives restricting themselves to follow hierarchical government structures, it was realized that technology-enabled improvements which are focusing on individual agencies are of limited value [8]. As a result, the emphasis is currently shifting towards enabling collaboration and networking between agencies, focusing on the delivery of seamless services.

Seamless services allow citizens or businesses to specify a certain need towards their government, in terms of a life event or a business episode, and obtain a service to fulfill this need without knowing which agency or level of government should be contacted. Usually, several agencies at different levels of the government may be involved without a citizen being even aware of this. The delivery of such services is based on collaborations between organizations from various

C.B. Jones, Z. Liu, J. Woodcock (Eds.): Bjørner/Zhou Festschrift, LNCS 4700, pp. 217–236, 2007.
© Springer-Verlag Berlin Heidelberg 2007

levels and functional areas of government and between public and private sectors. However, this implementation faces various legal, budgetary, cultural and - the focus of this work - organizational and technical challenges. For instance, enabling collaborative relations between agencies at different level of the government, between public and private sectors, and between different administrations is a serious organizational challenge. The resulting technical challenges include [6]: providing one-stop access to public services, coordinating processes that deliver such services across agency boundaries, enforcing policies that govern how such services are delivered, integrating different agency systems that participate in various process steps, ensuring that such systems can interoperate both technically and semantically, and delivering services through multiple channels.

While existing Message-Oriented Middleware (MOM) [2] could provide partial solutions to many technical challenges, three issues make the application of MOMs to Electronic Government less than ideal: reliability, extensibility and genericity. First, in the absence of formal foundations that allow the underling messaging services to be rigorously developed, the reliability of electronic public services and the reputation of the providers of such services (governments) may be affected. Second, MOMs typically offer a fixed set of services, such as logging or validation of messages, while government applications face complex, evolving communication needs. Third, generic messaging do not address the problems peculiar to governments, such as accumulation of legacy systems, reliance on regulations and policies to drive operational behaviour, high rate of changes to such regulations and policies, and collaboration across agency boundaries.

The aim of this work is to build a foundation for programmable messaging, especially in the context of the delivery of seamless public services. A formal model is developed to show how messaging services can be described at different levels of abstraction, from specifications that capture observable effects of messaging services, through design of communication structures to enable such effects, to implementation of messaging behaviours along such structures. The underling operational model is based on asynchronous exchange of messages between registered members along dynamically created and subscribed communication channels. On top of this core messaging, various extensions can be specified and implemented, including extensions related to particular channels (horizontal) and extensions related to particular processes (vertical). Just like channel-based communication structures upon which they are build, the extensions can evolve over time. The concept of programmable messaging for Electronic Government was first introduced in [6] and the implementation was presented in [7].

The rest of the paper is organized as follows. Section 2 contains a brief introduction to Electronic Government. Section 3 presents an example of a typical Electronic Government Service - issuing business licenses - and describes the communication requirements raised by this service. Section 4 presents a formal foundation for the messaging infrastructure to fulfill such requirements, comprising models to express messaging behaviours at various levels of abstraction. Section 5 presents the application of the infrastructure to Electronic Government practice and justifies how the infrastructure can fulfill the requirements for the licensing service defined in Section 3. Section 6 describes the development and operations of a prototype software infrastructure that implements the models. Section 7 presents related work and explains the contribution of this work. The final Section 8 presents conclusions and draws some directions for future work.

## 2    Electronic Government

Electronic Government refers to the use of ICT, particularly the Internet, as a tool to achieve better government [8]. In particular, Electronic Government aims to: provide customer-focused, efficient and reliable public services delivered through a variety of traditional and electronic channels; engage citizens in two-ways interactions with their government; support internal government operations; and enable one-stop access to all public services.

Based on the extent of ICT support for the underlying government processes, Electronic Government enables the delivery of public services at different levels of automation. A model by UNPAN - United Nations Public Administration Network identifies the following five levels [18]:

1. *Emerging* - The entry level for online presence, it involves publishing static information on agency websites including information about public services.
2. *Enhanced* - Expanded on-line presence, with regular content updates, search services, and periodicals - publications, legislations and newsletters.
3. *Interactive* - Enabling two-way interaction - e-mail contacts with public officers, download and upload of forms, possibility to search databases, etc.
4. *Transactional* - Complete and secure transactions can be executed through the website in order to: renew passports, apply for licenses, pay taxes, etc. A user is able to complete the whole process, including payments electronically.
5. *Seamless* - Related services are offered across agency boundaries responding to the needs of citizens (life events) or businesses (business episodes).

The UNPAN and other service maturity models [8][23] all recognize seamless services as the highest level of service maturity. At this level, agencies share the data provided by customers and cooperate in delivering public services through the integration of operations across agency boundaries. For example, Section 3 presents a concrete business process for citizens to apply for business licenses, with several agencies collaborating in the delivery of this service.

## 3    Example - Electronic License Service

Local governments LG are responsible for issuing various types of business licenses: for selling goods, for establishing food and beverage activities, for advertising in public places, and others. LG can offer these licensing services by requesting government agencies to collaborate in the execution of the underlying business process: carry out inspections, provide technical opinions, and check conformance to the relevant regulations. For instance, here is a five-stage process to issue a license for establishing a food and beverage business, based on the service provided by Macao Government [12]:

1. *Submission* - This phase involves: submitting an application form and supporting documents by the applicant through the government portal, and forwarding the request to the licensing agency. The submission of supporting documents may involve several sessions. Supporting documents may include: location plans; technical plans for water, sewage and fire prevention; declaration of responsibility by project engineer; and the insurance policy.
2. *Completeness Assessment* - This phase comprises: checking completeness of the application form and supporting documents, and notifying the applicant about missing documents, if any.
3. *Evaluation* - This phase involves: requesting an opinion from the Labour Bureau LE about labour situation; requesting an opinion about infrastructure from the Public Works Bureau PW; requesting building inspection to check the state of fire prevention from the Fire Brigade FB; requesting an opinion about heritage preservation from the Cultural Bureau CA; and requesting an inspection to check sanitary conditions from the Health Bureau HB. Once the requests are sent, the process waits to receive all replies. The replies may include requests to coordinate inspections onsite with the applicant, particularly from FB and HB. LG follows up by: coordinating inspection dates and notifying FB and HB about the agreed dates. After both inspections are carried out, LG collects the remaining opinions from FB and HB.
4. *Decision-making* - This phase involves deciding by the agency authority about issuing or rejecting the application based on the opinions obtained.
5. *Follow-up* - The final phase includes notifying the applicant about the decision and upon positive outcome: issuing the license; informing the applicant about collection of the license; and providing the license to the applicant.

Figure 1 depicts the overall process, as described above. The process also illustrates how the applicant can track the progress of its application. Each time a tracking request is issued, LG notifies the applicant about the current status.

## 4  Programmable Messaging - Foundations

This section presents a fragment of a foundation for the software infrastructure enabling programmable messaging for Electronic Government. The foundation comprises models at various levels of abstraction, from state and state-changing operations, through messages, members and channels, to message exchange carried out by members over channels.

The rest of the section is organized as follows. Section 4.1 presents a model to underpin subsequent behavioural models, leading to the definition of a state. Section 4.2 presents a set of generic state-changing operations, including expressions to represent such operations syntactically, and their semantics. Section 4.3 defines the structure of messages using the state model in Section 4.1, while Sections 4.4 and 4.5 define member- and channel-related operations using the syntax of state-changing operations in Section 4.2. The final Section 4.6 defines the operations for members to exchange messages along channels. The foundation is still under development, and the current section represents work in progress.

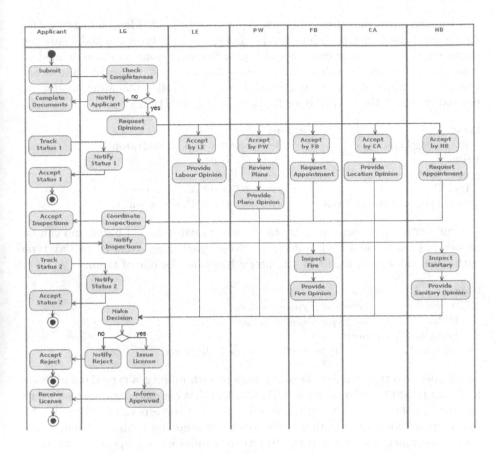

**Fig. 1.** Licensing food and beverage establishments - business process

## 4.1   State

The data model described here is the basis for expressing messaging behaviours in subsequent sections. Essentially, the model defines the notion of a state - a set of variables belonging to different members, and behavior models capture state changes caused by sending and receipt of messages. Variables and messages have the same internal structure - a set of parts of different categories, and a linear ordering on the parts of the same category. A type hierarchy is also defined to determine which parts are optional and which are mandatory inside a variable or a message, with subtyping relation defined between pairs of types. The top-level type requires all structures to contain three mandatory parts: an identifier to uniquely represent a structure, a type to determine the required composition of a structure, and a member to represent the owner of a variable or the sender of a message. Every part has a category and a value, with pairs of symmetric functions provided for each category to construct and deconstruct part values.

Formally, we define three abstract types to represent: identifiers Id, values Value and types Type, with initial value init, top-level type top and a subtype relation sub defined between pairs of types. Several axioms are also defined to constrain these values: sub is irreflexive, symmetric and transitive, and every type is a subtype of top, except itself. Here is the self-explanatory model expressed in RSL - the RAISE Specification Language [21][22]:

**type**
  Id, Value, Type
**value**
  init: Value,
  top: Type,
  sub: Type × Type → **Bool**

**axiom**
  ($\forall$ t: Type • t $\neq$ top $\Rightarrow$ sub(t, top)),
  ($\forall$ t, t', t'': Type •
    $\sim$sub(t, t) $\wedge$
    sub(t, t') $\wedge$ sub(t', t) $\Rightarrow$ t = t' $\wedge$
    sub(t, t') $\wedge$ sub(t', t'') $\Rightarrow$ sub(t, t''))

Identifiers, types, messages, etc. can represent categories of parts, and can be encoded as values, and back from values to original types. Here is the Cat type with three values and a pair of symmetric functions for one of them:

**type**
  Cat ==
    idCat |
    typeCat |
    mesCat | ...

**value**
  type2val: Type → Value,
  val2type: Value $\overset{\sim}{\to}$ Type
**axiom**
  ($\forall$ t: Type • val2type(type2val(t)) = t)

Lets define a type NatI of natural numbers with infinity, a type Cats of maps from Cat to NatI, and a function $\leq$ (is smaller) that compares two maps if every category in the first is also in the second, and the corresponding values in the first map are not greater than in the second; inf is greater than any number. We also define functions must and may to return mandatory and optional categories for a given type, such as: n(0) is not in the range of may, inf is not in the range of must, must is smaller than may for any type, may is smaller for a subtype than for a supertype, and must is smaller for a supertype than for a subtype.

**type**
  NatI == inf | n(val: **Nat**),
  Cats = Cat $\overset{}{m}$ NatI
**value**
  must, may: Type → Cats
**axiom**
  ($\forall$ t: Type • must(t) $\leq$ may(t) $\wedge$
    n(0) $\notin$ **rng** may(t) $\wedge$ inf $\notin$ **rng** must(t)
  ),
  ($\forall$ t, t': Type • sub(t, t') $\Rightarrow$
    may(t) $\leq$ may(t') $\wedge$ must(t') $\leq$ must(t)
  )

**value**
  $\leq$: Cats × Cats → **Bool**
  cs1 $\leq$ cs2 $\equiv$
    **dom** cs1 $\subseteq$ **dom** cs2 $\wedge$
    ($\forall$ c: Cat • c $\in$ **dom** cs1 $\Rightarrow$
      **case** (cs1(c), cs2(c)) **of**
      (inf, _) $\to$ cs2(c) = inf,
      (_, inf) $\to$ **true**,
      (n(n1), n(n2)) $\to$ n1 $\leq$ n2
    **end**
  )

The top type permits all categories in its may map, no number restriction imposed, and requires two must categories: typeCat - the required type of a structure and idCat - the identifier. These are mandatory for all types.

**axiom**
 must(top) = [typeCat ↦ n(1), idCat ↦ n(1)],
 may(top) = [c ↦ inf | c: Cat • **true**]

**Part** is an abstract type with functions **cat** and **val** to return the category and the value of a part. **Parts** contains lists of parts of the same category.

| **type** | **type** |
|---|---|
| Part | Parts = {| ps: Part* • iswf(ps) |} |
| **value** | **value** |
| cat: Part → Cat, | iswf: Parts' → **Bool** |
| val: Part → Value | iswf(ps) ≡ |
| | (∀ p1, p2: Part • |
| | p1 ∈ **elems** ps ∧ p2 ∈ **elems** ps ⇒ cat(p1) = cat(p2)) |

A structure **Struct** is a map from the type **Cat** to **Parts**. A structure is well-formed if and only if every part in the list has the category equal to the domain element, contains a part of the category **typeCat** and is valid with respect to this type: contains all optional categories and the number of parts for every category is between the minimum and the maximum determimed by this type.

**type**
 Struct' = Cat ⇉ Parts,
 Struct = {| s: Struct' • iswf(s) |}
**value**
 iswf: Struct' → **Bool**
 iswf(s) ≡ typeCat ∈ **dom** s ∧ s(typeCat) ≠ ⟨⟩ ∧ isValid(s, sType(s)) ∧
  (∀ c: Cat, p: Part • c ∈ **dom** s ∧ p ∈ **elems** s(c) ⇒ cat(p) = c),
 sType: Struct' ⥲ Type
 sType(s) ≡ val2type(val(s(typeCat)(1)))
  **pre** typeCat ∈ **dom** s ∧ s(typeCat) ≠ ⟨⟩
 isValid: Struct × Type → **Bool**
 isValid(s, t) ≡ **dom** s = **dom** may(t) ∧
  (∀ c: Cat • c ∈ **dom** must(t) ⇒ **len** s(c) ≥ val(must(t)(c))) ∧
  (∀ c: Cat • c ∈ **dom** s ⇒ may(t)(c) = inf ∨ **len** s(c) ≤ val(may(t)(c)))

**Var** is a structure that complies with the type **vType**, a subtype of **top** with an additional **id**-category part to idenfity the owner of a variable. Finally, a state is a map from identifiers to variables such that every variable has the value of the first id-category part equal to the values of the domain element.

**type**
 Var = {| s: Struct • sub(sType(s), vType) |},
 State' = Id ⇉ Var,
 State = {| s: State' • iswf(s) |}
**value**
 vType: Type •
  must(vType) = must(top) † [idCat ↦ n(2)] ∧ may(vType) = may(top),
 iswf: State' → **Bool**
 iswf(s) ≡ (∀ id: Id • id ∈ **dom** s ⇒ val2id(val(s(id)(idCat)(1))) = id)

## 4.2  State Changes

The initial state has no variables:

**value**
  init: State = [ ]

A state is subsequently build and modified through a series of basic operations to declare, undeclare and modify variables, as well as operations obtained from them by sequencing, concurrency, choice, etc. The type **StateX** represents such state-changing expressions and the function **exec** checks if a pair of states - initial and final state - are a possible effect of executing a given expression.

**type**
  StateX ==
    decl(StructX) | undecl(Id) | change(Id, StructX) |
    seq(StateX, StateX) | con(StateX, StateX) | test(BoolX, StateX, StateX)
**value**
  exec: StateX × State × State $\xrightarrow{\sim}$ **Bool**
  exec(sx, s, s′) ≡
    **case** sx **of**
      decl(tx) → decl(eval(tx, s), s, s′),
      undecl(id) → undecl(id, s, s′),
      change(id,tx) → change(id, eval(tx, s), s, s′),
      seq(sx1, sx2) → (∃ s″: State • exec(sx1, s, s″) ∧ exec(sx2, s″, s′)),
      con(sx1, sx2) → exec(sx1, s, s′) ∧ exec(sx2, s, s′),
      test(px, sx1, sx2) → **if** eval(px, s) **then** exec(sx1, s, s′) **else** exec(sx2, s, s′) **end**
    **end pre** iswf(sx, s)

For instance, here is a function **decl** to declare a variable. Its pre-condition **canDecl** checks if a given structure is a variable and its identifier is new.

**value**
  decl: Struct × State × State $\xrightarrow{\sim}$ **Bool**
  decl(v, s, s′) ≡ s′ = s ∪ [ val2id(val(v(idCat)(1))) ↦ v ] **pre** eval(canDecl(v), s),
  canDecl: Struct → BoolX
  canDecl(v) ≡ and(hasType(v, vType), not(hasVar(v)))

**StateX** depends on external expressions like **StructX** or **BoolX**. Here is the definition of **StructX** with operations to get, make and modify structures by adding or deleting their parts (all parts with a given category and value).

**type**
  StructX ==
    get(Id) |
    make(Struct) |
    add(PartX, StructX) |
    del(Cat, ValueX, StructX)

**value**
  eval: StructX × State $\xrightarrow{\sim}$ Struct
  eval(sx, s) ≡
    **case** sx **of**
      get(id) → s(id),
      make(st) → make(st),
      add(px, sx) → add(eval(px, s), eval(sx, s), s),
      del(c, vx, sx) → del(c, eval(vx, s), eval(sx, s), s)
    **end pre** iswf(sx, s)

For example, here is a function to add a part to a structure, by appending it at the end of its category list. Like `canDecl`, `canAdd` is expressed through a generated boolean expression `BoolX`, evaluated on the current state.

**value**
  add: Part × Struct × State $\xrightarrow{\sim}$ Struct
  add(p, st, s) ≡ st † [ cat(p) ↦ st(cat(p)) ⌢ ⟨p⟩ ] **pre** eval(canAdd(p, st), s),
  canAdd: Part × Struct → BoolX
  canAdd(p, st) ≡ and(
    isMay(cat(p),make(st)),
    isless(parts(make(st),cat(p)), may(make(st),cat(p))))

Similarly, we define types for other expressions. `PartX` includes operators to: make a part from a category and a value expression, get a part from a structure given a category and a number expression, and change the part value for given value and part expressions. `ValueX` includes operators to: make values, get values from parts, and obtain values from types, identifiers or messages. `NatX` includes operators to: make numbers, get numbers from the state - number of variables, number of categories in a structure, number of parts with a given category and value, number of mandatory and permissible parts - add them, etc.

| **type** | **type** | **type** |
|---|---|---|
| PartX == | ValueX == | NatX == |
| make(Cat, ValueX) \| | make(Value) \| | make(NatI) \| vars \| |
| get(StructX, Cat, NatX) \| | get(PartX) \| | cats(StructX) \| |
| change(ValueX, PartX) | id2val(Id) \| | parts(StructX, Cat) \| |
|  | type2val(Type) \| | may(StructX, Cat) \| |
|  | mes2val(Mes) | must(StructX, Cat) \| |
|  |  | add(NatX, NatX) |

Finally, the `BoolX` type contains a set of operators to make and combine boolean values and to check: if a structure exists in the state; if a structure contains parts of a given category; if a structure has a given type; if a given part is contained in a structure; if the part contained in a structure has a given category or value; if a value expression equals a given value; if a number expression equals a given number; if one number expression is less than another; if one type is a subtype of another; etc. We also present the signatures of `eval` functions for `PartX`, `ValueX`, `NatX` and `BoolX` expressions.

| **type** | **value** |
|---|---|
| BoolX == | eval: PartX × State $\xrightarrow{\sim}$ Part, |
| tt \| not(BoolX) \| and(BoolX, BoolX) \| | eval: ValueX × State $\xrightarrow{\sim}$ Value, |
| or(BoolX, BoolX)\| hasParts(Cat, StructX) \| | eval: NatX × State $\xrightarrow{\sim}$ NatI, |
| hasVar(StructX) \| hasType(StructX, Type) \| | eval: BoolX × State $\xrightarrow{\sim}$ **Bool** |
| hasPart(PartX, StructX) \| hascVar(Id) \| |  |
| hasCat(PartX, Cat) \| hasVal(PartX, ValueX) \| |  |
| isMay(Cat, StructX) \| isMust(Cat, StructX) \| |  |
| equal(ValueX, Value) \| equal(NatX, NatI) \| |  |
| isless(NatX, NatX) \| issub(Type, Type) |  |

## 4.3 Messages

Just like a variable which is a structure valid with respect to the vType type, a message is a structure which is valid with respect to the mType type. mType requires all messages to contain at least one type-category part and at least three id-category parts: message identifier, sender identifier and variable identifier. The following type Mes represents all messages.

**type**
  Mes = {| s: Struct • sub(sType(s), mType) |}
**value**
  mType: Type • may(mType) = may(top) ∧
    must(mType) = must(top) † [idCat ↦ n(3)]

The third required id-category part in a message identifies a variable that contains the identities of all recipients of the message. These address variables must have the type iType which requires precisely one type-category part and at least two id-category parts: variable identifier, owner identifier and any number, including zero, of member identifiers (recipients). If this number is zero, only the owner (sender) will receive the message. In addition to iType, we also define the type bType that requires zero or more parts of the mesCat category. Variables of this type will hold lists of messages send and received by members.

**value**
  iType: Type • may(iType) = [typeCat ↦ n(1), idCat ↦ inf] ...
  bType: Type • may(bType) = [typeCat ↦ n(1), idCat ↦ n(2), mesCat ↦ inf] ...

## 4.4 Members

Members are simply identified as the values of the type Id. Every variable in the state must belong to exactly one member, identified through the value of the second mandatory id-category part. A distinguished member, responsible among others for registration of other members, is admin. admin owns the variable reg that contains identities of all registered members. reg has the type iType just like address variables. In addition, every member must have two bType-variables to contain lists of incoming and outgoing messages for this member. Functions inb and outb return the identifiers of these two message variables, uniquely defined for every member identifier.

**value**
  admin, reg: Id,
  reg: Var •
    val2id(val(reg(idCat)(1))) = reg ∧
    val2id(val(reg(idCat)(2))) = admin ∧
    sub(sType(reg), iType)

**value**
  inb, outb: Id → Id
**axiom**
  (∀ id: Id • inb(id) ≠ outb(id)) ∧
  (∀ id, id': Id • id ≠ id' ⇒
    inb(id) ≠ inb(id') ∧
    outb(id) ≠ outb(id')
  ) ...

Below we define two functions to register and unregister members. Both functions generate StateX expressions, with preconditions expressed at BoolX expressions, according to the definitions in Section 4.2. The execution of both expressions is carried out through the corresponding eval functions.

1. register - The function carries out three operations concurrently: adding a part to the reg variable to identify a new member and declaring two bType-type variables - inbox and outbox - for the member. The precondition requires that the identifier of the new member does not belong to reg.

   **value**
   register: Id × State $\xrightarrow{\sim}$ StateX
   register(id, s) ≡
       **let**
           x1 = make(new(inb(id), bType, id)),
           x2 = make(new(outb(id), bType, id)),
           x3 = change(id, add(make(idCat, id2val(id)), get(reg)))
       **in** con(x3, con(decl(x1), decl(x2))) **end pre** eval(canRegister(id), s),
       canRegister: Id → BoolX
       canRegister(id) ≡ not(hasPart(make(idCat, id2val(id)), get(reg)))

2. unregister - The function carries out three operations concurrently: undeclares two bType-type variables of the unregistered member, and deletes the member's id-category part from the reg variable. The precondition checks that the reg variable contains the part that identifies the member, and the two bType-type variables for the member exist in the state.

   **value**
   unregister: Id × State $\xrightarrow{\sim}$ StateX
   unregister(id, s) ≡
       **let**
           x1 = con(undecl(inb(id)), undecl(outb(id))),
           x2 = change(id, del(idCat, id2val(id), get(reg)))
       **in** con(x1, x2) **end pre** eval(canUnregister(id), s),
       canUnregister: Id → BoolX
       canUnregister(id) ≡
       **let**
           x1 = hasPart(make(idCat, id2val(id)), get(reg)),
           x2 = and(hasVar(get(inb(id))), hasVar(get(outb(id))))
       **in** and(x1, x2) **end**

## 4.5   Channels

Channels are represented as variables of the iType type. That is, every channel variable contains identities of all members who are subscribers to this channel. The owner of the channel variable is also the owner of the channel itself, responsible for keeping the record of all subscribers. Below we define four functions to create and destroy channels, and subscribe and unsubscribe to channels.

3. **create** - The function takes two identifiers and declares a new channel variable (type **iType**) using the first identifier, to be owned by the member represented by the second identifier. The precondition requires that the member is registered and the variable identifier does not exist in the state.

**value**
 create: Id × Id × State $\overset{\sim}{\to}$ StateX
 create(cid, mid, s) ≡
  **let** x1 = make(new(cid, iType, mid)) **in** decl(x1) **end**
  **pre** eval(canCreate(cid, mid), s),
 canCreate: Id × Id → BoolX
 canCreate(chid, id) ≡
  **let** x = hasPart(make(idCat, id2val(id)), get(reg))
  **in** and(x, not(hasVar(get(chid)))) **end**

4. **destroy** - The function takes two identifiers as arguments and undeclares the variable represented by the first identifier. The precondition is that the variable exists in the state, that the second identifier represents the owner of the variable, and that the variable contains only two **id**-category parts - its own identifier and the owner identifier.

**value**
 destroy: Id × Id × State $\overset{\sim}{\to}$ StateX
 destroy(cid, mid, s) ≡
  undecl(cid) **pre** eval(canDestroy(cid, mid), s),
 canDestroy: Id × Id → BoolX
 canDestroy(cid, mid) ≡
  **let**
   x1 = hasVar(get(cid)),
   x2 = equal(parts(get(cid), idCat), n(2)),
   x3 = hasVal(get(get(cid), idCat, make(n(2))), id2val(mid))
  **in** and(x1, and(x2, x3)) **end**

5. **subscribe** - The function takes two identifiers - channel variable and member subscriber. It creates an **id**-category part with the new subscriber value, and adds this part to the channel variable. The precondition is that subscriber and channel exists, and channel variable does not contain such part.

**value**
 subscribe: Id × Id × State $\overset{\sim}{\to}$ StateX
 subscribe(cid, mid, s) ≡
  change(cid, add(make(idCat, id2val(mid)), get(cid)))
  **pre** eval(canSubscribe(cid, mid), s),
 canSubscribe: Id × Id → BoolX
 canSubscribe(cid, mid) ≡
  **let**
   x1 = hasVar(get(mid)),
   x2 = hasVar(get(cid)),
   x3 = hasPart(make(idCat, id2val(mid)), get(cid))
  **in** and(x1, and(x2, not(x3))) **end**

6. **unsubscribe** - The function takes two identifiers as arguments - a channel variable and a subscriber to this channel, and removes the **id**-category part with the subscriber value from the variable. The precondition says that the variable exists in the state and it contains a part representing the subscriber.

**value**
    unsubscribe: Id × Id × State $\xrightarrow{\sim}$ StateX
    unsubscribe(cid, mid, s) ≡
       change(cid, del(idCat, id2val(mid), get(cid)))
       **pre** eval(canUnsubscribe(cid, mid), s),
    canUnsubscribe: Id × Id → BoolX
    canUnsubscribe(cid, mid) ≡
      **let**
        x1 = hasVar(get(cid)),
        x2 = hasPart(make(idCat, id2val(mid)), get(cid))
      **in** and(x1, x2) **end**

## 4.6 Messaging

Messaging takes place by registered members exchanging messages along dynamically created and subscribed channels. Below we define three functions to send messages - a message is put into the inbox of the sender, receive message - a message is removed from the outbox of the recipient, and deliver messages - a message is moved from the inbox of the sender to the outbox of all recipients.

7. **send** - The function takes two arguments - the identifier of the sender and the message to be sent, and adds the message to the inbox of the sender. To this end, the message is first converted into a value throught the **mes2value** function, then this value is inserted into the inbox variable as a new **mesCat**-category part. The precondition check that the sender is properly recorded inside the message structure (equals to the value of the second **id**-category part), that the address variable (identified by the third **id**-category part) exists in the state, and that the sender of the message is identified in one of this variable's **id**-category parts.

**value**
    send: Id × Mes × State $\xrightarrow{\sim}$ StateX
    send(mid, m, s) ≡
      **let** x = make(mesCat, mes2val(m))
      **in** change(inb(mid), add(x, get(inb(mid)))) **end**
      **pre** eval(canSend(mid, m), s),
    canSend: Id × Mes → BoolX
    canSend(mid, m) ≡
      **let** cid = val2id(val(m(idCat)(3)))
      **in** and(hasVar(get(cid)), hasPart(make(idCat, id2val(mid)), get(cid))) **end**

8. `receive` - The function takes the identifier of the recipient as an argument and returns the message. It extracts the first message from the outbox of the recipient, applying `val2mes` and `make` to convert the value into a message and then into a structure. Subsequently, it removes the message from the outbox. The precondition states that the recipient exists and its outbox variable is non-empty.

> receive: Id × State $\overset{\sim}{\to}$ StateX × StructX
> receive(mid, s) **as** (s', m) **post**
>     **let** mp = get(get(outb(mid)), mesCat, make(n(1)))
>     **in**  m = make(val2mes(val(eval(mp, s)))) ∧
>         s' = change(outb(mid), del(mesCat, get(mp), get(outb(mid)))) **end**
>     **pre** eval(canReceive(mid), s),
> canReceive: Id → BoolX
> canReceive(id) ≡
>     **let**
>        x1 = hasPart(make(idCat, id2val(id)), get(reg)),
>        x2 = hasParts(mesCat, get(outb(id)))
>     **in** and(x1, x2) **end**

9. `deliver` - The function takes two arguments - the identifier of the sender and the message to be delivered. It removes the message from the inbox of the sender, and it adds the message to the outbox of the recipients. Function `recipients` provides a list of member identifiers who must receive the message on a given state. Recipients are calculated from the `idCat` parts of the variable representing the channel. In the current version of the model, we assume the list of recipients comprises only two members `id1` and `id2`. For adding the message into the outbox variables of the recipients, first the message is converted into a value throught the `mes2value` function, then this value is inserted as a new `mesCat`-category part. Function `deliver` is a total function modeling internal behaviour of the messaging infrastructure.

> **value**
>     deliver: Id × Mes × StateX → StateX
>     deliver(id, m, s) ≡
>     **let**
>            ⟨id1, id2⟩ = recipients(m, s),
>            x  = make(mesCat, mes2val(m)),
>            x1 = change(inb(id), del(mesCat, mes2val(m), get(inb(id)))),
>            x2 = change(outb(id1), add(x, get(outb(id1)))),
>            x3 = change(outb(id2), add(x, get(outb(id2))))
>     **in**  con(x1, con(x2, x3))
>     **end**

In a future version of the model we plan to include a recursive function on `StateX` providing an iterative behaviour. In particular, for delivering messages it will iterate over the list of recipients.

# 5    Example Revisited - Electronic License Service

The business process for licensing food and beverage establishments, described in Section 3, can be supported by the messaging services described in Section 4. However, basic messaging is insufficient to answer some concrete needs of the process, such as Authentication of members or Auditing, Validation, Encryption and Decryption of messages. Such needs can be addressed through so-called horizontal extensions, typically related to concrete channels. In addition, specific requirements of the business process can also be supported as so-called vertical extensions. For instance, assuring that the sequence of messages exchanged fulfills the definition of the process (Process-Enforcement), that the status of the process can be tracked (Tracking), that communication structures can be combined (Channel-Composition).

Figure 2 depicts the communication structures and some additional messaging services supporting the business process from Section 3. The graphical notation can be explained as follows: members are represented by ellipses labeled with member names; channels are represented as rectangles labeled with channel names; a solid line connects a channel with its owner; a dashed line connects a channel with its subscriber. Horizontal extensions applied to channels are shown within the box of the channel, identified with a special character: Logging by $\alpha$, Validation by $\nu$, Encryption/Decryption by $\epsilon$, and Authentication by $\sigma$. Vertical extensions are typically build using additional members and channels, all shown with different background colours.

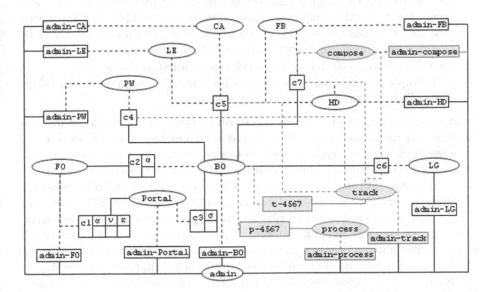

**Fig. 2.** Licensing food and beverage establishments - communication structure

Here is how messaging services support different stages of the process:

1. *Submission* - One member is registered for the one-stop portal (`Portal`) and one for the front-office application providing services through it (`FO`). The portal creates a channel (`c1`) to communicate with `FO`, and `FO` subscribes to it. Given this structure, each service request submitted through the portal is sent through the channel to the front-office application. The following horizontal extensions can be provided for the messages exchanged through `c1`: `Logging` to assess the number of applications submitted, `Validation` to assure that the front-office receives valid data, and `Encryption/Decryption` to protect the data transmitted through the net.

2. *Completeness Assessment* - The only communication required is notification to applicants in the case of incomplete documentation. Once complete, the application is forwarded to the back-office application. The `FO` member creates the channel `c2` for this purpose, and the back-office application registers a member `BO` who subscribes to this channel. In addition, the `Auditing` service can be provided for `c2` to keep track of the applications sent.

3. *Evaluation* - At this phase, collaborations from other agencies are required. Each agency registers a member - `PW`, `LE`, `CA`, `FB` and `HD`, and `LG` representing the licensing agency. `BO` creates the channels: `c4` to communicate with `PW`; `c5` to ask opinions from `LE`, `CA`, `FB` and `HD`; `c6` to communicate with `LG`; and `c7` to notify `FB` and `HD` about the inspection dates confirmed by the applicant and to receive the inspection results. `PW` subscribes to `c4`; `LE`, `CA`, `FB` and `HD` subscribe to `c5`; `LG` to `c6`; and `FB` and `HD` to `c7`. In addition, `BO` creates the channel `c3` to communicate the status of the process to `Portal`, who subscribes to it. The `Authentication` extension is enabled for `c3` to assure that the messages are sent by the `BO` application. The information sent by this channel is used when applicants track their applications.

4. *Decision-making* - No messaging service is required at this stage.

5. *Follow-up* - Notifications to applicants are the only communications taking place. They are provided by the infrastructure.

In order to support the correct execution of the process, the following vertical extensions are provided: `Process-Enforcement` to assure the sequence of messages exchanged through channels `c4` to `c7` conforms to the business process; `Tracking`, over the same channels, to enable `BO` to track the process execution; and `Channel-Composition` to link `c6` and `c7`. By enabling `Process-Enforcement`, a new member `process` is registered who creates the channel `p-4567`. All channel owners subscribe to `p-4567` to forward the messages received through their channels to `process`. Thus, `process` can control if the messages are sent in the correct sequence. By enabling `Tracking`, a new member `track` is registered who creates the channel `t-4567`. This member is subscribed to all tracked channels `c4` through `c7` to receive a copy of all messages exchanged through them, and therefore enable tracking. The extension is configured by specifying for each message exchanged what is the corresponding business step. By enabling `Channel-Composition`, member `compose` is registered and subscribed to `c6` and `c7`, responsible for forwarding all messages from `c6` to `c7`.

# 6    Programmable Messaging - Software

The concept of programmable messaging introduced in this paper was implemented into a prototype called G-EEG - Government-Enterprise Ecosystem Gateway. Serving research and validation purposes, the development of G-EEG followed a rigorous process relying on UML to express various development artifacts. For instance, we used domain class diagrams to describe and relate domain concepts, use case diagrams to depict functional requirements, and design class diagrams to elaborate on the components of the system and their relationships. Figure 3 below depicts the G-EEG design class diagram.

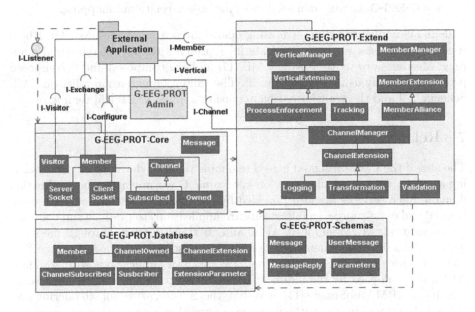

**Fig. 3.** G-EEG Design Class Diagram

The diagram shows a distributed architecture with four components in the business layer - G-EEG-Admin, G-EEG-Core, G-EEG-Extend and G-EEG-Schemas, and one in the persistence layer - G-EEG-Database, as follows:

1. G-EEG-Admin enables message exchange with the administrator.
2. G-EEG-Core provides basic messaging services. The component relies on the interface I-Listener implemented by external applications to receive messages and send acknowledgements, and offers three interfaces to such applications: I-Visitor to register members and recover member structures after restarting, I-Exchange to send and receive messages, and I-Configure to create and modify communication structures. The following classes are included in G-EEG-Core: Visitor and Member to implement the corresponding interfaces; Owned and Subscribed to implement operations defined in the

abstract class `Channel`; `Message` to compose and decompose messages; and `ServerSocket` and `ClientSocket` to send and receive messages by members.

3. `G-EEG-Extend` provides extended messaging services through the interfaces `I-Vertical`, `I-Member` and `I-Channel` to enable, configure, query and disable the three types of extensions. The component contains the following classes: `VerticalManager`, `MemberManager` and `ChannelManager` to manage these types of extensions, and abstract classes `VerticalExtension`, `ChannelExtension` and `MemberExtension` to define abstract operations that each extension must implement. Three channel-oriented extensions are currently implemented: `Auditing`, `Transformation` and `Validation`.

4. `G-EEG-Schemas` contains XML definitions for messages and parameter files, and `G-EEG-Database` defines classes for object-relational mapping.

`G-EEG` is implemented in Java using open-source technologies. MySQL [16] is used as a database engine. Hibernate [9] represents the object-relational mapping. Messages are written using XML [17] and are composed and decomposed programmatically using XMLBeans [3]. The validation extension relies on XML Schema [24] and the transformation extension applies XSLT [25] templates.

# 7 Related Work

The aim of the work presented here is to enable rigorous development of messaging services, with particular view on Electronic Government as the application domain. Such services are also provided by existing MOM solutions, both commercial and open-source, enabling software applications to produce and consume messages using MOM-supplied APIs, and to transfer them through messages queues. Concrete implementations of MOM include JMS - Java Message Service [19] which provides messaging services for Java applications with standard API widely adopted by the industry. Other MOM products include Microsoft's MSMQ [5], IBM WebSphere [11] or WebMethods Enterprise [26], all offering predefined functionality for authentication, encryption and routing of messages, among others. The limitations of existing MOM solutions include reliability - lack of formal models to enable rigorous development, extensibility - fixed functionality offered, and genericity - inability to address the problems peculiar to Electronic Government. These limitations were described in Section 1.

This work presents the formal model to serve as the foundation for messaging services. At the specification level, we followed a state-based paradigm to specify a set of basic operations to allow the definitions of syntax and semantics of messaging services. At this level, state-based languages such as VDM [13], B [1] or RSL [21] could be used; we opted for the last one. Our aim is to determine how to build and evolve communication structures through messaging, focusing on the expression of observables outcomes but ignoring implementation details. One important detail ignored at this stage is the distributed nature of the state, thus the inability for members to directly modify variables of other members.

At the implementation level, in contrast, remote state-changes can be only carried out through sending messages and processing such messages locally. At this level, we have distributed members exchanging messages, with service provision involving several members and messages. The behaviours could be specified following an action-based paradigm, making abstractions of the state changes of individual members, and focusing on the sequence of messages that are exchanged and how they are concurrently processed. In addition, behavioral properties express the results of exchanging series of messages. Thus, we may consider specification languages based on process algebras, particularly CSP [10] and CCS [14]. However, both CSP and CCS assume a fixed set of communication channels, which is incompatible with our approach. While pi-calculus [15] supports dynamically created channels, it is less convenient to express multicasting behaviours which are the cornerstone of our approach.

The main contribution of this work is the definition of a formal model constituting a foundation (or more precisely its fragment) for specifying messaging services. This foundation specifies a set of operations that can be later used as primitive operators for defining messaging services at different levels of abstraction. In particular, we specified a refinement of the abstract model based on communication channels, and defined an extensibility mechanism to build high-level communication services. We also demonstrated how this mechanism can address some requirements of the Electronic Government domain.

# 8    Conclusions

We presented the ongoing development of foundations to enable programmable messaging for Electronic Government. The motivation, existing solutions and their limitations were presented in Section 1, followed by a brief introduction to Electronic Government in Section 2. Section 3 introduced an example business process implementing cross-agency delivery of licensing services. The foundation for programmable messaging was presented in Section 4, from abstract state and state-changing operations, through messages, to concrete operations to register and unregister members, create and destroy channels, subscribe and unsubscribe to channels, and send and receive messages. The case study in Section 3 was revisited in Section 5 to explain how the messaging services introduced in Section 4 can support communication needs of the licensing process. Section 6 presented the design of prototype software implementing the concepts of programmable messaging. Related work was discussed in Section 7.

Future work includes completing the definition of the model for core messaging services, including the definition of iteration, specifying and implementing horizontal and vertical extensions based on core services, and verifying behavioral properties of such extensions and their compositions.

**Acknowledgments.** We wish to thank Adegboyega Ojo, Gabriel Oteniya and Pablo Fillottrani for collaboration and comments about this work. This work was partly supported by Macao S.A.R. Government under the e-Macao Program.

# References

1. Abrial, J.R.: The B Book. Cambridge Univeristy Press, Cambridge (1996)
2. Alonso, G., et al.: Web Services, Concepts, Architectures and Applications. Springer, Heidelberg (2004)
3. Apache.The Apache XML Project - XMLBeans, http://xmlbeans.apache.org
4. Derrick, J., Boiten, E.: Refinement in Z and Object-Z. Springer, Heidelberg (2001)
5. Dickman, A.: Designing Applications with MSMQ. Addison Wesley, Reading (1998)
6. Estevez, E., Janowski, T.: Government-Enterprise Ecosystem Gateway (G-EEG) for Seamless e-Government. In: 40th Hawaii International Conference on System Sciences, IEEE, Los Alamitos (2007)
7. Estevez, E., Janowski, T.: Building a Dependable Messaging Infrastructure for Electronic Government. In: 2nd International Workshop on Dependability and Security in e-Government, part of International Conference on Availability, Reliability and Security, IEEE, Los Alamitos (2007)
8. Field, T., Muller, E., Law, E.: The e-Government Imperative. Organization for Economic Co-operation and Development (OECD) (2003)
9. Hibernate. Relational Persistence for Java and .Net, http://www.hibernate.org
10. Hoare, C.A.R.: Communicating Sequential Processes. Prentice Hall, Englewood Cliffs (1985)
11. IBM. WebSphere, www.ibm.com/software/websphere
12. Ojo, A., Oteniya, G., Fong, C.K., Estevez, E., Janowski, T.: Electronic Delivery of Licensing Services - Development Document. Macao e-Government Project (e-Macao) (October 2005), http://www.emacao.gov.mo/documents/04/report5.pdf
13. Jones, C.: Systematic Software Development using VDM. Prentice Hall, Englewood Cliffs (1990)
14. Milner, R.: Communication and Concurrency. Prentice Hall International, Englewood Cliffs (1989)
15. Milner, R.: Communicating and Mobile Systems: the Pi-Calculus. Cambridge University Press, Cambridge (2000)
16. MySQL. MySQL Database Engine, http://www.mysql.org
17. Ray, E.: Learning XML. O' Reilly (2001)
18. Ronaghan, S.: Benchmarking e-Government: A Global Perspective. Assessing the UN Member States. United Nations Division for Public Economics and Public Administration and American Society for Public Administration (2002), http://unpan1.un.org/intradoc/groups/public/documents/UN/UNPAN021547.pdf
19. Sun Developer Network, Java Message Service, http://java.sun.com/products/jms
20. Texas Government. Seamless Government Issues (2000), www.dir.state.tx.us/taskforce/report/seamless.pdf
21. RAISE Language Group, T.: The RAISE Specification Language. BCS Practitioner Series. Prentice Hall, Englewood Cliffs (1992)
22. The RAISE Method Group.: The RAISE Development Method. BCS Practitioner Series. Prentice Hall, Englewood Cliffs (1995), ftp://ftp.iist.unu.edu/pub/RAISE/method_book
23. Turner, E., Nicoll, P.: Electronic Service Delivery, including Internet Use, by Commonweath Government Agencies. Australian National Audit Office (1999)
24. World Wide Web Consortium. XML Schema, Technical Report. (October 2004), http://www.w3.org/XML/Schema
25. World Wide Web Consortium. XSLT - XSL Transformations, http://www.w3.org/TR/xslt
26. WebMethods Enterprise. WebMethods, www.webmethods.com/meta/default/folder/0000005452

# Balancing Insight and Effort: The Industrial Uptake of Formal Methods

John Fitzgerald[1] and Peter Gorm Larsen[2]

[1] School of Computing Science, Newcastle University, UK
[2] Engineering College of Aarhus, Denmark
John.Fitzgerald@ncl.ac.uk, pgl@iha.dk

**Abstract.** Our goal is to help the developers of computer-based systems to make informed design decisions on the basis of insights gained from the rigorous analysis of abstract system models. The early work on model-oriented specification has inspired the development of numerous formalisms and tools supporting modelling and analysis. There are also many stories of successful industrial application, often driven by a few champions possessing deep a priori understanding of formalisms. There are fewer cases of successful take-up or adoption of the technology in the long term. We argue that successful industrial adoption of this technology requires that potential users strike a balance between the effort expended in producing and analysing a model and insight gained. In order to support this balancing act, tools need to offer a range of levels of effort and insight. Further, educators need to recognise that training in formal development techniques must support this trade-off process.

## 1 Introduction

"Start by being systematic. Specify crucial facets — of your application domain, your requirements and your software designs — formally. Then program (i.e., code) from there! ...

...a few customers are willing to accept today's rather high cost of formal development"

*Dines Bjørner [1]*

Formal methods are not immune from commercial reality [2,3,4,5]. They must be applied in a cost-effective manner so that the effort invested in building precise and abstract models yields insight that will "pay back" during system development [6]. We share with Dines Bjørner the position that even a little rigour, carefully applied, can bring substantial benefits. Yet, in order to give developers the option of applying "a little rigour", we must offer techniques and tools that are adaptable to lightweight or heavyweight use, as the application and business demand.

A development engineer is faced with a wide range of formal techniques and tools. Each demands a certain *effort*, by which we mean the combination of time and resources required to use the technique or tool. Each also promises some *insight* into the ways a

C.B. Jones, Z. Liu, J. Woodcock (Eds.): Bjørner/Zhou Festschrift, LNCS 4700, pp. 237–254, 2007.

particular system may behave and the mental energy that must be released to produce the final documented product. Generally, deeper insight demands greater effort; the skill is to balance the two, defining a systematic approach that yields sufficient insight for the task for a reasonable investment of effort. Beyond a certain level of effort, the gain in insight may not be valuable for the application, and the engineer should not be forced into unnecessary analysis or verification. The balance between effort and insight has been central to our work supporting industry adoption of formal techniques by evolutionary steps rather than revolutionary change. Although we are very positive about the benefits of formalism, we do see the overt (or covert) forcing of formal approaches into industrial practice as counterproductive [7].

In this paper, we examine a range of techniques and tools associated with model-oriented specification of the kind pioneered by Bjørner and many others. In each case, we review the effort/insight balance afforded by the technique and try to identify the future developments that will allow developers the freedom to choose the appropriate technology.

We have deliberately used the word *uptake* in the title of this paper in contrast to *application*. There are numerous successful applications of formal methods in many domains [8,9]. The approach with which we are most closely associated, VDM (the Vienna Development Method) has also seen some significant and instructive applications in recent years [10]. It is worth stressing that we are here interested in the long-term, sustainable industrial adoption of formally-based techniques than their successful application in isolated cases driven by specialist champions with deep a priori knowledge of specific methods. We freely admit to having been involved in many applications but few cases of take-up.

The formal methods community has developed a wide range of formalisms tailored to rather specific application environments and built on distinct semantic foundations. Our background is in model-oriented formalisms that emphasise precision obtained by applying (usually discrete) mathematics and logic to the semantics of languages used for expressing system models. The approach that we have developed, based on VDM, emphasises the use of abstract and rigorous models to help developers manage complexity and explore the consequences of alternative design decisions in early stages of the life cycle. Thus, abstraction and rigour in modelling have been more significant for us than code verification.

A good model guides your thinking, a bad one warps it.

*Brian Marick*

## Tools, Techniques, People and Processes

Successful systems development businesses need to recruit the right people, employ an appropriate development process and make use of the tools and techniques that fit the development challenge at hand. It is very hard to find companies that excel in all three areas at the same time. Typically, small specialist companies with a niche market can place an emphasis on special techniques, including formal ones. In such organisations,

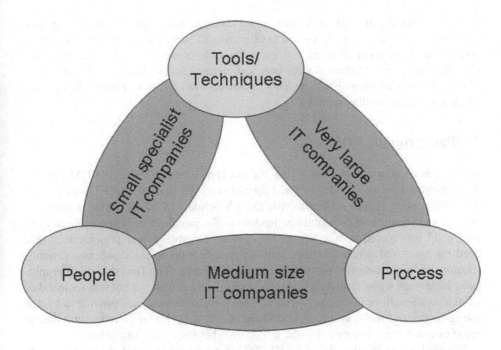

**Fig. 1.** The People, Process and Tools/Techniques Triangle

the focus is on the tools/techniques themselves and the highly skilled individuals who are needed to apply them. Medium sized software companies, where the distance from the bottom to the top of the corporate ladder is short, focus primarily on processes and the people. Very large software companies often focus on process and tools/techniques but from a long-term strategic perspective in which the dependence on small numbers of very highly skilled individuals is diminished. These are three rather independent dimensions are illustrated in Figure 1.

Formal methods form a part of the tools/techniques area of the picture, employed by good developers when it makes business sense to do so. Indeed, the proponents of formal methods may have concentrated too much of their efforts on tools and techniques at the expense of people (making methods accessible to the majority of professionals) and processes (integrating the technology with existing practice). Formal techniques may not always be the right choice for essential parts of systems, so it is important to have a good understanding of the interaction between a formally developed component and parts that are developed using other means. In addition entire systems are seldom developed from scratch. In many projects large legacy components form a part of the solution and so it is important to be able to easily understand how such legacy parts fit with a formal model.

In this paper, we consider this balance between effort and insight, especially as it has been found in model-oriented specification and in VDM. We first review our own involvement by giving a brief account of VDM and developments in the formalism in recent years (Section 2). In Section 3, we consider the range of tool features now becoming available. For each, we discuss the insights to be gained and the effort to be invested in using them. In Section 4 we discuss the consequences for education and training if future generations of engineers and research scientists are to take advantage of the full range of formalisms and tools becoming available now. Finally in Section 5 we give a few concluding remarks.

## 2  Background: VDM

We have been active in the use of the Vienna Development Method (VDM), one of the longest established model-oriented formalisms. We studied under Dines Bjørner and Cliff Jones[1]. Larsen studied in "the Danish School" of VDM, which emphasised explicit specification of functionality, leading to the possibility of executable models. Fitzgerald was rooted in "the British School" which gave greater prominence to the need for proof and, where possible, implicit specification by postconditions denoting relations on inputs, results and persistent state variables. The Danish School emphasised large-scale systems and compiler technology; the British School was focussed on validation through proof and refinement-based development. Jones provides an interesting account of the scientific development of VDM [11]. Our collaboration has, so some extent, been the story of an accommodation between these two schools.

We worked together briefly on the BSI/ISO standardisation panel of VDM's specification language (VDM-SL) [12,13]. Larsen took a leading role in completing the denotational semantics of the full language [14]. He went on to pioneer the development of industry-strength tool support for VDM-SL in IFAD. Fitzgerald was meanwhile working on the interaction between modular structuring mechanisms and user-guided proof in the typed Logic of Partial Functions [15] and started work with the British Aerospace Dependable Computing Systems Centre at Newcastle University.

Our first close collaboration was on the ConForm project funded under the European Systems and Software Initiative and conducted at British Aerospace Systems and Equipment (as it then was) in Plymouth. The project involved the concurrent development of a security-related software component using, in one stream, current best practice and, in the other stream, model-oriented specification. The specification was developed in VDM-SL by BAe engineers, with the IFAD tools and several ad hoc tools to integrate the formal model with structured methods already in use in the company. A study of the two parallel developments, while far from being a controlled experiment, indicated how formally-based tools might be used in practice. As a consequence of our logging all queries raised against the requirements documents, the study also provided evidence of the kinds of insight that arise when formal models are constructed [16].

The ConForm experience led us to develop a lightweight and tool-supported approach to formal modelling that we first presented in 1998 [17]. Subsequently both of us have used VDM with many different industrial users in various application domains. Some of the work has been reported in public, e.g. [18,19,20,21].

---

[1] Variously referred to as "the VDM twins" and, with Peter Lucas, as "the Ancient Greeks" behind the original VDM, latterly FME and FM, Symposia! Both of them frequently emphasise the crucial contributions of Lucas, Bekič and many others to the foundations of VDM.

Fitzgerald spent most of the following ten years in academia working with the aerospace industry and, for a couple of years, in a start-up company, Transitive. Larsen, by contrast, spent most of his time in industry at IFAD and Systematic, recently joining academia at the Engineering College of Aarhus. IFAD, the company that developed the original VDM tools [22], sold the technology on to the major Japanese company CSK [23]. The tools remain under very active support and development today. The new Overture initiative [24] is developing an open-source tools platform and plug-ins to deliver at least the same functionality as the rather more monolithic VDMTools.

VDM today is a well-established formal method based on the ISO standardised specification language VDM-SL [12] and its object-oriented extension VDM++ [25]. Further extensions have provided facilities for description and analysis of distributed real-time embedded systems [26,27,28], including explicit modelling of alternative system architectures and deployment of functionality to computation and communication resources.

We have reported elsewhere on the current state of VDM's tools and given data on industrial applications [10]. However, it is worth briefly reviewing a leading current application as an indication of how VDM is used today. FeliCa Networks Inc.[2] has been developing a next generation mobile integrated circuit chip, based on a contactless card technology developed and promoted by Sony [29]. The specification development process was carried out in three phases:

1. Writing an informal definition of the requirements in Japanese (383 pages).
2. Creating UML diagrams based on this document.
3. Modelling the system in VDM++ with over 100kLOC of VDM++ (677 pages).

Validation of the VDM++ model involved over 10 million tests. During phases 1 and 2 reviews found only 93 contradictions and faults in requirements and specifications in total. In phase 3, 162 faults were found through the process of writing and reviewing the VDM++ model. In addition 116 faults were found by executing the formal model in VDMTools. Finally, an extra 69 faults were found by combining the evaluation team and the specification writing teams in reviews. The discovery of these faults are all examples of insight gained by the formulation of the abstract model and the analysis on it. No refinement or formal verification has taken place, but the use of formal modelling has been viewed by the company as a considerable success, so balance of effort and insight seems to have been appropriate. The FeliCa development team included more than 50 people and the three year project has been completed on time, which is remarkable in itself. The product is produced in high volume, with potentially high recall costs in case of defects. By the end of November 2006 more than one million chips had been shipped.

# 3    A Tools Viewpoint

Developing and maintaining good industry-strength tool support is extremely time consuming. The formal methods community has spread its effort over many different formalisms. For the developers of the large number of specialised tools, integration with

---

[2] www.felicanetworks.co.jp

industrial users, tools and processes has not been of great importance. Thus, it is rare to find a level of tool support that is comparable with the standards for the industrial leading software development tools [30].

Tools have a strong influence on modelling style [31]. Interestingly model-oriented formalisms with similar semantic foundations such as VDM, Z [32] and B [33] have very different tool support. For VDM emphasis has been placed on the provision of an executable subset of the modelling language and, consequently, on validation of abstract models using testing techniques [34,35,36]. For Z the focus has been to a greater extent on proof support [37,38,39]. For B effort has been directed at providing automated proof support for refinement and code generation [40,41]. These approaches strike different balances between insight and effort, and between insight and concrete results such as code. In this section we review the different kinds of feature that can be included in a tool to support formal modelling and analysis, commenting on the balance for each of these.

## 3.1  Static Analysis Features

Very good tools now exist for efficiently developing parsers for formal languages. Once the conformance of a formal model to the language grammar has been confirmed, a variety of static checks can be performed. Probably the best known static analyser from the programming world is Lint [42] which performs simple static tests that identify potential code defects. The popularity of Lint and tools like it is partly down to the excellent balance between insight and effort. The effort is limited to running the analyser and subsequently examining the suspicious constructs 'flagged' by the tool. Provided the number of false positives is tolerable, the insight gained in spotting these defects is valuable. Similar 'push-button' technology has been advocated for formal methods tools for some time and is now becoming a reality [43,44,45,46].

The availability of a formal semantics for the modelling language enables a wide range of automatic or semi-automatic static analysis tools:

**Type checkers:** This kind of feature is a pure push-button technology where all the errors reported must be fixed by the user [47]. This kind of feature is always worthwhile because the cost of the analysis is low and the results identify genuine defects. The level of insight gained is rather shallow: a type correct model is a long way short of being validated! In languages like VDM++, in which type membership may be restricted by arbitrarily complex invariants, the full type-checking task involves the generation of proof obligations.

**Proof obligation generators:** In order to ensure internal consistency of a formal model it is typically possible to formulate a collection of "proof obligations" that indicate potential defects in a formal model [48]. Many of these surround the potential mis-application of partial operators (a kind of 'run-time error'). More subtle proof obligations also arise such as the necessity to prove that defined operations denote non-empty relations. Assuming that all of these obligations can be discharged the formal model is guaranteed to be internally consistent, i.e. it has a meaning. However, this is no guarantee that it is describing the "right" thing. The current VDM-Tools technology stops at this level, but push-button proof of obligations has been demonstrated and the technology to support this, using HOL, is once again under active development. Proof obligation generation is automatic and hence low-cost. Discharging of obligations can not be completely automated; tools that use this approach must provide a form of interactive prover unless unproved obligations are to be left for inspection. The level of insight gained is correspondingly higher in that failure to discharge an obligation may suggest a more subtle defect than can be identified by type checking alone.

**Assertions in program code:** In-line specification of contracts (including VDM-like invariants, preconditions and postconditions) provides an opportunity for enhanced static checks on program code. This kind of approach has a long history [49] and current initiatives around Java look particularly promising [50,51]. The strength of these features are that, by spending the effort in developing the assertions, the static analysis can typically provide deeper insight into subtle errors in the code that can then easily be fixed.

**Model checkers:** The model-checking concept is general and applies to many logics and models. Its particular benefit is the production of a counterexample in the case where a checked property is not satisfied. A simple model-checking problem is testing whether a given formula in the propositional logic is satisfied by a given model [52,53]. This very powerful technique is fully automated and so has potential for giving a very good balance between effort and insight. However, formulating the model in order to support efficient checking may require high effort. There are many stand-alone model checkers and increasing interest in combining them with other analysis tools. More recently small but powerful combinations of model-checking techniques have been applied in Alloy [54], so far on relatively small examples.

## 3.2 Dynamic Analysis of Formal Models

Models are not necessarily executable [55] but formal semantics for modelling languages make their symbolic execution [56] possible, albeit at high cost. It is possible to define executable subsets within which dynamic behaviour can be explored. The danger of restriction to an executable subset is that the model's abstraction level gets too low, hampering the insight gained from analysis. Our experience is that the use of an executable subset can still provide many benefits to a user with a training in abstraction [57]. Indeed, the borderline of executablity is not as clear as one might expect [58].

Dynamic analysis of formal models comes in several forms:

**Interpreters:** Interpreters are available for executable subsets of several modelling languages, including VDM [34]. Some of these tools also provide debugging capabilities similar to those provided by programming environments already familiar to software developers. The non-exhaustive testing supported by an interpreter helps a user to step into the evaluation of an unexpected result. Typically an interpreter feature is easy to use and gives deep insight into the subtleties of a formal model so although one must manually produce the test arguments to exercise there is normally a good balance between effort and insight here.

**Test case generation:** Where the use of an executable subset enables testing of models, it can also be valuable to automate the testing process in different ways. Automatic generation of test cases [59,60] can produce entire test suites [61]. Considering the balance between effort and insight, this kind of enhancement to the automation of testing is almost always favourable, particularly when the generated test cases can be used for testing the final implementation.

**Test analysis support:** In order to provide further insight into the quality of the test set used on a model, it is possible to display the coverage of the tests carried out, for example by using colour in ways similar to those used for programming languages [62]. Alternatively graphical overviews of executions can be used to give the user a deeper understanding for what is going on [27]. Depending upon the time that must be spent creating this kind of feature, it is typically worth the low effort required to monitor the coverage of tests on a model. The insight into the functional characteristics of the model is very limited, but it may lead to improved test sets that themselves prove worthwhile.

### 3.3 Verification of Formal Models

The expressiveness of formal modelling languages places limits on the extent to which analyses can be automated. For realistic industrial applications one must normally settle for as much automation as possible and then provide support for manual analysis [63]. In the area of formal verification one can divide features into those that support formal refinement and those that support formal proof:

**Formal refinement support:** Many formal modelling languages have an associated notion of refinement enabling the description of successively more concrete models, with a formal relationship between each of them [64]. Many different tools are able to support this process [65]. Typical approaches involve the definition of a refinement relation [66,67] between concrete and abstract models. The balance between effort and insight gained here is problematic from an industrial perspective unless either there is substantial automation or the correctness of the application is sufficiently important to warrant the extra cost in such a fully formal development [33,68]. However, there is also work towards automated support for refinement [69].

**Theorem provers:** The ultimate advantage of using a formal over an informal model is the ability to verify its properties to a high level of rigour [70], even for infinite state systems. Given our concern to balance effort and insight, some degree of automation is required here [71]. A complete reliance on proof automation may lead to the use of a notation that lacks expressiveness [72]. In reality, for many formal modelling applications, we would not wish to compromise the accessibility of the modelling language in order to support a certain level of automated analysis. The balance between the formalism and the extent of automation is crucial. It depends on the projects needs: are these to ensure internal consistency by discharging as many consistency proof obligations as possible, or are they to prove system-level properties (we have used the term validation conjectures)? In the former case a high level of automation may be desirable. In the latter the real insight gained by guiding a proof may help understanding of the rest of the model, in particular detecting and eliminating defects [73,74].

Until recently, we have not seen a strong enough industrial case for bringing proof support into VDMTools because of the computational overheads and also the possibility of having to build an interface for user guidance of the specialised proof process. Our experience with manual proof support for the proof theory of VDM-SL [15] indicated that many proof obligations are generated by even a simple model and it is vital to be able to discharge as many of these as possible without user guidance. In the PROSPER project [75], it was possible to discharge the vast majority of generated proof obligations automatically (up to 90 % for a railway application [76]) and we are now working on reproducing this for VDM++ using HOL4. We leave undischarged obligations for inspection, but view the development of good human-guided but machine-assisted proof tools (based on an appreciation of the cognitive aspects of proof) as an essential research goal.

### 3.4   Connection to the Development Environment

Modelling and analysis techniques based on formal notations will rarely be used for the development of an entire system, so their products should fit with the results of applying other techniques, as well as with the processes employed in the development team. In order to balance the effort spent on producing the formal models with the insight gained this is clearly one of the areas with potential for payback in terms of minimising the time that needs to be spent in the final implementation phases. Supporting this for VDMTools meant spending major efforts on tasks that formalists might find uninteresting, but which are essential for deployment. For example, we have had to develop interfaces to proprietary WYSIWYG document editors, use ASCII syntax, build code generators, application programmer interfaces and even links to UML tools! Here we list some of the features that we consider particularly significant in connecting our tools to people and processes in the development environment.

**Code generators:** If a formal modelling language has an executable subset, there is also potential for automating a part of the coding process. This adds value to the formal models being produced and thus affects the balance between the effort spent producing the model and its value as a basis for an implementation. Generated code will rarely be as efficient as a hand-coded implementation. However, given a reliable code generator, there is some confidence that the generated code accurately reflects the properties of the model. Critical applications demand the use of certified code generators [77]. The use of code generation for production code comes at a price in terms of the degree of abstraction that can be permitted in the model.

**Combination with other notations:** It is essential for industrial uptake that a tool for formal modelling is able to support whatever standards for processes and other tools are being used. It is even better if users are able to move back and forth between the various models and notations that are used, seeing updates in model reflected consistently in others. Considerable work has gone into developing appropriate couplings between formal methods tools and UML, the de-facto standard in large parts of the industry [78]. Such a bi-directional link with developed for VDM-Tools to support interaction with the Rose UML tool. The effort/insight balance is improved by linkage between informal and formal tools. However the links do not simply have to be with classical software design tools. For example, integration with a continuous time simulator is a promising vehicle for collaboration between systems and software engineers [79], both working in different, but both formal, spheres.

**Combination with Development Environments:** Companies have development environments that must be used for for integrating the final system. It is also likely that the implementation derived from a formal model will need to be integrated with code that is developed differently (e.g. for existing GUI or legacy code). Here the effort/insight balance is affected by the ease of doing this kind of integration. Features for combining existing code with a formal model may prove valuable [80], as may facilities for combining with a GUI interface [81].

## 3.5 Past and Future for Formal Methods Tools

Tools for formal modelling and analysis have come a long way since work began on VDM-SL parsers, but competition with conventional tools is hard. In the 1980s tools for formal specification were mainly limited to basic static checks for syntax- and type-correctness. At that time it was even possible to write PhD thesis about general formal methods tool support [82]. The 1990s saw an increase in the range of tools exploiting more of the formal semantics, in particular interpreters, code generators, test case generators, model checking and proof support. In addition many of the tools had support for combining formal models with informal, usually graphical, notations. At present, we conjecture that none of the formal methods tools are as highly featured as the leading industrial software development tools.

Open source platforms with potentially closed-source plug-ins offer a promising approach for delivering tools with the capabilities that we have discussed [83,24]. If this can be achieved tool builders will not have to start from scratch whenever tool support is to be developed for a new notation. Ideally, different views or parts of a system could be described in different formalisms and verification of properties could be performed by a variety of theorem provers in a compositional way. However, before this becomes a reality there are major theoretical challenges on semantic integration that must be addressed.

Our own experience with VDMTools and the Overture initiative leads us to want to address several areas:

- Co-simulation as an extension of executable specification and the use of interpreters for control applications in embedded real-time systems.
- Modelling faults and experimenting with alternative fault detection and tolerance mechanisms inside formal models.
- User-guided proof for gaining deep insight at a higher level than conventional theorem provers.

# 4 An Educational Viewpoint

> A fool with a tool is still a fool.
>
> *Grady Booch*

We have argued that successful industry adoption of formal techniques requires the balancing of effort and insight, and that tools and development environments should support this trade-off. No matter how advanced the tools, they can only achieve a measure of industry credibility if graduate engineers possess skills in abstraction and rigorous thinking, and are open to selecting the right techniques for the job. It therefore seems appropriate to ask how this should affect the aims, content and delivery of formal methods education.

We should not expect our students to share our motivations. In our experience, many students are driven by the need to develop skills that will be useful in pursuing a career and many are also driven by the satisfaction of building a working computer system and seeing it run. If we care about the industry uptake of formal techniques, we should care about all our students and not just the potential PhDs.

## 4.1 Aims

We suggest that the overriding aims of formal methods advocates in education should be: (i) to help students develop transferable skills of abstraction and rigorous modelling and analysis; and (ii) to develop the knowledge and skill needed to select tools and techniques on the basis of cost and potential effectiveness. These are not impossibly vague goals: Sobel's study [84], albeit the subject of a debate on experimental design [85,86], was a first attempt to assess whether a training in formal techniques may improve students' general analytic and problem solving skills [87]. In our teaching [88], with its origins in industrial courses, we have been led to ask whether we really know what skills we want to help our students develop and how we could establish whether our current courses are achieving this. Kramer has recently argued that abstraction skills are core to computing and that we should try to monitor the development of such skills through students' development [89]. It has been pointed out that the sorts of test we need are lacking, as most relevant tests focus on logical reasoning.

At a more practical level, we would like typical graduates, not only the most academically gifted, to at least know that next generation Integrated Development Environments will provide a higher static analysis capability than at present and will support expressive annotation-based languages in the manner of JML [50] and Spec# [90], allowing them to identify hitherto hard-to-detect errors in their code. We want them to be surprised when such technology is *not* deployed in the companies where they work and we would even like them to use it to get the edge on their fellow programmers! In that way we hope that they will be able to find an appropriate balance in the use of abstraction and rigour in their own work.

## 4.2 Content

Giving students a sense of the effort/insight trade-off means exposing them to a range of analysis techniques as well as offering them experiences that help them to see the insights that come from a range of analytic techniques, from manual to automated. In our own teaching experience [88], we apply a "lightweight" approach using VDM++. We emphasise practical applications, teaching through a range of examples derived from industry application. A strength of the approach is the relative familiarity of the structure of VDM++ to undergraduates already versed in object-oriented programming. However, analysis is so far limited to specification testing and proof obligation generation. Advanced techniques including proof and model checking, are taught separately. Practical experience, discussions centered around formal models and sharing of insights are central to the approach if we are to help students move from superficial and atomistic learning to a deeper appreciation of the costs and benefits of abstraction and rigour.

In a revision to its undergraduate curriculum in formal techniques, Newcastle is looking at beginning with JML (because Java is taught extensively in the first part of the curriculum), raising students' expectations about the forms of push-button analysis that can be applied to their programs. Similar concepts (pre-/post specification, use of invariants etc.) can then be lifted to the design level by teaching model-oriented specification in VDM++ with tool support and introducing validation through structured argument. At the final level, aimed at software engineering specialists who may well become tools developers themselves, we will introduce proof and model-checking as the technology that underpins the advanced analysis of both programs and design models.

### 4.3  Delivery

There has been much debate around the placing of formal methods in the wider computing curriculum. Should they be treated as a distinct discipline or should they be fully integrated with other material? van Lamsweerde [63] argues for the integration of formal methods into normal development activities. This surely suggests that training in formal techniques should be, to a large extent, part of the normal components of computer science and software engineering curricula. Wing's suggested approach [91] is to teach common elements (state machines, invariants, abstraction mappings, composition, induction, specification and verification) and to use tools to reinforce theory. She identifies the difficulty of winning fellow faculty members round as a real impediment to this [92].

Recent work [93] suggests that students' performance improves when they are provided with Integrated Development Environments encompassing specification support tools, static analysers and provers. It remains to be seen if this level of tooling deepens students' understanding of the models that they are creating and the formalism used. However, it may be seen as a step in the right direction by freeing students to concentrate on the meaning of a model rather than automatically checkable characteristics.

## 5  Concluding Remarks

Will formal methods remain niche technology with localised use dependent on energetic champions? We believe that some major changes are required to help the mainstream get the benefits of abstraction and rigour in system modelling and analysis. Tools are vital and, we have argued, a full range of tools have to be offered in a way that allows their gradual adoption into processes and by people already in place. This means much more collaboration between tools developers, very likely via open platforms, in order to give users the flexibility to balance effort and insight.

From a teaching perspective, we ought to be liberal in our use of a range of formalisms supported by tools in order to encourage the breadth of experience that will allow graduate engineers to select appropriate technology. We should not expect everyone to be interested in how we express formal semantics, but we should adopt course content and delivery styles that help them to feel the benefits of a little abstraction and rigour.

Formal approaches have been widely, but often quietly, adopted in modern programming languages and development environments. Industry-leading programming notations now include possibilities for increased abstraction through of abstract types such as sets, sequences and mappings and use of concepts such as invariants, pre and post-conditions formulated using predicates. None of these advances will be known as 'formal methods'. Dines Bjørner, Zhou Chaochen and so many others have worked to create technology so fundamental that it disappears into the fabric of software and systems engineering. Surely this is an achievement to be proud of.

**Acknowledgments.** We are grateful to the organisers of the Festschrift Symposium for the opportunity to prepare this paper, and most especially to Dines Bjørner for the lively inspiration, support and encouragement he has provided to us both over many years. As always we are grateful to our many colleagues involved in the current VDM Tools and Overture initiatives, especially Shin Sahara and Marcel Verhoef, for their contributions to the work reported in this paper and to Jeremy Bryans and Hugo Daniel Macedo for their helpful comments on a draft of this paper.

# References

1. Bjøorner, D.: Software Engineering 1: Abstraction and Modelling. Springer, Heidelberg (2006)
2. Hall, A.: Seven Myths of Formal Methods. IEEE Software 7(5), 11–19 (1990)
3. Bowen, J.P., Hinchey, M.G.: Ten Commandments of Formal Methods. IEEE Computer 28(4), 56–62 (1995)
4. Tretmans, J., Wijbrans, K., Chaudron, M.: Software Engineering with Formal Methods: The Development of a Storm Surge Barrier Control System Revisiting Seven Myths of Formal Methods. Form. Methods Syst. Des. 19(2), 195–215 (2001)
5. Bowen, J.P., Hinchey, M.G.: Ten Commandments of Formal Methods. Ten Years Later. IEEE Computer 39(1), 40–48 (2006)
6. Larsen, P.G.: On the Industrial Value of Models. In: Duke, D., Evans, A. (eds.) 2nd BCS-FACS Norhern Formal Methods Workshop, Ilkley, BCS-FACS, Springer, Heidelberg (1997)
7. Glass, R.L.: The Mystery of Formal Methods Disuse. Communications of the ACM 47(8), 15–17 (2004)
8. Dan Craigen, S.G., Ralston, T.: An International Survey of Industrial Applications of Formal Methods. vol. 1, Purpose, Approach, Analysis and Conclusions. U.S. Department of Commerce, Technology Administration, National Institute of Standards and Technology, Computer Systems Laboratory, Gaithersburg, MD 20899, USA (March 1993)

9. Rushby, J.: Formal Methods and the Certification of Critical Systems. Technical Report CSL-93-7, Computer Science Laboratory, Menlo Park CA 94025 USA (December 1993)
10. Fitzgerald, J.S., Larsen, P.G.: Triumphs and Challenges for the Industrial Application of Model-Oriented Formal Methods. In: Margaria, T., Philippou, A., Steffen, B. (eds.) Proc. 2nd Intl. Symp. on Leveraging Applications of Formal Methods, Verification and Validation (ISoLA 2007) (2007) (Also Technical Report CS-TR-999, School of Computing Science, Newcastle University)
11. Jones, C.B.: Scientific Decisions which Characterize VDM. In: Wing, J.M., Woodcock, J.C.P., Davies, J. (eds.) FM 1999. LNCS, vol. 1708, pp. 28–47. Springer, Heidelberg (1999)
12. Larsen, P.G., Hansen, B.S., Brunn, H., Plat, N., Toetenel, H., Andrews, D.J., Dawes, J., Parkin, G., et al.: Information technology – Programming languages, their environments and system software interfaces – Vienna Development Method – Specification Language – Part 1: Base language (December 1996)
13. Plat, N., Larsen, P.G.: An Overview of the ISO/VDM-SL Standard. Sigplan Notices 27(8), 76–82 (1992)
14. Larsen, P.G., Pawłiowski, W.: The Formal Semantics of ISO VDM-SL. Computer Standards and Interfaces 17(5-6), 585–602 (1995)
15. Bicarregui, J., Fitzgerald, J., Lindsay, P., Moore, R., Ritchie, B.: Proof in VDM: A Practitioner's Guide. In: FACIT, Springer, Heidelberg (1994)
16. Larsen, P.G., Fitzgerald, J., Brookes, T.: Applying Formal Specification in Industry. IEEE Software 13(3), 48–56 (1996)
17. Fitzgerald, J., Larsen, P.G.: Modelling Systems – Practical Tools and Techniques in Software Development, The Edinburgh Building. Cambridge University Press, Cambridge (1998)
18. Devauchelle, L., Larsen, P.G., Voss, H.: PICGAL: Practical Use of Formal Specification to Develop a Complex Critical System. In: Fitzgerland, J., Jones, C.B., Lucas, P. (eds.) FME 1997. LNCS, vol. 1313, pp. 221–236. Springer, Heidelberg (1997)
19. Fitzgerald, J., Jones, C.: Proof in the validation of a formal model of a tracking system for a nuclear plant. In: Bicarregui, J. (ed.) Proof in VDM: Case Studies. FACIT Series, Springer, Heidelberg (1998)
20. Smith, P.R., Larsen, P.G.: Applications of VDM in Banknote Processing. In: Fitzgerald, J.S., Larsen, P.G. (eds.) VDM in Practice: Proc. First VDM Workshop 1999, (September 1999), available at www.vdmportal.org
21. Mukherjee, P., Bousquet, F., Delabre, J., Paynter, S., Larsen, P.G.: Exploring Timing Properties Using VDM++ on an Industrial Application. In: Bicarregui, J., Fitzgerald, J. (eds.) Proceedings of the Second VDM Workshop, (September 2000), available at www.vdmportal.org
22. Elmstrøm, R., Larsen, P.G., Lassen, P.B.: The IFAD VDM-SL Toolbox: A Practical Approach to Formal Specifications. ACM Sigplan Notices 29(9), 77–80 (1994)
23. CSK: VDMTools homepage. (2007), http://www.vdmtools.jp/en/
24. Overture-Core-Team: Overture Web site (2007), http://www.overturetool.org
25. Fitzgerald, J., Larsen, P.G., Mukherjee, P., Plat, N., Verhoef, M.: Validated Designs for Object–oriented Systems. Springer, New York (2005)
26. Verhoef, M., Larsen, P.G., Hooman, J.: Modeling and Validating Distributed Embedded Real-Time Systems with VDM++. In: Misra, J., Nipkow, T., Sekerinski, E. (eds.) FM 2006. LNCS, vol. 4085, pp. 147–162. Springer, Heidelberg (2006)
27. Verhoef, M., Larsen, P.G.: Interpreting Distributed System Architectures Using VDM++ – A Case Study. In: Sauser, B., Muller, G. (eds.) 5th Annual Conference on Systems Engineering Research (March 2007), http://www.stevens.edu/engineering/cser/
28. Fitzgerald, J., Larsen, P.G., Tjell, S., Verhoef, M.: Validation Support for Distributed Real-Time Embedded Systems in VDM++. Technical Report CS-TR:1017, School of Computing Science, Newcastle University (April 2007)

29. Kurita, T., Oota, T., Nakatsugawa, Y.: Formal specification of an embedded IC for cellular phones. In: Proceedings of Software Symposium 2005, Software Engineers Associates of Japan, pp. 73–80 (June 2005) (in Japanese)
30. Holloway, M., Butler, R.W.: Impediments to Industrial Use of Formal Methods. IEEE Computer 29(4), 25–26 (1996)
31. Fitzgerald, J., Larsen, P.: Formal Specification Techniques in the Commercial Development Process. In: Wirsing, M. (ed.) Position Papers from the Workshop on Formal Methods Application in Software Engineering Practice, International Conference on Software Engineering (ICSE-17), Seattle (1995), http://home0.inet.tele.dk/pgl/icse.pdf
32. Woodcock, J., Davies, J.: Using Z – Specification, Refinement, and Proof. Prentice Hall International Series in Computer Science, Englewood Cliffs (1996)
33. Abrial, J.R.: The B Book - Assigning Programs to Meanings. Cambridge University Press, Cambridge (1996)
34. Larsen, P.G., Lassen, P.B.: An Executable Subset of Meta-IV with Loose Specification. In: VDM '91: Formal Software Development Methods, VDM Europe, Springer, Heidelberg (1991)
35. Mukherjee, P.: Computer-aided Validation of Formal Specifications. Software Engineering Journal , 133–140 (July 1995)
36. Larsen, P.G.: Ten Years of Historical Development: "Bootstrapping" VDMTools. Journal of Universal Computer Science 7(8), 692–709 (2001)
37. Houston, I.: The IBM Z Tool. In: Prehn, S., Toetenel, H. (eds.) VDM 1991. LNCS, vol. 552, pp. 691–692. Springer, Heidelberg (1991)
38. Saaltink, M.: Z and EVES. In: Nicholls, J. (ed.) Z User Workshop, York 1991. Workshops in Computing, pp. 223–242. Springer, Heidelberg (1991)
39. Toyn, I., J.: CADiZ: an Architecture for Z tools and its Implementation. Softw.-Pract. Exp (UK) 25(3), 305–330 (1995)
40. Lee, M., Sørensen, I.: B-tool. In: Prehn, S., Toetenel, W. (eds.) VDM 1991. LNCS, vol. 552, pp. 695–696. Springer, Heidelberg (1991)
41. Clearsy: Atelier B Web site (2007), http://www.atelierb.societe.com/index_uk.htm
42. Johnson, S.: Lint, a C Program Checker. Computer Science 65, Bell Laboratories (December 1977)
43. Rushby, J.: Model Checking and Other Ways of Automating Formal Methods. In: Software Quality Week, San Francisco, CA (May 1995) (Position paper for panel on Model Checking for Concurrent Programs)
44. Heitmeyer, C.L.: On the Need for Practical Formal Methods. In: Ravn, A.P., Rischel, H. (eds.) FTRTFT 1998. LNCS, vol. 1486, pp. 18–26. Springer, Heidelberg (1998)
45. Heitmeyer, C.: A Panacea or Academic Poppycock: Formal Methods Revisited. In: High-Assurance Systems Engineering, 2005. HASE 2005. Ninth IEEE International Symposium, pp. 3–7. IEEE, Los Alamitos (2005)
46. Heitmeyer, C.: Developing Safety-Critical Systems: the Role of Formal Methods and Tools. In: SCS '05: Proceedings of the 10th Australian Workshop on Safety Critical Systems and Software, Darlinghurst, Australia, pp. 95–99. Australian Computer Society, Inc., Australia (2006)
47. Pierce, B.C. (ed.) Advanced Topics in Types and Programming Languages. MIT Press, Cambridge (2005)
48. Aichernig, B.K., Larsen, P.G.: A Proof Obligation Generator for VDM-SL. In: Fitzgerald, J.S., Jones, C.B., Lucas, P. (eds.) FME 1997. LNCS, vol. 1313, pp. 338–357. Springer, Heidelberg (1997)
49. Luckham, D.C., von Henke, F.W.: An Overview of Anna, A Specification Language for Ada. In: IEEE Software, pp. 9–22. IEEE Computer Society Press, Los Alamitos (1985)

50. Burdy, L., Cheon, Y., Cok, D., Ernst, M.D., Kiniry, J.R., Leavens, G.T., Leino, K.R.M., Poll, E.: An overview of JML Tools and Applications. Intl. Journal of Software Tools for Technology Transfer 7, 212–232 (2005)
51. Chalin, P., Hurlin, C., Kiniry, J.: Integrating Static Checking and Interactive Verification: Supporting Multiple Theories and Provers in Verification. In: Proceedings of Verified Software: Tools, Technologies, and Experiences (VSTTE) (2005)
52. Clarke, E., Emerson, E., Sistla, A.: Automatic Verification of Finite-State Concurrent Systems Using Temporal Logic Specifications. ACM Transactions on Programming Languages and Systems 8(2), 244–263 (1986)
53. McMillan, K.L.: Symbolic Model Checking. PhD thesis, Carnegie Mellon University, School of Computer Science. Kluwer Academic Publishers, Dordrecht (1992)
54. Jackson, D.: Software Abstractions: Logic, Language, and Analysis. MIT Press, Heyward Street, Cambridge, MA02142, USA (2006)
55. Hayes, I., Jones, C.: Specifications are not (Necessarily) Executable. Software Engineering Journal, 330–338 (November 1989)
56. Kneuper, R.: Symbolic Execution as a Tool for Validation of Specifications. PhD thesis, Department of Computer Science, Univeristy of Manchester (March, Technical Report Series UMCS-89-7-1 (1989)
57. Andersen, M., Elmstrøom, R., Lassen, P.B., Larsen, P.G.: Making Specifications Executable – Using IPTES Meta-IV. Microprocessing and Microprogramming 35(1-5), 521–528 (1992)
58. Fröhlich, B.: Towards Executability of Implicit Definitions. PhD thesis, TU Graz, Institute of Software Technology (September 1998)
59. Dick, J., Faivre, A.: Automating the Generation and Sequencing of Test Cases from Model-Based Specifications. In: Larsen, P.G., Woodcock, J.C.P. (eds.) FME 1993. LNCS, vol. 670, pp. 268–284. Springer, Heidelberg (1993)
60. Gaudel, M.C.: Testing can be formal, too. In: Mosses, P., Schwartzbach, M., Nielsen, M. (eds.) CAAP 1995, FASE 1995, and TAPSOFT 1995. LNCS, vol. 915, pp. 82–96. Springer, Heidelberg (1995)
61. Burdonov, I., Kossatchev, A., Petrenko, A., Galter, D.: KVEST: Automated Generation of Test Suites from Formal Specifications. In: Wing, J.M., Woodcock, J.C.P., Davies, J. (eds.) FM 1999. LNCS, vol. 1708, pp. 608–621. Springer, Heidelberg (1999)
62. TestingFaqs.org: Test Coverage Tools (2007), http://www.testingfaqs.org/t-eval.html
63. van Lamsweerde, A.: Formal Specification: a Roadmap. In: ICSE '00: Proceedings of the Conference on The Future of Software Engineering, pp. 147–159. ACM Press, New York (2000)
64. Back, R.J.: On the Correctness of Refinement Steps in Program Development. PhD thesis, Åbo Akademi, Department of Computer Science, Helsinki, Finland Report A–1978–4 (1978)
65. Carrington, D., Hayes, I., Nickson, R., Watson, G., Welsh, J.: A Review of Existing Refinement Tools. SVRC TR-94-8, University of Queensland (1994)
66. Jones, C.B.: Systematic Software Development Using VDM, 2nd edn. Prentice-Hall International, Englewood Cliffs, New Jersey (1990)
67. Ah-Kee, J.: Operation Decomposition Proof Obligations. PhD thesis, University of Manchester (1989)
68. Badeau, F., Amelot, A.: Using B as a High Level Programming Language in an Industrial Project: Roissy VAL. In: Z to B Conference / Nantes, pp. 334–354 (2005)
69. Burdy, L., J.M.: Automatic Refinement. In: Woodcock, J.C.P., Davies, J., Wing, J.M. (eds.) FM 1999. LNCS, vol. 1709, Springer, Heidelberg (1999)

70. Leavens, G.T., Abrial, J.R., Batory, D., Butler, M., Coglio, A., Fisler, K., Hehner, E., Jones, C., Miller, D., Peyton-Jones, S., Sitaraman, M., Smith, D.R., Stump, A.: Roadmap for Enhanced Languages and Methods to aid Verification. In: Proceedings of the 5th International Conference on Generative Programming and Component Engineering, pp. 221–236. ACM Press, New York (2006)

71. Owre, S., Rushby, J.M., Shankar, N.: PVS: A Prototype Verification System. In: Kapur, D. (ed.) Automated Deduction - CADE-11. LNCS, vol. 607, pp. 748–752. Springer, Heidelberg (1992)

72. Paulson, L.C.: Generic automatic proof tools. In: Veroff, R. (ed.) Automated Reasoning and its Applications: Essays in Honor of Larry Wos, pp. 23–47. MIT Press, Cambridge (1997)

73. Harper, R.: Proof-directed debugging. Journal of Functional Programming 9(4), 463–469 (1999)

74. Dennis, L.A., Monroy, R., Nogueira, P.: Proof-directed Debugging and Repair. In: Nilsson, H., van Eekelen, M. (eds.) Seventh Symposium on Trends in Functional Programming 2006, pp. 131–140 (2006)

75. Dennis, L.A., Collins, G., Norrish, M., Boulton, R., Slind, K., Robinson, G., Gordon, M., Melham, T.: The PROSPER Toolkit. In: Schwartzbach, M.I., Graf, S. (eds.) ETAPS 2000 and TACAS 2000. LNCS, vol. 1785, Springer, Heidelberg (2000)

76. Terada, N., Fukuda, M.: Application of Formal Methods to the Railway Signaling Systems. Quarterly Report of RTRI 43(4), 169–174 (2002)

77. Dion, B., Gartner, J.: Efficient Development of Embedded Automotive Software with IEC 61508 Objectives using SCADE Drive. In: VDI 12th International Conference: Electronic Systems for Vehicles, VDI (October 2005)

78. Snook, C., Butler, M.: UML-B: Formal modeling and design aided by UML. ACM Trans. Softw. Eng. Methodol. 15(1), 92–122 (2006)

79. Verhoef, M., Peter Visser, J.H., Broenink, J.: Co-simulation of Real-time Embedded Control Systems. In: IFM 2007: Integrated Formal Methods. LNCS, Springer, Heidelberg (2007)

80. Fröhlich, B., Larsen, P.G.: Combining VDM-SL Specifications with C++ Code. In: Gaudel, M.-C., Woodcock, J. (eds.) FME 1996. LNCS, vol. 1051, pp. 179–194. Springer, Heidelberg (1996)

81. Hekmatpour, S., Ince, D.C.: A Formal Specification-Based Prototyping System. In: Barnes, D., Brown, P. (eds.) Software Engineering 1986, pp. 317–335. Peter Peregrinus Ltd., London (1986)

82. McParland, P.J.: Software Tools to Support Formal Methods. PhD thesis, Queen's University Belfast (October 1989)

83. RODIN-Project-Members: RODIN (2007), http://rodin.cs.ncl.ac.uk/

84. Sobel, A.E.K., Clarkson, M.R.: Formal Methods Application: An Empirical Tale of Software Development. IEEE Trans. Software Engineering 28(3), 308–320 (2002)

85. Berry, D.M., Tichy, W.F.: Comments on Formal Methods Application: An Empirical Tale of Software Development. IEEE Transactions on Software Engineering 29(6), 567–571 (2003)

86. Sobel, A.E.K., Clarkson, M.R.: Response to Comments on Formal Methods Application: An Empirical Tale of Software Development. IEEE Trans. Software Engineering 29(6), 572–575 (2003)

87. Sobel, A.E.K.: Empirical Results of a Software Engineering Curriculum Incorporating Formal Methods. In: Proceedings of SIGCSE 2000, ACM, pp. 157–161. ACM Press, New York (2000)

88. Larsen, P.G., Fitzgerald, J.S., Riddle, S.: Learning by Doing: Practical Courses in Lightweight Formal Methods using VDM++. Technical Report CS-TR:992, School of Computing Science, Newcastle University (December 2006)

89. Kramer, J.: Is Abstraction the Key to Computing? Communications of the ACM 50(4), 37–42 (2007)

90. Barnett, M., Leino, R.M., Schulte, W.: The Spec# Programming System: An Overview. In: Barthe, G., Burdy, L., Huisman, M., Lanet, J.-L., Muntean, T. (eds.) CASSIS 2004. LNCS, vol. 3362, Springer, Heidelberg (2005)

91. Wing, J.: Weaving Formal Methods into the Undergraduate Computer Science Curriculum. In: Rus, T. (ed.) AMAST 2000. LNCS, vol. 1816, Springer, Heidelberg (2000)

92. Palmer, T.V., Pleasant, J.C.: Attitudes Toward the Teaching of Formal Methods of Software Development in the Undergraduate Computer Science Curriculum: a Survey. SIGCSE Bulletin 27(3), 53–59 (1995)

93. Skevoulis, S., Makarov, V.: Integrating Formal Methods Tools into Undergraduate Computer Science Curriculum. In: Frontiers in Education Conference, 36th Annual, ASEE, pp. 1–6. IEEE Computer Society Press, Los Alamitos (2006)

# Proving Theorems About JML Classes

Leo Freitas and Jim Woodcock

Department of Computer Science
University of York, UK
{leo,jim}@cs.york.ac.uk

**Abstract.** We present an initial link between Z and JML that has enabled us to use Z/Eves to prove theorems about JML classes. We have applied this to the JML type system and the Java `HashMap` class from the *Java Collections Framework*. We present and discuss the issues behind a more general strategy for translation in both directions between Z and JML. This work is a contribution to the *Verified Software Repository*, part of the *Grand Challenge in Verified Software*.

**Keywords:** Grand Challenge in Verified Software, JML, Java Collections Framework, Java HashMap class, Java Modeling Language, formal specification, linking theories, mechanical theorem proving, software verification, Verified Software Repository, Z, Z/Eves.

*On the occasion of the 70th birthdays of Dines Bjørner and Zhou Chaochen.*

## 1  On Linking Z and JML

The *Java Modeling Language* (JML) [3] is a language used to specify more clearly than informal documentation the behaviour of Java programs [12] by using annotations as Java comments. These annotations not only document the code, but also enable static checking, run-time assertion checking, and other verification tasks to be performed on the target code, such as loop invariant detection [16,4]. The JML toolset contains a number of other tools, such as an annotation parser and typechecker, an HTML (`JavaDOC`-style) documentation generator for JML annotations, an automatic unit test set generator, and so on. In various syntactic forms, JML annotations are predicates specifying declarative behaviour, such as pre- and postconditions, class and instance invariants, modifiable-variable frames, concurrent and real-time behaviour, resource allocation in terms of memory and computational time, and so on [24]. JML supports a lightweight style of specification, where annotations start as quite trivial predicates, and are then enriched over time by adding extra constraints.

The Z notation [34] is a formal specification method that has enjoyed a certain acceptance amongst academic and industrial practitioners for more than two decades [36,42,18], and was standardised by ISO in 2002 [20]. Z is useful for specifying abstract data types and their corresponding operations, as well as for proving data refinement from an abstract specification to a concrete implementation [41], at which point a refinement calculus [1,25,6] can be used to reach a

C.B. Jones, Z. Liu, J. Woodcock (Eds.): Bjørner/Zhou Festschrift, LNCS 4700, pp. 255–279, 2007.

language of guarded commands [7] that is close to actual code in general-purpose programming languages.

In this paper we demonstrate the benefits of a link with Z that goes beyond using pure JML. We do this: (i) by using a mechanical theorem prover to verify some properties of a JML specification expressed in Z; and (ii) by pinpointing the issues for the definition of a more systematic translation strategy between Z and JML, and *vice versa*. The JML annotation syntax is divided into different language levels; lower levels are mandatory, but higher levels are optional [24, Sect. 2.9]. Starting from these lower levels, we concentrate on JML's specification of abstract data types, leaving out other important aspects of JML annotations as future work.

In [10], we formally specified in Z a hash map data type, an extension of the work originally done in [11]. The Z hash map was used as a concrete refinement for an abstract specification of the Unix filing system in [26]. We chose hash maps because they provide constant-time performance for most operations, including search and insertion. Although the Z hash map was tailored to the needs of the filing system, we based it on the requirements from the Java documentation and the JML specification. We took into account the essential properties hash maps ought to have, such as strategies for resolving clashes of hash keys. The choice for HashMap here remains an interesting proposition since it is widely used in Java programs, and is among one of the most complex data structures within the *Java Collections Framework*.[1]

Some other classes have been subjected to this kind of scrutiny before. Huisman [17] has shown that the Java Set implementation (version 1.3) is not guarded against Russell's paradox [31]). Earlier work verified the vector class [15] and aspects of the JavaCard API [29,39]. Our translation is similar in spirit to those between Z and BON/Eiffel [28] and BON and Object-Z [27].

## 2    JML Specifications

In this section, we give a brief overview of JML to help explain the HashMap specification. Suppose P, Q, and R are boolean JML expressions (*i.e.*, Java expressions with bounded quantifiers and mathematical sets), L is a list of locations (*i.e.*, object attribute names, or an abstract collection of names), and E is some checked Java Exception (*i.e.*, those exceptions that are part of a method signature). The JML specification for a method m() is given as

```
/*@ assignable L;
  @ requires P;
  @ ensures Q;
  @ signals (E) R; */
public void m() throws E { ... };
```

JML annotations are like Java comments but with an added "@" sign. Apart from the signals clause, this specification is like a specification statement in

---

[1] See java.sun.com/docs/books/tutorial/collections.

Morgan's refinement calculus [25] (*i.e.*, L : [P, Q]). The list of locations L is the frame; the precondition P is a predicate on the before-state; the postcondition Q is a predicate on both the before and the after-states. Both conditions can refer to attributes outside the frame, but the postcondition cannot change them. A before-variable x in L appearing in Q is represented as \old(x) where an after-variable is just x. In the signals clause, R represents the postcondition whenever m() throws the exception E. This enables the specification of error cases much like that in Z, where schema disjunction is used to combine error-free behaviour with error handling (see the *Disjoin Errors* Z specification pattern in [37, p. 63]).

Default values are widely used in the case where some of JML clauses are absent. In this way, no matter how minimal the given specification is, there is always a version of it that JML tools can infer; this transformation of the various syntaxes is known in the JML literature as "desugaring" [30]. We see the link with Z as "sweetening" JML with ("calorie free") results from proven theorems.

## 2.1 JML Type System

JML annotations include all expressions available in Java together with bounded quantifiers. This includes reference to object attributes and some methods and constructors, important since JML annotations were tailored for the Java programmer. Evaluating such expressions must not change the underlying object state; otherwise they would compromise the Java code they are supposed to specify. To help write side-effect free predicates, JML provides a meta-type system with useful side-effect free data types defined as Java classes. This is based on the JMLType class, which is the superclass of all meta-type systems. This makes it possible to have sets, sequences, bags, and other mathematical objects within JML annotations and quantifiers, just like one would expect to find in other formal notations, such as Z's mathematical toolkit [34, Chap. 4].

One concern JML needs to address is how the various forms of object equality in Java relate to the set-theoretic notion of equality. The two most important notions of equality in Java are object identity equality (*i.e.*, o1 == o2), which is like Leibniz's equality, and structural type equality (*i.e.*, o1.equals(o2)), where the former is usually stronger than the latter (o1 == o2 ⇒ o1.equals(o2)). Other notions of equality are also important, such as serial (marshalled) equality when object instances are represented as binary data files implementing the Serializable interface, but we are not concerned with this for now. Structural equality should be both symmetric and side-effect free, but this may not be the case. A structural equality test may inadvertently cause side effects on the object state; an alarming thought, since multiple consecutive calls to equals ought to produce the same result.

The JML type system provides implementations that use both forms of equality. These facilities are essential in order to extend Java expressions with quantifiers and set comprehension. Among these implementations, there are also versions of sets that are "mathematical sets", as opposed to a "collection of objects". That is, the JML type system offers for each meta-type, say a set, four different implementations: collections of Object elements compared using identity (==) equality (named `JMLObjectSet`), or structural (`equals`) equality (named `JMLEqualsSet`); and mathematical sets of `JMLType` elements compared with structural equality (named `JMLValueSet`). The collection of objects uses aliasing for the elements, whereas the mathematical set uses cloned (shallow copied) versions of the elements. The `JMLValueSet` class is used as a JML meta-specification for extending JML's type system, whereas the `JMLEqualsSet` and `JMLObjectSet` are aimed at JML specifications from practical users, where the same applies for other mathematical entities like sequences and bags. These internal JML classes also contain JML annotations. As the JML annotated version of Java `HashMap` uses `JMLEqualsSet`, we give some more detail on it in Sect. 2.

A final concern when implementing `equals` is its relationship with the Java "`int hashCode()`" method, which provides a unique hash code for object instances. The Java documentation states that structurally equivalent objects must have the same hash code.

$$o1.\texttt{equals}(o2) \Rightarrow o1.\texttt{hashCode}() = o2.\texttt{hashCode}()$$

The reverse is not required, but is desirable since it improves the performance of `HashMap` implementations. Ideal implementations of these two methods are available for the unaware programmer, such as the `EqualsBuilder` and `HashCode-Builder` classes of the *Jakarta Commons* Apache library,[2] which provide adequate solutions as suggested in [2].

## 2.2 Abstraction Mechanisms

JML allows specification abstraction through the definition of model fields and methods. These are specification devices that exist only as JML annotations and do not have a direct counterpart in Java code, but can be used as part of the annotations specifying concrete Java methods. For instance, the `Object` class specification has one model field representing the (abstract) object state

```
1 //@ public model non_null JMLDataGroup objectState;
```

This model field is a placeholder to represent whatever attributes derived classes might have. A `JMLDataGroup` is an abstraction device representing a set of locations that can appear in `assignable` clauses. Data groups are particularly useful in allowing different visibilities among model fields: it is possible to state that private and protected instance fields used to compute public model fields are `assignable`. The `Object` class also has an example of a model method that raises our interest

```
1 // The value produced by hashCode() but without any side effects.
2 //@ ensures (\forall Object o; this.equals(o)
3 //                ==> \result == o.hashValue());
4 //@ public pure model int hashValue();
```

The `hashValue()` model method is a side-effect free version of the `hashCode()` method that obeys the Java documentation requirement that structurally equivalent objects must have the same hash code. For clarity of presentation, we add

---

[2] See `jakarta.apache.org/commons`.

to the left-hand side of JML specifications line numbers, which are often referred to within the text. We also follow the convention to use arabic numerals for the specifications copied from the JML distribution, and roman numerals for specifications resulting from our experiments with Z.

## 2.3  Equational Theory

JML type system classes use an equational theory specified as a model method. The equational theory for `JMLEqualsSet` specifies seventeen properties, which are essentially some restricted forms or known set-theoretical laws [34, Chap. 4], such as cardinality of empty sets ($S = \varnothing \Leftrightarrow \#S = 0$) or set containment over set union ($e \in S1 \cup S2 \Leftrightarrow e \in S1 \vee e \in S2$). We pay careful attention to this equational theory for such JML sets since they are often used as model fields of actual JML specifications, such as the one for `HashMap`.

```
1 //@ public model instance non_null JMLEqualsSet theMap;
2 //@                                         in objectState;
```

This model field (abstractly) represents the map as a set of `Object` instances structurally equated with `equals`, which belongs to the data group of the general `Object` state. By understanding how JML sets interpret equality, it is possible to relate JML sets with the set-theoretical data types and notion of equality in Z, as shown below for Z hash maps (see Sect. 3).

## 2.4  Nullability and Instance Cloning

Another concern within JML is the "nullability" of method parameters and results, and object attribute initialisations. The JML type system provides facilities to handle `null` objects so that equality tests on sets (and other data structures) containing `null` objects are well defined and do not throw exceptions, such as in the `JMLNullSafe` class. We assume in this paper that no hash key or associated value within the Z hash map will ever be `null`. The effect of relaxing this assumption is a more verbose and laborious specification, without much insight or novelty added. Thus, we have traded the treatment of `null` for the investigation of additional properties of hash maps and automation mechanisation rules, as present in Sect. 3.4.

JML addresses object cloning via the specification of the `clone()` method for the `Object` class. It specifies how cloned object instances preserve the original class type, general (attribute) structure, and produce no side effects. In Java, only objects that implement the `Cloneable` interface can be cloned. In general, for any `Object` that implements the `Cloneable` interface, `clone()` is side-effect free, and has a non-null result of the same dynamic type as the cloned object.

```
1 /*@ protected normal_behavior
2   @    requires this instanceof Cloneable;
3   @    assignable \nothing;
4   @    ensures \result != null && \typeof(\result) == \typeof(this);
5   @    ensures (* \result is a clone of this *);
6   @*/
```

The `normal_behaviour` keyword is for exception-free postconditions. Cloned arrays must preserve all elements: all cloned array elements have the same object identity, and clone is specified as a shallow copy.

```
 7 /*@ ...
 8   @ requires this.getClass().isArray();
 9   @ ensures (\forall int i; 0 <= i && i < ((Object[])this).length;
10   @                ((Object[])\result )[i] == ((Object[])this)[i]);
11   @*/
12 protected /*@non_null*/ Object clone() throws ...;
```

A similar specification is added for other primitive array types. As `Object` itself does not implement `Cloneable`, this specification lays the foundation but cannot be used yet. Derived classes that implement `Cloneable` usually add a further (standard) postcondition, like the one below for `HashMap`, which strengthens dynamic typechecking (line (4)), guarantees structural equality (but not object equality) with `this` (line (5)), and is side-effect free (line (3)).

```
1 /*@ also
2   @   public normal_behavior
3   @     assignable \nothing;
4   @     ensures \result instanceof Map && \fresh(\result)
5   @         && ((Map)\result).equals(this);
6   @   ensures_redundantly \result != this;
7   @*/
8 public Object clone();
```

The `also` keyword conjoins this specification for `HashMap` with the one inherited from `Object`. The `ensures_redundantly` clause (line (6)) states a direct consequence of the previous postcondition that is useful for automatic tools that might not be able to deduce this directly. As object cloning is a low-level implementation issue, it does not quite have a direct correspondence in a Z specification, unless one is concerned with memory management. As our focus is to investigate the `HashMap` functionality, we do not consider cloning any further.

### 2.5   JML Invariants

JML also provides instance or class (`static`) invariants. These are predicates that always hold for visible object states [24, Sect. 8.2]. In JML's terminology [24, p. 50–51], invariants can be *assumed*, *established*, or *preserved*. For each method and constructor, class invariants can be assumed by the class type at visible pre-states and are established at visible post-states. Instance invariants are similar. Invariants that are both assumed and established are preserved.

For instance, Java models `HashMap` as an array of `Entry` objects as key-value pairs, where the following instance invariants about type consistency among `Entry` in `theMap` model field holds.

```
1 // only standard JML tools understand *+@ annotations
2 /*+@ public instance invariant
3   @      (\forall Object o; theMap.has(o); o instanceof Map.Entry);
```

```
4    @*/
5 /*+@ public instance invariant
6    @         (\forall Object o1, o2; theMap.has(o1) && theMap.has(o2);
7    @                         o2!=o1 ==> !JMLNullSafe.equals(o2,o1));
8    @*/
```

It specifies that `theMap` elements are a subtype of `Entry` (lines (2–4)), and that different `Entry` elements (by object identity) within `theMap` cannot be structurally equivalent (lines (5–8)), bearing in mind the treatment of equality among `null` objects through the `JMLNullSafe` class. As the specification of `equals` for `Entry` below relies on the implementation of `equals` for the key and the value, this second class invariant is more interesting: it enforces that key-value pairs within different entries properly implement their structural equivalence algorithm (in lines (4–6) below); and that they are side-effect free (with `pure` keyword in line (9)); the keyword `pure` is an abbreviation for `assignable \nothing`.

```
1 /*+@ also
2    @    public normal_behavior
3    @      requires o instanceof Entry;
4    @      ensures \result ==
5    @        (JMLNullSafe.equals(((Entry)o).abstractKey, abstractKey)
6    @      && JMLNullSafe.equals(((Entry)o).abstractValue,
7    @                            abstractValue) );
8    @+*/
9 /*@ pure @*/ public boolean equals(/*@ nullable @*/ Object o);
```

The specification for equality between map entries relies on the structural equality of the array of `Entry` as the key-value pairs it represents. This care with structural equality is needed since the equational theory used in the JML specification of `theMap` model field is the one from the `JMLEqualsSet` class. JML also allows the declaration of class axioms. The JML tools within the standard distribution usually ignore these axioms [3], but theorem provers within some more powerful JML tools [16,4] assume them as lemmas.

## 3  Formalising Java `HashMaps` in Z

With this basic introduction to JML, we start linking the JML specification of Java's `HashMap` with an extended Z hash map from [8,11]. The JML specification for `HashMap` encompasses the specifications of its inheritance tree: the `Object`, `AbstractMap`, and `HashMap` classes; and the `Map`, `Cloneable`, and `Serializable` interfaces. As mentioned above, we are not interested for now in object cloning or serialisation, and hence we concentrate on the other classes and interfaces. We are also not concerned here with specification for nullability or exception handling, and hence we omit them. Some of the JML specifications for `Object` and `Map` were already introduced in the previous section. The other JML elements we consider are detailed below together with their corresponding Z counterparts. They are the invariants, assignable variables, method preconditions, and exception-free method postconditions (*i.e.*, `ensures` rather than `signals` clauses).

In presenting the Z material, we follow the bottom-up style of the Z/Eves theorem prover [32] that we use to define the Z hash map. All material presented here has been mechanically verified, and the conjectures proved as theorems. We point out opportunities for completing the JML annotations, either with theorems developed in Z, or directly with definitions drawn from the Java documentation. These are merely suggestions, since we have not yet established how to formally link Z and JML (see discussion in Sect. 4), but we find them useful.

### 3.1   Java HashMap Design in Z

In Java, a HashMap represents Object keys mapped to Object values, where the key's hashCode() method is used to uniquely index entries of key-value pairs into an underlying array-like data structure. This array of Entry objects within the map is functional (*i.e., Key* $\nrightarrow$ *Value*). The map has two parameters allowing trade-off between operations performance: an initial capacity and a load factor. The capacity is the length of the array of entries, whereas the load factor measures how full the map may get before its capacity is automatically increased.

This design provides constant-time performance for basic query and insert operations, assuming the hash function disperses the elements properly. Iteration over the map requires time proportional to the capacity (the initial array size), plus the number of actual key-value pairs. When the number of map entries exceeds the product of these parameters, the array is rehashed to allow room for further entries. In this way, these two parameters can be used to trade-off performance between get/put and iteration operations. As Object instances are given as map keys, care must be taken if their structure (the result of their equals method) could change whilst within the map. Map keys are not immutable and may suffer from side effects, in which case the behaviour of the map is not specified. Thus, maps themselves should never be keys, and if they are values in Entry, the equals and hashCode methods of the map would no longer be well-defined.

**Hash Code Values.** The hash code integer ($\mathbb{Z}$) from a map key (o1) is normalised to a strictly positive integer ($\mathbb{N}_1$) via a hashing function (*hf*), taking into account the map's capacity.

$$i.e., \text{map.put(o1, v1)} \rightsquigarrow (hf \, (\text{o1.hashCode()}, \text{capacity}) \mapsto \text{v1})$$

As map keys are Object instances, we need to consider the Object JML specification for hashCode()

```
1 // for subclasses with benevolent side effects
2 /*@   public behavior
3   @     assignable objectState;
4   @     ensures (* \result is a hash code for this object *);
5   @ //ensures \result == hashValue();
6   @*/
7 /*+@ also
```

```
 8    @    public code normal_behavior
 9    @       assignable \nothing;
10    @+*/
11 public int hashCode();
```

This is a loose specification that permits the hash code calculation to have "benevolent side effects" on the objectState model field, and should rely on the hashValue() model method (see Sect. 2.2). The ensures clause (line (4)) is simply informal text, as meta-comments just evaluate to true. Although it not quite clear what it means for side effects to be "benevolent", one could argue that they would be related to unobservable by external clients, such as caching schemes. It is also not quite clear what the motivations were for not enforcing in the postcondition the invariant (line (5)) as defined by the hashValue() model method (see Sect. 2.2). There are two problems with this under-specification: (i) hashCode is not side-effect free, since the second behaviour (lines (7–10)) has no postcondition; and (ii) even if one agrees that there is a case for "benevolent side effects", nothing is given to enforce the invariant between hashCode and equals (see Sect. 2.1). Perhaps, this choice is based on some undisclosed technicality, or is still under development. We think a more intuitive specification would be:

```
  i /*@  public behavior
 ii   @     assignable \nothing;
iii   @     ensures (* \result is a hash code for this object *);
 iv   @     ensures \result == hashValue();
  v   @*/
 vi /*@ pure @*/ public int hashCode();
```

As the map implementation is modelled as an array of Entry, its hash code specification is also important. Despite this fact, there is no JML specification for it. The Java documentation says that provided the key-value is not null (which in our case we assume to always be *true*), then the hash code of an Entry e is the *bitwise exclusive or* (*xor*) integer operator between the hashCode of key and value (lines (v–vi)). So, a candidate JML specification would be

```
  i /*@ also
 ii   @ public normal_behaviour
iii   @    assignable \nothing;
 iv   @    requires getKey() != null && getValue() != null;
  v   @    ensures (\result == getKey().hashValue() ^
 vi   @                        getValue().hashValue());
vii   @*/
viii /*@ pure @*/ public int hashCode();
```

We inherit the specification from Object with also (line (i)), and add the expected side-effect free (in line (iii)) postcondition (line (v)), provided the Entry has non-null elements (line (iv)). This keeps the equals/hashCode invariant among any Entry within the map implementation. If hashCode was specified as pure in Object, we could have used getKey().hashCode() instead.

**Handling Clashes.** Clashes can happen either when there are more entries than room available, in which case the map could expand (and be rehashed), or when badly programmed hash codes provide duplicates for different keys, and so compromise the hash function. In both cases, Java's robust solution is to have a linked list at the points of clash, so that in the worst case one gets a *"spiked"* map, where the clashing entries grow outwards as linked lists. So, from the previous insertion example, in the case of a clash with another value,

```
o1 != o2 && hf(o1.hashCode(), capacity) = hf(o2.hashCode(), capacity)
```

an update would become

$$\texttt{map.put(o2, v2)} \rightsquigarrow (hf\,(\texttt{o2.hashCode()}, \texttt{capacity}) \mapsto \langle v1, v2 \rangle)$$

Thus, a `HashMap` is like an injection from hash codes (generated by *hf* from `hashCode()` considering the map capacity) into a sequence of abstractly defined *VALUE*s, as roughly drafted in Z below

$$[VALUE]$$

$$\text{``} HashMap \ == \ hf\,hashCode \rightarrowtail \text{seq } VALUE \text{ ''}$$

We need to model in Z the Java hashing and clashing mechanisms described above. We start defining the auxiliary structures that are the basis of a Z hash map. This mechanised specification grew out of the original work done in [10,11], and is slightly modified here for ease of presentation. Moreover, we assume maps are neither keys nor values within other maps, as these would be special cases (see Sect. 3.1). Nevertheless, they can be modularly handled later following some Z specification patterns, as in [37].

A candidate hash function is trivially defined using integer division remainder, bearing in mind the strictly positive capacity of the map involved.

$$hf : \mathbb{Z} \times \mathbb{N}_1 \to \mathbb{N}$$

$\langle\!\langle$ disabled rule dHashFcn $\rangle\!\rangle$
$\forall hck : \mathbb{Z}; \ n : \mathbb{N}_1 \bullet$
$\quad hf\,(hck, n) = \textbf{if}\ (hck \geq 0)\ \textbf{then}\ (hck \bmod n)\ \textbf{else}\ -(hck \bmod n)$

This provides separation of concerns, so that different implementations can provide more efficient hashing mechanisms without changing the clashing mechanism and other mapping operations.

As most objects that are meant to be map keys have individual `hashCode()` implementations, it is beside the point to specify them here. Instead, we abstract hash code key generation below with the *HashAlgo* schema.

$$[OID, VID]$$

$$HashAlgo \ \hat{=} \ [\,algo : OID \rightarrowtail \mathbb{Z}\,]$$

We define the given set *OID* as an abstract representation of object identifiers that are meant to be map keys. Those identifiers are either immutable objects or do not structurally change (*i.e.*, keep the results of `equals`) whilst being a map key. Equality between elements of this given set is interpreted as Java structural equality

$$(o1 \in OID \land o2 \in OID \land o1 = o2) \Leftrightarrow \texttt{o1.equals(o2)}$$

Similarly, the given set $VID$ is an abstract representation of object identifiers that are mapped values, where we use the same interpretation of equality as $OID$. These interpretations are important since the model field representing the array of $\texttt{Entry}$ in $\texttt{HashMap}$ ($\texttt{theMap}$) is an instance of $\texttt{JMLEqualsSet}$ (see Sects 2.1 and 2.3 above).

The schema $HashCode$ represents the abstraction of the $\texttt{hashCode()}$ algorithm as an injection from the object instance ($OID$) to the corresponding hash code value. It abstractly defines the behaviour of the $\texttt{hashCode()}$ method in Z.

---
$HashCode$

$HashAlgo$; $this?$ : $OID$ ; $result!$ : $\mathbb{Z}$

---
$result! = algo\ this?$

---

From a given object instance $this?$, the hash code $result!$ is output as the hash value of the algorithm for that instance ($i.e.$, $result! = this?.\texttt{hashCode()}$). With the abstract specification of $algo$ as an injection, we can further refine it to particular concrete implementations as needed, by coming back from generated hash codes to the object instances that generated them.

Next, we model the underlying $\texttt{Entry}$ for key-value pairs considering the clashing mechanisms described above as

$Entry$ ==
$\{\, s : \text{iseq}\,(OID \times VID) \mid$
$\quad \forall o : OID \,;\ v1, v2 : VID \mid o \mapsto v1 \in \text{ran}\ s \land o \mapsto v2 \in \text{ran}\ s \bullet v1 = v2 \,\}$

Whenever two different object ids $o1$ and $o2$ have the same normalised hash code, a clash will happen and an entry may grow like in the example above. In such cases, this "spiked" $Entry$ specification enforces that: (i) no key-value pairs are repeated in the list (iseq); and (ii) no clashes on different values can happen for the same key object instance, the clashed pairs of $Entry$ are functional on the keys. The first property is defined in JML as an axiom, and we have proved it as a trivial theorem based on our definition. In both cases, this theorem/axiom is used to avoid a key being associated with different values. The second property not only follows the $\texttt{HashMap}$ contract, but it also enforces that $\texttt{Entry}$ keys properly implement $\texttt{hashCode}$ by keeping hash keys immutable. It also serves as a soundness invariant for the $\texttt{hashCode()}$ of entries, whenever they are values in other maps themselves. Also, the sequences $s$ of $Entry$ that are entries represent ordering for clashes, where the injectivity (uniqueness) is an optimisation for storage. This (uniqueness) restriction is indirectly enforced in JML by the equational theory used in $\texttt{theMap}$ model field. This model also captures the efficiency concerns for Java $\texttt{HashMap}$ lifted from its JML specification. As $\texttt{Entry}$ is the most fundamental data structure to build a hash map, we see the finding and interpretation of such invariants as very useful. But they didn't appear by magic: they were discovered by using the theorem prover in the refutatory style advocated in the classical style [23, p.127], in order to reach an elegant specification that is amenable for mechanisation.

The JML axiom about the functionality of entries is given in the specification of the Map interface that HashMap implements in terms of the contains model methods, as transcribed below

```
1  /*@ public normal_behavior
3   @     requires e != null;
4   @     ensures \result <==> contains(e.getKey(),e.getValue());
5   @ public pure model boolean contains(Entry e);
7   @
8   @ public pure model boolean contains(Object key, Object value);
9   @
10  @ axiom (\forall Map m; (\forall Object k, v, vv;
11  @     (m.contains(k,v) && m.contains(k,vv)) ==>
12  @             JMLNullSafe.equals(v,vv)));
13  @*/
```

The model method in line (8) is important since its use is propagated throughout most of the HashMap specification. Despite this fact, it has no explicit specification, which means it has just the trivial postcondition *true*, whatever the given Entry. As theMap model field used to represent the array of entries implements an equational theory for structural equality (*i.e.*, JMLEqualsSet), we were surprised it was not linked with contains. This link was hinted at as one of the class invariant examples mentioned earlier (see Sect. 2.5), since the has() method is defined in terms of the right equational theory.

```
1  /*+@ public instance invariant
2   @   (\forall Object o1, o2; theMap.has(o1) && theMap.has(o2);
3   @                    o2!=o1 ==> !JMLNullSafe.equals(o2,o1));
4   @*/
```

We are not certain if this would enforce the right specification for containment. We suggest to explicitly add a link between theMap and contains, as

```
  i  /*@ public normal_behavior
 ii   @     requires e != null;
iii   @     ensures \result <==> theMap.has(e) ;
 iv   @ public pure model boolean contains(Entry e);
  v   @
 vi   @ public normal_behaviour
vii   @     requires key != null && value != null;
viii  @     ensures \result <==> contains(e.getKey(), e.getValue());
 ix   @ public pure model boolean contains(Object key, Object value);
  x   @*/
```

For JML, the restriction on non-null key/value could be relaxed or generalised to handle null.

**Z State Schema and Initialisation.** The state schema *HM* for Java `HashMap` in Z is given below.

```
┌─ HM ─────────────────────────────────────────────────
│  hm : ℕ ⤔ Entry ;   HashAlgo
│  idx, size : ℕ;  capacity, loadfactor : ℕ₁
├──────────────────────────────────────────────────────
│  dom hm = 0 .. capacity − 1
│  size ≤ capacity ∗ (loadfactor div 100)
│  idx ∈ dom hm
│  ∀ o : OID ; i : ℕ | i ∈ dom hm • i = hf (algo o, capacity)
```

It uniquely maps indexes into the entries array as the partial function *hm*, where all such indexes are valid within the map's *capacity*. Indexes are the result of the hashing function (*hf*), which uses the object instance (*o*) hash code result (from *algo o*) modulo the initial *capacity* of the map. This establishes the link between hash code indexes within the map ($i \in$ dom *hm*), and object instances (*o*) whose `hashCode()` algorithm we are interested in. The *hm* injection is representing `theMap` JML model field in our Z model. It also represents the design from the `Map` interface as an array of entries. Furthermore, *idx* defines the current allocation position some mapping operations require. The *loadfactor* is useful to balance the performance of the map for query, insertion, or iteration operations adequately. In Java, *loadfactor* is given as a floating-point number supposed to represent a percentage, but Z/Eves does not have floats. To accommodate this, we normalise its value with integer division by 100, where the discrepancies should be minor, since one usually uses whole integer percentages (*e.g.*, the default value is 75%). The few extra class invariants about *capacity* and *loadfactor* that we have not mentioned already are given below.

```
1 //@ public model int initialCapacity;
2
3 // loadFactor is spec_public below
4 //@ public invariant initialCapacity >= 0;
5 //@ public invariant loadFactor > 0;
```

We are puzzled by the JML invariant for initial capacity allowing zero capacity maps. Although the Java documentation says that the capacity should be a power of 2 (and zero certainly is), we think it is of little use to specify a map that can never hold any element. Also, to avoid rehashing, we add an invariant that the maximum *size* (or number of elements) the map can take is smaller than the *capacity* multiplied by the (normalised) *loadfactor*. As *size* is loosely defined, it follows the Java documentation suggestion that *"if many mappings are to be stored in a HashMap, creating it with a sufficiently large capacity will allow the mappings to be stored more efficiently than letting it perform automatic rehashing as needed to grow"*. Thus we changed the range of *capacity* in *HM*, and the relationship between *size*, *capacity*, and *loadfactor* accordingly.

In JML, initialisation takes place at class constructors. In our case, we need to consider the constructors for `Object` and `HashMap`, as `AbstractMap` and the implemented interfaces have no constructor specification. The default/implicit constructor from `Object` is trivial. Like a $\Xi$ schema in Z, it just states no attributes are modified.

```
1 /*@ public normal_behavior
2   @   assignable \nothing;
3   @*/
4 public /*@ pure @*/ Object();
```

`HashMap` has various constructors, which could all be related to one single version that we transcribe below.

```
1 /*@ public normal_behavior
2   @   requires initialCapacity >= 0;
3   @   assignable theMap, this.initialCapacity, this.loadFactor;
4   @   ensures theMap != null && theMap.isEmpty();
5   @   ensures this.initialCapacity == initialCapacity
6   @       && this.loadFactor == loadFactor;
7   @*/
8 public HashMap(int initialCapacity, float loadFactor);
```

It just initialises the *capacity* and *loadfactor*, and guarantees that `theMap` model field is non-null and empty. For the Z state schema, initialisation is also trivial, but slightly different.

$$
\begin{array}{l}
\hline
InitHM \\
\hline
HM\,'; \; c?, l? : \mathbb{N}_1 \\
\hline
algo' \neq \varnothing \wedge hm' = \varnothing \\
capacity' = c? \wedge loadfactor' = l? \\
size' = idx' = 0 \\
\hline
\end{array}
$$

We must also ensure that there is always an algorithm to go from an *OID* to its corresponding `hashCode()` (*i.e.*, $algo' \neq \varnothing$), which is trivially *true*, since *algo* is total, and we can assume *OID* to be a non-empty type.

## 3.2   Map Operations

Now we can define the map operations in Z from the JML specification of `HashMap` methods. We define some useful schemas shared among the operations.

$$HashOp \,\hat{=}\, [\,\Delta HM; \; key? : OID; \; result! : \mathbb{Z} \mid HashCode[key?/this?]\,]$$

$$KeyQueryOp \,\hat{=}\, (HashOp \wedge \Xi HM)$$

$$ValQueryOp \,\hat{=}\, [\,\Xi HM; \; val? : VID\,]$$

The *HashOp* schema represents all operations involving hash keys (*key?*), where the resulting `hashCode()` value is calculated via the *HashCode* schema, and is output in *result!*. Query ($\Xi$) operations in Z are those that do not change the state. We define one for keys (*KeyQueryOp*) and one for values (*ValQueryOp*), where the former requires a key and produces a hash code, whereas the latter requires an object identifier for mapped values (*val?*). This reuse via schema inclusion is useful in simplifying proofs from unrelated predicates, and it keeps the specification modular.

Next, we specify `HashMap` containment queries for keys and values within the map. Key containment is a query operation that ascertains that there exists an entry in `theMap` model field such that the given key is structurally equivalent to the given key. This operation is specified in the `Map` interface as

```
1 /*+@ public normal_behavior
2 @      ensures \result <==>
3 @          (\exists Map.Entry e; theMap.has(e) && e != null;
4 @              JMLNullSafe.equals(e.abstractKey, key));
5 @+*/
6 /*@ pure @*/ boolean containsKey(/*@ nullable @*/ Object key);
```

The Z equivalent is a bit different from the JML version. Instead of having an existential postcondition being equivalent to a boolean value (*i.e.*, a *false* result could still be a *true* postcondition), it explicitly mentions the key containment condition within the hash map. We make sure this difference is harmless by proving the **ensures** clause above as a theorem in Sect. 3.4. The next schema specifies the hash key containment query operation.

$$ContainsKey \; \widehat{=} \; [\, KeyQueryOp \mid key? \in \text{dom} \, (\text{ran} \, (hm \; idx)) \,]$$

It has the signature of *KeyQueryOp*, where the input *key?* is within the appropriate projection in `theMap` (represented by *hm*). The universally quantified invariant in *HM* allows us to link hash map (array) indexes (*idx*), in this case calculated from *key?*, with the hash code algorithm (*algo*), in this case stored in *result!*. When we apply *idx* to *hm*, we get an *Entry*, which is an injective sequence where the range is (*OID* × *VID*) pairs. From these pairs, we check whether the given *key?* is present in the map or not using dom. The JML specification for value containment is very similar, and we omit it here. The Z schema is also very similar and is given below.

$$\begin{array}{|l}
\hline
ContainsValue \underline{\hspace{4cm}} \\
ValQueryOp \\
\hline
val? \in \text{ran} \, (\text{ran} \, (hm \; idx)) \\
\hline
\end{array}$$

The same principle applies, but now we are interested in projecting the values (*val?*) from the (*OID* × *VID*) pairs from the *Entry* at *idx* in *hm*. Thus, we just use ran instead of dom.

The emptiness operation does not produce side effects and relates the hash map array *hm* with *size*. If the array is empty, then *size* must be zero. Yet if the *size* is zero, the Java documentation does not insist the array should be initialised as empty.

$$IsMapEmpty \; \widehat{=} \; [\, \Xi HM \mid hm = \varnothing \Rightarrow size = 0 \,]$$

The JML specification is similar.

```
1 /*+@ public normal_behavior
2    @    ensures \result <==> theMap.isEmpty();
3    @ implies_that
4    @+*/
5 /*@ public normal_behavior
6    @    ensures \result <==> (size() == 0);
7    @*/
8 /*@ pure @*/ boolean isEmpty();
```

Unfortunately, the `implies_that` keyword is not documented in [24] or [30].

Another query operation retrieves the mapped value associated with a given *key?*, provided the key is contained in the map. The actual value (*val!*) is the result of applying the *key?* to the *Entry* injective sequence returned by the map at the given index. As the pairs within ran *s* are functional, where $s \in Entry$, we can apply it to *key?* to retrieve the associated value. This creates interesting (and possibly general) proof obligations about the result of ran, which is defined as a relation, to be functional, so that application to *key?* is well-defined.

$$
\begin{array}{|l}
\hline
\textit{GetValue} \underline{\hspace{7cm}} \\
\textit{KeyQueryOp; val!} : \textit{VID} \\
\hline
\textit{ContainsKey} \\
\textit{val!} = (\text{ran}\,(hm\ idx))\,\textit{key?} \\
\hline
\end{array}
$$

Its JML specification is similar to the containment operations, but with the extra requirement for key containment.

```
1 /*+@
2    @    public normal_behavior
3    @      requires containsKey(key);
4    @      ensures (\exists Entry e; theMap.has(e); e != null
5    @              && JMLNullSafe.equals(e.abstractKey, key)
6    @              && \result.equals(e.abstractValue));
7    @*/
8 /*@ pure @*/ Object get(/*@ nullable @*/ Object key);
```

The obvious difference is that now there is an extra equality condition (line (6)) about the method result (*val!*) being the mapped value. As we are not considering `null` keys, we omit that part of the specification. Like in the key-value containment operations, it is not quite clear why the **ensures** clause needs the existential quantifier for a non-boolean method. We believe that is because there was no specification for the model method **contains** mentioned above. We would still need to investigate further with the JML community to clarify this precisely.

Similarly as before, we define general schemas now for insertion operations with the *MapOp* schema.

$$\boxed{\begin{array}{l} \underline{\phantom{x}MapOp}\phantom{xxxxxxxxxxxxxxxxxxxxxxxxxxxxxxxxxxxx} \\ HashOp \\ \hline idx' < capacity \\ capacity' = capacity \\ loadfactor' = loadfactor \end{array}}$$

This states that the map parameters cannot change and that the current index being modified is within the map capacity, since we insist in no rehashing. Operations also require a value ($val?$) with which to associate a key ($key?$):

$$ValMapOp \; \widehat{=} \; [\, MapOp; \; val?, val! : VID \,]$$

To associate a value with a key, we define the *Put* operation below. An *Entry* is added into the map, hence it must be able to increase, and the current index is the result of the hashing function on the given $key?$.

$$\boxed{\begin{array}{l} \underline{\phantom{x}Put}\phantom{xxxxxxxxxxxxxxxxxxxxxxxxxxxxxxxxxxxxxx} \\ ValMapOp \\ \hline idx' = hf\,((algo\;key?),\,capacity) \\ hm' = hm \oplus \{\,(idx',(hm\;idx'\,\frown\,\langle(key?,val?)\rangle))\,)\,\} \\ size' = size + 1 \end{array}}$$

The effect is to update the map at the given index with the given ($key?$, $val?$) pair. This operation is more complex than it seems. There are at least three easy cases to explain: (i) when *key* is not in any *Entry* in the map; (ii) when a *key?* with a consistent hash code and its mapping is being updated (*i.e.*, change of an available mapping within an *Entry*); and (iii) when a clash happens due to a *key?* that generates an inconsistent hash code, which leads to a "spiked" *Entry* in the map. A further hidden complexity is about the injectivity of $hm$ and its entries. That creates an opportunity for general laws associating relational overriding ($\oplus$) for injective functions, as well as injective sequence concatenation ($\frown$), where the range of such a sequence has key-value pairs that are functional. This leads to quite complex proof obligations and precondition calculation. As for Java, the *HM* invariant on *size* should be relaxed to allow rehashing, so that clashes could also happen whenever the map's *capacity* is exceeded.

The JML specification for the `put` method from the `Map` interface without considering exceptional postconditions is given as

```
1 /*+@ public behavior
2 @      assignable objectState;
3 @      ensures (\exists Entry e; theMap.has(e); e != null
4 @              && JMLNullSafe.equals(e.abstractKey, key)
5 @              && JMLNullSafe.equals(e.abstractValue, value));
6 @ also
7 @+*/
8 /*@ public behavior
```

```
 9  @    assignable objectState;
10  @    ensures (\exists Entry e; contains(e);
11  @               nullequals(e.abstractKey, key)
12  @             && nullequals(e.abstractValue, value));
13  @    ensures (\forall Entry e; \old(contains(e)) ==> contains(e));
14  @    ensures (\forall Entry e; contains(e) ==>
16  @             (\old(contains(e)) || (e.getKey() == key &&
17  @                      e.getValue() == value)));
18  @    ensures \result == \old(get(key));
19  @*/
20 public Object put(/*@ nullable @*/ Object key,
21                   /*@ nullable @*/ Object value);
```

As the **theMap** model field is contained within the data group of the more general **objectState** model field, the assignable clause is simply saying other fields from the object could be modified as a result of changing the map. Although this is reasonable for a general implementation, as JML allows heterogeneous frames, we could not follow precisely why it is that **theMap** was not used directly, instead. Again the use of an existential quantifier, and the **has** method of **theMap**, instead of the **contains** model method as a precondition (lines (3–5)) was surprising. The postcondition specifies (line (13)) that all old entries be still in the map. In lines (14–17), the specification states that known entries either did not change, or were modified according to the new given key-value mapping parameters. These two postconditions are consistent with the use of relational overriding (⊕) in the Z model. Still, as the **contains** model method specification is empty, these two postconditions on old entry containment are meaningless. The last postcondition (line (18)) states that the result is the old value stored under the given key. If there were no mappings for the key, or if the key is **null**, the result is **null**. Otherwise, the result is the previous value stored under the given key. Furthermore, it seems that JML does not specify any concern with respect to the two levels of injectivity that *hm* and *Entry* capture from the Java documentation. As it involves handling **null** objects, this is the only place where the Z model does not enforce one of the JML postconditions. Despite this fact, we could easily add this with an additional predicate in the *Put* schema, such as

$$ContainsKey \Rightarrow GetValue$$

provided we added an additional *val!* ∈ *VID* output variable to the *Put* declaration list.

## 3.3   Operation Preconditions

The preconditions for operations are summarised in Table 1 below. Apart from initialisation, the map operations rely on the *HM* invariant holding as part of their precondition. That is, if the **HashMap** can be instantiated at all, then those are the preconditions for the operations. The interesting and less obvious precondition is for the hash map initialisation. It requires the existence of a map

**Table 1.** Operations precondition table

| InitHM | $(\exists\, m : \mathbb{N} \rightarrowtail Entry;\ a : OID \rightarrowtail \mathbb{Z};\ c? : \mathbb{N}_1$ |
|--------|----------------------------------------------------------------------------------------------|
|  | $\bullet\ \text{dom}\ m = 0\,..\,c? - 1 \wedge a \neq \varnothing$ |
|  | $\wedge\ (\forall\, o : OID;\ i : \text{dom}\ m\ \bullet$ |
|  | $i = hf\left((a\,o), c?\right)\,)\,)$ |
| ContainsKey | $key? \in \text{dom}\,(\text{ran}\,(hm\ idx))$ |
| Contains Value | $val? \in \text{ran}\,(\text{ran}\,(hm\ idx))$ |
| IsEmpty | true |
| GetValue | pre ContainsKey |
| Put | $size < capacity * (loadfactor\ \text{div}\ 100)$ |

$(m)$ instantiated with enough room for the given (strictly positive) capacity $(c?)$, as well as a valid `hashCode()` algorithm $(a \neq \varnothing)$ mapping object instances $(o)$ spread across the `HashMap` array indexes $(i \in \text{dom}\ m)$. The strictly positive capacity and `hashCode()` algorithm availability are trivially *true* in practice, since a boundary check $(c? \geq 1)$ is made at instantiation time, and all Java `Object` instances have a default `hashCode()` implementation as their (unique) object address in memory. Nevertheless, this default value might not always be the best one from an implementation point of view, as `hashCode()` implementations ought to be consistent with respect to `equals`. It is also nice to confirm that the precondition for *GetValue* was indeed what the JML `requires` clause says it is: the precondition for *ContainsKey*.

Not surprisingly, the most complex proof was the one for the *Put* operation. That is because there are far too many cases to consider: when the key is within the map or when it is a new one; when clashes happen; and so on. Also, relational overriding and sequence concatenation over injections require a great deal of machinery and ingenuity in order to finish the proof. Thanks to previous work done for a similar operation on injections in Mondex [42], the work here was considerably reduced. That is both because of general proof strategies that have been reused, and because additional Z toolkit laws for injections and injective sequences were added. This is positive and encouraging evidence of what can be generally achieved with the pilot project verification experiments, and verified components: reusable toolkit laws and proof strategies.

As the JML specifications for the boolean operations were given as existentially quantified postconditions over a key-value pair in an *Entry* within the map, we decided to prove additional theorems to show that such a specification is as good as the one we found. This is defined in the next two theorems

**theorem** tContainsKeyPRE2
  $\forall\, HM;\ key? : OID \mid (\exists\, val : VID \bullet (key?, val) \in \text{ran}\,(hm\ idx))\ \bullet$
    pre *ContainsKey*

**theorem** tContainsValuePRE2
  $\forall\, HM;\ val? : FILE \mid (\exists\, key : OID \bullet (key, val?) \in \text{ran}\,(hm\ idx))\ \bullet$
    pre *Contains Value*

They specify that on the assumption of an initialised (instantiated) map ($HM$) and an appropriate $key?/val?$, the JML (postcondition) specification of the corresponding boolean operation holds, provided there exists a counterpart identifier within the map at a known $Entrye$ index.

### 3.4 Theorems and Automation Rules

In order to make sure our Z specification indeed meets the expected JML postconditions, we prove their **ensures** clauses as Z theorems. The JML **ensures** clause for the `containsKey` method is

```
1  @  ensures \result <==>
2  @     (\exists Map.Entry e; theMap.has(e) && e != null;
3  @        JMLNullSafe.equals(e.abstractKey, key));
```

where the Z theorem showing that it holds is given next.

>　**theorem** tContainsKeyEnsures
>　　$\forall\ ContainsKey \bullet \exists\, val : VID \bullet (key?, val) \in \operatorname{ran}(hm\ idx)$

That is, if the $ContainsKey$ operation is successful, then that means there must exist some value $val$ for which the contained $key?$ is within the map $hm$ at the index $idx$ calculated via $algo$ in $HM$. Similarly, the JML specification for the `get` method postcondition is

```
1  @ ensures (\exists Entry e; theMap.has(e); e != null
2  @       && JMLNullSafe.equals(e.abstractKey, key)
3  @       && \result.equals(e.abstractValue));
```

where the Z theorem ensuring that for the given $key?$, the result ($val!$) is indeed a mapping within the map ($hm$) is given as.

>　**theorem** tGetValueEnsures
>　　$\forall\ GetValue \bullet (key?, val!) \in \operatorname{ran}(hm\ idx)$

One can carry on doing this for the other operations until the complete set of **ensures** clauses have been proved. For class invariants that have not already been given as definitions, we would need to prove a theorem for every operation, where we could assume the operation and we needed to show that the invariant holds. Fortunately, as the `Map` axiom about functionality of key-value pairs is given in the definition of $Entry$, and the other class invariants are related to equality and type consistency, we have proved all the theorems about map instance invariants.

The successful mechanisation of a JML-inspired Z hash map heavily depends on a good set of automation rules that are tailor-made to the complexity of the data structure being manipulated, in this case an injective map of $Entry$. For instance, the maximal type of $hm \in \mathbb{N} \nrightarrow Entry$ is as follows

$$hm \in \mathbb{P}\,(\mathbb{Z} \times \mathbb{P}\,(\mathbb{Z} \times (OID \times VID)))$$

During proofs, it often happens that one gets different versions of this type as proof obligations, such as

(a)  $hm \in \mathbb{Z} \leftrightarrow \mathbb{P}(\mathbb{Z} \times (OID \times VID))$
(b)  $hm \in \mathbb{N} \rightarrowtail (\mathbb{Z} \nrightarrow (OID \times VID))$

These proof obligations depend on the nature of the Z toolkit operators and laws that have been used. For instance, when applying relational overriding to $hm$ in the *Put* operation the proof obligation (a) is generated, or when applying some laws on injections, such as

$$\forall f : X \rightarrowtail Y \bullet \forall x : \mathrm{dom}\, f \bullet f^{\sim}(f\,x) = x$$

another proof obligation (b) is generated. Other examples of proof obligations that are not related to type checking are what in Z/Eves is known as *forward rules*. They expose some important property $P$ of a schema $S$, which is usually easy to prove, without requiring further proofs involving $S$ and assuming $P$ to expand $S$, hence cluttering the goal with unnecessary detail. For instance, this happens often with state schemas, where the state invariant is needed to finish some proof about an operation over the map. Again, this is a general lesson previously learned from earlier work [42].

It is through these and other kinds of proof obligations arising whilst manipulating goals that we found problems in the original design, as well as interesting/reusable lemmas for similar problems. This is the major benefit of such mechanisation efforts: they produce reusable general theories that can benefit other future verification experiments and verified components. For the experiment explained in this paper, we relied on around 85–95 of these lemmas and rules, from which around 8–10 could be generally reused in any context, and many more that could be reused whenever injections and injective sequences are involved. Fortunately, most of this essential machinery was already available. From [42], we got most of the general material on injections and sequences. In [11], most of the specific rules for *Entry* and *HM* were provided. Thus, we reused quite a large number of lemmas, resulting in a much lower burden of proof. In this particular case, that low burden is because the work in [11] was already targeted at hash maps. Obviously, in general the reuse is not always that high, yet as the number of experiments grows, the richer the set of general theories becomes, hence the greater the chances of having higher reuse rates.

# 4  Conclusions

There are many opportunities for profitable interaction between JML and different mechanised formalisms: this paper describes just the tip of the iceberg.

## 4.1  Verifying the JML Type System

JML and its tools rely on the correctness of annotations, which in turn rely on the underlying JML meta-type system to provide functionalities, such as side-effect free bounded predicates and varied equational theories. So subjecting the type system to the scrutiny of mechanical theorem proving is likely to be beneficial. And JML already goes in this direction: there are quite detailed annotations within the meta-type system.

## 4.2    Strengthening JML Annotations

We can use the same approach to the JML specifications available for the Java libraries. What we did here with `HashMap` and part of the JML type system could be done again for other parts of the *Java Development Kit* (JDK), and this has already been done before for `AbstractCollection` with positive results [17]. The research community can now take the opportunity to systematically verify the JML specification of the entire JDK, and the same could be said for the JML specifications of other frameworks, such as the Java cards API [29,39].

Another interesting point about linking Z and JML in this way is that we can draw inspiration from concrete implementations specified in JML up to Z specifications of similar concepts. That is exactly what happened in the work done in [11,10]. We started by mechanising a well-known abstract specification of a filing system given in [26], assumed that a hash map would be a good implementation candidate and started doing the concrete specification. At this point, when we needed to think how to model a hash map in Z, we drew inspiration from the available JML specification for the Java `HashMap` class. This was also helpful in finding the right retrieve relation to prove the refinement between abstract and concrete Z specifications. The same route could be repeated for other important data types.

## 4.3    JML to Z

A step forward beyond verification of class libraries and frameworks would be the verification of the JML semantics itself. This would provide a basis for a logic for reasoning about JML specifications. For that we need more than what Z offers: the specification of abstract data types. JML has specification facilities for real-time, concurrency, and resource allocation, which could be captured within Hoare and He's *Unifying Theories of Programming* [14]. As mentioned above, JML is divided into language levels [24, Sect. 2.9], where there are minimum, desirable, and "exocentric" language features to be considered. The behavioural part that Z can capture is definitely the very basic/core part of JML, hence the most obvious place to start. The next step would be to combine JML concurrency features with Java models for CSP, which are also already available. The obvious path is the to add a systematic formal translation from JML to these different formalisms. Although this is a more ambitious project, it is a feasible (and promising one) nevertheless.

## 4.4    Z to JML

The other way round, from concrete Z specifications down to JML specifications, would also be very interesting. It would enable the prototyping of Z specifications in Java, which we believe will be attractive. There is already ongoing work in this direction in *Community Z Tools* (CZT).[3] Another interesting possibility

---

[3] See `czt.sourceforge.net`.

is to have JML as a target language for the refinement calculus [25] (or even the Z refinement calculus [6]). As there are available refinement tools for the refinement calculus that have other target languages rather than Java, we think this is also a profitable way forward.

This is a more modest endeavour than going from JML to Z, yet there are still interesting issues to tackle. One example is the treatment of undefined expressions in JML. Moreover, some of the quite powerful abstraction mechanisms available in Z would be difficult to directly translate to JML, like given sets and loosely defined paragraphs. Like in [37], we would obviously need to adhere to some Z specification patterns prior to translation to JML.

An important issue still to be considered in such a development is how to tackle the object-oriented features of JML. One could argue that Object-Z [33] would be a better candidate to aim for. Nevertheless, as there is no agreeable notion of refinement for Object-Z, we would rather prefer to stick to Z itself, perhaps using the solutions already described in [38].

### 4.5   Finally

In this paper we emphasise the benefits of proving theorems about JML specifications using the Z notation. We focus on the specification of the Java `HashMap` class, and parts of the JML meta-type system classes. This reveals interesting opportunities to improve JML specifications, uncovering some problems and strengthening the JML specifications with theorems from Z.

In linking Z and JML, we are paving the way towards providing formally documented components for the Verified Software Repository that others will find useful. Java's `HashMap` architect Joshua Bloch once said [2]

> Writing reusable software components is a bit like being a plumber. It's a critical but largely thankless task. No one says, "Gosh, your plumbing is really great!" But you can bet they would complain if it leaked.

## Acknowledgements

We would like to thank the *Software Assurance Group* at QinetiQ Malvern for their long-term funding and support for our research group. We are grateful to Zheng Fu for his work with the formalisation of a Z hash map for a POSIX filing system specification and verification. Finally, we are grateful to Gary Leavens and the JML community list for the various discussions during the development of the paper.

## References

1. Back, R.J., von Wright, J.: Refinement Calculus: A Systematic Introduction. In: Graduate Texts in Computer Science, Springer, Heidelberg (1998)
2. Bloch, J.: Effective Java Programming Language Guide. Prentice Hall, Englewood Cliffs (2001)

3. Burdy, L., Cheon, Y., Cok, D.R., Ernst, M.D., Kiniry, J.R., Leavens, G.T., Leino, K.R.M., Poll, E.: An overview of JML tools and applications. STTT 7(3), 212–232 (2005)
4. Burdy, L., Requet, A., Lanet, J.-L.: Java applet correctness: a developer-oriented approach. In: Araki, K., Gnesi, S., Mandrioli, D. (eds.) FME 2003. LNCS, vol. 2805, pp. 422–439. Springer, Heidelberg (2003)
5. Butterfield, A., Woodcock, J.: Formalising flash memory: first steps. In: 12th IEEE International Conference on Engineering of Complex Computer Systems (ICECCS'07), Auckland, New Zealand, July 11-14, 2007, IEEE Computer Press, Los Alamitos (2007)
6. Cavalcanti, A.L.C.: A Refinement Calculus for Z. DPhil Thesis. University of Oxford (1997)
7. Dijkstra, E.W.: A Discipline of Programming. Prentice-Hall, Englewood Cliffs (1976)
8. Freitas, L., Cavalanti, A.L.C., Woodcock, J.C.P.: Taking our own medicine: applying the refinement calculus to state-rich refinement model checking. In: Liu, Z., He, J. (eds.) ICFEM 2006. LNCS, vol. 4260, pp. 697–716. Springer, Heidelberg (2006)
9. Freitas, L., et al.: Verified Software Repository @ SourceForge (2006), vsr.sourceforge.net
10. Freitas, L., Fu, Z., Woodcock, J.: POSIX file store in Z/Eves: an experiment in the verified software repository. In: 12th IEEE International Conference on Engineering of Complex Computer Systems (ICECCS'07), Auckland, New Zealand, July 11–14, 2007, IEEE Computer Press, Los Alamitos (2007)
11. Fu, Z.: A Refinement of the UNIX Filing System using Z/Eves. Master's thesis, University of York (2006)
12. Gosling, J., Joy, B., Steele, G., Bracha, G.: The Java Language Specification, 3rd edn. Addison Wesley, Reading (2005)
13. Hoare, T.: The Verifying Compiler Software Grand Challenge. Journal of the ACM 50(1), 63–69 (2003)
14. Hoare, C.A.R., He, J.: Unifying Theories of Programming. International Series in Computer Science. Prentice-Hall, Englewood Cliffs (1998)
15. Huisman, M., Jacobs, B., van den Berg, J.: A Case study in class library verification: Java's Vector class. In: Moreira, A.M.D., Demeyer, S. (eds.) Object-Oriented Technology. ECOOP'99 Workshop Reader. LNCS, vol. 1743, pp. 109–110. Springer, Heidelberg (1999)
16. Huisman, M.: Reasoning about Java Programs in Higher-Order Logic using PVS and Isabelle. PhD thesis, Universiteit Nijmegen (2001)
17. Huisman, M.: Verification of Java's AbstractCollection class: a case study. In: Boiten, E.A., Möller, B. (eds.) MPC 2002. LNCS, vol. 2386, pp. 175–194. Springer, Heidelberg (2002)
18. IBM: CICS Application Programming Interface Release 3. Technical Report SC33-1688-01, IBM Hursley Park (1999)
19. Intel Corp.: Open NAND Flash Interface Specification. Open NAND Flash Interface Consortium (2007), http://www.onfi.org/
20. ISO/IEC 13568: Information Technology—Z Formal Specification Notation—Syntax, Type System and Semantics. First edn. ISO/IEC (2002)
21. Josey, A. (ed.): The Single UNIX Specification Version 3. Open Group (2004), ISBN (1931)62447X
22. Joshi, R., Holzmann, G.J.: A mini-challenge: build a verifiable filesystem. In: Verified Software: Theories, Tools, Experiments (VSTTE), IFIP Working Conference, Zurich (In press)

23. Lakatos, I.: Proofs and Refutations: The Logic of Mathematical Discovery. Cambrdige University Press, Cambrdige (2005)
24. Leavens, G. T., Poll, E., Clifton, C., Cheon, Y., Ruby, C., Cok, D., Müller, P., Kiniry, J., Chalin, P.: JML Reference Manual. Iowa State University. Revision 1.200 (2007)
25. Morgan, C.: Programming from Specifications. Prentice-Hall, Englewood Cliffs (1994)
26. Morgan, C., Sufrin, B.: Specification of the UNIX filing system. IEEE Transactions on Software Engineering SE-10, 128–142 (1984)
27. Paige, R.F., Brooke, P.J.: Integrating BON and Object-Z. Journal of Object Technology 3(3), 121–141 (2004)
28. Paige, R.F., Ostroff, J.S.: From Z to BON/Eiffel. In: ASE, pp. 209–212 (1998)
29. Poll, E., van den Berg, J., Jacobs, B.: 3. In: Specification of the JavaCard API in JML. Smart Card Research and Advanced Applications. In: Proceedings of the Fourth Working Conference on Smart Card Research and Advanced Applications, CARDIS 2000, September 20-22, 2000. Bristol. IFIP Conference Proceedings, vol. 180, pp. 135–154. Kluwer, Dordrecht (2000)
30. Raghavan, A.D., Leavens, G.T.: Desugaring JML Method Specifications. Technical Report TR#00-03e, Iowa State University, Department of Computer Science 226 Atanasoff Hall Ames Iowa 50011-1041, USA (2005)
31. Russell, B.: Recent Work in Philosophy of Mathematics. International Monthly (1901) Reprinted in Mysticism and Logic and Other Essays (p.59–74) Barnes & Noble (1976)
32. Saaltink, M.: Z/Eves 2.0 User's Guide. ORA Canada, TR-99-5493-06a (1999)
33. Smith, G.: The Object-Z Specification Language. Advances in Formal Methods. Kluwer Academic Publishers, Dordrecht (2000)
34. Spivey, J.M.: The Z Notation: A Reference Manual. Prentice-Hall, Englewood Cliffs (1998)
35. SRI: Workshop on the Verification Grand Challenge (2005), http://www.csl.sri.com
36. Stepney, S., Cooper, D., Woodcock, J.: An Electronic Purse: Specification, Refinement, and Proof. Technical Monograph PRG-126, University of Oxford (2000)
37. Stepney, S., Polack, F., Toyn, I.: A Z Patterns Catalougue: volume 1. Technical Report YCS349, Department of Computer Science, University of York (2003)
38. Utting, M., Wang, S.: Object orientation without extending Z. In: Bert, D., Bowen, J.P., King, S. (eds.) ZB 2003. LNCS, vol. 2651, pp. 319–338. Springer, Heidelberg (2003)
39. van den Berg, J., Jacobs, B., Poll, E.: Formal specification and verification of JavaCard's Application Identifier class. In: Attali, I., Jensen, T. (eds.) JavaCard 2000. LNCS, vol. 2041, pp. 137–150. Springer, Heidelberg (2001)
40. Woodcock, J.C.P., Cavalcanti, A.L.C.: A concurrent language for refinement. In: 5th Irish Workshop on Formal Methods, IWFM 2001, Dublin, Ireland, 16–17 July 2001. BCS Workshops in Computing (2001)
41. Woodcock, J., Davies, J.: Using Z: Specification, Refinement, and Proof. International Series in Computer Science. Prentice-Hall, Englewood Cliffs (1996)
42. Woodcock, J., Freitas, L.: Z/Eves and the Mondex Electronic Purse. In: Barkaoui, K., Cavalcanti, A., Cerone, A. (eds.) ICTAC 2006. LNCS, vol. 4281, pp. 15–34. Springer, Heidelberg (2006)

# Specification for Testing

Chris George[1], Padmanabhan Krishnan[2],
P.A.P. Salas[2], and J.W. Sanders[1]

[1] United Nations University International Institute for Software Technology, Macao
[2] School of Information Technology, Bond University, Australia

**Abstract.** The success of model-based testing, in automating the testing of an implementation given its state-based (or model-based) specification, raises the question of how best the specification can be tweaked in order to facilitate that process. This paper discusses several answers. Motivated by an example from web-based systems, and taking account of the restriction imposed by the testing interface, it considers both functional and non-functional properties. The former include laws, implicit system invariants and other consistency conditions whilst the latter include security leaks. It concludes that because of the importance of the link between specification and implementation in the testing process, there is a trade-off between genuinely useful testing information and the incorporation of some degree of information about the link, not normally regarded as part of the specification.

## 1  Introduction

(Formal) specifications and implementations are normally viewed as being poles apart. After all, a specification captures requirements by expressing what a system should achieve, whilst the purpose of an implementation is to be executed and so it contains much detail whose concern is computational efficiency; the connection is of course that the implementation conforms to the specification—ideally! They might also be viewed as being poles apart because, after all, much of the process of system development lies between a specification and an implementation.

Because that conformance *is* only ideal, testing is required. All testing presupposes *a priori*, an oracle, knowledge for interpreting test outcomes: of which tests pass and which fail. That knowledge constitutes, for any system of realistic size, only partial information about the specification. But it demonstrates an unbreakable link between specification and testing.

The advent of the important area of model-based testing, MBT, [7,9,26] forges an even stronger link. Its primary importance is the complete automation of validation testing, subject to control by the test engineer of those features of the system being tested, of coverage criteria and so on. As pointed out by Utting [25], MBT relies on *redundancy* between the test specification and the implementation; and then it is equally likely to reveal errors in each.

Over the past couple of decades, considerable experience has been gained in specification. The cost of the time spent on specification during the critical early stages of the development cycle can be partly amortized over the later activity of testing using MBT.

C.B. Jones, Z. Liu, J. Woodcock (Eds.): Bjørner/Zhou Festschrift, LNCS 4700, pp. 280–299, 2007.

However the precise difference between a (standard) specification and one that serves as a model for MBT is still unclear. That is the topic of this paper. More specifically, its purpose is to consider the following question, particularly in the context of web-based systems:

> What can a specifier do, when constructing a (state-based, or model-based) specification, to facilitate the subsequent task of testing, particularly by automated techniques like MBT?

The nature of testing has changed as a result of specification. One of the benefits of specification is that it provides notation and a place in the development cycle to make precise conditions that once were routinely incorrect in code; then they were picked up only by testing. Perhaps the best examples of that nature are boundary conditions: indices out of bounds, loops iterating too many or too few times, *etc*. Of course the specifier might still get those details wrong, but with MBT the mistake is likely to be picked up in the model rather than in the implementation.

One of the strengths of MBT is that the model and tests generated from it can be reused even when the implementation changes. This means that MBT is useful in black-box testing, whose focus is on the properties of the system rather than the low-level coding details. This facilitates the development of a model that is abstract and is derived only from observable behaviour. This is not to say that MBT cannot be used in whitebox testing. But the more details of the implementation are exposed, the less abstract the model—and hence the less reusable—it becomes.

In this paper, however, it is argued that some implementation details have to be exposed for certain types of property. The properties addressed include standard 'functional' properties like laws between operations, system invariants, confidence conditions (like pre- and postcondition analysis), boundary analysis; and they include 'nonfunctional' properties like security leaks.

For MBT to be really useful, the tests generated from the model must be linked to the implementation. The link must provide sufficient information to automate the process of testing the implementation from the model. It acts as an 'action refinement', translating test sequences obtained from the model into suitable test sequences for the implementation. The *action word* approach [6,5] has been proposed as a simple way to establish the link. This approach applies naturally to models which are labelled transition systems whose labels represent aspects of functionality that are to be tested. The link then associates code, which actually performs the testing, to the label. For example, if the link associates the code ca to the label $a$ and cb to the label $b$, then the test sequence $ab$ results in execution of the code ca $_9^o$ cb. Usually the oracle is built into the code.

## 1.1  Related Work and Outline

The study of the interplay between specifications and testing is far from new. Of the many contributions which predate MBT, a large number can with hindsight be seen as precursors. *Specification-based testing* is a term that has for long been used to describe the 'generation' of tests from a (formal) specification.

Some work has focused on the animation of specifications, either by choice of specification notation [7,13,14,15,18] or by translating the specification into executable form

[11,12,19]. Incorporation of the notion of testing into the framework of Formal Methods, and the refinement calculus in particular, has been accomplished by Aichernig [1]. Testing the kind of system considered here, specifically to reactive systems, has been the subject of a Dagstuhl meeting [4].

In outline, the paper proceeds as follows. In Section 2 a case study is presented of a web-based network-management system, and in Section 3 the manner in which it is linked to an implementation is discussed. Then three kinds of functional property are considered for the generation of extra-specification tests, in Sections 4, 5 and 6. In Section 7 a non-functional property, security, is considered. The case study is used illustratively throughout.

## 2    Case Study

This section describes a web-based network-management system that helps to illustrate the key issues discussed in this paper. The system is based on a real web application, whose testability has been determined by the interface available.

First, a brief informal overview of the system behaviour is given (Section 2.1) and supplemented (in Section 2.2) with a formalisation in ObjectZ. Then follows (in Section 3) a discussion of those issues in the model that are relevant to testing; that is followed (in Section 3.5) by a brief discussion of problems related to testability.

### 2.1    Overview

The system consists of a simple web-based system for managing a network of machines remotely. It is based on a network of clients and their users. There are two special kinds of user: administrators and managers. Although both are users, no user is both an administrator and a manager.

The system requires users to authenticate themselves by logging on in the usual manner. For security purposes, three consecutive unsuccessful logins result in the user's account being locked; this level of abstraction overlooks the details of how that is undone by a manager or administrator). A user can log on to only one client at a time.

An administrator (and only an administrator) can create a client, provided it is not already present and provided that a manager is assigned to it. An administrator can remove a client, provided there are no users logged on there. An administrator can select a client and see its details, consisting of the client's manager and the users currently logged on there. An administrator can also see the details of a user, consisting of its password, whether it is logged on and if so where, how many consecutive unsuccessful attempts it has currently made, and email it has sent and received. Finally, an administrator can broadcast mail to all users, and can send mail to a specific user as if from another specific user.

A manager (and only a manager) can create a user account, provided the user is not already registered. A manager can remove a user, provided it is not logged on, is not itself a manager or administrator, and provided mail it has received is also removed. After an administrator or manager logs out the functionality associated with its roles cannot be invoked.

Other users have very limited capabilities (at this level of abstraction). They can log in on any client, read their messages and send messages to other users and log out. But they cannot manage users or clients.

Initially there is at least one administrator and at least one manager (just because this level of abstraction abstracts the actions that change those sets), there are no other users, no user is logged in nor has tried to log in, and there is no post. It is arbitrary where the administrators and managers are initially logged in.

## 2.2   Model: Webbo

The model of that web-based network-management system is called Webbo. The specification below is approximately ObjectZ [8] but uses dependent types in order to shorten schema invariants and uses $C \sqcup D$ to stand for the disjoint union of $C$ and $D$ (*i.e.* the union in which the invariant $C \cap D = \{\}$ holds).

These generic types are assumed: *Users* for the set of possible users; *Clients* for the set of possible clients; *Mess* for the set of email messages; and *Pass* for the set of all possible passwords, both valid and invalid (thus *Pass* might well consist of the set of all character strings constrained in some way by length; but such detail is ignored at this level of abstraction).

These schemas are required and defined in the specification. *Loginfo* provides for each user: the number *no* of putative logins in the current sequence of attempts by that user; the user's password *pd*; a Boolean *in* which is true iff the user is currently logged in; the client *at* at which, if *in* is true, the user is logged in; and a Boolean *lock* which is true iff the user's account is locked (thus *lock* is a redundant observable, equivalent to $(no = 3)$).

State is described by sets: $U$ of users, $A$ of system administrators, $M$ of managers of clients, $C$ of clients; by a function *mng* which assigns a manager to each client (so is a total function), a function *log* which assigns *Loginfo* to each user, and a relation *post* between a sender-receiver pair and messages that is in general many-to-many. See Figure 1.

An administrator can create a client, with operation *CreateClient*, only if logged in, the client is not already in the network, and by assigning a manager to the client. Removal of a client, by operation *RemoveClient*, is similar, except that for a client to be removed it must have no users logged in there. See Figure 2.

With operation *AdminClient*, an administrator *a*? can receive information about the manager *man*! of a client *c*? and about which users, *users*!, are logged in there. With operation *AdminUser* an administrator can receive information about a user *u*?. See Figure 3.

An administrator *a*? sends post either by broadcasting a message *p*? to all users from itself, with operation *AdminPostAll*, or by sending it to just a single recipient *r*? from user *u*?, with operation *AdminPostOne*. See Figure 4.

The 'management' of users extends that of clients, because when a user is removed by a manager, its email is also removed; the user must not be logged in, and must not be an administrator or manager. This description abstracts the initial choice of a client's password. See Figure 5.

$\boxed{\begin{array}{l} \underline{\text{WebboState}} \\[4pt] \boxed{\begin{array}{l} \underline{\text{Loginfo}} \\[2pt] no : \mathbb{N} \\ pd : Pass \\ at : C \\ in, lock : \mathbb{B} \\ \hline no \le 3 \\ in \;\Rightarrow\; (no = 0) \\ lock \;\Leftrightarrow\; (no = 3) \end{array}} \\[4pt] \boxed{\begin{array}{l} \underline{\text{State}} \\[2pt] U, A, M : \mathbb{P}\, Users \\ C : \mathbb{P}\, Clients \\ mng : C \to M \\ log : U \to Loginfo \\ post : U \times U \leftrightarrow Mess \\ \hline A \sqcup M \subseteq U \end{array}} \quad \boxed{\begin{array}{l} \underline{\text{Init}} \\[2pt] State \\ \hline A \neq \{\} \\ M \neq \{\} \\ U = A \cup M \\ \forall u : U \cdot log(u).no = 0 \wedge \neg log(u).in \\ post = \{\} \end{array}} \end{array}}$

**Fig. 1.** State for the model Webbo

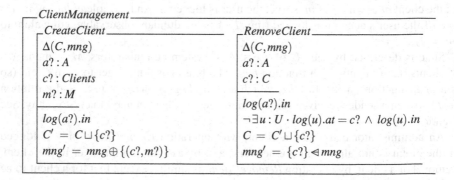

$\boxed{\begin{array}{l} \underline{\text{ClientManagement}} \\[4pt] \boxed{\begin{array}{l} \underline{\text{CreateClient}} \\[2pt] \Delta(C, mng) \\ a? : A \\ c? : Clients \\ m? : M \\ \hline log(a?).in \\ C' = C \sqcup \{c?\} \\ mng' = mng \oplus \{(c?, m?)\} \end{array}} \quad \boxed{\begin{array}{l} \underline{\text{RemoveClient}} \\[2pt] \Delta(C, mng) \\ a? : A \\ c? : C \\ \hline log(a?).in \\ \neg \exists u : U \cdot log(u).at = c? \wedge log(u).in \\ C = C' \sqcup \{c?\} \\ mng' = \{c?\} \vartriangleleft mng \end{array}} \end{array}}$

**Fig. 2.** Client management in Webbo

A user $u?$ who is logged in may send a message, with operation *UserPost*, to a named user $r?$; or may read mail without deleting it (an easy modification updates the state to remove read post), by outputting the mail in the set *ms!* of messages. Reading mail does not change the system state; sending it updates only the state component *post*. See Figure 6.

But the most subtle action is that of logging in. A user may (attempt to) log in only if not already logged in. The attempt fails if the input password *id?* is wrong; on the third consecutive failed attempt the user is locked out, but otherwise another attempt is permitted. A successful attempt returns the count *no* to 0 and changes the status of the

```
┌─AdminClient──────────────────        ┌─AdminUser─────────────────────
│ Ξ                                     │ Ξ
│ a? : A                                │ a? : A
│ c? : C                                │ u? : U
│ man! : M                              │ info! : Loginfo
│ users! : ℙU                           │ sent!, rec! : ℙMess
├─────────────────────────────         ├──────────────────────────────
│ log(a?).in                           │ log(a?).in
│ man! = mgr(c?)                        │ info! = log(u?)
│ users! = {u : U | ( log(u).at = c? )} │ sent! = {m : M | ∃v : U · post(u?,v,m)}
│                    ( log(u).in     )  │ rec! = {m : M | ∃v : U · post(v,u?,m)}
└─────────────────────────────         └──────────────────────────────
```

**Fig. 3.** Administrative information in Webbo

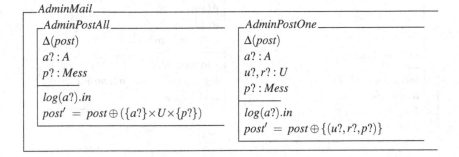

```
┌─AdminMail──────────────────────────────────────────────────────────
│ ┌─AdminPostAll───────────────          ┌─AdminPostOne──────────────
│ │ Δ(post)                               │ Δ(post)
│ │ a? : A                                │ a? : A
│ │ p? : Mess                             │ u?, r? : U
│ ├──────────────────────────            │ p? : Mess
│ │ log(a?).in                           ├──────────────────────────
│ │ post' = post ⊕ ({a?} × U × {p?})      │ log(a?).in
│ └──────────────────────────            │ post' = post ⊕ {(u?, r?, p?)}
│                                         └──────────────────────────
└────────────────────────────────────────────────────────────────────
```

**Fig. 4.** Administrative posting in Webbo

```
┌─UserManagement─────────────────────────────────────────────────────
│ ┌─CreateUser─────────────────          ┌─RemoveUser────────────────
│ │ Δ(U, log)                             │ Δ(U, log, post)
│ │ m? : M                                │ m? : M
│ │ u? : Users                            │ u? : U
│ ├──────────────────────────            ├──────────────────────────
│ │ log(m?).in                           │ log(m?).in
│ │ ∀v : U · v ≠ u? ⇒ log(v)' = log(v)    │ u? ∉ A ∪ M
│ │ U' = U ⊔ {u?}                         │ ¬log(u?).in
│ │ ¬log(u?).in'                          │ U = U' ⊔ {u?}
│ │ log(u?).no' = 0                       │ log' = {u?} ⊴ log
│ └──────────────────────────            │ post' = {(v, w, p) : post | w ≠ u?}
│                                         └──────────────────────────
└────────────────────────────────────────────────────────────────────
```

**Fig. 5.** User management in Webbo

$$\boxed{\begin{array}{l} \textit{UserMail} \\[4pt]
\boxed{\begin{array}{l} \textit{UserPost} \\[2pt]
\Delta(post) \\
u?, r? : U \\
m? : Mess \\ \hline
log(u?).in \\
post' \; = \; post \oplus \{(u?, r?, m?)\}
\end{array}}
\quad
\boxed{\begin{array}{l} \textit{UserRead} \\[2pt]
\Xi \\
u? : U \\
ms! : \mathbb{P}\,Mess \\ \hline
log(u?).in \\
ms! \; = \; \{m : Mess \mid \exists s : U \cdot (s, u?, m) \in post\}
\end{array}}
\end{array}}$$

**Fig. 6.** Sending and reading post in Webbo

$$\boxed{\begin{array}{l} \textit{LoggingIn} \\[4pt]
\boxed{\begin{array}{l} \textit{OK} \\[2pt]
\Delta(log) \\
u? : U \\
c? : C \\
ack! : ok \mid fail \\ \hline
log(u?).no' \; = \; 0 \\
log(u?).in' \\
log(u?).at' \; = \; c? \\
ack! \; = \; ok
\end{array}}
\quad
\boxed{\begin{array}{l} \textit{Fail} \\[2pt]
\Delta(log) \\
u? : U \\
ack! : ok \mid fail \\ \hline
\neg log(u?).in' \\
log(u?).no' \; = \; log(u?).no + 1 \\
ack! \; = \; fail
\end{array}} \\[4pt]
\boxed{\begin{array}{l} \textit{Login} \\[2pt]
\Delta(log) \\
u? : U \\
c? : C \\
id? : Pass \\
ack! : ok \mid fail \\ \hline
\neg log(u?).in \\
log(u?).no < 3 \\
log(u?).pd' \; = \; log(u?).pd \\
log(u?).pd = id? \; \Rightarrow \; OK \\
log(u?).pd \neq id? \; \Rightarrow \; Fail \\
\forall v : U \cdot v \neq u? \; \Rightarrow \; log(v)' = log(v)
\end{array}}
\end{array}}$$

**Fig. 7.** Logging on in Webbo

user to being logged in. A successful login returns an *ok* acknowledgement whilst an unsuccessful one returns *fail*. Operation *Login* is described in Figure 7.

Logout_____

$\Delta(log)$

$u? : U$

_____

$log(u?).in$

$\neg log(u?).in'$

$log(u?).pd' = log(u?).pd$

$log(u?).no = log(u?).no'$

$\forall v : U \cdot v \neq u? \Rightarrow log(v)' = log(v)$

_____

**Fig. 8.** Logging out in Webbo

Webbo_____

Webbo*State*

*ClientManagement*

*AdminClient*

*AdminUser*

*AdminMail*

*UserManagement*

*UserMail*

*LoggingIn*

*Logout*

_____

**Fig. 9.** The overall system Webbo

Logging out is straightforward and is described in Figure 8. User $u?$ is logged in before the operation but not after it; its password remains unchanged as does its number of unsuccessful login attempts (at 0); however $log(u?).at$ is left arbitrary.

Overall Webbo is specified with a class that combines the previous descriptions; see Figure 9.

## 3   Linking Model to Implementation

This section outlines how the link between the model and the implementation can be developed for the purposes of testing. Several examples are presented to illustrate the main issues, since a complete description lies beyond the scope of this paper.

### 3.1   Testing Language

General purpose programming languages are in general used to test systems (*e.g.*, Java is used in the Korat framework [3] and Ruby/Watir is used for testing web based systems [16]). This ensures that the expressive power of the tester is not restricted. But the implementation must provide sufficient information to the tester otherwise the expressive power of the testing language cannot be utilised.

For example, the Ruby/Watir framework uses the Internet Explorer's Component Object Model (COM) interface to access objects of interest. However if the HTML does not name the objects it is often difficult to pick the right object [16] and verify its state. In object-oriented approaches information hiding can restrict the ability of a tester to control and observe the state of the computation [2]. The implementation must provide an interface which can be used to inspect the values of relevant variables in the testing process.

In the present paper no particular testing language is assumed, though the constraints just mentioned will play a deciding role.

### 3.2 Action Words

The approach taken here to linking the specification and implementation is that of 'action words' due to Buwalda and Kasdorp [5,6]. It may be described, in the current context, as follows.

The atomic input action $pd$? : *Pass* is interpreted in the implementation as a succession of keyboard inputs, via a web page, as defined by a finite automaton. The automaton ensures that the password has length within an allowable range and so is legal.

Whilst the abstract event is atomic its concrete translation is not, since it now has several states (to reflect the length of legal passwords) and the possibility of being interrupted. Nonetheless the result is a bijective representation of *Pass*, that forms the link which is animated by code.

Before providing examples, the appropriate notion of oracle must be defined.

### 3.3 Oracle

An operation applied inside its precondition and producing a result within its postcondition is thought of as forming a 'positive' transition whilst one applied outside its precondition or producing a result outside its postcondition is 'negative'. Extending that idea to sequences of operations defines the oracle, which provides the required notion of a test that passes (all components in the trace are positive) and one that fails (at least one is negative).

For example, the (positive) transition `login(u,up)` indicates that one can log in as u with password up. For this, the initial web page must be at starting page and the result must be the page that is displayed after a successful login. As indicated above, the link between the model and the implementation translates the user name u and putative password up to appropriate text fields and the process of logging in involves clicking the button. It also links input of up to a succession of keystrokes (and perhaps to an acknowledging output, audible and visible). For this link to be useful in test automation, methods to access the text fields and buttons are assumed to be made available by the COM structure.

The model also contains (negative) transitions of the form `loginFail(i,p)` which indicate that the user i with putative password p fails the login. While the link for the process of logging in is the same as for `login`, the linking of the results is quite different. When login succeeds, the web page has the menu item with the appropriate functionality; whilst if the login fails, the web page does not have the menu item but goes back to the retry page (that is, until the user is locked out). This again assumes availability of the appropriate methods to inspect the resulting web page.

## 3.4   Link Issues for Testing

The model exhibits the behaviour that three consecutive `loginFail(i,_)` result in locking the user's account. To build the oracle into the action word, one might use `loginLock(i,p)`. Again the link has to translate the login process as before, but with a different check on the outcome.

The implementation may have state variables such as Booleans `auth` and `lock` which may not be directly accessible from the web page. In this particular case the implementation generates output on the web page by setting the title to "Not Logged in" or "Logged in".

If the link has only a method to examine the title, it is not possible to determine if the account is locked. That is, both `loginFail(i,p)` and `loginLock(i,p)` may be forced by the link into checking the title to "Not Logged in".

Either the title has to change or a method to examine `locked` is essential. If there were a message displaying 'locked' then the web page can be tested by checking its contents.

Sometimes there are popups (say created by Javascript) that require confirmation. In the model there are transitions of the form `clickOK`. They need to be translated into a number of operations—getting a handle of the javascript window, clicking the okay button there, waiting for that window to disappear and the main window to go to the desired page.

Usually all, or anyway most, of the methods are available or can be made available but if the web page does not provide that information, testing fails.

## 3.5   Problems with Test Automation

The purpose of this section is to show that developing a model and a link from the model to the implementation cannot automate all aspects of testing. The standard black box testing approach to web systems is thus not sufficient.

The first problem arises since an administrator can send, with operation *AdminPostOne*, a message on behalf of a user. The precondition for this operation is that the user posting the message should be an administrator and the message should be addressed to an existing user from an existing user. The model also defines the expected result of the operation: the message should be added to the pool of messages (various designs for which are discussed in Section 5.6).

Assume that an administrator *a* posts a message on behalf of the user *u* to *r*. After posting the message the system returns *a* to the web page from where the messages can be managed. Administrator *a* has no direct way of verifying that the message has been added to the post. That is, it is not possible to define a link using the methods made available by the web system.

The link needs to include steps such as logging out from administrator $a$'s account, logging in to user $u$'s account, opening the post and then viewing the message. Those steps assume that the tester (or the test execution engine) knows the password of $r$'s account. If this assumption is false, the situation cannot be tested. If the password is not known, the test case for the *CreateMessage* function can define a series of preparatory steps that includes the creation of a specific dummy user for whom the tester should record the password to be used later. Administrator $a$ then creates a message for this dummy user. However, the testing is restricted to just that dummy user.

A similar situation exists while creating a client. The implementation does not provide any actual information about the status of the operation. There is no way way of verifying that the client has indeed been created and users for it can be created. The link must try to add a user to the client and then delete the user. If this succeeds the client has been created. In this case the person creating the client is an administrator and does not have the right to create a user. Hence the test script needs to logout and login as manager to test the creation of a client. The system must allow this process for the testing to be automated.

Such situations are now examined in a more systematic fashion and it is shown how these problems lead to a tradeoff between specification and implementation.

# 4  Laws

State-based specifications and algebraic specifications feature quite different styles of requirements capture. Nonetheless the state-based specifier is typically aware of laws relating the operations being described in the state-based notation. For example, a 'do' operation is often accompanied in a system by an 'undo', in which case their composition—perhaps under some assumption, or by abstracting some components of state—leaves state unchanged. The following examples demonstrate those ideas using Webbo.

## 4.1  Laws in Webbo

Creation of a client followed by its removal leaves the state of Webbo unchanged. Conversely, removal of a client followed by its creation may not leave state invariant because the manager assigned during client creation may not coincide with that just deleted in client removal; but other state components are unchanged.

For this some notation is required. Suppose that (state) schema $S$ includes an observable $a : A$. Then the schema with that observable abstracted, and its identity function, are defined:

$$State_a = \exists a : A \cdot State$$
$$\text{id}[State_a] = \lambda s : State_a \cdot s.$$

(In practice it may be simpler to list, as subscripts there, the state components that are present rather than those that are not; but this notation is more convenient in theory.)

Now the previous laws can be expressed:

$$CreateClient \; \fatsemi \; RemoveClient = \text{id}$$
$$RemoveClient \; \fatsemi \; CreateClient = \text{id}[\text{Webbo}State_{mng}].$$

Creation followed immediately by removal of a user does not change the system state. But conversely, removal followed by creation of a user may result in a different password $log(u?).pd$ and a different $log(u?).at$. Continuing the subscript convention, that is expressed

$$CreateUser \ {}_9^9 \ RemoveUser = \text{id}$$
$$RemoveUser \ {}_9^9 \ CreateUser = \text{id}[WebboState_{pd,at}].$$

Further laws in Webbo follow from the following observations. The action of a user posting mail to another does not have the same effect as that of an administrator performing an analogous *AdminPostOne*. For it is a precondition of the former but not the latter that sender $u?$ be logged in, and a precondition of the latter but not the former that administrator $a?$ be logged in; but otherwise the effects are the same.

From a fresh start, $log(u?).no = 0$, three unsuccessful logins of user $u?$ leave the system in a state in which all components are the same except that $log(u?).no = 3$, $log(u?).lock$ holds and $log(u?).at$ is arbitrary.

A successful login of a user followed by its logout thus leaves state unchanged except for the $log(u?).at$ component. However a logout followed immediately by a login of the same user leaves state unchanged only if $u?$ was originally logged in and at the same client as the login.

All provide opportunities, subject to the qualification above about implementation detail, for testing; and all suggest information that can be provided by the specifier.

## 4.2 Reality Check

However in real systems the check for identity requires the checking of all system components. For example, it requires checking that the database has all and only the information that was present at the start of the operations. Expense precludes this from being part of the testing process. But worse, such simple identities are almost never true. Databases and other applications (such as the authentication engine) keep log files for rollback and forensics. As these log files do not affect the functionality they rarely feature in specifications.

Thus for testing purposes it is essential to specify explicitly the components that are used (or not used) for the calculation of the identity relation; hence our use of the notation above. In practice that requires a combination of knowledge of both specification (to determine which components to observe) and link (how they are represented in the implementation).

## 5 Testing Consistency

Different (state-based) specification notations employ slightly different styles and hence place emphasis on slightly different concepts. A state invariant in Z (like the three explicit predicates that constrain *Loginfo*[1] or the single explicit predicate that constrains

---

[1] The statement $at : C$ provides an implicit constraint since it expands to the type statement $at : Client$ with explicit constraint $at \in C$.

*State*) constitutes a sub-type in RAISE. Because of their importance in testing, both approaches are considered here.

## 5.1  Invariants

System invariants can be thought of as generalising algebraic laws. They are strictly more general: a property may hold after an operation is invoked even though it may not be captured in a law. As has just been seen, Webbo contains both explicit and implicit invariants. A further type of implicit invariant holds not from the expansion of a dependent type but from a property that holds initially and is maintained by all operations. An example is the nonemptiness of $A$. In principle each invariant provides an important test (if it can be achieved in the web-based implementation). This is something the specifier is in a position to provide, and will typically have considered either making explicit in the specification, or proving is a consequence of it.

An example of a restriction on testing imposed by the web-based interface is in testing the (explicit) invariant

$$\forall u : U \cdot log(u).no \leq 3 .$$

That cannot be tested directly without access to the internal variable that records the number of consecutive failed logins (something the web-based interface does not allow). For instance, in most applications we cannot directly test if $log(u).no$ has the value 2 after two unsuccessful logins. Thus the invariant must be changed, to incorporate

$$log(u).lock \Rightarrow \texttt{LoginFail(u,\_)} .$$

This can be tested at the state where the lock is first set (when $log(u).no$ equals 3). At this point any attempt to invoke *Login* on that user account should fail. The fact that the account is locked can be obtained in most implementations.

Another kind of invariant is that subtypes are used in a consistent manner: if an operation with inputs or states in a subtype is supposed to preserve that subtype (in the sense that outputs or state after also lie in the subtype), then it actually does so.

Less comprehensive invariants, nonetheless important for testing, are typically conveniently expressed in temporal logic. It has been shown [17] that in some circumstances such temporal formulae can replace the model-based specification for the purposes of testing. But in general just as a state-based specification can be complemented by algebraic laws—or refinements, *i.e.* one-sided laws—so too it can be complemented by temporal properties that the specifier is in a position to posit.

## 5.2  Confidence Conditions

*Confidence conditions*[2] are certain kinds of condition on a specification whose failure, it has been found by experience, often indicate error. They need be neither necessary

---
[2] The term was coined in the RAISE project [20,21].

nor sufficient for consistency[3], but their truth provides a degree of confidence in the specification.

Confidence conditions therefore provide some opportunities for verification activities. The RAISE tools, for example, allow them to be generated and inspected, to be generated and proved (in PVS), to be model checked (in SAL), and to be included in executable code produced by translators. Confidence conditions are used in two ways: to look for inconsistencies in the specification and also as hints for possible extra code in the implementation, to be switched on during testing and possibly also to aid in debugging. In this paper it is the second usage that is of particular interest.

In (sequential) RSL the main confidence conditions are:

- subtypes are not empty
- arguments to functions are in subtypes
- results of functions are in subtypes
- assignments to variables are in subtypes
- preconditions of functions are satisfied by invocations
- postconditions of functions are satisfied by invocations
- case expressions are complete.

Here 'functions' include built-in functions and operators, like division (perhaps by zero) or taking the head of a list (perhaps empty).

Although those conditions might be expressed slightly differently in Z (schemas are satisfiable, and functions and expressions are well defined at both their points of definition and of use) they are equally important. The same ideas can be applied to any specification language, but the possibilities will change with the language. In general, there is a tendency for Z specifications to involve less redundancy than RSL ones, and so the possibility for generating confidence conditions may be reduced. The next section applies the idea of confidence conditions to Webbo.

### 5.3  Confidence Conditions in Webbo

*Loginfo*, with its three-predicate invariant, forms an RSL subtype. The *State* definition has an invariant consisting of one explicit and one implicit predicate (the implicit predicate $mng : C \to M$ expands to the type statement $mng : Clients \nrightarrow M$ with an explicit constraint $\text{dom}(mng) = C$), and so also forms an RSL subtype. Thus obvious checks are

- Operations generate states consistent with the *State* predicate (which includes the *Loginfo* predicates on each value in the range of *log*)
- Outputs of type *Loginfo* satisfy the *Loginfo* predicates.

The specification Webbo is written in a largely implicit style. Thus in *RemoveClient*, the condition $C = C' \sqcup \{c?\}$ defines $C'$ implicitly whereas the equivalent $C' = C \setminus \{c?\}$

---

[3] Lack of sufficiency is obvious. They need not be necessary because of limitations in the static analysis that generates them; for example the (low-level, but consistent) expression 'if false then 1/0 else 1 fi' might generate the confidence condition that the divisor 0 is not 0, which fails to hold.

does so explicitly (but by violating the symmetry with *CreateClient*). Implicit descriptions are typically more abstract and aimed at establishing properties (for which purpose symmetry is helpful), whilst explicit descriptions are typically closer to code; most specification notations permit both styles, for use as appropriate in the development cycle.

Since an implementation models all the predicates in its specification, it is difficult to see, of an implicit-style specification, where possible inconsistencies come from: if a function is defined by a postcondition the confidence condition becomes an assertion that a result satisfying the postcondition, plus any relevant subtype condition, exists. This does not tend to be very helpful in discovering errors. But when an explicit style is used then a test can be run to check that a result lies in the appropriate subtype.

In a notation (like RSL) whose explicit functions may also have postconditions, the redundancy permits a much stronger confidence condition to be generated. Similarly with explicit preconditions (like RSL, VDM or the refinement calculus), which permit a check that the explicit precondition is strong enough to ensure the preconditions of functions and operators used in the definition. (The calculation of preconditions in Z provides no redundancy, although it may introduce mistakes in the specification—an inconsistency[4] between the calculated precondition and the implicit one—to be picked up in testing [25].)

So it is seen that in Webbo the subtype checks are not so useful as checks on the specification, although they do provide checks to be included in the implementation. The checks will probably need to be optional, as some will be computationally expensive, but they can be used in testing and debugging.

## 5.4  Partial Operators

The appearance of disjoint union, $\sqcup$, in Webbo exhibits the use that can be made of partiality. It appears in several operations in the form

$$S' = S \sqcup T$$

from which follows the precondition that $S$ and $T$ are disjoint. It also appears in the form

$$S = S' \sqcup T$$

from which follows the postcondition that $S'$ and $T$ are disjoint, though that is subsumed in the more general postcondition which is the whole equality.

## 5.5  Are Equalities Assignments?

When a specifier in ObjectZ writes

$$e0 = e1$$

---

[4] Typically because the specifier does not do the calculation carefully enough, relying on intuition for the answer.

where $e0$ and $e1$ are general expressions, then the confidence condition that one might generate is that there is a non-empty intersection between the possible sets of values for $e0$ and $e1$. But when the left-hand side of the equality is $x!$ or $x'$, where $x$ is a variable whose type is a subtype, the equality can be regarded as an explicit specification of an assignment in the implementation, in which case the stronger check can be introduced that the value of the expression on the right-hand side lies within the variable's subtype.

## 5.6 Guide to Implementers

A number of checks can therefore be generated to apply as optional code in the final implementation. However their execution requires:

- Equality functions on all types are needed. Since, as mentioned elsewhere, the finally implemented types are typically richer, an abstract equality needs to be implemented which is obviously defined in terms of the (abstract) equalities on the components
- In general, the constituents of the specification need to be implemented, or some means found to express the conditions in terms of the implementation.
  For example, the relation *post* is unlikely to be held as a set: it will be calculable (in theory) as such a relation from, perhaps, individual mail boxes for recipients like one which associates to each receiver a set consisting of pairs comprising a sender and a message

  $$postbox : U \to \mathbb{P}(U \times Mess)$$

  subject to the coupling invariant

  $$post = \{(u,r,m) : U \times U \times Mess \mid u \in U \ \wedge \ (r,m) \in postbox(u)\}.$$

  Then the assertion that a message exists with someone as recipient is easy to implement. The assertion that some message exists with a given sender would be harder (unless the implementation followed a design in which each user kept an analogous *outbox* of sent post).
- Following from the previous point, it is clear that the code used to implement these checks will often break properties such as security that need to be imposed on user-accessible functions. How to deal with this is unclear. For example one user ought not to be able to access another's post (except perhaps the sender, if the *outbox* design is used). Yet to test the operations of *AdminPost* and *UserMail*, just such probing is necessary. However this treatment has stopped short of security and other such properties.

## 6  Boundaries

Boundary value testing is an important technique that has been adopted in MBT [24]: each operation is tested at each state that is (reachable and) extreme in a sense defined by the tester. In Webbo, boundary testing focuses on the extreme values of the *Loginfo* observable $no = 0, 3$, on both values of any Boolean variable, on the initial values of the set *State* observables, on the empty and full cases of *post*, and so on.

The specifier is in a position to define appropriate boundary functions, which the tester might not think of. For that purpose it is sometimes easier (compared with the method used in [24]) to define an order (like set inclusion or ordering on integers) and to identify a boundary with its extreme points. That yields all the examples mentioned above.

One interesting, less systematic, example already considered is identification of a dummy user to include as a boundary point, as discussed in Section 3.5. But this is information a specifier has only if familiar with the test constraints.

Another example is provided by the important operation of logging in. There are potentially infinitely many ways in which the login operation can yield *Fail*. Of course in testing, a suitable subset of inputs must be found to trigger that behaviour. However, the model does not explicitly state which inputs to consider. Again, it is appropriate for the specifier to augment the specification with information to aid testing. For instance, a suitable function $f$ can be defined with the property that if Login(u?,id?) succeeds then Login(u?,f(id?)) should fail.

Similarly, tests Login(ux,idx) can be generated where ux is not a valid user, by specifying rules for ux. Such tests should of course fail for any value of idx, and rules for choice of idx can be specified. An alternative is to specify sets *Uinvalid* and *Pinvalid* and generate all tests for

$$(ux, idx) : Uinvalid \times Pinvalid .$$

# 7   Intermediate States

So far only functional properties, like those exemplified by Webbo, have been considered. But it is important for a specifier, and tester, to take account of so-called 'nonfunctional' properties like security, non-interference, distribution and even efficiency. This section considers one common situation that is typically a source of insecurity in the sense of exposing information that ought to remain concealed.

## 7.1   Sequential Components

The linking of the code to the model implicitly involves different levels of atomicity. It may be convenient, for example, to implement an operation *op* with a sequential composition $op = op0 \, \S \, op1$ where *op0* is responsible for some of the I/O and *op1* for the others. However such a factorisation may result in a security leak.

For example, the login operation of Webbo assumes that the system responds, atomically, only after both the user name and password have been input and the login button has been clicked. But in some implementations, login could be achieved as the sequential composition of two 'sub'-operations the first of which provides the user with information about the success of part of the process. If that information ought to be secure, then this factorisation of login should be flagged as a security hazard.

More explicitly, login may be expressed as a check that the user identified by input $u?$ is valid, *i.e.* $u? \in U$, (with no output but with a Boolean variable to record $(u? \in U)$

for use by the second sub-operation) followed by a check that if so then the password provided is correct, *i.e. log(u?).pd = p?*, (with appropriate change of state and output *ack!*) then an opportunity is provided for a malicious user to obtain information about *U* by probing with the first sub-operation.

Assume that `loginFail(u?,p?)` is linked to

```
enter_text(:name,u?);
enter_text(:password,p?);
login.click();
check-not-logged-in();
```

with the assumption only that the user u? and the password p? do not tally. It is desired also to check that if u? is not a valid user, no message is returned. To simplify the specification of the link, `loginFail(u?,p?)` is split into a sequential composition

```
loginFailName(u?) ; loginFailPassword(p?).
```

The code that links the action word `loginFailName(u?)` to the system is

```
enter_text(:name,u?);
check-no-message();
```

and the code that links the action word `loginFailPassword(p?)` to the system is

```
enter_text(:password,u?);
login.click();
check-not-logged-in();
```

An alternative solution to this problem is to have another action word `loginFailNoUser`. But that complicates the specification of the model and the link between the model and code.

## 7.2  Principle

In general if the code associated with an action word a is of the form b0;b1,

```
a ⤳ b0;b1,
```

where b0 represents a desired behaviour in itself, it is better to split a into a0;a1 and associate a0 with b0 and a1 with b1

```
a = a0;a1,    where  a0 ⤳ b0  and  a1 ⤳ b1.
```

Similarly, if the code associated with an action word a is of the form b0;b1 where b1 is associated with another action word b, it is better to associate a with only b0 and change the model by replacing the a transitions with a;b transitions.

## 8   Conclusion and Further Work

A model, in the form of a (state-based) specification, together with a link is able to generate tests of a putative implementation. It has been seen that, roughly, the more detailed a test is, the more information the tester needs to have of the link. Thus laws concerning the operations may involve little information beyond the specification; but they might require knowledge of how the link represents the system state in the implementation. The trade-off between specification and implementation knowledge has already been revealed by Stocks [22,23], so it is not surprising that it has reappeared here.

A specifier might ask the question: what extra functional information am I in a position to provide about the system that yields the kind of redundancy necessary for testing? Various answers have been discussed here, including: system invariants (explicit or implicit), further confidence conditions, partiality of operators, boundary testing and 'nonfunctional' properties like security.

The specifier is well placed to augment the specification with various pieces of information—along those lines—to generate tests. But the more detailed the test, the more information is required beyond mere specification information. For otherwise the result might be a test which is not able to be executed due to restrictions on the testing interface. That is particularly true of web-based systems of the kind represented by Webbo.

This paper represents work very much in progress. It is hoped to continue it by formalising the action-word approach to linking specification with implementation (using the concepts of data simulation and process algebra), automating the ideas contained here, applying them to Webbo to determine the nature of the tests generated, and identifying conditions sufficient for a test interface to execute a given family of tests.

## References

1. Aichernig, B.K.: Test-design through abstraction — A systematic approach based on the refinement calculus. Journal of Universal Computer Science 7(8), 710–735 (2001)
2. Binder, R.V.: Design for testability in object-oriented systems. Commun. ACM 37(9), 87–101 (1994)
3. Boyapati, C., Khurshid, S., Marinov, D.: Korat: automated testing based on Java predicates. In: Proceedings of the International Symposium on Software Testing and Analysis (ISSTA 2002), Rome, Italy, 22–24, IEEE, Los Alamitos (2002)
4. Broy, M., Jonsson, B., Katoen, J.-P., Leucker, M., Pretschner, A. (eds.): Model-Based Testing of Reactive Systems. LNCS, vol. 3472. Springer, Heidelberg (2005)
5. Buwalda, H.: Action Figures. Software Testing and Quality Engineering, 42–47 (2003)
6. Buwalda, H., Kasdorp, M.: Getting automated testing under control. Software Testing and Quality Engineering , 39–44 (November/December, 1999)
7. Dick, J., Faivre, A.: Automating the generation and sequencing of test cases from model-based specifications. In: Larsen, P.G., Woodcock, J.C.P. (eds.) FME 1993. LNCS, vol. 670, pp. 268–284. Springer, Heidelberg (1993)
8. Duke, R., Rose, G.: Formal Object-Oriented Specification Using Object-Z. Macmillan Press, NYC (2000)
9. El-Far, I.K., Whittaker, J.A.: Model-based software testing. In: Marciniak, J.J. (ed.) Encyclopedia of Software Engineering, vol. 1, pp. 825–837. Wiley-Interscience, Chichester (2002)

10. http://portal.etsi.org/mbs/Testing/conformance/conformance.asp

11. Hayes, I.J.: Specification directed module testing. IEEE Transactions on Software Engineering, SE-12(1):124–133 (1986), See also the 2006 revision
http://www.itee.uq.edu.au/~ianh/Papers/spectest.pdf

12. Helke, S., Neustupny, T., Santen, T.: Automating test case generation from Z specifications with Isabelle. In: Till, D., Bowen, J.P., Hinchey, M.G. (eds.) ZUM 1997. LNCS, vol. 1212, pp. 52–71. Springer, Heidelberg (1997)

13. Hörcher, H.-M., Peleska, J.: The role of formal specifications in software testing. In: Naftalin, M., Bertran, M., Denvir, T. (eds.) FME 1994. LNCS, vol. 873, Springer, Heidelberg (1994)

14. Hörcher, H.-M.: Improving software tests using Z specifications. In: Bowen, J.P., Hinchey, M.G. (eds.) ZUM 1995. LNCS, vol. 967, pp. 152–166. Springer, Heidelberg (1995)

15. Hörcher, H.-M., Peleska, J.: Using formal specifications to support software testing. Software Quality Journal 4, 309–327 (1995)

16. Kohl, J., Rogers, P.: Watir Works. Better Software, 40–45 (April 2005)

17. Krishnan, P.: Uniform descriptions for model based testing. In: Proceedings of the 2004 Australian Software Engineering Conference (ASWEC'04), IEEE, Los Alamitos (2004),
http://epublications.bond.edu.au/infotech_pubs/8

18. Li, D., Aichernig, B.K.: Automatic Test Case Generation for RAISE. Technical Report 273, UNU-IIST, P.O.Box 3058, Macao (January 2003)

19. Mikk, E.: Compilation of Z specifications into C for automatic test result evaluation. In: Bowen, J.P., Hinchey, M.G. (eds.) ZUM 1995. LNCS, vol. 967, pp. 167–180. Springer, Heidelberg (1995)

20. The RAISE Languager Group.: The RAISE Specification Language. BCS Practitioner Series. Prentice Hall, Englewood Cliffs (1992)

21. The RAISE Method Group.: The RAISE Development Method. BCS Practitioner Series. Prentice Hall, Englewood Cliffs (1995), available by ftp from ftp://ftp.iist.unu.edu/pub/RAISE/method_book

22. Stocks, P.A.: Applying Formal Methods to Software Testing. PhD thesis, Department of Computer Science, The University of Queensland, St. Lucia 4072, Australia (1993)

23. Stocks, P.A., Carrington, D.A.: A Framework for Specification-based Testing. IEEE Transactions in Software Engineering 22(11), 777–793 (1996)

24. Legeard, B., Peureux, F., Utting, M.: Automated boundary testing from Z and B. In: Meersman, R., Tari, Z. (eds.) On the Move to Meaningful Internet Systems 2004: CoopIS, DOA, and ODBASE. LNCS, vol. 3291, pp. 21–40. Springer, Heidelberg (2004)

25. Utting, M.: Position paper: model-based testing. Verified Software: Theories, Tools, Experiments. ETH Zürich, IFIP WG 2.3 (2005)

26. Utting, M., Legeard, B.: Practical Model-Based Testing: A Tools Approach. Morgan-Kaufmann, San Francisco (2007)

# Semantics and Verification of a Language for Modelling Hardware Architectures*

Michael R. Hansen, Jan Madsen, and Aske Wiid Brekling

Informatics and Math. Modelling, Technical University of Denmark
Ricard Petersens Plads, DK-2800 Lyngby
mrh@imm.dtu.dk, jan@imm.dtu.dk, awb@imm.dtu.dk

**Abstract.** In this paper we consider a high-level hardware description language Gezel, from which hardware can be synthesized through a translation to VHDL. The language is equipped with a simulator and supports exploration of hardware designs. The language has no semantics and it is difficult to get a deep understanding of many of the constructions. We therefore give a semantic domain for Gezel. Aiming at automated verification we relate this domain to the timed-automata model and we have experimented with verification of Gezel-specifications using the Uppaal system. In particular, we have proven the correctness of a hardware specification of the Simplified DES algorithm. We have also used Uppaal for small experiments of verifying resource usage.

**Keywords:** Hardware descriptions, semantics, verification, model-checking.

## 1   Introduction

As the complexity of chips grows, the methodology to build chips has to evolve. Today, chips are largely synthesized from high-level architectural descriptions which hide low-level details such as the physical characteristics of a transistor or how to build a flip-flop. This applies to chips ranging from small scale, specialized chips to be produced in modest quantities to highly complex ones of general computers for mass production. Today, the majority of hardware designs are done using the most common hardware description languages, VHDL [18] or Verilog [16]. Both languages support high-level architectural descriptions, but allow hardware designers to incorporate low-level details in order to optimize for a particular hardware technology. Although this makes it possible to produce highly optimized chips it also ties the hardware description to a particular technology or set of technologies.

It is possible to synthesize chips directly from VHDL and Verilog using a restricted subset of the languages. However, chips may also be synthesized from

---

* This work has been partially funded by The Danish Council for Strategic Research under project **MoDES**, the Danish National Advanced Technology Foundation under project **DaNES**, and ARTIST2 (IST-004527).

C.B. Jones, Z. Liu, J. Woodcock (Eds.): Bjørner/Zhou Festschrift, LNCS 4700, pp. 300–319, 2007.

software based models in much the same way as compilers produce executable code. Examples of such languages are Esterel, Lustre and Signal, see e.g. [2].

In this paper, we will use Gezel [12,15] as our choice of language for hardware models. It depends on reasonably few, simple and clean concepts, and it strikes a balance between software and hardware concerns that we believe suits the needs for a modern top-down approach to hardware design. Gezel is based on an execution model which resembles the synchronous model of Esterel, but unlike Esterel, the language of Gezel contains constructs for hardware design. Compared to VHDL and Verilog, Gezel may be considered to be at a higher abstraction level without any explicit timing constructs. This allows Gezel to be truly independent of any implementation technology.

The advantage of Gezel is that the language has simple parts with a clear hardware meaning, e.g. registers, controllers, synchronous execution. There are simulators for Gezel, and, furthermore, the language is designed so that it can be mapped to a synthesizable subset of VHDL. But the language has no formal semantics, and it is difficult to get a clear understanding of some of the more advanced constructs.

In this paper, we will give a semantics domain which can be used for hardware design languages like Gezel. With this semantics, we believe, that a new Gezel-like language could be defined, where the syntax reflects the semantics in a direct manner. We also show how the semantics can be used in connection with verification by relating the semantical domain to timed-automata [1]. We have experimented with verification of some examples, e.g. the Simplified Data Encryption Standard Algorithm [11], using the Uppaal system [4].

## 2   Gezel Specifications

The specification language Gezel [13,14] is used to express models of hardware. It comes with an interpreter as well as a translator with VHDL as its target language. The interpreter provides means for simulation and debugging. The language does not have a formal semantics, and there is no tool for the verification of Gezel specifications.

A Gezel specification describes a number of *components* and their *interconnections*. A Gezel component consists of a *datapath* providing a set of named actions, called signal flow graphs (sfg), and a *controller* expressed as a finite state machine which may execute one or more actions in each state transition. This model is called *finite state machine with datapath* [8], or FSMD in short. Fig. 1 shows the elements and structure of an FSMD, while Fig. 2 shows the pattern for the most essential parts of a Gezel specification.

A Gezel component models a piece of hardware which is always active. Such components operate in parallel and do not depend on resource allocations. The expressiveness of the FSMD model allows any type of digital hardware architecture to be modelled, from dedicated hardware devices to full micro processors. The execution semantics of Gezel is that of complete synchrony, i.e. every FSMD of a Gezel specification makes exactly one transition in every clock cycle.

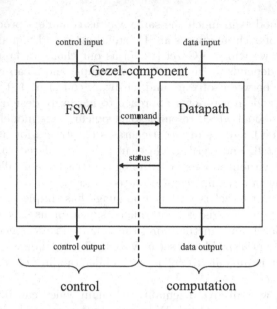

**Fig. 1.** The FSMD model

*(Datapath:*

```
dp Name₀(port list) {
  local register and signal   declarations
  sfg name₁ { (non-branching)  actions }
  sfg name₂ { (non-branching)  actions }
  ...
}
```

+

*Control:*                                                    *) ... + Composition:*

```
fsm controller_name (Name₀) {
  initial state declaration
  auxiliary state declarations
  @state₀ transition₀
  @state₁ transition₁
  ...
}
```

```
system id {
  Name₀ (n₀,₀ , n₀,₁ , ... );
  Name₁ (n₁,₀ , n₁,₁ , ... );
  ...
}
```

Composition in terms of *nets*
(implicitly introduced $n_{i,j}$)

**Fig. 2.** Pattern for a Gezel program

The FSMD model in which control and computation are separated as illustrated in Fig. 1, is a powerful abstraction which allows translation of programs into FSMD models and further into assembly code or synchronous hardware. Furthermore, it supports systematic testing and formal verification.

## 2.1 Extracting FSMD from Programs

An imperative program may be split into *basic blocks*, i.e. a maximal sequence of assignments (without any control statement), and its control flow. A program may then be represented as a graph, with edges mapping into basic blocks and nodes into control points, typically conditional jumps. Such a graph corresponds to a finite state machine of Mealy type. This graph is translated to the FSMD model as follows: each basic block forms an action of the datapath and the finite state machine becomes the controller of the FSMD, which executes exactly one basic block in each transition.

Fig. 3 shows the pseudo-code for a greatest common divisor (gcd) algorithm and its corresponding Gezel specification. Five basic blocks, named bb0 to bb4, are extracted from the gcd-program and the controller consists of 4 states and 6 transitions. Using Gezel all outputs must be given well-defined values in every transition. This is captured by the action update, which makes sure that the output c is always given the value of res. Registers, declared as reg, store values

```
gcd(a,b) =
   while a!=b
   do {
      if a<b
      then b:=b-a;
      else a:=a-b;
   };
   c:=a;
```

```
dp gcd(in a,b: ns(8);
       out c: ns(8)) {
   reg x, y, res: ns(8);
   reg xlessy, xneqy: ns(1);

   sfg bb0{ x=a; y=b; xneqy=(a!=b); }
   sfg bb1{ xlessy=(x<y); }
   sfg bb2{ y=y-x; xneqy=(x!=y-x); }
   sfg bb3{ x=x-y; xneqy=(x-y!=y); }
   sfg bb4{ res=x; }
   sfg update{ c=res; }
}

fsm gcd_ctl(gcd) {
   initial s0;
   state s1, s2, s3;

   @s0 (bb0, update)        -> s1;
   @s1 if (xneqy)
       then (bb1, update) -> s2;
       else (bb4, update) -> s3;
   @s2 if (xlessy)
       then (bb2, update) -> s1;
       else (bb3, update) -> s1;
   @s3 (bb4, update)        -> s3;
}
```

**Fig. 3.** An imperative program for gcd and a corresponding Gezel program for a 8-bit version of the gcd

between transitions. They are the only way for the controller to test conditions and make branching transitions.

## 2.2   Constructing Hardware from an FSMD

The translation of an FSMD model into hardware is done by translating the controller part into its hardware representation, and creating the hardware datapath as a parallel composition of all basic blocks, where in each basic block all operators are implemented by a hardware component. Finally, the components of the hardware datapath and the hardware controller are connected by appropriate signals.

Although this translation may seem straightforward, several optimizations may be applied in order to arrive at a more efficient hardware implementation:

- As only one transition is taken in any given cycle, hardware resources may be shared between different transitions.
- The number of operators may be reduced further by splitting a transition into a sequence of transitions as explained below.

The actual execution time of a program depends on the number of cycles to be executed and the time taken to execute a single cycle. The minimum cycle time is determined by the longest path through the hardware of any of the basic blocks. There is, therefore, a tradeoff between few transitions and long cycle time and many transitions with faster cycle time. By splitting a basic block with a long path through the hardware over two or more transitions, more resource sharing may be obtained, resulting in less area requirements, while the overall system performance may be the same if, for instance, the number of cycles have been doubled while the cycle time has been halved.

| Program text | Basic blocks | Mealy graph |
|---|---|---|
| int n, f0, f1;<br>n := N;<br>f0 := 0; f1 := 1;<br>while (n>0) do<br>    f1 := f0+f1;<br>    f0 := f1-f0;<br>    n  := n-1;<br>od<br>output f1; | A: n := N;<br>    f0 := 0;<br>    f1 := 1;<br>    n>0<br>B: f1 := f0+f1;<br>    f0 := f1-f0;<br>    n := n-1;<br>    n>0<br>C: output f1; | A<br>B<br>C |

**Fig. 4.** From a program text to a state transition graph

Fig. 4 shows an example of a program where the basic blocks form a set of parallel assignments. Fig. 5 shows two possible schedules of the computation in basic block B from Fig. 4. The left schedule computes in one cycle but then requires two arithmetic units (ALU's), while the right schedule requires two cycles but only one ALU as the two operations (Add and Sub) are executed in different cycles and hence may share the same resource.

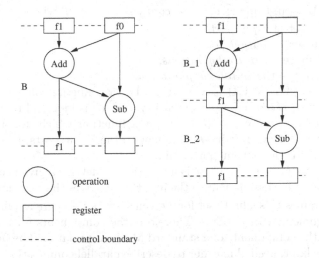

Fig. 5. Scheduling operations in the datapath

# 3   The Module Concept

In this section we will present the semantics domain for Gezel, where the aim is to make it clear in which way this domain extends the theory of automata. To this end we introduce the concept a *module*.

Modules shall constitute the building blocks for systems, and the module concept is defined to facilitate hierarchical constructions. In terms of Gezel, a *basic module* is constructed from a component of a controller and a datapath, and modules can be combined in parallel using a single assignment program to describe the combinatorial circuit connecting the ports of the modules.

We will not aim at a semantics for full Gezel. In particular, in Gezel a variety of shorthand notations are introduced with the consequence that it is difficult to get a clear semantical understanding of the language. Examples of such constructs are hardwired controllers, sequencer controllers, and the use-construct. We will not address these constructs. Furthermore, we will not address a type discipline (as in Gezel, where a type could be **unsigned** of length 64). A type discipline is important, but adding types to our framework will not be difficult.

We suppose that a set $V$ of *values* is given. $V$ can be thought of as a set of bit-vectors. We assume that $0 \in V$ and that every bit-vector with 0's only is a representation of 0. Furthermore, we suppose that a set of *variables Var* is given comprising input and output ports, signals, and registers. A *value assignment* $\sigma$ is a partial function:

$$\sigma : Var \xrightarrow{\sim} V \, ,$$

which associates values to a finite subset of the variables. Let *VA* denote the set of all value assignments.

A *module* $M$ is an tuple $(\bar{i}, \bar{o}, Conf, conf_0, \underline{p}, out, next)$, where

- $\bar{i}$ is a finite set of *input ports*,
- $\bar{o}$ is a finite set of *output ports*,
- $Conf$ is a finite set of *configurations*,
- $conf_0 \in Conf$ is the *initial configuration*,
- $\underline{p} : Conf \rightarrow (VA \rightarrow VA)$ is a function. For a configuration $conf$ and value assignment $\sigma$, $\underline{p}(conf)$ $\sigma$ is an extension of $\sigma$ (or is identical to $\sigma$),
- $out : Conf \times (\bar{i} \rightarrow V) \rightarrow (\bar{o} \rightarrow V)$ is a function which, for a given configuration and a given value assignment to the input ports, gives the value assignment for the output ports, and
- $next : Conf \times (\bar{i} \rightarrow V) \rightarrow Conf$ is a function, which for a given configuration and a given value assignment to the input ports, gives the next configuration.

The set of values $V$ is a finite set for a given system, i.e. there is a finite number of value assignments to the ports. Therefore, the components for a module excluding $\underline{p}$ are the components of a standard Mealy automaton. The function $\underline{p}$ is, as we shall see later, needed in order to describe parallel composition of modules, where values to some input ports may be computed by other components.

## 3.1  Top-Level Modules

A "running module" $M = (\bar{i}, \bar{o}, Conf, conf_0, \underline{p}, out, next)$, also called a *top-level module*, will be given a semantics in terms of a transition system. We shall describe the *computations* of $M$ by a *transition system*, $\mathcal{T_S}$, with initial configuration $conf_0$, where

$$\mathcal{T_S} \subseteq Conf \times (\bar{i} \rightarrow V) \times (\bar{o} \rightarrow V) \times Conf .$$

We use $conf \xrightarrow{\sigma_{\bar{i}}, \sigma_{\bar{o}}}_M conf'$ as an abbreviation for $(conf, \sigma_{\bar{i}}, \sigma_{\bar{o}}, conf') \in \mathcal{T_S}$, and we define that $conf \xrightarrow{\sigma_{\bar{i}}, \sigma_{\bar{o}}}_M conf'$, if and only if,

$$next(conf, \sigma_{\bar{i}}) = conf' \qquad \text{and} \qquad out(conf, \sigma_{\bar{i}}) = \sigma_{\bar{o}} .$$

# 4  Basic Modules

A basic module will be defined as a pair consisting of a *controller* and a *datapath*. The controller is basically a finite state machine, and the datapath consists of input ports, output ports, signals, registers, and a set of actions. We will not go into a concrete syntactical level like that of Gezel specifications; rather the presentation with be based on an abstract syntax, on which we can address well-formedness conditions such as freeness from *combinatorial loops*.

## 4.1  Abstract Syntax of Datapaths

A *variable signature for a datapath* consists of

- a finite set $\bar{r}$ of *registers*,
- a finite set $\bar{i}$ of *input ports*,

- a finite set $\bar{o}$ of *output ports*, and
- a finite set $\bar{s}$ of *local signals*.

Registers are special in the sense that they keep their values throughout a clock cycle, and a register will keep its value from one cycle to the next if the register is not changed. Therefore, we introduce a new variable $r'$ for the next value of every register $r \in \bar{r}$. Let $\bar{r}' = \{r'|r \in \bar{r}\}$ be the set of these "primed variables".

These five sets are assumed to be mutually exclusive, and we shall use the term *variable* for an element of one of these sets:

$$Var \mathbin{\widehat{=}} \bar{r} \cup \bar{r}' \cup \bar{i} \cup \bar{o} \cup \bar{s} .$$

Let $C \subseteq V$ be a set of constants, and $F$ a set of function symbols equipped with *arities*. Then, the set of expressions $e \in Expr$ is generated from constants and variables using functions and a kind of McCarthy conditional, as expressed in the following abstract grammar:

$$e ::= c \mid x \mid f^n(e_1, \ldots, e_n) \mid e?e_1, e_2 ,$$

where $c \in C, x \in Var/\bar{r}'$, and $f^n \in F$ is an $n$-ary function symbol. Notice that primed registers cannot occur in expressions.

For a given variable signature, an *action* is a pair $(an, p)$, where $an$ is the name of the action and $p$ is a *single assignment program*, where registers, output ports and signals only can be assigned a value. We shall model $p$ as a partial mapping from $\bar{r} \cup \bar{o} \cup \bar{s}$ to *Expr*:

$$p \in (\bar{r} \cup \bar{o} \cup \bar{s}) \xrightarrow{\sim} Expr .$$

We shall consider $p$ a set of equations, which defines values for output ports, signals and next values for registers on the basis of values for input ports and previous values for registers.

If $p(x) = e$, then the *associated equation* is $x = e$ if $x$ is not a register, $x' = e$ if $x$ is a register. Let $eqs_p$ be *the set of equations associated with $p$*. We shall occasionally omit the subscript $p$ when it is easily derivable from the context.

We shall now define the *dependency graph* of variables in a single-assignment program $p$ in order to formalize a well-formedness condition expressing that there is no circular definition of variables in $p$. Intuitively, $y$ *depends on* $x$, if the value of $x$ is must be computed in the computation of a value for $y$. The dependency graph for $p$, denoted by $\prec_p$ or just $\prec$, is a subset of $(\bar{i} \cup \bar{o} \cup \bar{s}) \times (\bar{r}' \cup \bar{o} \cup \bar{s})$ and it is defined as the set of pairs $(x, y)$ for which:

$$y = e \ \in eqs_p \text{ and } x \text{ occurs in } e .$$

We shall write $x \prec y$ if $(x, y) \in \prec$.

Constants do not occur the in the graph (their values are always present), neither do the variables for the previous values of registers (i.e. those occurring at the right-hand sides of equations), because these values are always known.

An action $(an, p)$ (and a single assignment program $p$) is called *well-formed* if the dependency graph $\prec_p$ is acyclic, and has input ports only as its sources. All variables of $\prec_p$, which are not input ports, are called *assigned variables*. We call such dependency graphs for well-formed.

A *datapath* consists of a finite set $Act = \{(an_1, p_1), \ldots, (an_n, p_n)\}$ of well-formed actions with unique names, i.e. $an_i = an_j$ implies $i = j$.

By the *signature for the actions* we understand an association of the appropriate dependency graph:

$$\mathrm{graph}(an_i) = \prec_{p_i} ,$$

with every action name.

We shall call a subset $as \subseteq \{an_1, \ldots, an_n\}$ of action names for *consistent*, if the corresponding dependency graphs have disjoint sets of assigned variables. For a consistent set of action names, the single assignment program obtained by joining all single assignment programs of the elements, will be a well-formed single assignment program.

Furthermore, $as$ is called *complete* if every output port is an assigned variable of some dependency graph of an element in $as$.

## 4.2   Semantics of Datapaths

In order to define the meaning of a datapath, we must define the meaning of variables, expressions and actions.

We assume that $\underline{F}$ is an assignment of a function:

$$\underline{f^n} \in V^n \to V ,$$

with every $n$-ary function symbol $f^n \in F$. Furthermore, let $V_\perp \;\hat{=}\; V \cup \{\perp\}$, where $\perp$ is a special element denoting undefined.

**Semantics of Expressions:** The semantics of an expression $e$ is a function: $\mathcal{E}[\![e]\!] \in VA \to V_\perp$, defined inductively as follows:

$$\mathcal{E}[\![c]\!]\sigma = c$$

$$\mathcal{E}[\![x]\!]\sigma = \begin{cases} \sigma(x) & \text{if } x \in \mathrm{dom}\,\sigma \\ \perp & \text{otherwise} \end{cases}$$

$$\mathcal{E}[\![f^n(e_1, \ldots, e_n)]\!]\sigma = \begin{cases} \underline{f^n}(v_1, \ldots, v_n) & \text{if } \perp \neq v_i = \mathcal{E}[\![e_i]\!]\sigma, \text{ for } i = 1, \ldots n \\ \perp & \text{otherwise} \end{cases}$$

$$\mathcal{E}[\![e?e_1, e_2]\!]\sigma = \begin{cases} \mathcal{E}[\![e_2]\!]\sigma & \text{if } 0 = \mathcal{E}[\![e]\!]\sigma \\ \mathcal{E}[\![e_1]\!]\sigma & \text{if } 0 \neq \mathcal{E}[\![e]\!]\sigma \in V \\ \perp & \text{otherwise.} \end{cases}$$

**Semantics of Single Assignment Programs and Actions:** A view of a well-formed single-assignment program $p$ is that it maps value assignments for input ports to value assignments for the assigned variables. We shall, however, take a more general approach which will be useful when we consider parallel composition: $p$ denotes a function on *consistent value assignments*.

An assignment $\sigma$ is *consistent* wrt. a single assignment program $p$, if for every equation $x = e$ in $eqs_p$, we have that $\mathcal{E}[\![x]\!]\sigma = \mathcal{E}[\![e]\!]\sigma$, when $x$ and $e$ are both defined for $\sigma$.

The idea behind the semantics of $p$ is simple: extend a value assignment by one iteration through the equations and add a binding for every assigned variable, where a value has been computed. This process is repeated until no further binding is obtained. The number of iterations needed is bounded by the depth of the dependency graph for $p$.

This idea is formalized by two function:

$$\mathcal{I}[\![eqs_p]\!] \in VA \to VA$$
$$\mathcal{P}[\![p]\!] \quad \in VA \to VA \,,$$

where we assume that $\sigma$ is consistent with $p$ in $\mathcal{I}[\![eqs_p]\!]\sigma$ and $\mathcal{P}[\![p]\!]\sigma$. The functions are defined below such that they preserve this consistency.

The function $\mathcal{I}$ is defined as follows:

$$\mathcal{I}[\![\{\,\}]\!]\sigma \qquad\qquad = [\,]$$
$$\mathcal{I}[\![\{x = e\}]\!]\sigma \qquad\qquad = \begin{cases} [\,] & \text{if } x \in \operatorname{dom}\sigma \text{ or } \mathcal{E}[\![e]\!]\sigma = \bot \\ [x \mapsto \mathcal{E}[\![e]\!]\sigma] & \text{otherwise} \end{cases}$$
$$\mathcal{I}[\![\{x_1 = e_1, \ldots, x_n = e_n\}]\!]\sigma = \mathcal{I}[\![\{x_1 = e_1\}]\!]\sigma + \cdots + \mathcal{I}[\![\{x_n = e_n\}]\!]\sigma \,,$$

where $+$ is the override function on maps. Observe that the resulting value assignment is consistent because the $x_1, x_2, \ldots, x_n$ are mutually distinct variables.

The function $\mathcal{P}$ is defined by:

$$\mathcal{P}[\![p]\!]\sigma \;=\; \bigcup_{i=0}^{d} \mathcal{I}[\![eqs_p]\!]^i \sigma \,,$$

where $d$ is the depth of the dependency graph for $p$ and $g^j(x)$ denotes the $j$-fold iteration of the function $g$, i.e. $g^0(x) = x$ and $g^{j+1}(x) = g(g^j(x))$.

If we order the equations $eqs_p$ into a sequence according to the dependency graph $\prec_p$, so that $x = e_1$ comes before $y = e_2$ whenever $y$ depends on $x$, i.e. $x \prec_p y$, then one iteration through the equations will suffice, as the dependency graph is acyclic.

For every well-formed action $(an, p)$, let $\underline{an}$ denote the function $\mathcal{P}[\![p]\!]$. Furthermore, a consistent set of actions $as$ denotes the function $\underline{as} = \mathcal{P}[\![as]\!]$, which is defined element-wise by:

$$\mathcal{P}[\![as]\!]\sigma \;=\; \underline{an}_a(\sigma) + \cdots + \underline{an}_k(\sigma) \,,$$

for $as = \{an_a, \ldots an_k\}$.

## 4.3   Abstract Syntax for Controllers

The abstract syntax for a controller is defined on the basis of a given datapath. The controller is essentially a deterministic finite state automaton, where a consistent and complete set of actions from the datapath is executed on a transition. Since actions are described by single assignment programs, i.e. without use of a construct for unbounded iterations, a finite set of actions is a convenient abstraction for an operation which can be performed in a bounded amount of time, such as during a clock cycle.

Each transition is guarded by a *condition* on the registers of the datapath. We let *Cond* denote the subset of *Expr* which is generated from registers (excluding the primed ones) and constants only, using functions and the conditional $e?e_1, e_2$, i.e. input and output ports and signals cannot occur in conditions. A condition with value $v$ (for a given value assignment to registers) is considered false if $v = 0$, and true otherwise.

A *controller* is defined by

- a finite set of *states* $S$,
- an initial state $s_0 \in S$, and
- a set of *transitions* $T \subseteq S \times Cond \times 2^{Act} \times S$, where $Act$ is the set of actions from the datapath.

We shall require that a controller is *deterministic*, i.e. for every state $s$, the set of conditions on transitions leaving $s$ are mutually exclusive and complete. Thus, for any state and any value assignment to the registers, there is precisely one *enabled* transition with true condition leaving that state. For Gezel specifications this comes for free due to the if-then-else construction used in connection with conditional transitions.

Furthermore, for any $(s, c, as, s') \in T$, we require that $as$ is a consistent and complete set of actions, i.e. every output port is assigned a value when the transition is taken.

## 4.4   Semantics of Basic Modules

The semantics of a basic module $B$, i.e. a well-formed controller with datapath as defined in the previous two sections, can now be defined. To this end, let $r_0$ be the value assignment where every register has the value 0.

The semantics of $B$ is the tuple $(\bar{i}, \bar{o}, Conf, conf_0, \underline{p}, out, next)$, where

- $Conf = S \times (\bar{r} \to V)$,
- $conf_0 = (s_0, \underline{r}_0)$, and
- the functions *next*, *out* and $p$ are defined as follows: Consider an arbitrary configuration $(s, \sigma_{\bar{r}})$ and let $(s, e, as, s') \in T$ be the uniquely determined transition which is enabled in that configuration, i.e. where $\mathcal{E}[\![e]\!]\sigma_{\bar{r}} \notin \{0, \bot\}$. Then

$$\begin{aligned}
\underline{p}(s, \sigma_{\bar{r}})\, \sigma &= \underline{as}(\sigma_{\bar{r}} + \sigma) \\
out((s, \sigma_{\bar{r}}), \sigma_{\bar{i}}) &= (\underline{p}(s, \sigma_{\bar{r}})\, \sigma_{\bar{i}}) \mid \bar{o} \\
next((s, \sigma_{\bar{r}}), \sigma_{\bar{i}}) &= (s', update(\sigma_{\bar{r}}, \underline{p}(s, \sigma_{\bar{r}})\, \sigma_{\bar{i}})
\end{aligned}$$

where $\sigma \mid A$ denotes the value assignment obtained from $\sigma$ by restricting its domain to the set $A$, and $update(\sigma_{\bar{r}}, \sigma) \in \bar{r} \to V$ is the value assignment to registers which is defined by:

$$update(\sigma_{\bar{r}}, \sigma)\, r = \begin{cases} \sigma(r') \text{ if } r' \in \text{dom}\,\sigma \\ \sigma_{\bar{r}}(r) \text{ otherwise,} \end{cases}$$

for $r \in \bar{r}$.

# 5 Composition of Modules

We shall now describe how modules can be combined in parallel (thereby forming new modules) using single assignment programs to connect their ports.

## 5.1 Abstract Syntax for Composition of Modules

Assume that a composition $M$ of modules is given by:

- sets of input ports $\bar{i}$, output ports $\bar{o}$, signals $\bar{s}$, and registers $\bar{r}$,
- a single assignment program $p \in (\bar{o} \cup \bar{s} \cup \bar{r}) \xrightarrow{\sim} Expr$, and
- a finite collection of modules $m_1, \ldots m_k$, where module $m_j$, for $1 \leq j \leq k$, is given by $m_j = (\bar{i}_j, \bar{o}_j, Conf_j, conf_{0j}, \underline{p}_j, out_j, next_j)$.

In order to express the well-formedness of $M$, we associate the *trivial dependency graph* $\text{graph}(m_j) = triv_j$ with every module $m_j$, where $(i, o) \in triv_j$, for every $i \in \bar{i}_j$ and $o \in \bar{o}_j$, i.e. we consider a module a black-box and assume as little as possible, i.e. that an output port depends on every input port.

The *composition $M$ is well-formed*, if the following conditions hold:

- no output port of $m_j$ is an assigned variable of $p$, i.e. $\bar{o}_j \cap \text{dom}\,p = \emptyset$, for $1 \leq j \leq k$,
- the modules $m_1, \ldots, m_k$ have disjoint sets of output ports, i.e. $\bar{o}_j \cap \bar{o}_l = \emptyset$, for $i \neq l$, and
- the dependency graph of $M$, denoted $\text{graph}(M) = \prec_p \cup \bigcup_{j=1}^k \text{graph}(m_j)$, is acyclic, has $\bar{i}$ only as its sources, and $\bar{o}$ is included in the nodes of the graph.

These conditions are sufficient to exclude what often is called combinatorial loops.

## 5.2 Semantics for Composition of Modules

The semantics for $M$ is defined by (a kind) of product automata construction. It is the module $(\bar{i}, \bar{o}, Conf_M, conf_{0M}, \underline{p}_M, out_M, next_M)$, where

- $Conf_M = Conf_1 \times \cdots \times Conf_k \times (\bar{r} \to V)$,
- $conf_{0M} = (conf_{01}, \ldots, conf_{0k}, \underline{r}_0)$,

– the function $\underline{p}_M : Conf_M \to (VA \to VA)$ is defined by:

$$\underline{p}_M(conf)\sigma = \bigcup_{i=1}^{d} \mathcal{I}(conf)^i \sigma, \quad \text{where}$$
$$\mathcal{I}(conf)\sigma = \underline{p}_1(conf_1)\sigma + \cdots + \underline{p}_k(conf_k)\sigma + \underline{p}(\sigma_{\bar{r}} + \sigma),$$
$$conf = (conf_1, \ldots, conf_k, \sigma_{\bar{r}}),$$

and $d$ is the depth of graph($M$),
– the function $out_M : Conf_M \times (\bar{i} \to V) \to (\bar{o} \to V)$ is defined by:

$$out_M(conf, \sigma_{\bar{i}}) = (\underline{p}_M(conf)\sigma_{\bar{i}}) \,|\, \bar{o}, \quad \text{and}$$

– the function $next_M : Conf_M \times (\bar{i} \to V) \to Conf_M$ is defined by:

$$next_M(conf, \sigma_{\bar{i}}) = (next_1(conf_1, \sigma_{\bar{i}}), \ldots, next_k(conf_k, \sigma_{\bar{i}}), update(\sigma_{\bar{r}}, \sigma')),$$

where $conf = (conf_1, \ldots, conf_k, \sigma_{\bar{r}})$ and $\sigma' = \underline{p}_M(conf)\sigma_{\bar{i}}$.

## 6    Representing Modules in Uppaal

In this section we will consider automated verification of modules. Since modules basically are finite automata, there are many ways to address this problem. In an initial study we experimented with using monadic second-order logics [6,7] for expressing the semantics and using the MONA tool [10] for verification. For the semantical part the experiment was promising, and it has the nice property that second-order quantification can be used to express hiding and refinement of modules can be expressed by implication. For the verification part we did, however, only succeed with very small examples. The problem is that $n$ second-order variables are necessary to model an $n$-bit Gezel variable.

In the next experiments Uppaal [4] was used. Uppaal is a model-checking tool based on timed automata [1]. Even though we have no real-time notions in modules, there was several reasons for experimenting with Uppaal: In other discrete models for embedded systems [5,9] Uppaal has proven to be a powerful tool. Furthermore, a timed-automata based approach to verification of modules would prepare for later real-time extensions.

### 6.1    Main Idea of the Uppaal Representation

In the Uppaal model of timed automata, a system consists of a parallel composition of $n \geq 1$ timed automata. These timed automata can communicate by synchronous communication over channels and by using shared variables. Transitions of a timed automaton can be guarded by a Boolean expression, and a statement of a simple imperative programming language can be executed when a transition is taken. Furthermore, real-valued clocks are used to express real-time properties. For further introduction to Uppaal we refer to [4].

Consider a module $M = (\bar{i}, \bar{o}, Conf, conf_0, \underline{p}, out, next)$. We shall construct an Uppaal model for $M$ such that a transition

$$conf_1 \xrightarrow{\sigma_{\bar{i}}, \sigma_{\bar{o}}}_M conf_2$$

of $M$ is simulated by a sequence of transitions:

$$c_1 \xrightarrow{\text{input?}} c'_1 \xrightarrow{\text{progress?}} c'_2 \xrightarrow{\text{progress?}} \cdots \xrightarrow{\text{progress?}} c'_n \xrightarrow{\text{sync?}} c_2 \,,$$

in the timed-automata model, where the Uppaal states $c_1$ and $c_2$ correspond to $conf_1$ and $conf_2$, respectively, and the *broadcast* channels input?, progress? and sync? have the following roles:

- All component modules synchronize on input? to initiate the start of a clock cycle simultaneously.
- Each component module, which has not yet definitions for all its assigned variables, synchronizes on progress?. Each such synchronization initiates an attempt to compute values for undefined variables. Hence, $\underline{p}(conf_1)\sigma_{\bar{i}}$ is computed in the $n$ steps from $c_1$ to $c'_n$.
- All component modules synchronize on sync? to complete a clock cycle simultaneously.

We shall sketch the timed-automata construction for basic modules and composition of modules below. These timed automata run in parallel with a top-level timed automaton *Top* shown in Fig. 6, which controls the synchronization in the system.

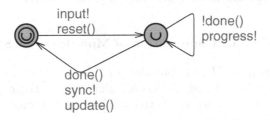

**Fig. 6.** The Timed Automaton *Top*

The three procedures **reset**, **done** and **update** have the following explanations:

- The function **reset** has type **void** and it sets a status field for every assigned variable in the system to undefined.
- The Boolean function **done** is true when all component modules have definitions for their assigned variables.
- The function **update** has type **void** and updates the register values as defined by the function *update* in the definition of *next* in Sect. 4.4.

## 6.2   Construction for Basic Modules — a Sketch

Consider a basic module $B$ as described in Sect. 4. We shall assume that there is a declaration of a global Uppaal variable for every variable in the signature for the datapath including the primed register variables. Furthermore, for every primed register, output port and signal (i.e. the assignable variables) there is a status field describing whether or not the variable is defined.

For every expression $e$ occurring as a guard in a transition of the controller there is corresponding local Boolean Uppaal function $G_e$ implementing $\mathcal{E}[\![e]\!]$, and for every set of actions $as$ occurring in a transition of the controller, there is a local Uppaal function $P_{as}$ of type void, which corresponds to the function $\underline{as}$, i.e. it can compute values for assigned variables whenever this is possible.

Every state $s$ of the controller corresponds to a location (also called $s$) of the timed automaton, and for every transition $(s_1, e, as, s_2)$ of the controller, a fresh timed-automaton location $s'$ is introduced as shown in Fig. 7.

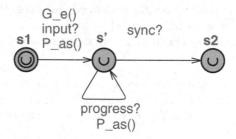

**Fig. 7.** Timed-automaton representation of the transition $(s_1, e, as, s_2)$

## 6.3   Construction for Composition of Modules — A Sketch

Consider a composition $M$ of $k$ modules $m_1, \ldots, m_k$ using a single assignment program $p$ as described in Sect. 5. Assume that $T_1, \ldots, T_k$ are timed-automata representations of $m_1, \ldots, m_k$, respectively. The timed automaton for $M$ is given by the parallel composition:

$$T_1 \parallel \cdots \parallel T_k \parallel T_p \, ,$$

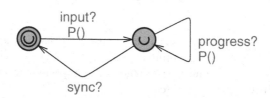

**Fig. 8.** Timed-automaton representation of the single assignment program $p$

where $T_p$ is the timed automaton for the single assignment program $p$ presented in Fig. 8. The local procedure $P$ corresponds to the function $\underline{p}_M$ in Sect. 5.2. Actually, this automaton is just a special case of the transition shown in Fig. 7, where the is no guard on the transition and $s_1 = s_2$.

# 7  Examples: Verification of Gezel Specification

In this section we will provide verification examples of high-level hardware designs. The specifications were described as modules and translated into Uppaal as shown in Sect. 6. We neither give the modules nor the timed automata.

The three examples are specifications of two different greatest common divisor (gcd) algorithms and a specification of a simplified DES (SDES) algorithm [11]. The aim of the verification is to guarantee certain properties of the underlying algorithm, e.g. a correct output for every input, an upper bound for the number of clock cycles needed to compute the output, and an upper bound on the changes of register values before the algorithm can provide an output — the last being an indicator of the energy consumption.

## 7.1  First gcd-Algorithm

This first gcd-algorithm is a simple algorithm based in repeated subtraction as shown in the following pseudo-code:

```
while a != b
do { if a < b then b := b-a; else a := a-b };
c := a;
```

where a and b are the input ports and c is the output port. A Gezel specification is found in Fig 3.

## 7.2  Second gcd-Algorithm

This second gcd-algorithm, in Fig. 9, is a recursive version, see [17], where even(x) is true iff x is even. A Gezel specification is found in Appendix A.

## 7.3  Verification of gcd-Specifications

The hardware specifications for the two gcd-algorithms were translated (by hand) to the Uppaal models, following the principle from Sect. 6. Each timed-automata model was put in parallel with a timed automaton for the environment, where the environment automata provides the input for gcd on the first *input* synchronization. In Uppaal, the input from the environment is chosen by the use of a select statement, which for verification purposes means that any input is attempted.

A query for verifying that for all combinations of inputs an output is generated (i.e. the automaton gcd reaches a final state final) is as follows:

```
    GCD(a,b) =
      if even(a) & even(b)
      then 2 * GCD(a/2, b/2)
      else if even(a) & !even(b)
           then GCD(a/2, b)
           else if !even(a) & even(b)
                then GCD(a, b/2)
                else if a > b              (* a and b are both odd *)
                     then GCD(a-b,b)
                     else GCD(a,b-a)
```

**Fig. 9.** Recursive gcd-algorithm

```
A<>gcd.final
```

which reads: "for all (A) paths, there exists a state (<>) where the gcd automaton is in state final.

Verifying that correct output is produced for any input combination is done by comparing the result with that of a proven correct implementation (igcd) of the greatest common divisor. This query is specified as follows:

```
A[]gcd.final imply (igcd(a,b)==c)
```

where [] reads "for all states on a path".

Two extra variables (regUpdate and cycle) are added to the specifications to keep track of the number of changes in register values and the number of clock cycles. Examples of queries are:

```
A<>gcd.final && regUpdate <= r
```

```
A<>gcd.final && cycle <= x
```

where r and x are upper-bound candidates for the number of register changes and the number of clock cycles needed, respectively.

### 7.4   Verification of SDES Specification

We have also verified a Gezel specification for the Simplified DES algorithm (SDES) [11]. The Gezel specification is too elaborate to give here, as the encryption controller, for example, has 10 states and 9 actions. Encryption takes an 8 bit plaintext and a 10 bit key and produces an 8 bit ciphertext. Decryption takes the 8 bit ciphertext and the same 10 bit key and produces the original 8 bit plaintext.

Verifying that the hardware design is correct is done in two steps. First, it is verified that for all input combinations the final state (final) of the decryption automaton is reached:

```
A<>decryption.final
```

Second, it is verified that the input to the encryption automaton is the same as the output of the decryption automaton:

```
A[]decryption.final imply encryption.input == decryption.output
```

## 7.5  Results and Analysis of Verification

The examples provided in this section have all been verified using Uppaal. One verification showed that the specification of the first gcd-algorithm did not work when one of the inputs were zero. In that case, the controller loops without reaching the state final.

Verification of the upper bound on the number of clock cycles and changes in register values showed that for 8 bit inputs the first algorithm maximally uses 511 clock cycles and 261 register value changes to calculate the greatest common divisor, the second algorithm maximally uses 26 clock cycles and 25 register value changes to calculate greatest common divisor. All these upper bounds are actually least upper bounds, as, for example, 25 clock cycles are shown, using Uppaal, not to be an upper bound for the number of clock cycles for the second gcd-algorithm.

Verification of the SDES algorithm showed that for all combinations of plaintexts and keys, an encryption followed by a decryption yields the original plaintext. However, it was also verified that not all combinations of plaintexts and keys had a changed ciphertext after encryption (e.g. plaintext 7 and key 0 gives ciphertext 7). This of course is a property of the algorithm.

Each of the aforementioned Gezel specifications (i.e. the two different gcd- and the SDES specifications) has been verified in less than 25 minutes on a SUN Fire 3800 with 1.2GHz CPUs running Solaris 10. We have not yet done anything particular to tune the verification.

## 8  Conclusion

We have clarified the semantical domain for the hardware specification language Gezel. Besides giving a much better understanding of the language itself, a clear semantical model allows for a seamless transition into automated verification of hardware specifications. In this way we have related the semantical domain of Gezel to the timed-automata model and we have experimented with the Uppaal system, showing the correctness of small, but interesting Gezel examples. Although functional correctness is of primary importance, we have also considered the analysis of resource usage which for instance may guide the hardware designer in choosing the most power efficient algorithm among a set of possible algorithmic implementations of a given specification.

We are currently using Gezel as a way to introduce software engineering students to hardware design and, in particular, to combined hardware/software codesign needed to deal with the challenges of embedded systems. Clarifying the semantical domain of Gezel have pointed to issues which are difficult for students to comprehend. Hence, a next step is to redefine the language so that the semantical concepts are reflected in the language in a direct manner. This may also provide a more elegant translation into the synthesizable subset of VHDL.

Although the initial results of automated verification are promising, verifying large hardware specifications is still a major challenge which most likely will require a compositional approach. The clear semantical model gives us some indications of how to approach this problem and this is currently one of our primary research objectives.

# References

1. Alur, R., Dill, D.L.: A theory of timed automata. Theoretical Comput. Sci. 126(2), 183–235 (1994)
2. Berry, G.: The Foundations of Esterel. In: Plotkin, G., Stirling, C., Tofte, M. (eds.) Proof, Language and Interaction: Essays in Honour of Robin Milner, MIT Press, Cambridge (1998)
3. Ashenden, P.J.: The Designer's Guide to VHDL Morgan Kaufmann Technology & Industrial Arts (2002)
4. Bengtsson, J., Larsen, K., Larsson, F., Pettersson, P., Yi, W.: Uppaal – a tool suite for automatic verification of real-time systems. In: Alur, R., Sontag, E.D., Henzinger, T.A. (eds.) Hybrid Systems III. LNCS, vol. 1066, pp. 232–243. Springer, Heidelberg (1996)
5. Brekling, A.W.: A Timed-Automata Semantics for a System-Level MPSoC model. Master's Thesis. Informatics and Mathematical Modelling, Technical University of Denmark (2006)
6. Buchi, J.: Weak second-order arithmetic and finite automata. Z. Math. Logik Grundl. Math 6, 66–92 (1960)
7. Elgot, C.: Decision problems of finite automata design and related arithmetics. Transactions of the American Mathematical Society 98, 21–52 (1961)
8. Gajski, D.D., Ramachandran, L.: Introduction to High-Level Synthesis. IEEE Des. Test 11(4), 44–54 (1994)
9. Ellebæk, J., Knudsen, K.S., Brekling, A.W., Hansen, M.R., Madsen, J.: MOVES – a tool for modelling and verification of embedded systems. In: DATE'07, University Booth (2007)
10. Klarlund, N., Møller, A.: Mona version 1.4: User manual, BRICS, Department of Computer Science, University of Aarhus, Denmark, http://www.brics.dk/mona
11. Schaefer, E.: A Simplified Data Encryption Standard Algotrihm. Cryptologia 20(1), 77–84 (1996)
12. Schaumont, P., Verbauwhede, I.: Domain Specific Tools and Methods for Application in Security Processor Design. Design Automation for Embedded Systems 7, 365–383 (2002)
13. Schaumont, P., Verbauwhede, I.: A Component-based Design Environment for Electronic System-level Design. In: IEEE Design and Test of Computers Magazine, special issue on Electronic System-Level Design, pp. 246–338 (2006)
14. Schaumont, P., Ching, D., Verbauwhede, I.: An interactive codesign environment for domain-specific coprocessors. ACM Transactions on Design Automation for Embedded Systems 11(1), 70–87 (2006)

15. Schaumont, P., Ching, D.: GEZEL version 2 (2006),
    http://rijndael.ece.vt.edu/gezel2/index.php/Main_Page
16. Thomas, D.E., Moorby, P.R.: The Verilog Hardware Description Language. Kluwer
    Academic Publishers, Dordrecht (1998)
17. Stein, J.: Journal of Computational Physics 1(3), 397–405 (1967)
18. IEEE Standard VHDL Language Reference Manual, IEEE Std 1076-2000 (2000)

# A    Gezel Specification of a gcd-Algorithm

```
dp gcd(in   a, b    : ns(8);
       out c        : ns(8)) {
  reg x, y, factor  : ns(8);
  reg done          : ns(1);

  sfg init    { x = a; y = b; factor = 0; done = 0; c = 0; }
  sfg shiftx  { x = m >> 1; }
  sfg shifty  { y = n >> 1; }
  sfg reduce  { x = (x >= y) ? x - y : x;
                y = (y >  x) ? y - x : y; }
  sfg shiftf  { factor = factor + 1; }
  sfg outidle { c = 0; done = ((x == 0) | (y == 0)); }
  sfg complete{ c = ((x > y) ? x : y) << factor; }
}

fsm gcd_ctl(gcd) {
  initial s0;
  state s1, final;

  @s0 (init, outidle) -> s1;
  @s1 if (done)                     then (complete)            -> final;
      else if ( x[0] &  y[0]) then (reduce, outidle)  -> s1;
      else if ( x[0] & ~y[0]) then (shifty, outidle)  -> s1;
      else if (~x[0] &  y[0]) then (shiftx, outidle)  -> s1;
                              else (shifty, shiftx,
                                    shiftf, outidle)  -> s1;
  @final (outidle) -> final;
}
```

# A Domain-Oriented, Model-Based Approach for Construction and Verification of Railway Control Systems

Anne E. Haxthausen[1] and Jan Peleska[2]

[1] Informatics and Mathematical Modelling
Technical University of Denmark, Lyngby, Denmark
ah@imm.dtu.dk
[2] TZI, Universität Bremen, Germany
jp@tzi.de

**Abstract.** This paper describes a complete model-based development and verification approach for railway control systems. For each control system to be generated, the user makes a description of the application-specific parameters in a domain-specific language. This description is automatically transformed into an executable control system model expressed in SystemC. This model is then compiled into object code. Verification is performed using four main methods applied to different levels: (0) The domain-specific description is validated wrt. internal consistency by static analysis. (1) The crucial safety properties are verified for the SystemC model by means of bounded model checking. (2) The object code is verified to be I/O behavioural equivalent to the SystemC model from which it was compiled. (3) The correctness of the hardware/software integration is checked by automated testing.

**Keywords:** domain engineering, domain-specific languages, code generation, formal methods, verification, railway control systems.

*Dedicated to Dines Bjørner and Zhou Chaochen, for their 70th birthdays.*

## 1   Introduction

**Motivation.** The development of modern railway and tramway control systems represents a considerable challenge to both systems and software engineers: The goal to increase the traffic throughput while at the same time increasing the availability and reliability of railway operations leads to a demand for more elaborate safety mechanisms in order to keep the risk at the same low level that has been established for European railways until today. The challenge is further increased by the demand for shorter time-to-market periods and higher competition among suppliers of the railway domain; both factors resulting in a demand for a higher degree of automation for the development, verification, validation and test phases of projects, without impairing the thoroughness of safety-related quality measures and certification activities. Motivated by these

C.B. Jones, Z. Liu, J. Woodcock (Eds.): Bjørner/Zhou Festschrift, LNCS 4700, pp. 320–348, 2007.
© Springer-Verlag Berlin Heidelberg 2007

considerations, this paper describes an approach for the construction, verification and validation of railway control systems which has been elaborated by the authors and their collaborators during the last decade.

**Two Problem Categories.** A closer analysis shows that the problems to be solved can be structured according to two main categories: (1) The design of novel *generic control algorithms* is stimulated by the availability of innovative technologies offering new possibilities for safe and reliable train control mechanisms. In this category the objective is to elaborate *generic theories*, that is, collections of theorems whose assumptions and implications are universally quantified over, say, railway networks of a certain type. As an example, we mention the investigation of distributed train control algorithms stimulated by the advent of mobile communication technologies, now allowing to develop alternatives to the centralised interlocking paradigm. For the verification of these algorithms mechanised (first-order or higher-order logic) proof support is desirable.

(2) The development and verification of *concrete system configurations* addresses a problem frequently arising in conventional developments: Typically, railway control systems are nowadays constructed following the principles of object orientation and generics: The system is designed as a generic collection of classes, structured according to certain design patterns, collaborations and frameworks enforcing proven design principles and facilitating the utilisation of specific hardware technology. Concrete systems are instantiated from the generic collection using configuration data specifying the network to be controlled, available track elements (signals, sensors, points) etc. In spite of the elegance of this approach, it suffers from the flaw that – when conventionally tested for a limited number of different configurations – some software bugs are only revealed when new configuration variants are used. Additionally, the verification of configuration data requires a considerable effort, often necessitating customised verification tool sets which in turn have to be qualified. As a consequence, also minor configuration changes, induced, for example, by construction work on certain track sections, require complex verification processes. The solution to these problems would be an automated verification suite allowing to *verify each concrete system instance together with its configuration*. Here, automation is a crucial requirement, since the conventional verification process currently only exercised once on generic system level would be far too time-consuming and expensive to be repeated on every concrete system instance. In this problem category, verification does not involve universal quantification, since all configuration aspects are completely determined. As a consequence, model-based development combined with model or property checking, validated compilers or object code verifiers are the technical means of choice for the development and verification process.

In this article, we focus on the second problem category, for a detailed description of the first, the reader is referred to [21] and further references listed there.

**Domain-specific Approach.** In recent years, domain-specific methods for software development have gained wide interest. One of the main objectives addressed by these techniques is the possibility for a given domain to reuse various assets when developing software, e.g. to develop a generic system from which one can instantiate concrete systems. Additionally, the use of domain-specific languages (DSLs) as front-ends for development tools is advocated. In contrast to general-purpose specification and programming languages, DSLs facilitate their utilisation by domain experts who are not specialists in the field of information technology, because they use the terminology of the application domain.

Inspired by these considerations, we have suggested an approach for efficient *construction* of a family of similar tramway or railway control systems in [23,24] and exemplified it for a class of route-based tramway control systems. The idea is to provide a framework consisting of (1) a generic control system that can be instantiated with configuration data, (2) a DSL front-end for specifying application-specific parameters and (3) a generator from domain-specific descriptions into configuration data and instantiation rules for the concrete system. Hence, for each control system to be developed, application-specific parameters are described in the domain-specific language and from this specification a control system can automatically be generated. An advantage of the front-end consists in the fact that it is much simpler to specify the parameters of a system in the domain-specific language and then apply the generator, than it is to program the configuration data directly. This speeds up the production time and reduces the risk of errors; furthermore, it can be done by domain experts without requiring the assistance of programming specialists.

While this approach clearly offers advantages, it requires careful work to *develop* such a language, generator and generic control system and to *automatically verify* that generated control systems are safe. For this purpose we use formal methods.

**Automated Verification Approach.** As "programming" language for the control systems we have chosen SystemC [19] that allows for formal reasoning based on an operational transition system semantics. SystemC serves both as a compilation target from semi-formal DSL descriptions to semantically well-founded formal specifications and as high-level programming language which can be compiled into executable code. Our development approach prescribes that each time a SystemC control system model is generated and compiled into object code, verification shall be performed at two levels: (1) The SystemC control system model is verified to be safe by means of bounded model checking combined with an inductive proof strategy, and (2) the object code is verified to be a correct implementation of the SystemC control system model. For this purpose, the framework provides support tools: a proof obligation generator and an object code verifier.

**Development of Languages and Tools.** For the development of a domain-specific language and support tools our suggestion is to follow the TripTych dogma by Dines Bjørner (see for instance [9]) making a domain model describing the concepts of the application domain prior to the actual development of applications. Apart from separating the concern of describing *what there is* from the concern of describing *what there should be* (the applications), this ensures that different applications are based on the same conceptual understanding. Then from the domain-model one can establish a model of domain-specific descriptions and their static semantics, a model of the application generators and a model of the code verifier. For the case study we have formulated such models in the formal RAISE Specification Language, RSL, [33].

**Related Work.** The overview given in this paper is based on results published in [21,26,28,22,23,25,24,17,20,29,3,30]. Our work has been inspired by Dines Bjørner's TripTych dogma and formal techniques for software development described in [7,8,9,4,10,11].

The domain model used in our case study only includes aspects needed for our development framework. For domain models capturing a much broader collection of aspects for railways we consider Dines Bjørner's formal railway domain models (see e.g. [6,12]) as very promising candidates.

Object code verification has been investigated by several authors, see [32] for an approach that has influenced our work in a considerable way. While our results have a similar formal basis – for example, our notion of I/O-equivalence is a specialisation of the "correct implementation relation" defined in [32] – we exploit the specific restrictions of our model-based development framework in order to simplify the equivalence proofs in a considerable way.

For other complementary and competing approaches for the development and verification of railway control systems the reader is referred to the contributions in [37,35,36,15], and for a survey of new results and current trends the reader is referred to the paper [5].

**Paper Overview.** First, in *Sections* 2–3, we give an overview of our approach and informally describe a case study used to illustrate our approach. Then, in *Section* 4, we outline how a domain-specific description language for our case study can be formally developed from a static domain model. Next, in *Section* 5, we outline the development of application generators. In *Section* 6, we explain how the safety requirements can be verified. After that, in *Section* 7, we outline our approach for object code verification and we sketch how an associated code verifier can be formally developed. Finally, in *Section* 8, we discuss the work presented in this paper.

## 2   Method and Toolchain – Overview

Our approach requires a domain-specific language DSL and tools supporting the language. The main tool components required are:

1. A *data collector* for producing syntactically correct DSL text documents.
2. A *static semantics checker* for DSL documents.
3. *Generators* parsing DSL documents in order to create (1) executable controller models with transition system semantics (expressed in SystemC), (2)

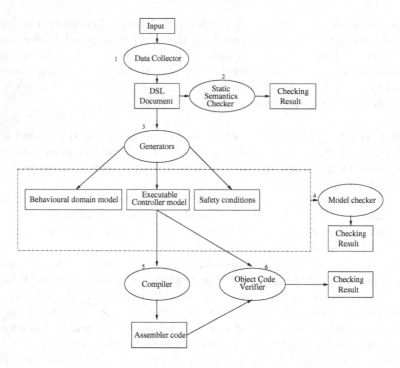

**Fig. 1.** Toolchain overview

behavioural physical domain models with transition system semantics (SystemC), and (3) safety conditions for the concurrent composition of these two models.

4. A *bounded model checker* capable of verifying properties of composed controller and physical domain models written in SystemC.
5. A *compiler* for translating SystemC models into assembler code (since SystemC is embedded into C++, conventional compilers can be used for this task).
6. An *object code verifier* which, given a SystemC controller model and associated assembler code, verifies that the latter is a correct implementation of the former.

To create and verify a new control system users should apply these tools to go through the following steps illustrated in Fig. 1:

1. The railway specialists use the data collector to produce a syntactically well-formed DSL description $\mathcal{D}$ of domain-specific details of the system to be developed.
2. The static semantics checker checks that $\mathcal{D}$ is statically well-formed.

3. The generators automatically transform the domain-specific description $\mathcal{D}$ into a behavioural controller model $\mathcal{M}$, a behavioural physical domain model $\mathcal{P}$ (describing how uncontrolled physical devices are behaving) and a set of verification obligations $\Phi$ (safety properties as, for example, the requirement that trains should never meet within a track segment or on a point).

4. It is proved that the controller model $\mathcal{M}$ in concurrent combination with the physical model $\mathcal{P}$ satisfies the obligations $\Phi$. This is done by means of an inductive proof strategy, where the induction step is performed using bounded model checking techniques.

5. The controller model $\mathcal{M}$ is compiled into object code and data with conventional C/C++ compilers. This results in an assembler "model" $\mathcal{A}$.

6. The assembler "model" $\mathcal{A}$ is verified to be behaviourally equivalent to the controller model $\mathcal{M}$ using the object code verifier.

7. Finally the correctness of the hardware/software integration is automatically tested, following the concepts described in [2].

# 3   A Case Study

In a case study we have applied our approach to construct and verify a family of route-based tramway control systems. In particular we designed a domain-specific language and a SystemC model generator. In later sections we explain how these were developed. Below, we first informally explain the required behaviour of the generated control systems and the contents of domain-specific descriptions, and then we outline the SystemC models that the generator produces.

## 3.1   Domain-Specific Description

The basic requirements for avoiding tram collisions are that trams must only drive on predefined routes previously reserved and that two conflicting (overlapping) routes must not be reserved at the same time. As a consequence, controllers built to enforce these requirements depend on the railway network to be controlled and on a selection of predefined routes through that network. This implies that the associated domain-specific description should include network specifications and interlocking tables describing the routes.

Fig. 2 shows a DSL representation of a sample network, consisting of the following track components:

- *sensors*: G20.0,... ,G25.1
- *controllable points*: W100, W102, W118
- *non controllable points*: W120, W121, W122
- *signals*: S20, S21, S22
- *track segments*: (G20.0,G20.1), (G20.1,G20.2), ..., shown as solid lines between two sensors

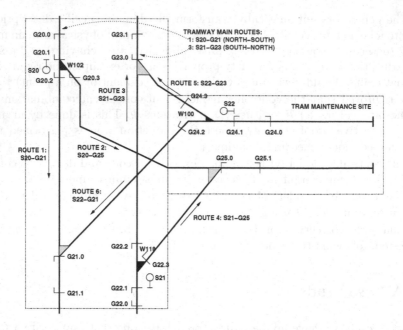

**Fig. 2.** The sample network

| Route Definition Table | |
| --- | --- |
| Route Id | Sensor List |
| R1 | <G20.1,G20.2,G21.0,G21.1 > |
| R2 | <G20.1,G20.3,G25.0,G25.1 > |
| R3 | <G22.1,G22.2,G23.0,G23.1 > |
| R4 | <G22.1,G22.3,G25.0,G25.1 > |
| R5 | <G24.1,G24.3,G23.0,G23.1 > |
| R6 | <G24.1,G24.2,G21.0,G21.1 > |

| Route Conflict Table | | | | | | |
| --- | --- | --- | --- | --- | --- | --- |
| Route Id | Conflicts with | | | | | |
| | R1 | R2 | R3 | R4 | R5 | R6 |
| R1 | - | o | - | - | - | x |
| R2 | o | - | x | x | - | x |
| R3 | - | x | - | o | x | x |
| R4 | - | x | o | - | - | - |
| R5 | - | - | x | - | - | o |
| R6 | x | x | x | - | o | - |

| Point Position Table | | | |
| --- | --- | --- | --- |
| Route Id | W100 | W102 | W118 |
| R1 | - | STRAIGHT | - |
| R2 | - | TURN | - |
| R3 | - | - | STRAIGHT |
| R4 | - | - | TURN |
| R5 | TURN | - | - |
| R6 | STRAIGHT | - | - |

| Signal Setting Table | | |
| --- | --- | --- |
| Route Id | Signal Id | Signal Setting |
| R1 | S20 | GO |
| R2 | S20 | GO |
| R3 | S21 | GO |
| R4 | S21 | GO |
| R5 | S22 | GO |
| R6 | S22 | GO |

**Fig. 3.** Interlocking tables

The *interlocking tables*, which are also part of the DSL, comprise four items: (1) a *route definition table* specifying admissible routes through the network, (2) a *route conflict table* describing the routes not to be simultaneously allocated (because they overlap in one of two ways[1] ), (3) a *point position table* describing for each route how points should be set for its traversal, and (4) a *signal setting table* specifying for each route the name of its entry signal and the aspect it should be set to, in order to indicate that a tram is allowed to enter the route. In Fig. 3 the graphical representation of some sample interlocking tables for the network given in Fig. 2 are shown.

## 3.2   Generated SystemC Models

The generator creates SystemC models from DSL descriptions as depicted in Fig. 2 and 3, together with the associated interface specifications and safety-related proof obligations $\Phi$. For this purpose, the generator utilises a library of design patterns, so that architectural aspects, physical model, controller model and proof obligations are elaborated according to pre-defined schemes.

**Interfaces.** Interfaces are modelled according to the shared variable paradigm, to be realised using DMA or dual-ported RAM technology on all hardware interfaces (Fig. 4). Signal and point interfaces, for example, consist of three data fields: The requested state (controller $\rightarrow$ signal/point), the actual state (controller $\leftarrow$ signal/point) and the switching deadline used to detect failed track elements.

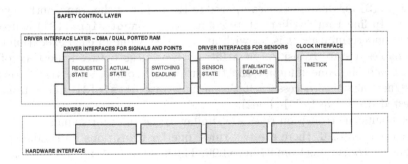

**Fig. 4.** Layered architecture and interfaces

**SystemC Model for Controller.** The basic behavioural patterns of a control system generated for such a network and collection of routes are as follows: When a tram approaches the network, a route is requested to be reserved. The control system makes a reservation for that route if no conflicting route has already been reserved. Then it allocates the route by requesting points to be switched

---

[1] For a description of this, see [23].

into positions that allow traversal of the chosen route (as described by the point position table), and when the points have been switched it requests the entry signal to show a GO aspect (as described by the signal setting table) indicating that the tram may enter the route. As soon as the tram has passed the entry signal, the signal is requested to show STOP, and when the tram has left the route, the route is deallocated by removing its reservation.

Each control system is implemented using a main loop, so that each execution cycle has four phases: In the *input phase* all current values of input interfaces (actual states) are copied to (global) shadow variables, in the *processing phase* interfaces are neither read nor updated, but global or local variables are processed. In the *wait phase* the system "spins" in an *active wait* loop without side effects (this is to ensure constant loop frequency), and in the *output phase* the states of global variables shadowing outputs are copied to the corresponding output interfaces (requested states).

**SystemC Model for Physical Domain.** For each signal S there is a transition rule instantiated from the following pattern:

```
1    if ( ((t >= reqsigtm[S] + delta_s) || (nondet_signal[S]))
2        && (reqsig[S] != actsig[S20]) ) {
3        actsig[S] = reqsig[S];
4    }
```

It states that the signal actsig[S] ( *"actual state"*) has to switch to the new state reqsig[S] ( *"requested state"*) issued by the controller (line 3). A signal without failures has to switch within the specified switching deadline delta_s. To determine whether delta_s time units have elapsed, the time of the request reqsigtm[S] for this signal is compared to the time t of the tram control system (line 1). In line 1 an auxiliary state component (nondet_signal[S]) is used to model nondeterminism: It is set with an arbitrary value in each execution cycle and enables a state transition at arbitrary time ticks between the time of the request and the time limit for the transition. Of course, state transitions for the signals are only necessary if the actual state actsig[S] differs from the requested state reqsig[S] (line2).

For points the transition rules are similar to the rules for signals.

For each sensor G, there are two rules, one for transitions from LOW to HIGH and one for transitions from HIGH to LOW. The HIGH to LOW rule has the following form:

```
1    if ( (sen[G] == SEN_HIGH) && (t>=delta_l + sentm_G) ) {
2        sen[G] = SEN_LOW;
3    }
```

It states that the sensor has to be stable in state HIGH for exactly delta_l time units (line 1) (so that the controller is able to recognise the HIGH state) before going from state HIGH to state LOW.

The conditions in the LOW to HIGH rule depend on the sensor location. We do not report all these conditions here.

# 4   From Static Domain Model to Domain-Specific Language

In this section we explain how a domain-specific description language for our case study can be formally developed from a static domain model using RSL. At the end of this development process, the RSL model obtained represents the *abstract syntax* and *static semantics* of the DSL under construction. It then only remains to associate the abstract syntactic elements with *concrete* syntax, in order to complete the DSL definition: The *behavioural semantics* is defined in a transformational way by means of the generator translating DSL specifications into SystemC.

## 4.1   RSL Static Domain Model

We start by describing how a domain model can be established. The domain model covers the concepts of railway networks and routes. More general models would typically cover further aspects like time tables, but here we only present those concepts that are relevant for the development of the application considered in this paper. The model of each concept is *generic* (algebraic) in the sense that it defines *which* properties any concrete instance of the concept should have. The generic model can be instantiated to produce a *concrete* one defining *what* the specific properties are for that specific instance.

**Generic Network Model.** Any concrete network model should describe the topology of a railway network consisting of the physical components: segments, sensors, signals and points.

In the generic model, for each kind of component, an abstract type of identifiers for its components is declared:

**type** Sensor, Point, Signal, Segment

Furthermore, signatures for functions that describe the relationship between the components are given. For instance, the following function gives the sensor at which a given signal is placed:

**value** sensor_of : Signal → Sensor

Finally, a number of axioms express requirements to these functions, i.e. impose restrictions on which network topologies are allowed. For instance, the following axiom requires that any two distinct signals are placed at distinct sensors:

$$\forall \; s1, s2 : Signal \bullet s1 \neq s2 \Rightarrow sensor\_of(s1) \neq sensor\_of(s2)$$

To describe a *concrete network*, the elements of the types should be specified and the functions should be explicitly defined in such a way that the axioms are satisfied.

**Generic Route Model.** An abstract type of identifiers for routes is declared:

**type** Route

We state the signature for a function that for a given route returns a list of those sensors which have to be passed in the stated order when travelling along the route:

**value** sensors_of : Route → Sensor*

A number of axioms express requirements to this function, i.e. impose restrictions on what is an allowed route. For instance, there must be a signal at the first sensor of any route:

$$\forall\ r : \text{Route} \bullet \exists\ s : \text{Signal} \bullet \text{sensor\_of}(s) = \mathbf{hd}\ \text{sensors\_of}(r)$$

## 4.2  Domain-Specific Language

**RSL Specification.** The domain model is now extended with value declarations for each element to be part of a domain description. For each kind of physical component there is an element (all together providing a network description):

**value**
  sensors : Id-**set**,
  points : Id $\underset{m}{\rightarrow}$ ...,
  signals : Id $\underset{m}{\rightarrow}$ Sensor,
  segments : Id $\underset{m}{\rightarrow}$ ...

and for each kind of interlocking table there is an element[2]:

**value**
  rdt : Id $\underset{m}{\rightarrow}$ Sensor*,
  rct : Route → Route-**set** × Route-**set**,
  ppt : Route → Point $\underset{m}{\rightarrow}$ PointPosition,
  sst : Route → Signal × SignalSetting

We chose identifiers to be texts:

**type** Id = **Text**

The declarations give each element a name and a model-oriented type and hence provide an *abstract syntax* for the elements. As an example, the abstract syntax for the *signals* element is $Id \underset{m}{\rightarrow} Sensor$, and the intension is that a *signals* element should map any signal identifier to the identifier of that sensor at which it is placed.

Now, the *Signal* type can be explicitly defined as containing the identifiers of the domain of the *signals* element:

**type** Signal = {| id : Id • id ∈ **dom** signals |}

The *Sensor*, *Point*, *Segment* and *Route* types can be defined in a similar way.

---

[2] *rdt* for route definition table, *rct* for route conflict table, *ppt* for point position table, and *sst* for signal setting table.

All functions from the domain model can now be explicitly defined in terms of the element values. In this way the axioms (that refer to these functions) from the domain model now impose well-formedness conditions on the elements of a language description. Additional axioms that impose well-formedness conditions on the *rct*, *ppt* and *sst* values are added, so that these axioms provide a *static semantics* for the DSL.

**Concrete Syntax and Data Collector Implementation.** Two alternative solutions to the implementation of the concrete DSL have been made using the Extensible Markup Language *XML* [39] and the Unified Modelling Language *UML* [34], respectively. Below we outline the XML solution that is documented in [14]. In [3] it is described how the DSL is defined by a UML 2.0 profile in the second solution.

The *concrete syntax* of the language has been defined by an XML document type definition (DTD). For the elements of the RSL abstract syntax, corresponding XML elements are defined. The *static semantics* has been implemented using the extensible style sheet language XSL [40]. In a systematic way each RSL axiom expressing a well-formedness requirement has been transformed into a template that tests whether the requirement is fulfilled.

A GUI based *data collector* for creating DSL descriptions in the required XML syntax has been developed using XForms [38].

For the convenience of users, a *graphical representation* of DSL descriptions (XML documents) has been developed. This was done using XSLT and HTML. In Fig. 3 the graphical representation of some sample interlocking tables for the network given in Fig. 2 are shown.

# 5   Generating Applications from Domain-Specific Descriptions

According to our method three generators taking a statically well-formed DSL description $\mathcal{D}$ as argument are required (Fig. 1). The primary one is the generator producing a control system model $\mathcal{M}$. The second generator produces the behavioural model $\mathcal{P}$ of the physical environment and the third one generates the safety properties $\Phi$, to be checked to hold for the concurrent composition of the control system model $\mathcal{M}$ and the physical model $\mathcal{P}$. In this section we outline the basic concepts of the generator for $\mathcal{M}$. The other generators are developed in a similar way.

**Components of the Controller Model Generator.** The implemented generator for controller models consists of two parts:

1. A configurable library of generic code that is re-usable for all control systems to be generated: The code comprises generic versions of the control algorithms, the data structures carrying dynamic state information needed for performing control decisions, and the static configuration data structures.

2. A parser that takes a domain-specific description as input and returns concrete configuration data and instantiation parameters for the generic algorithms.

We have selected SystemC [19] as the target language for the generators, since it is associated with a formal transition system semantics and can be directly compiled into executable code [29,3]. As a consequence, the original DSL descriptions "inherit" formal behavioural semantics from the transformations performed by the generators.

**Generic Configurable Library.** Since the SystemC code is automatically generated, the emphasis of the coding structure – whose layout is already fixed in the configurable library – lies on easy verifiability and efficient executability: Configuration data is encoded in global arrays of integers, and the control structures of the algorithms are in one-one-correspondence with the safety properties $\Phi$, while controlling signal and point states: For example, if allocation of route $r_i$ excludes simultaneous allocation of routes $r_\ell$ and requires point states $p_j(r)$ and signal states $s_k(r)$, then the allocation is guarded by code structures like

```
bool mayAllocate = true;
for (int l = 0; l < m1; l++)
    mayAllocate = mayAllocate and not allocated(r[i][l]);
for (int j = 0; j < m2; j++)
    mayAllocate = mayAllocate and p[i][j];
for (int k = 0; k < m3; k++)
    mayAllocate = mayAllocate and s[i][k];
if ( mayAllocate )
    allocate(i);
```

This also ensures a close relationship between SystemC and assembler code which facilitates the object code verification in a considerable way.

The generic parameters referenced in the control algorithms of the library are of a very simple nature: They comprise number parameters, specifying the concrete quantities of sensors, signals, points and routes to be fixed for each system and offset parameters used for looking up specific routes and track elements in the static configuration data or in the dynamic control states.

The most important aspect of the static configuration data is the description of available track elements and route specifications. Routes are represented as sequences of index references to track elements, together with information about the required signal and point states to be enforced when allocating a route to a tram. An additional integer array is used for specifying the conflict relations between routes.

**DSL → SystemC Parser.** The parser for producing concrete SystemC code from DSL descriptions proceeds in two passes: First, the number parameters are determined from the DSL and represented as C constant declarations. As a result the dimensions of all arrays used for storing static configuration data and dynamic state information are fixed.

In the second pass the parser generates constant C array assignments carrying the configuration data and auxiliary offset information for looking up routes and track elements.

# 6    Safety Requirements and Their Verification

**Verification Objectives.** Our verification strategy is driven by the following boundary conditions:

- DSL specifications inherit their formal behavioural semantics from the SystemC models which are automatically generated. As a consequence, no refinement proofs are required to ensure consistency between internal SystemC models and high-level DSL descriptions.
- No assumptions about the correctness of the generators are made.
- No assumptions about the correctness of interlocking tables are made.
- It is assumed that the railway network description (Fig. 2) is complete and correct.
- The rules how trains can move in the uncontrolled network (physical model $\mathcal{P}$) are complete and correct.
- The safety conditions $\Phi$ are complete and correct.
- Trains stop at signals in HALT state.

Under these assumptions our verification objective is to show that all possible $\mathcal{P}$ executions, when controlled by the model $\mathcal{M}$ executed in parallel, respect safety conditions $\Phi$.

Observe further that, since we are not assuming that generators and interlocking tables are correct, an universal "once-and-for-all" verification is impossible: Each system instance has to be verified with its concrete configuration data. As a consequence, it is desirable to elaborate a verification strategy which can be executed in an automated way.

**Verification Method.** With respect to full automation the property checking approach for $(\mathcal{P} \parallel \mathcal{M})$ **sat** $\Phi$ seems attractive. It is well known, however, that conventional model checking would lead to state explosions for train control tasks of realistic size. As a consequence, we have adopted a *bounded model checking* strategy combined with inductive reasoning: Instead of elaborating a complete system model $((\mathcal{P} \parallel \mathcal{M})$ in our case), bounded model checking starts in an arbitrary system state $s$ which may be additionally restricted by some auxiliary property $\Psi$, and *unwinds* the model, thereby obtaining all possible transitions emanating from $s$ *for a bounded number of* $n > 0$ *discrete time steps*. The property $\Phi$ is checked in each state reachable by means of this unwinding.

For the verification task at hand, auxiliary property $\Psi$ mainly states relationships between sensor events and associated updates of internal counters performed within the controller $\mathcal{M}$. We prove that $\Phi \wedge \Psi$ holds in the initial state of $(\mathcal{P} \parallel \mathcal{M})$. Next it is shown that, provided $\Phi \wedge \Psi$ holds in some state $s$, it will also hold for the next $n > 0$ discrete time steps. As property specification language we use a subset of the widely known industrial standard PSL from Accellera [1] and the property checker [13]. A detailed explanation of how the case study has been model checked using this approach can be found in [29,31].

# 7  Object Code Verification

In this section we outline our approach for object code verification that is described in detail in [30], and we sketch how an associated code verifier can be formally developed.

## 7.1  Motivation

Automated object code verification for safety-critical control systems is motivated by the fact that applicable standards for these safety-critical applications, e.g. for railways [16], require a substantial justification with respect to the consistency between high-level software code and the object code generated by the applied compilers.

## 7.2  Approach

The conventional approach for this is *compiler validation*: "Once-and-for-all" it is validated that the compiler for any input produces object code that is a correct implementation of that input. However, such an approach is very time-consuming, especially if it should be done formally (see e.g. [18] for techniques for that), and furthermore it has to be performed again whenever modifications of the compiler have been performed. An alternative to compiler validation is *object code validation*: Each time object code is generated (by an arbitrary compiler), the generated object code is verified to be a correct implementation of the high-level software code. Object code verification has the advantage that it is independent of changes in the compiler and it can be fully automated and reasonably fast, if the compiled code originates from high-level programs strictly adhering to certain programming patterns as it is the case for our generated SystemC models.

Our specific approach to object code verification is as follows: To prove that an assembler program (object code) $\mathcal{A}$ is a correct implementation of the SystemC controller model $\mathcal{M}$ from which it is generated, one should map (see Section 7.5) $\mathcal{A}$ and $\mathcal{M}$ to their behavioural models $\mathcal{T}(\mathcal{A})$ and $\mathcal{T}(\mathcal{M})$ given in terms of some common semantic foundations (I/O-Safe Transition Systems to be explained in Section 7.3) and then prove that $\mathcal{T}(\mathcal{A})$ and $\mathcal{T}(\mathcal{M})$ are I/O equivalent (modulo a variable renaming) by applying transformations that have been proved "once-and-for-all" to preserve I/O behaviour (see Section 7.4).

## 7.3  Common Semantic Foundations: I/O-Safe Transitions Systems

In this section we introduce our notion of *I/O-safe transitions systems (IOTS)* and our notion of *I/O equivalence* between IOTS'es.

I/O-safe transitions systems remind about usual transitions diagrams (as defined e.g. in [27]) consisting of (1) a set of variables for which initial values are given by an initial state, (2) a set of locations one of which is designated as the initial location $l_0$, and, (3) a set of transition rules. Variables are classified into input, output and processing variables. A transition rule from one location $l_1$ to another location $l_2$ is specified by a guard that is a quantifier-free predicate over the variables and by a multiple assignment $(v_1, \ldots, v_n) := (e_1, \ldots, e_n)$, where $v_1, \ldots, v_n$ are variables and $e_1, \ldots, e_n$ are expressions over the given set of variables. However, as a new thing, for an IOTS we also divide the locations into pairwise disjoint sets of input, output and processing locations, and we put further constraints on the allowed use of variables in guards and expressions in an IOTS: guards must only use processing variables, for transitions into input locations the assignments must only read input variables and make assignment to processing variables, for transitions into processing locations the assignments must only read processing variables and make assignment to processing variables, and, for transitions into output locations the assignments must only read processing variables and make assignment to output variables.

One can obviously specify an abstract syntax of IOTS'es in RSL :

**type**
  IOTS ::
    vars : Var-**set**
    initstate : State
    locs : Loc-**set**
    initloc : Loc
    trans : TransitionRel-**set**,
  TransitionRel = Loc $\times$ Guard $\times$ Assign $\times$ Loc,
  Assign :: al : (Var $\times$ Expr)*,
  Expr ==
    mk_Const(i : **Int**) | mk_Var(v : Var) | mk_Sum(e1 : Expr, e2 : Expr) | ...,
  Guard == TRUE | ...,

where *Guard* and *Expr* are the abstract syntaxes of guards and expressions, respectively, for space reasons not completely specified here.

For variables and locations two abstract types are used, each having an observer function *mode* that informs about the mode (input, output or processing) of variables and locations, respectively:

**type** Var, Loc
**value** mode : Var $\rightarrow$ Mode, mode : Loc $\rightarrow$ Mode,
**type** Mode == IN | OUT | PROC

We also introduce a well-formedness predicate for IOTS'es formalising all the conditions on the use of variables and locations stated informally above:

**value**
  is_wff : IOTS $\rightarrow$ **Bool**
  is_wff(iots) $\equiv$
    **dom** initstate(iots) = vars(iots) $\wedge$ initloc(iots) $\in$ locs(iots) $\wedge$ ...

For instance, the predicate checks that the initial state of an IOTS gives initial values to the variables in its variable set and that the initial location is in its location set.

We are now going to define a notion of I/O equivalence of IOTS'es. In order to do that, first we need a to define an operational semantics of IOTS'es involving states. A state $\sigma$ for an IOTS is a valuation of its variables.

**type** State = Var $\xrightarrow{m}$ Int

Each transition relation specification of an IOTS denotes a state transformer:

**value**
    eval : TransitionRel $\rightarrow$ (State $\rightarrow$ State)
    eval(l, g, a, l')($\sigma$) $\equiv$
      **if** eval(g)($\sigma$) **then** eval(a)($\sigma$) **else** $\sigma$ **end**

Here $eval(g)(\sigma)$ and $eval(a)(\sigma)$ are the standard extensions of the valuation $\sigma$ to guards $g$ and assignments $a$.

The *semantics* of an IOTS is the set of its possible runs. A possible *run* of an IOTS is a non-empty sequence of pairs of locations and states such that the first location is its initial location, the first state is its initial state, and that for each consecutive pairs in the list there is a transition relation in the IOTS from the location of the first pair to the location of the second pair so that the associated state transformer maps the state of the first pair to the state of the second pair:

**type** Run = (Loc $\times$ State)*

**value**
    eval : IOTS $\rightarrow$ Run-**set**
    eval(iots) $\equiv$
      { r | r : Run •
        **len** r > 0 $\wedge$
        **let** (l0, $\sigma$0) = **hd** r **in**
          l0 = initloc(iots) $\wedge$ $\sigma$0 = initstate(iots)
        **end** $\wedge$
        ($\forall$ i : **Int** • i > 0 $\wedge$ i < **len** r $\Rightarrow$
          **let**
            (l_i, $\sigma$_i) = r(i), (l_i', $\sigma$_i') = r(i+1)
          **in**
            ($\exists$ (l, g, a, l') : TransitionRel •
            (l, g, a, l') $\in$ trans(iots) $\wedge$
            l = l_i $\wedge$ l' = l_i' $\wedge$
            eval(l, g, a, l')($\sigma$_i) = $\sigma$_i')
          **end**
        )
      }

An *I/O restriction* of a run is the restriction of the run to pairs where the location is an input or output location, and for these pairs the states are restricted to input and output variables only:

IOrestrict : Run → Run
IOrestrict(r) ≡
  ⟨ (l, σ / { v | v : Var • mode(v) ∈ {IN,OUT} }) |
    (l,σ) **in** r • mode(l) ∈ {IN,OUT} ⟩,

An *I/O map* $\rho$ is a bijective, mode preserving variable mapping between I/O variables:

**type** IOMap = {| $\rho$ : Var $\overrightarrow{m}$ Var • bijective($\rho$) ∧ IOmodepreserving($\rho$) |}
**value**
  bijective : (Var $\overrightarrow{m}$ Var) → **Bool**
  bijective($\rho$) ≡
    (∀ v2 : Var • v2 ∈ **rng** $\rho$ ⇒ (∃! v1 : Var • v1 ∈ **dom** $\rho$ ∧ $\rho$(v1) = v2)),

  IOmodepreserving : (Var $\overrightarrow{m}$ Var) → **Bool**
  IOmodepreserving($\rho$) ≡
    (∀ v : Var • v ∈ **dom** $\rho$ ⇒
      IOmode($\rho$(v)) = mode(v) ∧ mode(v) ∈ {IN,OUT})

Two runs are *I/O equivalent* wrt. an I/O map if their I/O restrictions have (1) the same length, (2) the same order of input locations and output locations, and (3) their states agree on input variables and output variables modulo the I/O map:

equiv : Run × Run × IOMap → **Bool**
equiv(r1, r2, $\rho$) ≡
  **let** r1_io = IOrestrict(r1), r2_io = IOrestrict(r2) **in**
    **len** r1_io = **len** r2_io ∧
    (∀ j : **Int** • j > 0 ∧ j ≤ **len** r1_io ⇒
      **let** (l1, σ1) = r1_io(j), (l2, σ2) = r2_io(j) **in**
        mode(l1) = mode(l2) ∧
        σ1 = σ2 ° $\rho$
      **end**
    )
  **end**,

Finally, we can define two IOTS'es to be *I/O behavioural equivalent* wrt. an I/O map, if there is a bijection $\gamma$ between I/O equivalent runs of the two IOTS'es:

equiv : IOTS × IOTS × IOMap $\overset{\sim}{\to}$ **Bool**
equiv(iots1, iots2, $\rho$) ≡
  (∃ $\gamma$ : Run $\overrightarrow{m}$ Run •
    **dom** $\gamma$ = eval(iots1) ∧ **rng** $\gamma$ = eval(iots2) ∧
    (∀ r1, r2 : Run • r1 ≠ r2 ⇒ $\gamma$(r1) ≠ $\gamma$(r2)) ∧

$(\forall\ r : Run \bullet equiv(\gamma(r), r, \rho))$
)
**pre dom** $\rho = iovars(iots1) \wedge$ **rng** $\rho = iovars(iots2)$,

iovars : IOTS $\rightarrow$ Var-**set**
iovars(iots) $\equiv \{v \mid v : Var \bullet v \in vars(iots) \wedge mode(v) \in \{IN,OUT\}\}$,

For the identity variable mappings *id* we just write *equiv(iots1, iots2)* rather than *equiv(iots1, iots2, id)*.

## 7.4   IOTS Transformation Rules

We have developed a collection (see [30]) of transformation rules between IOTS patterns and proved by hand that any instance of the rules gives rise to a transformation that preserves I/O behaviour. The RSL formulation of the IOTS concepts in previous section now makes it possible to make the proofs formal.

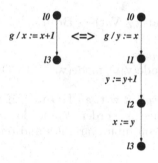

**Fig. 5.** A transformation rule

As an example, there is a rule stating that an IOTS *iots1* can be transformed into an equivalent IOTS *iots2* by replacing the transition shown on the left hand side of Fig. 5 with the three transitions shown on the right hand side of Fig. 5, or vice versa, provided that (1) *l1* and *l2* are not locations of *iots1*, *x* and *y* are local variables, and (2) in any path emanating from location *l3*, the variable *y* is assigned before read. The rule is generic in locations *l0*, *l1*, *l2*, *l3*, variables *x* and *y*, and, guard *g*.
   Proving this rule correct, amounts to prove:

$\forall$  iots1, iots2 : IOTS, l0, l1, l2, l3 : Loc, g : Guard, x, y : Var $\bullet$
   $\{x, y\} \subseteq$ vars(iots1) $\wedge$ mode(x) = PROC $\wedge$ mode(y) = PROC $\wedge$
   $\{l0, l3\} \subseteq$ locs(iots1) $\wedge$ l1 $\notin$ locs(iots1) $\wedge$ l2 $\notin$ locs(iots1) $\wedge$
   (l0, g, mk_Assign($\langle\langle$(x, mk_Sum(mk_Var(x), mk_Const(1)))$\rangle\rangle$), l3)
      $\in$ trans(iots1) $\wedge$
   vars(iots2) = vars(iots1) $\wedge$
   initstate(iots2) = initstate(iots1) $\wedge$
   locs(iots2) = locs(iots1) $\cup$ {l1, l2} $\wedge$

initloc(iots2) = initloc(iots1) ∧
trans(iots2) =
   trans(iots1) \
      {(l0, g, mk_Assign(⟨(x, mk_Sum(mk_Var(x), mk_Const(1)))⟩), l3)}
   ∪
   {(l0, g,  mk_Assign(⟨(y, mk_Var(x))⟩), l1),
    (l1, TRUE,  mk_Assign(⟨(y, mk_Sum(mk_Var(y), mk_Const(1)))⟩), l2),
    (l2, TRUE,  mk_Assign(⟨(x, mk_Var(y))⟩), l3)
    } ∧
assigned_before_read(iots1, l3, y)


⇒


equiv(iots1, iots2)

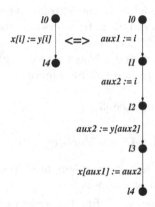

**Fig. 6.** Another transformation rule

Another example of a transformation rule is one stating that an IOTS *iots1* can be transformed into an equivalent IOTS *iots2* by replacing the transition shown on the left hand side of Fig. 6 with the four transitions shown on the right hand side of Fig. 6, or vice versa, provided that (1) *l1*, *l2* and *l3* are not locations of *iots1*, *aux1* and *aux2* are local variables, and (2) in any path emanating from location *l4*, the variables *aux1* and *aux2* are assigned before read. The rule is generic in locations *l0*, *l1*, *l2*, *l3* and *l4*, and variables *aux1*, *aux2*, *x* and *y*.

## 7.5 IOTS Semantics of the Source and Target Languages

In [30] it is explained how to derive the IOTS semantics for generated SystemC models and assembler code. This can be formalised in RSL by defining abstract syntaxes *Ccode* and *AssemblerCode* for the generated SystemC models and AssemblerCode, respectively, and defining evaluation functions $T$:

**type** Ccode = ...
**type** AssemblerCode = ...

**value** $T$ : Ccode → IOTS ...
**value** $T$ : AssemblerCode → IOTS ...

## 7.6    Abstraction Mappings

When a SystemC model $M$ is compiled into an assembler program $A$, there is a 1-1 correspondence between SystemC variable symbols and assembler variable symbols (e.g. for each SystemC array element $x[n]$ there is a corresponding assembler array element $x(, n, 4)$), except that $A$ contains additional local variables: flags, registers and stack addresses.

We define a SystemC model $M^+$ that extends $M$ with local variable symbols corresponding to the additional flags, registers and stack addresses in $A$. E.g. we add `eax` corresponding to the flag `%eax`.

Then one can obviously define a bijective map $\alpha^M$ from the variables in $A$ to the variables in $M^+$. This map will also serve as a map between the variable sets in $T(A)$ and $T(M^+)$.

For the detailed definitions, see [30].

## 7.7    Implementation of a Code Verifier

Currently the code verifier is being implemented in C++. The implementation consists of the following major components:
- an implementation of the two $T$ functions yielding IOTS generators for SystemC and assembler code, respectively,
- a library of transformation rules, and
- an IOTS transformer that given an IOTS and a transformation rule is able to apply the transformation rule.

A mechanised proof of the equivalence between an assembler program $A$ and the SystemC controller model $M$ from which it is generated is automatically performed according to the following procedure: The SystemC controller model $M$ is now mapped to its behavioural IOTS model $T(M)$, and $A$ is mapped to its model $T(A)$ as well, using the semantic rules for SystemC and assembler statements, respectively. Next, the symbols of $T(A)$ are changed to C-style notation according to mapping $\alpha^M$ defined above – this results in $T^1$. Also, the variable symbol space of $T(M)$ is extended to $T(M^+)$, so that $T^1$ and $T(M^+)$ can be directly compared with respect to their variable symbols. Then the mechanised proof generator analyses $T^1$ with respect to applicable patterns in the transformation rules. Each pattern application results in a I/O-equivalent transformation $T^1 \mapsto T^2 \mapsto \ldots$ until the last transformation results in $T(M^+)$, whereupon the proof generator terminates.

## 7.8 Example

We illustrate the mechanised proof procedure explained above using a fragment of the SystemC controller code from our case study. Here global shadow variables `reqsigNext[i]` (the new state required for signal $i$) and `reqptNext[j]` (the new state required for point $j$ are copied to output signals `reqsig[i]` (set-state request to signal $i$) and `reqpt[j]` (set-state request to point $j$) during the output phase of a main loop cycle. Consider the following fragment from the output phase of a SystemC controller $\mathcal{M}$:

```
for ( int i=0; i<NUM_SIGNALS; i++)
  reqsig[i] = reqsigNext[i];
for ( int j=0; j<NUM_POINTS; j++)
  reqpt[j] = reqptNext[j];
```

The concrete configuration data for this controller instance defines NUM_POINTS=3 and NUM_SIGNALS=3. From that the compiler[3] generates the following assembler fragment of $\mathcal{A}$:

```
  movl $0, i
  jmp  .L103
.L104:
  movl i, %edx
  movl i, %eax
  movl reqsigNext(,%eax,4), %eax
  movl %eax, reqsig(,%edx,4)
  movl i, %eax
  incl %eax
  movl %eax, i
.L103:
  movl i, %eax
  cmpl $2, %eax
  jle  .L104
  movl $0, j
  jmp  .L106
.L107:
  movl j, %edx
  movl j, %eax
  movl reqptNext(,%eax,4), %eax
  movl %eax, reqpt(,%edx,4)
  movl j, %eax
  incl %eax
  movl %eax, j
.L106:
  movl j, %eax
  cmpl $2, %eax
  jle  .L107
```

---

[3] We have used gcc 4.0.2 for this example.

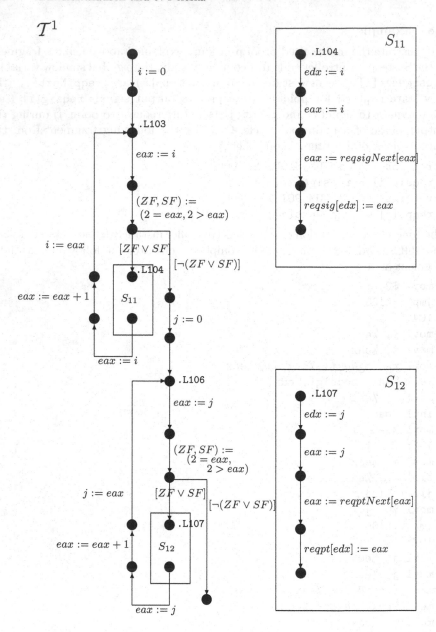

**Fig. 7.** IOTS $\mathcal{T}^1$ associated with $\mathcal{A}$ after renaming of variables

Now the mechanised equivalence proof is constructed as follows: (1) the be-
havioural IOTS model $\mathcal{T}(\mathcal{A})$ of $\mathcal{A}$ is constructed by using the semantic rules
for assembler instructions. After changing the names of assembler variables to
C-style notation according to mapping $\alpha^{\mathcal{M}}$ explained above, this results in an
IOTS $\mathcal{T}^1$ which is depicted in Fig. 7. (2) Applying the transformation rule shown

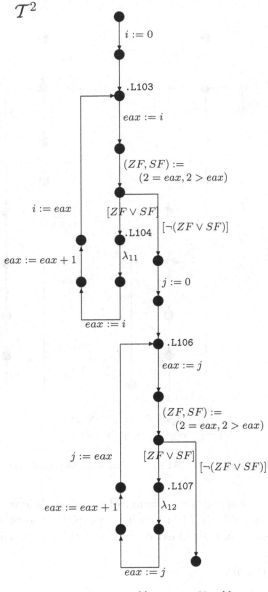

$$\lambda_{11} =_{def} reqsig[i] := reqsigNext[i]$$
$$\lambda_{12} =_{def} reqpt[j] := reqptNext[j]$$

**Fig. 8.** $\mathcal{T}^1 \mapsto \mathcal{T}^2$: I/O-equivalent transformation

in Fig. 6 to the regions $S_{11}$ and $S_{12}$ of $\mathcal{T}^1$ results is an I/O-equivalent IOTS $\mathcal{T}^2$ depicted in Fig. 8. (3) Twofold application of other transformation rules on $\mathcal{T}^2$ results in I/O-equivalent IOTS $\mathcal{T}^3$ shown on the left-hand side of Fig. 9.

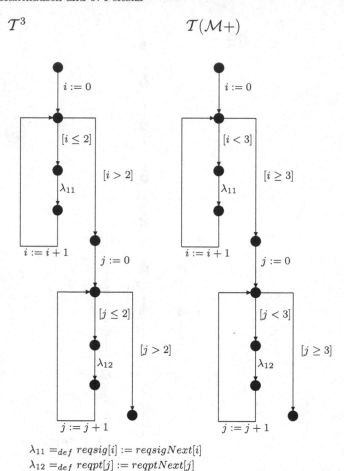

$$\lambda_{11} =_{def} reqsig[i] := reqsigNext[i]$$
$$\lambda_{12} =_{def} reqpt[j] := reqptNext[j]$$

**Fig. 9.** $\mathcal{T}^3 \mapsto \mathcal{T}(\mathcal{M}+)$: I/O-equivalent guard transformation

Finally, a valuation-preserving change of guard conditions ($[i \leq 2] \mapsto [i < 3], [i > 2] \mapsto [i \geq 3]$ etc.) yields $\mathcal{T}(\mathcal{M}+)$ which completes the proof, as far as the code fragments shown here for illustration purposes are concerned.

## 8   Conclusion

In this paper we have given an overview of a complete model-driven development and verification approach for railway and tram control systems. The approach provides a framework consisting of

1. a domain-specific language,
2. a collection of tools, including (a) syntax and static semantics checkers for the language, (b) generators producing executable models of the control system and its physical environment as well as proof obligations, (c) a bounded model checker and (d) an object code verifier,

3. a method for using these tools to construct and verify a family of similar control systems.

For each control system to be generated, the user makes a description of the application-specific parameters in the domain-specific language and checks the description by means of the syntax and static semantics checker. Then from this description the generators produce models of the control system and its physical environment, together with the safety requirements which are automatically verified using the bounded model checker in combination with an inductive proof strategy. Finally – since the formal controller model can be directly compiled – object code is generated by a conventional compiler, and it is checked by the object code verifier that the object code is behaviourally equivalent to the control system model. In this way it is ensured that the safety properties established for the control system model also hold for the object code.

The development of the framework was formalised by using the RAISE formal method, thereby providing complete and precise specifications of the tools as well as the domain-specific language. This provides a sound basis for tool implementation and allows for formal verification of algorithms.

# References

1. Accellera. Property Specification Language Version 1.1 (2004)
2. Badban, B., Fränzle, M., Peleska, J., Teige, T.: Test automation for hybrid systems. In: Proceedings of the Third International Workshop on SOFTWARE QUALITY ASSURANCE (SOQUA 2006), Portland Oregon, USA, November 2006 (2006)
3. Berkenkötter, K.: OCL-based validation of a railway domain profile. In: OCLApps 2006 - OCL for (Meta-)Models in Multiple Application Domains, October 2006 (2006)
4. Bjørner, D.: Domain Engineering: A "Radical Innovation" for Software and Systems Engineering? A Biased Account. In: Dershowitz, N. (ed.) The Zohar Manna Intl.Symp. on Verification: Theory & Practice, Heidelberg, Germany, Springer, Heidelberg (2003)
5. Bjørner, D.: New Results and Current Trends in Formal Techniques for the Development of Software for Transportation Systems. In: Proceedings of the Symposium on Formal Methods for Railway Operation and Control Systems (FORMS'2003),, Budapest/Hungary, May 15-16 2003, L'Harmattan Hongrie (2003)
6. Bjørner, D.: Railways systems: Towards a domain theory. Technical report, Informatics and Mathematical Modelling, Technical University of Denmark, Building 322, Richard Petersens Plads, DK-2800 Kgs.Lyngby, Denmark (2003)
7. Bjørner, D.: Software Engineering. Abstraction and Modelling. Texts in Theoretical Computer Science, vol. 1, Springer, Heidelberg (2006)
8. Bjørner, D.: Software Engineering. Specification of Systems and Languages. Texts in Theoretical Computer Science, vol. 2, Springer, Heidelberg (2006)
9. Bjørner, D.: Software Engineering. Domains, Requirements and Software Design. Texts in Theoretical Computer Science, vol. 3, Springer, Heidelberg (2006)
10. Bjørner, D.: The Rôle of Domain Engineering in Software Development. Invited keynote paper and talk: IPSJ/SIGSE Software Engineering Symposium 2006, Tokyo (October 2006)

11. Bjørner, D.: Domain Engineering. In: reprinted March 2007. To appear as a chapter in a book based on the BCS FACS Evening Seminars to be published by Springer (UK), Springer, Heidelberg (2006)
12. Bjørner, D., George, C.W., Stig Hansen, B., Laustrup, H., Prehn, S.: A railway system, coordination'97, case study workshop example. Technical Report 93, UNU/IIST, P.O.Box 3058, Macau (1997)
13. Drechsler, R., Große, D.: System level validation using formal techniques. IEE Proc.-Comput. Digit. Tech. 152(3), 393–406 (2005)
14. Dyhrberg, R., Christensen, N.: A Domain-Specific Language for Tramway Control Systems. Master's thesis, Informatics and Mathematical Modelling, Technical University of Denmark, DTU (May 2004)
15. Ehrig, H., Damm, W., Desel, J., Große-Rhode, M., Reif, W., Schnieder, E., Westkämper, E. (eds.): Integration of Software Specification Techniques for Applications in Engineering. In: Ehrig, H., Damm, W., Desel, J., Große-Rhode, M., Reif, W., Schnieder, E., Westkämper, E. (eds.) Integration of Software Specification Techniques for Applications in Engineering. LNCS, vol. 3147, pp. 3–540. Springer, Heidelberg (2004)
16. European Committee for Electrotechnical Standardization. EN 50128 - Railway applications - Communications, signalling and processing systems - Software for railway control and protection systems. CENELEC, Brussels (2001)
17. Gjaldbæk, T., Haxthausen, A.E.: Modelling and Verification of Interlocking Systems for Railway Lines. In: Proceedings of the 10th IFAC Symposium on Control in Transportation Systems, Elsevier, Amsterdam (2003)
18. Goos, G., Zimmermann, W.: Verification of compilers. In: Correct System Design, pp. 201–230. Springer, Heidelberg (1999)
19. Grötker, T., Liao, S., Martin, G., Swan, S.: System Design with SystemC. Kluwer Academic Publishers, Dordrecht (2002)
20. Haxthausen, A.E., Christensen, N., Dyhrberg, R.: From Domain Model to Domain-specific Language for Railway Control Systems. In: Proceedings of Formal Methods for Automation and Safety in Railway and Automotive Systems (FORMS/FORMAT 2004), Braunschweig, Germany (2004)
21. Haxthausen, A.E., Peleska, J.: Formal Development and Verification of a Distributed Railway Control System. IEEE Transaction on Software Engineering 26(8), 687–701 (2000)
22. Haxthausen, A.E., Peleska, J.: Formal Methods for the Specification and Verification of Distributed Railway Control Systems: From Algebraic Specifications to Distributed Hybrid Real-Time Systems. In: Forms '99 - Formale Techniken für die Eisenbahnsicherung Fortschritt-Berichte VDI, Reihe 12, Nr. 436, pp. 263–271. VDI-Verlag, Düsseldorf (2000)
23. Haxthausen, A.E., Peleska, J.: A Domain Specific Language for Railway Control Systems. In: Proceedings of the Sixth Biennial World Conference on Integrated Design and Process Technology (IDPT2002), Pasadena, California, June 23-28 2002 (2002)
24. Haxthausen, A.E., Peleska, J.: Automatic Verification, Validation and Test for Railway Control Systems based on Domain-Specific Descriptions. In: Proceedings of the 10th IFAC Symposium on Control in Transportation Systems, Elsevier, Amsterdam (2003)
25. Haxthausen, A.E., Peleska, J.: Generation of Executable Railway Control Components from Domain-Specific Descriptions. In: Proceedings of the Symposium on Formal Methods for Railway Operation and Control Systems (FORMS'2003), Budapest/Hungary, May 15-16 2003, pp. 83–90. L'Harmattan Hongrie (2003)

26. Lindegaard, M.P., Viuf, P., Haxthausen, A.E.: Modelling Railway Interlocking Systems. In: Proceedings of the 9th IFAC Symposium on Control in Transportation Systems 2000, Braunschweig, Germany, June 13-15, 2000, pp. 211–217 (2000)

27. Manna, Z., Pnueli, A.: The Temporal Logic of Reactive and Concurrent Systems. Springer, Heidelberg (1992)

28. Peleska, J., Baer, A., Haxthausen, A.E.: Towards Domain-Specific Formal Specification Languages for Railway Control Systems. In: Proceedings of the 9th IFAC Symposium on Control in Transportation Systems 2000, Braunschweig, Germany, June 13-15, 2000, pp. 147–152 (2000)

29. Peleska, J., Große, D., Haxthausen, A.E., Drechsler, R.: Automated verification for train control systems. In: Schnieder, E., Tarnai, G. (eds.) Proceedings of the FORMS/FORMAT 2004 - Formal Methods for Automation and Safety in Railway and Automotive Systems, pp. 252–265. Technical University of Braunschweig (2004) (ISBN 3-9803363-8-7)

30. Peleska, J., Haxthausen, A.E.: Object Code Verification for Safety-Critical Railway Control Systems. In: Proceedings of Formal Methods for Automation and Safety in Railway and Automotive Systems (FORMS/FORMAT 2007), Braunschweig, Germany, GZVB e.V. (2007) (ISBN 13:978-3-937655-09-3)

31. Peleska, J., Haxthausen, A.E., Kinder, S., Drechsler, R.: Model-driven development and verification in the railway domain (To be submitted) (2007)

32. Pnueli, A., Shtrichman, O., Siegel, M.: The code validation tool CVT: Automatic verification of a compilation process. International Journal on Software Tools for Technology Transfer 2(2), 192–201 (1998)

33. The RAISE Language Group.: The RAISE Specification Language. The BCS Practitioners Series. Prentice-Hall, Englewood Cliffs (1992)

34. Rumbaugh, J., Jacobson, I., Booch, G.: The Unified Modeling Language - Reference Manual, 2nd edn. Addison-Wesley, Reading (2004)

35. Schnieder, E., Tarnai, G.: Proceedings of Formal Methods for Automation and Safety in Railway and Automotive Systems (FORMS/FORMAT 2004), Braunschweig, Germany, (Technical University of Braunschweig (December 2004)

36. Schnieder, E., Tarnai, G.: Proceedings of Formal Methods for Automation and Safety in Railway and Automotive Systems (FORMS/FORMAT 2007), Braunschweig, Germany. GZVB e.V (2007) ISBN 13:978-3-937655-09-3

37. Tarnai, G., Schnieder, E.: Proceedings of the Symposium on Formal Methods for Railway Operation and Control Systems (FORMS'2003), Budapest. L'Harmattan Hongrie (2003)

38. XForms 1.0, available under `http://www.w3.org/TR/xforms`

39. Extensible Markup Language (XML), available under `http://www.w3.org/XML/`

40. The Extensible Stylesheet Language Family (XSL), available under `http://www.w3.org/Style/XSL`

# A Laudatio to Dines Bjørner from Anne Haxthausen

It is indeed a great honour to contribute to the celebration of Dines Bjørner. Dines and his family have mattered so much to me.

First, his sister, Elisabeth Bjørner Søe, was my math teacher in Ingrid Jespersens Private School. She taught me the beauty of mathematics and gave me the skills and interest in mathematics and science that led me to study at the Technical University of Denmark (DTU).

Then Dines took over and with such a great competence taught me how to apply mathematical modelling in computer science that this has been my main interest since then (for more than 20 years). I must say that I was fascinated listening to Dines' lectures where scientific pearls were interspersed with anecdotes. Throughout my career Dines has given me so much inspiration, challenges and support. Indeed this has meant a lot for my career and my life.

Later, closing the circle, I had the pleasure of teaching Nikolaj, Dines son.

Thanks, Dines, for offering me to be a Ph.D. student, for recommending me to be employed at DDC and to work on the RAISE projects, and for encouraging me to come back to DTU. Also thanks for inviting me to write papers with you and for sharing courses. A thing I like very much about you, Dines, is the fatherly way that you care about your colleagues and students. You do not only care about their careers, but also about their personal lives. Thanks, to you and your lovely wife, Kari, for inviting me home at many occasions.

Thank you, Dines, I am deeply indebted for all what you have done for me!

# Compensable Programs

He Jifeng[*]

Software Engineering Institute
East China Normal University, Shanghai

**Abstract.** Transaction-based services are increasingly being applied in solving many universal interoperability problems. Compensation is one typical feature for long-running transactions. This paper presents a design matrix model for specifying the behaviour of compensable programs and provides new healthiness conditions to capture these new programming features. The new model for handling exception and compensation is built as conservative extension of the standard relational model in the sense that the algebraic laws presented in [14] remain valid. The paper also shows that the design matrix model is a retract of the design model.

## 1 Introduction

With the development of Internet technology, web services and web-based applications play an important role to information systems. The aim of web services is to achieve the universal interoperability between different web-based applications. Due to the provided interface, web services can be invoked across the Internet. In recent years, in order to develop web-based information systems and describe the infrastructure for carrying out business transactions, various business modelling languages have been introduced, such as XLANG, WSFL, BPEL4WS (BPEL) and StAC [24,15,9,7].

Compensation is one typical feature for long-running transactions. Butler *et al.* have investigated the compensation feature in the style of process algebra CSP [6,7,8], namely *compensating* CSP. The operational semantics and trace semantics have been studied [8]. The compensation is expressed as $P \div Q$, where $P$ is the forward process and $Q$ is its associated compensation behaviour. StAC (Structured Activity Compensation) [6] is a business process modelling language, where compensation acts as one of its main features. Its operational semantics has also been studied in [7]. Meanwhile, the combination of StAC and B method has been explored, which can provide the precise description of business transactions. Further, Bruni *et al.* have studied the transaction calculi for StAC programs. The long-running transactions were discussed, and a process calculi was provided in the form of Java API, namely Java Transactional Web Services [4]. Qiu *et al.* have provided a deep formal analysis of the fault behaviour for BPEL-like processes [22]. Pu *et al.* have formalized the operational semantics for BPEL [21], where bisimulation has been considered.

---

[*] This work was supported by the National Basic Research Program of China (Grant No. 2005CB321904).

C.B. Jones, Z. Liu, J. Woodcock (Eds.): Bjørner/Zhou Festschrift, LNCS 4700, pp. 349–363, 2007.

The $\pi$-calculus has been applied in describing various compensable program models. Lucchi and Mazzara formalised the semantics of BPEL within the framework of the $\pi$-calculus [18]. Laneve and Zavattaro explored the application of the $\pi$-calculus in the formalisation of the compensable programs and the standard pattern of compisition [16].

This paper is an attempt at taking a step forward to gain some perspectives on compensable programs within the design calculus [14] as well as to identify the links among various models for the following language features

- Exception handling
- Compensation mechanism

Our contributions include

- providing a conservative extension of the standard relational model to deal with fault handling and compensation, which can be characterised by additional halthiness conditions.
- exploring the algebraic system for exception handling and compensation.
- constructing a Galois connection (retract) to link the new model with the design model.

The paper is organised as follows: Section 2 defines the merge combinator of designs, which is used later to construct design matrix in describing the dynamic behaviour of compensable programs. It also investigates the algebraic properties of the merge operator. Section 3 presents the new healthiness conditions to capture the exception handling and compensation features of compensable programs, and introduces a new notion **design matrix**. It also explores the Galois link between the design model with the design matrix model. Section 4 gives an observation-oriented semantics to compensable programs. We explore the algebraic properties of exception handler and compensation mechanism in Section 5. The paper concludes with a short discussion on the linking theories.

## 2 Preliminaries

This section introduces some notations which will be used in constructing design matrix in the next section.

**Definition 2.1** (Merge)

Let $P$ and $Q$ be designs. The notation $P \oplus Q$ denotes the program which merges the outcomes of $P$ and $Q$.

$$P \oplus Q =_{df} \textbf{if} (\textbf{pre}.P \rightarrow P, \textbf{pre}.Q \rightarrow Q)\textbf{fi}$$

where **pre**.$P$ stands for the precondition of Design $P$:

$$\textbf{pre}.P =_{df} \neg P[true, false/ok, ok']$$

**Theorem 2.1.** $(b \vdash S) \oplus (c \vdash T) =_{df} (b \vee c) \vdash (b \wedge S \vee c \wedge T)$

The merge operator is idempotent, symmetric and associative. It distributes over both nondeterministic choice and conditional.

**Theorem 2.2**

(1) $P \sqcap (Q \oplus R) = (P \sqcap Q) \oplus (P \sqcap R)$

(2) $(P \vartriangleleft b \vartriangleright Q) \oplus R = (P \oplus R) \vartriangleleft b \vartriangleright (Q \oplus R)$

(3) $(P \oplus Q) \vartriangleleft b \vartriangleright R = (P \vartriangleleft b \vartriangleright R) \oplus (Q \vartriangleleft b \vartriangleright R)$

**Proof.** Let $P =_{df} (b \vdash S)$ and $Q =_{df} (c \vdash T)$ and $R =_{df} (d \vdash U)$.

(1)  $LHS$ ⠀⠀⠀⠀⠀⠀⠀⠀⠀⠀⠀⠀⠀⠀⠀⠀⠀⠀⠀⠀⠀⠀⠀⠀⠀⠀⠀⠀⠀⠀⠀⠀⠀⠀⠀⠀ {Def of $\oplus$}

⠀⠀$= P \sqcap (c \lor d) \vdash (c \land T \lor d \land U)$ ⠀⠀⠀⠀⠀⠀⠀⠀⠀⠀⠀⠀⠀ {def of $\sqcap$}

⠀⠀$= (b \land (c \lor d)) \vdash (b \land S) \lor (c \land T) \lor (d \land U)$ ⠀⠀ {Ordering of designs}

⠀⠀$= b \land (c \lor d) \vdash$

⠀⠀⠀⠀$(b \land (c \lor d) \land S \lor (b \land c) \land T \lor b \land d \land U)$ ⠀⠀⠀⠀ {Def of $\oplus$}

⠀⠀$= (b \land c) \vdash (S \lor T) \oplus (b \land d) \vdash (S \lor U)$ ⠀⠀⠀⠀⠀⠀⠀ {def of $\sqcap$}

⠀⠀$= RHS$

**Definition 2.2** (Strong refinement)

Design $D_1 = b \vdash S$ is a strong refinement of design $D_2 = c \vdash T$, denoted by $D_1 \geq D_2$, if

$$[c \Rightarrow (b \land (S \equiv T))]$$

**Example.** Let $F(X) =_{df} (P; X) \vartriangleleft b \vartriangleright \textbf{skip}$. Then

$$F^{n+1}(\textbf{true}) \geq F^n(\textbf{true})$$

$\oplus$ plays the same role as the angelic choice in the refinement ordering.

**Theorem 2.3.** $D_1 \geq D_2$ iff $D_1 \sqsupseteq D_2$ and $D_1 \oplus D_2 = D_1$

**Proof.** Let $D_1 = (b \vdash S)$ and $D_2 = (c \vdash T)$

⠀⠀$D_1 \geq D_2$ ⠀⠀⠀⠀⠀⠀⠀⠀⠀⠀⠀⠀⠀⠀⠀⠀⠀⠀⠀⠀⠀⠀⠀⠀⠀⠀⠀⠀⠀⠀⠀⠀ {Def 2.2}

$\equiv [c \Rightarrow b]$ **and** $[c \Rightarrow (S \equiv T)]$ ⠀⠀⠀⠀⠀⠀⠀⠀⠀⠀⠀⠀ {predicate calculus}

$\Rightarrow [c \Rightarrow b]$ **and** $[(c \land S) \Rightarrow T)]$ **and** $[(c \land T) \Rightarrow S]$ ⠀⠀ {Def of $\oplus$}

$\Rightarrow (D_1 \sqsupseteq D_2)$ **and** $(D_1 \oplus D_2 = D_1)$ ⠀⠀⠀⠀⠀⠀⠀⠀⠀⠀⠀ {Def of $\oplus$}

$\Rightarrow [c \Rightarrow b]$ **and** $[(c \land S) \Rightarrow T)]$ **and**

⠀⠀$[(b \land S \lor c \land T) \equiv (b \land S)]$ ⠀⠀⠀⠀⠀⠀⠀⠀⠀⠀⠀⠀⠀⠀⠀⠀ {Def of $\geq$}

$\Rightarrow D_1 \geq D_2$

**Definition 2.3**

Designs $D_1$ and $D_2$ are domain-disjoint if

$$\textbf{pre.}D_1 \land \textbf{pre.}D_2 = false$$

**Theorem 2.4**

If $P$ and $Q$ are domain-disjoint, then

(1) $P \oplus Q = P \sqcup Q$

(2) $(P \oplus Q); R = (P; R) \oplus (Q; R)$

**Proof**

$$
\begin{aligned}
& (1) \ RHS && \{\text{refinement calculus}\} \\
&= (b \vee c) \vdash ((b \Rightarrow S) \wedge (c \Rightarrow T)) && \{\text{ordering of designs}\} \\
&= b \vee c \vdash (b \vee c) \wedge (\neg c \wedge S \vee \neg b \wedge T) && \{b \wedge c = false\} \\
&= LHS
\end{aligned}
$$

$$
\begin{aligned}
& (2) \ LHS && \{\text{def of } \oplus\} \\
&= (b \vee c) \vdash (b \wedge S \vee c \wedge T); R && \{\text{refinement calculus}\} \\
&= (b \vee c) \wedge \neg((b \wedge S \vee c \wedge T); \neg d) \vdash (b \wedge S \vee c \wedge T); U && \{b \wedge c = false\} \\
&= b \wedge (\neg(b \wedge S); \neg d) \vee c \wedge \neg((c \wedge T); \neg d) \vdash \\
& \quad (b \wedge S \vee c \wedge T); U && \{\text{def of } \oplus\} \\
&= b \wedge \neg((b \wedge S); \neg d) \vdash (b \wedge S); U \oplus \\
& \quad c \wedge \neg(c \wedge T); \neg d)) \vdash (c \wedge T); U && \{\text{refinement calculus}\} \\
&= RHS
\end{aligned}
$$

**Theorem 2.5**

If $R = true \vdash U$, then $(P \oplus Q); R = (P; R) \oplus (Q; R)$.

# 3   Design Matrix

In this section we work towards a precise characterisation of the class of *designs* [14] that are most useful in exception handling and compensation.

A subclass of designs may be defined in a variety of ways. Sometimes it is done by a syntactic property. Sometimes the definition requires satisfaction of a particular collection of algebraic laws. In general, the most useful definitions are these that are given in many different forms, together with a proof that all of them are equivalent.

To handling exception requires a more explicit analysis of the phenomena of program execution. We therefore introduce into the alphabet of our designs a pair of Boolean variables to denote the relevant observations.

**Definition 3.1** (*eflag* and *eflag'*)

*eflag* records the observation that the program is asked to start when the execution of its predcessor halts due to an exception.

*eflag'* records the observation that an exception occurs during the execution of the program.

The introduction of error states has implication for sequential composition: all the exception cases of program $P$ are of course also the exception cases of $P; Q$. Rather than change the definition of sequential composition given in [14], we enforce these rules by means of a healthiness condition. If the program $Q$ is asked to start in an exception case of its predecessor, it leaves the state unchanged

**Definition 3.2** (Healthiness Condition)

$(\mathbf{Req_1})\ Q\ =\ II \lhd eflag \rhd Q$

when the design $II$ adopts the following definition

$$II =_{df}\ true \vdash (s' = s)$$

where $s$ denotes all the state variables in the alphabet of $Q$.

A design is $\mathbf{Req_1}$-healthy if it satisfies the healthiness condition $\mathbf{Req_1}$. Define

$$\mathcal{H}_1 =_{df} \lambda Q \bullet (II \lhd eflag \rhd Q)$$

Clearly $Q$ is $\mathbf{Req_1}$ healthy if and only if $Q$ lies in the range of $\mathcal{H}_1$.

The following theorem indicates $\mathbf{Req_1}$-healthy designs are closed under conventional programming combinators.

**Theorem 3.1**

(1) $\mathcal{H}_1(P \sqcap Q)\ =\ \mathcal{H}_1(P) \sqcap \mathcal{H}_1(Q)$

(2) $\mathcal{H}_1(P \lhd b \rhd Q)\ =\ \mathcal{H}_1(P) \lhd b \rhd \mathcal{H}_1(Q)$

(3) $\mathcal{H}_1(P; \mathcal{H}_1(Q))\ =\ \mathcal{H}_1(P); \mathcal{H}_1(Q)$

The basic concept of a $\mathbf{Req_1}$-healthy design deserves a notation of its own.

**Definition 3.3** (Design Matrix)

Let $D_1 = (b_1 \vdash R_1)$ and $D_2 = (b_2 \vdash R_2)$ be designs of the same alphabet which contains neither $eflag$ nor $eflag'$. Define

$$\begin{pmatrix} D_1 \\ D_2 \end{pmatrix} =_{df} \mathcal{H}_1((D_1\ ;\ \mathbf{succ_1}) \oplus (D_2\ ;\ \mathbf{error_1}))$$

where

$$\mathbf{succ_1} =_{df} true \vdash (v' = v \wedge \neg eflag')$$

$$\mathbf{error_1} =_{df} true \vdash (v' = v \wedge eflag')$$

where $v$ and $v'$ are the variables in the alphabet of $D_1$ and $D_2$.

This definition states that

- if the program starts in a state satisfying $b_1$, it will terminate successfully on states satisying $R_1$.
- if it is activated in a state satisfying $b_2$, an exception case may occur during its execution and $R_2$ will hold when the program halts.

To equip a program with compensation mechanism, it is necessary to characterise the cases when the control has to be passed to the compensation components. Following the line adopted by the fault handling model, we introduce a new logical variable *forward* to describe the status of control flow of the execution of a program:

- *forward'* = *true* indicates successful termination of the execution of the forward activity of a program. In this case, its successor will carry on with the initial state set up by the program.
- *forward'* = *false* indicates it is required to undo the effect caused by the execution of the forward activity. In this case, the installed compensation module will be invoked.

As a result, when a program $Q$ is asked to start in a state where *forward* = *false*, it has to meet the following healthiness condition:

**Definition 3.4** (Healthiness Condition)

$(\textbf{Req}_2)\ Q\ =\ II \lhd \neg forward \rhd Q$

This condition can be identified by the following mapping

$$\mathcal{H}_2(Q)\ =_{df}\ II \lhd \neg forward \rhd Q$$

in the sense that a program satisfies $\textbf{Req}_2$ iff it is a fixed point of $\mathcal{H}_2$

**Theorem 3.2**

$\mathcal{H}_2 \circ \mathcal{H}_1\ =\ \mathcal{H}_1 \circ \mathcal{H}_2$ where $\circ$ denotes functional composition.

**Proof.** From the fact that

$$\mathcal{H}_1(\mathcal{H}_2(Q))\ =\ II \lhd eflag \vee \neg foward \rhd Q\ =\ \mathcal{H}_2(\mathcal{H}_1(Q))$$

Define

$$\mathcal{H}\ =_{df}\ \mathcal{H}_1 \circ \mathcal{H}_2$$

**Theorem 3.3**

A design satisfies both $\textbf{Req}_1$ and $\textbf{Req}_2$ iff it is a fixed point of $\mathcal{H}$.

Like the mapping $\mathcal{H}_1$, $\mathcal{H}$ is also a homomorphism.

**Theorem 3.4**

(1) $\mathcal{H}(P \sqcap Q)\ =\ \mathcal{H}(P) \sqcap \mathcal{H}(Q)$

(2) $\mathcal{H}(P \lhd b \rhd Q)\ =\ \mathcal{H}(P) \lhd b \rhd \mathcal{H}(Q)$

(3) $\mathcal{H}(P; \mathcal{H}(Q))\ =\ \mathcal{H}(P); \mathcal{H}(Q)$

**Definition 3.5** (Design Matrix for exception and rollback)

Define

$$\begin{pmatrix} D_1 \\ D_2 \\ D_3 \end{pmatrix}\ =_{df}\ \mathcal{H}((D_1; \textbf{succ}) \oplus (D_2; \textbf{error}) \oplus (D_3; \textbf{rollback}))$$

where

$$\mathbf{succ} =_{df} (\mathbf{succ}_1 \parallel (true \vdash forward'))$$

$$\mathbf{error} =_{df} (\mathbf{error}_1 \parallel (true \vdash forward'))$$

$$\mathbf{rollback} =_{df} true \vdash ((v' = v) \wedge \neg forward')$$

where $\parallel$ stands for the disjoint parallel operator [14]

$$(b \vdash R) \parallel (c \vdash S) =_{df} (b \wedge c) \vdash (R \wedge S)$$

We introduce the following mappings to link the design matrix model with the design model. For any design $D$ and design matrix $Q$, define

$$\mathcal{G}(D) =_{df} \mathcal{H}(D; \mathbf{succ})$$

$$\mathcal{F}(Q) =_{df} Q[true, false/forward, eflag]; ((forward \wedge \neg eflag) \vdash (v' = v))$$

**Theorem 3.5**

$$(1)\ \mathcal{G}(b \vdash R) = \begin{pmatrix} b \vdash (R \wedge \neg eflag' \wedge forward') \\ true \\ true \end{pmatrix}$$

$$(2)\ \mathcal{F} \begin{pmatrix} c_1 \vdash S_1 \\ c_2 \vdash S_2 \\ c_3 \vdash S_3 \end{pmatrix} = (c_1 \wedge \neg c_2 \wedge \neg c_3) \vdash S_1$$

$\mathcal{G}$ distributes over the standard programming combinators.

**Theorem 3.6** (Homomorphism)

(1) $\mathcal{G}(D_1; D_2) = \mathcal{G}(D_1); \mathcal{G}(D_2)$

(2) $\mathcal{G}(D_1 \sqcap D_2) = \mathcal{G}(D_1) \sqcap \mathcal{G}(D_2)$

(3) $\mathcal{G}(D_1 \lhd b \rhd D_2) = \mathcal{G}(D_1) \lhd b \rhd \mathcal{G}(D_2)$ provided that $b$ is well-defined.

**Proof** $\mathcal{G}(D_1 \lhd b \rhd D_2)$                          {Def of $\mathcal{G}$}

$= \mathcal{H}((D_1 \lhd b \rhd D_2); \mathbf{succ})$                   {; distributes over $\lhd b \rhd$}

$= \mathcal{H}((D_1; \mathbf{succ}) \lhd b \rhd (D_2; \mathbf{succ}))$            {Theorem 3.4}

$= \mathcal{G}(D_1) \lhd b \rhd \mathcal{G}(D_2)$

$\mathcal{F}$ and $\mathcal{G}$ form a retraction

**Theorem 3.7** (Retraction)

$(\mathcal{F}, \mathcal{G})$ is a Galois connection, satisfying

(1) $\mathcal{F}(\mathcal{G}(D)) = D$

(2) $\mathcal{G}(\mathcal{F}(Q)) \sqsubseteq Q$

## 4    Compensable Programs

The ability to declare compensation logic alongside forware-working logic is the underpinning of the application-controlled error-handling framework of WS-BPEL. This section will provide a model for compensable programs which consist of forward activity (for application task), backward activity (for compensation) and exception handling component.

A compensable program will be identified as a healthy design with the alphabet containing the following variables to record the status of the holder of compensation program and the values of program variables:

1. $x$ and $x'$: to stand for the initial value and the final value of variable $x$ respectively.
2. $Cseq$: to keep the compensation programs installed so far.
3. $Cpens$: to record the named compensation programs. It is a mapping from the scope names to their corresponding compensation programs.

### 4.1    Primitive Commands

The chaotic program $\perp$ is defined as usual

$$\mathbf{beh}(\perp) \ =_{df} \ \begin{pmatrix} \mathbf{true} \\ \mathbf{true} \\ \mathbf{true} \end{pmatrix}$$

The execution of skip terminates successfully, leaving both the contents of the holder of compensation programs and the values of program variables and target lables unchanged.

$$\mathbf{beh}(\texttt{skip}) \ =_{df} \ \begin{pmatrix} true \vdash Identity \\ \mathbf{true} \\ \mathbf{true} \end{pmatrix}$$

where the binary relation $Identity$ is defined by

$$Identity \ =_{df} \ (v' = v) \wedge (Cpens' = Cpens) \wedge (Cseq' = Cseq)$$

The program fail stops the execution indicating the failure of the forward activity.

$$\mathbf{beh}(\texttt{fail}) \ =_{df} \ \begin{pmatrix} \mathbf{true} \\ \mathbf{true} \\ true \vdash Identity \end{pmatrix}$$

There is a class of programs which never end the execution with a meaningful outcome. The assignment $x := 1/0$ belongs to this category. We use the notation halt to denote the program which always throws an exception case, and leaves all variables unchanged.

$$\mathbf{beh(halt)} =_{df} \begin{pmatrix} \mathbf{true} \\ true \vdash Identity \\ \mathbf{true} \end{pmatrix}$$

The definition of the assignment needs to take into account the possibility that evalation of the expression is undefined..

For each expression $e$ of a reasonable programming language, it is possible to calculate a condition $\mathcal{D}(e)$, which is true in just those circumstances in which $e$ can be successfully evaluated [20]. For example

$$\begin{aligned}
\mathcal{D}(17) &= true \\
\mathcal{D}(true) &= \mathcal{D}(false) = true \\
\mathcal{D}(b \vee c) &= \mathcal{D}(b) \wedge \mathcal{D}(c) \\
\mathcal{D}(x) &= true \\
\mathcal{D}(e + f) &= \mathcal{D}(e) \wedge \mathcal{D}(f) \\
\mathcal{D}(e/f) &= \mathcal{D}(e) \wedge \mathcal{D}(f) \wedge f \neq 0 \\
\mathcal{D}(e \triangleleft b \triangleright f) &= (b \Rightarrow \mathcal{D}(e)) \wedge (\neg b \Rightarrow \mathcal{D}(f)) \quad \text{if } b \text{ is well-defined}
\end{aligned}$$

For any expression $e$, $\mathcal{D}(e)$ is a well-defined Boolean expressuion.

Successful execution of an assignment relies on the assumption that the expression will be successfully evaluated. So we formulate our definition of assignment

$$\mathbf{beh}(x := e) =_{df} \begin{pmatrix} \mathcal{D}(e) \vdash Identity[v \oplus \{x \mapsto e\}/v] \\ \neg\mathcal{D}(e) \vdash Identity \\ \mathbf{true} \end{pmatrix}$$

Expressed in words, this definition states that

- Either the initial values of the variables are such that evaluation of $e$ fails $(\neg\mathcal{D}(e))$, and the execution halts with all variables unchanged.
- or the program terminates successfully, and the value of $x'$ is $e$, and the final values of all the other variables are the same as their initial values.

## 4.2 Programming Combinators

The nonderterminic choice and sequential composition have exactly the same meaning as operators on the single predicates defined in [14].

$$\mathbf{beh}(P; Q) =_{df} \mathbf{beh}(P); \mathbf{beh}(Q)$$
$$\mathbf{beh}(P \sqcap Q) =_{df} \mathbf{beh}(P) \vee \mathbf{beh}(Q)$$

The definition of conditional takes the well-definedness of its Boolean test into account

$$\mathbf{beh}(P \lhd b \rhd Q) =_{df} \left( \begin{array}{l} \mathcal{D}(b) \Rightarrow (b \wedge \mathbf{beh}(P) \vee \neg b \wedge \mathbf{beh}(Q)) \wedge \\ \neg \mathcal{D}(b) \Rightarrow \mathbf{beh}(\mathtt{halt}) \end{array} \right)$$

Let $\{b_i \mid 1 \le i \le n\}$ be a set of boolean expressions, and $\{P_i \mid 1 \le i \le n\}$ a set of programs. The guarded choice construct if $b_1 \to P_1, .., b_n \to P_n$ fi is defined by

$$\mathbf{beh}(\text{if } b_1 \to P_1, .., b_n \to P_n \text{ fi}) =_{df} \left( \begin{array}{l} \bigvee_i (b_i \wedge \mathcal{D}(b) \wedge \mathbf{beh}(P_i)) \vee \\ (\bigwedge_i \neg b_i) \wedge \mathcal{D}(b) \wedge \mathbf{beh}(\bot) \vee \\ \neg \mathcal{D}(b) \wedge \mathbf{beh}(\mathtt{halt}) \end{array} \right)$$

The following theorem enables us to focus on the guarded choices with well-defined boolean guards in the rest of this section.

**Theorem 4.1**

if$(b_1 \to P_1, ..., b_n \to P_n)$fi $=$

if$((b_1 \lhd \mathcal{D}(b) \rhd false) \to P_1, .., (b_n \lhd \mathcal{D}(b) \rhd false) \to P_n, \neg \mathcal{D}(b) \to \mathtt{halt})$fi

where $b =_{df} \bigvee_i b_i$.

**Definition 4.1** (Total assignment)

An assignment is a total one if all the variables of the program appear on the left hand side in some standard order

$$x, y, .., z := e, f, .., g$$

and all the expressions on the right hand side are well-defined.

We can transform an assignment into a total one by using guarded choice.

**Theorem 4.2**

$$x := e = \text{if} \left( \begin{array}{l} \mathcal{D}(e) \to x := (e \lhd \mathcal{D}(e) \rhd x), \\ \neg \mathcal{D}(e) \to \mathtt{halt} \end{array} \right) \text{fi}$$

Total assignments satisfy the algebraic laws given in [14], for example

(1) $\mathtt{skip} = (v := v)$

(2) $(v := e; v := f) = (v := f(e))$

(3) $v := e; \text{if} \left( \begin{array}{l} b_1(v) \to P_1, \\ .., \\ b_n(v) \to P_n \end{array} \right) \text{fi} = \text{if} \left( \begin{array}{l} b_1(e) \to (v := e; P_1), \\ ..., \\ b_n(e) \to (v := e; P_n) \end{array} \right) \text{fi}$

## 4.3   Scope

Let $A$, $C$ and $F$ be programns, and let $n$ be a name. The named scope $\{A? C, F\}_n$ has $n$ as its name, and $A$, $C$ and $F$ as its forward activity, backward activity and exception handler. It runs $A$ first. If $A$ terminates successfully, it installs program $C$ that can later be invoked by a undo command to compensate the effect caused by the execution of $A$. Otherwise it passes the control to $F$ to deal with the exception case.

$$\mathbf{beh}(\{A?\,C,\ F\}_n) \ =_{df} \ \mathcal{H}\begin{pmatrix}\mathbf{beh}(A); \\ \mathbf{install}(C); \\ \mathbf{set}(n,\ C); \\ \mathbf{exception}(F)\end{pmatrix}$$

where

$$\mathbf{install}(C) =_{df} \begin{pmatrix}true \vdash \begin{pmatrix}v' = v \wedge Cpens' = Cpens \wedge \\ Cseq' = (Cseq \cdot < C > \triangleleft C \neq \epsilon \triangleright Cseq)\end{pmatrix} \\ true \\ true\end{pmatrix}$$

$$\mathbf{set}(n,\ C) =_{df} \begin{pmatrix}true \vdash \begin{pmatrix}v' = v \wedge Cseq' = Cseq \wedge \\ Cpens' = Cpens \oplus \{n \mapsto C\}\end{pmatrix} \\ true \\ true\end{pmatrix}$$

$$\mathbf{exception}(F) =_{df} ((\mathbf{beh}(F)[false/eflag]; \mathbf{beh}(\mathtt{halt})) \triangleleft eflag \triangleright \mathbf{beh}(\mathtt{skip}))$$

where $\epsilon$ stands for the empty text.

The unnamed scope $\{A?,\ C,\ F\}$ behaves the same as the named scope except that it does not install a named compensation.

$$\mathbf{beh}(\{A?\,C,\ F\}) \ =_{df} \ \mathcal{H}\begin{pmatrix}\mathbf{beh}(A); \\ \mathbf{install}(C); \\ \mathbf{exception}(F)\end{pmatrix}$$

## 4.4   Compensation

**compensate**$(n)$ activates the compensation program associated with the scope $n$.

$$\mathbf{beh}(\mathbf{compensate}(n)) \ =_{df} \ (\mathbf{beh}(Cpens(n)) \triangleleft n \in \mathbf{domain}(Cpens) \triangleright \mathbf{beh}(\mathtt{throw}))$$

The execition of the command undo switches the direction of control flow by invoking the compensation program stored in $Cseq$.

$$\mathbf{beh}(\mathtt{undo}) \ =_{df} \ \mathbf{beh}(Cseq); \mathbf{beh}(\mathtt{fail})$$

Let $P$ be a program. The notation $\mathtt{undo} \triangleright P$ represents the program which runs $P$ first, then behaves like $\mathtt{undo}$.

$$\mathtt{undo} \triangleright P \ =_{df} \ \mathbf{beh}(P); \mathbf{beh}(\mathtt{undo})$$

# 5   Algebraic Properties

The model we provide for compensable programs can be seen as a conservative extension of the design model for the imperative language discussed in [14]. In particular, sequential composition, conditional and nondeterministic choice satisfy the same laws as given in [14]. This section will investigate the algebraic properties of the new features of compensable programs.

## 5.1   Composition

Sequential composition has undo and halt as its left zeroes.

(seq-1) undo ; $Q$ = undo

(seq-2) halt ; $Q$ = halt

## 5.2   Exception Handler

The exception handler $\mathcal{E}$ is defined as a binary operator of programs.

$$P \, \mathcal{E} \, F \; =_{df} \; \{P \, ? \, \epsilon, \, F\}$$

$\mathcal{E}$ distributes leftward over all programming combinators.

($\mathcal{E} - 1$) $(P_1 \sqcap P_2) \mathcal{E} \, F = (P_1 \mathcal{E} \, F) \sqcap (P_2 \mathcal{E} \, F)$

($\mathcal{E} - 2$) $(P_1 \, ; \, P_2) \mathcal{E} \, F = (P_1 \mathcal{E} \, F) \, ; \, (P_2 \mathcal{E} \, F)$

($\mathcal{E} - 3$) If the Boolean expression $b$ is well-defined, then

$$(P_1 \lhd b \rhd P_2) \mathcal{E} \, F = (P_1 \mathcal{E} \, F) \lhd b \rhd (P_2 \mathcal{E} \, F)$$

It is also disjunctive on its right operand.

($\mathcal{E} - 4$) $P \mathcal{E} \, (F_1 \sqcap F_2) = (P \mathcal{E} \, F_1) \sqcap (P \mathcal{E} \, F_2)$

$\mathcal{E}$ has skip and throw as its right units.

($\mathcal{E} - 5$)

(1) $P \mathcal{E} \, \text{skip} = P$

(2) $P \mathcal{E} \, \text{halt} = P$

The following laws enable us to merge the consecutive exception handlers.

($\mathcal{E} - 6$) $(P \mathcal{E} \, \text{halt}) \mathcal{E} \, F = P \mathcal{E} \, F$

($\mathcal{E} - 7$) $(P \mathcal{E} \perp) \mathcal{E} \, F = P \mathcal{E} \perp$

$\mathcal{E}$ can be eliminated using the following laws.

($\mathcal{E} - 8$) $\text{halt} \, \mathcal{E} \, F = F ; \text{halt}$

($\mathcal{E} - 9$) $\text{skip} \, \mathcal{E} \, F = \text{skip}$

($\mathcal{E} - 10$) $\perp \mathcal{E} \, F = \perp$

($\mathcal{E} - 11$) $\text{undo} \, \mathcal{E} \, F = \text{undo}$

A named scope can be converted into an exception handler.

$(\mathcal{E} - 12)$ $\{A? C, F\}_n = (A; \{C\}_n) \mathcal{E} F$, where

$$\{C\}_n =_{df} \{\texttt{skip}? C, \texttt{halt}\}_n$$

Similar to unnamed scope we adopt the following notation for a unnamed compensation program.

$$\{C\} =_{df} \{\texttt{skip}? C, \texttt{halt}\}$$

No exception occurs during the execution of a total assignment, or installation of a compensation program.

$(\mathcal{E} - 13)$ $(v := e; P) \mathcal{E} F = (v := e); (P \mathcal{E} F)$

$(\mathcal{E} - 14)$ $(\{C\}_n; P) \mathcal{E} F = \{C\}_n; (P \mathcal{E} F)$

$(\mathcal{E} - 15)$ $(\{C\}; P) \mathcal{E} F = \{C\}; (P \mathcal{E} F)$

## 5.3   Compensation

Installation of a compensation program can be postponed.

(cpens-1)

(1) $\{C\}_n; (v := e) = (v := e); \{C\}_n$

(2) $\{C\}; (v := e) = (v := e); \{C\}$

(cpens-2) If $b$ is well-defined, then

(1) $\{C\}_n; (P \triangleleft b \triangleright Q) = (\{C\}_n; P) \triangleleft b \triangleright (\{C\}_n; Q)$

(2) $\{C\}; (P \triangleleft b \triangleright Q) = (\{C\}; P) \triangleleft b \triangleright (\{C\}; Q)$

It becomes void to install a compensation program before a undo command.

(cpens-3)

(1) $\{C\}_n; (\texttt{undo} \triangleright P) = \texttt{undo} \triangleright (P; C)$

(2) $\{C\}; (\texttt{undo} \triangleright P) = \texttt{undo} \triangleright (P; C)$

Consecutive unnamed compensations can be merged.

(cpens–4) $\{C\}; \{D\} = \{D; C\}$

## 6   Conclusion

A theory of programming is intended to support the practice of programming by relating each program to the specification of what it is intended to achieve. An unifying theory is one that is applicable to a general paradigm of computing, supporting the classification of many programming languages as correct instances ofthe paradigm. This paper indicates that the UTP approach is effective in the following aspects

– a new model can be built by adding healthiness conditions:
1. the model of designs is characterised by the left zero law $\bot; P = \bot$ and the unit laws $\texttt{skip}; P = P = P; \texttt{skip}$
2. the model of $\mathbf{Req_1}$-healthy designs is captured as a subset of designs that meet the new left zero law $\texttt{halt}; P = \texttt{halt}$
3. the model in dealing with compensation is seen as a submodel of the $\mathbf{Req_1}$-healthy designs which satisfies the left zero law $\texttt{fail}; P = P$.
– the model extension is ecnomical since the original algebraic laws remain valid.

# References

1. Abadi, M., Gordon, A.D.: A calculus for cryptographic protocols: The spi calculus. Information and Computation 148(1), 1–70 (1999)
2. Alonso, G., Kuno, H., Casati, F., et al.: Web Services: Concepts, Architectures and Applications. Springer, Heidelberg (2003)
3. Bhargavan, K., et al.: A Semantics for Web Service Authentication. Theoretical Computer Science. 340(1), 102–153 (2005)
4. Bruni, R., Montanari, H.C., Montannari, U.: Theoretical foundation for compensation in flow composition languages. In: Proc. POPL 2005, 32nd ACM SIGPLAN-SIGACT symposium on principle of programming languages, pp. 209–220. ACM, New York (2004)
5. Bruni, R., et al.: From Theory to Practice in Transactional Composition of Web Services. In: Bravetti, M., Kloul, L., Zavattaro, G. (eds.) Formal Techniques for Computer Systems and Business Processes. LNCS, vol. 3670, pp. 272–286. Springer, Heidelberg (2005)
6. Bulter, M.J., Ferreria, C.: A process compensation language. In: Grieskamp, W., Santen, T., Stoddart, B. (eds.) IFM 2000. LNCS, vol. 1945, pp. 61–76. Springer, Heidelberg (2000)
7. Bulter, M.J., Ferreria, C.: An Operational Semantics for StAC: a Lanuage for Modelling Long-Running Business Transactions. In: De Nicola, R., Ferrari, G.L., Meredith, G. (eds.) COORDINATION 2004. LNCS, vol. 2949, pp. 87–104. Springer, Heidelberg (2004)
8. Butler, M.J., Hoare, C.A.R., Ferreria, C.: A Trace Semantics for Long-Running Transactions. In: Abdallah, A.E., Jones, C.B., Sanders, J.W. (eds.) Communicating Sequential Processes. LNCS, vol. 3525, pp. 133–150. Springer, Heidelberg (2005)
9. Curbera, F., Goland, Y., Klein, J., et al.: Business Process Execution Language for Web Service (2003), http://www.siebei.com/bpel
10. Dijkstra, E.W.: A Discipline of Programming. Prentice-Hall, Englewood Cliffs (1976)
11. Gordon, A.D., et al.: Validating a Web Service Security Abstraction by Typing. Formal Aspect of Computing 17(3), 277–318 (2005)
12. Jifeng, H., Huibiao, Z., Geguang, P.: A model for BPEL-like languages. Frontiers of Computer Science in China 1(1), 9–20 (2007)
13. Hoare, C.A.R.: Communicating Sequential Language. Prentice Hall, Englewood Cliffs (1985)
14. Hoare, C.A.R., Jifeng, H.: Unifying theories of programming. Prentice Hall, Englewood Cliffs (1998)

15. Leymann, F.: Web Service Flow Language (WSFL1.0). IBM (2001)
16. Laneve, C., et al.: Web-pi at work. In: De Nicola, R., Sangiorgi, D. (eds.) TGC 2005. LNCS, vol. 3705, pp. 182–194. Springer, Heidelberg (2005)
17. Jing, L., Jifeng, H., Geguang, P.: Towards the Semantics for Web Services Choreography Description Language. In: Liu, Z., He, J. (eds.) ICFEM 2006. LNCS, vol. 4260, pp. 246–263. Springer, Heidelberg (2006)
18. Lucchi, R., Mazzara, M.: A Pi-calculus based semantics for WS-BPEL. Journal of Logic and Algebraic Programming (in press)
19. Milner, R.: Communication and Mobile System: the $\pi$-calculus. Cambridge University Press, Cambridge (1999)
20. Morris, J.M.: Non-deterministic expressions and predicate transformers. Information Processing Letters 61, 241–246 (1997)
21. Geguang, P., et al.: Theoretical Foundation of Scope-based Compensation Flow Language for Web Service. In: Ning, P., Qing, S., Li, N. (eds.) ICICS 2006. LNCS, vol. 4307, pp. 251–266. Springer, Heidelberg (2006)
22. Qiu, Z.Y., et al.: Semantics of BPEL4WS-Like Fault and Compensation Handling. In: Fitzgerald, J.A., Hayes, I.J., Tarlecki, A. (eds.) FM 2005. LNCS, vol. 3582, pp. 350–365. Springer, Heidelberg (2005)
23. Tarski, A.: A lattice-theoretical fixpoint theorem and its applications. Pacific Journal of Mathematics 5, 285–309 (1955)
24. Thatte, S.: XLANG: Web Service for Business Process Design. Microsoft, Redmond, Washington (2001)

# Deriving Specifications for Systems That Are Connected to the Physical World

Cliff B. Jones[1], Ian J. Hayes[2], and Michael A. Jackson[3]

[1] School of Computing Science,
Newcastle University, NE1 7RU, England
cliff.jones@ncl.ac.uk
[2] School of Information Technology and Electrical Engineering,
The University of Queensland, Brisbane, 4072, Australia
Ian.Hayes@itee.uq.edu.au
[3] 101 Hamilton Terrace, London NW8 9QY, England
jacksonma@acm.org

**Abstract.** Well understood methods exist for developing programs from formal specifications. Not only do such methods offer a precise check that certain sorts of deviations from their specifications are absent from implementations but they can also increase the productivity of the development process by careful use of layers of abstraction and refinement in design. These methods, however, presuppose a specification from which to begin the development. For tasks that are fully described in terms of the symbolic values within a machine, inventing a specification is not difficult but there is an increasing demand for systems in which programs interact with an external physical world. Here, the task of fixing the specification for the "silicon package" can be more challenging than the development itself. Such applications include control programs that attempt to bring about changes in the physical world via actuators and measure things in that external (to the silicon package) world via sensors. Furthermore, most systems of this class must tolerate failures in the physical components outside the computer: it then becomes even harder to achieve confidence that the specification is appropriate. This paper offers a systematic way to *derive* the specification of a control program. Furthermore, our approach leads to recording assumptions about the physical world. We also discuss separating the detection and management of faults from system operation in the absence of faults. This discussion is linked to the distinction between "normal" and "radical" design.

## 1 Introduction

This paper is intended to contribute to the formal development of computer systems by showing how one might obtain the starting specification for an important class of problems. The applications of interest are those whose function is best understood by describing behaviour in the physical world. Of course, computers can only receive and transmit signals; they cannot directly affect

C.B. Jones, Z. Liu, J. Woodcock (Eds.): Bjørner/Zhou Festschrift, LNCS 4700, pp. 364–390, 2007.

their external world. What connects the signals from (what we call) the "silicon package" to the physical world is a collection of sensors and actuators. We show how it is possible to derive a specification of the silicon package from a description of the desired behaviour of the overall system in the physical world. We do this *without* building a complete model of the external components; the method does however leave a clear record of assumptions which are crucial to safe deployment.

As computers become cheaper and smaller, they are increasingly connected to devices that sense and affect the physical world. Such applications of general purpose digital computers include "control programs". We do not restrict what we have to say to control programs in the narrow sense; but they furnish an important –and convenient– example of systems connected to the physical world.[1] The broad class of "open systems", which receive input from the physical world via sensors and influence it via actuators, is both large and important. Such open systems are often deployed in safety-critical environments.[2]

It is often difficult to develop the specification of an open system because the devices to which it is connected are themselves complex. The task of developing an appropriate specification is further complicated by the fact that the physical devices are subject to failure. We outline our approach to deriving formal specification of control systems and argue that it extends to more general open systems.[3]

Notice that the observations above affect any specification whether it is formal or informal. It is expected that –as with other formal methods– the ideas will inspire less formal approaches as well.

This paper develops the ideas presented in our earlier paper [HJJ03]. As there, our ideas are presented using the example of a controller for an irrigation sluice gate. Section 2 begins with the overall requirement for an ideally reliable sluice gate and develops a specification for its controller. In Section 3 we consider faults in the problem world. This is one area where our thinking has developed since the earlier paper. Another development is our more explicit recognition of the influence of the distinction between "normal" and "radical" design (see Section 3.8).

---

[1] In fact, we hope to extend (see Section 4.2) our area of application to systems where humans play a significant part. We have, for example, studied advisory systems, which are in some respects similar to the control systems we discuss here, but whose purpose is to provide advice to a human operator who makes final decisions.

[2] The most common argument used for replacing custom designed control hardware with software running in a general purpose processor is that flexibility for change is offered; it is not the intention here to argue whether or not the claims justify the use of software-controlled systems.

[3] There is a considerable literature on the development of control systems in particular (more generally, "hybrid systems"); representative publications are cited and compared in Section 4.1. It is important to understand that our interest here is in *obtaining* the initial specification of the silicon package. In some senses, the work on ISAC [Lan73,BB87] is a closer pre-cursor to our work than the research on developing reactive systems.

## 1.1    Outline of Our Method

Our method is conceptually simple: we ground our view of a desired computer system (or "silicon package") in the external physical world. This is the *problem world* whose phenomena are to be measured and influenced by the overall system. Having agreed with the customer the desired behaviour in the problem world, we record –and again obtain conformation of acceptability– assumptions about the physical components outside the computer itself. Only then do we *derive* the specification of the software to run in the computer.

To some developers, it may seem surprising to begin by discussing external physical phenomena most of which the pro          n influence only indirectly. Programs can only receive and send signals: they do not *directly* experience or control any other phenomena of the problem world. So our message can be stated negatively: the method discourages designers from jumping too early into writing a specification of the control software.

To use our method a number of technical issues have had to be settled. How these are resolved is discussed in Section 1.3.

As indicated, our proposed approach is first to specify the requirements of the overall system in the physical (problem) world; then to determine –and record as *rely conditions*– necessary assumptions about components of that physical world; and only then to derive a specification of the computational part of the control system (the symbolic world). See Figure 1.

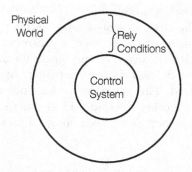

**Fig. 1.** A representation of the overall method

Most open systems must be designed to tolerate failures in the physical components — both in the sensors and actuators, and in other components not directly interfaced to the computer. This requirement for fault-tolerance complicates the problem of deriving a specification by introducing conflicting needs into the development process. On the one hand, it is necessary to understand and capture enough of the complexity of the possible problem world behaviours to accommodate a sufficient class of faults to achieve the desired degree of fault-tolerance. On the other hand, it is important to maintain clarity in the set of assumptions that underpins the specification of control program behaviour in normal fault-free operation. This conflict cannot be conveniently resolved in a unitary top down development process in which a single specification of problem properties is elaborated to accommodate both faulty and fault-free operation. Our approach is to treat faulty and fault-free operation as distinct *subproblems*, to be solved separately and subsequently combined. We address a number of issues relating to the treatment of faults in Section 3 and return to the problem of relating fault-tolerant behaviour to normal and radical design in Section 3.8. This is one area where our understanding has progressed substantially beyond the ideas in [HJJ03] but as we explain in Section 4.3 there is more work required in this area and we are looking at the connection with the "Time Bands" ideas in [BHBF05].

There are two key advantages of starting with a specification that describes problem world phenomena more generally (rather than restricting it to those phenomena which cross the interface to the computer as input or output signals):

- the problem world requirements are meaningful to the customer, and so are likely to be better understood; and
- the process forces the developer to articulate *and record* clear assumptions about the problem world properties, which must be checked before any deployment of the control software.

Of course, we make no claim that systems can be made perfectly safe; we aim only to offer a method that will make it easier to identify the assumptions about the physical components of the system and to ensure that they are formally documented.

There is a problem with this wider view: it would be unreasonable to ask system developers to build models of all of the physical components of a system. In particular, components which have extremely complex behaviour –for example, airflow over an aircraft wing– might defy adequate formal description. Our approach here is to record only the assumptions (which we record as *rely conditions*) on which the development is based. These assumptions will often hold for a range of possible devices, enlarging the range of environments in which the developed control software can be deployed.

It might be useful to contrast our approach with Dines Bjørner's notion of "domain modelling". In [Bjø06, Chapter 10], he uses formal specification techniques to describe the physical world in which the silicon package will be embedded. Our purpose is rather to see "how little can one say"; our rely-conditions provide a "separation of concerns" *without* modelling the whole of the physical system. Crucially, our approach does leave a record of assumptions which have been made. An instructive experiment would be to compare a fully worked out version of [Bjø06, Example 10.4] (which addresses RADAR inaccuracy) with our approach. It might well be the case that general properties of the domain are useful to build an overall picture but that our approach would put clearer bounds on the concerns relevant to specific systems.

## 1.2   A Micro Example

A simple illustration of the envisaged method can be given for a room heating system [MH91a]. We argue that one should not jump at once into a specification of the control program — stating what corrective action should follow when the value read from the temperature sensor indicates that some limit value has been exceeded. Instead one should first specify the desired relationship between the actual room temperature and the target temperature set on the control knob: this is the *requirement* in the problem world.

A control program cannot detect the actual temperature so a realisable specification must record, in rely conditions, the properties of those components which link the control system to the physical world: that is, the *assumptions* made about the accuracy of the sensors and about the causal chain connection between sending signals to the heating equipment and changes in the actual room temperature. Proceeding in this way is likely to pinpoint assumptions about the extremes and rate of change of external temperature. Once these assumptions have been recorded and authorised, it is possible to derive the specification of the control program.

Perhaps most importantly, the assumptions are recorded for anyone who is considering deploying the control system.

## 1.3   Technical Tools

In clarifying the understanding of a system, one essential tool is the use of *problem diagrams* [Jac00]. A problem diagram shows the customer's requirement, the problem world, the computer (which we refer to as *the machine*), and the interfaces among them. A problem diagram represents these elements explicitly and so helps to provide a firm basis both for exploring the problem scope and for identifying the parts of the problem world that must be specified and the phenomena that must be related by those specifications. A simple example of a problem diagram is given in Figure 3.

We are of the firm opinion that handling complex systems requires formal notation. We do not rehearse the arguments for formal methods here beyond saying that reasoning requires formal notation.

A number of methods exist for developing sequential programs from formal specifications; two which embrace the "posit and prove" idea are [Jon90,Abr96]. A posit and prove method identifies proof obligations to be discharged at each development step: if all such proof obligations are satisfied, one class of error has been excluded from the final program. Notice that we are not claiming that the system will perform, in some sense, perfectly. For one thing, any reasoning about the text of a program is done with respect to assumptions about faithful implementation of the assumed semantics. There are also the questions of "clean termination" discussed in [Sit74]. For the current concerns however, the crucial gap is that the specification (however formal) might not accord with the real needs of a system — proving that a program satisfies a specification in no way guarantees that the specification itself is perfect (cf. [Jon90, Postscript]). It is against this last doubt that the current paper tries to offer some way to gain reassurance.

Although such formal methods are not universally practised, their existence shows that a class of errors can be eliminated from program design. Methods which use a *posit and prove* approach are particularly useful because they combine the predisposition of an engineer to introduce decisions one at a time with the possibility to verify one design decision before moving on to base further work on that decision. Such approaches use the essential ideas of redundancy and diversity and thus minimise the amount of scrap and rework.

A development method that can scale up to deal with realistic problems must be *compositional* in the sense that the specification of a subsystem is a complete statement of its required properties. For sequential programs, various forms of precondition and postcondition specifications satisfy this requirement. For concurrent programs, the task of finding tractable compositional methods has proved more challenging; but even here, techniques like *rely and guarantee* specifications (see [Jon96, further references therein] and [MH92,BS01]) offer compositional methods.

It is worth emphasising the difference in nature between rely and guarantee conditions because it clarifies their use in our approach. Guarantee conditions are obligations on the code that is to be created: the program is obliged to behave in a certain way. Rely conditions give permission to the developer to ignore possible uses: the program is under no obligation if it is used in an environment in which the rely condition is not true. There is of course an exact correspondence here with preconditions and postconditions: the precondition on a square root function tells the developer that –since the input can be assumed to be positive– imaginary number results are outside the scope; but for positive numbers, the bounds on the accuracy of the result must be respected by any valid implementation.

Since, in general, a program cannot directly monitor or control all the phenomena of interest in the problem world, satisfaction of the customer's requirement must be achieved indirectly, relying on causal properties of the problem world. We therefore use rely and guarantee conditions in the following way. The machine and the problem world are related by mutual rely and guarantee conditions: each one guarantees to satisfy certain conditions provided that it can rely on the guarantees of its partner. On this basis we can prove that the parallel composition of the machine with the problem world satisfies the specification of the whole system. The rely and guarantee conditions remain explicit in the specification documents as a reminder and a warning: they must be checked for safe deployment.

Properties of a control system must, in general, be specified over time intervals: in particular, the time interval, and its subintervals, over which the system operates. In addition, properties may relate behaviour in one subinterval to behaviour in an adjoining interval. We follow the approach of explicitly quantifying over such intervals [MH91b,MH92] (the notation is similar to the Duration Calculus [CHR91]).

## 1.4  Fault Tolerance

Armed with the technical ideas of the previous section, it is possible to undertake the approach of deriving specifications of the silicon package from a description of the required behaviour of the overall system. This process is illustrated in Section 2.

The approach to describing fault-tolerant behaviour is less firm but a number of ideas are explored in Section 3. Our basic hope is to be able to formalise a notion of layered specifications in which one can for example state the behaviour desired in the absence of component failures (with one set of rely/guarantee predicates) separately from a description of (presumably) more restricted behaviour in the presence of faults. (There might of course be several layers of such fault-tolerance.) The motivation here is very like that for VDM's "error conditions" (see [Daw91]) but we discuss in Section 4.3 why the notion of changing from the well-behaved to the fault-tolerant phase is difficult (and the direction in which we are seeking a resolution of the difficulty.)

## 2   The Sluice Gate Example

The example considered in detail in this paper concerns a sluice gate (as introduced in [Jac00]) designed to control the flow of water in a farm irrigation channel. The gate is pictured in Figure 2; it consists of a barrier sliding in vertical guides and positioned across the flow of water in the irrigation channel. The barrier is raised and lowered by a reversible motor which drives a rack-and-pinion mechanism engaging with the guide at each side. When the barrier is fully raised it is open and the flow of water is unimpeded; when the barrier is fully down it is closed and the flow of water is blocked. The guides are equipped with stops that prevent the barrier from moving beyond the guide limits. There are top and bottom sensors which should be set on when the barrier is fully raised or fully down respectively.

The idea outlined in Section 1.1 is to write an initial specification based on a wide view of a *system*, including both the *machine* and the *problem world*. The machine is the computer, executing the control program to be developed. The problem world is that part of physical reality in which the problem resides and in which the effects of the system, once installed and set in operation, will be evaluated.

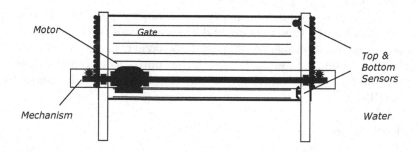

**Fig. 2.** A representation of a sluice gate

Drawing the boundaries of the problem world demands a judgment based on the responsibilities and the scope of authority of the customer for the system (we return to this topic in Section 2.1).

One view is that it is the customer's responsibilities that bound the effects to be evaluated in the problem world, while the customer's scope of authority bounds the freedom of the developers in aiming to achieve those effects.

The customer's requirement is that the gate should be *open* or *closed* according to a certain regime intended to ensure appropriate irrigation of the fields. The problem is to develop the controller that will impose this regime. The problem is depicted in the problem diagram in Figure 3. The two rectangles represent the two physical *domains* of this problem. One is the Control Machine, which is the computer executing the control program that we are to develop. It is marked with a double stripe; this indicates that it is the *machine domain* in the problem. The other is the Sluice Gate with its sensors and drive motor, the plain rectangle indicating that it is a *problem domain*, which in the software development we regard as given.[4]

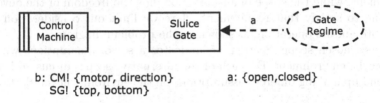

b: CM! {motor, direction}          a: {open,closed}
SG! {top, bottom}

**Fig. 3.** The machine, the problem world and the requirement

In this diagram there is only one problem domain; it is frequently the case that there are two or more, interacting with each other and with the machine domain. We refer to the problem domains collectively as the *problem world*, distinguishing them from the machine. The *requirement* is represented by the dashed ellipse; the requirement is to impose the desired regime on the gate. The *requirement phenomena* –that is the phenomena in terms of which the requirement is expressed– are represented by the arrow marked *a*, and listed in the text below the diagram. The *specification phenomena* –that is, the shared phenomena of the interaction between the machine and the problem world — are represented by the line marked *b*, and listed in the text below the diagram. The notations "CM!" and "SG!" indicate that the Control Machine and Sluice Gate respectively *control* the annotated phenomena: the machine can switch the *motor* on and off and set its *direction*, while the *top* and *bottom* sensors are controlled by the sluice gate. The requirement phenomenon is expressed in terms of periods in which the gate is either *open* or *closed*.

---

[4] It is important that we are concerned with *software* development, and that we regard the problem domain as *given*: that is, we are not free to replace the sluice gate equipment with different equipment better suited to our needs. We must develop a control program for the sluice gate with which our customer presents us.

## 2.1   The Scope of the Problem

By drawing the problem diagram as we have done we have identified the scope of
the problem: it is restricted to operation of the sluice gate. We might instead have
broadened the scope to include the irrigation channel. The diagram would then
have shown the Irrigation Channel as an additional domain of the problem world,
interacting with the Sluice Gate; and the requirement would have been expressed
in terms of a required flow of water in the channel. Any broadening or narrowing
of the problem world will, of course, be reflected in a change in the requirement
phenomena, and *vice versa*. A further broadening would include the fields and
their crops as a part of the problem world. Each of these expansions would give
rise to new assumptions (expressed as rely-conditions) about those things which
are beyond the control of the silicon package. Drawing the boundaries of the
problem world in this way demands an inescapable judgment: the whole universe
cannot be encompassed in a single problem. This judgment must be based on
an understanding of the responsibilities and scope of authority of the customer
for the system. The customer's responsibilities place an upper bound on the
requirement, while the scope of authority bounds the freedom of the developers
in aiming to satisfy that requirement. Here we limit our consideration to the
sluice gate and its operation, as shown in the problem diagram.

For the chosen scope, Section 2.5 indicates a set of assumptions which are
made on the environment. For each of the alternative scopes discussed here, one
would end up making different assumptions on the environment (cf. Section 4.2).

## 2.2   Formalising the Problem Requirement

The requirement is that –over the whole time of system operation– the time
when the gate is fully closed should be in a certain ratio to the time when it is
fully open.[5] Specifically, the ratio between the time the gate is in its *closed* : *open*
states should approximate 5 : 1 over any substantial period of time. Evidently
we must make this requirement more formal and more precise.

To formalise the requirement we begin by recognising that the gate is not
always open or closed: it can sometimes be in intermediate positions. Let the
variable *pos* denote the position of the gate. This variable is of type *Height*:

   *pos* : *Height*

where *Height* is defined as[6]

   *Height* $\widehat{=}$ CLOSED | NEITHER | OPEN.

The position is determined by the Sluice Gate, interacting with the Control
Machine. We initially focus on the trace of *pos* values over time. Hence, in

---

[5] Remember that this initial specification is about an idealised world in which fault-
tolerant issues are postponed.

[6] It is worth observing here that this definition –with only three distinct positions of
the gate– may prove to be too abstract. We return to this point in Section 2.5, when
we discuss the physical properties of the sluice gate.

predicates, *pos* will be treated as a function of time: that is, $pos(t)$ gives the position of the gate at time $t$. A *timed predicate* of the form $P$ **over** $I$ states that the predicate $P$ holds for every instant of time in the interval $I$. For example,

$$(pos = \text{OPEN}) \textbf{ over } I$$

is equivalent to $(\forall t : I \bullet pos(t) = \text{OPEN})$. The operator **over** binds more tightly than binary logical operators. The operator '$\#$' gives the size of an interval. The integral of a predicate over an interval $I$, such as $\int_I (pos = \text{OPEN})$, treats the predicate, $pos = \text{OPEN}$, as a function of time (because *pos* is a function of time); it treats a true value as 1 and a false value as 0 (as in the Duration Calculus [CHR91]). In short, the two integrals in the formalisation *SluiceGateRequirement* below give the total time in the interval $I$ for which the variable *pos* is equal to CLOSED and OPEN respectively. The notation $Interval(T)$ stands for the set of all contiguous finite non-empty intervals that are subsets of the time interval $T$. The parameter $T$ should be thought of as the time interval over which the system is operating.

Informally, it is stated above that the ratio of closed to open times should be "approximately 5 : 1". Specifying this precisely requires some care. One must remember to allow for the time the gate is in movement and thus in neither stable position. Furthermore there is a risk that the pattern is too rigidly fixed because all intervals of time are considered. The specification must obviously be agreed with the customer and it is likely that the most intuitive way to convey this is to have some reasonable period of several hours and to introduce specific numbers.[7] The notation $x \pm e$ stands for the set of times from $x - e$ to $x + e$. The range for the error bounds below are given as a fraction, ERROR, of the interval size. The constants MAX_OPEN and MAX_CLOSED allow for the end effects of the interval $I$ only containing part of an open/closed cycle. Suitable values for MAX_OPEN, MAX_CLOSED and ERROR might be 15 minutes, 75 minutes, and 0.05 (i.e. a 5% cumulative error).

$$
\begin{aligned}
&SluiceGateRequirement \; \widehat{=} \\
&\quad \lambda\, T : Interval(\,Time) \bullet \\
&\qquad \forall I : Interval(T) \bullet \#I \geq 6hours \Rightarrow \\
&\qquad\quad \textstyle\int_I (pos = \text{OPEN}) \in \frac{1}{6} * \#I \pm (\text{MAX\_OPEN} + \#I * \text{ERROR}) \land \\
&\qquad\quad \textstyle\int_I (pos = \text{CLOSED}) \in \frac{5}{6} * \#I \pm (\text{MAX\_CLOSED} + \#I * \text{ERROR})
\end{aligned}
$$

This requirement suffices for the discussion which follows but it is clear that some issues may arise at this point, demanding early resolution. In particular, the requirement describes a behaviour over time of the sluice gate, but the sluice gate may perhaps not be capable of this behaviour. For example, if the sluice gate position cannot change between OPEN and CLOSED without dwelling for 200 minutes in the NEITHER position, then the requirement will not be satisfiable. This issue clearly depends on the physical properties of the sluice gate and we return to this topic in Section 2.5.

---

[7] See Section 4 for an alternative approach using timebands.

## 2.3    Initial Combined System Specification

The specification of the whole system, consisting of the Control Machine and the Sluice Gate connected together and operating in parallel, is that it must satisfy the requirement above:

$$CMSGSystem \; \widehat{=} \; \textbf{system}$$
$$\textbf{output } pos : Height$$
$$\textbf{rely } true$$
$$\textbf{guar } SluiceGateRequirement$$

We regard the subject of each specification of this kind as a *system*. The system *CMSGSystem* specifies the requirement on the combined system. A system specification explicitly lists its inputs and outputs, any assumptions on which it relies about its environment and the conditions it guarantees to establish. In this case there are no assumptions and there are no inputs: the overall specification is concerned only with the gate position, which is an output.

Evidently, the combined system can satisfy its specification only if the Sluice Gate and the Control Machine satisfy appropriate conditions. In the case of the Control Machine, which is the *machine* in the problem diagram shown in Figure 3, our assumptions describe the properties with which the machine must be endowed by virtue of the software it will be executing. In the case of the Sluice Gate, by contrast, our specification describes the properties with which the sluice gate is assumed to be endowed by virtue of its physical construction. The description does not however attempt to describe everything that could be known about the gate in question; we attempt to determine a minimal set of assumptions in Section 2.5.

The assumptions on the Sluice Gate specification must be developed first; the specification of the Control Machine, which is to be built, will be derived from it. Even here there can be a degree of iteration in the development. The problem world may offer a rich set of properties from which the developer may be able to select different subsets as sufficient assumptions for developing the machine. In making this selection it may be reasonable to pay some attention to considerations of program specification and design.

## 2.4    The Shape of the Specification of the Control System

The next objective is to arrive at a specification of the control system. It would obviously be possible to jump straight to an outline *algorithm* which indicated, say, that each hour the control system should open the sluice gate; pause 9 minutes; then move the gate down; pause for about 45 minutes; etc. Any temptation to specify the control system in this way should be resisted. One argument is that many other patterns (e.g. a 5/23 minute pattern each half hour) would satisfy the user's requirements as documented.

The aim here is to derive an implicit specification of the control system from an understanding of the components. This identifies the assumptions clearly and ensures that they are recorded. Our approach is to look at the consequences of putting the onus for meeting the system specification on the control system. We could specify the Control Machine as a system:

$Controller \; \widehat{=}$ **system**
      **external** $pos : Height$
      **input** $top, bot :$ Boolean
      **output** $motor :$ ON | OFF, $dir :$ UP | DOWN
      **rely** ??
      **guar** $SluiceGateRequirement$

It is of course clear that the *Controller* cannot achieve this guarantee condition unless its developer can make assumptions: to give just one example, the *Controller* cannot directly cause *pos* to change because it is in the physical world.

The next section explores assumptions which need to be made to ensure that the above outline can be completed to a realisable specification.

### 2.5 Assumptions About the Problem World

The Control Machine's inputs are the states of the sensors, its outputs are signals to the motor controls. To achieve the overall specification, the control program relies on the sensors and the motor working correctly (the question of which sorts of faults can be tolerated is considered in Section 3). The first set of assumptions needs to relate *pos* being CLOSED or OPEN with the inputs to the *Controller* (sensor values *top* and *bot*).

At the interface $b$ in Figure 3, the Sluice Gate controls the states of the sensors *top* and *bot*, while the Control Machine can set the motor direction control, *dir*, to either UP or DOWN and can switch the motor by setting *motor* to either ON or OFF. We describe the phenomena of the interface more precisely as follows:

    *Control Machine* ! {$dir :$ UP | DOWN; *motor* : ON | OFF}
    *Sluice Gate* ! {$top, bot :$ Boolean}

The states of the two sensors, *top* and *bot*, can be formalised as Boolean functions of time. The sensors detect when the gate is OPEN (*top*) or CLOSED (*bot*). We formalise this property in the following definition *SensorProp*. In the definition, $T$ is the whole time interval over which the system operates.

$SensorProp \; \widehat{=}$
    $\lambda \, T : Interval(Time) \; \bullet$
        $(((pos = \text{OPEN}) \Leftrightarrow top) \wedge ((pos = \text{CLOSED}) \Leftrightarrow bot))$ **over** $T$

As shown in Figure 2, the sluice gate is driven by a motor that raises or lowers the gate through a pair of mechanisms. At the interface $b$, the Control Machine (see Figure 3) can send signals that are intended to switch the motor on or off, and can set the *dir* signal. To achieve our specification we need to make assumptions about what changes arise in the problem world when these signals are sent.

To capture these assumptions about the motor's effect on the gate, we begin by introducing some derived properties that indicate when the gate is being *lifted* or *lowered* by the motor and when the gate is *moved*. These derived properties will form our vocabulary for discussing motor properties. They can be used throughout the specification to simplify its presentation. The property that the gate is *moved* includes the time MOTOR_DECEL over which it is decelerated when the motor is turned off.

$$lifted \;\widehat{=}\; \lambda\, t : Time \bullet motor(t) = \text{ON} \wedge dir(t) = \text{UP}$$
$$lowered \;\widehat{=}\; \lambda\, t : Time \bullet motor(t) = \text{ON} \wedge dir(t) = \text{DOWN}$$
$$moved \;\widehat{=}\; \lambda\, t : Time \bullet (\exists\, J : Interval(Time) \bullet$$
$$sup(J) = t \wedge \#J \leq \text{MOTOR\_DECEL} \wedge (motor = \text{ON})\ \textbf{in}\ J)$$

The supremum, $sup(J)$, of a set of times $J$ is the least upper bound of $J$, and the infimum, $inf(J)$, is the greatest lower bound. A predicate, $P$, holds within a set of times $J$, written $P$ **in** $J$, if there exists a time within $J$ at which $P$ holds. We also introduce an ordering, *lower*, on the gate position and its reflexive transitive closure, *lower\**. This allows us to express the property that the gate is either rising (monotonically upwards) or falling (monotonically downwards).

$$lower \;\widehat{=}\; \{\text{CLOSED} \mapsto \text{NEITHER}, \text{NEITHER} \mapsto \text{OPEN}\}$$
$$monotonic\_up \;\widehat{=}\; \lambda\, I : Interval(Time) \bullet$$
$$\forall\, t_1, t_2 : I \bullet t_1 \leq t_2 \Rightarrow lower^*(pos(t_1), pos(t_2))$$
$$monotonic\_down \;\widehat{=}\; \lambda\, I : Interval(Time) \bullet$$
$$\forall\, t_1, t_2 : I \bullet t_1 \leq t_2 \Rightarrow lower^*(pos(t_2), pos(t_1))$$

If the motor has been on in the direction UP for at least some constant UPTIME, the gate will have reached the open position. A similar condition applies for downward travel.[8] The gate remains stationary after the motor has been turned off for time MOTOR_DECEL. After the motor has been turned off the gate can only continue its travel in the direction in which it was going (for at most MOTOR_DECEL). In the definition, an interval $I$ adjoins an interval $J$, written $I$ **adjoins** $J$, if the supremum of $I$ is equal to the infimum of $J$, i.e. $sup(I) = inf(J)$. Infix relations, such as **adjoins**, bind more tightly than binary logical operators.

$$MotorOperation \;\widehat{=}\; \lambda\, T : Interval(Time) \bullet$$
$$\forall\, I : Interval(T) \bullet$$
$$((lifted \wedge pos \neq \text{OPEN})\ \textbf{over}\ I \Rightarrow \#I \leq \text{UPTIME}) \wedge$$
$$((lowered \wedge pos \neq \text{CLOSED})\ \textbf{over}\ I \Rightarrow \#I \leq \text{DOWNTIME}) \wedge$$
$$(((\neg\ moved)\ \textbf{over}\ I) \Rightarrow (\exists\, p : Height \bullet (pos = p)\ \textbf{over}\ I))$$
$$\wedge$$
$$\forall\, I, J : Interval(T) \bullet I\ \textbf{adjoins}\ J \Rightarrow$$
$$(lifted\ \textbf{over}\ I \wedge (motor = \text{OFF})\ \textbf{over}\ J \Rightarrow$$
$$monotonic\_up(I \cup J))$$
$$(lowered\ \textbf{over}\ I \wedge (motor = \text{OFF})\ \textbf{over}\ J \Rightarrow$$
$$monotonic\_down(I \cup J))$$

---

[8] Because we chose to describe *pos* as having only three values, rather than giving it a numeric value, we now naturally describe the gate's speed of movement only in terms of the travel time between the extreme positions.

At this point we can fill in the rely condition in the specification outlined in Section 2.4.

$Controller \mathrel{\widehat{=}}$ **system**
    **external** $pos$ : $Height$
    **input** $top, bot$ : Boolean
    **output** $motor$ : ON | OFF, $dir$ : UP | DOWN
    **rely** $SensorProp \wedge MotorOperation$
    **guar** $SluiceGateRequirement$

Both $SensorProp$ and $MotorOperation$ are predicates parameterised by the time interval over which the system operates; in $SensorProp \wedge MotorOperation$ the operator "$\wedge$" is a lifted conjunction, that is, it means

$$\lambda\, T : Interval(Time) \bullet SensorProp(T) \wedge MotorOperation(T)$$

However, this specification is still not complete because we need to review a general concern (that of assumptions on equipment to avoid breakage); we have used this to illustrate the symmetric way in which assumptions are made.

## 2.6 Avoiding Breakage

The properties that are important in the problem world are not yet complete. The sluice gate does exhibit the properties we have described here, but only if certain restrictions are observed on its operation. In a control problem such as we are discussing here, it is necessary to ensure that the machine itself does not cause failure of any part of the problem domain by ignoring known restrictions on its use. This is the *breakage concern* of [Jac00]. For example, checking the motor equipment manual, we might learn that the motor will be damaged if it is switched between directions without being brought to rest in between: for any period over which the gate is moved, the direction must be constant. Recall that the definition of *moved* above includes periods when the motor is on as well as periods when it has been on recently (within MOTOR_DECEL).

$MotorDirectionStable \mathrel{\widehat{=}} \lambda\, T : Interval(Time) \bullet$
  $\forall I : Interval(T) \bullet$
    $(moved \textbf{ over } I \Rightarrow ((dir = \text{UP}) \textbf{ over } I \vee (dir = \text{DOWN}) \textbf{ over } I))$

Note that, because this condition involves only the variables $motor$ and $dir$, the controller can satisfy this requirement without relying on any properties of the sluice gate. Hence the rely condition associated with this condition is just *true*. By requiring that the controller always maintain this property, even if the sluice gate is not working correctly, we ensure the controller won't break the motor by switching direction while the motor is turned on or shortly after a period where it has been on. Of course if the sluice gate is broken in a manner that means the the motor is actually running even when turned off by the controller, the change of direction can still damage the motor/gears.

A second restriction applies when the motor has driven the gate to the open or closed position. It must then be switched off soon enough to avoid straining the motor and mechanism when the gate reaches the end of its vertical travel and further movement is impossible; MOTOR_LIMIT is the maximum time the motor can be on with the direction UP (DOWN) when the gate has reached the OPEN (CLOSED) position.

$$
\begin{aligned}
MotorOffAtLimit \;\widehat{=}\; &\lambda\, T : Interval(\,Time) \;\bullet \\
&\forall\, I : Interval(\,T) \;\bullet \\
&\quad ((pos = \text{OPEN}) \;\textbf{over}\; I \Rightarrow \\
&\qquad \textstyle\int_I (motor = \text{ON} \wedge dir = \text{UP}) \le \text{MOTOR\_LIMIT}) \;\wedge \\
&\quad ((pos = \text{CLOSED}) \;\textbf{over}\; I \Rightarrow \\
&\qquad \textstyle\int_I (motor = \text{ON} \wedge dir = \text{DOWN}) \le \text{MOTOR\_LIMIT})
\end{aligned}
$$

As this condition refers to the gate position ($pos$), the controller needs to assume that the sensors are operating correctly in order to satisfy this requirement. Hence the rely condition associated with this condition is $SensorProp$.

Only if it respects both $MotorDirectionStable$ and $MotorOffAtLimit$ can the Control machine rely on the behaviour described in $MotorOperation$.

## 2.7   Derived Specification of the Control Machine

As we made clear in Section 2.4, it is the purpose of the Control Machine to satisfy $SluiceGateRequirement$; and this is, essentially, its specification. The previous two sections have recorded enough about the problem world to enable us to write a realisable specification.

We can specify the Control Machine as a system:

$$
\begin{aligned}
Controller1 \;\widehat{=}\; &\textbf{system} \\
&\textbf{external}\; pos : Height \\
&\textbf{input}\; top,\, bot : \text{Boolean} \\
&\textbf{output}\; motor : \text{ON} \mid \text{OFF},\, dir : \text{UP} \mid \text{DOWN} \\
&\textbf{rely}\; SensorProp \wedge MotorOperation \\
&\textbf{guar}\; SluiceGateRequirement \\
&\textbf{rely}\; SensorProp \\
&\textbf{guar}\; MotorOffAtLimit \\
&\textbf{rely}\; true \\
&\textbf{guar}\; MotorDirectionStable
\end{aligned}
$$

An implementation of $Controller1$ is required to simultaneously satisfy all three rely/guarantee pairs. If the sluice gate satisfies both $SensorProp$ and $MotorOperation$ then the controller must ensure $SluiceGateRequirement$ but, even if the sluice gate does not satisfy these properties, the controller must always ensure $MotorDirectionStable$ and it must ensure $MotorOffAtLimit$ while $SensorProp$ holds, even if $MotorOperation$ doesn't hold.

The use of separate pairs of rely/guarantee conditions is a change from our earlier paper [HJJ03] in which there was a single rely/guarantee pair with the rely and guarantee consisting of the conjunction of the above relies and the conjunction of the above guarantees, respectively. This is a subtle but significant difference in approach, especially when specifying safety-critical systems. Wherever possible, the controller should avoid unsafe modes of operating the equipment, regardless of whether the equipment is working correctly. In some cases (e.g. *MotorDirectionStable*) this is possible irrespective of the behaviour of the equipment, while in other cases (e.g. *MotorOffAtLimit*) the rely condition to ensure safe operation may be weaker than that required for normal operation. Overall the new approach leads to a stronger and safer specification of the controller.

## 2.8   Taking Stock

At this stage one could implement the above controller specification, provided the equipment satisfies the rely conditions. It is important to note that the specification is still an *implicit* specification: it does not give an explicit algorithm to be executed by the Control Machine but leaves the programmer to devise an algorithm that will satisfy the specification. We consider this an important characteristic of the specification, retaining all the well-known advantages of implicit over explicit specification. In *MotorOperation*, *MotorOffAtLimit* and *MotorDirectionStable* the specification embodies just those problem domain properties on which we expect the programmer to rely in the further refinement to a program text of the Control Machine. A control program derived from this specification could be used with a different sluice gate, provided only that this different sluice gate offered the same interface to the Control Machine and exhibited the physical properties specified in *MotorOperation*, *MotorOffAtLimit* and *MotorDirectionStable*.

To make the observation clear, there is nothing above which prevents connecting the signals going out from the *control* program to indicator lights to which a human operator reacts to achieve the gate adjustments by manually moving the gate; the operator would finally push the *top* button when the alloted task was complete. Perhaps less fancifully, the *control* program could be connected to a simulator which fully exercised its function in a world without sluice gates (in this case *pos* has to be reinterpreted as the simulated position).

In developing our specification we have made and exploited more assumptions than are embodied in its final form *Controller1*. We know more, so to speak, about the problem world than we have chosen to convey to the programmer. One example is the whole set of assumptions on which we based our original problem domain specification *MotorOperation*. In effect, we have assumed that the sluice gate mechanism is sufficiently reliable (subject to *MotorOffAtLimit* and *MotorDirectionStable*) to satisfy *SensorProp* and *MotorOperation*, and hence to allow *SluiceGateRequirement* to be satisfied by the Control Machine we have finally specified. Because the sluice gate is a physical device that may fail, such an assumption would be unwise.

# 3  Addressing Component Failures

In a critical system –or any system in which it is important to limit the possible damage to the equipment– all assumptions must be systematically questioned. Potential faults must be identified and the software must deal with them appropriately.

It is pointed out in Section 1.4 that it is desirable to layer a specification by separating the behaviour under different sets of assumptions: the most optimistic (no faults in external components) through to minimal behaviour which might involve setting off alarms.

One way to undertake such a division is to treat the separate systems as different problems and to look at their combination with programming combinators. In the world of "normal design" such decompositions might be standard and the choice of components be so accepted that one could indeed just use the techniques presented so far to specify the individual problems.

Computer technology has however developed so fast that many problems fall into the "radical design" category. We should in any case like to be *able* to deduce properties of an overall system. The source of the difficulty with which we have struggled is the continuous time specifications which our applications have forced us to employ. It is not difficult to describe normal behaviour as in Section 2; describing fault-tolerant behaviour uses similar notation plus the ideas in this section. The key issue is how to describe the handover between the normal and fault-tolerant phases of operation. Our ideas for this will appear elsewhere but an indication of the approach is given in Section 4.3.

## 3.1  Faults in the Sluice Gate System

In our treatment of the sluice gate example so far, we have focused on the situation where all of the (physical) components operate faultlessly. We now consider what sorts of issues arise when trying to cope with component failure.

In the sluice gate problem, components like sensors can fail; for example, they can become stuck false or they can become stuck true. Moreover, the motor could burn out and no longer be able to move the gate when power is applied to it. Such component failures are faults in the larger system and a useful control program will limit their impact even if it cannot meet the original requirements.

In [Jac00] this obligation is called the *reliability concern*. If a faulty component is detected, the Control Machine should, perhaps, switch off the motor and turn on an alarm to indicate that the system needs attention from the maintenance engineer and that the irrigation requirement is no longer being satisfied.

It will become clear that it is more difficult to maintain our isolation from details of the physical world when we examine fault-tolerance but we will examine ways in which such considerations can be brought in gradually.

It would be possible to follow the method described above with weaker assumptions about the physical components (and additional requirements with respect to alarms) but the resulting specification might become opaque because it would lack structure. One would like to achieve a structure which preserved the distinction between normal and abnormal operation in the specification. Sections 3.2–3.6 explore various forms of fault-tolerant behaviour and how it might be specified; we discuss the problems of structuring in Section 3.7 but concede that further research is required here; the question of implementation is touched on in Section 4.3.

## 3.2  Making the System More Robust

It is clear that one needs to understand more about the external equipment in order to discuss fault tolerance than to describe healthy behaviour; but it is also advantageous to identify any general tactics which come from a formal analysis rather than specific instances. This section and the next indicate two ideas which appear to work in general.

It is known from work on the (formal) specification of sequential (closed) programs that a system can be made more "robust" by widening its precondition; the same holds, *mutatis mutandis*, for the weakening of rely conditions. Just as with widened preconditions, the process of making a program more robust might result in different obligations.

Returning our attention to the sluice gate example, the case of not getting an expected signal that a sensor has become *true* after the expected traversal time fits the category of something suggested by looking at *MotorOperation* (cf. Section 2.5). But there are several physical problems that might give rise to this rely condition not being satisfied:

- the sensor in question becomes stuck false and fails to signal the arrival of the gate at its extremity;
- the gate becomes jammed (perhaps –in the downward direction– because a log has become wedged under it); or
- the motor has burned out and is not driving the gate; or
- a blown fuse is preventing power getting to the motor;
- etc.

Given the paucity of the equipment envisaged in the sluice gate system of Section 2, these different physical problems cannot be distinguished. This is precisely why one might wish to add new equipment.

For brevity we do not present the full formalisation of the conditions under which the sluice-gate/sensors/motor is faulty. Given suitable declarations of duration constants for the criteria of fault-free operation in the domain we obtain a definition of the faulty state. Here we consider the situations where the gate fails to rise (fall) when driven up (down). Recognition of the state is triggered by an interval $J$ in which a fault condition is detected.

$$
\begin{aligned}
Faulty\_GSM \triangleq{}& \lambda\, J : Interval(\,Time) \bullet \\
& \exists\, I : Interval(\,Time) \bullet I \text{ \bf adjoins } J \land \\
& \begin{pmatrix} (motor = \text{ON}) \text{ \bf over } I \land (dir = \text{UP}) \text{ \bf over } (I \cup J) \land \\ \#I > \text{HEALTHY\_RISE\_TIME} \land (\lnot\, top) \text{ \bf over } J \end{pmatrix} \lor \\
& \begin{pmatrix} (motor = \text{ON}) \text{ \bf over } I \land (dir = \text{DOWN}) \text{ \bf over } (I \cup J) \land \\ \#I > \text{HEALTHY\_FALL\_TIME} \land (\lnot\, bot) \text{ \bf over } J \end{pmatrix}
\end{aligned}
$$

Here HEALTHY_RISE_TIME (HEALTHY_FALL_TIME) represents the maximum time that the sluice should take to rise (fall). We require that a healthy sluice gate should satisfy the condition *MotorOperation* given in Section 2.5, and hence, for example, that HEALTHY_RISE_TIME < UPTIME. The choice of the constant HEALTHY_RISE_TIME may depend on the particular equipment being used, whereas UPTIME is a requirement on any equipment.

The general point here is that one class of potential enhancements toward a fault-tolerant system can be motivated by a formal analysis of the idealised specification. Systematically looking at rely conditions to see what behaviour might be achieved when clauses fail looks like a useful heuristic for developing specifications of fault-tolerant systems.

### 3.3   New Equipment/Requirements

In many cases, fault spotting and warning will be associated with extra equipment. Such new equipment clearly changes the problem and requires a new problem diagram and new requirements. In the sluice gate system, one could for example consider adding a temperature sensor to the motor. This would require a revision of the problem diagram in Figure 3 and a description of what would constitute "overheat" and the action required;[9] this would probably involve signalling an alarm.

For the purposes of this paper, we stick to our resolve that no such new sensors are available and confine the discussion to what can be done with the existing equipment.

### 3.4   Looking for "Drift"

The idea of finding "patterns" for extensions to the specification for a system by formal means without having to delve into details of the external equipment is attractive because it can lead to heuristics which apply to a class of problems. Another idea which works on the sluice gate example and appears to be general is to look for "drift" toward unacceptable behaviour.

For the sluice gate, for example, if the time to raise the gate is getting longer on each use, this might suggest that the moment is approaching (but has not yet arrived) when the rely condition will not be satisfied. Physically, some malfunction is getting closer in time and a warning could be issued. Care should however be exercised in distinguishing cyclic patterns (e.g. the grease getting more viscous in lower night-time temperatures) from long-term decay. We do not present the formulae for this example.

### 3.5   Looking at the External Equipment

Just formal analysis of the specification is not sufficient for locating problems with the equipment. One also needs to analyse the way the equipment operates. Examples are:

---

[9] See also the discussion of transience in Section 3.6.

- it is clear from understanding its function that the state of the *bottom* sensor should become false after the motor has been set to drive the gate upward for some (short) period of time;
- again from the physical components, one can see that the state of the target sensor should not become *true* too quickly after starting a traversal in the direction of the target sensor from the opposite extreme.

Such cases are extra requirements and give rise to new specifications. One would want to ask what reaction is expected (and this would likely involve extra alarms — see Section 3.3). It would also be necessary to think about how far one would go and different answers are likely in the sluice gate system and a nuclear reactor protection system.[10] The objective of this section is just to make the point that some forms of fault tolerance can only be sorted out by looking at the physical environment.

To give one example in formulae, consider raising a warning if the gate is slow leaving the closed position or the bottom sensor is faulty.

$Slow\_Leaving\_Closed \mathrel{\widehat{=}} \lambda I : Interval(\mathit{Time}) \bullet$
$\qquad (\mathit{lifted} \wedge \mathit{bot}) \textbf{ over } I \wedge \#I > \text{RISE\_DEPART\_TIME}$

## 3.6   Transient Errors

There is another generic question which has come up in our study of fault-tolerant behaviour and that is *transience*. Since there is a useful way of specifying such issues, it is worth describing it here. We take as a representative example, from the sluice gate system, the issue of checking that "both sensors should not be on simultaneously". If this situation occurred for an extremely short period of time (and then rectified itself), a control program *might* sense it and be in a position to set whatever alarm was required to be triggered. Such transient errors do occur within physical systems and, if the period of time is extremely short, the execution cycle for checking might well fail to detect the event. There will, however, be a notion (in any particular case) of a problem becoming a "hard fault" if it has persisted for at least some stated period of time. In this case, one would presumably require that the control program detect the situation. Thus we might say

$(\forall \mathit{long} : Interval(T) \bullet$
$\qquad \#\mathit{long} \geq \text{RESPONSE} \wedge Faulty\_GSM(\mathit{long}) \Rightarrow$
$\qquad\qquad (\forall I : Interval(T) \bullet sup(\mathit{long}) \leq inf(I) \Rightarrow ErrorIndicated(I)))$

but prevent this being met by always turning on the error indication by adding

$\forall I : Interval(T) \bullet$
$\quad ErrorIndicated(I) \Rightarrow$
$\qquad (\exists \mathit{short} : Interval(\mathit{Time}) \bullet sup(\mathit{short}) \leq inf(I) \wedge$
$\qquad\qquad\qquad\qquad\qquad\qquad Faulty\_GSM(\mathit{short}))$

---

[10] It was precisely the worry about abstraction levels that discouraged one of the authors from publishing earlier work on rely conditions for ISAT [SW89].

In fact, the question of transience is even more delicate because the same reasoning that causes us to recognise transience as an issue means that "simultaneous" actually means "within a small time interval". It is issues like these which have prompted the second author of this paper to consider "time bands" [BHBF05] — see further discussion in Section 4.3.

## 3.7  Combining Specifications

In [Jac00], the reliability concern is normally handled by introducing new subproblems. The way in which such subproblems can be specified is indicated in Sections 3.3–3.6 and within "normal design" one might use a standard pattern for combining solutions to the subproblems. Thus the notation described in Section 2 would suffice. But one would also wish to draw conclusions about combinations of machine descriptions. In the same spirit, there are issues concerning "phases" of operation (one example of which is the special problems that arise during system initialisation) which prompt us to want to reason about combinations of machine descriptions.

Thus the desire to specify a fault-tolerant system in a structured way necessitates a semantics for combinators over machine specifications. This applies even if we consider the problem of detecting faults as a separate issue from the "healthy" behaviour. Consider a single machine description and recall the comment in Section 1.2 about the conceptual distinction between rely and guarantee conditions (the former are to be viewed as permissions to the designer to ignore certain potential deployments; the latter are obligations on the code created by the designer). We should not therefore expect to find code in the program developed from *this specification* that will check on the truth of the rely condition. Instead, the created program must not be deployed in contexts where the rely condition is not satisfied. We are then obliged either to use *Controller*1 only in situations where its inputs satisfy the rely condition or, perhaps, to ignore its outputs where they do not.

It is however clear that, if we wish to *detect* faults, there might have to be code in another subproblem which monitors the rely condition. The argument in Section 3.2 is that the closer the rely condition of an overall system can be made to *true* the more robust a system will be. Furthermore, the extra code that is required is more complicated than the case with a simple precondition where one only needs check a parameter: the truth of a rely condition can only be determined over a period of time. It is the need to combine machines (developed with simple rely conditions) with machines which monitor for a healthy environment that points to the need to be able to reason about combinations of machine descriptions and this introduces some technical issues which require further research (the authors are working on a further paper on this topic).

## 3.8  Normal and Radical Design

An aspect of system development that is less often discussed than it should be is what Vincenti [Vin90] calls *normal design*. Normal design is what an engineer does when designing a product for which there are well established standards and norms, both in the design process and in the product's structure and implementation. In Vincenti's words:

> ... the engineer knows at the outset how the device in question works, what are its customary features, and that, if properly designed along such lines, it has a good likelihood of accomplishing the desired task.

Normal design is contrasted with *radical design*, in which:

> ... how the device should be arranged or even how it works is largely unknown. The designer has never seen such a device before and has no presumption of success. The problem is to design something that will function well enough to warrant further development.

Normal design is specialised to each class of system, or product, or device, and evolves over a long period in a community of designers or engineers who specialise in the class in question. The design of cars, for example, has evolved over 120 years since Karl Benz's first model of 1886. Many features have now become standard that were unknown and even unimaginable to Benz: front wheel brakes, unitary body, and automatic gearbox are just three of a huge number of features that make modern cars safe, convenient, and reliable. Normal design allows such inventions to be evaluated by experience, and the results of experience to be shared and exploited by all members of the particular design community.

Even more important is the effect of a normal design discipline on less obvious aspects of development. Specification of any system or product is inevitably partial, even for a product as small as an integer function. Specifying the function value in terms of its arguments may be straightforward, but this specifies only the abstraction. In constructing the real program to satisfy the abstraction, a perverse programmer can easily frustrate the specifier's intentions: by devising a novel algorithm that causes arithmetic overflow in an intermediate result; by using a memo-style design that can demand an impossibly large amount of storage; by starting a new thread; by gratuitously accessing the web; and in many other ways. Normal design excludes such perverse choices, because it allows the specification of a normal device or product to imply an additional set of unstated conditions.

For a software-intensive system, where the computer interacts with the physical world, the importance of normal design is even greater. The physical world has an unbounded capacity for unexpected failures, and only experience can teach which failures are more likely, and therefore more necessary to handle. For example, Section 3 discussed the treatment of certain equipment faults, and pointed out that many faults demand not only an analysis of the rely-condition of fault-free operation, but also a careful examination of the equipment itself and of the many ways in which it can fail.

The impact of normal design –or, rather, its lack– can be seen also in the formalisation of the *SluiceGateRequirement*. The informally stated requirement was that the gate should be closed for approximately five sixths of the time over any substantial period. The formalisation makes this precise in a certain sense.

It states a necessary condition for acceptability of the developed system, but inevitably omits other important conditions that are left implicit. For example, the gate should be opened and closed often enough to ensure that the humidity gradient in the irrigated soil is reasonably smooth, but seldom enough to avoid unnecessary wear and tear in the equipment. In the absence of a normal design discipline it is not easy to make these judgments at the outset of development. The "posit and prove" approach, mentioned earlier in connection with program development to meet formal specifications, applies equally to system development to meet implicit criteria of acceptability.

The relationship of the non-formal aspects of normal design disciplines to the formal development of software-intensive systems is a topic that merits further investigation. The dependability that we seek for critical systems must be a product of their marriage, not of either one alone, divorced from the other.

## 4    Conclusions

This section looks at what remains to be done and compares our approach to related publications.

### 4.1    Related Research

There are many excellent papers on notations for writing specifications of "hybrid" or "reactive systems" and a considerable literature on development from such specifications. Here we list a short but representative sample before contrasting with our objectives [LL95,SR96,Hoo91,CZ97,BS01].

As is mentioned above, what distinguishes our objectives from most of this line of research is that we are interested in *deriving* the initial specification of the "silicon package". In fact, one of the earliest reactions against just starting with a specification was when one of the authors heard Anders Ravn present the ProCoS Boiler example: a treatment more in our style is available as [Col06]. Another example which has been influential because it has been tackled in many notations is the "Production Cell" (cf. [LL95]): again, our approach to this problem takes a wider view; in particular we seek to distinguish more clearly –than in for example [MC00]– the assumptions on the equipment and the requirements on the control program.

Closer in the spirit of our approach are the papers by Fred Schneider and colleagues [MSB91,FS94a,FS94b]; these publications have also considered systems which are similar to those that we hope to encompass. We find their approach interesting and somewhat different from ours. One point of difference is that they place variables corresponding to physical phenomena in the program state so that they can use a (combined) state invariant where we use rely conditions. They can then play the real world forward in time by showing the rates of change. Our task has been to look at ways of "deriving" specifications of control systems. Their operations need to discuss how "reality" changes; our rely conditions might provide a more natural description. Similar comments on the overall direction could be applied to Parnas's "Four Variable model" [PM95].

## 4.2   How General Is Our Approach?

One way to look at the generality of the idea of starting with a description of the required phenomena and then deriving the specification of the inner system is to reconsider the scope of the sluice gate system.

Sections 2 and 3 above focus on a requirement restricted to the gate position. This view could be broadened:

- If the requirement were to deliver a certain flow of water, we would have to make assumptions about the available water flow.[11]
- A yet wider system might be concerned with the humidity of the soil in the fields being irrigated, leading to assumptions about the weather, plant physiology and the effects of irrigation.
- A requirement to maximise farm profits would lead to assumptions about a wide range of factors including prices and even (in Europe) the Common Agricultural Policy.

The responsibilities and authority of the customer were both assumed to be bounded by the sluice gate itself and its stipulated operation. The effects of the irrigation schedule on the crops and and the farm profits were firmly outside our scope.[12] But the ability to force attention on the assumptions being made appears to be a major advantage of our method.

The Sluice Gate problem has proved to be stimulating and we have tried to expose the issues it has thrown up rather than modify the problem to fit our evolving method. For example, the third author has on occasions played the role of our customer and has always refused requests to acquire new sensors to simplify the task of specifying and implementing the system.

There are, of course, many other dependability issues which could be considered. Examples include: the power supply to the motor; the maximum load of the motor; and the running state revolutions per minute. While we believe that such points do not bring in fundamentally different technical requirements, they should be categorised as an indication that nothing has been hidden.

Outside the sluice gate system we (and others) have already experimented with this technique on other examples (e.g. [Col06]). The "Dependability IRC" project (see www.dirc.org.uk) considers computer-based systems whose dependability relies critically on human (as well as the mechanical) components. A first indication of extensions in this direction was given by one of the current authors in an invited talk to the DSVIS-05 event in July 2005.

One of the referees of [HJJ03] raised the interesting point of the "evolvability" of a system. The authors agree that this is an important issue; evolution is in fact a major strand of work within the Dependability IRC (see [BGJ06, Chapter 3]).

---

[11] This would, furthermore, force us to record assumptions about the flow of water while the gate is moving.

[12] There is also a technical argument for narrowing, rather than widening, the scope of the system to be considered: one might question any set of assumptions which referred to widely disparate phenomena.

In the current paper, the reliance on rely conditions about equipment, rather than a detailed description of the characteristics of particular equipment allows for the replacement of the equipment, provided the new equipment meets the rely conditions. On the other hand, monitoring of the healthiness of the equipment may well (and probably should) be dependent on the detailed characteristics of the particular equipment. By factoring out this aspect in the specification, the specification can be more easily revised. A study of the contribution of other research on "evolvability" to the issues of this paper will be undertaken in the future. We wonder if there might be a way of using layers of rely conditions where one set expresses things whose change would be disastrous while another level is "anticipated evolutions".

### 4.3 Further Developments

Our research contributes to the creation of specifications but it is informative to look at how such specifications might be implemented. We know from sequential programs that combining clauses of postconditions with *and* and *not* logical operators provides a valuable way of recording "what" is required without saying "how" it should be done. For example, the postcondition for a *Sort* routine can be elegantly expressed as a conjunction of *InputPermutation* and *Ordered*. From the discussion in Section 3.7 above, it looks as though one needs the full power of a conventional programming language in order to "combine the machines" from the various subproblems. One wonders whether new programming paradigms could offer more natural "combinators" for such situations. (Another issue is whether conventional programming languages like Ada or Java are ideal for combining the sort of monitoring implied by the discussion in Section 3.6).

The research on "time bands" in [BB06,BHBF05] is extremely interesting and we are already looking at ways in which time bands might help to achieve a better structure for our specifications.

Another major avenue which we hope to pursue with our DIRC collaborators Bloomfield, Littlewood and Strigini is handling stochastic assumptions and requirements.

## Acknowledgements

All three authors received support from the (UK) EPSRC funding of *Dependability Interdisciplinary Research Collaboration (DIRC)*: the first listed author was directly involved and the last two authors are Senior Visiting Fellows to DIRC. In addition, the second author's research has been partially supported by the Australian Research Council (ARC) Centre for Complex Systems, and the first author's research has been partially supported by European IST RODIN Project (IST 2004-511599). The first author now has funding from EPSRC under the "TrAmS" Platform Grant and the EU's RODIN project.

We have derived great benefit from technical discussions with: Alan Burns, Joey Coleman, Tom Maibaum and Jim Woodcock.

# References

[Abr96]    Abrial, J.-R.: The B-Book: Assigning programs to meanings. Cambridge University Press, Cambridge (1996)

[BB87]     Blokdijk, A., Blokdijk, P.: Planning and Design of Information Systems. Academic Press, London (1987)

[BB06]     Burns, A., Baxter, G.: Time bands in systems structure. In: Besnard, et al. (eds.), pp. 74–90 [BGJ06]

[BGJ06]    Besnard, D., Gacek, C., Jones, C.B.: Structure for Dependability: Computer-Based Systems from an Interdisciplinary Perspective. Springer, Heidelberg (2006)

[BHBF05]   Burns, A., Hayes, I.J., Baxter, G., Fidge, C.J.: Modelling temporal behaviour in complex socio-technical systems. Technical Report YCS 390, Department of Computer Science, University of York (2005)

[Bjø06]    Bjørner, D.: Software Engineering 3: Domains, Requirements, and Software Design. Springer, Heidelberg (2006)

[BS01]     Broy, M., Stølen, K.: Specification and Development of Interactive Systems. Springer, Heidelberg (2001)

[CHR91]    Chaochen, Z., Hoare, C.A.R., Ravn, A.P.: A calculus of durations. Information Processing Letters 40, 269–271 (1991)

[Col06]    Coleman, J.W.: Determining the specification of a control system: an illustrative example. In: Butler, M., Jones, C., Romanovsky, A., Troubitsyna, E. (eds.) Rigorous Development of Complex Fault-Tolerant Systems. LNCS, vol. 4157, pp. 114–132. Springer, Heidelberg (2006)

[CZ97]     Cau, A., Zedan, H.: Refining interval temporal logic specifications. In: Rus, T., Bertran, M. (eds.) AMAST-ARTS 1997, ARTS 1997, and AMAST-WS 1997. LNCS, vol. 1231, pp. 79–94. Springer, Heidelberg (1997)

[Daw91]    Dawes, J.: The VDM-SL Reference Guide. Pitman (1991)

[FS94a]    Fix, L., Schneider, F.B.: Reasoning about programs by exploiting the environment. In: Shamir, E., Abiteboul, S. (eds.) ICALP 1994. LNCS, vol. 820, pp. 328–339. Springer, Heidelberg (1994)

[FS94b]    Fix, L., Schneider, F.B.: Hybrid verification by exploiting the environment. In: Langmaack, H., de Roever, W.-P., Vytopil, J. (eds.) Formal Techniques in Real-Time and Fault-Tolerant Systems. LNCS, vol. 863, pp. 1–18. Springer, Heidelberg (1994)

[HJJ03]    Hayes, I., Jackson, M., Jones, C.: Determining the specification of a control system from that of its environment. In: Araki, K., Gnesi, S., Mandrioli, D. (eds.) FME 2003. LNCS, vol. 2805, pp. 154–169. Springer, Heidelberg (2003)

[Hoo91]    Hooman, J.: Specification and Compositional Verification of Real-Time Systems. Springer, Heidelberg (1991)

[Jac00]    Jackson, M.: Problem Frames: Analyzing and structuring software development problems. Addison-Wesley, Reading (2000)

[Jon90]    Jones, C.B.: Systematic Software Development using VDM. Prentice-Hall, Englewood Cliffs (1990)

[Jon96]    Jones, C.B.: Accommodating interference in the formal design of concurrent object-based programs. Formal Methods in System Design 8(2), 105–122 (1996)

[Lan73]    Langefors, B.: Theoretical Analysis of Information Systems. Studententlitteratur, Sweden (1973)

[LL95]     Lewerentz, C., Lindner, T. (eds.): Formal Development of Reactive Systems. LNCS, vol. 891. Springer, Heidelberg (1995)

[MC00]     MacDonald, A., Carrington, D.: Some elements of Z specification style: Structuring techniques. Journal of Universal Computer Science 6(12), 1203–1225 (2000)

[MH91a]    Mahony, B.P., Hayes, I.J.: A case study in timed refinement: A central heater. In: Proc. BCS/FACS Fourth Refinement Workshop, Workshops in Computing, pp. 138–149. Springer (January 1991)

[MH91b]    Mahony, B.P., Hayes, I.J.: Using continuous real functions to model timed histories. In: Bailes, P.A. (ed.) Proc. 6th Australian Software Engineering Conf (ASWEC91), pp. 257–270. Australian Comp. Soc., Australian (1991)

[MH92]     Mahony, B.P., Hayes, I.J.: A case-study in timed refinement: A mine pump. IEEE Trans. on Software Engineering 18(9), 817–826 (1992)

[MSB91]    Marzullo, K., Schneider, F.B., Budhiraja, N.: Derivation of sequential, real-time process-control programs. In: Foundations of Real-Time Computing: Formal Specifications and Methods, pp. 39–54. Kluwer Academic Publishers, Dordrecht (1991)

[PM95]     Parnas, D.L., Madey, J.: Functional documentation for computer systems engineering. Sci. Comput. Program 25, 41–61 (1995)

[Sit74]    Sites, R.L.: Some thoughts on proving clean termination of programs. Technical Report STAN-CS-74-417, Computer Science Department, Stanford University (May 1974)

[SR96]     Schenke, M., Ravn, A.P.: Refinement from a control problem to programs. In: Abrial, J.-R., Börger, E., Langmaack, H. (eds.) Formal Methods for Industrial Applications. LNCS, vol. 1165, pp. 403–427. Springer, Heidelberg (1996)

[SW89]     Smith, I.C., Wall, D.N.: Programmable electronic systems for reactor safety. Atom 395 (1989)

[Vin90]    Vincenti, W.G.: What Engineers Know and How They Know It. The John Hopkins University Press, Baltimore, MD (1990)

# Engineering the Development of Embedded Systems

Mathai Joseph

Tata Consultancy Services
1 Mangaldas Road
Pune 643101 India
m.joseph@tcs.com

## 1 Inter Alia

Fifteen years ago, it would have been hard to predict just how large a role the software industry would play in the life of a developing country. True, the sale of PC's had started to grow and access to the Internet was slowly spreading but these were trends in the developed world, far remote from the cities, towns and villages of developing countries. It was in this world of promise and uncertainty that a few pioneers set out on their mission to create for the developing world an Institute that would provide them with knowledge, training and experience. It was not an attempt to transfer trade information on the use of this or that software package or even to train people in programming skills, both of which would certainly have found ready acceptance. Instead, it was to share the conviction that a mathematical understanding and definition of *what* a program was to achieve would be the way of the future, bringing abstractness and precision to a field that was otherwise distinguished more by the scale and detail of *how* a program performed its tasks.

Most of the software systems developed at that time (and indeed many developed even later) have become part of the unwieldy heritage that the industry struggles to 'modernize' today. By comparison, the work of this Institute has acquired even greater importance today than in the past. Formal techniques, whose propagation in developing countries has been the major mission of this Institute, have come of age with routine use in many application areas. Few people would today design a chip or build onboard software for a car without using tools that unobtrusively help them to perform the complex mathematical reasoning that gives them the assurance that the programs they are constructing will meet their objectives. From cautious and curious scientific exploration, formal techniques have now become a widening part of an engineering discipline.

This *Festschrifft* for Dines Bjorner and Zhou Chaochen is also an apt celebration of the International Institute for Software Technology that they helped to found and which has made a place for itself in the software techniques community. Both of them had long and illustrious careers before coming to Macau but perhaps it will be for what they achieved here that they will be most remembered.

The informal paper that follows is a reminder that a great deal still remains to be done. Some of the problems in constructing correct and reliable embedded systems have been solved but many still remain. In fact, there are strong arguments (e.g. [Lee 2005] [Henzinger & Sifakis 2006]) that solving the remaining problems will need some major breakthroughs.

C.B. Jones, Z. Liu, J. Woodcock (Eds.): Bjørner/Zhou Festschrift, LNCS 4700, pp. 391–398, 2007.

The problems discussed in this paper are related to two of the long term interests of Dines Bjørner, on domain specific languages, and Zhou Chouchen on real-time specification and timing logics.

## 2  Embedded Real-Time Systems

Embedded systems are in such widespread use, often hidden in controllers for a wide variety of devices or providing the interface for controlling a device, that they are now taken for granted. Few people will know just how many embedded systems there are in the cars that they drive or the washing machines they use. Yet, the extent of their use should not hide the fact that embedded systems are complex and hard to reason about; they may need to combine the control of discrete and continuous systems and their performance depends on the allocation and use of physical resources. They are also remarkably hard to design and build correctly (some evidence suggests that more embedded software projects fail than any other kind of software projects).

There has been a great deal of progress in constructing embedded systems. Development environments like Scade, Rhapsody/StateMate and MATLAB/Simulink are widely used in industry and help to separate the specification, design and program construction phases. There have been major advances in computer science relating to real-time and embedded systems: timed specification techniques are well understood and there are many different timed semantic models. There is much better understanding of hybrid systems and advances in model-checking have made it possible to verify the properties of large and complex designs.

The problems start to emerge because formal analysis, reasoning and design stop at some level of abstraction. The next step is often dismissed as 'an implementation problem'. So, for example, mapping programming operations to compact and verified code, proving that timing properties are satisfied by the code and proving that execution of the code of each operation in the program will terminate while the execution of the whole program will continue endlessly are not problems that are solved at the specification level.

It is here that major difficulties arise: the model used when reasoning about the specification will usually differ from the implementation: further,

- The code model will differ from the design model,
- Timings used in the specification may not correspond exactly with machine level execution timings,
- The operating system and run-time operations such as garbage collection may cause variations in the execution timing of the program, and
- The properties of the platform (e.g. the use of pipe-lining, cache memories, etc.) may add further to the uncertainties in timing.

Advances in processor speed will not make these problems insignificant. Improvements in performance are invariably overtaken by the competitive pressures to incorporate new features into embedded devices. And the problems are compounded for mixed continuous and discrete control with the lack of a common framework for reasoning.

# 3 Abstractions and Reality

An idealized view of the development of a real-time program would consist of the following steps:

1. Requirements engineering: formalization of the properties and operations of the system in a domain specific language,
2. Transformation of the requirements definition into a program specification,
3. Refinement of the program specification into a program expressed in a real-time programming language, and
4. Implementation and testing of the real-time program.

However, none of these steps can actually be carried out completely with rigour and precision. Domain-specific languages and methods of reasoning are, at best, available in very limited forms. There is no *method* by which a domain-specific requirements definition can be transformed into a timed program specification, and no method to convert the specification into a real-time program.

Semantic models for real-time programs (e.g. [Henzinger et al 1991]) are usually constructed to simplify analysis and reasoning; they are chosen to be appropriate for representing the problems to be solved and they provide an abstraction over the hardware platform. There is no suggestion that the models are suitable for mapping directly to the hardware: the logic for specifying and reasoning over real-time programs applies over the abstract semantic model.

Real-time programming languages typically do not provide features for explicit timing or for controlling the allocation and release of physical resources. They provide a level of 'platform independence' but this means that timing and resource control can only be done at the level of the platform, perhaps by an operating system or real-time executive. Finally, as Lee points out ([Lee 2005]), the execution time of an operation of a program is often determined by the actual interleaving of executions of the program processes as this will determine what information is in the cache memory (and hence available for quick access) and what has to be retrieved from slower memories; processor pipelining can further affect execution times. And the interleaving of process executions may be controlled by their relative priorities, which may be fixed or variable.

Given the difficulty in computing such basic data as the execution times of a program operation, it is surprising that so many real-time embedded systems work as well as they do. A lot of this apparent reliability may be because (a) systems are designed very conservatively and make minimal use of advanced processor features, (b) much of the code for an embedded application is derived from existing code, and (c) there is extensive testing, both before release and in the field: when millions of copies of a system are in widespread use (e.g. as with mobile telephones), the chances of design and coding errors being detected and eventually corrected are high, though at a price.

# 4 Requirements

There is increasing evidence that errors in defining requirements continue to be the largest cause of software errors. [Marasco 2006] shows that while other causes of errors are reducing, errors due to incorrect requirements remain steady at 50% of the total.

Much of this could be addressed by developing better domain specific languages. In fact, development systems such as MATLAB/Simulink are remarkably effective where they apply and [Henzinger et al 2003] have shown how to add timing control to such programs. However, where there is mixed continuous and discrete control, as in many practical applications, this is insufficient. [Henzinger & Sifakis 2006] describe this as the problem of combining equational and abstract computational reasoning.

Even where there is just discrete control, there are difficulties with ensuring that requirements are consistent and as complete as possible. [Sukumaran et al 2006] describe a relatively simple but very effective method of checking requirements formally by verifying that system invariants are preserved over all operations. Their method is capable of handling practical data models in an object oriented framework. They show how to produce visual representations of *scenarios* and to create *prototypes* that can be checked to reveal problems.

An important part of any successful requirements definition method is the ability to incrementally handle *changes* which will take place right through the design cycle of a system. Minimizing the cost of checking that changes preserve system properties is crucial to having the method used in practice.

Equally important is the capability to handle *product lines*, as most embedded systems not only incorporate code from previous versions and models but are also part of a family of related products; changes made for one version may need to be integrated into all versions of the product.

## 5   Requirements, Program Specification and Design

However well requirements are defined and checked, there remains the crucial steps of transforming requirements into program specifications and elaborating this into a design. These are all difficult steps and very little work has been done to formalize any of them for a program of practical size.

It is here especially that formalizing combined discrete and continuous control poses basic problems. While the models used for control will differ, so will the methods of reasoning: equational and quantitative in one case and in terms of a programming logic in the other. Henzinger and Sifakis ([Henzinger & Sifakis 2006]) describe the difficulties and point out that solving them will need basic advances in computer science.

Recent work ([Sharma et al 2006, Chakravorty & Pandya 2003, Pandya et al 2007], [Agrawal et al 2006, Agrawal & Thiagarajan 2005]) suggests that discrete sampling of continuous systems may provide a sufficient approximation for the precise control of mixed systems. Incorporating such techniques into a specification method will make it possible to consider their use for practical applications.

## 6   Progress: Termination

A real-time program is usually designed to execute without termination. The program will consist of a number of concurrent operations that perform different functions. So while the program as a whole should be non-terminating, each operation of the program is expected to terminate within a specified time time bound (thus enabling the program to meet its timing constraints. Using automated methods for proving termination of such operations (and non-termination of the main program) is difficult; informal arguments have usually been made and supported by extensive testing.

Cook *et al* have shown ([Cook et al 2006]) how termination can be proved for parts of concurrent programs. They use an automated technique which both constructs a number of possible termination conditions by simple path analysis of the execution and checks that they compute a function that monotonically decreases on every execution. This is done for all finite execution sequences. Using this technique, they have proved termination conditions for a number of device drivers in the Windows operating system. In later work ([Cook et al 2007]), they have extended the results for proving termination of threads.

There are strong similarities between devices drivers and the processes that perform the operations of a real-time program: both of them usually interface with physical devices and are part of a concurrent program. It should be possible to use very similar techniques for proving the termination of code used for the operations.

# 7 Implementation

## 7.1 Priorities

For many decades, the use of hardware-arbitrated priorities has been a feature of real-time systems: the classic work by Liu & Layland ([Liu & Layland 1973]) contains an analysis of the use of such priority mechanisms, providing the starting point for a great deal of subsequent work in the area (e.g. [Joseph & Pandya 1986]).

The basic assumption is that the real-time program is divided into N concurrent processes, or tasks, each of which is executed at a unique priority level. During execution, the processor is allocated to the executable (i.e. non-blocked) process of the highest priority. Such priority mechanisms effectively impose an N-way partition over the execution of the program. The major advantage of fixed priority allocation is that it permits the *schedulability* of the program to be statically analyzed before execution.

Using a fixed N-way partition is practical for some applications (e.g. multi-channel analyzers) which are used for applications like data-logging where each channel may have an independent process and there is no inter-process communication. But most real-time programs require communication between its processes and this will impose another order over the execution. Conflicts may then occur, e.g. resulting in deadlock, or priority *inversion* (where a lower priority process may block the execution of an unblocked higher priority process).

A solution to this conflict is to restrict communication and synchronisation between processes so that the order they impose conforms to the order resulting from the hardware priority arbitration mechanism: the use of the priority ceiling protocol is one such solution.

The major advantage of such restrictions is that the schedulability of a program can be analyzed statically. However, the limitations in the possible program structures may make such techniques unsuitable for many applications. Moreover, the analysis requires use of the *worst-case* timing for operations, which is pessimistic and often inapplicable. Further, the method is not suitable for handling the dynamic changes which are often required, e.g. for changes in the operating conditions for different modes of execution, or for fault-tolerance.

It has long been known that dynamic allocation of priorities is better suited for handling changes in the operating environment. The disadvantage is that schedulability can no longer be analyzed statically.

Recent studies ([Gossler & Sifakis 2000]) have shown how to combine proof of timed program properties with the use of dynamic priorities. There are still a number of questions about efficient implementation of dynamic priorities and under what conditions schedulability analysis will still be possible.

## 8    A New Generation

The embedded systems described here so far are the 'traditional' ones where there is centralized or distributed control of an application. In this, control is intended to be precise and provided by software executing on a reliable hardware system. This requires the use of relatively complex processors with a large complement of supporting hardware.

Two directions of development throw open a whole new range of problems that require radically different techniques for analysis. The first is an evolution of the current mobile technology for large-scale data analysis and control ([Stankovic et al 2005]) on a geographic level. The second relates to recent work on devices such as the Berkeley Mote ([Warneke et al 2002]) which are intended for large-scale distribution.

In both cases, single nodes are not expected to be fully reliable or to have long lifetimes; in fact, the Berkeley Mote has inherent limitations of power that mean that each node will cease operation in a relatively short time. Single nodes have very simple functionality yet the ensemble of nodes as a whole must be capable of computing accurate results. A great deal of work will be needed for the analysis of such systems and very little of the existing methods of analysis for embedded systems is likely to be of use here.

## 9    Testing

There is an inevitability about testing which transcends any disapprobation from the formal techniques community. All systems must be tested because there is no other way of discovering remnant errors during the development cycle, from the requirement to the coding stage. This is even more so of embedded systems because it is only by testing them *in situ* that it is possible to exercise the code in a realistic environment.

However, such operational testing will be inherently limited: the more realistic the testing environment, the less control and repeatability there will be and therefore the harder to discover the causes of errors. So any reduction in the need for operational testing is of major importance.

Much work has been done on the use of program analysis for static testing of programs. While a great deal of progress has been made on static testing, especially for unit testing, such methods are inherently limited:

1. Unit testing requires a test harness to be created to substitute for the actual execution environment of the unit;
2. Representative test values need to be computed to ensure that all control paths in the unit are traversed.

Both of these are time-consuming, even if done using a test generation tool. There is therefore a strong temptation to do perfunctory unit test, or to skip the stage altogether.

Unit testing must be followed by module and system testing, where new test data must be generated. This is altogether more difficult because it involves testing the functionality of the program as execution passes through various modules and units. Systematic test may attempt to be comprehensive but still fail to perform the boundary tests (the *corner* cases) which are often the cause of errors.

[Godefroid et al 2005] show how dynamic testing can be used for testing software. The method automatically generates a test harness for the program, randomly generates test values and analyses the results to be able to generate new values that will exercise the program in different ways. Later work ([Godefroid 2007]) extends the results to allow testing to be done compositionally, by testing a unit in a test environment that makes use of the results of the tests of the other units in the program. This makes testing truly scalable, since it allows testing of new or modified units without re-testing of all the units with which it interfaces.

Godefroid's techniques for random testing could be used to develop an effective method for testing an embedded program statically, before it is integrated into a system and tested.

# 10 Conclusions

The field of embedded systems has grown enormously over the past two decades with a wide variety of applications. Programming techniques have also developed but there are several areas where formal analysis is still very difficult or not possible at all using current methods. There are numerous problems that need further study, ranging from requirements validation to processor design.

It would be an apt tribute to the work initiated here by Dines Bjørner and Zhou Chaochen to embark on an investigation of these problems.

# Acknowledgements

A number of people have commented on an earlier version of this material which was presented as an invited talk at the First Conference on Theory and Applications of Software Engineering in Shanghai [Joseph 2007]. I have benefited from discussions with R. Venkatesh, Vivek Diwanji and Zhiming Liu. Joseph Sifakis has sent a number of very useful comments. My thanks to all of them.

# References

[Lee 2005] Lee, E.: Absolutely, positively on time: What would it take? IEEE Computer, 85–87 (2005)

[Godefroid et al 2005] Godefroid, P., Klarlund, N., Sen, K.: DART: Directed Automated Random Testing. In: Proc. ACM PLDI, Chicago, pp. 213–223 (2005)

[Godefroid 2007] Godefroid, P.: Compositional dynamic test generation. In: Proc. ACM POPL, Nice, pp. 47–54 (2007)

[Joseph 2007] Joseph, M.: Abstractions for real-time systems. In: Proc. TASE, p. 22 (2007)

[Cook et al 2007] Cook, B., Podelski, A., Rybalchenko, A.: Proving thread termination. In: Proc. ACM PLDI, San Diego (2007)

[Cook et al 2006] Cook, B., Podelski, A., Rybalchenko, A.: Termination proofs for systems code. In: Proc. ACM PLDI, Ottawa, pp. 415–426 (2006)

[Henzinger & Sifakis 2006] Henzinger, T.A., Sifakis, J.: The embedded systems design challenge. Invited paper, Formal Methods (2006)

[Henzinger et al 1991] Henzinger, T.A., Manna, Z., Pnueli, A.: Temporal proof methodologies for timed transition systems. Inf. & Control 112(2), 273–337

[Marasco 2006] Marasco, J.: Software development productivity and project success rates: are we attacking the right problem? http://www-128.ibm.com/developerworks/rational/library/feb06/marasco/index.html

[Sukumaran et al 2006] Sukumaran, S., Sreenivas, A., Venkatesh, R.: A rigorous approach to requirements Validation. In: Proc. SEFM 2006, IEEE Press, Los Alamitos (2006)

[Agrawal et al 2006] Agrawal, M., Stephan, F., Thiagarajan, P.S., Yang, S.: Behavioural approximations for restricted linear differential hybrid automata. In: Hespanha, J.P., Tiwari, A. (eds.) HSCC 2006. LNCS, vol. 3927, pp. 1–18. Springer, Heidelberg (2006)

[Agrawal & Thiagarajan 2005] Agrawal, M., Thiagarajan, P.S.: The discrete time behaviour of lazy linear hybrid automata. In: Hespanha, J.P., Tiwari, A. (eds.) HSCC 2006. LNCS, vol. 3927, pp. 1–18. Springer, Heidelberg (2006)

[Stankovic et al 2005] Stankovic, J.A., Lee, I., Mok, A., Rajkumar, R.: Opportunities and obligations for physical computing systems. IEEE Computer, 23–31 (November 2005)

[Sharma et al 2006] Sharma, B., Pandya, P., Chakraborty, S.: Bounded validity checking of interval duration logic. In: Kalviainen, H., Parkkinen, J., Kaarna, A. (eds.) SCIA 2005. LNCS, vol. 3540, pp. 301–316. Springer, Heidelberg (2005)

[Chakravorty & Pandya 2003] Chakravorty, G., Pandya, P.: Digitizing interval duration logic. In: Proc. CAV, Boulder, pp. 167–179 (2003)

[Pandya et al 2007] Pandya, P., Krishna, S.N., Loya, K.: On sampling abstraction of continuous time logic with durations. In: Grumberg, O., Huth, M. (eds.) TACAS 2007. LNCS, vol. 4424, pp. 246–260. Springer, Heidelberg (2007)

[Liu & Layland 1973] Liu, C.L., Layland, J.: Scheduling algorithms for multiprogramming in a hard-real-time environment. J. ACM 20(1), 46–61 (1973)

[Gossler & Sifakis 2000] Gössler, G., Sifakis, J.: Priority Systems. In: de Boer, F.S., Bonsangue, M.M., Graf, S., de Roever, W.-P. (eds.) FMCO 2003. LNCS, vol. 3188, pp. 314–329. Springer, Heidelberg (2004)

[Henzinger et al 2003] Henzinger, T., Kirsch, C.M., Sanvido, M.A.A., Pree, W.: From control models to real time codes using Giotto. IEEE Contr.SYS., February, 50–64

[Joseph & Pandya 1986] Joseph, M., Pandya, P.K.: Finding response times in a real-time system. Comp.J., 29(5), 390–395.

[Warneke et al 2002] Warneke, B., Last, M., Liebovitz, B., Pister, K.S.J.: Smart dust: communicating with a cubic millimetre computer. IEEE Computer, 44–51 (2001)

# Design Verification Patterns

John Knudsen, Anders P. Ravn, and Arne Skou

Department of Computer Science
Aalborg University
Fredrik Bajers Vej 7E
DK-9220 Aalborg, Denmark
apr@cs.aau.dk

**Abstract.** Design Verification Patterns are formal specifications that define the semantics of design patterns. For each design pattern, the corresponding verification pattern give a set of proof obligations. They must be discharged for a correct implementation of the pattern. Additionally there is a set of properties that may be used in the design and verification of applications that employ the pattern. The concept is illustrated by examples from general software engineering and more specialised properties for embedded software.

## 1 Introduction

Engineers design; thus software engineering is a discipline that systematizes knowledge about procedures for designing software. This is evident from the structure of Dines Bjørner's volume on the subject [2]: After a careful analysis of the application domain and a systematic elicitation of requirements, the remaining task is design with implementation. Like in any other engineering discipline software design is based on reuse of patterns and well known components. However, unlike other disciplines, software engineering does not systematically use the patterns and components to analyse properties of the resulting system. Software is generally built without systematic analyses. Throughout the ProCoS project [8,14] it was the ambition to improve on this state of affairs, and through numerous case studies, we demonstrated that is was feasible, see for instance [24,23].

Yet, application of formal techniques have not spread dramatically, and it is rather clear that it is so difficult that it will remain a specialist activity even with better integrated notations like those developed in Oldenburg [21,13] and at UNU/IIST [9,16]. Perhaps a remark from control engineering colleagues helps to clarify, how difficult it is to work rigorously from basics: "Either you choose a PID controller or you have to get a PhD-controller." Yet, we cannot expect every engineer to have skills at a PhD level, therefore we must rely on standard components that we know well, and where there are standard procedures for tuning them and *checking their properties*. Design Verification Patterns is an attempt at defining properties for the standard design patterns for software engineering.

C.B. Jones, Z. Liu, J. Woodcock (Eds.): Bjørner/Zhou Festschrift, LNCS 4700, pp. 399–413, 2007.

The idea is rather natural, and one may wonder why it has not been done already. Here it helps to look at history: In the 1990ies, software was coded using languages like c, and systematic designs were very hard to discover in the programs that resulted from this activity. Components were statements, and analysis would be at a similar low level; it would focus on programming language semantics and the corresponding program correctness theories as for instance consolidated in Hoare and He's "Unified Theory of Programming" [11].

Since then, the demand for more software to increasingly efficient computers that find applications in the most diverse areas - ubiquitous computing - means that the level of abstraction is lifted. There is increased use of object oriented languages and design notations like UML [25,7], beginning experiments with reuse of components [28], and concern for architecture [1]. These ideas are combined with formal techniques and gains increasing popularity through efforts of Meyer [19], which are continued in tool developments like JML [3].

Thus, modern software relies on datatypes and common functions as embodied in the standard class libraries of objected oriented programming languages. A corresponding level of structuring constructs comes with the practical use of design patterns [15,6]. They may be the "PID"s for the practicing software engineer, but what are their properties, and how may these properties be used to analyze applications?

**A Design Verification Pattern.** As an introduction to properties of design patterns, we may look at the ancestor to all design patterns: The *procedure pattern*. A (side-effect free) procedure $p$ has an input or value parameter $x$ and computes an output or result $y$:

$$p(value\ x;\ result\ y)$$

With axiomatic semantics, we know that it may be fully specified in terms of two predicates, a pre- and a post-condition: $p.pre(x)$ and $p.post(x, y)$, where the pre-condition specifies the domain of the procedure, and the post-condition specifies the effect in the form of an input-output relation.

**Analysing Properties.** It is also clear that an implementer of $p$ has an obligation to *guarantee* the post-condition, but only when one can *rely* on the precondition. This is the basis for verifying correctness of the component $p$. From our point of view, it is also the *design verification pattern*. The lemmas that can be used in an application. Just before a call $p(e, r)$, the application must *assert* that the the procedure can relay on the pre-condition with $e$ for $x$, $p.pre[e/x]$. Then, after the call, it is legitimate to *assume* the post-condition with a similar substitution,$p.post[e/x, r/y]$, and use it in an analysis of application properties.

Much research in verification has focused on the obligations of the implementors. We are less concerned with this, because with increasing reuse, components are developed by specialists - the PhDs, who should be able to deal with the task. In contrast, the components are used in many contexts, so the lemmas formulated in the assert and assume conditions are a higher level start for verifying applications. They may form the basis for harnessing theories for tool support [17], a point we will return to in the concluding Section 4.related work.

**Beyond Functional Aspects.** In the more complex setting of objects or components, the verification must go beyond pure functional properties as expressed in the pre- post-condition paradigm. There is a state component as well that enters in the post-condition and which satisfies some *invariant*. Furthermore, many applications are reactive systems where the properties are protocols, that is constraints on *behaviours* of concurrent processes. An additional aspect occurs with embedded systems where *real-time properties* are important. In Section 2 we will introduce suitable notation for expressing such non-functional aspects, before we exemplify in Section 3 with conventional design patterns and extends it with a discussion of timing properties which are important for embedded software systems.

## 2 Background

In the following we introduce verification patterns more formally after defining the notations that are used to define properties. Settling on notation is a matter of preference, but it is important that the chosen notation conveniently can express what is required and that it is well established so that it is easily understood. The most widely used notation for design patterns today is UML [25] so UML class diagrams are the syntax in the following. To enable formal specification and reasoning, the UML diagrams must be given semantics. The formalism chosen to serve this purpose is the CSP-OZ-DC combination of Oldenburg [12,21,20] as elaborated in Hoenicke's dissertation [13]. The CSP [10] part hereof allows specification of processes, Object Z (OZ) [26] allows specification of functional aspects for operations on objects, and Duration Calculus (DC) [31,30] enables reasoning about time aspects.

**OZ.** Here, we are not going to go into syntactical and semantical details of OZ, but just note that a class $C$ corresponds to a Z schema, a method $m$ to an operation on the schema, and that an object $o$ of the class $C$ is a *reference* to a value of the schema.

**CSP.** The *communication events* are elaborated such that a channel is associated with each public method and thereby with the corresponding schema operation. A method call to an object, say with input parameter $x$, actual argument $e$, and output parameter $y$ of type $T$, is written $o.m!(x == e)?(y : T)$, cf. [13]. Otherwise, we have the usual syntax for CSP processes which syntactically are added as constraints to OZ schemas, or in UML as constraints in a *responsibility* part of a class or object. For convenience, we list the CSP operators:

$$P ::= \text{STOP} \mid \text{SKIP} \mid ce \rightarrow P \mid P \square P \mid P \sqcup P \mid P \| P \mid P; P$$

where STOP is the deadlocked process, SKIP is the terminating process, $ce \rightarrow P$ communicates event $ce$ and continues as $P$, $P \square P$ is external choice, $P \sqcup P$ is non-deterministic choice, $P \| P$ is parallel composition, and $P; P$ is sequential composition. As usual, recursive definition of processes is allowed.

**Duration Calculus.** Duration Calculus formalizes dynamic systems properties. The basis is the well-known *time-domain model*, where a system is described by a collection of *states* which are functions of time (the non-negative real numbers). The state names are here the variables in a given schema, which clearly vary over time.

A *behaviour* of a system is thus an assignment of state functions to the names of elementary states, An *observation of a behavior* is a restriction of such an assignment to a bounded interval; it can be illustrated by a timing diagram. Boolean values and thus the value of state predicates are by convention represented by 0 (*false*) and 1 (*true*).

For a given observation interval $[b, e]$ of a predicate $P$, the *duration*, denoted $\int P$ is simply the integral $\int_b^e P(t) \, dt$; it measures the fraction of time $P$ holds in the interval.

*Duration terms* are built from durations, logical variables and real numbers and closed under arithmetic operators and arithmetic relations. *Duration formulas D* are built from duration terms of Boolean type and closed under propositional connectives, the Interval Temporal Logic [22] "chop" connective, and quantification over rigid variables and variables of duration terms.

A duration formula $D$ *holds* in $[b, e]$ if it evaluates to true. For the predicate $P$, it is obvious that it holds (almost everywhere) in the interval, just when the duration $\int P$ is equal to the length of the interval. The length is the duration of the constant function 1 ($\int 1$). This duration is often used, so it is abbreviated ($\ell$), pronounced 'the length'. The property that $P$ holds is thus given by the atomic formula $\int P = \ell$. This holds trivially for a point interval, so we consider proper intervals of a positive length. These two properties are combined in the abbreviation

$$\lceil P \rceil == (\int P = \ell) \wedge (\ell > 0)$$

read as '$P$ holds'.

Given formulas $D$ and $E$, the binary "chop" connective can combine them to $D; E$ which holds on $[b, e]$ when there exists a $m$ such that $D$ holds on $[b, m]$ and $E$ holds on $[m, e]$. A simple example is the valid equivalence $\lceil P \rceil = \lceil P \rceil; \lceil P \rceil$.

With CSP, we include event based reasoning by defining that for an event $ce$, the formula $\uparrow ce$ holds exactly when the event occurs at the beginning of the interval. Thus we can specify an interval where $ce$ does not occur in the open interval by the counterexample formula

$$\overline{ce} == \neg(\ell > 0; (\uparrow ce); \ell > 0))$$

## 2.1   Verification of Design Patters

In describing the relation between the syntactic language of UML and the semantics of the formal description language package from Oldenburg, the CSP-
OZ-DC it is now possible to illustrate the idea of using verification patterns in
the software development process graphically, as seen in Figure 1.

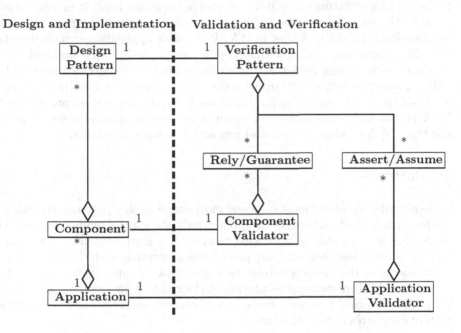

**Fig. 1.** The framework of Component Based Development using Design Patterns and
Verification Patters

Figure 1 represents the framework for Component Based Development using
Design Patterns and Verification Patterns. The framework extend what is considered ordinary software development efforts by explicitly emphasising the use
of design patterns and by illustrating the associated validation possibilities that
verification patterns offer.

Design patterns are usually applied in a context similar to the one illustrated
in the *Design and Implementation* part of Figure 1. Design patterns provides
guides on how to develop good designs to well known design challenges and
components that must address one or more of these challenges can then be
designed using the respective design patterns. That the component is designed
and implemented using certain design patterns can be useful for the system
developer that later will embed the component in a system design. Most design
patterns, however, contains more useful information that can be exploited, as
illustrated in the *Validation and Verification* part of Figure 1. For each design
pattern a verification pattern, which is a range of rely/guarantee pairs, can be
specified reflecting the different aspects of the pattern. The specification can

be used either as test and verification of the component, or in a test driven applicaition development process model as assert/assume pairs for verification, monitoring or for developing tests.

## 2.2   Related Work

There is a rich literature on verification, and patterns are implicit in many proof rules, yet the idea of combining architectural patterns with verification occurs, to our knowledge for the first time in [4,5]. It develops application specific pattern for collision avoidance. A somewhat similar idea is to develop refinement rules or conditions for design patterns; this is explored in [18]. Finally we mention [27] which approaches design patterns with the same mission to delimit the responsibilities of the developer and define the rewards for the application programmer. Their proposal for formalization, however, does not distinguish between aspects and thus require coding behavioural properties as state invariants.

## 3   Patterns

We begin with one of the most used and most simple design patterns; the Singleton pattern. A good example of its application is the control module for a ship's rudders. A modern ship is controlled from several stations, but it is essential that the rudders have one and only one common interface, such that clients that needs access to the rudders access the same software unit. If different clients have or create their own representation of the rudders, the representations are hard, if not impossible to keep consistent. A correct instantiation of a Singleton pattern eliminates such behaviour.

### 3.1   Singleton Pattern

The intent of the Singleton pattern is to ensure that there can only be one instance of the Singleton class and to provide global access to this instance [6].

**Fig. 2.** The Singleton pattern as an UML class diagram

Figure 2 shows the UML class diagram for the Singleton pattern. Note that the instance attribute has a − prefix, indicating that it is private to the class, i.e. only accessible through methods/operations of the class. For the Singleton class a protected constructor operation, ♯ Singleton(), is given and the public operation + Instance().

The pattern description provide information that can be very useful in verifying that an actual design or implementation actually is in accordance with the intent of the pattern.

*Implementation:* A Singleton is usually implemented as a class with a *protected* constructor as the only constructor. This should prevent external use of *new* to generate more instances. The instance of the Singleton is created first time the Instance() method is called. This call looks up the private instance attribute to see if it exists, and if it is not an instance is created, assigned and returned to the caller. For future calls the instance is returned.

*Functional Verification Conditions:* The Singleton pattern is a creational pattern, where there as such is not much to verify. There is an *invariant* stating that the instance reference is valid and that it is not changed unless it is *null* by the Instance operation. The pre-condition for the Instance operation is trivially *true* and the post-condition states that the result of the operations is a copy of the reference to this instance.

*Behavioural Verification Conditions:* There is one specified behaviour

$$main == s.Instance!(y == s.instance) \rightarrow main$$

When applying a singleton pattern with class $s$, we do not have to take any special precautions, the *assert* is trivially *true*. At any point, we can *assume* that there is at most one instance of the class and that this instance remains the same, i.e. it is not overwritten. Thus combining the functional and behavioural condition, we can prove that an application satisfies the property that

$$(s.Instance?y : Singleton \rightarrow P(y)) \| ((s.Instance?y : Singleton \rightarrow Q(y))$$

is equivalent with

$$(s.Instance?y : Singleton \rightarrow (P(y)) \| Q(y))$$

Thus, we can eliminate or introduce (using CSP laws) multiple calls of *Instance*.

The idea of exploiting a design using design patterns to extract verification lemmas is in Example 1 made less abstract as the use of a Singleton patterns is embedded in a design.

*Example 1.* On a modern ship the rudder can be manipulated and monitored from various stations on the ship. Here it is relevant to consider the rudder controller as a Singleton. In this example the rudder can be manipulated from the ship bridge and from the machine room.

In Figure 3 the UML diagram illustrates a design where the classes **Bridge** and **Machine** both have a **RudderSingleton** object. Although UML allows specification of the arity between objects by annotating the edges between them, in Figure 3 by 1's at the RudderSingleton class, this only states that one Bridge

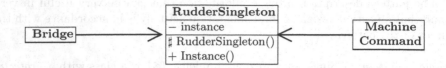

**Fig. 3.** UML class diagram showing a rudder control design

object has one RudderSingleton and one Machine object should have one Rudder Singleton and not that it should be the same object. However, the verification pattern allows us to deduce that.

Also, depending on the structure of the application, it may show us that the Machine and the Bridge has simultaneous access to the rudders, and that may lead to some conflicts about who controls the ship; but such a source conflict is not handled by the Singleton pattern. It only ensures that there is a single control object with atomic operations.

*Timing Verification Condition:* In embedded applications, the only timing condition we can think of in connection with the Singleton pattern is the (worst case) execution time for the method. It produces a rely condition, which is an invariant that the application has to satisfy:

$$(\uparrow \mathit{Instance} \land \ell > 0)\,;\,(\uparrow \mathit{Instance}) \Rightarrow \int Active(p) \geq WCET_{Instance}$$

here, *Active* is for each process a state variable which is true exactly when the process is executing. A naive formulation would use $\ell$ for $\int Active(p)$ but that would assume a dedicated processor for each process. The *Active* variable is manipulated by scheduling mechanisms which may be specified by duration formulas [29].

## 3.2   Observer Pattern

A more intricate example is the Observer pattern. It is often used in embedded systems to signal changes in an environment.

*Intent:* The intent of the observer pattern is to define a one to many dependency on objects, so that when one object changes state, all its dependents are notified.

*Motivation:* Partitioning leads to a need to maintain consistency between objects without tight coupling for reusability. Observers are updated when the subject changes state. The key objects in the Observer pattern are *observer* and *subject*. A subject may have any number of dependant observers, where all observers are notified when the subject has changed state. The subject sends its notifications without knowing its observers.

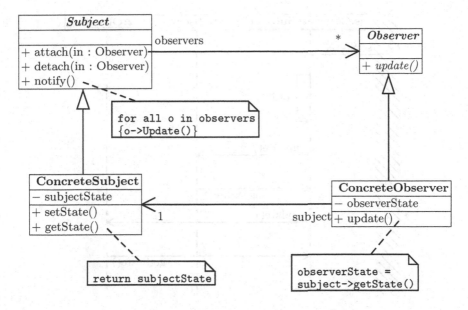

**Fig. 4.** A UML class diagram of the Observer pattern

*Structure:* The class structure of the Observer pattern is illustrated by the class diagram in Figure 4. The Observer pattern is modeled with the above mentioned classes *Subject* and *Observer* as abstract classes with a directed association from *Subject* to *Observer*, indicating that the subject is capable of calling the *Update* operation on observer objects. The two abstract classes each have a concrete counterpart, *ConcreteSubject* and *ConcreteObserver*, that inherit from the respective abstract classes. Between the *ConcreteSubject* and *ConcreteObserver* classes a directed association towards the *ConcreteSubject* lets concrete observer objects call the *getState* operation on concrete subjects to get its state.

*Participants:* *Subject* knows its observers. Any number of observers can observe a subject. *Observer* defines an updating interface for objects that should be notified of changes in a subject. *ConcreteSubject* stores the state of interest to the *ConcreteObserver* and sends a notification to its observers when the state is changed. The *ConcreteObserver* maintains a reference to a *ConcreteSubject* object and stores the state of it to stay consistent. A sequence diagram illustrating interactions of the participants is given in Figure 5.

**Verification Conditions for the Observer pattern:** The structure of the Observer pattern, as given in Figure 4, imply a CSP-OZ translation as in Figure 6 which gives the functional verification conditions. The *Observer* and *Subject* classes are both specified as abstract classes with an association that is navigable form *Subject* to *Observer*. The association implies a data structure in a *Subject* object containing *Observer* objects. This is to register the objects that attach

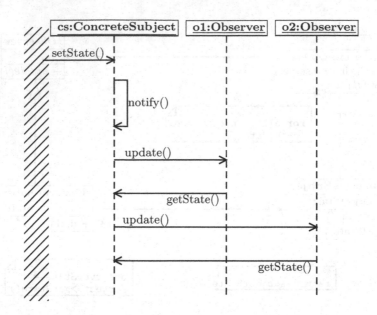

**Fig. 5.** Interactions between the participants in the Observer pattern

themselves as observers. As the classes are declared abstract this is not really going to be the case, but the concrete "children" objects, objects of the classes that inherit from the respective abstract classes have to posses these properties.

The classes *ConcreteSubject* and *ConcreteObserver* are the classes that inherit from respectively the *Subject* and *Observer* classes. The *ConcreteObserver* is related to the *ConcreteSubject* by an association that is navigable towards the *ConcreteSubject*. This means that a *ConcreteObserver* object will have an attribute of type *ConcreteSubject*, which store the object to which it is attached.

In [6] the *notify* operation has a note which says that the operation should implement a sequential call of the *update* operation on all attached observers. The *update* operation in the *Observer* class has no attached specification, and do as such only specify an interface to the concrete observer. Perhaps a use of the UML interface class to represent the observer would have been more appropriate, as the *update* operation is declared as abstract, leaving it to the inheriting classes to implement the operation body.

*Behavioural Verification Condition* The original specification of the Observer pattern do not provide any information on the events of a process encapsulating the pattern. The behaviour that is *guaranteed* is

$$\texttt{main} \stackrel{c}{=} Subject.setState \rightarrow Subject.Notify \rightarrow (\|_x : o \bullet x.Update \rightarrow SKIP); \texttt{main}$$

The purpose of the observer pattern is as stated to notify observers of state changes to some subject. This assumption can be analyzed by investigating

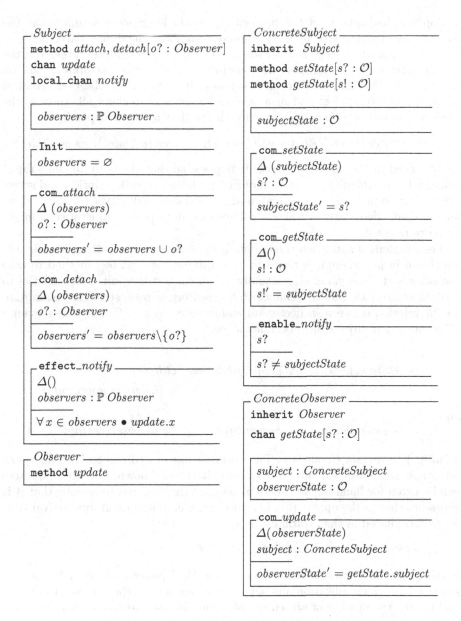

**Fig. 6.** The structure of the observer pattern as CSP-OZ schemata

possible method call sequences. For observers $o_1, \ldots, o_n$ and a concrete subject object $cs$ a state change must be recognized as following sequence:

$$cs.Attach(o_1); \ cs.Attach(o_3); \ \ldots;$$
$$cs.setState(); \ cs.Notify(); \ o_1.Update(); \ o_2.Update(); \ \ldots .$$

Popular descriptions of the pattern indirectly let readers assume that the consistency is guaranteed by the proposed design and the design pattern is motivated by a need to keep observer states consistent with subject states. Yet, the design pattern description puts no constraints on observers' $getState()$ calls on the subject. This may lead to inconsistency. If $o_s$ is a slow observer attached to $cs$, a concrete subject and $o_s$ as a data logger must register all states of the subject, the following possible sequence shows that $o_s$ is not dependable:

$$\ldots;\; cs.setState();\; cs.Notify();\; o_s.Update();\; \ldots;\; cs.setState();\; cs.getState()$$

As observed in the above sequence, it is possible that the state of the subject changes before the observers have finished updating. The description and structure of the observer pattern as stated above has data pull characteristics, where for i.e. embedded systems and control systems data push characteristics might be more relevant.

The problem of data push versus data pull of the observer pattern was already addressed in [6], where it is noted that modifying the $Update()$ method to take the subject state as parameter actually would convert the pull characteristics to push characteristics. Such a change to the pattern allow a stronger assumption on the relation between subject state and observer state. We have the sequence after interested objects have been attached:

$$\ldots;\; cs.setState();\; cs.Notify();\; o_1.Update(subjectState);$$
$$o_2.Update\;(subjectState);\; \ldots$$

and

$$cs.subjectState = o_1.observerState = \ldots = o_n.observerState$$

*Timing Verification Conditions* The observer pattern corresponds to an aperiodic task in a hard-real time setting, and it is well known that no guarantees can be given for handling all events of such a task. One has to assume that it is sporadic, that is the application has to guarantee a minimum interarrival time $T$, as formulated in the invariant:

$$(\uparrow setState \wedge \ell > 0)\,;\, (\uparrow setState) \Rightarrow \ell \geq T$$

Furthermore, the worst case execution time for Update leads to a further assumption on the application analogous with the one for the Singleton Pattern, and finally, the number of attached tasks must be used to define an assumption linking $T$ and the worst case execution time for the set of Updates.

If the ConcreteObserver is designed according to the data pull variant of the Observer Pattern, following constraint must hold to ensure consistency between a concrete subject and concrete observers:

$$(\uparrow Update \wedge \ell = 0)\,;\, (\overline{Update} \wedge \overline{getState})\,;\, (\uparrow getState \wedge \ell = 0) \Rightarrow \ell \leq T$$

It says that the elapsed time between two consecutive *Update*, *getState* events is less than mimnimum interarrival time.

### 3.3   Summary

We have illustrated that it is feasible to specify both functional, behavioural and timing conditions that form design verification patterns. A few other patterns have been investigated and give similar reasonably succinct conditions. Yet, there is much more work to do. Some particularly interesting questions are to what extent the verification patterns can be made complete for a given design pattern, that is they give a precise characterization of the pattern. For the functional and behavioural properties, we think they can be made complete, however, we are not sure that that can be done for the timing properties, because these are dependent on the underlying execution platforms.

## 4   Conclusion

We have developed the concept of a verification pattern, the semantic twin to syntactic design patterns. They are based on conventional rely-guarantee conditions for an implementation which are used as assert-assume lemmas for the application that uses them. The concept has been illustrated with functional, behavioural and timing specifications for conventional patterns.

**Discussion.** The application of Design Patterns in practical design of embedded systems is still at a early stage but as the complexity increase and the object oriented paradigm gains ground in this field, so will the application of technologies known from this field. A substantial part of the research in Design Patterns has focus on efficient solutions to architectural design challenges, and although designers of embedded systems are faced with such challenges also, more effort on researching Design Patterns for the special challenges that characterise embedded systems is needed.

In a case study of control software for marine diesel engines, that spurred our research of Verification Design Patterns, we encountered behavioral challenges typically encountered in control engineering that could be candidates for Design Patterns and Verification Design Patterns in embedded software systems.

One such challenge was the modelling of the *JetAssist*, a system that assist a turbo charger in optimizing the the fuel consumption and reduce $CO_2$ emission levels. For the JetAssist the specification explicitly stated that the system should have a *hysteresis* behaviour, i.e. the behavior of the system must by increasing and decreasing temperature, in respective overlapping intervals displaying different temperatures. That is, by measuring the temperature alone, is is not possible to predict the behavior of the JetAssist. Hysteresis is known from a variety of control and processing systems. Around this hysteresis pattern we found a number of well-known conventional patterns, exemplified by those described in this paper. It was clear to us that if we are to prove proerties of the *JetAssist* in a way that is comprehensible to engineers, we would have to structure the arguments - thus the patterns.

**Acknowledgement.** The first author wishes to thank CISS for funding his work on the topic, and menbers of the "Correct System Design" group, in particular Professor Olderog, for hospitality during extended stays. The second and third author acknowledge the inspiration fromk CISS' industrial collaborators to pursue this line of research.

# References

1. Bass, L., Clements, P., Kazman, R.: Software Architecture in Practice. Addison-Wesley, Reading (1999)
2. Bjørner, D.: Software Engineering. In: Bjørner, D. (ed.) Domains, Requirements and Software Design. Texts in Theoretical Computer Science, vol. 3, Springer, Heidelberg (2006)
3. Chalin, P., Kiniry, J.R., Leavens, G.T., Poll, E.: Beyond assertions: Advanced specification and verification with JML and ESC/Java2. In: de Boer, F.S., Bonsangue, M.M., Graf, S., de Roever, W.-P. (eds.) FMCO 2005. LNCS, vol. 4111, pp. 342–363. Springer, Heidelberg (2006)
4. Damm, W., Hungar, H., Olderog, E.-R.: On the verification of cooperating traffic agents. In: de Boer, F.S., Bonsangue, M.M., Graf, S., de Roever, W.-P. (eds.) FMCO 2003. LNCS, vol. 3188, pp. 77–110. Springer, Heidelberg (2004)
5. Damm, W., Hungar, H., Olderog, E.-R.: Verification of cooperating travel agents. International Journal of Control 79(5), 395–421 (2006)
6. Gamma, E., Helm, R., Johnson, R., Vlissides, J.: Design Patterns. Addison-Wesley, Reading (1995)
7. Object Management Group. Unified Modeling Language: Superstructure, version 2.0, final adopted specification, http://www.omg.org/uml/, formal/05-07-04, 2005
8. He, J., Hoare, C.A.R., Fränzle, M., Müller-Olm, M., Olderog, E.-R., Schenke, M., Hansen, M.R., Ravn, A.P., Rischel, H.: Provably correct systems. In: Langmaack, H., de Roever, W.-P., Vytopil, J. (eds.) Formal Techniques in Real-Time and Fault-Tolerant Systems. LNCS, vol. 863, pp. 288–335. Springer, Heidelberg (1994)
9. He, J., Li, X., Liu, Z.: rCOS: A refinement calculus for object systems. Theoretical Computer Science 365(1-2), 109–142 (2006)
10. Hoare, C.A.R.: Communicating Sequential Processes. Prentice-Hall, Englewood Cliffs (1985)
11. Hoare, C.A.R., He, J.: Unifying Theories of Programming. Prentice-Hall, Englewood Cliffs (1998)
12. Hoenicke, J., Olderog, E.-R.: Combining Specification Techniques for Processes Data and Time. In: Butler, M., Petre, L., Sere, K. (eds.) IFM 2002. LNCS, vol. 2335, pp. 245–266. Springer, Heidelberg (2002)
13. Hoenicke, J.: Combination of Processes, Data, and Time. PhD thesis, Fachbereich Informatik Universitt Oldenburg (2006)
14. Langmaack, H., Ravn, A.P.: The procos project: Provably correct systems. In: Bowen, J. (ed.) Towards Verified Systems. Real-Time Safety Critical Systems, ch. Appendix B. vol. 2, Elsevier, Amsterdam (1994)
15. Larman, C.: Applying UML and Patterns: An Introduction to Object-Oriented Analysis and Design and the Unified Process, 2nd edn. Prentice-Hall, Englewood Cliffs (2001)

16. Liu, Z., He, J., Li, X.: rCOS: A relational calculus of components. In: Mathematical Frameworks for Component Software, pp. 207–238. World Scientific, Singapore (2006)
17. Liu, Z., Mencl, V., Ravn, A.P., Yang, L.: Harnessing theories for tool support. In: Proceedings of International Symposium on Leveraging Applications of Formal Methods, Verification and Validation (ISoLA 2006), November 2006 (2006) (An extended version is found as UNU-IIST Technical Report 335, August 2006)
18. Long, Q., Qiu, Z., Liu, Z., Shao, L., He, J.: POST: a case study for an incremental development in rCOS. In: Van Hung, D., Wirsing, M. (eds.) ICTAC 2005. LNCS, vol. 3722, pp. 485–500. Springer, Heidelberg (2005)
19. Meyer, B.: Object-oriented software construction, 2nd edn. Prentice-Hall, Englewood Cliffs (1997)
20. Meyer, R., Faber, J., Rybalchenko, A.: Model checking duration calculus: A practical approach. In: Barkaoui, K., Cavalcanti, A., Cerone, A. (eds.) ICTAC 2006. LNCS, vol. 4281, pp. 332–346. Springer, Heidelberg (2006)
21. Möller, M., Olderog, E.-R., Rasch, H., Wehrheim, H.: Linking CSP-OZ with UML and Java: A case study. In: Boiten, E.A., Derrick, J., Smith, G.P. (eds.) IFM 2004. LNCS, vol. 2999, Springer, Heidelberg (2004)
22. Moszkowski, B.: A temporal logic for multilevel reasoning about hardware. Computer 18(2), 10–19 (1985)
23. Olderog, E.-R., Ravn, A.P., Skakkebæk, J.U.: Refining system requirements to program specifications (chapter 5). In: Heitmeyer, C., Mandrioli, D. (eds.) Formal Methods in Real-Time Systems. Trends in Software-Engineering, pp. 107–134. Wiley, Chichester (1996)
24. Rischel, H., Cuellar, J., Mørk, S., Ravn, A.P., Wildgruber, I.: Development of safety-critical real-time systems. In: Bartosek, M., Staudek, J., Wiedermann, J. (eds.) SOFSEM 1995. LNCS, vol. 1012, pp. 206–235. Springer, Heidelberg (1995)
25. Rumbaugh, J., Jacobson, I., Booch, G.: The Unified Modelling Language Reference Manual. Addison-Wesley, Reading (1999)
26. Smith, G.: The Object-Z specification language. Kluwer Academic Publishers, Norwell, MA, USA (2000)
27. Soundarajan, N., Hallstrom, J.O.: Responsibilities and rewards: specifying design patterns. In: Proceedings 26th International Conference on Software Engineering, ICSE 2004, May 2004, pp. 666–675. IEEE Computer Society Press, Los Alamitos (2004)
28. Szyperski, C.: Component Software: Beyond Object-Oriented Programming. Addison-Wesley, Reading (1997)
29. Zhou, C., Hansen, M.R., Ravn, A.P., Rischel, H.: Duration specifications for shared processors. In: Vytopil, J. (ed.) Formal Techniques in Real-Time and Fault-Tolerant Systems. LNCS, vol. 571, pp. 21–32. Springer, Heidelberg (1991)
30. Zhou, C., Hansen, M.R.: Duration Calculus: A Formal Approach to Real-Time Systems. In: Monographs in Theoretical Computer Science. An EATCS Series, Springer, Heidelberg (2004)
31. Zhou, C.C., Hoare, C.A.R., Ravn, A.P.: A calculus of durations. Information Processing Letters 40(5), 269–276 (1991)

# On Revival of Algol-Concepts in Modern Programming and Specification Languages*

Hans Langmaack

Institut für Informatik
Christian-Albrechts-Universität zu Kiel
Olshausenstr. 40, D-24118 Kiel, Germany
hl@informatik.uni-kiel.de

**Abstract.** Appearance of computing machines dates back to the 1940s and their corresponding scientific disciplines, computer science resp. informatics, have arisen in the 1960s. Nevertheless, fighting for appropriate programming and specification languages has not yet come to an end: The Java-programming language and the Abstract State Machines ASM are new and representative specimens which have arisen recently. These languages are even advancing and improving themselves: Original Java 1996, a flat language language without class nestings, towards more modern Java 2000 with nested classes, and Basic ASM resp. Evolving Algebras 1988/91 towards Turbo ASM 2003 where machines and rules show new features like naming, parameterizing, local states and recursive calls. These transitions inside Java resp. ASM remind at a much earlier transition from Fortran and Algol 58 to Algol 60 with its block concept and nested, parameterized, recursive and formal procedures. Aim of the present essay is to show that many of those new concepts incorporated in new Java and Turbo ASM were already available in Algol60.

**Keywords:** Programming language, Algol, Java, block concept, formal procedure, class, object, structural simulation, specification language, Abstract State Machine ASM, recursive procedure and rule, semantics, verification.

## 1 Introduction

Appearance of electronic universal computing machines dates back to the 1940s and their corresponding scientific disciplines, computer science resp. informatics, have arisen in the 1960s. Nevertheless, fighting for appropriate programming and specification languages has not yet come to an end. On the contrary: The Java-programming language and the Abstract State Machines ASM are new and representative specimens which have arisen just recently in the 1990s. And we realize that these languages are advancing and improving: Original Java

---

* This essay is a contribution to the Festschrift Symposium at UNU/IIST Macao, devoted to our dear colleagues Dines Bjørner and Zhou Chaochen on behalf of their 70th birthdays. Macao, 24th - 25th of September 2007.

C.B. Jones, Z. Liu, J. Woodcock (Eds.): Bjørner/Zhou Festschrift, LNCS 4700, pp. 414–434, 2007.
© Springer-Verlag Berlin Heidelberg 2007

1996 [GJS96] which is a flat language without class nestings towards more modern Java 2000 [GJSB00] with nested classes, and Basic ASM resp. Evolving Algebras 1988/91 [Gur88, Gur91] towards Turbo ASM 2003 [BoB03, FrS03, BoS03] where machines and rules show new features like naming, parameterizing, local states, return values and recursive calls of rules. These transitions inside Java resp. ASM remind at a much earlier transition from programming languages like Fortran [Bac57] and Algol58 [Sam57, PeS59] to Algol60 [SaB59, Nau60] with its block concept (vigorously promoted by committee member K. Samelson [Lan02]) and its nested, parameterized and recursive procedures, especially with formal procedure identifiers as parameters and with possible return values.

Aim of our present essay is to show that many of those new concepts which have been incorporated in new Java 2000 and in Turbo ASM 2003 were already available in Algol60, a language designed 40 years earlier. This fact is well documented in the literature, but is often unaware because Algol60 has not found enough industrial support.

Our essay is firstly, in section 2, dealing with programming language Java. We are reasoning on the concept of formal Algol-procedures versus classes and objects. Object orientation does not generate better intelligible program structures than formal procedures do, contrary to K.Nygaard's apodictic opinion. In section 3 the essay is dealing with ASMs where the authors of Turbo ASM [BoS03] are stating: "We extend Basic ASMs by parameterized submachines which may recursively call themselves and thus genuinely enrich the notational macroshorthand". The authors of Fortran [Bac57] and of Algol58 [PeS59] in the 1950s saw their functions resp. procedures in a similar manner only as comfortable shorthand notations for macro-expanded programs which have no (function) procedures. We see that ASM is taking over aspects of VDM's specification style [BjJ78, Jon89].

## 2  Formal Procedures Versus Classes and Objects

### 2.1  Introduction to the Problem

O.-J. Dahl and K. Nygaard are the great initiators of object orientation in programming. In 1967 they invented the object oriented programming language Simula67 [DaN67, Dah01] and they created important notions like class, object and inheritance. In 2002 O.-J. Dahl died, unfortunately. After his burial the author of this essay had a long conversation with K. Nygaard on the latter's scientific motivations. [1] A main motivation to introduce the concept of objects was the

**Thesis 1** of K. Nygaard: Algol60's concept of formal procedures [Nau60] as a means of program structuring is not intelligible and not communicable as compared to object orientation.

---

[1] The author would like to mention that Dines Bjørner and he himself attended Ole-Johan Dahl's burial ceremony in Asker near Oslo. Since Kristen Nygaard died only a few weeks later the author is remembering the conversation so intensively.

Nygaard's thesis is a harsh critics towards Algol and a praise of object oriented languages among which Java [GJSB00] is a prototypical and most widely used one today. The statement seems to be apodictic, but is rather informal and intuitive. Good scientific tradition obliges surviving colleagues to make the thesis more precise and more formal such that a convincing, rigorous proof or disproof of Nygaard's thesis is possible.

In [Goe05] W. Goerigk came up with a theorem which can be considered to be a disproof :

**Theorem 2:** Algol60-programs, even with nested and formal procedures, can be simulated by object oriented Java-programs in a structurally equivalent manner.

In other words: For every well-formed Algol60-program there can be constructed a well-formed Java-program with an essentially equal formal execution (call) tree. The latter notion was introduced in [Lan73a, Lan73b, Lan74, Old79, LaO80, Old81a, Old81b] in order to prove structural equivalence of Algol-like programs with procedures and of correctness and relative completeness of Hoare-like proof calculi [Hoa69]. With some care the notion can be extended to Java-like programs. Structurally equivalent programs are especially functionally equivalent (have the same input-output behaviour) independently of the interpretation of data constants and data operators, even for non-constructive data and operations. There is no Gödel-numbering used, there is not employed any Java-written interpreter which interprets Algol60-programs.

Since Algol60 is an untyped language, whereas Java is typed, we have to require that well-formedness (static semantical correctness) of Algol60-programs is slightly more stringent than the Algol60-report demands. The programs have to be typable in the sense of Algol68 [Wij+69] , i.e. the system of type equations associated to procedure declarations and calls has to be solvable.

Goerigk's strutural simulation allows to formulate the following

**Counterthesis 3** to K.Nygaard: The structure of object oriented programs is *not at all* more intelligible than the structure of procedure oriented programs.

Every structural complication (which, by definition, is representing itself in formal execution trees), especially if generated by use of formal Algol-procedures and of formal global variables, transfers also to Java with its object orientation. Thus object orientation does not lower down the complications. The unpleasant structure properties of Algol60 in Nygaard's sense are straight forwardly transferred to Java by Goerigk's structural simulation; object orientation does not prevent the unpleasanties.

From [Lan73b] we know that Algol60-programs can simulate Turing-machines without employment of data like numbers and of conditional statements and expressions although Algol60-procedures have no functional results as we have them in $\lambda$-calculus [CuF68], Lisp [McC65, Ste84], Algol68 or StandardML [MTH90]. This simulation is performed purely by procedure declarations, their nestings, non-formal and formal procedure calls and their call-by-name parameter transmissions. So formal termination (finiteness of formal execution trees) of Algol60-programs is algorithmically undecidable. It is merely semi-decidable, i.e. formal non-termination is not recursively enumerable. In other words: If we would try to decide e.g. formal termination using the techniques of abstract interpretation [CoC77], then for full Algol with nested procedures and global formal variables we are not able to define an appropriate abstract domain, whereas for unnested (flat) C-like programs we are.

We do not say that we consider the mentioned properties of Algol60-programs and of their simulating Java-programs (which form a sublanguage of Java) only as unpleasant. The properties demonstrate a surprisingly high computational power of Algol60. Steering (controlling) of Algol60-computations can be done both by (general recursive) arithmetics, but also by equivalently powerful procedure parameter transmissions [Lan73a]. The specific field of application decides which (mixture) of both techniques is yielding most efficient and adequate programs.

To the best knowledge of the author, before [Goe05]'s structural simulation there seems to be no work which shows: It is possible to write Java-programs which generate non-regular, general recursive execution paths and trees without employment of any arithmetics, just by class instantiations, method invocations and parameter transmissions.

We should remind the reader that Algol60's structural power is due to the so called static scoping or binding of identifiers which is subjected to the following defining phrases inside section "4.7.3. Semantics" of the Algol60-report [Nau60, Nau63]:

"*4.7.3.2. Name replacement* (call by name). ⋯ Possible conflicts between identifiers inserted through this process and other identifiers already present within the procedure body will be avoided by suitable systematic changes of the formal or local identifiers involved."

*4.7.3.3. Body replacement and execution.* ⋯ If the procedure is called from a place outside the scope of any non-local quantity of the procedure body [a so called global parameter] the conflicts between the identifiers inserted through this process of body replacement [copying] and the identifiers whose declarations are valid at the place of the procedure statement [procedure call] or function designator [function procedure call] will be avoided through suitable systematic changes of the latter identifiers."

Note that the meaning of a procedure call is defined by a copy of the corresponding procedure body. The above phrases explain how to avoid so called local binding errors when actual parameters (arguments), i.e. identifiers or expressions, are substituting applied occurrences of corresponding formal parameters and how to avoid so called global binding errors when a modified procedure body substitutes a procedure call.

In the past several programming language researchers have overlooked these two phrases or have (unwillingly) misunderstood them. Maybe the researchers have thought that just one initial renaming is sufficient so that no further renamings are necessary during runs of computations. Before Algol60 came up continued renamings were known in $\lambda$-calculus derivations ($\alpha$- and $\beta$-reductions).

But if we don't do any renamings, i.e. if we perform so called dynamic scoping and binding of identifiers, we would arrive at a semantics of Algol60-programs which is different from Algol60's static scope semantics defined in the report. Every dynamic scope formal execution tree is regular [Old81b], whereas static scope formal execution trees may be irregular [Lan74, Old81b]. Consequence: Algol60 with dynamic scope semantics has a correct and relatively complete Hoare-like proof calculus, whereas there does not exist any such calculus for the full static scope Algol60-language [Lan73b, Cla79, LaO80]. In case of static scoping we have such calculi only for certain sublanguages, e.g. of those programs with regular formal execution trees [Old81a, Old81b], especially of those programs sufficing the so called formal "most recent"-property [Kan74], or of those programs with finite procedure types (Pascal-like) if the latter have only simple sideeffects [Old84, Lan85, CGH83, Hun90].

C [KeR78] and Ada [Ich80] do not support procedure nesting. From a software engineering viewpoint, though, nesting (with static scoping) is a key technique for information hiding: It reduces the number of global dependencies and helps to encapsulate and to handle implementation decisions more abstractly. It is well-known that object oriented programs can be simulated by imperative languages. Late binding can either be implemented by generic procedures, which perform a runtime dispatch on the type of message receiver objects [Goe93], or by procedure variables (formal procedures) as part of the receiver's class object [Bla03]. Thus Algol-like programs are sufficiently expressive to support simulation of object oriented programs.

Note that, in the present essay, we are interested in the opposite direction of simulation.

## 2.2 On Reasons Why Proper Understanding of Formal Algol60-Procedures and Their Static Scope Semantics Has Been so Intricate

After a discussion of Bauer, Dijkstra, Paul and Samelson in Copenhagen in 1959, Dijkstra [Dij60] extended operator and number cellar (Operator- und Zahlkeller) of Bauer and Samelson [SaB59] towards a runtime stack with procedure activation records (procedure stack frames) as information units which contain

- local and auxiliary variables,
- intermediate results,
- local parameters (arguments),
- return address,
- dynamic pointer $DV$ to the frame of the most recently called and not yet completed procedure,
- static pointer $SV$ to a certain frame of the statically (lexicographically) enclosing procedure in order to have access to global parameters.

The latter three entries form the so called procedure link of a frame (Anschlussteil in [SaB59]). The special parameter "Beginn freier Speicher" in [SaB59] is exactly the administrative quantity "stack pointer" in [Dij60] which always points to the first free place in the memory reserved for the stack. [2]

The notion static pointer is due to Algol60's new language feature, namely the block (nesting) concept. Dijkstra formulated a statement in [Dij60] to determine the static pointer $SV$:

"$SV$ points to the *most recent*, not yet completed, activation of the first block that lexicographically encloses the block of the subroutine called in."

In [KaL74, Kan74] this statement is called the *"most recent"-property* of an Algol-program. But: Is this property really a logical consequence constituted by Algol60's static scope copy rule semantics for all programs?

McGowan [McG72] contradicts this consequence and speaks of Dijkstra's *"most recent"-error*. In [GHL67] there is a first example $\pi_1$ of an Algol60-program which does not meet the *"most recent"*-property. Nevertheless, Dijkstra's claim has been around for a long time. E.g. in the book on compiler construction [WiM92] we find the following statement together with a so called proof of assurance (Sicherstellungsbeweis) which is obviously incorrect:

"(Invariant ISV) In every stack frame provided for the incarnation of a procedure $p$ the static pointer $SV$ is pointing to the stack frame of the *most recent*, still living incarnation of that program unit which is directly enclosing $p$" (translated from German).

The program example $\pi_1$ in [GHL67], page 108/109, which does not satisfy the "most recent"-property has the following substructure:

```
proc P(F, G) {
    proc Q(R, S) {
        . . . } end Q

    . . .
    F(Q, F)
    . . . } end P
. . .
P(P, P)
. . .
```

The *"most recent"*-error shows up already in that linear subtree inside the formal execution tree which is generated by this substructure. In the following we show a simplified example $\pi_2$ [Goe05] (compare the simplified examples in [KaL74, Kan74])

```
proc p(f,g) {
    proc q(r,s) { print(g) }
    f(q,false) }
p(p,true)
```

---

[2] Already in [Sam57] K. Samelson discribes how to execute closed parameterized subroutines by help of the fixed variable "Anfang (=Beginn) freier Speicher" where repeatedly called subroutines are to be provided with parameters, return informations and auxiliary storage places before earlier calls have been completely executed.

with its associated (linear) formal execution tree generated by successive applications of the static scope copy rule:

```
    |
    { proc q'(r', s') { print(true) }
      p(q', false) }
      |
      |
    { proc q''(r'',s'') {print(false)}
      q'(q'', false) }
      |
      |
    {print(true)}
```

We use primes ' , '', ... to indicate the necessary renamings of identifiers. This formal execution tree consists of four incarnations constituting the nodes of the tree (the main program's incarnation is contributing also). The final call q'(q'', false) which generates the fourth incarnation is bound to the procedure declaration q' in the *second* incarnation; the primes of q', q'' are indicating static pointers $SV$. If program $\pi_2$ would really satisfy the *"most recent"*-property, as Dijkstra claims, then q' should be bound to procedure q'' in the *third* incarnation.

If we would apply the copy rule without any renamings we would perform so called dynamic binding or scoping. Then in fact the final call q(q, false) would be bound to the *most recent* procedure declaration q in the *third* incarnation. Then false would be printed, which is quite different from the static scope result true.

The type $\tau_p, \tau_q, \tau_f$ and $\tau_r$ of p, q, f and r is an infinite procedure type, solves the type equation

$$\tau = \text{proc}(\tau, \text{bool})$$

and is equal to

$$\text{proc}(\text{proc}(\dots,\text{bool}),\text{bool})$$

whereas $\tau_q$ and $\tau_s$ are equal to bool. But infinity of procedure types is by no means the source of the *"most recent"*-error. Look at the following Pascal-like program $\pi_3$

```
    proc p(f,g) {
        proc q(s) { print(g) }
        if g
        then p(q, false)
        else f(false)
        fi }
    proc h(i) {}
    p(h, true)
```

where $\tau_p$ is proc(proc(bool),bool), $\tau_q$, $\tau_f$ and $\tau_h$ are proc(bool) and $\tau_i, \tau_s$ and $\tau_g$ are bool. Static scoping yields the result true as intended by the Algol60- and Pascal-reports [Nau60, Nau63, JeW75] whereas dynamic scoping yields the different result false.

Wilhelm's and Maurer's runtime system described in [WiM92] is working correctly in the sense of Algol60's static scoping. The same seems to hold for the Dijkstra/Zonneveld Algol60-compiler on the Electrologica X1-machine as F.E.J. Kruseman Aretz has found out by emulation [KrA06]. Our impression is that the *"most-recent"*-property of static pointers has grown out of a wishful thinking of the authors of [Dij60, WiM92] towards a simple formula, similar to number theorists who are lenging for a simple formula to determine the $n$-th prime number.

## 2.3 On Another Misunderstanding of Static Binding Towards Dynamic Binding

In 1965 McCarthy published his Lisp1.5-Programmer's Manual [McC65]. Lisp1.5 is a functional programming language, an extension of the applied $\lambda$-calculus [CuF68]. What was new? Lisp's semantics was defined by an interpreter formulated in Lisp itself. In fact there were two interpreters, one on page 13 for Lisp1.5 without functional arguments, one on page 70/71 for Lisp1.5 with functional arguments.

A language semantics defined by an interpreter written in the same language is absurd in general. But not in Lisp1.5's case. The two interpreters were formulated as systems of non-nested recursive function definitions for which a semantics can be defined independently [LoS84].

The Lisp1.5-manual shows the following curiosity: Bound renaming of identifiers in given Lisp-programs might lead to deviating results, a fact which is in strict opposition to bound renaming in $\lambda$-calculus expressions. Round about 1983 (as C.A.R.Hoare reported to H.Langmaack [Hoa90]) McCarthy apologized: The interpreters had just a few simple programmer's errors.

In his lectures on Higher Programming Languages in 1971 at the University of the Saarland the author of this essay repaired McCarthy's interpreters in the spirit of Algol60 and called the modified semantics Lisp's *natural semantics* [LKK76]. In his book "Common Lisp - The Language" [Ste84] G.L.Steele jr. changed Lisp's semantics towards static scoping. During the years 1965 to 84 there were presented many conference lectures to overcome the difficulties and inefficiencies in shallow binding as prescribed by Lisp1.5's interpreters. Searching for most recent entries requires searching processes which are not necessary for static scoping.

Inconsistencies between Algol60's static scope semantics and several Algol60-implementations which obeyed Dijkstra's dynamic scope advice how to determine the static pointer $SV$ had unfortunate consequences for the progress of programming language developments. Ichbiah [Ich80] disallowed procedures as parameters and formal procedure calls in Ada. He considered formal procedures to be a too difficult concept as G. Goos reported to the author of this essay.

Kernighan and Ritchie [KeR78] disallowed nestings of function declarations in C. Both decisions lead to language restrictions of full Algol60. Static and dynamic scope semantics coincide in these sublanguages [Old81a, Old81b].

## 2.4  Structural Simulation of Algol60-Programs with Nested and Formal Procedures by Object Oriented Java-Programs

This essay is not the right place to present a full explicit definition of a transformation [Goe05] from Algol60-programs $\pi$ to Java-programs $\pi'$ which shows up the desired structural simulation.

In a way we may say that a transformed Algol60-program $\pi'$ is a macro-expanded Java-program which is done by a moderate syntactic sugaring. Java's new language specification [GJSB00] with its nested (inner) classes makes that possible. Java's old and original specification [GJS96] has no nested (no inner) classes. So the transformation $\pi_2'$ of our program example $\pi_2$ looks as follows:

```
interface tau { public void call ( tau f , boolean g ) ; }
class p  { tau f ; boolean g ;
     class q {  tau r ; boolean s ;
         public q ( tau r , boolean s ) {
             this.r = r ; this.s = s ;
             System.out.println ( ∇ g ) ; }}
     class %q implements tau {
         public void call ( tau r , boolean s ) {
             ∇ new q ( r , s ) ; }}
     public p ( tau f , boolean g ) {
         this.f = f ; this.g = g ;
         f .call ( ∇ new %q ( ) , false ) ; }}
class %p implements tau {
         public void call ( tau f , boolean g ) {
             new p ( f , g) ; }}
class π₂'  {
     public static void main ( String[ ] args ) {
         new p ( new %p ( ) , true ) ; }}
```

A few comments:
1. The interface is realizing the recursive type equation $\tau = \mathtt{proc}\,(\tau, \mathtt{bool})$.
2. The extra classes %p and %q are required to simulate formal calls of procedure p and procedure q.
3. $\nabla$ denotes a free place which later is filled by so called elaboration $\varepsilon$ prior to compilation to a Java-program without nested classes.

We abstain from explicit proving that $\pi$ and $\pi'$ have essentially equal formal execution trees, i.e. that $\pi$ and $\pi'$ are structurally equivalent. We should mention that, due to [IgP02], nested Java-programs are to be elaborated before proper semantics definition can be done. The elaboration $\varepsilon$ refines program $\pi'$ towards

$\pi'^\varepsilon$ and, in essence, adds Dijkstra's display vector components explicitly, an Algol60-implementation idea not mentioned in [GJSB00] nor in [IgP02].

Instead of semantics we shall study the preprocessor of the new Java-compiler as described by [IgP02]. The preprocessor performs a denesting | | of Java-programs $\pi_J$. $\pi_J$ and | $\pi_J$ | have essentially equal formal execution trees; work in [IgP02] may be considered as (or may be modified towards) a proof of this fact. If we look closer at a denested Java-program | $\pi'^\varepsilon$ | we see that | $\pi'^\varepsilon$ | is essentially a description of how an Algol60-runtime system as in [GHL67] or [WiM92] is executing an implemented Algol60-program $\pi$. This implies that $\pi$ and | $\pi'^\varepsilon$ | have essentially equal formal execution trees, i.e. that | $\pi'^\varepsilon$ | is structurally simulating $\pi$. A closer discussion is following:

## 2.5  On Denesting of Algol60-Procedures and Java-Classes

The preprocessor's denesting of Java is quite surprising compared to experiences in Algol60. For Algol60 we have

**Theorem 4:** Algol60 with non-nested procedures has regular formal execution trees only. Algol60 in general has also irregular ones [Lan73b, Lan74, Old81b].

Consequence: In Algol60 there is no denesting of procedures possible such that the formal execution trees are essentially equal, i.e. such that original and denested programs are structurally simulating each other. Reason: Algol60 has no functional results of procedures, there is no partial evaluation, such that denested programs could structurally simulate all programs. [Lan73b, Lan74] define a slightly generalized language, Algol60-G, which allows partial evaluation in a restricted form and therefore facilitates denesting (modularizing). Look at program example $\pi_2$ as a denested program $\pi_{2G}$ and at the associated formal call tree generated by generalized copy rule applications and ending up with four nodes as for $\pi_2$ earlier:

```
proc p ( f , g ) {
      f ( q < g > , false ) }
proc q < g > ( r , s ) {
      print ( g ) }
p ( p , true )
      |
      |
{ p ( q < true > , false )  }
      |
      |
{ q < true > ( q < false > , false ) }
      |
      |
{ print ( true ) }
```

Observe the clarity of acting of Algol60-G even in comparison to Algol60.

The preprocessor's transformation from Java to non-nested Java as described in [IgP02] has two steps, first a so called elaboration $\varepsilon$ as mentioned above, and then a compilation | | .

In this paper we need not talk about elaboration of types since our Java-programs $\pi'$ originate from distinguished Algol60-programs $\pi$. Inheritance is trivial here, the only superclass is Object which needs not be mentioned explicitly. So, if an applied occurrence of a field or formal parameter $f$ is declared non-locally in an enclosing class named $p^e$ then

$f$ is elaborated to $p^e$.this.$f$ .

If a method $m$ in a method call $m($ is declared in a class named $p^e$ then

$m($ is elaborated to $p^e$.this.m( .

If a class $p$ in an instantiation new $p($ is an inner class and is declared in its enclosing class named $p^e$ then

new $p($ is elaborated to $p^e$.this.new $p($ .

See [IgP02] for a more complete system of elaboration rules.

We illustrate the effect of elaboration in our Java-program example $\pi'_2$ : The three free places (indicated by $\nabla$) in front of g , new q( and new %q( are to be filled by p.this. . Variables like p.this inside (inner) classes like q or %q denote components of the display vector (resp. of the static chain) of q or %q [Dij60, GHL67]. It is a crucial problem how the runtime system has to determine the values of these components in a right way. See the indications after Theorem 5.

For a description of the preprocessor's compilation | | we restrict to Java-program constructs which are resulting from Goerigk's transformation ' in subsection 2.4 and from Igarashi's and Pierce's elaboration $\varepsilon$ above.

For illustration we show the transformed | $\pi'^\varepsilon_2$ | of our Algol60-program example $\pi_2$:

```
interface tau {
    public void call ( tau f , boolean g ) ;  }
class p {
    tau f ; boolean g ;
    public p ( tau f , boolean g ) {
        this.f = f ; this.g = g ;
        f.call ( new %q (this),false); }}
class %p implements tau {
    public void call ( tau f , boolean g ) {
        new p ( f , g ) ; }}
class q {
    tau r ; boolean s ;
    p this$$q ;
    public q ( tau r , boolean s , p this$$q ) {
        this.r = r ; this.s = s ;
        this.this$$q = this$$q
        System.out.println ( this.this$$q.g ); }}
```

```
class %q implements tau {
   p this$$q ;
   public void call ( tau r , boolean s ) {
      new q ( r , s , this.this$$%q ) ; }
   public %q ( p this$$%q ) {
      this.this$$%q = this$$%q ; }}
class | π₂'ᵉ | {
   public static void main ( String[] args ) {
      new p ( new %p ( ) , true ) ; }}
```

The formal execution tree of $| \pi_2'^\varepsilon |$ is a collection of addressed stack frames which represent instances of classes p , %p , q  and %q and activation records of method invocations call and println.

```
0: main program stack frame
   |                        \
   |                         1: %p ( )
2: p ( 1 , true)
   |                \
   |                 3: %q ( 2 )
4: call₁ ( 3 , false)
   |
5: p ( 3 , false)
   |                \
   |                 6: %q ( 5 )
7: call₃ ( 6 , false )
   |
8: q ( 6 , false , 2 )
   |
9: System.out.println (true)
```

The stack frames form four groups 0, 1 to 2, 3 to 5 and 6 to 9 which correspond to the four execution tree nodes of $\pi_2$ and $\pi_{2G}$ before. The pointers 2, 1, 5, 3, 2 are the associated static pointers $SV$ of the entries 3:%q(2), 4:call₁(3,false), 6:%q(5), 7:call₃(6,false), 8:q(6,false,2). Observe that the static pointer 2 (third actual parameter) in 8:q(6,false,2) is pointing to 2:p(1,true) (as q' in the formal execution tree of $\pi_2$ does), a *non-most recent* activation record of p ! 5:p(3,false) would be the *most recent* one. This again demonstrates Dijkstra's *"most recent"*-error.

After elaboration and denesting the resulting unnested Java-program $| \pi_2'^\varepsilon |$ implements the Algol60-program $\pi_2$ in a very detailed manner: In fact, the actions of an Algol60-static scoping runtime system are explicitly incorporated as macros. This is an indication of a proof of

**Theorem 5:** New Java with nested classes as presented in [GJSB00] instantiates and executes its classes due to the Algol60-like static scope strategy. Methods remain executed due to the dynamic scope strategy.

In order to achieve a static scope implementation it is crucial to generate appropriate actual parameter information when a non-formal inner procedure identifier is occurring as an actual parameter. In our program example $\pi_2$ it is q inside call f(q,false). The actual parameter information for q is generated by new %q(this) which yields a coupling of the identifier q and of a reference to an instance of the enclosing procedure (class) p. So 3 in 5: p(3,false) is pointing to 3:%q(2) and 6 in 8:q(6,false,2) to 6:%q(5).

If we compare to results on denesting of Algol60-programs it seems surprising that Java's classes can be denested and that the original Java of 1996 is in a way as powerful as the new Java of 2000. On the other hand, one should not forget that methods are declared inside classes. So, honestly, original Java has a nesting level 2, in a sense. This corresponds to a result in [LiS73] which says that Algol60-programs of any nesting level can be denested towards level 2 in a structurally equivalent manner (but not lower down to level 1 due to [Lan74]).

There is another interesting situation where Java-researchers could have learnt from investigations on Algol. Apt's and Olderog's ingenious soundness definition [Apt79, Old79] of Hoare's proof rule for recursive procedure calls [Hoa71] was reinvented by A. Poetzsch-Heffter and P. Müller [PHM99] when they developed a programming logic for sequential Java. See also the later subsection 3.2.

# 3   Algol60 and Turbo ASM

## 3.1   Corresponding Notions and Phrases

We have realized that the modern extension [GJSB00] of original Java [GJS96] has adopted essential language concepts and implementation techniques from Algol60 (without explicit mentioning, perhaps unconsciously). We see a similar phenomenon at the specification language ASM, especially at the transition from Basic ASM to Turbo ASM. There are a good few corresponding notions and phrases which sound differently, but mean the same concepts:

| Turbo ASM | Algol60 |
|---|---|
| 1. 0-ary static function | standard constant |
| 2. $n \geq 1$-ary static function | standard function |
| 3. 0-ary dynamic function | simple variable |
| 4. $n \geq 1$-ary dynamic function | $n \geq 1$-dimensional array |
| 5. location | simple or subscripted variable |
| 6. skip rule | dummy statement |
| 7. update rule | assignment statement |
| 8. conditional rule | conditional statement |
| 9. sequence rule | compound statement |
| 10. let rule | block as a procedure body with call-by-value parameters |

11. local rule with local named block with local procedures,
    rules and functions      simple variables and arrays
12. named rule with formal    procedure declaration with formal
    parameters            call-by-name parameters
13. body as right hand side    procedure body
    of a named rule
14. call rule              procedure statement or call
15. formal call rule       formal procedure statement or call
16. actual parameter      actual call-by-name parameter

These language constructs, cum grano salis, are already available in Basic ASM, but Turbo ASM has a considerably richer semantics. Namely, Basic ASM does not allow that submachines (named rules) may call themselves recursively. I.e. submachines and phrases 11. to 16. are used only as a notational macro-shorthand in Basic ASM.

The syntax of an abstract state machine $M$ consists of three components, 1. a signature (vocabulary) $\Sigma_M$, 2. a set (an environment) $E_M$ of named rule declarations and 3. a distinguished 0-ary main rule name $r_M$. Static semantics requires that every free function name is used due to its classification in $\Sigma_M$ and that there are no free logical variables (let-variables etc.). In order to demonstrate close neighbourhood of Algol60 and Turbo ASM we present the Algol60-program example $\pi_2$ of section 2.2 in the shape of two named rules in $E_{M_{\pi_2}}$ :

```
p(f,g) = {
     local q(r,s) = { print(g) }
     f(q,false) }
rM_π2  = {p(p,true)}
```

We interpret the transition from Basic ASM to Turbo ASM with its named recursive rules as a clear indication that ASM has taken over aspects of VDM's specification style, see [BjJ78, Jon89].

## 3.2  Dynamic Semantics

The informal semantics and execution explanation of procedures and their calls in Algol60 (see the copy rule sections 4.7.3.2 and 4.7.3.3 in [Nau60, Nau63] and in subsection 2.1 of this essay) and of named rules and their calls (see pages 73 and 170 in [BoS03]) are very similar although there is no explicit mentioning of the Algol60-report in [BoS03]. On page 73 we read:

"Rules [ $r(x_1, \ldots, x_n) = P$ ] are called *by name*. This means that in a call $r(t_1, \ldots, t_n)$ the [ free occurrences of the ] variables $x_1, \ldots, x_n$ are [textually] replaced in the body $P$ by the parameters $t_1, \ldots, t_n$ . The parameters are not evaluated in the state where the rule is called, but only later when they are used in the body .... In the extension of ASMs each formal parameter of a rule declaration is either a logical variable ... or a location variable or a rule variable."

On page 170 we read:

"We assume that there are no name clashes for local functions [plus local named rules] between different incarnations of the same rule (i.e. each rule incarnation has its own local dynamic functions [and local named rules])."

Börger and Stärk [BoS03] present an inductive definition of the dynamic semantics of Turbo ASM rules in the manner of a derivation calculus for the so called *yields*-relation

$$yields(E \mid Q, \; \mathcal{A}, \; \zeta, \; U \;)$$

where $E$ is an environment of named rules, $Q$ is an unnamed rule, $E \mid Q$ is a rule unit, $\mathcal{A}$ is a state, i.e. an assignment of values to all locations given by a signature $\Sigma$, $\zeta$ is an assignment to logical variables and $U$ is an update set. The copy rule of Algol60 with its implicit bound renamings is turned into the following derivation rule for Turbo ASM's call rule (please, be carefull and differ between "ASM rule" and "derivation rule"):

$$\frac{yields(E \mid P_{\frac{t_1}{x_1} \; \cdots \; \frac{t_n}{x_n}}, \; \mathcal{A}, \; \zeta, \; U \;)}{yields(E \mid r(t_1,\ldots,t_n), \; \mathcal{A}, \; \zeta, \; U \;)}$$

– where $r(x_1,\ldots,x_n) = P$ is a named Turbo ASM-rule from the environment $E$ in which all rule names $r$ are assumed to be pairwisely different,
– where name clashes in the substituted $P_{\frac{t_1}{x_1} \; \cdots \; \frac{t_n}{x_n}}$ are avoided by implicit bound renamings of names (identifiers) which are declared and bound inside $P$.

In case we have a program-like abstract state machine $M$, i.e. one where the environment does not interfere internal states of $M$, then dynamic semantics of $M$ is defined as follows: If

$$yields(E_M \mid r_M, \; \mathcal{A}, \; \emptyset, \; U)$$

with a consistent update set U is derivable then a run of $M$, applied to initial state $\mathcal{A}$, is called *successfully (regularly) terminating in resulting state* $\mathcal{A} + U$. Since logical variables in the named rules of $E_M$ are not free $\zeta$ is allowed to be the empty assignment $\emptyset$.

A Turbo ASM's macro- and micro-computation steps have their analoga in Algol-implementation. N.G.Fruja and R.F.Stärk do an interesting investigation [FrS03] on the hidden computation steps of Turbo ASMs by the help of so called PAR/SEQ-trees. So the specification language Turbo ASM has not only a natural big step operational semantics, defined by the *yields*-relation, there is also an equivalent small step structural operational semantics [Plo81]. An Algol60-program corresponds to a purely sequential Turbo ASM. Such a program has PAR/SEQ-trees as well. They are tail constituents of runtime stack contents of nested procedure incarnations as we find them in the program's formal execution tree [Lan73a, Old81a, Lan04].

Furtheron, there is a connecting view of big step operational and denotational semantics of Algol-programs and Turbo ASMs [Sco70, MiSt76, Bak80]. The denotational style to define semantics of a given program or machine $M$ with recursive procedures or named rules is to search for a continuous functional $\Phi$

such that its least fixed point $\mu\Phi$ is the essence of dynamic semantics of $M$ with its components $\Sigma_M$, $E_M$ and $r_M$, i.e. $\mu\Phi$ $((E_M \mid r_M, \Sigma_M, \emptyset))$ is the state-update function $[[E_M \mid r_M]]$ ( $[[E \mid Q]]_\zeta^{\mathcal{A}} \triangleright U$ is a notational variant of $yields(E \mid Q, \mathcal{A}, \zeta, U)$ [BoS03]).

## 3.3  Verification

Denotational semantics, especially its fixed point theorem $\mu\Phi = \bigsqcup_{\nu \geq 0} \Phi^\nu(\bot)$ with its approximating semantics $\Phi^\nu(\bot)$, is showing a way towards logic and verification of ASMs in an area where ASM-literature is sparse, but where looking at Algol-like programming might be helpful. ASM-logic is similar to dynamic logic [Har79] or algorithmic logic [Sal70, MiSa87]. Completeness results in [BoS03] are presented only for hierarchical ASMs, i.e. ASMs without recursions where call graphs have no cycles. The machines' analoga in Algol are so called macro-programs the formal execution trees of which are finite.

In order to prove Algol-like programs with recursive procedures partially correct C.A.R.Hoare presented his proof rule for recursive procedures [Hoa71]. The rule has, beside a conclusion and a premis, also a so called assumptions set. It took quite a while until soundness and completeness results on Hoare's extended calculus came up. E.M.Clarke [Cla79] gave an intricate soundness proof of Hoare's calculus, Clarke had not yet available an appropriate definition of soundness of Hoare's proof rules with the decisive property: If all proof rules in the calculus are sound then the whole calculus is sound.

1979 K.Apt and E.-R.Olderog [Apt79, Old79] independently came up with the same idea how to define soundness of proof rules by help of approximating semantics $\Phi^\nu(\bot)$, specifically in the shape of a syntactical representation. It is holding

$$[[E_M \mid r_M]]_\nu = \Phi^\nu(\bot)((E_M \mid r_M, \Sigma_M, \emptyset))$$
$$= [[\mathcal{R}(\mathcal{C}_\nu^{stat}(\textbf{local } E_M \ r_M))]].$$

$\mathcal{C}_\nu^{stat}(\textbf{local } E_M \ r_M)$ is forming the formal execution tree (or a congruent version) of $\textbf{local } E_M \ r_M$ up to level $\nu$. This means: Apply the copying process $\mathcal{C}^{stat}$ in a simultaneous parallel manner $\nu$-times to all rule calls outside any rule body in a static scope manner, i.e. by avoiding name clashes by appropriate bound renamings. In a next step $\mathcal{R}$ reduces the resulting tree by erasing all named rules and replacing all remaining rule calls by **abort**. $E \mid$ **abort** "*yields*" the bottom (undefined) update set which originates in $\bot$ mentioned in the fixed point theorem. $\bot$ interpretes every rule call $E \mid r(t_1, \ldots, t_n)$ by the totally undefined state-update function.

Apt's and Olderog's inductive soundness proof of Hoare's proof rule for recursive calls is a highlight in any course on program verification. We have mentioned already in subsection 2.1 that there is no sound and relatively complete proof calculus for the full static scope Algol60-language. This is holding for full Turbo ASM as well. We have seen that such calculi are available only for certain sublanguages. It would be very illuminating to investigate how completeness results of the kind above and those from algorithmic logic [MiSa87] transfer to ASM-logic. Furtheron: Parallel and concurrent executions are not yet integrated in the above mentioned completeness results. See [Lan04] for more detailed expositions.

# 4    Conclusion

It is the systematic usage of the block concept with its far reaching consequences for nested, recursive and formal procedures what is distinguishing Algol60 as compared to its language predecessors Fortran and Algol58. Algol60's progress was so dramatic that later language developers in the 1970s to 1990s were very hesitant to allow an unrestricted block concept. We see this attitude even in the 1990s with the authors of original Java [GJS96] and of Basic ASM [Gur88, Gur91]. After several years of experience both Java- and ASM-researchers found out that they should allow the block concept together with recursion at any reasonable place of a program or specification. The researchers could have had an easier and more continuous approach to semantics definitions, implementation techniques and verification methods if they would have respected more closely all the experiences with Algol in the 1960s and 1970s. Nevertheless revival of Algol-concepts demonstrates their inherant importance.

The author of this essay would like to thank for being invited to contribute to the Festschrift to honour our colleagues Dines Bjørner and Zhou Chaochen. Furtheron the author would like to thank Annemarie Langmaack for typesetting of this essay.

# References

[Apt79]     Apt, K.R.: Ten years of Hoare's logic, a survey, part I. ACM Transactions on Programming Languages and Systems 3, 431–483 (1981) (Tech. Report, Fac. of Economics, Erasmus Univ. Rotterdam, April 1979)

[Bac57]     Backus, J.W., et al.: The FORTRAN Automatic Coding System. Proc. Western Joint Computing Conf. 11, 188–198 (1957)

[Bak80]     de Bakker, J.: Mathematical Theory of Program Correctness. Prentice Hall, Englewood Cliffs (1980)

[BjJ78]     Bjorner, D., Jones, C.B. (eds.): The Vienna Development Method: The Meta-Language. LNCS, vol. 61. Springer, Heidelberg (1978)

[Bla03]     Blaue, C.: Anforderungen bei industriellem Softwareengineering, Procedurale Implementierungstechniken im objektorientierten Entwicklungsprozeß. Diss. Tech. Fak. CAU Kiel (2003), pp. 205, dissertation.de-Verlag im Internet, Berlin (2004)

[BoB03]     Börger, E., Bolognesi, T.: Remarks on Turbo ASMs for Functional Equations and Recursion Schemes. In: Börger, E., Gargantini, A., Riccobene, E. (eds.) ASM 2003. LNCS, vol. 2589, pp. 218–228. Springer, Heidelberg (2003)

[BoS03]     Börger, E., Stärk, R.: Abstract State Machines. Springer, Heidelberg (2003)

[Cla79]      Clarke, E.M.: Programming language constructs for which it is impossible to obtain good Hoare–like axioms. J. Assoc. Comp. Mach. 26, 129–147 (1979)

[CGH83]      Clarke, E.M., German, S.M., Halpern, J.Y.: Effective Axiomatizations of Hoare Logics. JACM 30, 612–636 (1983)

[CoC77]      Cousot, P., Cousot, R.: Abstract interpretation: a unified lattice model of static analysis of programs by construction or approximation of fixpoints. In: Proc. ACM Symp. POPL, pp. 238–252 (1977)

[CuF68]      Curry, H.B., Feys, R.: Combinatory Logic, vol. I. North–Holland, Amsterdam (1968)

[Dah01]      Dahl, O.-J.: The Roots of Object Orientation: The Simula Language. In: Broy, M., Denert, E. (eds.) Software Pioneers, Contributions to Software Engineering. sd & m Conf. on Software Pioneers, Bonn 2001, pp. 79–90. Springer, Heidelberg (2002)

[DaN67]      Dahl, O.-J., Nygaard, K.: Class and Subclass Declarations. In: Buxton, J.N. (ed.) Simulation Programming Languages. Proc. IFIP Work. Conf., pp. 158–174. North Holland, Amsterdam (1968)

[Dij60]      Dijkstra, E.W.: Recursive Programming. Num. Math. 2, 312–318 (1960)

[FrS03]      Fruja, N.G., Stärk, R.F.: The Hidden Computation Steps of Turbo Abstract State Machines. In: Börger, E., Gargantini, A., Riccobene, E. (eds.) ASM 2003. LNCS, vol. 2589, pp. 244–262. Springer, Heidelberg (2003)

[GJS96]      Gosling, J., Joy, B., Steele, G.: The Java Language Specification, 1st edn. Addison-Wesley, Reading (1996)

[GJSB00]      Gosling, J., Joy, B., Steele, G., Bracha, G.: The Java Language Specification, 2nd edn. Addison-Wesley, Reading (2000)

[GHL67]      Grau, A.A., Hill, U., Langmaack, H.: Translation of ALGOL60. In: Samelson, K. (ed.) Handbook for Automatic Computation Ib, Springer, NewYork (1967)

[Goe93]      Goerigk, W.: Korrektheit der Übersetzung objektorientierter Wissensrepräsentationssprachen mit statischer Vererbung. Diss. Math.-Nat. Fak., Bericht 9304, Inst. Inf. Prakt. Math. CAU Kiel, 1–105 (1993)

[Goe05]      Goerigk, W.: On Simulating Nested Procedures by Nested Classes. In: Czaja, L. (ed.) Proc. Worksh. Concurrency, Specification & Programming, Rucine 2005, p. 10. Warsaw (2005)

[Gur88]      Gurevich, Y.: Logic and the challenge of computer science. In: Börger, E. (ed.) Current Trends in Theoretical Computer Science, pp. 1–57. Computer Science Press (1988)

[Gur91]      Gurevich, Y.: Evolving algebras. A tutorial introduction. Bull. EATCS 43, 264–284 (1991)

[Hoa69]      Hoare, C.A.R.: An axiomatic basis for computer programming. Comm. ACM 12, 576–580 (1969)

[Hoa71]      Hoare, C.A.R.: Procedures and parameters: An axiomatic approach. In: Engeler, E. (ed.) Symposium on semantics of algorithmic languages. Lecture Notes in Mathematics, vol. 188, pp. 102–116. Springer, Heidelberg (1971)

[Hoa90]      Hoare, C.A.R.: Personal communications. EU-ESPRIT-BRA-Projekt Provably Correct Systems - ProCoS, Oxford (1990) Cambridge (2001)

[Har79]      Harel, D.: First Order Dynamic Logic. In: Harel, D. (ed.) LNCS, vol. 68, Springer, Heidelberg (1979)

432     H. Langmaack

[Hun90]      Hungar, H.: Über Komplexitätsfragen Hoarescher Beweissysteme:
             Effiziente Beweiserstellung und komplexitätsbedingte Grenzen bes-
             timmter Systeme. Bericht 9007, Inst. Inf. Prakt. Math., CAU Kiel,
             p. 140 (1990)
[Ich80]      Ichbiah, J.D.: Ada Reference Manual. In: The Programming Language
             Ada. LNCS, vol. 106, Springer, Heidelberg (1981)
[IgP02]      Igarashi, A., Pierce, B.C.: On Inner Classes. Information and Compu-
             tation 177, 56–89 (2000)
[JeW75]      Jensen, K., Wirth, N.: PASCAL User Manual and Report. Springer,
             Heidelberg (1975)
[Jon89]      Jones, C.B.: Systematic Software Development using VDM, 2nd edn.
             Prentice Hall, Englewood Cliffs (1989)
[KaL74]      Kandzia, P., Langmaack, H.: On a theorem of McGowan concerning
             the "most recent"-property of programs. Bericht A 74/07, Fachb. Ang.
             Math. Inf., Univ. Saarland, p.19 (1974)
[Kan74]      Kandzia, P.: On the "most recent"-property of ALGOL–like programs.
             In: Loeckx, J. (ed.) Automata, Languages and Programming. LNCS,
             vol. 14, pp. 97–111. Springer, Heidelberg (1974)
[KeR78]      Kernighan, B.W., Ritchie, D.M.: The C Programming Language. Pren-
             tice Hall, Englewood Cliffs (1978)
[KrA06]      Kruseman  Aretz,  F.E.J.:  Personal  communication.  Organizer:
             G.Alberts,
             Pioneering Software in the 1960s in Germany, The Netherlands, and
             Belgium. Conf. CWI Amsterdam (November 2-4, 2006)
[Lan73a]     Langmaack, H.: On Correct Procedure Parameter Transmission in
             Higher Programming Languages. Acta Informatica 2(2), 110–142
             (1973)
[Lan73b]     Langmaack, H.: On procedures as open subroutines I, II. Acta Infor-
             matica 2, 311–333 (1973) and Acta Informatica 3, 227–241 (1974)
[Lan74]      Langmaack, H.: Zum Begriff der Modularität von Programmier-
             sprachen. In: Schlender, B., Frielinghaus, W. (eds.) GI - 3. Fachta-
             gung über Programmiersprachen. LNCS, vol. 7, pp. 1–12. Springer,
             Heidelberg (1974)
[Lan85]      Langmaack, H.: A new transformational approach to partial correct-
             ness proof calculi for ALGOL68–like programs with finite modes and
             simple side–effects. Annals of Discrete Mathematics 24, 73–102 (1985)
[Lan02]      Langmaack, H.: Klaus Samelsons frühe Beiträge zur Informatiken-
             twicklung. Informatik Spektrum 18, 132–137 (2002)
[Lan04]      Langmaack, H.: An Algol-View on Turbo ASM. In: Zimmermann, W.,
             Thalheim, B. (eds.) ASM 2004. LNCS, vol. 3052, p. 20. Springer, Hei-
             delberg (2004)
[LaO80]      Langmaack, H., Olderog, E.R.: Present–day Hoare–like systems for
             programming languages with procedures: power, limits and most likely
             extensions. In: de Bakker, J.W., van Leeuwen, J. (eds.) Automata,
             Languages and Programming. LNCS, vol. 85, pp. 363–373. Springer,
             Heidelberg (1980)
[LKK76]      Langmaack,  H.,  Kröger,  H.,  Kölsch,  R.-T.:  Scriptum  zum
             Compilerbau-Praktikum SS 1975 u. WS 1975/76. Inst. f. Infor-
             matik U. Prakt. Math., CAU zu Kiel, p. 68 (1976)

[LiS73]     Lippe, W.M., Simon, F.: A Formal Notion for Equivalence of ALGOL–
            like Programs. In: Robinet, B. (ed.) Transformationes de Programmes,
            3e coll. int. sur la programmation, Paris 1978, pp. 141–156, Dunod,
            Paris (1978)

[LoS84]     Loeckx, J., Sieber, K.: The Foundations of Program Verification. Wiley,
            Chichester (1984)

[McC65]     McCarthy, J., et al.: Lisp 1.5 Programmer's Manual. The M.I.T. Press,
            Cambridge Mas (1965)

[McG72]     McGowan, C.L.: The "most recent"-error: its causes and correction.
            Proc. ACM Conf. on Proving assertions about programs. SIGPLAN
            Notices 7(1), 191–202 (1972)

[MiSa87]    Mirkowska, G., Salwicki, A.: Algorithmic Logic. D.Reidel Publ. Comp.
            Dordrecht, PWN–Polish Scient. Publ. Warsaw (1987)

[MiSt76]    Milne, R., Strachey, C.: A Theory of Programming Language Seman-
            tics, parts a, b. Chapman and Hall, Sydney, Australia (1976)

[MTH90]     Milner, R., Tofte, M., Harper, R.: The Definition of ML. MIT Press,
            Cambridge (1990)

[Nau60]     Naur, P., et al.(ed.) Report on the Algorithmic Language ALGOL60.
            Num. Math. 2, 106–136 (1960)

[Nau63]     Naur, P., et al.(ed.) Revised Report on the Algorithmic Language AL-
            GOL60. Num. Math. 4, 420–453 (1963)

[Old79]     Olderog, E.R.: Korrektheits- und Vollständigkeitsaussagen über
            Hoarsche Ableitungskalküle. Diplomarbeit, Christian-Albrechts-Univ.
            Kiel (1979)

[Old81a]    Olderog, E.R.: Sound and Complete Hoare–like Calculi Based on Copy
            Rules. Acta Informatica 16, 161–197 (1981)

[Old81b]    Olderog, E.R.: Characterisierung Hoarescher Systeme für ALGOL–
            ähnliche Programmiersprachen. Dissertation, Inst. f. Informatik u.
            Prakt. Math., Univ. Kiel, Bericht 5/81 (1981)

[Old84]     Olderog, E.R.: Correctness of Programs with Pascal–like Procedures
            without Global Variables. Theoretical Computer Science 30, 49–90
            (1984)

[PeS59]     Perlis, A.J., Samelson, K.: ACM Comunittee on Programming Lan-
            guages and GAMM Comittee on Programming. Report on the Algo-
            rithmic Language ALGOL. Num.Math. 1, 41–60 (1959)

[PHM99]     Poetzsch-Heffter, A., Müller, P.: A Programming Logic for Sequential
            Java. In: Swierstra, S.D. (ed.) ESOP 1999 and ETAPS 1999. LNCS,
            vol. 1576, pp. 162–176. Springer, Heidelberg (1999)

[Plo81]     Plotkin, G.D.: A structural approach to operational semantics. Tech-
            nical Report DAIMI FN-19, Comp. Sc. Dept., Aarhus, Denmark (Sep-
            tember 1981)

[SaB59]     Samelson, K., Bauer, F.L.: Sequentielle Formelübersetzung. Elektr.
            Rechenanl 1(4), 176–182 (1959)

[Sco70]     Scott, D.S.: Outline of a Mathematical Theory of Computation. In:
            Proc. 4th Annual Princeton Conference on Information Sciences and
            Systems, pp. 169–176. Princeton, Princeton (1970)

[Sal70]     Salwicki, A.: Formalized Algorithmic Logic. Bull.PAS 18, 227–332
            (1970)

[Sam57]     Samelson, K.: Probleme der Programmierungstechnik. In: Int. Koll.
            ü. Probleme d. Rechentechnik, Dresden 1955, pp. 61–68. Berlin: VEB
            Deutscher Verlag der Wissenschaften (1957)

[Ste84]         Steele jr, G.L.: CommonLisp: The Language. Digital Press (1984)
[Wij+69]       van Wijngaarden, A., Mailloux, B.J., Peck, J.E.L., Koster, C.H.A.(ed.)
               Report on the Algorithmic Language ALGOL68. Num. Math. 14, 79–
               218 (1969)
[WiM92]        Wilhelm, R., Maurer, D.: Übersetzerbau. Theorie, Konstruktion,
               Generierung. Springer, Heidelberg (1992)

# Design in CommUnity with Extension Morphisms

Xiang Ling[1], Tom Maibaum[1], and Nazareno Aguirre[2]

[1] Department of Computing and Software, McMaster University
1280 Main St West, Hamilton ON, Canada L8S 4K1
lingx@univmail.cis.mcmaster.ca, tom@maibaum.org
[2] Departamento de Computación, FCEFQyN, Universidad Nacional de Río Cuarto, Ruta 36
Km. 601, Río Cuarto (5800), Córdoba, Argentina
naguirre@dc.exa.unrc.edu.ar

**Abstract.** We have been engaged over the past few years in studying and formalizing software architecture concepts such as hierarchical design, dynamic
reconfiguration and the application of the concept of aspects to software architecture descriptions. Our attention has focused on the language CommUnity,
developed by Fiadeiro and Maibaum, and an extension that we call DynaComm
that incorporates support for dynamic reconfiguration, hierarchical design, a
general notion of connector and other supporting mechanisms. In applying DynaComm, we have found that the relationships normally used in CommUnity,
i.e., regulative superposition (used to regulate the behaviour of a component)
and refinement (used to instantiate a role in a higher order connector) are not
sufficient for dealing with some required changes to a software architecture or a
component that we would like to be able to affect. To this end, we have defined
the concept of *extension morphism* between two components. Such morphisms
do not preserve encapsulation of components, as do regulative superpositions
and refinements, but they do give us substitutability, in the sense of object-
oriented systems, and, hence, a basis of predictability about its application
to designs. In this paper, we describe the nature of extension morphisms and
illustrate their use by means of a non trivial example.

## 1 Introduction

### 1.1 Motivation and Background

Software architecture research is directed at addressing the high-level decomposition
and organization of systems, where component interactions are incorporated into the
notion of connectors and identified as first-class design entities. Architecture description languages (ADLs) have been proposed to provide formal modelling notations,
analysis and development tools to support architecture-based development, which
focuses on the system's high-level structure rather than the implementation details of
any specific modules [33].

There has been some work in surveying ADLs providing broad comparisons. The
survey in [33] compared ADLs with respect to their ability to model components,
connectors and configurations, as well as their tool support for analysis and refinement. The survey in [13] focused on the characteristics of different ADLs supporting

C.B. Jones, Z. Liu, J. Woodcock (Eds.): Bjørner/Zhou Festschrift, LNCS 4700, pp. 435–466, 2007.
© Springer-Verlag Berlin Heidelberg 2007

self-managing architectures, which not only implement the concept of dynamic change, but also initiate, select and assess the change itself without the assistance of an external user. We are currently interested in ADLs with support for dynamic software architectures and that also support the essential engineering concept of hierarchical design. Examples of ADLs, which support such a view, are Dynamic Wright [11], Darwin [31] and Dynamic Acme [19][38]. An assessment of these languages can be found in [13] and a more thorough review of their language constructs, associated styles of specification and mechanisms to achieve dynamic reconfiguration can be found in [27]. However, these ADLs have important shortcomings in relation to their support for hierarchical design and having a formal semantics that enable us to perform useful analyses.

CommUnity [15, 29, 30] was designed to study the problem of the 'magic step' from specification to program, in the context of component based design using temporal and multi modal logics for component specification. It is always the case that the languages used for specifications and programs are ontologically very different. Specifications are about properties, whilst programs are about operational behaviour, even if this behaviour is described abstractly. For one thing, a programming language has no facility to express *properties* of programs; a meta language of properties is required for this. So, programs and specifications occupy different conceptual worlds and there is not a simple notion of homomorphism or refinement that relates them directly: hence the reference to the 'magic step' above. What *is* the relationship between specifications and programs and how can one remove the magic? We cannot talk about the program being a refinement of a specification, as refinement is an internal notion in the language of component specifications. We might introduce a notion of *realization*, which relates a program to its specification by assigning to the program a minimal (not unique and minimum) specification, which *is* a refinement of the specification.

CommUnity explored this space and addressed the important issue of compositionality in this context: when can we say that a program constructed from parts, where each part is a correct realization as a program of the corresponding specification part, is correct with respect to the specification constructed from the component specifications in a way that mimics the construction of the program? Not too surprisingly, compositionality in this sense is not an easy property to achieve. Given an arbitrary specification language and some programming language, not every program constructed from parts is correct with respect to the corresponding specification. This is not surprising, as the structural properties of the specification category may not mimic that of the category of programs, or *vice versa*.

We have been extending CommUnity to encompass features we regard as essential for architecture based design, namely hierarchical organization of subsystems and dynamic reconfiguration [26]. However, in this paper the new features of DynaComm are not essential for the presentation, so, for the sake of clarity, we avoid the presentation of its extra details and features.

Recently, we have been exploring the issue of 'early aspects' [39], attempting to see if these ideas can be rationalized, based on traditional software engineering principles of modularity and hierarchy, by analyzing them at the architectural level. After numerous case studies, we have come to the conclusion that aspects are just the soft goals or non functional requirements traditionally found in requirements engineering, and that they can be handled uniformly at the architectural level by formalizing a specific aspect as an architectural pattern used to replace an existing pattern in the underlying architecture (by means of, for example, a graph transformation). Then, aspect weaving is achieved by the colimit construction used to obtain the semantics of any architectural configuration, the latter being defined as a categorical diagram of component objects and relationships between them. Aspect composition then becomes the sequential application of different transformations, corresponding to the different aspects, to the underlying diagram depicting the original architecture. As with features, there may be (unforeseen) interactions between different aspects and the order of application is crucial to achieving the right system. Many aspects require the replacement of a component in the original architecture by another, closely related, component that is a subtype of the original component, in the sense of object-oriented design. This requires a formal relationship between components that involves breaking encapsulation of the original component in the design. We have developed the notion of extension as a realization of this controlled breaking of encapsulation. The application of extension morphisms in the construction of software architectures is the aim of this paper.

## 1.2 Introducing CommUnity

CommUnity was developed to explore the relationships between specifications and programs in a component based development setting. José Fiadeiro and his (former) students developed the language extensively in the interim [18,29,30], making of CommUnity a (proto) ADL. A review of CommUnity and its semantics are given, and, in particular, we rehearse the idea that the notion of superposition can be formalized as a morphism between designs in CommUnity. The concept of superposition is defined as a structure preserving transformation on designs through the extension of their state space and control activity while preserving their properties [29,30]. So, a regulative superposition morphism is proposed in CommUnity as a means of augmenting an existing component by superposing a regulator over it while preserving its functionality, thus supporting a layered approach to system design. In addition, several different kinds of morphisms (other than regulative superposition morphisms) between designs as well as their relationships are also investigated to explain the language's well-founded support for compositionality, reusability, and enforcement of design principles.

The syntax of a CommUnity design is:

```
design component P
out out(V)
in in(V)
prv prv(V)
init I
do
     [prv] g[D(g)] : L(g), U(g) -> R(g)
endofdesign
```

A fixed collection of data types (say S) is assumed to be given by a first-order algebraic specification and the design is defined over such data types. Because data types chosen in the design determine the nature of the elementary computations that can be performed locally by the components, the emphasis in the language is put on the co-ordination mechanisms between system components rather than data refinement, which focuses on computational aspects. As a result, CommUnity does not support polymorphism directly.

In the above example, V is the set of *channels* in the design P. Each channel v is typed with a sort from S. in(V) represents input channels, which read data from the environment of the component and the component has no control over them. out(V) and prv(V) are output channels and private channels, respectively. They are controlled locally by the component. Output channels allow the environment to read data produced by the component, while private channels support internal activity that does not involve the environment. We use loc(V) to represent out(V) $\cup$ prv(V). The formula I constrains potential initial states of the corresponding program. I is a formula in first-order logic over the channels of the design.

For any action g, D(g) is a subset of loc(V) consisting of the local channels that can be written to by action g (we call it the write frame of g). U(g) is a progress condition, which establishes the upper bound for enabledness and L(g) indicates the lower bound. In a program, L(g) = U(g), so the guards in a design define the "interval" within which the guard of the action in a program implementing the design must lie. R(g) is a condition on V and D(g)', where by D(g)' we mean the set of primed channels from D(g). Primed channels account for references to the values of channels after the execution of an action. The condition is a first-order logic formula built from V and D(g)'. Usually, we define it as a conjunction of implications of the form pre $\Rightarrow$ post, which corresponds to a pre/post condition specification in the sense of Hoare and where pre does not contain primed channels. Using this form, the number of conjuncts in the formula will correspond to the number of channels in the write frame of g, so that we can understand the meaning of the action fairly easily. Moreover, it will be convenient for us to calculate the colimit of the diagram if we have put all the designs in this form.

In order to study the relationship between designs, we need the formal definition for designs as follows:

**Definition 1.** A *design signature* is a tuple (V, $\Gamma$, tv, ta, D) where:

- V is the set of *channels*, which is an S-indexed family of mutually disjoint sets. The channel is typed with sorts in S, which is a fixed set of data types specified as usual via a first-order specification.
- $\Gamma$ is a finite set of actions.
- tv is a total function from V to {prv, in, out}, which partitions V into three disjoint sets of channels, namely private, input and output channels, respectively. Loc(V) represents the union of private and output channels.
- ta is a total function from $\Gamma$ to {sh, prv}, which divides $\Gamma$ into private and shared actions. Only shared actions can serve as the synchronization points with other designs.
- D is total function from $\Gamma$ to $2^{loc(V)}$. The write frame of action g is represented by D(g).

All these sets of symbols are assumed to be finite and mutually disjoint. Channels are used as atoms in the definition of terms:

**Definition 2.** Given a design signature θ=(V, Γ, tv, ta, D), the language of *terms* is defined as follows: for every sort s ∈ S,

- $t_s ::= a$ , where $a \in V$ and of type s
- $t_s ::= c$, where c is a constant with sort s
- $t_s ::= f(t_1,...,t_n)$, where $t_1: s_1,..., t_n: s_n$ and $f:s_1 \times ... \times s_n \rightarrow s$

The language of *propositions* is defined as follows:

- $\phi ::= (t_{1s}\ p_s\ t_{2s}) \mid \phi_1 \Rightarrow \phi_2 \mid \phi_1 \wedge \phi_2 \mid \neg\phi$

where $p_s$ is a binary predicate defined on sort s. The set of predicates defined on sort s must contain $=_s$.

Having defined the signature of designs and given the language of terms and propositions, we can formalize the notion of designs as follows:

**Definition 3.** A *design* is a pair (θ, Λ), where θ = (V, Γ, tv, ta, D) and Λ is (I, R, L, U) where:

- I is a proposition defined on θ, which constrains the values of the channels when the program is initialized.
- R assigns to every action $g \in \Gamma$ an expression R(g).
- For every action $g \in \Gamma$, L(g) assigns the enabling guard to it and U(g) assigns the progress guard.
- For every action $g \in \Gamma$, for any $a \in D(g)$, tv(a) ∈ {prv, out}.

Recall that R(g) specifies the effect of action g on its write frame. For any channel $a \in D(g)$, we will use R(g,a) to denote the expression that represents the effect of action g on channel a.

Before we define the semantic structures for a design, a model for the abstract data type specification (S) needs to be introduced. The model is given by a Σ-algebra $U$, i.e., a set $s^U$ is assigned to each sort symbol s ∈ S, a value in $s^U(c^U)$ is assigned to each constant symbol c of sort s, a (total) function $f^U : s_1^U \times ... \times s_n^U \rightarrow s^U$ is assigned to each function symbol f in S, and a relation $p_s^U \subseteq s \times s$ is assigned to each binary predicate $p_s$ defined on sort s.

The semantic interpretation of designs is given in terms of transition systems:

**Definition 4.** A *transition system* (W, $w_0$, E, →) consists of:

- a non-empty set W of states or possible worlds
- $w_0 \in W$, the initial state
- a non-empty set E of events
- an E-indexed set of partial functions → on W, W → (E → W), defines the state transition performed by each event.

Having transition systems to represent the state transitions of a design, we can interpret the signature of a design with the following structure:

**Definition 5.** A *θ-interpretation structure* for a signature θ=(V, Γ, tv, ta, D) is a triple (*T*, *A*, *G*) where:

- *T* is a transition system (*W*, $w_0$, *E*, →)
- *A* is an S-indexed family of maps $A_s$: $V_s$ → (*W* → $s^U$).
- *G*: Γ → $2^E$.

That is to say, *A* interprets attribute symbols as functions that return the value that each attribute takes in each state, and *G* interprets the action symbols as sets of events -- the set of the events during which the action occurs.

It is possible that no action will take place during an event. Such events correspond to environment steps, which means steps performed by the other components in the system. Interpretation structures are intended to capture the behavior of a design in the context of a system of which it is a component. Because environment steps are taken into account, state encapsulation techniques can be formalized through particular classes of interpretation structures.

**Definition 6.** A *θ-interpretation structure* (*T*, *A*, *G*) for a signature θ=(V, Γ, tv, ta, D) is called a *locus* iff, for every a ∈ loc(V) and w, w'□ ∈ *W*, if (w, e, w') is in →, and for any g ∈ D(a), e ∉ G(g), then *A*(a)(w') = *A*(a)(w).

This means a *locus* is an interpretation structure in which the values of the program variables remain unchanged during events in which no action occurs that contains them in their write frame.

Having defined the interpretation structures for designs and the model for the abstract data type specification (S), we are able to give the semantics of the terms and propositions in the language given by the design signature.

**Definition 7.** Given a signature θ = (V, Γ, tv, ta, D) and a *θ-interpretation structure* *S*= (*T*, *A*, *G*), the semantics of terms (for every sort s, term t of sort s and w ∈ *W*, $[t]^s$(w) ∈ $s^U$, the value taken by t in the world w, is defined as follows:

- if t is a ∈ $A_s$, $[a]^s$(w) = *A*(a)(w)
- if t is a constant c, $[c]^s$(w) = $c^U$
- if t is $f^U$ : $s_1^U$ ×...× $s_n^U$ → $s^U$, $[f(t_1,t_2,...,t_n)]^s$(w) = $f^U$($[t_1]^s$(w), $[t_2]^s$(w), ..., $[t_n]^s$(w))

The semantics of propositions is defined as:

- (*S*,w) ⊢ ($t_1$ =$_s$ $t_2$) iff $[t_1]^s$(w) = $[t_2]^s$(w)
- (*S*,w) ⊢ ($t_1$ $p_s$ $t_2$) iff $[t_1]^s$(w) $p_s^U$ $[t_2]^s$(w)
- (*S*,w) ⊢ $\phi_1$ ⇒ $\phi_2$, iff (*S*,w) ⊢ $\phi_1$ implies (*S*,w) ⊢ $\phi_2$
- (*S*,w) ⊢ (¬$\phi$) iff ¬((*S*,w) ⊢ $\phi$)

Now on the semantic level, we can represent whether a proposition (in a signature) is true or valid in the interpretation structure of the signature:

**Definition 8.** A *θ-proposition* $\phi$ is *true* in an *θ-interpretation structure* *S*, written *S* ⊢ $\phi$, iff (*S*,w) ⊢ $\phi$ at every state w. A proposition $\phi$ is *valid*, written ⊢ $\phi$, iff it is true in every interpretation structure.

Having introduced the above concepts, we can now define when an interpretation structure is a model of a design.

**Definition 9.** Given a design $(\theta, \Lambda)$, where $\theta = (V, \Gamma, tv, ta, D)$ and $\Lambda$ is a triple $(I, R, L, U)$, a *model* of $(\theta, \Lambda)$ is an interpretation structure $S=(T, A, G)$ for $\theta$, such that:

- $(S, w_0) \models I$
- for every $g \in \Gamma$, $a \in D(g)$, $e \in G(g)$, and $(w, e, w') \in \rightarrow$, then $A(a)(w')= [R(g,a)]^s(w)$
- for every $w \in W$ and $g \in \Gamma$, if $e \in G(g)$ and for some $w' \in W$, $(w, e, w') \in \rightarrow$, then $(S,w) \models L(g)$.

That is to say, a *model* of a design is an interpretation structure for its signature that enforces the assignments, only permits actions to occur when their enabling guards are true, and for which the initial state satisfies the initialization constraint.

A model is said to be a *locus* if it is a locus as an interpretation structure, which enforces the encapsulation of local attributes.

This classification of models reflects the existence of different levels of semantics for the same design (taken as a set of models), depending on which subset of the set of its models is considered. These different semantics are associated with different notions of superposition (design morphism) that have been used in the literature, namely regulative, invasive and spectative. This means that there is no absolute notion of semantics for designs: it is always relative to the use one makes of designs. This corresponds to the categorical way of capturing the "meaning" of objects through the relationships (morphisms) that can be defined between them.

### 1.3 The Morphisms Between Designs

The concept of superposition has been proposed and used as a structuring mechanism for the design of parallel programs and distributed systems. Structure preserving transformations are usually formalized in terms of morphisms between the objects concerned, thus justifying the formalization of superposition in terms of morphisms of designs in CommUnity.

Having defined designs over signatures in the above section, we first introduce signature morphisms as a means of relating the "syntax" of two designs.

**Definition 10.** A *signature morphism* $\sigma$ from a signature $\theta_1=(V_1, \Gamma_1, tv_1, ta_1, D_1)$ to $\theta_2=(V_2, \Gamma_2, tv_2, ta_2, D_2)$ consists of a total functions $\sigma_\alpha: V_1 \rightarrow V_2$, and a partial mapping $\sigma_\gamma: \Gamma_2 \rightarrow \Gamma_1$ such that:

- For every $v \in V_1$, $\sigma_\alpha(v)$ has the same type as $v$.
- For every $o \in out(V_1)$, $\sigma_\alpha(o) \in out(V_2)$.
- For every $p \in prv(V_1)$, $\sigma_\alpha(p) \in prv(V_2)$.
- For every $i \in in(V_1)$, $\sigma_\alpha(i) \in out(V_2) \cup in(V_2)$.

For every $g \in \Gamma_2$, such that $\sigma_\gamma(g)$ is defined:

- $g \in sh(\Gamma_2)$, then $\sigma_\gamma(g) \in sh(\Gamma_1)$.
- $g \in prv(\Gamma_2)$, then $\sigma_\gamma(g) \in prv(\Gamma_1)$.
- $\sigma_\alpha(D_1(\sigma_\gamma(g))) \subseteq D_2(g)$.

A signature morphism maps attributes of a design to attributes of the system of which it is a component, and the direction of the mapping is reversed for actions. The first condition enforces the preservation of the type of each attribute by the morphism. Output and private attributes of the component should keep their classification in the system, while input attributes may be turned into output attributes, when they are synchronized with output channels of other components and thus represented as output channels of the system. The restriction over action domains means that the type of each action is preserved by the morphism. In other words, the images of the write frame of an action in the source program must be contained in the write frame of the corresponding action in the target program. Notice that more attributes may be included in the domain of the target program's action via a morphism. This is intuitive because an action of a component may be shared with other components within a system and, hence, has a larger domain.

Signature morphisms provide us with the means for relating a design with its superpositions. However, superposition is more than just a relationship between signatures on the level of syntax. To capture its semantics, we need a way of relating the models of the two designs as well as the terms and propositions that are used to build them.

Signature morphisms define translations between the languages associated with each signature in the obvious way:

**Definition 11.** Given a signature morphism $\sigma$: $\theta_1 \rightarrow \theta_2$, we can define translations between the languages associated with each signature:

- if t is a term:
  $\sigma(t) ::= \sigma(a)$ if t is a variable a
  c if t is a constant c
  $f(\sigma(t_1),\ldots, \sigma(t_n))$ if $t= f(t_1,\ldots, t_n)$
- if $\phi$ is a proposition:
  $\sigma(\phi) ::= \sigma(t_1) = \sigma(t_2)$ if $\phi$ is $t_1 = t_2$
  $\sigma(t_1) \, p_s \, \sigma(t_2)$ if $\phi$ is $t_1 \, p_s \, t_2$
  $\sigma(\phi_1) \Rightarrow \sigma(\phi_2)$ if $\phi$ is $\phi_1 \Rightarrow \phi_2$
  $\sigma(\phi_1) \wedge \sigma(\phi_2)$ if $\phi$ is $\phi_1 \wedge \phi_2$
  $\neg\sigma(\phi')$ if $\phi$ is $\neg\phi'$

**Definition 12.** Given a signature morphism $\sigma$: $\theta_1 \rightarrow \theta_2$ and a $\theta_2$–interpretation structure $S = (T, A, G)$, its $\sigma$-reduct, $S|_\sigma$, is the $\theta_1$–interpretation structure $(T, A|_\sigma, G|_\sigma)$, where $A|_\sigma(a) = A(\sigma(a))$, $G|_\sigma(g) = \cup \, G(\sigma^{-1}(g))$.

That is, we take the same transition system of the target design and interpret attribute symbols of the source design in the same way as their images under $\sigma$, and action symbols of the source design as the union of their images under $\sigma^{-1}$. Reducts provide us with the means for relating the behavior of a design with that of the superposed one. The following proposition establishes that properties of reducts are characterized by translation of properties.

**Proposition 1.** Given a $\theta_1$ proposition $\phi$ and a $\theta_2$–interpretation structure $S=(T, A, G)$, we have for every $w \in W$: $(S, w) \, t \, \sigma(\phi)$ iff $(S|_\sigma, w) \, t \, \phi$.

Superposition morphisms that preserve locality are called *regulative* superposition morphisms and are defined as follows:

**Definition 13.** A *regulative superposition morphism* σ from a design $(\theta_1, \Lambda_1)$ to another design $(\theta_2, \Lambda_2)$ is a signature morphism $\sigma: \theta_1 \to \theta_2$ such that:

0     $\vdash (I_2 \Rightarrow \sigma(I_1))$.

1     If $v \in loc(V_1)$, $g \in \Gamma_2$ and $\sigma_\alpha(v) \in D_2(g)$, then g is mapped to an action $\sigma_\gamma(g)$ and $v \in D_1(\sigma_\gamma(g))$.

For every $g \in \Gamma_2$ for which $\sigma_\gamma(g)$ is defined,

3     If $v \in loc(V_1)$ and $g \in D_2(\sigma_\alpha(v))$, then $\vdash (R_2(g, \sigma_\alpha(v)) \Leftrightarrow \sigma_\alpha(R_1(\sigma_\gamma(g), v)))$.

4     $\vdash (L_2(g) \Rightarrow \sigma(L_1(\sigma_\gamma(g))))$.

5     $\vdash (U_2(g) \Rightarrow \sigma(U_1(\sigma_\gamma(g))))$.

Notice that we do not require $\sigma_\alpha$ to be injective, and two channels of the same category (output/private/input) in the source design can be mapped to one channel of the target design. Because we only consider the actions in the target design mapped to the source design, $\sigma_\gamma$ does not need to be surjective.

The second condition implies that actions of the system in which a component C is not involved cannot have local channels of the component C in their write frame, which corresponds to the locality condition: new actions cannot be added to the domains of attributes of the source program. The justification is as follows: suppose system action g has $\sigma_\alpha(v)$ in its write frame, $v \in loc(V_1)$, then $\sigma_\gamma(g)$ must be defined, and $\sigma_\gamma(g) \in D_1(v)$. Therefore, component C is involved in the system action.

Regulative superposition morphisms require that the functionality of the base design in terms of its variables be preserved (the underspecification cannot be reduced) and allows for the enabling and progress conditions of its actions to be strengthened. Strengthening of the lower bound reflects the fact that all the components that participate in the execution of a joint action have to give their permission for the action to occur. On the other hand, the progress of a joint action can only be guaranteed when the involved components can locally guarantee so. Regulative superpositions preserve encapsulation and do not change the actions themselves, as far as they relate to the basic variables.

**Proposition 2.** Let $\sigma: (\theta_1, \Lambda_1) \to (\theta_2, \Lambda_2)$ be a regulative superposition morphism. Then the reduct of every model of $(\theta_2, \Lambda_2)$ is also a model of $(\theta_1, \Lambda_1)$.

We find that in the proof of proposition 2.2, we do not use condition 2 of regulative superposition morphism, which means this proposition will hold without enforcing the encapsulation principle. When we consider condition 2 and the definition of signature morphism, we will have the following assertion:

**Proposition 3.** If $v \in loc(V_1)$, then $D_1(v) = \sigma_\gamma(D_2(\sigma_\alpha(v)))$.

This result implies the following property:

**Proposition 4.** Let $\sigma: (\theta_1, \Lambda_1) \to (\theta_2, \Lambda_2)$ be a regulative superposition morphism; then the reduct of every locus of $(\theta_2, \Lambda_2)$ is also a locus of $(\theta_1, \Lambda_1)$.

The reason is that through regulative superposition, the domains of the attributes remain the same up to translation, as stated above. Therefore, it will prevent "old attributes" from being changed by "new actions", i.e., actions of the target design not mapped to the source design.

Now we will introduce the notion of extension morphism, related to ideas of model-expansiveness. The motivation for extension morphisms originated from the substitutability principle from object oriented program design, which says if a component $P_2$ extends another component $P_1$, then we can replace $P_1$ by $P_2$ and the "clients" of $P_1$ must not perceive the difference. This principle cannot be characterized by regulative superpositions or refinement morphisms, as we may want to extend the component by breaking encapsulation. This controlled breaking of encapsulation is necessary when dealing with many aspects.

**Definition 14.** An *extension morphism* $\sigma$ from a design $(\theta_1, \Lambda_1)$ to another design $(\theta_2, \Lambda_2)$ is a signature morphism $\sigma$ such that:

1     $\sigma_\gamma$ is surjective.
2     $\sigma_\alpha$ is injective.
3     There exists a formula $\beta$, which contains only channels from $(V_2 - \sigma_\alpha(V_1))$, such that $\beta$ is satisfiable and $\vdash I_2 \Leftrightarrow \sigma(I_1) \wedge \beta$.

For every $g \in \Gamma_2$ for which $\sigma_\gamma(g)$ is defined,

4     If $v \in loc(V_1)$ and $g \in D_2(\sigma_\alpha(v))$, then there exists a formula $\beta$, which contains only primed channels from $(V_2' - \sigma_\alpha(V_1)')$, and $\beta$ is satisfiable and such that $\vdash \sigma (L_1(\sigma_\gamma(g))) \Rightarrow (R_2(g, \sigma_\alpha(v)) \Leftrightarrow \sigma_\alpha(R_1(\sigma_\gamma(g), v)) \wedge \beta)$.
5     If $v \in loc(V_1)$, $g \in D_2(\sigma_\alpha(v))$, then $v \in D_1(\sigma_\gamma(g))$.
6     $\vdash (\sigma(L_1(\sigma_\gamma(g))) \Rightarrow L_2(g))$.
7     $\vdash (\sigma(U_1(\sigma_\gamma(g))) \Rightarrow U_2(g))$.

This definition of extension morphism was first given [8]. Because we expect that the extended design can replace the original design in a system and the clients of the original component should not perceive any difference, the first two conditions ensure the preservation of its interface. The initialization condition of the original design can be strengthened in its extended version, while respecting the initialization of the channels of the original component, as required in the third condition. The fourth condition indicates that the actions corresponding to those of the original design should preserve the assignments to old channels and the assignments to new channels must be realisable, when the safety guards of their image actions in the original design are satisfied. The fifth condition establishes that for each action of the extended design that is mapped to an action of the original design, it can only modify old channels that have been modified by the corresponding action of the original design. The last two conditions indicate that both the enabling and progress guards can be weakened, but not strengthened.

Because an extension morphism relaxes the enabling guard of the source design, the reduct of a model of the target design may not be a model of the source design. However, the model-expansive property holds for extension morphism [8], which means the extended design can replace the source design and the clients of the original design will not perceive the difference.

**Proposition 5.** Let $\sigma$ be an extension morphism from a design $(\theta_1, \Lambda_1)$ to another design $(\theta_2, \Lambda_2)$. Then, every model of $(\theta_1, \Lambda_1)$ can be expanded to a corresponding model of $(\theta_2, \Lambda_2)$.

The rationale behind the definition of extension morphisms is the characterization of the substitutability principle (a property that can be shown to fail for invasive super-position, a more general and less predictable way of breaking encapsulation, as defined in [15]). The above result shows that, if there exists an extension morphism $\sigma$ between two designs $(\theta_1, \Lambda_1)$ and $(\theta_2, \Lambda_2)$ (and this extension is realisable), then all behaviours exhibited by $(\theta_1, \Lambda_1)$ are also exhibited by $(\theta_2, \Lambda_2)$. Since superposition morphisms, used as a representation of "clientship" (strictly, the existence of a super-position morphism between two designs indicates that the first is part of the second, as a component is part of a system when the first is used by the system), restrict the behaviours of superposed components, it is guaranteed that all behaviours exhibited by a component when this becomes part of a system will also be exhibited by an extension of this component, if replaced by the first one in the system. Of course, one can also obtain *more behaviours*, and this is the intention behind the definition of extension morphisms, resulting from the explicit use of new actions of the component. But if none of the new actions are used, then the extended component behaves exactly as the original one did.

Now we introduce the relationship of refinement between two components, which we need to enable us to use the architectural concept of connector.

**Definition 15.** A *refinement morphism* $\sigma$ from a design $(\theta_1, \Lambda_1)$ to another design $(\theta_2, \Lambda_2)$ is a signature morphism $\sigma: \theta_1 \to \theta_2$ such that:

1   For every $i \in in(V_1)$, $\sigma_\alpha(i) \in in(V_2)$.
2   $\sigma_\alpha$ is injective on input and output channels.
3   $\sigma_\gamma$ is surjective on shared actions in $\Gamma_1$.
4   $t\ (I_2 \Rightarrow \sigma(I_1))$.
5   If $v \in loc(V_1)$, $g \in \Gamma_2$ and $\sigma_\alpha(v) \in D_2(g)$, then $g$ is mapped to an action $\sigma_\gamma(g)$ and $v \in D_1(\sigma_\gamma(g))$.

For every $g \in \Gamma_2$ where $\sigma_\gamma(g)$ is defined,

6   If $v \in loc(V_1)$ and $g \in D_2(\sigma_\alpha(v))$, then $t\ (R_2(g, \sigma_\alpha(v)) \Rightarrow \sigma_\alpha(R_1(\sigma_\gamma(g), v)))$.
7   $t\ (L_2(g) \Rightarrow \sigma(L_1(\sigma_\gamma(g))))$.

For every shared action $g \in \Gamma_1$,

8   $t\ (\sigma(U_1(g)) \Rightarrow \wedge U_2(\sigma_\gamma^{-1}(g)))$.

A refinement morphism identifies a way in which design $(\theta_1, \Lambda_1)$ is refined by a more concrete design $(\theta_2, \Lambda_2)$. The first three conditions must be established to ensure that refinement does not change the interface between the system and its environment. Notice that we do not require $\sigma_\gamma$ to be injective because the set of actions in the target design that are mapped to action $g$ of the source design can be viewed as a menu of refinements that is made available for implementing g. Different choices can be made at different states to take advantage of the structures available at the more concrete level.

As for the "old actions", the last two conditions in the refinement morphism definition require that the interval defined by their enabling and progress conditions must be preserved or reduced. This is intuitive because refinement should reduce underspecification, so the enabling condition of any implementation must lie in the "old interval": the lower bound cannot be weakened and the upper bound cannot be strengthened. This is also the reason why the underspecification regarding the effects of the actions of the more abstract design are intended to be reduced.

**Proposition 6.** The structure composed of CommUnity designs and superposition/refinement/extension morphisms constitutes a category SUP/REF/EXT, respectively, where the composition of two morphisms $\sigma_1$ and $\sigma_2$ is defined in terms of the composition of the corresponding channel and action mappings of $\sigma_1$ and $\sigma_2$.

So, we can build superpositions/refinements/extensions incrementally. Most importantly, SUP has finite colimits, i.e., we can compute the system corresponding to a configuration of CommUnity designs whose channels and actions are synchronized via cables and superposition morphisms. So called *higher order connectors* [29] are defined in CommUnity to enable designers to use complex connectors between components, in the style of software architecture approaches. These higher order connectors are just CommUnity designs in which some components play a designated *role*, namely stating minimum requirements of actual components to be connected by the connector in question. One can instantiate a role with a 'real' component by defining a refinement from the role to the component. Thus, when designing a system using components and connectors, we may end up with a configuration in which we see both regulative superpositions and refinements. In order to calculate the intended system form this configuration, we must eliminate the refinements and thus get a configuration in SUP.

Luckily, we have the following crucial result about the joint use of refinement and superposition morphisms. If we restrict the kinds of components used to interconnect components to so called *cables*, we can combine superposition morphisms from such a cable with a refinement. A cable is a design containing only input channels and its actions having the following form g: true -> skip. We only expect input channels in the cable, which can be used to interconnect designs, because output channels cannot be used to connect the input channel of one design with the output channel of another design, and it will make no sense to interconnect output channels of different designs. Also we set the enabling guard and progress guard of each action in the cable to true and set R(g) to skip (by skip we mean this action has no effects on the local channels of the design), which is good enough to synchronize the actions.

**Proposition 7.** Suppose m is a regulative superposition morphism from cable $\theta$ to design $C_i$ and n is a refinement morphism from design $C_i$ to design $E_i$; there exists a regulative superposition morphism n' from cable $\theta$ to design $E_i$ such that n'=n•m.

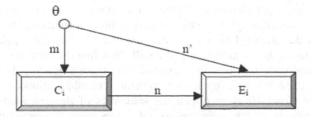

**Fig. 1.** Combining regulative superposition and refinement morphisms

## 2 CommUnity and Extension Morophisms

It has been shown in [5] that higher-order connectors provide a very convenient basis for enhancing the behavior of an architecture of component designs, by the superimposition of aspects, such as fault tolerance, security, monitoring, compression, etc. Owing to the coordination mechanism of CommUnity, which externalizes completely the definition of interaction between components, the coupling between the components has been reduced to a minimum so that we can superimpose aspects on existing systems through replacement, superposition and refinement of components. However, higher-order connectors are not powerful enough for defining various kinds of aspects, because some of them require *extensions* of the components and connectors [8], which break encapsulation of the extended component, though in a controlled and predictable way. (The usual relationships used in CommUnity, i.e., regulative superposition and refinement, preserve encapsulation: channels (attributes) of the original component are not modified by new actions of the new component and actions of the original component can only have their enabling guards and effects strengthened in the new component.) Hence, we defined an extension morphism as a mechanism for modifying/adapting components, in a way that satisfies the notion of substitutability arising in the context of object oriented design and programming [8], enables us to predict properties of extended components in a safe manner and enables the design of various aspects [8].

This means that in a well-formed configuration diagram we should be able to replace component C by its valid extension, component C', and preserve the well formedness (our ability to compute the colimit) of the diagram. We prove this property in the next section. To illustrate the application of this principle in designing systems with the CommUnity language, a vending machine system example will be discussed below to show how we can combine regulative superpositions with extension morphims to derive an "augmented" version of the original system, where the modified system is not simply a refinement of the original, nor is it a regulated version of the original obtained by the use of regulative superpositions (the usual structuring relationship in CommUnity).

### 2.1 Combining Regulative Superpositions with Extension Morphisms

In this section we will consider the case where, in a well-formed configuration diagram, one component is extended by a design through an extension morphism. Since we know that, in a well formed configuration diagram, all the components are interconnected by cables through regulative superposition morphisms, the component to be replaced by the extended design is connected to a cable by the regulative superposition morphism, as shown in Figure 2. We will show that the regulative superposition can be combined with the extension morphism to obtain a new regulative superposition from the cable to the extended component. This then allows us to apply the mechanisms of CommUnity to obtain the semantics of the extended configuration diagram, the colimit, which again consists of components connected through cables and superposition morphisms. Again, it is crucial to have the notion of cables to interconnect the components, to ensure that the composition of regulative superposition and extension morphism will give a new regulative superposition.

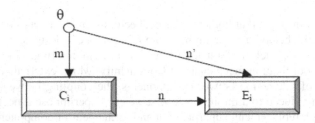

**Fig. 2.** Combining regulative superposition and extension morphisms

**Proposition 8.** Suppose m is a regulative superposition morphism from cable $\theta$ to design $C_i$ and n is an extension morphism from design $C_i$ to design $E_i$; there exists a regulative superposition morphism n' from cable $\theta$ to design $E_i$ such that n'=n•m.

*Proof*
The morphism n' is defined as follows:

- n'$_\alpha$ is a total function: for every channel v in $\theta$, n'$_\alpha$(v) = $n_\alpha(m_\alpha(v))$.
- n'$_\gamma$ is a partial mapping: for every action g in $E_i$, if n$_\gamma$(g) is defined and m$_\gamma$(n$_\gamma$ (g)) is also defined, n'$_\gamma$(g) = m$_\gamma$(n$_\gamma$ (g)); otherwise, it is undefined.

Since an extension morphism is also a signature morphism, we know n' is a signature morphism. To check if n' is a regulative superposition morphism, we need to check the following conditions:

- $I_{Ei} \Rightarrow$ n'($I_\theta$ ).

Because n is an extension morphism, there exists a formula $\alpha$, using only channels contained in ($V_{Ei}-n_\alpha(V_{Ci})$), and $\alpha$ is satisfiable, $\vdash I_{Ei} \Leftrightarrow n(I_{Ci})\wedge\alpha$.
We have $I_{Ei} \Rightarrow n(I_{Ci})$, $I_{Ci} \Rightarrow m(I_\theta)$, so $n(I_{Ci}) \Rightarrow n(m(I_\theta)) \Leftrightarrow$ n'($I_\theta$), and $I_{Ei} \Rightarrow$ n'($I_\theta$ ).

- If $v \in loc(\theta)$, $g \in \Gamma_{Ei}$ and n'$_\alpha$(v) $\in D_{Ei}$(g), then g is mapped to an action n'$_\gamma$(g) and v$\in D_\theta$(n'$_\gamma$(g)).
- For every $g \in \Gamma_{Ei}$ where n'$_\gamma$(g) is defined, if $v \in loc(\theta)$ and $g \in D_{Ei}$(n'$_\alpha$(v)), then $R_{Ei}$(g, n'$_\alpha$(v)) $\Leftrightarrow$ n'$_\alpha$($R_\theta$(n'$_\gamma$(g),v)).

Because $\theta$ only contains input channels, loc($\theta$) is empty, so these two conditions hold.

- $L_{Ei}(g) \Rightarrow n'(L_\theta(n'_\gamma(g)))$.
- $U_{Ei}(g) \Rightarrow n'(U_\theta(n'_\gamma(g)))$.

From our definition of "middle" design, $L_\theta(n'_\gamma(g)) \Leftrightarrow$ true, $U_\theta(n'_\gamma(g)) \Leftrightarrow$ true, so these two conditions hold.

With this property, in a well-formed configuration diagram, we are able to replace a component by its extension component, by combining the regulative superposition from the cable to the old component with the extension morphism between the old component and its extension, to obtain a new regulative superposition from the cable to the extended component. If we build several extensions, each built on top of the previous one, then the fact that extensions compose in the category of CommUnity designs and extension morphisms guarantees that this composition is an extension. Hence, the above result still applies when we build extensions incrementally. Therefore, we reach the conclusion that in a well-formed configuration diagram of a system, we can extend any subcomponents of the system (through extension morphisms), and thus obtain an updated well-formed configuration diagram only containing regulative superpositions, through which the semantics of the new system can be derived from its colimit. Moreover, it can be shown that the colimit of the new configuration diagram is an extension of the colimit of the old configuration diagram [8].

By examining the proof of proposition 8, we can see that, if $\theta_i$ is not a cable, the composition of a regulative superposition and an extension morphism may not give a regulative superposition. Therefore, it is necessary to enforce designs to be interconnected by cables in a well-formed configuration diagram, so that the colimit will exist after extending any of the designs in the diagram through extension morphisms. (This result mimics the properties of refinements in the context of cables and regulative superpositions.)

## 3   An Example Vending Machine System

Now we want to model a system consisting of a customer and a vending machine with the DynaComm language, to illustrate the use of hierarchical design and then to illustrate the use of extension morphisms to enable us to modify our design in a way not allowed by refinements and regulative superpositions. The requirement of this system is described as follows: *The vending machine maintains a list of items, along with the price and amount of each item. The customer can place an order by inputting the name of the item and the payment to the vending machine. Initially, we only allow the customer to order one item in a transaction; this will be extended later. The vending machine will check the price of the item and decide if the order is accepted. If so, it will deliver the item along with the change to the customer; otherwise, the payment is returned to the customer. Initially, the vending machine will only accept payment comprised of nickels, dimes, quarters and loonies (Canadian single dollars using the image of a local bird), so it will refuse the order if the customer puts a one cent piece in the payment slot. Meanwhile, if the vending machine is not able to make the change, it will also refuse the order and return the payment.*

### 3.1 The Design of the Customer

We consider the machine's interface, operated by the customer, as the simulation of the customer's behavior. To make the system simple and general at first, the interface is divided into two parts: the buttons and the slot. The names of different items label the corresponding item buttons, and after the customer presses one of them, other item buttons will be disabled, so that he can only choose one item in an order. Then the customer can choose the "confirm" button to continue the order, where the slot will indicate to him to put the coins in and the complete order will be sent to the vending machine. If the customer chooses the "cancel" button, all the item buttons will be enabled and he can start another order.

The vending machine will check the price of this order and whether the ordered item is still available in its storage. If so, it will ask the slot to make the change. Then the vending machine will deliver the product to the slot and enable the item buttons, if the change can be made. Otherwise, the order will be refused and the payment is returned to the customer.

#### 3.1.1 The Interface Controller

According to the above requirement, the customer places his order of an item through the buttons (including the item buttons and the command buttons: confirm and cancel) on the machine's interface, so we design an interface controller to model these buttons, as well as the customer's interaction with the interface of the machine. A finite set of actions for the item buttons and "confirm", "cancel" buttons are specified in the following design. The slot_get and slot_ret actions are designed to interact with the slot component to obtain the payment from the customer. Meanwhile, we use the order action to send the complete order to the vending machine, and after the order has been processed by the vending machine, the order_ret action will be called to reset the controller.

```
design component controller
in      // the customer's payment in the slot
        i_pay: int
prv     b_item: array(int);
        bt_g: bool;   //guard for item buttons
        bt_confirm: bool;   //guard for confirm/cancel buttons
        slot_g: bool;   // guard for slot get action
        s_req: bool;
        ord_g: bool;   // guard for order action
        o_req: bool
out     // order to vending machine
        c_item: list (int);
        c_pay: int
init    ord_g = false ∧ o_req = false ∧ bt_g = true ∧ bt_confirm
        = false ∧ slot_g = false ∧ s_req = false ∧ c_item = NULL
actions
        button_select(id: int)[bt_g,c_item,bt_confirm]: bt_g,
        false ->
        bt_g' = false ∧ c_item' = c_item * b_item [id] ∧
        bt_confirm' = true
```

```
[] button_confirm[bt_confirm,slot_g]: bt_confirm, false ->
   bt_confirm' = false ∧ slot_g' = true
[] button_cancel[bt_confirm,bt_g,c_item]: bt_confirm, false
   -> bt_g' = true ∧ bt_confirm' = false ∧ c_item' = NULL
[] slot_get[slot_g,s_req]: slot_g, false ->
   slot_g' = false ∧ s_req' = true
[] slot_ret[c_pay, s_req, ord_g]: s_req, false ->
   c_pay' = i_pay ∧ s_req' = false ∧ ord_g' = true
[] order[o_req,ord_g]: ¬o_req ∧ ord_g, false ->
   o_req' = true ∧ ord_g' = false
   // enable all the item buttons
[] order_ret[o_req, bt_g, c_item]: o_req, false ->
   o_req' = false ∧ bt_g' = true ∧ c_item' = NULL
endofdesign
```

The input channel i_pay indicates the payment received from the customer. A finite set of item button actions (button_select) are defined, which correspond to the sequence of item buttons on the machine's interface. These actions are examples of *schema actions* indexed by the id (in the above sequence) of the item buttons. Such schema actions may be used to describe succinctly a finite set of related actions, distinguishable by means of some index set. See [27] for a full explanation of such families of actions and their precise semantics. We use a fixed size array b_item to store the item's index in the storage of the vending machine, and the index of array b_item will correspond to the id of the item button, e.g., the second item button b_item[2] may correspond to the item index 6 in the item list of the vending machine's storage.

The workflow of the controller component is described as follows. After one item button is selected, the guard bt_g is set to false to disable all the item buttons, so that the customer can only choose buttons confirm or cancel (as the enabling guards of other actions are disabled). If he chooses the confirm button, the guard slot_g is enabled and the slot_get action will be executed to request the customer's payment in the slot component. If the cancel option is selected, the controller will enable all the item buttons and wait for the customer's input of a new transaction. After the payment is obtained from the slot, the order action will be called and it will send the order

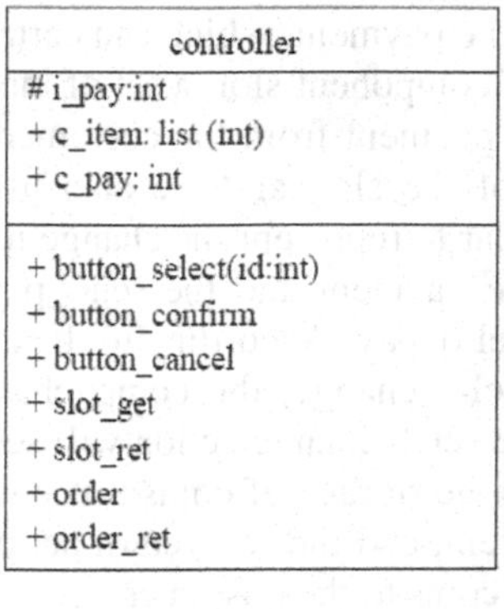

| controller |
|---|
| # i_pay:int |
| + c_item: list (int) |
| + c_pay: int |
| + button_select(id:int) |
| + button_confirm |
| + button_cancel |
| + slot_get |
| + slot_ret |
| + order |
| + order_ret |

**Fig. 3.** Graphical representation of the controller component

(c_item, c_pay) to the vending machine, then wait for the result of the order. After the vending machine processes the order and indicates the result to the order_ret action of the controller, the order_ret action will reset the item buttons and the c_item list, to be ready to accept another order. The graphical notation for the (syntax of the) controller component is shown in Figure 3 (we suppress private channels and actions):

Notice that we use a number of guards to control the sequence of actions in the controller, and the correctness of our design can be ensured by maintaining the right workflow of the component through the appropriate use of these guards. We also use the list data structure to record the ordered items, although currently only one item is allowed in the order. The reason is that in the different kinds of design morphisms we have discussed so far, the mapping of channels requires the types of channels to be preserved. (Refinement morphisms do not support data refinement, so a refinement solution to get around this problem is not available.) If we use one channel of integer type to record the ordered item now and there is a new requirement to allow the customer to select multiple items in an order, we have to add new channels to the component and modify the corresponding actions as well, which seems awkward. Therefore, we choose the list data structure for the ordered items and the corresponding actions are designed to process the list of items.

We have also designed a pattern for a pair of actions of one component (e.g. slot_get and slot_ret), which sends a request to another component and waits for its response to proceed. The trick is to assign a guard (initialized to be false) to the callback action to make sure that it will not be called arbitrarily in an unexpected situation, and it will only be enabled in the request action.

### 3.1.2 The Slot

The slot component takes care of the acceptance of the customer's payment and decides if the correct change can be made depending on its current store of coins. When the interface controller requests the payment from the customer, the slot will distinguish the various kinds of coins and it will refuse the payment and indicate this event to the controller if there exists an illegal coin in the customer's input. Otherwise, it will store the coins and send the payment amount to the controller. Regarding the function for making the change, the slot is able to compute the composition of coins for the amount of change requested by the vending machine, based on its current store. If the computation is not successful, the vending machine will refuse the order and inform the slot to return the payment, which can certainly be made.

In the following design of component slot, a set of input channels such as i_dollar, i_quarter, etc. represents the payment from the customer, a set of private channels is included as the coin store of the slot, and we also use output channels o_nickel, o_dime, o_quarter and o_dollar to represent the change made by the slot. The get_pay action stores the coins in the payment and the send_pay action puts the amount of payment in the output channel o_pay. According to the amount of change that should be made in the input channel r_change, the comp_change action will compute the composition of coins, and the send_change action will send the result of the computation (change_res) and update the storage of coins if needed. While the ordered item is accepted by the action rec_item, and the rec_return action receives the returned payment amount and returns the coins to the customer.

```
design component slot
in      // input coins from customer
        i_cent: int;
        i_nickle: int;
        i_dime: int;
        i_quarter: int;
        i_dollar: int;
        // received change amount and items from vending machine
        r_change : int;
        r_item: list(ITEM)
prv     // coins storage
        s_nickle: int;
        s_dime: int;
        s_quarter: int;
        s_dollar: int;
        // guards for action sequence
        get_g: bool;
        change_g:bool;
        item_g: bool
out     // changes made by the slot
        o_nickle: int;
        o_dime: int;
        o_quarter: int;
        o_dollar: int;
        s_item: list (ITEM);   // items to slot
        o_pay: int; // payment amount to the controller
        change_res: bool
init    get_g = true ∧ change_g = true ∧ change_res = false ∧
        item_g = false
actions
        get_pay[get_g, s_nickle, s_dime, s_quarter, s_dollar]:
        get_g ∧ i_cent = 0, false ->
        get_g' = false ∧ s_nickle' = s_nickle + i_nickle ∧
        s_dime' = s_dime + i_dime ∧ s_quarter' = s_quarter +
        i_quarter ∧ s_dollar' = s_dollar + i_dollar
   []   send_pay[get_g, o_pay]: ¬ get_g, false ->
        get_g' = true ∧ o_pay' = 100*i_dollar + 25*i_quarter +
        10*i_dime + 5*i_nickle
   []   comp_change[change_g, change_res]: change_g, false ->
        get_changed ∧ change_g' = false
   []   send_change[change_g]: ¬change_g, false ->
        change_g' = true ∧ (change_res = true ⇒  item_g' = true ∧
        s_nickle' = s_nickle - o_nickle ∧ s_dime' = s_dime -
        o_dime ∧ s_quarter' = s_quarter - o_quarter ∧ s_dollar' =
        s_dollar - o_dollar)
   []   rec_item[s_item, item_g]: item_g, false ->
        s_item' = r_item ∧ item_g' = false
   []   rec_return[ret_g, s_item,]: true, false ->
        s_item' = NULL ∧ get_changed
endofdesign
```

In the above design, we assume the function to compute the composition of change, namely get_change, has already been defined, which takes r_change as input and computes the number of nickels, dimes, quarters and dollars. If the computation is successful, it will set change_res to be true and the output channels for the change. Otherwise, change_res is set to false and this event is sent to the vending machine. Actually, get_change solves a linear programming problem, which takes s_nickel, s_dime, s_quarter, s_dollar and r_change as parameters. To simplify the specification of the slot component, we do not describe the detailed procedure here.

The workflow of the slot component is described as below. When the interface controller requests the payment from the customer, the get_pay and send_pay actions will be executed to provide the payment amount to the controller. After the vending machine receives the order and recognizes that the payment is enough, it will ask the slot to compute the change. So, the comp_change action is called and the result of computation (change_res) is sent to the vending machine by the send_change action. If the result is successful, the change is given to the customer by the slot and the vending machine will send the product to the slot by means of the rec_item action. Otherwise, the rec_return action will get the amount of payment from the vending machine and give it back to the customer by calling the get_change function. The graphical notation for the slot component is as follows, where we again suppress the private channels and actions.

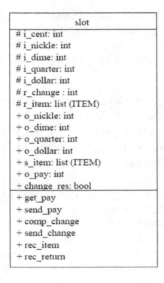

**Fig. 4.** Graphical representation of the slot component

## 3.2   The Design of the Vending Machine

Based on the functional requirement of the vending machine, we will divide it into two components: vender and inventory, where the vender is in charge of the interaction with the customer interface (controller and slot), and the inventory serves as a database for storing the actual products (items) and maintaining the price and amount of each item.

### 3.2.1  The Vender

The job of the vender is to accept the order from the customer (the accept action), ask the inventory to check the price and amount of the ordered item(s) (actions check_inv and check_ret), send the amount of change to the slot and ask if the change can be made (actions change and change_ret), request the item(s) from the inventory (actions req_item and req_return), deliver the item(s) to the customer (the delivery action) or return the payment (the return_ord action), and inform the interface controller to be reset to start a new order (the reset_controller action). The design of the vender component is as follows, the meaning of the channels being explained in the comments.

```
design component vender
in      // the ordered item(s) and payment from the controller
        in_item: list(int);
        in_pay: int;
        // the price of the ordered item(s) from the inventory
        inv_price: int;
        inv_item: list(ITEM);
        // the result of checking whether the change can be made
        from the slot
        chg_res: bool
prv     // the set of guards to control the sequence of actions
        ac: bool;
        ck: bool;
        cg: bool;
        rt: bool;
        rq:bool;
        rc: bool;
        dl:bool;
        // stores the requested item(s) from the inventory
        v_item: list(ITEM);
        // stores the order and payment from the customer
        ord_item: list(int);
        ord_pay: int
out     // the order and payment to be sent to the inventory
        ck_item: list(int);
        ck_pay: int;
        // the amount of change to be sent to the slot
        chg_amt: int;
        // the ordered item(s) sent to the customer
        out_item: list(ITEM);
        // the returned amount of payment to be sent to the slot
        ret_amt: int
init    ac' = false ∧ ck' = false ∧ cg' = false ∧ rt' = false ∧
        dl' = false ∧ rq' = false ∧ rc' =false
actions
        [ac, ord_item, ord_pay, ck]: ¬ac, false ->
        ac' = true ∧ ord_item' = in_item ∧ ord_pay' = in_pay ∧ ck'
        = true
```

```
[]   check_inv[ck, ck_item, ck_pay]: ck, false ->
     ck_item' = ord_item ∧ ck_pay' = ord_pay ∧ ck' = false
[]   check_ret[cg, rt, v_item]: true, false ->
     (inv_price >= 0 ⟹ cg' = true) ∨ (inv_price = 0 ⟹ rt' =
     true)
[]   change[cg, chg_amt]: cg, false ->
     chg_amt' = ord_pay − inv_price ∧ cg' = false
[]   change_ret[rq, rt ]: true, false ->
     (chg_res = true ⟹ rq' = true) ∨ (chg_res = false ⟹ rt'
     = true)
[]   req_item[rq, ck_item]: rq, false ->
     ck_item' = ord_item ∧ rq' = false
[]   req_return[v_item, dl]:true, false ->
     v_item' = inv_item ∧ dl' = true
[]   return_ord[rt, ret_amt, out_item, ac, rc]: rt, false ->
     rt' = false ∧ ret_amt' = ord_pay ∧ out_item' = NULL ∧
     rc' = true
[]   delivery[dl, ac, out_item]: dl, false ->
     dl' = false ∧ out_item' = v_item ∧ rc' = true
     // inform the controller to accept another order
[]   reset_controller[rc]: rc, false ->
     rc' = false ∧ ac' = false
endofdesign
```

According to the initialization condition of this design, only the accept action is enabled and it is synchronized with the order action of controller to accept the order of the customer. It also sets the guard ck to be true, so that the check_inv action will be executed to ask the inventory to check the price and amount of the ordered item(s). The check_ret action waits for the response from the inventory: if inv_price>=0, it means that the transaction can continue and this action sets the guard cg to be true, to call the slot to check if the change can be made; otherwise, it enables the guard rt to call the return_ord action, if any item is not available or the payment is not enough.

If the order can continue, the change action is synchronized with the comp_change action of the slot to make the appropriate change to the customer. Then the change_ret action will wait for the response from the slot indicated by the input channel chg_res: if the change can be made, the vender will request the item from the inventory using the req_item action, which is synchronized with the rec_req action of the inventory; otherwise, the return_ord action is called to return the payment. After the vender receives the requested item from the inventory using the req_return action, the delivery action will be called, which is synchronized with the rec_item action of the slot to deliver the item. Otherwise, the action return_ord will be executed and the slot's action rec_return will be synchronized to return the payment to the customer. Finally, the vender will call the reset_controller action to synchronize with the order_ret action of the controller to inform it that the next order can now be taken.

The graphical notation for the vender component is depicted in Figure 5 below (we ignore private channels and actions).

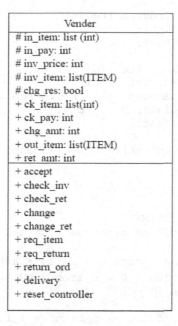

**Fig. 5.** Graphical representation of the vender component

Again, we use a set of guards to control the sequence of actions in the vender component, and, in the above explanation of the component's work mechanism, we are able to control the right workflow of the design through the appropriate use of these guards, so that the correctness of our design can be ensured.

### 3.2.2 The Inventory

The inventory component maintains a list of items along with their price and remaining amount: (item_id:int, item:ITEM, price:int, amount:int), where item_id is the item's index in the storage and item represents the real item product. We use an array db (with a fixed size) to store this list of items, and the index of this array corresponds to item_id. Meanwhile, we assume functions first, second and third have been defined to return the first, second and third member of db, respectively.

The private action count_item calculates the amount of each ordered item and stores it in the channel s_item. It also computes the total price of the order. The check_price action goes through the inventory database and compares the amount of each ordered item with the amount of that item in the storage. If the storage is not enough or the payment is less than the price of the order, the output channel will be set to 0; otherwise, it will set to the value in p_price. The get_item action will retrieve the items from the storage according to the order and update the db channel. The specification of the inventory component is as follows:

```
design component inventory
in      // the ordered item(s) and payment from the vender
        i_item: list (int);
        i_pay: int
```

```
prv     // stores the ordered item(s)
        p_item: list (int);
        r_item: list (int);
        p_price: int;
        // array index is item id
        db: array (ITEM, int, int);
        // stores the amount of each ordered item, all the en-
        tries are initialized to be 0.
        s_item: array (int);
        j :int;
        // the guards to control the sequence of actions
        price_g: bool;
        amt_g: bool;
        ret_g: bool;
        send_g : bool
out     o_item: list (ITEM);
        // the price of the order sent to the vender
        o_price: int
init    p_item = NULL ∧  price_g = false ∧ amt_g = false ∧ ret_g
        = false ∧ o_price = 0 ∧ o_item = NULL ∧ r_item = NULL ∧
        send_g = false
actions
        check[]: true, false -> p_item' = i_item
   [] prv count_item[]: p_item != NULL, false ->
        s_item[head(p_item)]' = s_item[head(p_item)] + 1 ∧
        p_price' = p_price + second(db[head(p_item)]) ∧ p_item' =
        tail(p_item) ∧ (tail(p_item) = NULL ⇒ price_g' = true)
   [] prv check_price[: price_g, false ->
        price_g' = false ∧ ((i_pay >= p_price ⇒ amt_g' = true ∧ j'
        = 1) ∨ (i_pay < p_price ⇒ ret_g' = true ∧ o_price' = 0))
   [] prv check_amt[]: amt_g ∧ (j <= sizeof(db)) , false ->
        ((s_item[j] <= third(db[j])) ⇒ j' = j + 1 ∧ (j =sizeof(db)
        ⇒ ret_g' = true ∧ o_price' = p_price)) ∨ (s_item[j] >
        third(db[j]) ⇒ amt_g' = false ∧ o_price' = 0 ∧ ret_g' =
        true))
   [] inv_ret[]: ret_g, false -> ret_g' = false
   [] rec_req[]: true, false -> r_item' = i_item
   [] prv get_item[]: r_item != NULL, false -> o_item ' =
        o_item * first(db[head(r_item)]) ∧
        third(db[head(r_item)])' = third(db[head(r_item)])-1 ∧
        r_item' = tail(r_item) ∧ (tail(r_item) = NULL ⇒ send_g'
        = true)
   [] send_item[]: send_g, false -> send_g' = false
endofdesign
```

The workflow of this component is as follows. First, the check action is called to enable the guard of the count_item action. Then the action check_price is called to decide if the total price is less than ck_pay. If so, the inv_ret action will be enabled to return the result (inv_price) to the vender. Otherwise, the check_amt action is executed to check if the amount of each ordered item in the inventory is greater than the number of this item requested in the order. If so, it will call action inv_ret to return inv_price > 0 (the total price of the items in ck_item); otherwise, it will return inv_price = 0 in the inv_ret action. After the vender verifies that the change can be made, it will call the req_item action, which is synchronized with the rec_req action of the inventory, to get the ordered items and update the storage, and the inventory has the send_item action to send the ordered items back to the vender.

Notice that in the count_item action we use the guard p_item != NULL to iterate through the list of ordered items. It can be generalized as a mechanism to implement the loop structures in the DynaComm language. (See future work.)

### 3.2.3  The Vending Machine Subsystem

According to our design of the vender and inventory components and the discussion of their interactions, we can put them together by interconnecting the vender and the inventory through a cable. The CommUnity Workbench like notation of Figure 5 describes the configuration diagram of the vending machine subsystem. The solid circles attached to a component description represent elements of the interface of that component. A line connecting two such interface elements, say sync1 of cable and chaeck_inv of Vender, indicate that in the categorical diagram corresponding to that of Figure 5, the regulative superposition from cable to Vender maps the action sunc1 to the action check_inv. So, this configuration diagram corresponds exactly to a well defined and well formed diagram in the category of CommUnity designs and regulative superposition morphisms. The colimit of this categorical diagram is the intended semantics of the configuration.

The specification of the vending machine subsystem can be obtained easily from the above configuration diagram and we do not describe it in detail here. We can also determine the interface of this subsystem by looking at the left part interface of the vender component in the diagram, which will interact with the interface controller and the slot.

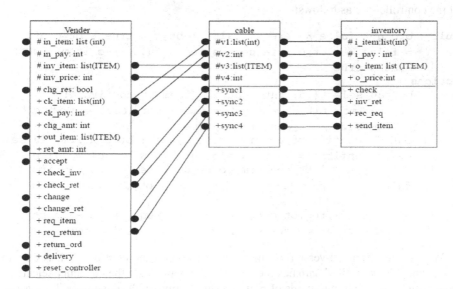

**Fig. 6.** Configuration diagram of the vending machine subsystem

Now we can put the vending machine subsystem together with the interface part (the controller and slot) to obtain the required vending machine system, which satisfies the design requirements, and the morphims between them are described in the configuration diagram depicted in Figure 6.

The interface of the vending machine system is shown in the left interface section of the controller component and the right interface section of the slot component, in which the controller provides the buttons for the customer to select his favorite item and confirm or cancel the order, and the slot indicates to the customer to put the coins in and to get his ordered item and change.

### 3.3 The Extended Vending Machine System

Now we want to add more behaviors to the vending machine system to improve the quality of its service. There are two extensions to be made, one for allowing a customer to order more than one item in a single transaction and the other to allow more kinds of coins to be used in payments, and we will show that they can only be achieved by the usage of extension morphisms.

#### 3.3.1 The Extension Allowing Multiple Items in an Order

One extension we want to make is to allow the customer to select more than one item in an order, which should be done in the controller component. We must modify the actions of item buttons to achieve this effect. First, we will extend the controller component and show there is an extension morphism from the old controller to this extended new component. Then a proof is given to justify that it is impossible to regulate or refine the controller to obtain the required functionality and the extension morphism is necessary for our purpose.

We introduce a new channel ac: bool (initialized to be true) and weaken the guards of item buttons actions by taking the disjunction of ac with bt_g. The modified actions of the controller are as follows:

```
init    ord_g = false ∧ o_req = false ∧ bt_g = true ∧ bt_confirm
        = false ∧ slot_g = false ∧ s_req = false ∧ c_item = NULL
        ∧ ac = true
actions
        button_select(id: int) [bt_g,c_item,bt_confirm] :
        bt_g ∨ ac, false -> bt_g' = false ∧ c_item' = c_item *
        b_item [id] ∧ bt_confirm' = true
   [} button_confirm[bt_confirm,slot_g,ac] : bt_confirm, false
        -> bt_confirm' = false ∧ slot_g' = true ∧ ac' = false
   [] button_cancel[bt_confirm,ac,bt_g,c_item] : bt_confirm,
        false -> bt_g' = true ∧ ac' = true ∧ bt_confirm' = false ∧
        c_item' = NULL
   [] order_ret[o_req,bt_g,c_item,ac]: o_req, false -> o_req' =
        false ∧ bt_g' = true ∧ c_item' = NULL ∧ ac' = true
```

We call the extended version of the controller component controller'. It is easy to determine that controller' satisfies the new requirement. After the customer selects an item button, the enabling guards of button_select actions will remain true because ac

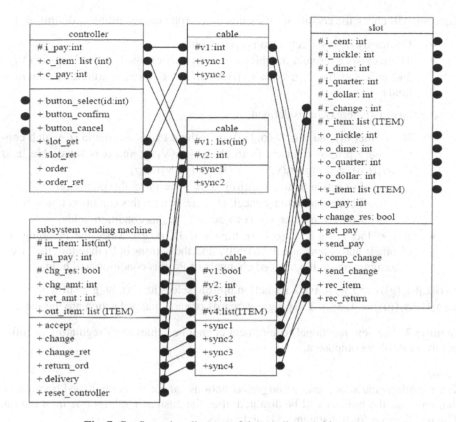

**Fig. 7.** Configuration diagram of the vending machine system

is true. They will not be disabled until the customer selects the confirm button, and after the vending machine subsystem informs the controller that the order has been processed by calling the order_ret action, all the item buttons will be reset.

We need to show that there exists an extension morphism from the old controller component (say $P_1$) to controller' (say $P_2$). The morphism $\sigma$ is defined as follows: the mapping of the channels $\sigma_\alpha$ will map each channels of $P_1$ to the identical channel of $P_2$, and $\sigma_\gamma$ defines the mapping of actions from each action in $P_2$, to the identical action in $P_1$.

**Lemma 1.** $\sigma$ is an extension morphism from $P_1$ to $P_2$.

*Proof*

First we will show that $\sigma$ is a signature morphism. Since the mappings of channels and actions are the identity, it is easy to see that all the conditions of a signature morphism are satisfied, except possibly for the condition $\sigma_\alpha(D_1(\sigma_\gamma(g))) \subseteq D_2(g)$. Since the actions in $P_2$ keep the effect of assignment to the mapped channels of $P_1$, this condition also holds. Therefore, $\sigma$ is a signature morphism.

Then we will check the conditions of extension morphisms according to definition 14:

- Obviously $\sigma_\gamma$ is surjective and $\sigma_\alpha$ is injective.
- There exists a formula $\alpha$, which contains only channels from $(V_2 - \sigma_\alpha(V_1))$, and $\alpha$ is satisfiable, $t \; I_2 \Leftrightarrow \sigma(I_1) \wedge \alpha$. As $\alpha \Leftrightarrow ac = true$, this condition holds.

For every $g \in \Gamma_2$ where $\sigma_\gamma(g)$ is defined,

- If $v \in loc(V_1)$ and $g \in D_2(\sigma_\alpha(v))$, then there exists a formula $\alpha$, which contains only primed channels from $(V_2' - \sigma_\alpha(V_1)')$, and $\alpha$ is satisfiable, $t \; \sigma$ $(L_1(\sigma_\gamma(g))) \Rightarrow (R_2(g, \sigma_\alpha(v)) \Leftrightarrow \sigma_\alpha(R_1(\sigma_\gamma(g), v)) \wedge \alpha)$.
  - o    For action button_confirm, $\alpha \Leftrightarrow ac' = false$, this condition holds.
  - o    For action button_cancel, $\alpha \Leftrightarrow ac' = true$, this condition holds.
  - o    For action order_ret, $\alpha \Leftrightarrow ac' = true$, this condition holds.
- If $v \in loc(V_1)$, $g \in D_2(\sigma_\alpha(v))$, then $v \in D_1(\sigma_\gamma(g))$. Since the mappings of channels and actions are the identity and the actions in $P_2$ maintain the effect of assignments to the mapped channels of $P_1$, this condition will hold.

$t \; (\sigma(L_1(\sigma_\gamma(g))) \Rightarrow L_2(g))$. For each action button_select(id: int), bt_g $\Rightarrow$ bt_g $\vee$ ac.
$t \; (\sigma(U_1(\sigma_\gamma(g))) \Rightarrow U_2(g))$. The progress guards of each mapped action are the same.

**Lemma 2.** The new functional requirement cannot be achieved by regulating or refining the controller component.

*Proof*
The enabling guards of these button_select actions cannot be strengthened because, in that case, all the buttons will be disabled after the customer selects one item button. The justification for this statement is as follows:

Suppose we have regulated or refined the controller component, then, in the target component, the enabling guards of the button_select actions will be strengthened; say one of the actions is g, its enabling guard is f and f $\Rightarrow \sigma$(bt_g) (bt_g must be translated). According to the definition of regulative superposition and refinement morphism, we have $R_2$(g, $\sigma$(bt_g)) $\Rightarrow \sigma(R_1(\sigma_\gamma(g), bt\_g))$. Since bt_g is set to false after the button_select action is called in the old controller, we know that $\sigma$(bt_g) should also be set to false after the execution of g in the extended controller. Because we have f $\Rightarrow \sigma$(bt_g) and it should hold all the time, if $\sigma$(bt_g)' is false, we know f' must be false. Therefore, after the button_select action is executed in the target component, this action will be blocked, which means this item button is disabled.

### 3.3.2   The Extension of Payment Options
We expect that instead of only accepting payment consisting of nickels, dimes, quarters and loonies, the vending machine system can also accept payment including one cent pieces and make the correct change. It is clear that we cannot refine or regulate component slot to achieve this goal, because we must modify its action get_pay and relax its enabling guard, which is not allowed in regulative superpositions and refinement morphisms. Therefore, we have to apply an extension morphism to the slot by modifying the get_pay action as follows and obtain the extended slot component.

```
get_pay [get_g, s_nickle, s_dime, s_quarter, s_dollar, s_cent]:
get_g, false -> get_g' = false ∧ s_nickle' = s_nickle + i_nickle
∧ s_dime' = s_dime + i_dime ∧ s_quarter' = s_quarter + i_quarter
∧ s_dollar' = s_dollar + i_dollar ∧ s_cent' = s_cent + i_cent
```

Notice that we need to add a new channel s_cent into the slot component to store the cents and make the corresponding assignment to this channel. However, based on the definition of extension morphism, there will exist an extension morphism from the old component to this extended component (the proof is similar to the case above). For the same reason, we can modify the following actions of the slot component as well (and add the channel o_cent):

```
send_pay [get_g, o_pay]:
¬ get_g , false -> get_g' = true ∧ o_pay' = 100*i_dollar +
25*i_quarter + 10*i_dime + 5*i_nickel + i_cent
```

```
send_change [change_g]:
¬change_g, false -> change_g' = true ∧ ( change_res = true ⇒
item_g' = true ∧ s_nickle' = s_nickle - o_nickle ∧ s_dime' =
s_dime - o_dime ∧ s_quarter' = s_quarter - o_quarter ∧
s_dollar' = s_dollar - o_dollar ∧ s_cent' = s_cent - o_cent)
```

Since we have divided the functionality of the system in an appropriate way, we can simply reuse the vending machine subsystem and the controller component.

# 4 Conclusions

Extension morphisms were originally motivated by their use in the application of aspects [8]. The examples developed in [8] were related to the application of a monitoring and a performance aspect to an unreliable communication system. We would like to impose behaviour on the existing architecture of an unreliable medium between a sender and receiver, to make the communication reliable by implementing a reset in the communication when packets are lost. The mechanism we used was very simple, and required a "reset" operation in the sender, which can be achieved by component extension. In order to complete the enhanced architecture to implement the reset acknowledgement mechanism, we need a monitor that, if it detects a missing packet, issues a call for reset. The idea is that, if a message is not what the monitor expected, then it will go to a "reset" cycle, and wait to see if the expected packet arrives. If the expected packet arrives, then the component will start waiting for the next packet. (Note that, since the superposed monitor is *spectative*, i.e., it has no effect on the underlying component – simply "observing" it.) Because of the properties of extension, we can guarantee that, if the augmented system works without the need for reset in the communication, i.e., no messages are lost, then its behaviour is exactly the same as the one of the original architecture with unreliable communication.

As we hope to have demonstrated in this paper, extension morphisms have a life of their own, independently of their usefulness in defining some aspects. They provide an interesting and predictable mechanism for software architects interested in change and evolution of their designs.

We have said very little about the new features of DynaComm, as this was unnecessary to talk about extensions. However, many aspects cannot be dealt with without hierarchical designs incorporating subsystem specific dynamic reconfigurability. This is what DynaComm sets out to provide. It also offers mechanisms to make design of architectures easier, such as the idea of indexed actions: a family of actions that "do the same thing" but to different elements, which can be indexed via a finite set of names. We are developing a DynaComm Workbench on the basis of experience with the CommUnity Workbench [37]. We are also putting together a catalogue of aspects and methods for developing formalizations of them. In particular, we are interested in reasoning about the applications of aspects to architectures to provide analyses for systems built in this way.

# References

1. Aguirre, N., Maibaum, T.: A Temporal Logic Approach to the Specification of Reconfigurable Component-Based Systems. In: ASE 2002, pp. 271–274 (2002)
2. Aguirre, N., Maibaum, T.: A Logical Basis for the Specification of Reconfigurable Component-Based Systems. In: Pezzé, M. (ed.) ETAPS 2003 and FASE 2003. LNCS, vol. 2621, pp. 37–51. Springer, Heidelberg (2003)
3. Aguirre, N., Maibaum, T.: Some Institutional Requirements for Temporal Reasoning on Dynamic Reconfiguration of Component Based Systems, Verification: Theory and Practice 2003, 407–435 (2003)
4. Aguirre, N.: A Logical Basis For the Specification of Reconfigurable Component Based Systems, Ph.D. Thesis, King's College London, Department of Computer Science (2004)
5. Aguirre, N., Alencar, P., Maibaum, T.: Aspect Modularity in a High-level Program Design Language. In: CASCON Workshop on Aspect Oriented Software Development, IBM (2005)
6. Aguirre, N., Regis, G., Maibaum, T.: Verifying Temporal Properties of CommUnity Designs. In: Davies, J., Gibbons, J. (eds.) IFM 2007. LNCS, vol. 4591, Springer, Heidelberg (2007)
7. Aguirre, N., Maibaum, T., Alencar, P.: Abstract Design with Aspects (submitted, 2007)
8. Aguirre, N., Maibaum, T., Alencar, P.: Extension Morphisms for CommUnity, Essays Dedicated to Joseph A. In: Futatsugi, K., Jouannaud, J.-P., Meseguer, J. (eds.) Algebra, Meaning, and Computation. LNCS, vol. 4060, pp. 173–193. Springer, Heidelberg (2006)
9. Allen, R., Garlan, D.: Formalizing Architectural Connections. In: ICSE'94, IEEE CS Press, Los Alamitos (1994)
10. Allen, R.J.: A Formal Approach to Software Architecture, Ph.D. Thesis, Carnegie Mellon University, School of Computer Science, available as TR# CMU-CS-97-144 (May 1997)
11. Allen, R., Douence, R., Garlan, D.: Specifying and Analyzing Dynamic Software Architectures. In: Astesiano, E. (ed.) ETAPS 1998 and FASE 1998. LNCS, vol. 1382, pp. 21–37. Springer, Heidelberg (1998)
12. Bicarregui, J.C., Lano, K.C., Maibaum, T.: Towards a Compositional Interpretation of Object Diagrams, Algorithmic Languages and Calculi, pp. 187–207. Chapman & Hall, Sydney, Australia (1997)
13. Bradbury, J.S., Cordy, J.R., Dingel, J., Wermelinger, M.: A survey of self-management in dynamic software architecture specifications, Workshop on Self-Healing Systems, ACM Digital Library (2004)

14. Corradini, A., Hirsch, D.: An Operational Semantics of COMMUITY Based on Graph Transformation Systems. Electr. Notes Theor. Comput. Sci. 109, 111–124 (2004)
15. Fiadeiro, J.L., Maibaum, T.: Categorical Semantics of Parallel Program Design, Technical Report, FCUL and Imperial College (1995)
16. Fiadeiro, J.L., Maibaum, T.: Design Structures for Object Based System, Formal Methods and Object Technology, pp. 183–204. Springer, Heidelberg (1996)
17. Fiadeiro, J.L., Maibaum, T.: Interconnecting Formalisms: Supporting Modularity, Reuse and Incrementality. In: FSE, pp. 72–80 (1995)
18. Fiadeiro, J.L.: Categories for Software Engineering. Springer, Heidelberg (2005)
19. Garlan, D., Monroe, R., Wile, D.: ACME: An Architecture Description Interchange Language. In: CASCON'97 (1997)
20. Garlan, D.: Software Architecture: A Roadmap, The Future of Software Engineering. In: Filkenstein, A. (ed.), ACM Press, New York (2000)
21. Georgiadis, I.: Self-Organising Distributed Component Software Architectures, Ph.D. Thesis, Imperial College of Science, Technology and Medicine, Department of Computing (2002)
22. Goguen, J.: Mathematical Representation of Hierarchically Organised Systems. In: Attimger, E. (ed.) Global Systems Dynamics, Krager, pp. 112–128 (1971)
23. Goguen, J., Ginali, S.: A Categorical Approach to General Systems Theory. In: Klir, G. (ed.) Applied General Systems Research, pp. 257–270. Plenum, New York (1978)
24. Goguen, J.: Categorical Foundations for General Systems Theory. In: Pichler, F., Trappl, R. (eds.) Advances in Cybernetics and Systems Research, Transcripta Books, pp. 121–130 (1973)
25. Kiczales, G.: An overview of Aspect J. In: Knudsen, J.L. (ed.) ECOOP 2001. LNCS, vol. 2072, Springer, Heidelberg (2001)
26. Larsen, K.G., Skou, A.: Bisimulation through probabilistic testing. Information and Computation 94, 1–28 (1991)
27. Ling, X.: DynaComm: The Extension of CommUnity to Support Dynamic Reconfiguration, MSc Thesis, McMaster University, available as SQRL Technical Report 40 (2007), http://www.cas.mcmaster.ca/sqrl/sqrl_reports.html
28. Liskov, B., Wing, J.: A Behavioral Notion of Subtyping, ACM Transactions on Programming Languages and Systems, vol. 16(6). ACM Press, New York (1994)
29. Lopes, A., Wermelinger, M., Fiadeiro, J.: Higher-Order Architectural Connectors. ACM Transactions on Software Engineering and Methodology 12(1) (2003)
30. Lopes, A., Fiadeiro, J.: Superposition: Composition vs. Refinement of Non-Deterministic, Action-Based Systems, Formal Aspects of Computing, vol. 16(1). Springer, Heidelberg (2004)
31. Magee, J., Kramer, J.: Dynamic Structure in Software Architectures. In: Gollmann, D. (ed.) Fast Software Encryption. LNCS, vol. 1039, pp. 24–32. Springer, Heidelberg (1996)
32. Manna, Z., Pnueli, A.: The Temporal Logic of Reactive and Concurrent Systems. Springer, Heidelberg (1991)
33. Medvidovic, N., Taylor, R.N.: A classification and comparison framework for software architecture description languages. IEEE Trans. on Software Engineering 26(1), 70–93 (2000)
34. Perry, D.E., Wolf, A.L.: Foundations for the study of software architectures. SIGSOFT Software Eng. Notes 17(4), 40–52 (1992)
35. Shaw, M., Garlan, D.: Software Architecture: Perspectives on an Emerging Discipline. Prentice Hall, Englewood Cliffs (1996)

36. Szyperski, C., Pfister, C.: Component–Oriented Programming: WCOP '96 Workshop Report, In: Cointe, P. (ed.) ECOOP 1996. LNCS, vol. 1098, pp. 127–130. Springer, Heidelberg (1996)
37. Wermelinger, M., Oliveira, C.: The CommUnity Workbench, ICSE. ACM Press, New York (2002)
38. Wile, D.S.: Using Dynamic Acme, Working Conference on Complex and Dynamic Systems Architecture, Brisbane, Australia (2001)
39. Early Aspects: Aspect-Oriented Requirements Engineering and Architecture Design: //www.early-aspects.net/

# Symbolic Test Generation Using a Temporal Logic with Constrained Events*

Daguang Liu[1,3], Peng Wu[2], and Huimin Lin[1]

[1] Lab of Computer Science, Institute of Software, Chinese Academy of Sciences,
Beijing 100080, China
[2] CNRS and LIX, Ecole Polytechnique, 91128 Palaiseau Cedex, France
`wu@lix.polytechnique.fr`
[3] Graduate School, Chinese Academy of Sciences, Beijing 100049, China
`{liudg,lhm}@ios.ac.cn`

**Abstract.** A temporal logic with constrained event modallities, TLCE, is proposed to represent test purposes for testing concurrent programs. The logic is capable can express not only temporal relationships among input and output events, but also data dependencies between event parameters. A TLCE-based test generation algorithm is developed to automatically derive symbolic test cases that incorporate given data dependency constraints as verdict conditions. The advantage of the approach is demonstrated with a case study on a cache coherence protocol.

## 1 Introduction

The symbolic test generation method was proposed for the conformance testing of reactive systems, where the models, test purposes and test cases are all represented as symbolic transition systems [RdBJ00, CJRZ02, RMJ04]. However, only the temporal relationships among input/output (I/O) events are concerned therein. This would result in less precise test cases, where the relevancy among event parameteres are ignored. [JJRZ05] improved the method with an approximate analysis on reachability/co-reachability. But in practice, it is still tedious and error-prone to represent test purposes as transition systems.

A predicate sequencing constraint logic (PSCL) was proposed in [WL05] as an alternative way to represent test purposes concerning data dependencies between event parameters. A PSCL-based symbolic test generation algorithm was also developed there. The approach allows automated test generation based on first-order temporal properties, and releases the effort in constructing transition systems for test purposes.

This paper presents a temporal logic with constrained events (TLCE) which refines PSCL, so that test purposes can be described in a simpler and more

---

* The work of Peng Wu was partially supported by the INRIA/ARC project ProNoBis. The work of Daguang Liu and Huimin Lin was partially supported by the National Science Foundation of China under Grant No. 60421001.

C.B. Jones, Z. Liu, J. Woodcock (Eds.): Bjørner/Zhou Festschrift, LNCS 4700, pp. 467–471, 2007.

natural manner. Moreover, we revise the algorithm of [WL05] to work for TLCE-based symbolic test generation, and present experimental results to demonstrate the effectiveness of our approach.

The rest of the paper is organized as follows. Section 2 presents TLCE with its syntax and semantics. The TLCE-based symbolic test generation algorithm is introduced in Section 3. Section 4 illustrates a case study on a cache coherence protocol. The paper is concluded with Section 5.

## 2   A Temporal Logic with Constrained Events

We presuppose the following syntactic categories: $Val$ is a set of values ranged over by $v$; $Var$ is a set of variables ranged over by $x, y, z$; a valuation is a total mapping from $Var$ to $Val$, denoted by $\rho$; a substitution $\bar{v}/\bar{z}$ maps $\bar{z}$ to $\bar{v}$. Let $b$ range over boolean expressions over $Val \cup Var$, and $c$ over channel names. The syntax of TLCE is given by the following BNF-definition:

$$\beta ::= c?\bar{z} \mid c!\bar{z}$$
$$\eta ::= \mathbf{G}\varphi \mid \varphi \mathbf{U}\varphi$$
$$\varphi ::= tt \mid \neg\, \varphi \mid \varphi \wedge \varphi \mid \mathbf{E}\eta \mid \mathbf{A}\eta \mid \langle \beta : b \rangle \varphi \mid [\beta : b]\varphi$$

TLCE can be seen as a first-order extension of CTL [CGP99]. The operators $\langle \beta : b \rangle$ and $[\beta : b]$ are *constrained input/output modalities*. Intuitively, $\langle c?\bar{z} : b \rangle$ specifies an input event on channel $c$ such that the received values, to be stored in the variables $\bar{z}$, satisfy $b$; similarly, $\langle c!\bar{z} : b \rangle$ says an output event must occur on channel $c$ such that the output values, stored in the variables $\bar{z}$, satisfying $b$. The semantics of TLCE is defined over a labeled transition system as follows:

| | |
|---|---|
| $s \vDash_\rho^M \langle c?\bar{z} : b \rangle \varphi$ | There exists a $s' \in S$ such that for any $\bar{v} \in Val^{|\bar{z}|}$ $(\rho\{\bar{v}/\bar{z}\} \vDash b)$, $s \xrightarrow{c?\bar{v}} s'$ and $s' \vDash_{\rho\{\bar{v}/\bar{z}\}}^M \varphi$. |
| $s \vDash_\rho^M \langle c!\bar{z} : b \rangle \varphi$ | There exist $s' \in S$ and $\bar{v} \in Val^{|\bar{z}|}$ $(\rho\{\bar{v}/\bar{z}\} \vDash b)$ such that $s \xrightarrow{c!\bar{v}} s'$ and $s' \vDash_{\rho\{\bar{v}/\bar{z}\}}^M \varphi$. |
| $s \vDash_\rho^M [c?\bar{z} : b]\varphi$ | For any $s' \in S, \bar{v} \in Val^{|\bar{z}|}$ $(\rho\{\bar{v}/\bar{z}\} \vDash b)$, if $s \xrightarrow{c?\bar{v}} s'$, then $s' \vDash_{\rho\{\bar{v}/\bar{z}\}}^M \varphi$. |
| $s \vDash_\rho^M [c!\bar{z} : b]\varphi$ | For any $s' \in S$, if there exists $\bar{v} \in Val^{|\bar{z}|}$ $(\rho\{\bar{v}/\bar{z}\} \vDash b)$ such that $s \xrightarrow{c!\bar{v}} s'$, then $s' \vDash_{\rho\{\bar{v}/\bar{z}\}}^M \varphi$. |
| $s \vDash_\rho^M \neg\, \varphi$ | $s \nvDash_\rho^M \varphi$. |
| $s \vDash_\rho^M \varphi_1 \wedge \varphi_2$ | $s \vDash_\rho^M \varphi_1$ and $s \vDash_\rho^M \varphi_2$. |
| $s \vDash_\rho^M \mathbf{E}[\mathbf{G}\ \varphi]$ | There exists a path $\pi$ from $s$ such that for all $j \geq 0$, $s_j \vDash_\rho^M \varphi$. |
| $s \vDash_\rho^M \mathbf{A}[\mathbf{G}\ \varphi]$ | For every path $\pi$ from $s$ and all $j \geq 0$, $s_j \vDash_\rho^M \varphi$. |
| $s \vDash_\rho^M \mathbf{E}[\varphi_1\ \mathbf{U}\ \varphi_2]$ | There exists a path $\pi$ from $s$ and a $k \geq 0$ such that $s_k \vDash_\rho^M \varphi_2$ and for all $0 \leq j < k, s_j \vDash_\rho^M \varphi_1$ |
| $s \vDash_\rho^M \mathbf{A}[\varphi_1\ \mathbf{U}\ \varphi_2]$ | For every path $\pi$ from $s$, there exists a $k \geq 0$ such that $s_k \vDash_\rho^M \varphi_2$ and for all $0 \leq j < k, s_j \vDash_\rho^M \varphi_1$ |

where $s \vDash_\rho^M \varphi$ means that $\varphi$ holds at state $s$ of labeled transition system $M$, under valuation $\rho$.

## 3   Symbolic Test Generation

In this section, we briefly introduce the TLCE-based symbolic test generation algorithm with a running example [JJRZ05], depicted in Fig. 1(a). The related details can be referred to [WL05].

Given a system model and a test purpose in TLCE, the workflow of our approach is as follows: (1) Make the system model deterministic by eliminating internal transitions and resolving conflict I/O transitions; (2) Slice the resulting model according to the specified temporal relationship in the test purpose; (3) Customize the resulting model slice as a symbolic test case according to the specified data dependency constraints in the test purpose.

The test purpose represented as a transition system in Fig. 2 of [JJRZ05] can be directly described as a TLCE formula $\mathbf{EF}(\langle a?x : x \leq 3\rangle\mathbf{EF}(\langle ok!p : p == 3\rangle tt))$, where $\mathbf{EF}(\varphi) = \mathbf{E}(tt \ \mathbf{U} \ \varphi)$. The corresponding model slice is shown in Fig. 1(b). Such a model slice can then be customized by setting the data dependency constraints as verdict conditions. The resulting symbolic test case is shown in Fig. 1(c), where $\delta$ represents the absence of the expected events, *Trap* indicates that some unexpected event or $\delta$ happens, and $ represents marks the end of testing with some verdict (*PASS, FAIL, INCONClusive*) assigned.

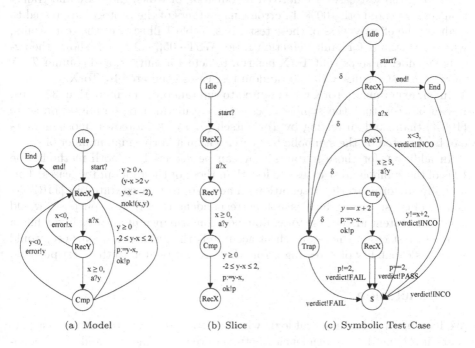

(a) Model          (b) Slice          (c) Symbolic Test Case

**Fig. 1.** Symbolic Test Generation

**Table 1.** Test Results

| No. | FD(%) | S | TorX | | No. | FD(%) | S | TorX | |
|-----|-------|---|------|---|-----|-------|---|------|---|
| | | | FD(%) | S | | | | FD(%) | S |
| 1 | 64.79 | 11.39 | 99.50 | 9.42 | 8 | 6.03 | 12.55 | - | - |
| 2 | 64.79 | 11.39 | 97.00 | 10.10 | 9 | 10.82 | 14.19 | 39.50 | 18.63 |
| 3 | 13.42 | 8.41 | - | - | 10 | 1.23 | 7.44 | 19.50 | 16.95 |
| 4 | 22.19 | 5.08 | - | - | 11 | 20.00 | 29.30 | - | - |
| 5 | 0.14 | 2.00 | - | - | 12 | 0.68 | 19.10 | 30.00 | 21.53 |
| 6 | 37.53 | 11.96 | 40.50 | 19.98 | 13 | 38.36 | 4.00 | - | - |
| 7 | 0.27 | 4.50 | 14.00 | 19.54 | 14 | 0.96 | 14.92 | 29.50 | 19.97 |

## 4  Case Study

We revise the symbolic test generation algorithm in [WL05] to adapt the syntax and semantics of TLCE. The TorX tool environment [TB02] is used as the execution engine for test campaigns.

A cache coherence protocol [GG04] is considered for a case study. The protocol aims to maintain the cache coherence among multi-processors with shared memory. We construct a system model with 3 processes, based on the formal description of the protocol presented in [PLL06], and design 6 test purposes in TLCE, concerning the features defined in the protocol specification.

In total 730 test cases are derived by our tool, of which the state and transition coverage are both 100%. 14 erroneous mutants of the protocol are tested to evaluate the effectiveness of these test cases. Table 1 illustrates the test results, where *FD* stands for fault detection ratio [WST+05], column *S* shows the average number of steps that TorX has run to detect a mutant, and column *TorX* shows the test results with 300 random test cases generated by TorX.

In our experiment, TorX is configured to run randomly no more than 35 steps. It can be seen that the symbolic test cases result in a better mutation score (100%) than random testing by TorX itself (57.14%). Moreover, most mutants can be detected by the symbolic test cases within a fairly small number of steps.

In addition, for those mutants that can be detected by both methods, the FDs of the symbolic test cases are less than those of the random test cases. This actually conforms to the observation on accurate test cases stated in [JJRZ05]. A random test case, which is not correspondent to any test purpose, would drive the system under test to exhibit non-conformance more possibly; while a symbolic test case, which can reflect accurately the guiding test purpose, would show less capability of detecting errors that are not related to that test purpose.

## 5  Conclusion

We have proposed a temporal logic with constrained events to express test purposes involving data dependencies between event parameters, and correspondingly developed a symbolic test generation algorithm. Case studies have shown the effectiveness and efficiency of our approach. As future work, we would like to investigate ways to embed our approach into the symbolic testing framework presented in [JJRZ05].

# References

[CGP99]    Clarke, E.M., Grumberg, O., Peled, D.A.: Model Checking. MIT Press, Cambridge (1999)

[CJRZ02]   Clarke, D., Jéron, T., Rusu, V., Zinovieva, E.: STG: A symbolic test generation tool. In: Katoen, J.-P., Stevens, P. (eds.) ETAPS 2002 and TACAS 2002. LNCS, vol. 2280, pp. 470–475. Springer, Heidelberg (2002)

[GG04]     German, S.M., Janssen, G.: Tutorial on verification of distributed cache memory protocols. In: Hu, A.J., Martin, A.K. (eds.) FMCAD 2004. LNCS, vol. 3312, Springer, Heidelberg (2004)

[JJRZ05]   Jeannet, B., Jron, T., Rusu, V., Zinovieva, E.: Symbolic test selection based on approximate analysis. In: Halbwachs, N., Zuck, L.D. (eds.) TACAS 2005. LNCS, vol. 3440, pp. 349–364. Springer, Heidelberg (2005)

[PLL06]    Pan, H., Lin, H.-M., Lv, Y.: Model checking data consistency for cache coherence protocols. J. of Computer Science and Technology 21(5), 765–775 (2006)

[RdBJ00]   Rusu, V., du Bousquet, L., Jéron, T.: An approach to symbolic test generation. In: Grieskamp, W., Santen, T., Stoddart, B. (eds.) IFM 2000. LNCS, vol. 1945, pp. 338–357. Springer, Heidelberg (2000)

[RMJ04]    Rusu, V., Marchand, H., Jéron, T.: Verification and symbolic test generation for safety properties. Technical Report 5285, INRIA (August 2004)

[TB02]     Tretmans, J., Brinksma, E.: Côte de Resyste – Automated Model Based Testing. In: Proc. of Progress 2002 – the 3rd Workshop on Embedded Systems, Utrecht, The Netherlands, pp. 246–255 (October 24, 2002)

[WL05]     Wu, P., Lin, H.: Model-based testing of concurrent programs with predicate sequencing constraints. In: Proc. of the 5th Int. Conf. on Quality Software (QSIC 2005), Melbourne, Australia, pp. 3–10 (September 19-20, 2005)

[WST+05]   Wu, P., Shi, X., Tang, J., Lin, H., Chen, T.Y.: Metamorphic testing and special case testing: A case study. J. of Software 16(7), 1210–1220 (2005)

# Expansive-Bisimulation for Context-Free Processes*

Xinxin Liu

Laboratory of Computer Science
Institute of Software, Chinese Academy of Sciences
P.O.Box 8718, 100080 Beijing, China
xinxin@ios.ac.cn

**Abstract.** Through the notion of expansive-bisimulation, in this paper we give a finite characterization of bisimulation equivalence for context-free processes, i.e. we show that two context-free processes are bisimulation equivalent if and only if there is a finite expansive-bisimulation which contains them. This immediately suggests the set of finite expansive-bisimulation as a complete class of verifiable evidence for bisimulation equality of context-free processes. Compared with the well known result that two context-free processes are bisimulation equivalent if and only if there is a finite self-bisimulation which relates them, the new result made improvement in the sense that whether a finite relation is an expansive-bisimulation is decidable while whether a finite relation is a self-bisimulation is only semi-decidable.

## 1   Motivation

Decidability results for bisimulation equivalence between context-free processes have been flourishing since Baeten, Bergstra and Klop [BBK87] first proved that bisimulation equivalence is decidable for normed BPA processes, a class of context-free processes. The same fact has been proved by a series of simpler proofs later by Caucal [Cau90], Hüttel and Stirling [HS91], and Groote [Gro91]. Also algorithms and various complexity results for deciding bisimilarity of normed context-free processes have been obtained by Huynh and Tian [DT94], Hirshfeld,Jerrum, and Moller [HJM96]. Finally, Christensen, Hüttel and Stirling [CHS92] demonstrated that bisimilarity is decidable not only for normed context-free processes but also for all context-free processes, and Burkart, Caucal and Steffen [BCS95] demonstrated an elementary decision procedure. There results were summarized in the survey article by Burkart, Caucal, Moller and Steffen in [BPS01]. Also Srba keeps an up-to-date summary of equivalence checking results for infinite-state systems [Srb].

However most of the above mentioned works put emphasis on checking bisimilarity. Works about a closely related problem, the problem of proving bisimilarity of context-free processes, seem to attract much less attention with relatively

---

* Supported by Chinese NSF grant 60496321 and 60173020.

C.B. Jones, Z. Liu, J. Woodcock (Eds.): Bjørner/Zhou Festschrift, LNCS 4700, pp. 472–482, 2007.

fewer results. Nevertheless this problem is also important. The decidability results for context-free processes settled the foundation for automatic tools to test if two context free processes are bisimulation equivalent. However, in general we want more than just a "YES" or "NO" answer from such an automatic tool. In particular, when told that two processes are equivalent we want to be convinced by some *verifiable* evidence. For finite state processes there are satisfactory solutions. For two finite state processes, if they are bisimulation equivalent then

1. a proof of their equality can be constructed in Milner's equational proof system for regular processes [Mil82]; and also
2. a finite bisimulation relation can be constructed which contains the pair of processes in question.

Clearly both a proof in Milner's equational proof system and a *finite* bisimulation can qualify as verifiable evidences. The situation for context-free processes is very different. First, no equational proof systems for context-free processes have been reported so far. Second, for two bisimulation equivalent context-free processes, there may not exist a *finite* bisimulation relation which contains them. Here it is important that we put emphasis on finiteness. If the relation is infinite, it can hardly be taken as an evidence because we do not have a general procedure to verify infinite bisimulation relations. So far, main results for proving bisimilarity of context-free processes include Hüttel and Stirling's tableau proof method and a sequent style proof system for *normed* context-free processes [HS91]. For the full class of context-free processes to the best of our knowledge no similar result is known. In [Cau90] Caucal first introduced the useful notion of self-bisimulation and showed that if two normed context-free processes are bisimilar then there is a finite self-bisimulation containing the two processes. Christensen, Hüttel and Stirling showed in [CHS92] that this also holds for arbitrary context-free processes. Unfortunately since checking whether a finite relation is a self-bisimulation is only semi-decidable, finite self-bisimulation falls short of a verifiable evidance.

In this paper we propose a notion of expansive-bisimulation, and with it we give a finite characterization of bisimulation equivalence for arbitrary context-free processes. More precisely, we show that two context-free processes are bisimulation equivalent if and only if there is a finite expansive-bisimulation which contains them. This immediately suggests a complete proof method for bisimilarity of context-free processes: in order to prove equality of two processes we just need to construct a finite expansive-bisimulation which contains the processes in question.

The paper is organized as follows. In section 2 we present the syntax and operational semantics of context-free processes, and study some important finiteness properties of such processes. Our presentation of this part is in a more direct approach compared with previous works. Section 3 contains the main technical contribution, where we study expansive-bisimulation. We conclude in section 4 with some discussions and possible future directions.

## 2   BPA Processes and Operational Semantics

Assume a set of variables $V$ and a set of actions $Act$, we consider the set of BPA expressions $\mathcal{E}$ given by the following syntax; we shall use $E, F, \ldots$ as metavariables over $\mathcal{E}$.

$$
\begin{aligned}
E ::= \quad & a && (\text{action, } a \in Act) \\
& |\; X && (\text{variable, } X \in V) \\
& |\; \Sigma_{i \in I} E_i && (\text{summation, } I \text{ is a finite set}) \\
& |\; E_1; E_2 && (\text{sequential composition}) \\
& |\; \mu X.E && (\text{recursion, } X \in V).
\end{aligned}
$$

We shall use $\mathsf{fv}(E)$ to stand for the set of variables occurring free (i.e., not bounded by $\mu$) in $E$. We shall write $E\{F/X\}$ for the result of substituting $F$ for each free occurrence of $X$ in $E$, renaming bound variables as necessary. BPA processes are closed BPA expressions, i.e. those $E \in \mathcal{E}$ with $\mathsf{fv}(E) = \emptyset$. Moreover (bound) variables in BPA processes must be guarded by action prefixing.

**Table 1.** Transition rules

$$
\text{act} \quad a \xrightarrow{a} \epsilon
$$

$$
\text{sum} \; \frac{E_j \xrightarrow{a} \alpha}{\Sigma_{i \in I} E_i \xrightarrow{a} \alpha} \; j \in I
\qquad
\text{seq} \; \frac{E \xrightarrow{a} \alpha}{E; F \xrightarrow{a} \alpha F}
$$

$$
\text{rec} \; \frac{E\{\mu X.E/X\} \xrightarrow{a} \alpha}{\mu X.E \xrightarrow{a} \alpha}
\qquad
\text{state} \; \frac{E \xrightarrow{a} \alpha}{E\beta \xrightarrow{a} \alpha\beta}
$$

The operational semantics of processes can be described by a labelled transition system

$$
\langle \mathcal{S}, Act, \longrightarrow \rangle
$$

where the state space $\mathcal{S}$ consists of finite sequences of BPA processes, and the transition relation

$$
\longrightarrow \subseteq \mathcal{S} \times Act \times \mathcal{S}
$$

is generated by the rules in Table 1, in which (as also later) we use Greek letters $\alpha, \beta, \ldots$ as meta variables ranging over elements of $\mathcal{S}$, write $\epsilon$ for empty sequence, write $E\alpha$ for the state starting with $E$ and followed by $\alpha$, write $\alpha\beta$ for the state obtained by concatenating the sequences $\alpha$ and $\beta$, write $\alpha \xrightarrow{a} \beta$ for $(\alpha, a, \beta) \in \longrightarrow$. We will write $\alpha \xrightarrow{a_1 \ldots a_n} \beta$ if $\alpha \xrightarrow{a_1} \alpha_1, \alpha_1 \xrightarrow{a_2} \ldots \xrightarrow{a_n} \beta$, and say $\beta$ is reachable from $\alpha$.

**Definition 1.** *A binary relation $R \subseteq S \times S$ is a bisimulation if for all $(\alpha, \beta) \in R$ the following hold:*

1. *$\alpha = \epsilon$ if and only if $\beta = \epsilon$;*
2. *whenever $\alpha \xrightarrow{a} \alpha'$, then $\beta \xrightarrow{a} \beta'$ for some $\beta'$ with $(\alpha', \beta') \in R$;*
3. *whenever $\beta \xrightarrow{a} \beta'$, then $\alpha \xrightarrow{a} \alpha'$ for some $\alpha'$ with $(\alpha', \beta') \in R$.*

*Two states $\alpha$ and $\beta$ are said to be bisimulation equivalent, written $\alpha \sim \beta$, if there is a bisimulation $R$ such that $(\alpha, \beta) \in R$.*

It is well know that $\sim$ is an equivalence relation between processes. Moreover it is a congruence with respect to concatenation of sequences of processes.

Note that in general clause 1. of Definition 1 is necessary. Since here we use the general summation notation $\Sigma$ to write expressions, and when the index set is empty, $\Sigma_{i \in \emptyset} E_i$ is the inactive process which should not be equated with $\epsilon$. Otherwise the congruence property of $\sim$ would fail. With clause 1. in Definition 1 this cannot happen.

An important notion in the study of bisimulation of context-free processes is that of self-bisimulation proposed by Caucal [Cau90].

**Definition 2.** *For any binary relation $R$ on $S$, we denote by $R^{\rightarrow}$ the least precongruence wrt sequential composition containing $R$, denote by $R^{\leftrightarrow}$ the symmetric closure of $R^{\rightarrow}$, denote by $R^{\leftrightarrow*}$ the reflexive and transitive closure of $R^{\leftrightarrow}$.*

**Definition 3.** *A binary relation $B \subseteq S \times S$ is a self-bisimulation if for all $(\alpha, \beta) \in B$, $\alpha = \epsilon$ just in case $\beta = \epsilon$ and moreover the following hold:*

1. *whenever $\alpha \xrightarrow{a} \alpha'$, then $\beta \xrightarrow{a} \beta'$ for some $\beta'$ with $(\alpha', \beta') \in B^{\leftrightarrow*}$;*
2. *whenever $\beta \xrightarrow{a} \beta'$, then $\alpha \xrightarrow{a} \alpha'$ for some $\alpha'$ with $(\alpha', \beta') \in B^{\leftrightarrow*}$.*

Note that for a finite relation, checking if it is a self-bisimulation is in general only semi-decidable since one needs to check membership of its congruence closure.

**Proposition 1.** [Cau90] *If $B$ is a self-bisimulation then $B^{\leftrightarrow*} \subseteq \sim$.*

Obviously $B \subseteq B^{\leftrightarrow*}$. Thus if $(\alpha, \beta)$ is contained in a self-bisimulation than $\alpha \sim \beta$.

For the process system $\langle S, Act, \longrightarrow \rangle$, an important finiteness property which forms the base of our discussion in the paper is that, although the number of reachable states from an arbitrary state $\alpha \in S$ can be infinite, the processes (closed expressions) that can occur in those reachable states must be from a finite set. Another important finiteness property of $\langle S, Act, \longrightarrow \rangle$ is finite branching, which says that for any $\alpha \in S$, the set

$$B(\alpha) = \{\beta \mid a \in Act, \alpha \xrightarrow{a} \beta\}$$

is a finite set. In previous works, for example in [CHS92], these properties are guaranteed by using results from [BBK87] that every BPA process is bisimulation equivalent to a process which is a solution to an equation system in Greibach Normal Form. Here we take a more direct approach to prove the properties directly for the labelled transition system.

For $E \in \mathcal{E}$, the closure set of $E$, written $\mathsf{cl}(E)$, is inductively defined on the structure of $E$ as follows:

$$\mathsf{cl}(a) = \mathsf{cl}(X) = \emptyset,$$
$$\mathsf{cl}(\Sigma_{i \in I} E_i) = \bigcup_{i \in I} \mathsf{cl}(E_i),$$
$$\mathsf{cl}(E; F) = \mathsf{cl}(E) \cup \mathsf{cl}(F) \cup \{F\},$$
$$\mathsf{cl}(\mu X.E) = \{E'\{\mu X.E/X\} \mid E' \in \mathsf{cl}(E)\}.$$

The following two lemmas are easily proved by direct structural induction.

**Lemma 1.** Let $E \in \mathcal{E}$, then $\mathsf{cl}(E)$ is a finite set.

**Lemma 2.** Let $E, F \in \mathcal{E}$. If $E \in \mathsf{cl}(F)$ then $\mathsf{fv}(E) \subseteq \mathsf{fv}(F)$.

For $\alpha \in \mathcal{E}^*$, its closure, also written $\mathsf{cl}(\alpha)$ (a harmless misuse of notation), is defined such that $\mathsf{cl}(\epsilon) = \emptyset$ and $\mathsf{cl}(E\alpha) = \mathsf{cl}(E) \cup \mathsf{cl}(\alpha)$. Now the finiteness property which we need to show is that if $E$ occurs in the sequence $\beta$ which is reachable from $\alpha$, then either $E$ occurs in $\alpha$ or $E \in \mathsf{cl}(\alpha)$. Thus such $E$ must be from a finite set, since obviously by Lemma 1 $\mathsf{cl}(\alpha)$ is a finite set, and the number of processes that occur in $\alpha$ is also finite.

**Lemma 3.** $\mathsf{cl}(E\{\mu X.E/X\}) \subseteq \mathsf{cl}(\mu X.E)$.

**Proof:** We prove by induction on the structure of $F$ the following inclusion:

$$\mathsf{cl}(F\{\mu X.E/X\}) \subseteq \{F'\{\mu X.E/X\} \mid F' \in \mathsf{cl}(F)\} \cup \mathsf{cl}(\mu X.E).$$

Then take $F$ to be $E$ we obtain the inclusion relation we want.

When $F \equiv F_1; F_2$ we have the following sequence of inclusions:

$\mathsf{cl}(F\{\mu X.E/X\})$

$= \mathsf{cl}(F_1\{\mu X.E/X\}; F_2\{\mu X.E/X\})$

$= \mathsf{cl}(F_1\{\mu X.E/X\}) \cup \mathsf{cl}(F_2\{\mu X.E/X\}) \cup \{F_2\{\mu X.E/X\}\}$        def. of cl

$\subseteq \{F'\{\mu X.E/X\} \mid F' \in \mathsf{cl}(F_1)\} \cup \{F'\{\mu X.E/X\} \mid F' \in \mathsf{cl}(F_2)\}$

$\quad \cup \mathsf{cl}(\mu X.E) \cup \{F_2\{\mu X.E/X\}\}$        ind. hyp.

$= \{F'\{\mu X.E/X\} \mid F' \in \mathsf{cl}(F_1; F_2)\} \cup \mathsf{cl}(\mu X.E).$        def. of cl

When $F \equiv \Sigma_{i \in I} E_i$ the calculation is similar to the case for $F_1; F_2$.

The key case is when $F \equiv \mu Y.F_1$, and without loss of generality we can assume that $Y$ does not occur free in $\mu X.E$. We calculate as follows:

$$\mathsf{cl}(F\{\mu X.E/X\})$$
$$= \mathsf{cl}(\mu Y.F_1\{\mu X.E/X\})$$
$$= \{F'\{\mu Y.F_1\{\mu X.E/X\}/Y\} \mid F' \in \mathsf{cl}(F_1\{\mu X.E/X\})\} \qquad \text{def. of cl}$$
$$\subseteq \{F'\{\mu Y.F_1\{\mu X.E/X\}/Y\}|$$
$$\qquad F' \in \{F_1'\{\mu X.E/X\} \mid F_1' \in \mathsf{cl}(F_1)\} \cup \mathsf{cl}(\mu X.E)\} \qquad \text{ind. hyp.}$$
$$= \{F_1'\{\mu X.E/X\}\{\mu Y.F_1\{\mu X.E/X\}/Y\} \mid F_1' \in \mathsf{cl}(F_1)\}$$
$$\qquad \cup \{F'\{\mu Y.F_1\{\mu X.E/X\}/Y\}| \ F' \in \mathsf{cl}(\mu X.E)\}$$
$$= \{F_1'\{\mu Y.F_1/Y\}\{\mu X.E/X\} \mid F_1' \in \mathsf{cl}(F_1)\}$$
$$\qquad \cup \{F' \mid F' \in \mathsf{cl}(\mu X.E)\} \qquad\qquad **$$
$$= \{F'\{\mu X.E/X\} \mid F' \in \{F_1'\{\mu Y.F_1/Y\} \mid F_1' \in \mathsf{cl}(F_1)\}\}$$
$$\qquad \cup \mathsf{cl}(\mu X.E)$$
$$= \{F'\{\mu X.E/X\} \mid F' \in \mathsf{cl}(\mu Y.F_1)\} \cup \mathsf{cl}(\mu X.E) \qquad \text{def. of cl}$$

Here we explain the step marked $**$ above, keep in mind that $Y$ does not occur free in $\mu X.E$. With such condition on variable, first by the well known substitution lemma in this case we have

$$F_1'\{\mu Y.F_1/Y\}\{\mu X.E/X\} = F_1'\{\mu X.E/X\}\{\mu Y.F_1\{\mu X.E/X\}/Y\}.$$

Second, for $F' \in \mathsf{cl}(\mu X.E)$ by Lemma 2 $\mathsf{fv}(F') \subseteq \mathsf{fv}(\mu X.E)$, thus $Y$ does not occur free in $F'$, so $F'\{\mu Y.F_1\{\mu X.E/X\}/Y\} = F'$.

Other cases are trivial. $\qquad\qquad\qquad\qquad\qquad\qquad\qquad\qquad\qquad\qquad\square$

When confusion is unlikely, for $\alpha \in S$ we will also write $\alpha$ to mean the set of expressions which occur in $\alpha$.

**Lemma 4.** If $\alpha \xrightarrow{a} \beta$ then $\beta \cup \mathsf{cl}(\beta) \subseteq \alpha \cup \mathsf{cl}(\alpha)$.

**Proof:** First, we have the fact: if $E \xrightarrow{a} \beta$ then $\beta \cup \mathsf{cl}(\beta) \subseteq \mathsf{cl}(E)$. This can be proved by induction on the rules of Table 2, where for rule rec we need to use Lemma 3.

Suppose $\alpha \xrightarrow{a} \beta$, then by the rules of Table 2 it must be that $\alpha = E\alpha'$, $\beta = \beta'\alpha'$, and $E \xrightarrow{a} \beta'$ for some $E, \alpha', \beta'$. By the fact above $\beta' \cup \mathsf{cl}(\beta') \subseteq \mathsf{cl}(E)$, thus $\beta \cup \mathsf{cl}(\beta) = \beta' \cup \alpha' \cup \mathsf{cl}(\beta') \cup \mathsf{cl}(\alpha') \subseteq \mathsf{cl}(E) \cup \alpha' \cup \mathsf{cl}(\alpha') \subseteq \alpha \cup \mathsf{cl}(\alpha)$. $\quad\square$

With this lemma, by transitivity it is easy to see that if $\beta$ is reachable from $\alpha$ then $\beta \cup \mathsf{cl}(\beta) \subseteq \alpha \cup \mathsf{cl}(\alpha)$, and in particular we have the following theorem which we aimed at from the beginning.

**Theorem 1.** If $\beta$ is reachable from $\alpha$ then $\beta \subseteq \alpha \cup \mathsf{cl}(\alpha)$.

With this theorem, when we discuss bisimulation equivalence of two states $\alpha, \beta \in S$ we know that the reachable state space is the part consisting of states in which only processes from a finite set $\alpha \cup \beta \cup \mathsf{cl}(\alpha) \cup \mathsf{cl}(\beta)$ can occur. Thus, in the discussion of the next section we can assume that the relevant state space $S$ is of this kind. That is there is a finite process set $\mathcal{P}$ such that $S \subseteq \mathcal{P}^*$.

Let $E$ be an expression and $F_1, F_2$ be two subexpressions occuring in $E$. We say that the occurrence of $F_1$ is before the occurrence of $F_2$ if there is a subexpression of the form $E_1; E_2$ in $E$ such that the occurrence of $F_1$ is in $E_1$ and the occurrence of $F_2$ is in $E_2$. We say that the occurrence of $F_1$ is unguarded if there is no subexpression which occurs before $F_1$, otherwise the occurrence of $F_1$ is called guarded. If $F$ occurs unguarded in $E$, the nesting depth of the occurrence is the number of subexpressions of the form $E_1; E_2$ where $E_1$ contains the occurrence.

**Lemma 5.** *If $E \xrightarrow{a} \alpha$, then there is an unguarded occurrence of $a$ in $E$ such that the length of $\alpha$ equals to the nesting depth of the occurrence.*

**Proof:** Induction on the rules in Table 2.                                        □

**Theorem 2.** *Every $\alpha \in S$ is finite branching.*

**Proof:** We need to show that the set $B(\alpha) = \{\beta \mid a \in Act, \alpha \xrightarrow{a} \beta\}$ is finite. If $\alpha = \epsilon$ then it holds trivially. If $\alpha = E\alpha'$, then by the rules of Table 2 $B(\alpha)$ has the same number of elements as $B(E) = \{\gamma \mid a \in Act, E \xrightarrow{a} \gamma\}$. Now by Theorem 1 if $E \xrightarrow{a} \gamma$ then the processes which can occur in $\gamma$ is from a finite set. Moreover by the previous lemma the length of $\gamma$ is bounded, thus $B(E)$ must be finite.                                        □

## 3   Expansive-Bisimulation

This section contains the main result of the paper, where we study expansive-bisimulation which gives a finite characterization of bisimilar BPA processes.

**Definition 4.** *A state $\alpha \in S$ is said to be normed if there exists a finite sequence of transitions from $\alpha$ to $\epsilon$. The norm of a process $\alpha$ is the length of the shortest transition sequence from $\alpha$ to $\epsilon$. We denote by $\mathcal{N}(\alpha)$ the norm of $\alpha$.*

It is easy to see that for normed processes $\alpha, \beta$ we have the following facts:

1. $\mathcal{N}(\alpha) = 0$ iff $\alpha = \epsilon$.
2. Norm is additive: $\mathcal{N}(\alpha\beta) = \mathcal{N}(\alpha) + \mathcal{N}(\beta)$.
3. $\sim$ preserves norms: If $\alpha \sim \beta$ then $\mathcal{N}(\alpha) = \mathcal{N}(\beta)$.

Clearly $\alpha$ is normed if and only if each process occurring in it is normed. We define a function $\lceil : S \to S$ such that for $\alpha \in S$, if $\alpha$ is normed then $\alpha\lceil = \alpha$, if $\alpha$ is un-normed then $\alpha\lceil$ is the least prefix of $\alpha$ which ends with an un-normed process. And we will call the part of $\alpha$ after $\alpha\lceil$ its tail. Thus the tail of any normed state is always $\epsilon$. We say that $\alpha$ is standard if $\alpha = \alpha\lceil$. In other words, a state is standard just in case its tail is $\epsilon$.

A straightforward consequence of the definition of having a norm is that if $\alpha$ is un-normed then $\alpha\beta \sim \alpha$ holds for any $\beta \in S$.

**Definition 5.** *A binary relation $R \subseteq S \times S$ is an expansive-bisimulation if for all $(\alpha, \beta) \in R$ it holds that either $\alpha = \beta$, or $\alpha\lceil = E\alpha_1, \beta\lceil = F\beta_1$ and there exist $\alpha_2, \beta_2, \gamma \in S$ such that $(\alpha_1, \alpha_2\gamma) \in R, (\beta_2\gamma, \beta_1) \in R$, and moreover the following hold:*

1. *if $E\alpha_2 \xrightarrow{a} \alpha'$, then $F\beta_2 \xrightarrow{a} \beta'$ for some $\beta'$ such that $(\alpha', \beta') \in R$;*
2. *if $F\beta_2 \xrightarrow{a} \beta'$, then $E\alpha_2 \xrightarrow{a} \alpha'$ for some $\alpha'$ such that $(\alpha', \beta') \in R$.*

It is not difficult to see that for a finite relation, whether it is an expansive-bisimulation is decidable.

**Proposition 2.** *If $R$ is an expansive-bisimulation, then $R \subseteq \sim$.*

**Proof:** Suppose $R$ is an expansive-bisimulation, then it is easy to check that $R \cup \{(\alpha, \beta) \mid \alpha, \beta \in S, \alpha\lceil = \beta\lceil\}$ is a self-bisimulation. Thus $R$ is included in a self-bisimulation, and then by Proposition 1 $R \subseteq \sim$. □

**Definition 6.** *When $E\alpha \sim F\beta$ we say that the pair $(E\alpha, F\beta)$ is decomposable if $E, F$ are normed and there is a $\gamma$ such that*

- *$\alpha \sim \gamma\beta$ and $E\gamma \sim F$ if $\mathcal{N}(E) \leq \mathcal{N}(F)$,*
- *$\gamma\alpha \sim \beta$ and $E \sim F\gamma$ if $\mathcal{N}(F) \leq \mathcal{N}(E)$.*

**Theorem 3.** *Let $\alpha, \beta \in S$, then $\alpha \sim \beta$ if and only if there exists a finite expansive-bisimulation which contains $(\alpha, \beta)$.*

**Proof:** The soundness part easily follows from Proposition 2.

Now suppose $\alpha_0 \sim \beta_0$, to show the completeness we will construct a finite expansive-bisimulation $R$ which contains $(\alpha_0, \beta_0)$. In order to construct such $R$, we rely on the following fact which was first proved in [CHS92] in the process of showing the existence of a complete finite self-bisimulation:

> There exists a finite relation $R_0 \subseteq S \times S$ such that if $(\alpha, \beta) \in R_0$ then $\alpha \sim \beta$ and moreover if $E\alpha, F\beta$ are standard and $E\alpha \sim F\beta$ is not decomposable, then there exists $(E\alpha', F\beta') \in R_0$ such that $\alpha \sim \alpha'$ and $\beta \sim \beta'$.

With this fact, our construction of $R$ is based on such $R_0$ as follows. Let

$$S_0 = \{\alpha_0, \beta_0\} \cup \{\gamma \mid \exists \alpha.(\alpha, \gamma) \in R_0 \text{ or } (\gamma, \alpha) \in R_0\}$$
$$\cup \{\gamma \mid \exists (\alpha, \beta) \in R_0, a \in Act.\alpha \xrightarrow{a} \gamma \text{ or } \beta \xrightarrow{a} \gamma\}.$$

Since $R_0$ is finite and every state is finite branching, $S_0$ is a finite set. Choose $n$ such that whenever $\gamma_0$ is a normed prefix of some $\gamma \in S_0$ then $\mathcal{N}(\gamma_0) \leq n$, obviously such $n$ exists as $S_0$ is finite. Let $S_1$ consists of those states $\gamma \in S$ of which the norm of its maximal normed prefix is less than or equal to $n$, and its tail is a tail of some $\gamma' \in S_0$. Then it is not difficult to see that $S_0 \subseteq S_1$. Moreover, note that the states in $S$ only contain processes from a finite set $\mathcal{P}$,

$S_1$ must be finite since for each element in it, the norm of the maximum normed prefix is bounded, and the tail is also from a finite set. Now construct

$$R = \{(\alpha, \beta) \mid \alpha, \beta \in S_1, \alpha \sim \beta\},$$

then $R$ is finite. The rest of the proof is to show that $R$ is an expansive-bisimulation, then since $\alpha_0, \beta_0 \in S_1$ and $\alpha_0 \sim \beta_0$, thus $(\alpha_0, \beta_0) \in R$ so we can conclude the completeness proof.

To show that $R$ is an expansive-bisimulation, take any $(\alpha, \beta) \in R$, and suppose $\alpha \neq \beta$, we will show that $\alpha\lceil = E\alpha_1, \beta\lceil = F\beta_1$ and there exist $\alpha_2, \beta_2, \gamma$ such that $(\alpha_1, \alpha_2\gamma) \in R$ and $(\beta_2\gamma, \beta_1) \in R$ and moreover

1. if $E\alpha_2 \xrightarrow{a} \alpha'$ then $F\beta_2 \xrightarrow{a} \beta'$ for some $\beta'$ such that $(\alpha', \beta') \in R$;
2. if $F\beta_2 \xrightarrow{a} \beta'$ then $E\alpha_2 \xrightarrow{a} \alpha'$ for some $\alpha'$ such that $(\alpha', \beta') \in R$.

Since $\alpha \sim \beta$ and $\alpha \neq \beta$, then it must be the case that neither of $\alpha, \beta$ is $\epsilon$, so $\alpha\lceil = E\alpha_1, \beta\lceil = F\beta_1$ for some $E, F, \alpha_1, \beta_1$, and obviously $E\alpha_1, F\beta_1$ are standard. If $E\alpha_1 \sim F\beta_1$ is not decomposable, then according to the property of $R_0$ there exists $(E\alpha_2, F\beta_2) \in R_0$ such that $\alpha_1 \sim \alpha_2$, $\beta_1 \sim \beta_2$, and now take $\gamma = \epsilon$ we can show that $\alpha_2, \beta_2, \gamma$ are just what we want. For that we need to show that $(\alpha_1, \alpha_2\gamma) \in R$, $(\beta_2\gamma, \beta_1) \in R$, and moreover requirements 1. and 2. above are satisfied. To see $(\alpha_1, \alpha_2\gamma) \in R$, just note that $E\alpha_1, E\alpha_2 \in S_1$ which implies $\alpha_1, \alpha_2 \in S_1$, and moreover $\alpha_1 \sim \alpha_2$, so $(\alpha_1, \alpha_2\gamma) = (\alpha_1, \alpha_2) \in R$. For the same reason $(\beta_2\gamma, \beta_1) \in R$. To see requirement 1. is satisfied, note that $E\alpha_2 \sim F\beta_2$, so for $E\alpha_2 \xrightarrow{a} \alpha'$ there must exist $\beta'$ such that $F\beta_2 \xrightarrow{a} \beta'$ and $\alpha' \sim \beta'$. According to the construction in this case $\alpha', \beta' \in S_1$, so $(\alpha', \beta') \in R$. In the same way we can show that 2. is also satisfied. Now if $E\alpha_1 \sim F\beta_1$ is decomposable, then both $E$ and $F$ are normed and there exists $\delta$ such that A: $E \sim F\delta$ and $\delta\alpha_1 \sim \beta_1$, or B: $E\delta \sim F$ and $\alpha_1 \sim \delta\beta_1$. If it is case A, then since $E \sim F\delta$ is not decomposable, there is $(E\xi, F\eta) \in R_0$ such that $\epsilon \sim \xi, \delta \sim \eta$. Now we can take $\alpha_2 = \epsilon, \beta_2 = \eta, \gamma = \alpha_1$, and we will show that $(\alpha_1, \alpha_2\gamma) \in R$, $(\beta_2\gamma, \beta_1) \in R$, and moreover requirements 1. and 2. above are satisfied. To see $(\alpha_1, \alpha_2\gamma) \in R$, note that $\alpha_1 \in S_1$ and $\alpha_2\gamma = \alpha_1$, thus $\alpha_2\gamma \in S_1$ and $\alpha_1 \sim \alpha_2\gamma$ thus $(\alpha_1, \alpha_2\gamma) \in R$. To see $(\beta_2\gamma, \beta_1) \in R$, note that $\beta_2\gamma = \eta\alpha_1 \sim \delta\alpha_1 \sim \beta_1$, $F\beta_1 \in S_1$ thus $\beta_1 \in S_1$, $E\alpha_1 \in S_1$, $E \sim F\delta \sim F\eta$ and $E$ is normed, so $\mathcal{N}(E) = \mathcal{N}(F\eta)$ and $F\eta\alpha_1 \in S_1$ thus $\eta\alpha_1 \in S_1$, we have $\beta_2\gamma = \eta\alpha_1 \in S_1$, so $(\beta_2\gamma, \beta_1) \in R$. To see 1. is satisfied, note that $(E\alpha_2, F\beta_2) \in R_0$, so $E\alpha_2 \sim F\beta_2$, and the reasoning is as in the previous case for non-decomposable $E\alpha_1 \sim F\beta_1$. The case B can be checked in the same way.  □

In proving decidability of bisimilarity of context-free processes [CHS92], Christensen, Hüttel, and Stirling proved that two context-free processes are bisimulation equivalent if and only if they can be generated by a finite (full) self-bisimulation. Based on their work, the last theorem gives a finite characterization of bisimulation equivalence for context-free processes in terms of expansive-bisimulation. In [BCS95], Burkart, Caucal and Steffen presented an elementary time algorithm that can compute a (full) self-bisimulation which can generate a given pair of bisimulation equivalent context-free processes. Comparing the results, note that whether a finite relation is an expansive-bisimulation is decidable while whether a finite relation is a self-bisimulation is only semi-decidable, thus our characterization result based on expansive-bisimulation implies a complete proof method in that in order to show bisimilarity of two context-free processes we can just present a finite expansive-bisimulation. In this respect it is an obvious advantage to the characterization result based on self-bisimulation.

Also from this characterization result semi-decidability of checking bisimilarity of arbitrary context-free processes is easily obtained. In this case one just need to enumerate all finite relations on $S$ and check if there is one which contains the pair of processes in question and which at the same time is an expansive bisimulation. Thus the dovetailing technique used in the proof in [CHS92] can be avoided.

## 4 Conclusion

In this paper we proposed a notion of expansive-bisimulation which is defined so that checking whether a finite relation is an expansive-bisimulation is decidable. We proved that for equivalent context-free processes finite expansive-bisimulations always exist. Thus expansive-bisimulation can also be considered as providing a witness or proof for bisimulation equivalence of two BPA processes.

To the best of our knowledge no other complete proof method for bisimulation of context-free processes is published. An ideal framework for such kind of proof method would be in the style of Milner's equational proof system for regular processes [Mil82]. However this is not been done even for normed context-free processes, and this could be a result to expect. For normed context-free processes there are Hüttel and Stirling's tableau proof method and a sequent style proof system. One can also seek to extend their results to deal with arbitrary context-free processes.

## References

[BBK87]  Baeten, J.C.M., Bergstra, J.A., Klop, J.W.: Decidability of bisimulation equivalence for processes generating context-free languages. In: de Bakker, J.W., Nijman, A.J., Treleaven, P.C. (eds.) PARLE Parallel Architectures and Languages Europe. LNCS, vol. 259. Springer, Heidelberg (1987)

[BCS95]  Burkart, O., Caucal, D., Steffen, B.: An elementary bisimulation decision procedure for arbitrary context-free processes. In: Hájek, P., Wiedermann, J. (eds.) MFCS 1995. LNCS, vol. 969, Springer, Heidelberg (1995)

[BPS01]  Bergstra, J., Ponse, A., Smolka, S.: Handbook of Process Algebra. Elsevier, Amsterdam (2001)

[Cau90]  Caucal, D.: Graphes canoniques de graphes algébriques. Theoret. Inform. and Appl. 24, 339–352 (1990)

[CHS92]  Christensen, S., Hüttel, H., Stirling, C.: Bisimulation equivalence is decidable for all context-free processes. In: Cleaveland, W.R. (ed.) CONCUR 1992. LNCS, vol. 630, Springer, Heidelberg (1992)

[DT94]      Huynh, D.T., Tian, L.: Deciding bisimilarity of normed context-free processes is in $\sigma_2^p$. Theoretical Computer Science 12, 183–197 (1994)

[Gro91]     Groote, J.F.: A short proof of the decidability of bisimulation for normed bpa-processes. Inform. process. lett. 42, 167–171 (1991)

[HJM96]    Hirshfeld, Y., Jerrum, M., Moller, F.: A polynomial algorithm for deciding bisimulation of normed context-free processes. Theoretical Computer Science 15, 143–159 (1996)

[HS91]      Hüttel, H., Stirling, C.: Action speaks louder than words: Proving bisimilarity for context-free processes. In: Proceedings on Logic in Computer Science (1991)

[Mil82]     Milner, R.: A complete inference system for a class of regular behaviours. CSR 111–82, University of Edinburgh, Department of Computer Science (1982)

[Srb]       Srba, J.: Roadmap of infinite results, http://www.brics.dk/~srba/roadmap

# VDM Semantics of Programming Languages: Combinators and Monads

Peter D. Mosses

Department of Computer Science, Swansea University, UK
p.d.mosses@swan.ac.uk
http://www.cs.swan.ac.uk/~cspdm/

**Abstract.** Although VDM semantic descriptions of programming language are denotational, they can be read quite operationally. After recalling the main features of denotational semantics, this paper examines the combinators of the VDM specification language, and relates them to the use of monads in the monadic style of denotational semantics. It also provides an overview of published VDM semantic descriptions of major programming languages. Familiarity is assumed with the basic concepts of formal specification.

## 1 Introduction

The Vienna Development Method, VDM, is a major framework for the formal specification and rigorous development of software systems. In this paper, we focus on the use of VDM for semantic description of programming languages, which was the original motivation for the framework.

VDM evolved from the operational semantics framework known as VDL, the Vienna Definition Language [1], in the early 1970s [2]. The main change in the transition from VDL to VDM was the adoption of the fundamental principles of denotational semantics, which had already been established by Scott and Strachey [3]. One of the innovations in the VDM style of denotational semantics was the introduction of a number of *combinators* having a fixed *operational* interpretation. We shall see that these combinators are closely related to the operations that later formed the basis for the monadic style of denotational semantics.

The rest of the paper proceeds as follows: Section 2 recalls the fundamental principles of denotational semantics. Section 3 illustrates the original style adopted in denotational descriptions at Oxford, both before and after the introduction of continuations. Section 4 illustrates the VDM style, and explains the main differences between it and the Oxford style. Section 5 presents the concepts and notation used in the monadic style of denotational semantics, and examines the claim that VDM is actually based on monads. Section 6 gives an overview of published VDM semantic descriptions of major programming languages, and proposes to establish an online repository for semantic descriptions of programming languages in all frameworks. A concluding section summarises the main

C.B. Jones, Z. Liu, J. Woodcock (Eds.): Bjørner/Zhou Festschrift, LNCS 4700, pp. 483–503, 2007.
© Springer-Verlag Berlin Heidelberg 2007

points, and acknowledges the major contributions to formal semantics of Dines Bjørner and his colleagues over more than three decades.

## 2    Denotational Semantics

Denotational semantics was initiated by Christopher Strachey in the 1960s [4,5]. Originally it was based on mapping phrases of programs to the untyped $\lambda$-calculus.[1] At the time, it was conjectured that there was no mathematical model of self-applicable functions, which were allowed by the untyped $\lambda$-calculus and used to define the so-called paradoxical combinator $Y$ (needed by Strachey for expressing the semantics of loops and recursive procedures). In 1969, Dana Scott discovered how to construct the missing model, and developed a theory of domains, providing solid foundations for denotational descriptions [3,7].

This section recalls the fundamental principles of denotational semantics. Details specific to the original Oxford style, and the differences between the VDM and Oxford styles, are covered in the following two sections.

A denotational semantics of a programming language maps each phrase of the language to its *denotation*. The denotation represents the contribution of the phrase to the overall behaviour of any complete program that contains it; in particular, the denotation of a complete program represents its entire behaviour when run with particular input. The denotation of a phrase is composed from the denotations of its subphrases, and is independent of its context.

A programming language is essentially just a set of strings (the texts of the syntactically legal programs) together with some criteria for implementations of the language to be regarded as conforming. A language can have many different denotational semantics, depending on the choice of:

- phrase structure: how programs can be uniquely decomposed into phrases;
- program behaviour: when programs are regarded as equivalent; and
- denotations: how contributions to behaviour are represented by abstract entities.

The above differences concern the semantic function that maps phrases to denotations, and are independent of the framework used to specify that function. Let us consider them in a bit more detail.

*Phrase structure:* A set of strings can have many different phrase structures. The choice of a particular phrase structure determines the compositional structure of denotations, which may in turn affect the possibilities for choosing denotations.

For example, consider the set of binary numerals: a string of 0s and 1s could be grouped to the left or to the right (or even both ways). Suppose that the leftmost digit of a binary numeral is the most significant, and that the 'behaviour' of a numeral is its numerical value; then grouping to the left is the obvious choice

---

[1] Peter Landin's approach [6] was superficially similar, but involved an extended $\lambda$-calculus with imperative features.

(since the value of a compound numeral such as 100 can then be computed by doubling the value of 10, whereas with grouping to the right the value of 100 depends on the length of 00 as well as on its value, so denotations would then be pairs of numbers).

Phrase structure for use in denotational semantics is specified by some form of context-free grammar, together with a correspondence relating program texts uniquely to derivation trees according to the grammar. The grammar could be an unambiguous concrete grammar, involving the symbols used in program texts; but usually it is an *abstract grammar*, defining a set of *abstract syntax trees* whose structure is significantly simpler than that of derivation trees for a concrete grammar. The relationship between program texts and abstract syntax trees is generally left to be inferred from the use of suggestive symbols in the abstract grammar, augmented by some informal explanations.

Semantic functions, mapping phrases to their denotations, are defined on abstract syntax trees. The semantic function for a particular language is specified inductively, by giving for each production of the abstract grammar a semantic equation of the form:

$$\mathcal{M}[\![ \cdots V_1 \cdots V_n \cdots ]\!] = f(\mathcal{M}[\![V_1]\!], \ldots, \mathcal{M}[\![V_n]\!]) \tag{1}$$

where $V_1, \ldots, V_n$ are metavariables ranging over sets of abstract syntax trees, and $f$ expresses how the denotations $\mathcal{M}[\![V_1]\!], \ldots, \mathcal{M}[\![V_n]\!]$ of the subphrases are composed to give the denotation of the phrase '$\cdots V_1 \cdots V_n \cdots$'. The double brackets '$[\![ \ldots ]\!]$' enclose the notation expressing syntactic phrases of the described programming language, separating it from the notation used for expressing the mathematical entities used as denotations.

*Program behaviour:* Program behaviour is an abstract representation of what is supposed to be *observable* when programs are compiled and run. It corresponds to the behaviour exhibited by conforming implementations of the programming language.

Compilation usually involves checking for consistency between declaration and use of identifiers throughout the program; the abstract behaviour might then include a list of error messages, or merely a boolean value.

When running the program, its input and output are regarded as observable, so its abstract behaviour always has to represent the input-output relationship. In contrast, potentially observable properties such as how long it takes to run the program (when it terminates), how much memory is required, which machine is used, etc., are generally regarded as irrelevant to the conformance of implementations, and therefore not included in the abstract behaviour of programs.

*Denotations:* After a phrase structure has been chosen, the denotations of phrases can be specified, subject only to the following constraints:

- the denotation of each phrase is composed from the denotations of its subphrases, and
- the abstract behaviour of each program is determined by its denotation.

Denotations are elements of *domains*. The mathematical nature of domains as partially-ordered sets is of much theoretical interest, but does not substantially affect how denotational semantic descriptions are formulated in practice. The crucial properties provided by Scott's domain theory [3,7] are that both domains and elements of domains can be defined recursively as the least solutions of systems of equations:

- Domain equations involve domain constructors (e.g., domains of continuous functions, tuples, tagged values) and given domains (truth values, integers, etc.). The least solution of a system of domain equations can be understood as the limit of a series of approximations, starting from trivial domains. Recursive domain equations are needed for denotations of phrases involving self-applicable procedures (which are found not only in the untyped $\lambda$-calculus, but also in many imperative programming languages).
- Element equations are expressed using $\lambda$-notation. The least solution of an element equation $x = f(x)$ in a domain $D$ is a fixed point of the function $f$ on $D$, and can be understood as the limit of the approximations $f^n(\perp_D)$, where $\perp_D$ is the least element of $D$, representing nontermination or undefinedness. The function $Y$ mapping each function $f$ on $D$ to its least fixed point $Y(f)$ corresponds to the paradoxical combinator used in Strachey's early work, and is needed for expressing the denotations of loops and recursive procedures.

Two phrases (of the same sort) are *interchangeable* when replacing one of them by the other in any program does not affect the overall program behaviour. Clearly, phrases that have the same denotation are necessarily interchangeable. In the other direction, denotations are said to be *fully abstract* when two interchangeable phrases always have the same denotation. When denotations are less than fully abstract, two phrases with different denotations may in fact be interchangeable. Although full abstraction is desirable, it can be difficult (sometimes even impossible) to obtain using standard frameworks for specifying denotations,[2] and lack of full abstraction does not prevent the use of denotational semantics for defining the class of conforming implementations of a language.

The denotation of a phrase is generally a function of an *environment* $\rho \in Env$ that represents the bindings created by the context of the phrase. Environments are themselves functions, mapping identifiers to the entities to which they are bound. Landin and Strachey's original approach in the 1960s was to map program identifiers to bound variables in the $\lambda$-calculus, and to map blocks with local declarations to applications of $\lambda$-abstractions; Scott suggested to use explicit environments in 1969, and they were introduced and illustrated in his seminal joint paper with Strachey in 1971 [3].

In the semantics of imperative languages, the denotation of a phrase is moreover a function of a *store* $\sigma \in S$ that represents the effects of assignments to variables. Stores generally include functions mapping each (currently allocated) location $\alpha \in L$ to the value $\beta \in V$ last stored in it. Simple variable declarations compute environments in which variable identifiers are bound to locations;

---

[2] Fully abstract denotations can always be defined as equivalence classes of phrases.

inspecting the value of a simple variable involves looking up the location to which the identifier is bound in the environment, then looking up the current value of that location in the store.

# 3   The Oxford Style

Strachey established the Programming Research Group in Oxford in 1965. He was already developing his own approach to semantics [4] (see also [5, Sect. 3.3]). Following Scott's discovery of a model for the untyped $\lambda$-calculus [7] while on sabbatical at Oxford in 1969, and Strachey's subsequent collaboration with Scott in the early 1970s [3], the development of denotational semantics accelerated rapidly. The group led by Strachey shared his firm conviction that the denotational approach would now do for semantics what BNF had done for syntax (as witnessed by the *Algol 60 Report* [8]) and that within a few years, all major programming languages should have been given a denotational semantics.

The distinctive Oxford style of denotational semantics (often referred to simply as Scott-Strachey semantics) is particularly concise, and has been followed in many textbooks and articles on semantics, e.g. [9,10,11,12]. The conciseness facilitates (pencil and paper) proofs about semantic properties and is strongly favoured by many theoreticians – but unfortunately, it does not appeal much to practitioners such as compiler writers and programmers. Let us look at some simple examples, which have been selected to illustrate the use of combinators in the Oxford style.

## 3.1   Abstract Syntax

Recall that abstract syntax trees are essentially derivation trees for an abstract context-free grammar. The Oxford style of specifying abstract syntax, illustrated in Fig. 1, is to give a simplified BNF-like grammar using the same terminal symbols as in concrete syntax: reserved words, mathematical signs, and separators. This makes the intended mapping from program texts to abstract syntax trees rather easy to imagine, even though there is usually some grouping ambiguity.

The nonterminal symbols of the grammar are written as metavariables ranging over the corresponding sets of abstract syntax trees; metavariables over the same set are distinguished by subscripts and/or primes. The style of the metavariables themselves varies considerably: Scott and Strachey [3] used lowercase Greek letters, Bob Tennent [12] and Joe Stoy [11] used uppercase Greek letters, Mike

$$\gamma \in \mathsf{Cmd} \qquad commands$$
$$\varepsilon \in \mathsf{Exp} \qquad expressions$$

$$\gamma ::= \mathsf{dummy} \mid \gamma_0 ; \gamma_1 \mid \varepsilon \text{->} \gamma_0 , \gamma_1 \mid \varepsilon_0 := \varepsilon_1 \mid \ldots$$
$$\varepsilon ::= \ldots$$

**Fig. 1.** Abstract syntax fragment, Oxford style

Gordon [13] and Dave Schmidt [10] used uppercase Roman letters, and other authors (including myself) have used abbreviated English words.

## 3.2  Domains and Operations

The domain constructors used in the Oxford style include:

- $A \times B$: product domain containing tuples $\langle a, b \rangle$;
- $A + B$: sum domain containing elements injected from $A$ and $B$;
- $A \to B$: function domain with elements expressed by $\lambda$-abstractions $\lambda a.b$. Note that $A \to B \to C$ groups as $A \to (B \to C)$, and $A \to B \times C$ groups as $A \to (B \times C)$.

The above domains are equipped with some natural operations. Scott and Strachey used the following:

- pairing and projection for product domains $D = A \times B$:
  $P : A \to B \to D$, $M_0 : D \to A$, $M_1 : D \to B$
- injection and projection for sum domains $D = A + B$:
  $\_|_A : D \to A$, $\_|_B : D \to B$, $\_\mathrm{in}\, D : A \to D$, $\_\mathrm{in}\, D : B \to D$
- least fixed points of functions on any domain $D$:
  $Y : (D \to D) \to D$; and
- identity function on any domain $D$:
  $I : D \to D$.

They also introduced a couple of combinators simply as abbreviations:

- composition $f \circ g = \lambda a.f(g(a))$:
  $f \circ g : A \to C$ when $f : B \to C$ and $g : A \to B$;
- composition $f * g = \lambda a.(\lambda b.f(M_0 b)(M_1 b))(g(a))$:
  $f * g : A \to C$ when $f : B_0 \to B_1 \to C$ and $g : A \to B_0 \times B_1$.

Finally, they introduced some operations in connection with the given domain $T$ of truth values and the (loosely specified) domain $S$ of stores:

- $Cond(a_0, a_1)$ mapping $true$ to $a_0$ and $false$ to $a_1$:
  $Cond : A \times A \to T \to A$;
- $Contents(\alpha)$ mapping $\sigma$ to the value stored in it at location $\alpha$:
  $Contents : L \to S \to V$;
- $Assign(\alpha, \beta)$ mapping $\sigma$ to $\sigma'$ such that the value stored at $\alpha$ in $\sigma'$ is $\beta$:
  $Assign : L \times V \to S \to S$.

(The definition of the domain $V$ of values returned by evaluating expressions depends on the language being described [14]; for the examples give here, we shall assume that it includes $L$ and $T$ as summands.) Later papers by other authors introduced considerably more auxiliary notation, mainly to improve the readability of the $\lambda$-expressions arising in the equations used to define denotations.

## 3.3    Denotations

Let us first recall how Scott and Strachey defined denotations in their joint paper in 1971 [3], before reviewing the more commonly-used continuation passing style.

**Direct Semantics.** Scott and Strachey's choice of denotations is called direct semantics. The basic idea is that denotations of commands are functions from environments to store transformers. The semantic function $\mathcal{C}$ maps commands to their denotations:

$$\mathcal{C} : Cmd \to Env \to S \to S \tag{2}$$

Similarly, the denotations of expressions (whose evaluations might have side-effects) should be functions from environments to value-returning store transformers. The semantic function $\mathcal{E}$ maps expressions to their denotations:

$$\mathcal{E} : Exp \to Env \to S \to V \times S \tag{3}$$

Thanks to the use of combinators, the denotations of various commands and expressions can be defined without explicit reference to the store $\sigma$:

$$\mathcal{C}[\![\gamma_0 ; \gamma_1]\!] = \lambda\rho.\ \mathcal{C}[\![\gamma_1]\!](\rho) \circ \mathcal{C}[\![\gamma_0]\!](\rho) \tag{4}$$

$$\mathcal{C}[\![\varepsilon\text{->}\gamma_0, \gamma_1]\!] = \lambda\rho.\ (\lambda\beta.Cond(\mathcal{C}[\![\gamma_0]\!](\rho), \mathcal{C}[\![\gamma_1]\!](\rho)(\beta|T)) * \mathcal{E}[\![\varepsilon]\!](\rho) \tag{5}$$

However, Scott and Strachey were apparently not satisfied with the relatively complicated notation required for expressing the denotations of assignment commands, and resorted to an informal explanation of the steps involved. Here is how they could have written the formal definition:[3]

$$\mathcal{C}[\![\varepsilon_0 := \varepsilon_1]\!] = \lambda\rho.(\lambda\beta_0.(\lambda\beta_1.Assign(\beta_0|L, \beta_1)) * \mathcal{E}[\![\varepsilon_1]\!](\rho)) * \mathcal{E}[\![\varepsilon_0]\!](\rho) \tag{6}$$

Reading the above equation operationally involves associating the values computed by the expressions $\varepsilon_0$ and $\varepsilon_1$ with the $\lambda$-abstractions on $\beta_0$ and $\beta_1$, which is not immediately obvious without close inspection of the grouping of the term.

Suppose, however, that we were to use variants $\hat{\circ}$ and $\hat{*}$ of the combinators $\circ$ and $*$, taking their operands in the reverse order:

- reverse composition $f \hat{\circ} g = \lambda a.g(f(a))$:
  $f \hat{\circ} g : A \to C$ when $f : A \to B$ and $g : B \to C$;
- reverse composition $f \hat{*} g = \lambda a.(\lambda b.g(M_0 b)(M_1 b))(f(a))$:
  $f \hat{*} g : A \to C$ when $f : A \to B_0 \times B_1$ and $g : B_0 \to B_1 \to C$.

The above definitions of denotations can now be written thus:

$$\mathcal{C}[\![\gamma_0 ; \gamma_1]\!] = \lambda\rho.\ \mathcal{C}[\![\gamma_0]\!](\rho) \hat{\circ} \mathcal{C}[\![\gamma_1]\!](\rho) \tag{7}$$

$$\mathcal{C}[\![\varepsilon\text{->}\gamma_0, \gamma_1]\!] = \lambda\rho.\ \mathcal{E}[\![\varepsilon]\!](\rho) \hat{*} \lambda\beta.Cond(\mathcal{C}[\![\gamma_0]\!](\rho), \mathcal{C}[\![\gamma_1]\!](\rho))(\beta|T) \tag{8}$$

---

[3] Let us assume here that any implicit dereferencing of variables is made explicit in the abstract syntax of expressions, in order to simplify the examples a bit.

$$\mathcal{C}[\![\varepsilon_0 := \varepsilon_1]\!] = \lambda\rho.\ \mathcal{E}[\![\varepsilon_0]\!](\rho) \mathbin{\hat{*}} \lambda\beta_0.\mathcal{E}[\![\varepsilon_1]\!](\rho) \mathbin{\hat{*}} \lambda\beta_1.Assign(\beta_0|L, \beta_1) \qquad (9)$$

This minor change of notation allows the terms to be read more operationally, from left to right, with the $\lambda$-abstractions simply naming the values computed by the preceding terms. (It also substantially reduces the number of required parentheses.) In Sect. 5 we shall compare the above formulation with the monadic style.

**Continuation Semantics.** Scott and Strachey's original denotations for commands and expressions, based on store transformers, can represent both normal termination and nonterminating behaviour. To represent abrupt termination, due to escapes (such as break or return) and jumps to labels, the denotations need to be enriched. The standard technique in the Oxford style (often used also for languages that do not involve abrupt termination) is to replace store transformers by *continuation* transformers, where continuations are themselves some kind of store transformers [15]. The semantics of abrupt termination involves ignoring the argument continuation and applying a different one. As we shall see in the next section, the VDM style avoids the use of continuations by letting store transformers return extra values that indicate whether termination is normal or abrupt, and by introducing combinators to propagate and detect the extra values; see [16] for a detailed comparison of the two techniques.

Any ordinary store transformer $\theta$ can be converted to a continuation transformer which, given a continuation $\theta'$, returns the continuation that maps any store $\sigma$ to the result of $\theta'(\theta(\sigma))$. This continuation transformer can be expressed by $\lambda\theta'.\theta' \circ \theta$. The original store transformer can be retrieved from the continuation transformer by applying it to the identity continuation.

Denotations of commands map environments to continuation transformers:

$$\mathcal{C}: Cmd \rightarrow Env \rightarrow C \rightarrow C \qquad (10)$$

where the domain $C$ of command continuations $\theta$ can be defined as $C = S \rightarrow S$. The denotation of command sequencing using continuations is defined as follows:

$$\mathcal{C}[\![\gamma_0;\gamma_1]\!] = \lambda\rho.\lambda\theta.\ \mathcal{C}[\![\gamma_0]\!](\rho)\{\mathcal{C}[\![\gamma_1]\!](\rho)\{\theta\}\}$$
$$= \lambda\rho.\ \mathcal{C}[\![\gamma_0]\!](\rho) \circ \mathcal{C}[\![\gamma_1]\!](\rho) \qquad (11)$$

The domain of expression continuations $\kappa$ is defined as $K = V \rightarrow C$: the continuation is to be applied to the value of the expression. Denotations of expressions are given by the semantic function:

$$\mathcal{E}: Exp \rightarrow Env \rightarrow K \rightarrow C \qquad (12)$$

The continuation semantics of conditional commands is defined by:

$$\mathcal{C}[\![\varepsilon\mathord{\rightarrow}\gamma_0,\gamma_1]\!] = \lambda\rho.\lambda\theta.\ \mathcal{E}[\![\varepsilon]\!](\rho)\{\lambda\beta.Cond(\mathcal{C}[\![\gamma_0]\!](\rho),\mathcal{C}[\![\gamma_1]\!](\rho))(\beta|T)\{\theta\}\}$$
$$= \lambda\rho.\ \mathcal{E}[\![\varepsilon]\!](\rho) \circ \lambda\beta.Cond(\mathcal{C}[\![\gamma_0]\!](\rho),\mathcal{C}[\![\gamma_1]\!](\rho))(\beta|T) \qquad (13)$$

and that of assignment commands by:

$$\mathcal{C}[\![\varepsilon_0 := \varepsilon_1]\!] =$$

$$\lambda\rho.\lambda\theta.\ \mathcal{E}[\![\varepsilon_0]\!](\rho)\{\lambda\beta_0.\mathcal{E}[\![\varepsilon_1]\!](\rho)\{\lambda\beta_1.Assign'(\beta_0|L,\beta_1)\}\}$$

$$= \lambda\rho.\ \mathcal{E}[\![\varepsilon_0]\!](\rho) \circ \lambda\beta_0.\mathcal{E}[\![\varepsilon_1]\!](\rho) \circ \lambda\beta_1.Assign'(\beta_0|L,\beta_1) \tag{14}$$

where $Assign' : L \times V \to C \to C$ is the continuation-passing version of $Assign$.

An alternative to the use of $\circ$ for avoiding deeply-nested braces is to introduce an infix combinator corresponding to application, but grouping to the right. Tennent [12] and Gordon [13] used semicolons for this purpose, writing e.g.:

$$\mathcal{C}[\![\gamma_0;\gamma_1]\!] = \lambda\rho.\lambda\theta.\ \mathcal{C}[\![\gamma_0]\!](\rho);\mathcal{C}[\![\gamma_1]\!](\rho);\theta \tag{15}$$

## 4   The VDM Style

This section focusses on the distinctive features of the VDM style of denotational semantics, which was already quite stable by 1974 [17]. The illustrations and explanations given here are based primarily on the presentation of VDM in the book by Dines Bjørner and Cliff Jones from 1982 [18], since it is essentially that version of the VDM specification language, known as *Meta-IV*, which has been used for almost all published VDM semantic descriptions of major programming languages (see Sect. 6 for references). A subsequent version, *VDM-SL*, was standardised by ISO in 1996 [19], and was used for defining the formal semantics of Modula-2 in its ISO standard [20]. Although there may be some significant differences between *Meta-IV* and *VDM-SL*, the combinators provided appear to be very similar. *Caveat:* The author has not followed the development of VDM at all closely since the end of the 1980s, and the explanations below should definitely not be regarded as authoritative.

In contrast to the Oxford style of denotational semantics, illustrated in the previous section, the VDM style is quite verbose, generally using (abbreviated) English words rather than single letters and mathematical signs. Another stylistic difference is that in VDM, the notation used for abstract syntax (inherited from VDL) does not involve the concrete symbols of the described language. The VDM style is clearly more appropriate than the Oxford style for describing larger programming languages.

### 4.1   Abstract Syntax

The VDM style of specifying abstract syntax is illustrated in Fig. 2. The absence of terminal symbols from the concrete syntax of the described language makes the mapping from program texts to abstract syntax trees somewhat less obvious than in the Oxford style, but the words used as nonterminal symbols in the abstract syntax are usually quite suggestive, and in practice it is not difficult to imagine the exact relationship to a concrete syntax.

Another difference from the Oxford style is that the nonterminal symbols of the abstract grammar are the names of the sets of abstract syntax trees themselves, rather than metavariables over those sets. Moreover, VDM requires a separate nonterminal to be introduced for each kind of statement, expression, etc. A grammar rule of the form $N = N1\ |\ \ldots\ |\ Nm$ defines $N$ to be the union

$$Stmt = Compound \mid If \mid Assign \mid \ldots$$
$$Expr = \ldots$$

$$Compound :: Stmt^*$$
$$If \qquad :: Expr\ Stmt\ Stmt$$
$$Assign \quad :: Expr\ Expr$$

**Fig. 2.** Abstract syntax fragment, VDM style

of $N1, \ldots, Nm$; in contrast, a rule of the form $N :: N1 \ldots Nm$ defines $N$ to be the set of trees constructed by terms of the form $mk\text{-}N(t1, \ldots, tm)$ – essentially, the nodes of the trees are labelled by $N$.

Clearly, VDM grammars for abstract syntax correspond closely to algebraic data type definitions in functional programming languages such as Standard ML and Haskell. The use of $Stmt^*$ in the abstract grammar is reminiscent of regular expressions in concrete syntax, but it is interpreted as the set of tuples of $Stmt$ trees, so the trees in the set $Compound$ are constructed by terms of the form $mk\text{-}Compound(s1, \ldots, sn)$ for all $n \geq 0$.

An interesting feature of the VDM treatment of abstract syntax (not illustrated here) is that it allows trees to have sets and maps as components, as well as tuples. Sets, specified by $N\text{-}set$, are used when the order of the components of a node is (semantically) irrelevant; maps are specified by $N1 \xrightarrow{m} N2$, and can be used to reflect that declarations or formal parameters bind distinct identifiers.

## 4.2  Domains and Operations

The domain constructions available in VDM include:

- $A \times B$: product domain containing tuples $<a,b>$;
- $A \mid B$: union domain;
- $[A]$: optional domain, containing the elements of $A$ and the special value $nil$ (which is used to indicate the absence of an optional value);
- $D :: A1 \ldots An$: domain of trees, containing elements $mk\text{-}D(a1, \ldots, an)$;
- $A \to B$ and $A \xrightarrow{\cdot} B$: total and partial function domains, containing elements expressed by $\lambda$-abstractions $\lambda a.b$;
- $A \xrightarrow{m} B$: domain of finite maps, with elements $[a1 \mapsto b1, \ldots, an \mapsto bn]$; and
- $A\text{-}set$: domain of finite subsets of $A$, with elements $\{a1, \ldots, an\}$.

VDM also provides the usual domains of boolean truth-values and integers.

A distinctive feature of VDM is its imperative combinators, which are used for expressing state transformations, i.e. functions from $STATE$ to $STATE$ (where $STATE$ generally includes $STORE$, mapping locations to their assigned values, as a component). Continuations are not normally used in VDM semantics [16].

A significant difference between these combinators and those introduced by Scott and Strachey for use in the Oxford style is that each combinator provided by VDM has a *fixed operational interpretation*, whereas its definition in $\lambda$-notation varies according to what kind of transformations are to be composed.

In contrast, each combinator used in the Oxford style has a *fixed definition*, but its operational interpretation varies. For example, the VDM combinator written '*s1;s2*' always represents sequential composition of state transformations, (starting from *s1*, and continuing with *s2* when *s1* terminates normally) and its definition depends on that of the domain of state transformations; in the Oxford style, the combinator $f \circ g$ is defined as an abbreviation for $\lambda x.f(g(x))$, and what it represents operationally varies, as illustrated in Sect. 3.3.

The abbreviation '=>' in VDM stands for the domain of pure transformations, and '=>R' stands for the domain of transformations that return values in *R*. The domain of functions from *D* to => is written *D*=>; similarly, the domain of functions from *D* to =>R is written *D*=>R. Below, assume *s* is in =>, *e* is in =>V, and *f* is in *V*=> or *V*=>R.

The main imperative combinators used in the VDM style of denotational semantics are as follows:

- sequencing '*def x: e; f(x)*' applies the transformation *e*, followed by the transformation obtained by applying *f* to the value *x* returned by *e*;
- '*return v*' simply returns the value *v* without transforming the state;
- '*I*' is the identity transformation on states;
- assignment '*r:=e*' first applies *e*, then replaces the component of the state selected by *r* by the value returned by *e*;
- contents '*c r*' returns the component of the state selected by *r* without transforming the state;
- sequencing '*s1; s2*' applies *s2* to the state obtained by applying *s1*;
- conditional '*if b then s1 else s2*' applies *s1* or *s2*, depending on whether the boolean value *b* is *true* or *false*;
- iteration '*for i = m to n do s(i)*' abbreviates '*sm;...;sn*'.

Some further combinators are used in connection with abrupt termination:

- '*exit v*' terminates abruptly, returning a non-*nil* abnormal value *v*;
- '*trap x with f(x) in s*' handles abrupt termination of *s* with the transformation obtained by applying *f* to the abnormal value *x* returned by *s*;
- '*tixe m in s*' handles abrupt termination of *s* by applying the transformation to which the abnormal value returned by *s* is mapped by *m* (repeatedly), propagating the abrupt termination if the value is not in the domain of *m*;
- '*always s2 in s1*' applies *s1*, then applies *s2*, regardless of whether termination of *s1* was normal or abnormal (*s2* is not supposed to terminate abnormally).

All the above combinators are defined by translation to $\lambda$-notation, making the state explicit. In the absence of abrupt termination, '=>' and '=>V' are:

$$\Rightarrow \quad = STATE \xrightarrow{\sim} STATE$$
$$\Rightarrow V \quad = STATE \xrightarrow{\sim} STATE \times V$$

When the possibility of abrupt termination is introduced, '=>' is redefined as:

$$\Rightarrow \quad = STATE \xrightarrow{\sim} STATE \times [ABNORMAL]$$

In the PL/I semantics [17], '$=>V$' is redefined using a *disjoint* union:

$=>V$ = $STATE \xrightarrow{\sim} STATE \times ($ $\underline{res}$ $V$ | $\underline{abn}$ $ABNORMAL)$

In [18], however, '$=>V$' is redefined somewhat differently:

$=>V$ = $STATE \xrightarrow{\sim} STATE \times [ABNORMAL] \times V$

Redefining '$=>$' and '$=>V$' requires redefinition of all the combinators, but their operational interpretation and usage in the semantic equations does not change.

In Sect. 5, we shall see that some of the combinators in VDM are closely related to standard operations of the *monads* used in the monadic style of denotational semantics. Moreover, the redefinitions required when abrupt termination is introduced correspond to the so-called *lifting* of operations when applying the standard *monad transformer* for exception-handling (at least with the definition of '$=>V$' used in the PL/I semantics [17]). Thus it appears that VDM, right from the start in the early 1970s, was already using significant elements of the monadic style that was developed by Eugenio Moggi in the late 1980s [21]. We shall examine this aspect of VDM further in Sect. 5.

### 4.3   Denotations

The following examples illustrate the use of the most basic VDM combinators for defining the denotations of the syntactic constructs shown in Fig. 2, which correspond directly to those used to illustrate the Oxford style in Sect. 3.

As in the Oxford style, denotations of statements (i.e. commands) are functions of environments. The semantic function $M$ maps statements to their denotations:

$M$ : $Stmt$ $->$ $ENV$ $=>$

The same semantic function also maps expressions to their denotations:

$M$ : $Expr$ $->$ $ENV$ $=>$ $VALUE$

The abbreviations '$=>$' and '$=>$ $VALUE$' indicate that both statements and expressions are modelled as state transformations. Whether these transformations involve the possibility of abnormal termination does not need to be specified until later, since it does not affect how denotations are expressed. However, to specify the denotations of assignment statements, we shall need to know how to select the store from a state. This is specified by indicating the name of the selector function next to the store component of the state:

$STATE$ :: $STR$:$STORE$ . . .

(The elided further components might support input and output.)

The denotation of a compound statement involves combining the denotations of an arbitrary number of sub-statements, which can be expressed using the VDM combinator corresponding to a definite iteration:

$M[mk\text{-}Compound(sl)](env)$ = $\underline{for}$ $i$ = $1$ $\underline{to}$ $\underline{len}$ $sl$ $\underline{do}$ $M[sl](env)$

The following is a special case of the above, and is directly comparable with defining binary statement sequencing in the Oxford style, as illustrated in the previous section:

$M[mk-Compound(<s1,s2>)](env) = M[s1](env); M[s2](env)$

Also the VDM definition of the denotations of conditional statements is rather similar to the corresponding definition in the Oxford style:

$M[mk-If(e,th,el)] =$
    $\underline{def}$ $b$: $M[e](env)$;
    $\underline{if}$ $b$ $\underline{then}$ $M[th](env)$ $\underline{else}$ $M[el](env)$

Our final illustration of the VDM style of denotational semantics is the assignment statement:

$M[mk-Assign(lrs,rhs)](env) =$
    $\underline{def}$ $l$: $M[lhs](env)$;
    $\underline{def}$ $v$: $M[rhs](env)$;
    STR := $\underline{c}$ STR + $[l \mapsto v]$

## 5   The Monadic Style

This style of denotational semantics was introduced by Eugenio Moggi at the end of the 1980s [21]. His original motivation was to generalise the categorical semantics of partiality to "other notions of computation"; he subsequently realised that it also allows a much higher degree of modularity and extensibility in semantic descriptions.

The main technical innovations were to let denotations be elements of *monads*, and to construct monads incrementally using *monad transformers*. Monads and monad transformers provide various combinators, which are closely related to some of those used by Scott and Strachey [3], and even more closely to some of those provided by VDM [18]. Like the latter, the monadic combinators have a simple operational reading. The monadic style of denotational semantics has been exploited in several theoretical studies, but it appears that, despite its clear mathematical foundations and advantages regarding modularity, it has not yet been used to describe any major programming language.

### 5.1   Domains and Operations

The monads used in the monadic style of denotational semantics provide the denotations of phrases of programs, and are generally defined in terms of domains.

**Monads.** A monad consists of a domain constructor $T$, mapping value domains $D$ to computation domains $T(D)$, together with two polymorphic operations:

- $Return: D \rightarrow T(D)$;
- $\ggg : T(A) \times (A \rightarrow T(B)) \rightarrow T(B)$

The trivial computation $Return(d)$ simply returns the value $d$ as its result. When the computation $e$ computes a value $a$ and $f$ is a function mapping values to computations, $e \ggg f$ follows the computation $e$ with the computation $f(a)$. (The symbol '$\ggg$', pronounced 'bind', is from the notation for monads provided by the language Haskell, which also allows $e_1 \ggg \lambda x.e_2$ to be written as '$x \leftarrow e_1; e_2$'.) The operations $Return$ and $\ggg$ are required to satisfy three laws:

$$(Return(d) \ggg f) \;=\; f(d) \tag{16}$$

$$(e \ggg Return) \;=\; e \tag{17}$$

$$((e \ggg f) \ggg g) \;=\; (e \ggg \lambda x.(f(x) \ggg g)) \tag{18}$$

where $x$ must not be free in $f$ or $g$ in the last law above.

The simplest possible example of a monad is the identity monad, where $T(D) = D$, $Return(d) = d$, and $e \ggg f = f(e)$.

Particular kinds of monads provide further operations. Such monads can often be constructed by applying standard monad transformers [21] to existing monads.

*Side-Effect Monads:* Given domains $L$ of locations and $V$ of values, a side-effect monad provides the operations:

- $Update : L \times V \to T()$
- $Inspect : L \to T(V)$

*Environment Monads:* Given a domain $Env$, an environment monad provides:

- $GetEnv : T(Env)$
- $UseEnv : Env \to T(D) \to T(D)$

*Exception Monads:* Given a domain $A$ of exception identifiers, an exception monad provides:

- $Raise : A \to T(D)$
- $Handle : A \times T(D) \times T(D) \to T(D)$

All the above operations satisfy some equational axioms, which allow algebraic reasoning about equivalence (and can even be used to define the respective monads [22]). In fact we have already seen some examples corresponding closely to such monads:

**Oxford style, direct semantics:** For an example of a side-effect monad, let $T(D) = S \to D \times S$, then define $Return(d) = \lambda\sigma.\langle d, \sigma\rangle$ and $e \ggg f = (\lambda\langle a, \sigma\rangle.f(a)(\sigma)) \circ e$. Scott and Strachey's combinators $P$ and $*$ are special cases of $Return$ and $\ggg$ (the latter with the arguments reversed). Defining $Update(l, v) = \lambda\sigma.\langle\langle\rangle, Assign(l, v)(\sigma)\rangle$ and $Inspect(l) = \lambda\sigma.\langle Contents(l), \sigma\rangle$ provides the required operations, and shows their close relationship to Scott and Strachey's combinators.

For an example of both an environment monad and a side-effect monad, take $T(D) = Env \to S \to D \times S$ with $Return(d) = \lambda\rho.\lambda\sigma.\langle d, \sigma\rangle$ and $e \ggg f = \lambda\rho.(\lambda\langle a, \sigma\rangle.f(a)(\rho)(\sigma)) \circ e(\rho)$. Then define $GetEnv = P$ and $UseEnv(\rho')(e) = \lambda\rho.e(\rho')$. Notice that $T(V)$ is the domain of expression denotations in direct semantics, and $T()$ is isomorphic to the domain of statement denotations. However, Scott and Strachey did not introduce combinators in connection with environments, preferring to exhibit the propagation of environments.

**Oxford style, continuation semantics:** A further example of both an environment monad and a side-effect monad is provided by $T(D) = Env \to (D \to C) \to C$ (where $C = S \to S$) with $Return(d) = \lambda\rho.\lambda\kappa.\kappa(d)$ and $e \ggg f = \lambda\rho.\lambda\kappa.e(\rho)(\lambda a.f(a)(\rho)(\kappa))$. (It could presumably be made into an exception monad by adding continuations corresponding to handlers to the environment.)

**VDM style, normal termination:** Let $T(D)$ be =>$D$, which, in the absence of abnormal termination, is $STATE \xrightarrow{\sim} STATE \times D$. Let $Return$ be the VDM combinator **_return_**, and let $e \ggg f$ be defined as **_def_** $x$: $e$; $f(x)$. This provides a monad. Assuming that the store component of the state is selected by STR, $Update(l, v)$ can be defined to be STR := (**_c_** STR)+[$l \mapsto v$], and $Inspect(l)$ to be **_return_**((**_c_** STR)($l$)). This gives a side-effect monad, which has been used in VDM since the early 1970s. It would be straightforward to make $Env$=>$D$ into an environment monad as well, but VDM does not provide combinators corresponding to $GetEnv$ and $UseEnv$.

**VDM style, abnormal termination:** The redefinition of =>$D$ to allow abrupt termination given in the PL/I semantics [17] is:

$$=>V = STATE \xrightarrow{\sim} STATE \times (\underline{res}\ V\ |\ \underline{abn}\ ABNORMAL)$$

where values are tagged with **_res_** or **_abn_** to distinguish between normal and abrupt termination. The redefined combinators **_return_** and **_def_** still provide a monad: this is essentially an instance of applying a monad transformer, and all the original combinators are 'lifted' to the new domains. Moreover, the resulting monad is easily made into an exception monad: define $Raise(a)$ to be **_exit_** $a$, and $Handle(a, b, c)$ as **_trap_** $a$ **_with_** $b$ **_in_** $c$. It is remarkable that VDM was already using these monads more than 15 years before the monadic style of denotational semantics was explicitly introduced.

However, it appears that the alternative redefinition of =>$D$ in *Meta-IV* [18]

$$=>V = STATE \xrightarrow{\sim} STATE \times [ABNORMAL] \times V$$

does *not* allow the combinators **_return_** and **_def_** to be redefined as a monad.[4] The problem is that $e \ggg f$ needs to be defined for all $e$ in =>$A$ and $f$ in $A$=>$B$, where $A$ and $B$ are generally different domains; in the case corresponding to abrupt termination of $e$, the third component of the resulting tuple needs to be mapped from $A$ to $B$. Simply mapping all elements of $A$ to the bottom element of $B$ would violate one of the laws for monads (equation 17 above).

---

[4] Thanks to Eugenio Moggi for drawing attention to this point.

## 5.2   Denotations

Let us conclude this section by showing how simple it can be to define the denotations of our illustrative phrases in the monadic style. We shall not bother to define the monad $T$, since the details of the definition do not affect how denotations are expressed, nor their operational understanding. We do however assume that $T$ is both a side-effect monad and an environment monad.

The semantic function $C$ maps commands to their denotations in $T()$, since commands do not compute values (which is represented by computing the null value).

$$C : Cmd \to T() \tag{19}$$

The semantic function $\mathcal{E}$ maps expressions to their denotations in $T(V)$, where $V$ is a domain of values whose definition depends on the language being described, but is here assumed to include both $L$ (locations) and $T$ (truth values) as summands.

$$\mathcal{E} : Exp \to T(V) \tag{20}$$

Thanks to the use of monadic notation, the denotations of various commands and expressions can be defined without notational clutter regarding appropriate propagation of the environment $\rho$ and the store $\sigma$ (not to mention details concerning the representation of abnormal termination):

$$C[\![\gamma_0 ; \gamma_1]\!] = C[\![\gamma_0]\!] \ggg \lambda(). \ C[\![\gamma_1]\!] \tag{21}$$

$$C[\![\varepsilon \text{->} \gamma_0 , \gamma_1]\!] = \mathcal{E}[\![\varepsilon]\!] \ggg \lambda\beta. \ Cond(C[\![\gamma_0]\!], C[\![\gamma_1]\!])(\beta | T) \tag{22}$$

$$C[\![\varepsilon_0 := \varepsilon_1]\!] = \mathcal{E}[\![\varepsilon_0]\!] \ggg \lambda\beta_0. \ \mathcal{E}[\![\varepsilon_1]\!] \ggg \lambda\beta_1. \ Update(\beta_0 | L, \beta_1) \tag{23}$$

The reader is invited to compare the above semantic equations with those given in the Oxford style (Sect. 3) and in the VDM style (Sect. 4). The basic monadic combinators provided in both those early styles allowed them to get close to the simplicity of the monadic style. VDM has the advantage of a fixed operational interpretation for its combinators, and originally used what is essentially a monad transformer when adding the possibility of abnormal termination.

# 6   Published VDM Semantic Descriptions

VDM was originally developed for giving a formal definition of PL/I and providing a formal basis for the development of a compiler [2]. Other major programming languages that have been described using VDM include Algol 60, Pascal, Ada, and Modula-2. The aim here is merely to give a general overview of the cited descriptions. In general, the descriptions are out of print; this section concludes by proposing the establishment of an online repository for semantic descriptions, so that these major contributions can be preserved and made more easily accessible to the research community.

*PL/I:* The technical report *A Formal Definition of a PL/I Subset* by Hans Bekič, Dines Bjørner, Wolfgang Henhapl, Cliff Jones, and Peter Lucas was published by the IBM Laboratory in Vienna in 1974 [17]. Covering 201 pages, its length was modest compared to the size of the language described (and to that of the earlier definition of PL/I given in the operational VDL framework). The described subset is essentially the version of PL/I described in the ECMA/ANSI standard (which does not include tasking) but omitting Input/Output. Section 4 of the chapter on Notation introduces and defines the VDM combinators concerned with state transformations, imperative variables, exit, and arbitrary ordering.

Although the original technical report is out of print, 61 pages from it were reprinted in a volume of LNCS containing a selection of papers by Hans Bekič, and is available online in pdf [17]. The development of a compiler based on the semantic description stopped in 1975, when IBM cancelled the project to build the intended target machine [2].

*Algol 60:* A VDM semantics for Algol 60 by Wolfgang Henhapl and Cliff Jones was published as Chapter 6 of the book *Formal Specification and Software Development* in 1982 [23]; it is a revision of a previous paper by the same authors published in the 1978 LNCS volume on VDM [24]. In 33 pages it specifies the abstract syntax and semantics of the language described in the 1975 *Modified Report* on Algol 60, and provides a list of abbreviations as well as an index of object and function definitions. The specifications of the abstract syntax, static semantics and dynamic semantics are interleaved, so that the static and dynamic semantics for the same construct are given close to each other.

The definition of the arbitrary order of evaluation allowed by Algol 60 is deliberately not addressed; a few other minor deviations from the intended semantics of Algol 60 are indicated in comments. Neither the concrete syntax nor its translation to the abstract syntax are given, although some of the comments refer to various expansions made by "the translator".

*Pascal:* A VDM semantics for Pascal by Derek Andrews and Wolfgang Henhapl was published as Chapter 7 of the book *Formal Specification and Software Development* in 1982 [25]. As with the VDM semantics for Algol 60 that it follows, it is a revision of a previous paper published in the 1978 LNCS volume on VDM [24]. After an introduction commenting on various aspects of the VDM semantics of Pascal, it takes 60 pages to specify the abstract syntax and semantics of the language described in the BSI/ISO Standard for Pascal.

In contrast to the VDM semantics of Algol 60, the specifications of the abstract syntax, static semantics, and dynamic semantics of Pascal are not interleaved. The abstract syntax was chosen to be "fairly close" to the concrete syntax of Pascal, making their relationship "more obvious". The specification of the abstract syntax is about 6 pages, including some detailed notes about the intended concrete to abstract translation (which involves the introduction of fresh identifiers "not used elsewhere"). The static semantics takes 22 pages, and the dynamic semantics 30 pages.

*Ada:* A VDM semantics for full Ada was initially developed by Dines Bjørner and several MSc students under his supervision at the Danish Technical University, and published as a volume of LNCS with the title *Towards a Formal Description of Ada* in 1980 [26]. This description was subsequently revised and finalised in a series of technical reports, published by Dansk Datamatik Center (DDC) in 1981–2, which provided the basis for the rigorous development of an Ada compiler [27]. The compiler was released in 1983, and became renowned not only for its quality, but also as commercially successful. The unqualified success of this application of VDM was a clear vindication of Dines Bjørner's trust in the suitability of the VDM specification language for describing the semantics of large languages such as Ada, as well as a welcome, highly visible demonstration of the potential usefulness of research in formal semantics.

VDM was later used also in the official *Draft Formal Definition of Ada*, but only for the static semantics [28]. The dynamic semantics [29,30] was specified using SMoLCS [31], which uses a "VDM-like" style of denotational semantics to map Ada programs into a semantic algebra, where behaviour (including concurrency) is specified using a combination of labelled transition rules and algebraic axioms. The semantic algebra includes the combinators used in VDM.

*Modula-2:* VDM was used, along with English text, for defining the semantics of Modula-2 in the ISO/IEC base standard, which was developed from 1987 to 1996. The formal definition and the English text are regarded as having equal importance. According to an article about the process of producing the standard [20], it contains about "200 type definitions, 1800 function and operation definitions and some 20,000 lines of VDM-SL code". All the VDM-SL specifications were "tested for syntactical accuracy and semantic constraints" using a front end for VDM-SL developed at Delft University of Technology. ISO/IEC did not allow publication of the standard on the web [32], although a draft version is available.[5]

*Online access:* The VDM Portal[6] provides online access to many VDM documents, including examples of specifications in VDM-SL and VDM++. However, it appears that only *two* VDM semantic descriptions of programming languages are currently available through the portal: one for a language called *NewSpeak* from 1994, the other for a tutorial-style example of static and dynamic semantics of a simple programming language.

One problem with providing online access to the VDM semantic descriptions cited above is that they are generally available only in printed form, and would need scanning to pdf (fortunately, this has already been done for parts of the PL/I semantics [17] – although it is frustrating not to have access to the rest of it at present – and for the semantics of Algol 60 and Pascal in [18]). It is conceivable that the original sources of some of the documents have been archived electronically, in which case it might be feasible to retrieve them and use them to generate searchable pdfs.

---

[5] ftp://ftp.mathematik.uni-ulm.de/pub/soft/modula/standard/draft4/
[6] http://www.vdmportal.org/

A different and more general problem with providing online access to large VDM specifications is to allow efficient *searching* for particular items of interest. For semantic descriptions of programming languages, it would be useful to search for the parts concerning particular (concrete or abstract) constructs. Searching for mathematical formulae is inherently difficult, and addressed on the web by using special markup languages such as MathML; but this would not help with existing, older documents. A possible solution might be to add bookmarks to pdfs, identifying the pages concerned with particular constructs.

There is also the issue of copyright. Presumably all authors of semantic descriptions would be happy to see their work made accessible online, but some publishers are unlikely to agree to free access. A compromise might be to provide free access only to summary information about semantic descriptions, sufficient to support searching for descriptions of particular constructs, but require login as a registered user to see the pdf of the description itself.

The author is currently investigating the possibility of establishing a repository for semantic descriptions of programming languages in *all* major frameworks; VDM would be among the first to be covered. Readers who have copies of significant semantic descriptions of programming languages (in any format) are kindly requested to contact the author, indicating what they could provide, and who holds the copyright.

## 7 Conclusion

The fundamental principles of denotational semantics were established by Scott and Strachey at Oxford in the early 1970s. VDM adopted these principles, but also introduced some innovations: in particular, VDM made much greater use of combinators than was usual in the original Oxford style. Significantly, each combinator in VDM has a fixed operational interpretation, whereas its definition in $\lambda$-notation can vary; see also [33]. We have seen that some of the VDM combinators introduced in the early 1970s correspond directly to operations provided in the monadic style of denotational semantics, which was developed at the end of the 1980s; moreover, the way their definitions vary corresponded to the lifting of operations by particular monad transformers.

VDM semantic descriptions of some major programming languages have been published, including PL/I, Algol 60, Pascal, Ada, and Modula-2. They are valuable sources of examples of how to describe a wide range of programming constructs using VDM, and deserve to be much more easily accessible to researchers and students than at present; including them in the proposed online repository of semantic descriptions would not only make them electronically available, but should also allow searching for descriptions of particular kinds of constructs.

*Acknowledgement.* Thanks to Cliff Jones and Eugenio Moggi for helpful comments on drafts of this paper, and to the organisers for the invitation to give a presentation at the symposium.

This paper was written in celebration of Dines Bjørner's 70th birthday. As one of the originators of VDM, through his many articles and books about VDM, and by his use of VDM in major projects such as the formal descriptions of PL/I and Ada, Dines has had a profound influence on the development and practical application of denotational semantics. Personally, I have benefited immensely from contact with him since we first met in the early 1970s. In particular, Dines arranged for me to be involved as an observer in DDC's project to develop an Ada compiler from its VDM semantics, and he helped me become a member of IFIP Working Group 2.2 (on *Formal Description of Programming Concepts*). His expertise, friendship and hospitality have always seemed limitless.

*Hjertelig tillykke med de 70 år, Dines!*

# References

1. Wegner, P.: The Vienna Definition Language. ACM Comput. Surv. 4(1), 5–63 (1972)
2. Jones, C.B.: The transition from VDL to VDM. J. UCS 7(8), 631–640 (2001)
3. Scott, D.S., Strachey, C.: Towards a mathematical semantics for computer languages. In: Proc. Symp. on Computers and Automata. Microwave Research Inst. Symposia, vol. 21, pp. 19–46. Polytechnic Institute of Brooklyn (1971) (Also Tech. Mono. PRG-6, Oxford Univ. Comp. Lab.) (August, 1971)
4. Strachey, C.: Towards a formal semantics. In: Steel Jr., T.B. (ed.) Formal Language Description Languages for Computer Programming, Proc. IFIP Work. Conf., Vienna, 1964, pp. 198–220. North-Holland, Amsterdam (1966)
5. Strachey, C.: Fundamental concepts in programming languages. Higher-Order and Symbolic Computation 13(1/2), 11–49 (2000) (Originally lecture notes, NATO Copenhagen Summer School, 1967)
6. Landin, P.J.: Correspondence between ALGOL 60 and Church's lambda-notation: Part I. Commun. ACM 8(2), 89–101 (1965)
7. Scott, D.S.: Outline of a mathematical theory of computation. In: Proc. Fourth Annual Princeton Conf. on Information Sciences and Systems, pp. 169–176. Princeton University (1970) (Superseded by Tech. Mono. PRG-2, Oxford Univ. Comp. Lab.)
8. Backus, J.W., Bauer, F.L., Green, J., Katz, C., McCarthy, J., Perlis, A.J., Rutishauser, H., Samelson, K., Vauquois, B., Wegstein, J.H., van Wijngaarden, A., Woodger, M.: Revised report on the algorithmic language ALGOL 60. Commun. ACM 6(1), 1–17 (1963)
9. Mosses, P.D.: Denotational semantics. In: van Leeuwen, J. (ed.) Handbook of Theoretical Computer Science, vol. B, Elsevier, Amsterdam (1990)
10. Schmidt, D.A.: Denotational Semantics: A Methodology for Language Development. Allyn and Bacon (1986), available at
    http://people.cis.ksu.edu/~schmidt/text/densem.html
11. Stoy, J.E.: Denotational Semantics: The Scott-Strachey Approach to Programming Language Theory. The MIT Press Series in Computer Science, vol. 1. MIT Press, Cambridge (1977)
12. Tennent, R.D.: The denotational semantics of programming languages. Commun. ACM 19(8), 437–453 (1976)
13. Gordon, M.J.C.: The Denotational Description of Programming Languages: An Introduction. Springer, Heidelberg (1979)

14. Strachey, C.: The varieties of programming language. In: Proc. Int. Computing Symp., Cini Foundation, Venice. (1972) 222–233 A revised and slightly expanded version is Tech. Mono. PRG-10, Oxford Univ. Comp. Lab. (March 1973)
15. Strachey, C., Wadsworth, C.P.: Continuations: A mathematical semantics for handling full jumps. Higher Order Symbol. Comput. 13(1-2), 135–152 (2000) (Originally published as Tech. Mono. PRG-11, Oxford Univ. Comput. Lab., January 1974)
16. Jones, C.B.: More on exception mechanisms [18], ch. 5, pp. 125–140
17. Bekič, H., Bjørner, D., Henhapl, W., Jones, C.B., Lucas, P.: On the formal definition of a PL/I subset (selected parts). In: Jones, C.B (ed.) Programming Languages and their Definition. LNCS, vol. 177, pp. 107–155. Springer, Heidelberg (1984), available at http://homepages.cs.ncl.ac.uk/cliff.jones/ home.formal/ftp-stuff/LNCS177-Bekic Full version published as Tech. Rep. 25.139, IBM Lab. Vienna (December 1974)
18. Bjørner, D., Jones, C.B.: Formal Specification and Software Development. Computer Science Series. Prentice-Hall, Englewood Cliffs (1982), available at http://homepages.cs.ncl.ac.uk/cliff.jones/home.formal/ftp-stuff/ BjornerJones1982/
19. Plat, N., Larsen, P.G.: An overview of the ISO/VDM-SL standard. SIGPLAN Not. 27(8), 76–82 (1992)
20. Pronk, C., Schönhacker, M.: ISO/IEC 105141, the standard for Modula-2: Process aspects. SIGPLAN Not. 31(8), 74–83 (1996)
21. Moggi, E.: An abstract view of programming languages. Technical Report ECS-LFCS-90-113, Edinburgh Univ. (1989)
22. Plotkin, G.D., Power, A.J.: Computational effects and operations: An overview. In: Proc. Workshop on Domains VI. Electr. Notes Theor. Comput. Sci., vol. 73, pp. 149–163. Elsevier, Amsterdam (2004)
23. Henhapl, W., Jones, C.B.: ALGOL 60. [18], ch. 6, pp. 141–173
24. Bjørner, D., Jones, C.B.: The Vienna Development Method: The Meta-Language. LNCS, vol. 61. Springer, Heidelberg (1978)
25. Andrews, D.J., Henhapl, W.: Pascal. [18], ch. 7, pp. 175–252
26. Oest, O.N., Bjørner, D.: Towards a Formal Description of Ada. LNCS, vol. 98. Springer, Heidelberg (1980)
27. Clemmensen, G.B., Oest, O.N.: Formal specification and development of an Ada compiler – a VDM case study. In: ICSE '84: Proc. 7th Int. Conf. on Software Engineering, pp. 430–440. IEEE Computer Society Press, Los Alamitos (1984)
28. Botta, N., Storbank Pedersen, J.: The draft formal definition of Ada, the static semantics definition, vol. 1–4. Technical report, Dansk Datamatik Center, Lyngby, Denmark (1987)
29. Bendix Nielsen, C., Karlsen, E.W.: The draft formal definition of Ada, the dynamic semantics definition, vol. 1–3. Technical report, Dansk Datamatik Center, Lyngby, Denmark (1987)
30. Giovini, A., Mazzanti, F., Reggio, G., Zucca, E.: The draft formal definition of Ada, the dynamic semantics definition, vol. 4, Technical report, Dansk Datamatik Center, Lyngby, Denmark (1986)
31. Astesiano, E., Reggio, G.: Direct semantics of concurrent languages in the SMoLCS approach. IBM J. Res. Dev. 31(5), 512–534 (1987)
32. Pronk, C., Schönhacker, M.: Formal definition of programming language standards. SIGPLAN Not. 38(8), 20–21 (2003)
33. Mosses, P.D.: Making denotational semantics less concrete. In: Proc. Int. Workshop on Semantics of Programming Languages, Bad Honnef. Bericht 41, Abteilung Informatik, Universität Dortmund, 102–109 (1977)

# Formal Approach to Railway Applications

Martin Pěnička

Czech Technical University, Department of Applied Mathematics, U611,
Na Florenci 25, CZ-11000 Prague, Czech Republic
penicka@fd.cvut.cz
http://www.fd.cvut.cz

**Abstract.** This paper names railway applications, where the basis of stable, underlying railway formal domain models can be successfully used. It is done with big care of a uniform treatment of two diverse issues of railway system: Allocation & Scheduling and Monitoring & Control applications. This uniform treatment allows us later on better, easier and deeper integrations of these applications.

**Keywords:** Railways, Planning, Timetabling, Rostering, Control, Interlocking, Signalling, Technique Integration.

## 1 Introduction

The problem which this paper addresses is that of understanding the railway application domain. One can use a basic core of such railway application domain to model various application from two different aspects of any railway system:

- Allocation & Scheduling and
- Monitoring & Control

The goal of the paper is to show that mathematically precise specification techniques allow a uniform treatment of these two diverse issues on the basis of stable, underlying models.

There are already papers on formal description of railway domain, see [14, 15, 16, 17, 18, 19, 21, 22, 23]. One can also find railway domain descriptions in PRaCoSy project [33, 103, 104, 105, 106, 107, 108, 109, 110, 116].

## 2 Issues of Scheduling and Allocation

### 2.1 Introduction

In this section we would like to provide a brief informal description of several issues of railway allocation & scheduling tasks. Each subsection in this paper gives a short railway application description and then a reference to formal solution to bibliography.

C.B. Jones, Z. Liu, J. Woodcock (Eds.): Bjørner/Zhou Festschrift, LNCS 4700, pp. 504–520, 2007.

## 2.2   Rail Net Development

The Rail Net Development System takes care of the rail net management. That is for instance insertion or removal of lines and stations, changing parameters (like speed) of lines, etc.

Chapter 8 in [118] shows how to generate optimum railway net layout and its timetable as an indivisible pair.

The problem can be also solved by Petri nets, see [12]. Formal representation of track topologies can be found in [68, 95]. For graphical systems for the visual simulation and control of railway network, see [27, 127].

## 2.3   Timetable Generation

Timetables belong to the most important entities in railway system from both the operator's and passenger's point of view. There are several different ways how to present timetable. From the operator's point of view the most important form of timetable is called 'running map' [13, 46, 131, 117, 111].

From the passenger's point of view timetable can be seen as a printed book, set of all departures/arrivers at stations, web-based travel planning application, train or lines booklets, etc.

Section 4.2.1 of the [118] gives a general formal model (data structure), from which all other forms can be easily derived. Also many others papers deals with timetabling from the formal point of view. We refer to some of them [45, 47, 67, 69, 70, 83, 102, 115, 129].

## 2.4   Scheduling and Rescheduling

One can talk about a traffic being on schedule or not. In particular one can talk about traffic being delayed. For a traffic to be on schedule, the traffic must be one of the traffics allowed by the schedule.

The whole chapter 15 in [118] deals with the rescheduling problem. Scheduling and rescheduling of trains from the formal point of view is also described in [20]. Usage of genetic algorithms in train scheduling problem can be found in [29]. A duration Model for Railway scheduling is shown in [34].

## 2.5   Other Resource Planning

Staff, monies, and auxiliary resources need also be managed.

Among auxiliary resources we include: car and wagon cleaning etc.; car and wagon maintenance and repair equipment; freight loading & unloading trucks; etc.

Their physical and temporal availability, i.e. allocation and scheduling, subject to various rules and regulations, is part of station management.

We refer to chapter 8 in [118] and to [28, 35] for more details about this topic.

## 2.6   Maintenance Planning

By maintenance we do not mean only regular check of all systems (assemblies, etc.) in the depot, but we present maintenance in a more general sense. We understand maintenance as a set of all activities, which must be done with rolling stock, regularly according to some rules, and which should be planned in advance except for the operation of rolling stock itself. Therefore we also include outside and inside cleaning of carriages, refueling diesel engines, refilling supplies into restaurant carriages, water and oil refilling, etc.

In the [118] whole chapter 9 deals with this task. We also refer to [64] that deals with application of genetic techniques to the planning of railway track maintenance work. Fuzzy neural networks for machine maintenance in mass transit railway systems are shown in [91].

## 2.7    Optimum Train Length

A determination of the train composition is another optimisation problem of railway allocation and scheduling. It deals with the maximum usage of available rolling-stock. The problem to be tackled is as follows: trains travel from station to station. Trains are composed of carriages. At stations trains may have carriages added (composed) to, or removed (decomposed) from the train. Station tracks may restrict train additions and removals to occur only at either the front, or at the back of a train. Given the requirements for trains to provide suitable load (for example passenger) capacity along a journey with such demands varying, the problem is now to plan that trains, during their journeys, have suitable assemblies added to or removed from the train.

The costs of coupling and decoupling have to be taken into account. There can be found graphical tools [38] that help dealing this task. We also refer to [52, 62, 78, 101].

## 2.8    Station Track Assignment

Track may be blocked for several trains. The planning and actual setting (i.e. signalling) of the corresponding unit states is an essential function of station management. Station management also involves determination of train positions.

Complexity issues of routing trains through railway stations can be found in [87]. A case study of railway station management from the formal approach is described in [50, 122].

## 2.9    Delay Train Management

In the everyday operation of a railroad, it is unfortunately not uncommon for a train to arrive at a station with a delay. In such a situation, some of the trains passengers may miss a connecting train, resulting in an even larger delay for them since they have to wait for the next train. If, on the other hand, the connecting train waits, then it is delayed itself, and so are all the passengers it is carrying. Delay management consists of deciding which connecting trains should wait for what delayed feeder trains, usually with the objective of minimizing the overall discomfort faced by the passengers. Although railway optimization and scheduling problems have been studied quite intensely over the past decade, the management of delayed trains has received much less attention.

Scheduling and rescheduling of trains from the formal point of view can be found in [20, 102].

## 2.10  Hub Location Problem

Hub location problems are likely to occur in any kind of logistic system. A hub is a special type of facility, which collects the flow from a set of other facilities, transfers it to other hub facilities and distributes it to its final destination.

A hub location problem consists of a location part, in which the locations of the hub nodes are selected, and an allocation part, in which every non-hub node is assigned to one ore more hub nodes [38, 49].

The hub center problem is to locate appropriate numbers of hubs and to allocate nonhub nodes to hub nodes so that the maximum travel time (or distance) between any origin-destination pair is minimized.

## 2.11  Automatic Train Control

State-of-the-art information and communication technologies allow for an automated driverless operation of insular mass transit systems. In the long term such options exist for railway operation in general. Energy efficiency effects can be achieved through general optimisation of driving style and traffic flows.

Finding the optimum energy-saving train run-curve is one of the issues. The optimisation is made by changing the speed-position profile with keeping the same running time. Analysis of the optimum 'energy-saving' train run-curve is one of the difficult research topics of train operation.

## 2.12  Train Dispatch

The Train Dispatch System handles the scheduling of train traffic. This includes the arrival and departure of trains from stations and may also include information on which lines to use when traveling between stations. We refer to [30, 71, 87, 115] for more details on distributed train dispatching system and its complexity issues.

## 2.13  Shunting and Marshalling

Given description of the status (whereabouts, availability, etc.) of rolling stock, including train bodies waiting to be decomposed, and given description of train bodies to be composed, shunting and marshalling implies both the planning for, and the execution of, plans of shunting and marshalling.

Shunting and marshalling involves route planning and signalling: i.e. the setting of unit states. Shunting and marshalling also involves determination of train body, car and wagon positions.

More information about this topic can be found in [21, 50, 87].

## 2.14  Passenger and Freighter Information

The main subject of railway information systems is a real-time dissemination of the time and other status of all incoming, arrived or departed trains, whether passenger or freight trains, and if the latter, what freight has been received or passed on, and then to where.

Passenger & freighter information systems are not the subject of the Thesis, instead we refer to [52, 77].

## 2.15   Line Capacity

Improving railway line capacity (the maximum number of trains which can be moved in each direction over a specified line in a 24 hour period) is another optimisation problem that can be solved with a significant help of computer calculation power.

This topic is also not a part of the Thesis, instead we refer to [1, 37, 84].

# 3   Issues of Train Monitoring and Control

## 3.1   Introduction

Railway monitor and control systems are systems used on railways to control traffic safely, for example, to prevent trains from colliding. Trains are uniquely susceptible to collision because, running on fixed rails, they are not capable of avoiding a collision by steering away, as can a road vehicle; furthermore, trains cannot decelerate rapidly, and are frequently operating at speeds where by the time the driver/engineer can see an obstacle, the train cannot stop in time to avoid colliding with it.

Most forms of train control involve messages being passed from those in charge of the rail network or portions of it (e.g., a stationmaster) to the train crew; these are known as 'signals' and from this the topic of train control is known as 'signalling'.

This chapter shows several examples of railway monitoring and control tasks with cross–references to other places in the Thesis and to bibliography. Formal verification of safety critical properties of railway monitoring and control issues can be found in [4, 6, 8, 39, 66, 85, 113].

## 3.2   Line Direction Agreement Device

Each line connects exactly two stations. At any point in time, the line can be open in at most one direction. This is a safety requirement to protect head-on train crashes on the line.

Formal models and verification of interlocking systems for railway lines can be found in [24, 63, 125]. In the Thesis whole chapter 13 in [118] describes line direction agreement devices in detail.

## 3.3   Station Interlocking

In railway signaling, an interlocking is an arrangement of signal apparatus that prevents conflicting movements through an arrangement of tracks such as junctions, crossings, and so forth. The signaling appliances and tracks are sometimes collectively referred to as an interlocking plant. An interlocking is designed so that it is impossible to give clear signals to trains unless the route to be used is proved to be safe.

A typical railroad definition of interlocking is "an arrangement of signals and signal appliances so interconnected that their movements must succeed each other in proper sequence."

The minimum interlocking consists of signals, but usually includes additional appliances like switches, derails, crossings at grade and movable bridges. Some of the fundamental principles of interlocking include:

- Signals may not be operated to permit conflicting train movements to take place at the same time.
- Switches and other appliances in the route must be properly 'set' (in position) before a signal may allow train movements to enter that route.
- Once a route is set and a train is given a signal to proceed over that route, all switches and other movable appliances in the route are locked in position until either the train passes out of the portion of the route affected, or the signal to proceed is withdrawn and sufficient time has passed to ensure that a train approaching that signal has had opportunity to come to a stop before passing the signal.

To cover that topic formally interlocking specification languages (ExSpect, EURIS, etc.) have been introduced [7, 11, 25, 54, 55, 56, 59, 60]. We also refer to other work concerning formal specification and modeling of railway interlocking systems [31, 53, 55, 58, 61, 73, 74, 75, 82, 98, 90, 119]. In the [118] in chapter 14 and in [128] the usage of Petri nets for modeling of station interlocking is shown.

## 3.4   Signalling

The purpose of signalling is to inform the train driver when it is safe to proceed on the line ahead. In early days the signalman was responsible for ensuring any switch was set correctly before allowing a train to proceed. Mistakes were made and accidents occurred, sometimes with fatalities. The concept of interlocking of points, signals, and other appliances was introduced to improve safety. Interlocking prevents the signalman from operating appliances in an unsafe sequence, such as setting the signal to clear while one or more points in the route the signal governs are improperly set. Early interlocking systems used mechanical devices both to operate the signalling appliances and ensure their safe operation, but the contemporary interlocking systems operate using complex electronic circuitry.

Application of formal methods to railway signalling on lines can be found in [41, 42, 43, 44, 51, 76].

*Dwarf Signals.* Dwarf Signals are station signals and can be located almost anywhere on a station, where a signal for switching or for flank protection is required. Dwarf Signal proceed aspects are only valid for switching, not for trains proceeding outside the station area.

Formal specification of the control process for a Dwarf signal can be found in [97, 96]. Dwarf signal controller was also formally specified in WDM [88], in B-method [89] and in RAISE [112]. A CSP Model of the Alcatel Dwarf signal can be found in [130].

*Signalling on Lines.* On the lines, automatic block signals (ABS) are commonly used. ABS systems consist of a series of signals that govern blocks of track between the signals. The signals are automatically activated by the conditions of the block beyond the signal. If a train is currently occupying a block, that block's signal will not allow a train in the previous block to proceed into the block, or will only allow it to proceed at a speed which allows the train to stop before colliding with the train or another object (also known as restricted speed).

Automatic block signals also detect the status of a following signal. If a signal is displaying a stop indication, the preceding signal will display an aspect that warns the train crew that the following signal may require the train to stop.

ABS systems detect track occupancy by passing a low-voltage current through the track between the signals and detecting whether the circuit is closed, open, or shorted. A train's metal wheels and axles will pass current from one rail to the other, thereby shorting the circuit. If the ABS system detects that the circuit is shorted between two signals, it understands that a train is occupying that block and will "drop" the signals (display a stop indication) on either side of that block to prevent another train from entering. ABS system electronics are also able to detect breaks in the rail or improperly-lined switches, which result in an open circuit. These will also cause the signal's aspect to drop, preventing any trains from entering the block and running the risk of bending, breaking, or overturning the rail and derailing or running through an improperly-lined switch.

In the Thesis the whole chapter 12 in [118] shows formal statechart model for ABS system. Usage of Petri nets in the railway signalling can be found in [92].

## 3.5    Level Railway Crossing

The term level railway crossing is a crossing on one level ("at-grade intersection") without recourse to a bridge or tunnel  of a railway line by a road, path, or another railroad.

Early level crossings had a flagman in a nearby booth who would, on the approach of a train, wave a red flag or lantern to stop all traffic and clear the tracks. Manual or electrical closable gates that barricaded the roadway were later introduced. With the appearance of motor vehicles, this barrier became less and less effective. Many countries therefore substituted the gated crossings with less strong but highly visible barriers and relied upon road users following the associated warning signals to stop.

The consensus in contemporary railway design is to avoid the use of level crossings. The use of level crossings contributes the greatest potential for catastrophic risk on the railways. Bridges and tunnels are now favoured.

There are several papers that deal with the level crossing in a formal way [48, 72, 99, 100, 126].

## 3.6    Interlocking Safety and Reliability

Railway monitoring and control system are safety-critical systems. It means that their failure could result in loss of life, significant property damage, or damage to the environment. The degree of safety is hard to identify. Computers are increasingly being embedded within safety systems [2, 4, 5, 40, 80]. That means that one has to compute probability of a failure of such system.

Using Z-specification for railway interlocking safety can be found in [3]. Formal verification process and proving safety can be found in [10, 36, 79, 81, 94, 114, 120, 121, 123, 124]. Examples of practical usage of formal methods in interlocking safety are shown in [32, 65, 93].

### 3.7 Automatic Train Control

An automatic train control system (ATC) is when the train receives data at all times in order to maintain the correct speed and prevent trains from passing stop signals if the driver should fail to react. Modelling and Simulation of train control systems can be done with Petri nets [132]. Using Prolog for a railway control system is shown in [9]. Other papers like [15, 26, 24] tackle automatic train control also formally. New generation of microcomputer-based operations control systems for high-speed rail TRANSRAPID can be found in [86].

### 3.8 European Rail Traffic Management System (ERTMS)

Over the past decade, industrial giants and European governments have strived to attain rail interoperability, so that trains can cross borders without stopping. Today, each country still has its own rail "language" for managing the movement of the trains on its network.

In order to redress these incompatibilities, the European Rail Traffic Management System project has been set up to create unique signaling standards throughout Europe called ETCS.

The ERTMS is the new signaling and management system for Europe, enabling interoperability throughout the European Rail network.

## 4   Discussion

We have tried to list several issues (not all) that need to be solved when one should take care about scheduling & allocation problems and about monitoring & control issues on railways. For each listed issue there is a reference solution done by formal way.

In the 2nd section there are many interesting operation researchers' problems. The most difficult issues are the complexity (most of shown application are MP-hard) and definition of appropriate optimisation function.

In the 3rd section we have listed several basic topics, that must be solved when one takes care about monitoring and control of railways. Not all possible railway applications were mentioned there. Several more could be covered, like breaking systems, door opening systems, train integrity control, telecommunications, detection of train position, etc.

Most of the issues can be covered by others formal methods like Petri net, statecharts or live sequence charts.

**Acknowledgments.** It is a pleasant aspect that I have now the opportunity to express my gratitude prof. Dines Bjørner. His kind invitation in 2003 to Danish Technical University and work at AMORE project basically started my interest in Computer Science, especially in Formal methods. In the end, thanks to him, I have returned to Denmark three times and most of the work on the Thesis was done and published during these stays. I have known Dines Bjørner as a sympathetic and methodical-centered person. His overly enthusiasm and integral view on research and his leadership capability has made a deep impression on me. I am and I always will be very grateful for him having shown me this way and this kind of research.

# References

1. Alle, P.: Improving rail transit line capacity using computer graphics. Logist. and Transp. Rev (Canada) 17, 429–442 (1981)
2. Amendola, A.M., Impagliazzo, L., Marmo, P., Poli, F.: Experimental evaluation of computer-based railway control systems. In: Proceedings of The Twenty-Seventh Annual International Symposium on Fault-Tolerant Computing (FTCS'97), Washington - Brussels - Tokyo, jun 1997, pp. 380–384. IEEE Computer Society Press, Los Alamitos (1997)
3. Anot, A.J.: Using Z Specification for Railway Interlocking Safety. Periodica Poly-technica, Transport Engineering Series 28(1–2), 39–53, Department of Information and Safety Systems Faculty of Electrical Engineering University of Zilina, Vel'ký diel, Zilina 010 26, Slovak Republic (2000)
4. Anselmi, A., Bernardeschi, C., Fantechi, A., Gnesi, S., Larosa, S., Mongardi, G., Torielli, F.: An experience in formal verification of safety properties of a railway signalling control system. In: Rabe, G. (ed.) SAFECOMP'95: 14th International Conference on Computer Safety, Reliability and Security, Belgirate, Italy, pp. 474–488. Springer, Heidelberg (1995)
5. Aprea, G., Colantuoni, P., Firpo, P., Lido, R., Pellegrino, D., Rapone, M., Senesi, F.: SIGAV, the italian high speed railway integrated management system: Safety and reliability overview. In: Schoitsch, E. (ed.) SAFECOMP'96: 15th International Conference on Computer Safety, Reliability and Security, Vienna, Austria, p. 250. Springer, Heidelberg (1996)
6. Bailey, C.(ed.) European Railway Signalling, London, England, Institution of Railway Signalling Engineers, A&C Black (1995)
7. Basten, T., Bol, R.N., Voorhoeve, M.: Simulating and Analyzing Railway Inter-locking in ExSpect. Technical Report 94-37, Department of Computing Science, Eindhoven University of Technology, P.O. Box 513, 5600 MB Eindhoven, The Netherlands (September 1994)
8. Basten, T., Bol, R.N., Voorhoeve, M.: Simulating and analyzing railway inter-lockings in ExSpect. IEEE Parallel & Distributed Technology: Systems & Applications 3(3), 50–62 (1995)
9. Bechina, A., Hermle, J., Siormanolakis, M.: Using Prolog for a railway control system. In: Fourth International Conference on the Practical Application of Prolog, London, UK, pp. 19–30. Practical Application Co., Blackpool, UK (1996)

10. Berg, A.: Adtranz Signal's Formal Verification Process: Safety Verification of Interlocking Functionality. In: Bjørner, D., Fahlén, M. (eds.) FME Rail Workshop # 4. FME, Rail Workshop, Stockholm, Sweden. FME,Rail Workshop # 4, vol. # 4, FME: Formal Methods Europe, Banverket, Falun, Sweden (May 12–14, 1999)
11. Berger, J., Middelraad, P., Smith, A.J.: The European railway interlocking specification. In: IRSE, pp. 70–82 (1993)
12. Billington, J., Janczura, C.: Removing Deadlock from a Railway Network Specification. In: Australian Engineering Mathematics Conference (AEMC'96), Sydney, Australia, July 1996, pp. 193–200. Australian Engineering Mathematical Society (1996)
13. Bjørner, D.: A Architecture for Running Map Systems. Technical Report db/arch/01, UNU/IIST, the UN University's International Institute for Software Technology, P.O.Box 3058, Macau (February 1994), E-Mail: library@iist.unu.edu
14. Bjørner, D.: Formal Software Techniques in Railway Systems. In: Schnieder, E. (ed.) 9th IFAC Symposium on Control in Transportation Systems, pp. 1–12, Technical University, Braunschweig, Germany, 13-15 June 2000. VDI/VDE-Gesellschaft Mess- und Automatisierungstechnik, VDI-Gesellschaft für Fahrzeug- und Verkehrstechnik (2000)
15. Bjørner, D.: Dynamics of Railway Nets: On an Interface between Automatic Control and Software Engineering. In: CTS2003: 10th IFAC Symposium on Control in Transportation Systems, Oxford, UK, August 4-6 2003, Elsevier, Amsterdam (2003)
16. Bjørner, D., Braad, J., Mogensen, K.S.: Models of Railway Systems: Domain (FME: Formal Methods Europe, Steria, France, September 22–24 1999.). In: Lecomte, T., Larsen, P.G. (eds.) FME Rail Workshop, FME,Rail Workshop # 5. FME, Rail Workshop, Toulouse, France, vol. # 5. FME: Formal Methods Europe, Steria, France (September 22–24, 1999)
17. Bjørner, D., Braad, J., Mogensen, K.S. (eds.): Models of Railway Systems: Requirements. In: Lecomte, T., Larsen, P.G. (eds.) FME Rail Workshop # 5. FME Rail Workshop, Toulouse, France, vol. # 4, FME: Formal Methods Europe, Steria, France (September 22–24, 1999)
18. Bjørner, D., George, C.W., Prehn, S.: Computing Systems for Railways — A Rôle for Domain Engineering. Relations to Requirements Engineering and Software for Control Applications. In: Kraemer, B., Petterson, J.C. (eds.) Integrated Design and Process Technology, P.O.Box 1299, Grand View, Texas 76050-1299, USA, 24–28 June 2002, Society for Design and Process Science (2002)
19. Bjørner, D., George, C.W., Hansen, B.S., Laustrup, H., Prehn, S., et al.: A Railway System, Coordination '97: Case Study Workshop Example. Technical Report 93, UNU/IIST, P.O.Box 3058, Macau (Spring 1997 – Fall 1998)
20. Bjørner, D., George, C.W., Prehn, S.: Scheduling and rescheduling of trains, p. 24. Academic Press, London (1999)
21. Bjørner, D., Lin, D.Y., Prehn, S.: Domain Analyses: A Case Study of Station Management. In: KICS'94: Kunming International CASE Symposium, Yunnan Province, P.R.of China,Software Engineering Association of Japan (November 16–20, 1994)
22. Bjørner, D., Prehn, S., George, C.W.: Formal Models of Railway Systems: Domains Technical report, Dept. of IT, Technical University of Denmark, Bldg. 344, DK–2800 Lyngby, Denmark (September 23, 1999)

23. Bjørner, D., Yulin, D.: Railway System Characteristic. Technical Report dyl/3/1, UNU/IIST, the UN University's International Institute for Software Technology, P.O.Box 3058, Macau (August 1993), E-Mail: library@iist.unu.edu
24. Bohn, J., Damm, W., Klose, J., Moik, A., Wittke, H.: Modeling and Validating Train System Applications Using Statemate and Live Sequence Chats. In: Ehrig, H., Krämer, B.J., Ertas, A. (eds.) Proceedings of IDPT2002 - Integrated Design and Process Technology, Society for Design and Process Science (2002)
25. Bol, R.N., Koorn, J.W.C., Oei, L.H., van Vlijmen, S.F.M.: Syntax and Static Semantics of the Interlocking Design and Application Language. Technical Report P9422, Programming Research Group, University of Amsterdam, Kruislaan 403, 1098 SJ Amsterdam, The Netherlands (November 1994)
26. Braad, J., Mogensen, K.S., Bjørner, D.: The Automatic Railway Case Based on [57]. In: Bjørner, D., Fahlén, M. (eds.) FME Rail Workshop # 4. FME Rail Workshop; Stockholm, Sweden, vol. # 4, FME: Formal Methods Europe, Banverket, Falun, Sweden (May 12–14, 1999)
27. Brand, R.A.: 3-D colour graphics for rail network simulation and control. In: First Australasian Conf. on Computer Graphics, pp. 38–48 (1983)
28. Brandes, U., Wagner, D.: Using Graph Layout to Visualize Train Interconnection Data. Research report, konstanz (1999)
29. Bud, A., Nicholson, A., Chandra, B.: Scheduling trains with genetic algorithms. Technical Report 96/250, Dept. Computer Science, Monash University, Australia 3168 (October 1996)
30. Bussieck, M.R., Kreuzer, P., Zimmermann, U.T.: Optimal lines for railway systems. Technical Report TR-95-01, MOTUBS (1995)
31. Canver, E., Gayen, J.T., Moik, A.: Formal specification of the controller software on railway switch example. Automatiserungs Praxis (1997)
32. Ceglowski, L., Lewinski, A.: Highly reliable microcomputer systems for railway control. In: SARSS'87: Achieving Safety and Reliability with Computer Systems, p. 182 (1987)
33. Chao, M.: PRaCoSy: Data Structures for Train Journeys. Technical Report mc/dstr1/1, UNU/IIST, the UN University's International Institute for Software Technology, P.O.Box 3058, Macau (May 1994), E-Mail: library@iist.unu.edu
34. Chaochen, Z., Huiqun, Y.: A duration Model for Railway scheduling. Technical Report 24b, UNU/IIST, P.O.Box 3058, Macau (May 1994)
35. Chow, T.W.S., Shuai, O.: Feedforward neural networks based input-output models for railway carriage system identification. Neural Processing Letters 5(2), 57–67 (1997)
36. Cichocki, T., Górksi, J.: Safety Assessment of Computerised Railway Signalling supported by Formal Methods. In: Lecomte, T., Larsen, P.G. (eds.) FME Rail Workshop # 5. FME, Rail Workshop; Toulouse, France, vol. # 5, FME: Formal Methods Europe, Steria, France (September 22–24, 1999)
37. Claessens, M.T., van Dijk, N.M.: A mathematical programming model to determine a set of operation lines at minimal costs. Technical report, University of Amsterdam (1994)
38. Crainic, T.G., Roy, J.: OR tools for tactical freight transportation planning. EU-JOR 33, 290–297 (1988)
39. Cribbens, A.H.: Solid Sate Interlocking (SSI): An integrated electronic signalling system for mainline railways. IEE Proceedings 134(3), 148–158 (1987)
40. Cullyer, J., Fairclough, J.: Safety critical systems - when computers might kill. Information Technology & Public Policy 11(1), 14–19 (1992)

41. Cullyer, J., Wai, W.: Application of formal methods to railway signalling - a case study. Computing & Control Engineering Journal 4(1), 15–22 (1993)
42. Cullyer, W.J., Wai, W.: A formal approach to railway signalling. In: Compass '90: 5th Annual Conference on Computer Assurance, Gaithersburg, Maryland, pp. 102–108. National Institute of Standards and Technology (1990)
43. Cullyer, W.J., Wise, J.W.: Application of formal methods to railway signalling. In: SARSS'89: Reliability on the Move, p. 11 (1989)
44. Damm, W., Klose, J.: Verification of a Radio-based Signaling System Using the Statemate Verification Environment. Formal Methods in System Design 19(2) (2001)
45. Danhua, J.: A First Mathematical Model of Train Time Tabling. Technical Report jdh/math/03, UNU/IIST, the UN University's International Institute for Software Technology, P.O.Box 3058, Macau (August 1994), E-Mail: library@iist.unu.edu
46. Danhua, J.: Running Map Display Transformation. Technical Report jdh/trans/02, UNU/IIST, the UN University's International Institute for Software Technology, P.O.Box 3058, Macau, (April 1994), E-Mail: library@iist.unu.edu
47. Danhua, J.: Second Math. Model of Train Time Tabling. Technical Report jdh/math/05, UNU/IIST, the UN University's International Institute for Software Technology, P.O.Box 3058, Macau (October 1994), E-Mail: library@iist.unu.edu
48. Dierks, H., Dietz, C.: Graphical specification and reasoning: Case study generalised railroad crossing. In: Fitzgerald, J., Jones, C.B., Lucas, P. (eds.) FME 1997. LNCS, vol. 1313, pp. 20–39. Springer, Heidelberg (1997)
49. Dipoppa, G., Bove, R.: Modelling a Railway Application in a Geographical and Textual Integrated Fashion. In: FME Rail Workshop 2, Via Anguillarese, 301 S.Maria di Galeria, I–00060 Roma, Italy, ENEA C.R.-CASACCIA (1998)
50. Dong, Y., Bjørner, D., Prehn, S.: Domain Analysis: A Case Study of Railway Station Management. Technical Report db/03/01, UNU/IIST, the UN University's International Institute for Software Technology, P.O. Box 3058, Macau; (November 12, 1994), E-Mail: library@iist.unu.edu
51. Doppelbauer, J.: Safety Considerations on Railway Signalling Systems — is there a Future for Formal Methods. In: Lecomte, T., Larsen, P.G. (eds.) FME Rail Workshop 5, FME Rail Workshop; Toulouse, France. FME: Formal Methods Europe, Steria, France, vol. 5 (September 22–24, 1999)
52. Dürr, E., Plat, N., de Boer, M.: CombiCom: Tracking and Tracing Rail Traffic using VDM++. In: Hinchey, M.G., Bowen, J.P. (eds.) Applications of Formal Methods, pp. 203–225. Prentice-Hall International, Englewood Cliffs (1995)
53. Eriksson, L.H.: Specifying railway interlocking requirements for practical use. In: Schoitsch, E. (ed.) SAFECOMP'96: 15th International Conference on Computer Safety, Reliability and Security, Vienna, Austria, p. 243. Springer, Heidelberg (1996)
54. Eriksson, L.H.: Formal Verification of Railway Interlockings. Technical Report 1997:4, Swedish National Rail Administration, Banverket HK, S–781 85 Borlänge, Sweden (December 1, 1997)
55. Eriksson, L.H.: Formalising Railway Interlocking Requirements. Technical Report 1997:3, Swedish National Rail Administration, Banverket HK, S–781 85 Borlänge, Sweden (December 1, 1997)
56. Eriksson, L.H.: Some Technical Aspects of an Interlocking Specification language. In: Bjørner, D., Fahlén, M. (eds.) FME, Rail Workshop, 4, FME, Rail Workshop; Stockholm, Sweden. FME: Formal Methods Europe, Banverket, Falun, Sweden, vol. 4 (May 12-14, 1999)

57. Feijs, L.M.G., Jonkers, H.B.M., Middelburg, C.A.: The Automatic Railway case, ch. 2. FACIT Series. Springer, Heidelberg (1994)
58. Fokkink, W.J.: Safety criteria for the vital processor interlocking at Hoorn–Kersenboogerd. In: Proceedings of the 5th Conference on Computers in Railways, COMPRAIL'96, Part I: Railway Systems and Management, Berlin, Computational Mechanics Publications, pp. 101–110, (1996)
59. Fokkink, W.J., Kolk, G.P., van Vlijmen, S.F.M.: EURIS, a specification method for distributed interlockings. In: Ehrenberger, W. (ed.) SAFECOMP 1998. LNCS, vol. 1516, Springer, Heidelberg (1998)
60. Fredholm, D.: Specifying an Interlocking System: The Alister Project. In: Bjørner, D., Fahlén, M. (eds.) FME, Rail Workshop #, 4, FME Rail Workshop; Stockholm, Sweden. FME: Formal Methods Europe, Banverket, Falun, Sweden, vol. # 4 (May 12-14, 1999)
61. Fringuelli, B., Lamma, E., Mello, P., Santocchia, G.: Knowledge-based technology for controlling railway stations. IEEE Expert 7(6), 45–52 (1992)
62. George, C.W.: A Theory of Distributed Train Rescheduling. In: Gaudel, M.-C., Woodcock, J.C.P. (eds.) FME 1996. LNCS, vol. 1051, pp. 499–517. Springer, Heidelberg (1996)
63. Gjaldbaek, T., Haxthausen A.E.: Modelling and verification of interlocking systems for railway lines. In: IFAC-CTS (2003)
64. Grimes, C.A.: Application of genetic techniques to the planning of railway track maintenance work. In: Zalzala, A.M.S. (ed.) First International Conference on Genetic Algorithms in Engineering Systems: Innovations and Applications, GALESIA, Sheffield, UK IEE, vol. 414, pp. 467–472 (September 12-14, 1995)
65. Groote, J.F., van Vlijmen, S.F., Koorn, J.W.C.: The safety guaranteeing system at station Hoorn-Kersenboogerd. In: COMPASS '95. Proceedings of the Tenth Annual Conference on Computer Assurance (Cat. No.95CH35802), Gaithersburg, MD, USA, pp. 57–68. IEEE, New York (1995)
66. Guiho, G., Mejia, L.-F.: Operational safety critical software methods in railways. In: Anon. (ed.) IFIP Transactions A (Computer Science and Technology) IFIP World Congress, Hamburg, Germany, pp. 262–269 (1984)
67. Guoqin, S.: Formal Models of Time-table Input Tool. Technical Report sgq/11/3, UNU/IIST, the UN University's International Institute for Software Technology, P.O. Box 3058, Macau (October 1994), E-Mail: library@iist.unu.edu
68. Guoqin, S.: PRaCoSy: Data Structures for Railway Networks. Technical Report sgq/3/1, UNU/IIST, the UN University's International Institute for Software Technology, P.O. Box 3058, Macau (June 1994), E-Mail: library@iist.unu.edu
69. Guoqin, S.: PRaCoSy: Data Structures for Time-table Projections. Technical Report sgq/4/1, UNU/IIST, the UN University's International Institute for Software Technology, P.O. Box 3058, Macau (July 1994), E-Mail: library@iist.unu.edu
70. Guoqin, S.: PRaCoSy: Time-Table Preparation Tool Scriptor. Technical Report sgq/12/1, UNU/IIST, the UN University's International Institute for Software Technology, P.O. Box 3058, Macau (October 1994), E-Mail: library@iist.unu.edu
71. Guoqing, S., Xin, L., Parthasarathy, S.: Global Data Flow Diagrams for Train Dispatch. Technical Report sgq/1/6, UNU/IIST, the UN University's International Institute for Software Technology, P.O. Box 3058, Macau (August 1994), E-Mail: library@iist.unu.edu
72. Haga, S.: Prevention of accidents at road-rail level crossings protected with automatic barriers. In: Proceedings of the Human Factors Society 32nd Annual Meeting, Safety: Transportation Safety, vol. 1, pp. 933–937 (1988)

73. Hansen, K.M.: Modeling Railway Interlocking Systems. In: FME Rail Workshop # 2. FME: Formal Methods Europe, Formal Systems (Europe) Ltd, Keble Court, 26 Temple Street, Oxford OX4 1JS, UK, vol. # 2 (October 1998)

74. Hansen, K.M.: Validation of a railway interlocking model. In: Naftalin, M., Denvir, T., Bertran, M. (eds.) FME '94: Industrial Benefit of Formal Methods. Second International Symposium of Formal Methods Europe. Proceedings, Barcelona, Spain. LNCS, pp. 582–601. Springer, Berlin (1994)

75. Hansen, K.M.: Modelling Railway Interlocking Systems. Technical Report ID-TR: 1996-167, Department of Computer Science, Technical University of Denmark, Building 344, DK-2800 Lyngby, Denmark (September 1995)

76. Haxthausen, A., Gjaldbæk, T.: Modelling and Verification of Interlocking Systems for Railway Lines. In: 10th IFAC Symposium on Control in Transportation Systems, Tokyo, Japan (August 4-6, 2003)

77. Hayashi, I., Itoh, K., Suzuki, S.: Man-machine interactive guidance for urban railway networks passenger information system. Computers and Graphics 7(1), 59–72 (1983)

78. Heinrichs, U., Moll, C.: On the scheduling of one-dimensional transport systems. Technical report, Mathematisches Institut, Universität zu Köln (1997)

79. Ingleby, M.: Safety properties of a control network: local and global reasoning in machine proof. In: Proceedings of Real Time Systems. Paris (January 1994)

80. Ingleby, M., Mee, D.J.: A calculus of hazard for railway signalling. In: Workshop on Industrial-Strength Formal Specification Techniques (Cat. No.95TH8051), Boca Raton, FL, USA, pp. 146–158. IEEE Comput. Soc. Press, Los Alamitos, CA (1995)

81. Ingleby, M., Mitchell, I.H.: Proving Safety of a Railway Signalling System Incorporating Geographic Data. In: Frey, H.H. (ed.) SAFECOM'92 Conference Proceedings of IFAC, Zürich (CH), pp. 129–134. Pergamon Press, Oxford (1992)

82. Jackson, D.: Mechanical Verification of British Rail Interlocking. In: FME, Rail Workshop #, 2, FME: Formal Methods Europe, Formal Systems (Europe) Ltd, Keble Court, 26 Temple Street, Oxford OX4 1JS, UK, vol. # 2 (October 1998)

83. Jelaska, M.: Computer elaboration of time-table for single railway line. In: Cea, J. (ed.) Optimization Techniques. Modeling and Optimization in the Service of Man 2. LNCS, vol. 41, pp. 657–675. Springer, Heidelberg (1976)

84. Jose, R.M.J., vom Scheidt, G., Boyce, J.F.: Application of connectionist local search to line management rail traffic control. In: Proceedings of the 3rd International Conference on the Practical Application of Constraint Technology, Blackpool, April 23-25, The Practical Application Ltd., pp. 193–212 (1997)

85. King, T.: Formalising British Rail's Signalling Rules. In: Bertran, M., Naftalin, M., Denvir, T. (eds.) FME 1994. LNCS, vol. 873, pp. 45–54. Springer, Heidelberg (1994)

86. Knigge, R., Eilers, H., Freitag, V.: New generation of microcomputer-based operations control systems for high-speed rail and guided transportation as demonstrated by TRANSRAPID. In: IFIP World Computer Congress, Hamburg IFIP, pp. 174–179 (1994)

87. Kroon, L.G., Romeijn, H.E., Zwanefeld, P.J.: Routing Trains through railway stations: complexity issues. European Journal of Operational Research 98, 485–498 (1997)

88. Larsen, P.G.: A VDM-SL Specification of the Dwarf Signal Controller. In: FME, Rail Workshop # 3, FME: Formal Methods Europe, vol. # 3 (February 1999)

89. Lecomte, T.: Dwarf Signal Formalisation in B. In: Lecomte, T., Larsen, P.G. (eds.) FME, Rail Workshop #, 5, FME, Rail Workshop; Toulouse, France. FME: Formal Methods Europe, Steria, France, vol. # 5 (September 22-24, 1999)

90. Lindegaard, M.P., Viuf, P., Haxthausen, A.: Modelling Railway Interlocking Systems. In: Proceedings of the 9th IFAC Symposium on Control in Transportation Systems 2000, June 13-15, 2000, Braunschweig, Germany, pp. 211–217 (2000)

91. Liu, J.N.K., Sin, K.Y.: Fuzzy neural networks for machine maintenance in mass transit railway systems. IEEE Transactions on Neural Networks 8(4), 932–941 (1997)

92. Malavassi, G., Ricci, S.: Petri Nets in the Railway Signalling Model. In: Lecomte, T., Larsen, P.G. (eds.) FME, Rail Workshop #, 5, FME, Rail Workshop; Toulouse, France. FME: Formal Methods Europe, Steria, France, vol. # 5 (September 22-24, 1999)

93. Meertens, J.: Verifying the safety guaranteeing system at railway station Heerhugowaard. Master's thesis, Utrecht University, Department of Philosophy, Faculteit Wijsbegeerte (August 1996)

94. Morley, M.J.: Safety in railway signaling data: A behavioural analysis. In: Joyce, J.J., Seger, C.-J.H. (eds.) HUG 1993. LNCS, vol. 780, pp. 465–476. Springer, Heidelberg (1994)

95. Montigel, M.: Formal representation of track topologies by double vertex graphs. In: Proceedings of Railcomp 92 held in Washington DC, Computers in Railways 3. Technology. Computational Mechanics Publications, vol. 2 (1992)

96. Montigel, M.: Formal Methods in Computer-based Safety Systems: Design of a Control Process for an Alcatel–like Dwarf Signal. In: Montigel, M. (ed.) FME, Rail Workshop # 3, FME, Rail Workshop; St. Pölten. FME: Formal Methods Europe, vol. # 3 (February 17-19, 1999)

97. Montigel, M.: Specification of the Control Process for a Dwarf Signal. In: Lecomte, T., Larsen, P.G. (eds.) FME Rail Workshop # 5, FME Rail Workshop; Toulouse, France. FME: Formal Methods Europe, vol. # 5 (September 22-24, 1999), also See fmews3:p4

98. Morley, M.J.: Modelling British Rail's Interlocking Logic: Geographic Data Correctness. Technical Report ECS-LFCS-91-186, University of Edinburgh (1991)

99. Mortimer, R.G.: Visual factors in rail-highway grade crossing accidents. In: Proceedings of the Human Factors Society 35th Annual Meeting, Forensics Professional: Real-World Problems and Practices in Forensics, vol. 1, pp. 600–602 (1991)

100. Mortimer, R.G.: Oh! say, can you hear that train coming to the crossing. In: Proceedings of the Human Factors and Ergonomics Society 38th Annual Meeting, SAFETY: Safety Potpourri II [Lecture], vol. 2, pp. 898–902 (1994)

101. Murphy, K., Ralston, E., Friedlander, D., Swab, R., Steege, P.: The scheduling of rail at Union Pacific Railroad. In: Proceedings of the 14th National Conference on Artificial Intelligence and 9th Innovative Applications of Artificial Intelligence Conference (AAAI-97/IAAI-97), Menlo Park, July 27-31, 1997, pp. 903–912. AAAI Press, Stanford (1997)

102. Nievergelt, J.: Thoughts on Traffic Scheduling and Time Table Design. Technical Report dyl/9/2, Swiss Federal Technical University, Zürich, Informatik, ETH, CH-8092 Zurich, Switzerland (January 1994)

103. Parthasarathy, S.: An Informal Definiton of the Scheduling Problem in PRaCoSy. Technical Report par/5/1, UNU/IIST, the UN University's International Institute for Software Technology, P.O. Box 3058, Macau (October 1993), E-Mail: library@iist.unu.edu

104. Parthasarathy, S.: PRaCoSy: An Executive Overview. Technical Report par/02/09, UNU/IIST, the UN University's International Institute for Software Technology, P.O. Box 3058, Macau (June 1994), E-Mail: library@iist.unu.edu
105. Parthasarathy, S.: PRaCoSy: Document Roadmap. Technical Report par/roadmap/2, UNU/IIST, the UN University's International Institute for Software Technology, P.O. Box 3058, Macau (June 1994), E-Mail: library@iist.unu.edu
106. Parthasarathy, S.: PRaCoSy Project Phase i: Revised Activity Plan. Technical Report par/plan/01, UNU/IIST, the UN University's International Institute for Software Technology, P.O. Box 3058, Macau (April 1994), E-Mail: library@iist.unu.edu
107. Parthasarathy, S.: PRaCoSy: Software Design Description. Technical Report par/sdd/2, UNU/IIST, the UN University's International Institute for Software Technology, P.O. Box 3058, Macau (July 1994), E-Mail: library@iist.unu.edu
108. Parthasarathy, S.: Episode Analysis — A Practical Approach for Temporal Reasoning in Automated Processes. Engineering Applications of AI (1995)
109. Parthasarathy, S., Bjørner, D.: PRaCoSy: Document Catalogue. Technical Report jdh/catal/05, UNU/IIST, the UN University's International Institute for Software Technology, P.O. Box 3058, Macau (July 1994), E-Mail: library@iist.unu.edu
110. Parthasarathy, S., Prehn, S., Bjørner, D.: PRaCoSy: Work-package Description. Technical Report par/03/03, UNU/IIST, the UN University's International Institute for Software Technology, P.O. Box 3058, Macau (January 1994), E-Mail library@iist.unu.edu
111. Parthasarathy, S., Prehn, S., Bjørner, D.: Running Map Display and Interactivity. Technical Report par/disply/03, UNU/IIST, the UN University's International Institute for Software Technology, P.O. Box 3058, Macau (March 1994), E-Mail: library@iist.unu.edu
112. Pedersen, J.S.: Specifying Aspects of a Dwarf Signal System Using RAISE. In: Lecomte, T., Larsen, P.G. (eds.) FME, Rail Workshop # 5, FME, Rail Workshop; Toulouse, France. FME: Formal Methods Europe, Steria, France, vol. # 5 (September 22-24, 1999)
113. Peleska, J., Haxthausen, A.: Formal Development and Verification of a Distributed Railway Control System. In: FME Rail Workshop # 1, FME: Formal Methods Europe, Utrecht, The Netherlands, vol. # 1 (June 1998)
114. Petersen, J.L.: Mathematical Methods for validating Railway Interlocking Systems. PhD thesis, Dept. of IT, Techn. Univ. of Denmark, Bldg. 344, DK–2800 Lyngby (February/November 1998)
115. Prehn, S.: Distributed Train Time-tables and Dispatching. Technical Report SP/13/2, UNU/IIST, the UN University's International Institute for Software Technology, P.O.Box 3058, Macau (July 1994), E-Mail: library@iist.unu.edu
116. Prehn, S.: PRaCoSy Document Standard. Technical Report sp/4/1, UNU/IIST, the UN University's International Institute for Software Technology, P.O. Box 3058, Macau (October 1993), E-Mail: library@iist.unu.edu
117. Prehn, S.: A Railway Running Map Design. Technical Report SP/12/3, UNU/IIST, the UN University's International Institute for Software Technology, P.O. Box 3058, Macau (July 1994), E-Mail: library@iist.unu.edu
118. Pěnička, M.: Towards a Theory of Railways. PhD thesis, Czech Technical University in Prague, Danish Technical University in Kgs. Lyngby (December 2006)

119. Roanes-Lozano, E., Laita, L.M., Roanes-Macias, E.: An Algebraic Model for Decision-taking in Railway Interlocking. In: Montigel, M. (ed.) FME Rail Workshop # 3, FME Rail Workshop; St. Pölten. FME: Formal Methods Europe, vol. # 3 (February 17-19, 1999)

120. Ropke, B., Seibel, W., Wozniak, A.: Verification and function test of electronic interlockings in the system test centre (rail traffic control). Signal und Draht 87(4), 120–122 (1995)

121. Rowden, N.: A safe, reliable control and supervisory system for railway networks. In: Schoitsch, E. (ed.) SAFECOMP'96: 15th International Conference on Computer Safety, Reliability and Security, Vienna, Austria, p. 266. Springer, Heidelberg (1996)

122. Savage, M.J.: Junction optimisation technique. The Computer Journal 12(3), 268–272 (1969)

123. Sethy, A.: Connection between reliability and signalling-safety in railway technology. In: Reliability and Maintainability Symposium, Las Vegas, Nevada USA, pp. 75–79 (1992)

124. Short, R.C.: Software validation for a railway signalling system. In: SAFECOMP'83, pp. 183–193. Pergamon Press, Oxford (1983)

125. Simpson, A.: A formal specification of an automatic train protection system. In: Naftalin, M., Bertran, M., Denvir, T. (eds.) FME 1994. LNCS, vol. 873, pp. 602–617. Springer, Heidelberg (1994)

126. Skakkebæk, J.U.: A Larger Case Study: Railway Crossing, chapter 7. Dept. of Computer Science, Techn. Univ. of Denmark, vol. I (1992)

127. Tsiflakos, K., Owen, D.B.: A graphical sytem for the interactive visual modelling of railway transportation layouts. COMPUGRAPHICS '91 I, 409–418 (1991)

128. van der Aalst, W.M.P., Odijk, M.A.: Analysis of railway stations by means of interval timed colored Petri Nets. Real-Time Systems 9(3), 241–263 (1995)

129. VanWezel, M.C., Kok, J.N., Van Den Berg, J., VanKampen, W.: Genetic improvement of railway timetables. In: Davidor, Y., Männer, R., Schwefel, H.-P. (eds.) Parallel Problem Solving from Nature - PPSN III. LNCS, vol. 866, pp. 566–575. Springer, Heidelberg (1994)

130. Woodcock, J.: A CSP Model of the Alcatel Dwarf Case Study. In: Lecomte, T., Larsen, P.G. (eds.) FME Rail Workshop # 5, FME Rail Workshop; Toulouse, France. FME: Formal Methods Europe, Steria, France, vol. # 4 (September 22-24, 1999)

131. Yulin, D.: Train Running Map. Technical Note dyl/8/1, UNU/IIST, the UN University's International Institute for Software Technology, P.O. Box 3058, Macau; (October 1993), E-Mail: library@iist.unu.edu

132. zu Hörste, M.M.: Modelling and Simulation of Train Control Systems with Petri Nets. In: FME Rail Workshop # 3. FME: Formal Methods Europe, vol. # 3 (February 1999)

# Services as a Paradigm of Computation

Wolfgang Reisig, Jan Bretschneider, Dirk Fahland, Niels Lohmann,
Peter Massuthe, and Christian Stahl

Humboldt-Universität zu Berlin, Institut für Informatik
Unter den Linden 6, 10099 Berlin, Germany
{reisig,bretschn,fahland,nlohmann,massuthe,stahl}@informatik.hu-berlin.de

**Abstract.** The recent success of service-oriented architectures gives rise
to some fundamental questions: To what extent do services constitute a
new paradigm of computation? What are the elementary ingredients of
this paradigm? What are adequate notions of semantics, composition,
equivalence? How can services be modeled and analyzed? This paper
addresses and answers those questions, thus preparing the ground for
forthcoming software design techniques.

**Keyword:** models of computation, services, SOA, open workflow nets.

## 1   The Demand for a New Paradigm of Computation

### 1.1   Shortcomings of the Classical Paradigm

The classical paradigm of computation characterizes the behavior of an information processing system as a function, $f$: A user of the system supplies an argument $x$ and expects to eventually receive the result $f(x)$ from the system.

Experience with distributed and reactive systems reveals the need for a more comprehensive paradigm. Among the many arguments for a new paradigm, the following may be the most striking one: A computation of a system does not necessarily receive all its input in the initial state, nor does it withheld all its output until it reaches a final state. Rather, a computation may start running with no or a first portion of input, and it may provide output whenever generated. In short, a computation may exchange messages with the systems' environment *during* its course. Examples of such systems include operating systems, any kind of technical control systems, and many forms of co-operating business processes. It is not too difficult to capture this kind of behavior in the framework of conventional programming, establishing communication of a program $P$ with its environment by help of special input and output procedures, variables shared by $P$ and its environment, and remote procedure calls. It took decades to acknowledge that this property of computations is not just a minor aspect, but that it affects (among other aspects, to be discussed elsewhere) our fundamental understanding of computation.

C.B. Jones, Z. Liu, J. Woodcock (Eds.): Bjørner/Zhou Festschrift, LNCS 4700, pp. 521–538, 2007.
© Springer-Verlag Berlin Heidelberg 2007

## 1.2   Proposals to Adjust the Classical Paradigm

Church's thesis has dominated the discussion on the limits of computation since this kind of discussion has started in the 1950ies. It is overwhelmingly agreed that this thesis is most convincing when it comes to the computation of functions over sequences of symbols (for more details on this discussion we refer to [1]).

Nevertheless, it has frequently been argued that the classical paradigm of computable functions does not comprise all important aspects of the expressive power of information technology. We have discussed one such aspect above already. Here we survey a number of system models, all contributing to the non-standard aspects of communication, synchronization, and reactivity.

*Petri nets*: With his seminal Ph.D. thesis "Communication with Automata" [2], Carl Adam Petri pointed at the fundamental role of asynchronous, communicating processes, already in the early 1960ies. This led to the development of Petri nets as a technique to model concurrent behavior.

The decisive aspect of Petri nets in this context is the local character of its transitions. A behavior then is not a sequence of global states and steps, but a set of transition occurrences partially ordered by the relation of causality. This perception brought new insights into the fundamental notions of nondeterminism, fairness, scenarios, and others.

*Omega-automata*: $\omega$-Automata [3] capture sequential, infinite computation in the late 1960ies already, laying ground for infinite, reactive computations.

*Stream processing functions*: The first proposals to model systems consisting of interacting components conceive a system component as a stream processing function (or, in the nondeterministic case, as a relation). This dates back to the early 1970ies already. As a typical example we refer to [4]. Streams (i.e. finite or infinite sequences) of data on the *input ports* of a stream processing function $f$ are transformed into streams of data on the *output ports* of $f$. One system's output stream may be an other system's input stream. The *FOCUS* formalism [5] pursues this line of research. Stream processing functions are most adequate to describe a single system's semantics in isolation. The formalism properly reflects that a system's intermediate output can affect later input, via cooperation with the environment.

*Process algebras*: First suggested by Robin Milner in the late 1970ies [6] process algebras capture synchronous communication. The fundamental question of equivalence between system models gave rise to the notion of simulation and bisimulation. It has been a matter of surprise that those notions can not be simply captured in terms of formal language containment or equality.

*Interface variables and remote calls*: In the framework of programming languages, reactive behaviour can easily be represented by help of variables, shared by the program and its environment. This has been done since the late 1960ies. It has later been adapted by specification techniques such as Lamport's Temporal Logic of Actions [7], as well as Gurevich's Abstract State Machines [8]. Fairly more expressive than shared variables is the technique of remote procedure calls, which is a fundamental principle of middleware systems, in particular CORBA. Misra and Cook in their *ORC* language recently generalized this principle, replacing the call of procedures by the call of services [9].

*Interacting and communicating systems*: Peter Wegner's contributions of the late 1990ies ([10,11]) boosted the awareness of a greater public, that interaction and communication was indeed a decisive argument to search for a new paradigm of computation. Many authors took up his arguments (as, e.g. in the volume [12]). Some authors extend the classical models, in particular Turing Machines (examples include [13] and [14]).

We follow this line in the sequel, too. To this end, we discuss some elementary aspects of the new paradigm in the next section, and pose some fundamental questions.

## 1.3 Aspects of the New Paradigm

The above described aspects models and representation techniques for information processing systems share a couple of aspects. Here, we focus just two of them.

Firstly, in the classical setting, non-termination of a computation denotes failure, as no output is generated in this case. Two different non-terminating computations cannot and need not to be distinguished in any respect. In contrast, in the new paradigm, a computation is in general not envisaged to terminate. Infinite computations are of utmost interest. Two different infinite computations in general very well exhibit different input/output behaviour. Interaction of services is usually split into finite slices: An instance of interaction is intended to terminate in a "reasonable" state. But a service is assumed "always on", capable to engage in interaction ad infinitum.

The second consequence of the new paradigm is related to the *composition* of systems. The classical setting offers *sequential composition* $A;B$ of two systems $A$ and $B$ as the only choice: $A$'s output is $B$'s input. In contrast, the new paradigm permits composed systems $A$ and $B$ to exchange data at any time during a computation.

Though we have identified only two aspects of the new paradigm, it is obvious that fundamentally new problems arise that cannot be identified, let alone be solved, in the framework of classical system models. Typical problems of systems that follow the new paradigm include:

- What kind of properties are important for such systems?
- Is there a canonical notion of *equivalence* for such systems?
- Can any two such systems be composed, at least syntactically, resulting in a (may be, futile) system?
- What, precisely, is refinement and abstraction, and which properties should refinement and abstraction preserve?
- How can the effect of such systems be abstractly described (in analogy to a function $f$ in the classical case)?

- What kind of formal representations of such systems are reasonable?
- How can the expressive power of formal description techniques of such systems be compared?
- Is there a "most general" class of "representable" such systems, in analogy to the class of computable functions in the classical setting?

## 2   Service-Oriented Computing and Service-Oriented Architectures

The above discussion focused communicating agents as a basic construct of the new paradigm. We suggest *services* as an adequate concretion for such agents. Services provide viable means to implement communicating agents. Furthermore, there exists a rich theory to handle services, and to answer the above questions. Details will be given in the next sections.

### 2.1   The New Paradigm in Practical Applications

Governed by practical needs, and not caring too much about theoretical aspects, systems following the new paradigm have been implemented for decades. Examples include operating systems, technical control systems, workflows etc. But only nowadays such systems are conceived as following a new paradigm. This may be due to the emerging problems that arise in the course of automatic *composition* of such systems, as required for computer based interorganizational business processes and new software architectures, such as "programming-in-the-world" or "programming on demand".

   In this context, systems that fit into the new paradigm are usually denoted as *services*. Their implementation in the framework of existing technologies evoked the concepts of *service-oriented computing* (SOC) and, as a principle of using SOC, the term of *service-oriented architectures* (SOA). We expand on those aspects in the sequel.

### 2.2   Service-Oriented Computing

Trying to identify what many different views, descriptions and definitions for services have in common, we can conclude that a service is a well defined, self-contained module that provides some concrete functionality to its environment. Consequently, the minimal requirements of a service include an *interface* and an *internal control*. An interface can usually be conceived as a set of *ports*, with each port capable to store *messages*. The internal control triggers the *actions* of the service. An action either sends a messages to a port or receives one from a port or operates locally. Hence, asynchronous communication is the usual communication mode of services. But other modes may be supported as well, such as synchronous (handshake) communication or lock step communication.

## 2.3    Web Services

Currently, the most prominent kind of services are *Web services*. A Web service is a functionality (e.g., a standard business function) provided at a unique network address, given as a URI. This functionality is described in a standard definition language, and available via various transport protocols, formats and profiles for quality of service. Today's implemented Web Services rely on highly distributable communication- and integration backbones (sometimes called "the Big Basic Bus", BBB). Each Web Service is addressed by its unique URI and is usable by other services along its – publically known – interface. A Web Service is assumed as "always on": A user does not have to create it, nor to care about destruction, etc. Several *instances* of a Web Service may exist concurrently, mimicking for each user exclusive access to the service. The language WS-BPEL established itself as a quasi-standard for the implementation of Web services.

## 2.4    Service-Oriented Architectures

Though independent of other services, a service is typically constructed with respect to other services: Purpose and use of a service is its *communication* with other services. Partners to communicate with may reside anywhere in the real world. For a Web service, any service on the web is a potential candidate to serve as a partner. A fundamental problem then is *service discovery*, i.e. for a service $P$ the problem to identify proper communication partners, and to establish communication with those partners. A *service-oriented architecture* (SOA) solves this problem by help of a scenario that assumes

– agents called *providers*: A provider offers services to the public, to be used by (i.e., to be composed with) other services. To this end, a provider *publishes* information about the services he offers.
– agents called *requesters*: A requester requests services, i.e. wants to *find* services it can use, as they are published by providers.
– agents called *brokers*: A broker collects information about the services provided by providers and the services wanted by requesters. Upon detecting services that would properly fit, the broker informs the requester about the provider, such that they can directly *bind* their services. In more elaborated variants, a broker may itself compose two or more provider services, and offer the composed service to a requester. Even more, a broker may observe that a provider service only "almost" fits to a requester service. In this case the broker may construct an *adapter* service to bridge the gap. Figure 1 shows the conventional outline of SOA, indicating the three agents and their pairwise activities.

SOC and SOA can be conceived as *virtualization*, viz. abstraction, from technical implementation details of services. SOA is an architectural style to realize SOC. This can be conceived an analogy to the client/server architectural style that realizes distributed computing.

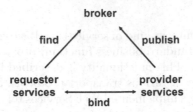

**Fig. 1.** The SOA triangle

The above described agents (provider, requester, and broker) may be likewise virtual. Usually there are no corresponding physical or implemented components in an SOA. It is the services themselves, that play the *role* of providers, requesters, and even brokers.

## 3   An Algebraic View on Services

Both, the foundational considerations of Sect. 1 and the applied aspects of Sect. 2 jointly establish principles of services. Here we introduce fundamental notions and their properties, as a nucleus for a rich conceptualization of "services as a paradigm of computation", to blossom in the sequel of this paper.

### 3.1   Composition of Services and "Reasonable" Services

As outlined in Sect. 2, a core aspect of services is their composition: Any two services $P$ and $R$ may be composed, resulting in a service $P \oplus R$. Of course, $P \oplus R$ is not always a very reasonable service, given "any" $P$ and $R$. In particular, $P \oplus R$ may deadlock or livelock; sent messages may remain in a buffer forever, etc. Conceiving $P \oplus R$ as a transition system $T$ with initial and final states, a typical requirement for $P \oplus R$ to be "reasonable" is *weak termination* of $T$: Each computation $s_0 s_1 \ldots s_k$ starting from an initial state $s_0$, can be extended to a computation $s_0 \ldots s_k \ldots s_n$ with a *final* state $s_n$. A final state does not necessarily deadlock; it may just indicate that one "round" of computation is finished and the service is prepared to launch into a new round. Instead of weak termination, any other predicate may characterize "reasonable" services. Typical examples are fair termination or strong termination, i.e. each (fair) computation eventually will reach a terminal state.

Formulated in an abstract setting, on the set $S$ of all services under consideration we assume a binary, symmetrical operator

$$\oplus : S \times S \to S$$

to compose services, and a distinguished predicate

$$\tau \subseteq S$$

to discriminate "reasonable" (e.g., terminating) services. $\oplus$ and $\tau$ lay the ground for a canonical, rich theory of services, covering a wealth of important notions, questions and properties, as they are particularly important in the framework of SOA.

## 3.2   The Strategies of a Service

One of the central ideas of SOA is the assumption of a *provider* agent, offering a service $P$ to the public. $P$ is intended to be engaged by *requester* agents. To engage $P$ means to follow a strategy to interact with $P$ in order to reach the requester's goal. In technical terms, a *strategy of* $P$ is an other service, $R$, such that the composition $P \oplus R$ of $P$ and $R$ is "reasonable", i.e. $P \oplus R \in \tau$. So, from the requester perspective, the most important aspect of $P$ is the set

$$Strat(P) =_{def} \{R \in \mathcal{S} \mid P \oplus R \in \tau\}$$

of all strategies of $P$. This set may be conceived as the semantics of $P$.

## 3.3   Simulation and Equivalence

The strategies of a service $P$ yield a canonical *generalization* relation

$$\leq \ \subseteq \mathcal{S} \times \mathcal{S}$$

on services: A service $P'$ *generalizes* $P$ if $P'$ preserves all strategies of $P$:

$$P \leq P' \text{ iff } Strat(P) \subseteq Strat(P').$$

A typical scenario including this relation is the provider of $P$ wanting to exchange $P$ by a service $P'$ without bothering the so-far users of $P$.

Consequently, two services $P$ and $P'$ are *equivalent* iff they generalize each other:

$$P \sim P' \text{ iff } Strat(P) = Strat(P').$$

This equivalence is in fact the canonical counterpart of functional equivalence in the classical setting: Two systems are equivalent iff their environment cannot distinguish them.

## 3.4   Brokering of Services

The handling of services includes ways to find an adequate provider services $P$ for given requester services, $R$. This basic problem gives rise to a lot of derived questions, including efficient decision procedures and construction algorithms. Many of them can be posed in the general framework as developed so far. More precisely, a given provider service $P$ rises the quest of

- *Controllability*: Does $P$ have a strategy at all, i.e. $Strat(P) \neq \emptyset$?
- *Compatibility*: For a given service $R$, is $R$ a strategy for $P$, i.e. $R \in Strat(P)$?

- *Public view*: The provider of the service $P$ may want to hide internal details of $P$, and describe only communication capabilities of $P$, i.e. an abstract version of $P$. Technically, we search to derive a canonical $P'$ such that $Strat(P') = Strat(P)$.
- *Operating guideline*: A requester of $P$ is usually interested in all potential strategies of $P$. Technically we search for a concise description of $Strat(P)$.

A given requester service $R$ rises a couple of questions at the broker's job, including

- *Efficient search*: The broker may administer a large provider repository $\mathcal{P}$ of provider services. Efficient algorithms are mandatory to find a service $P \in \mathcal{P}$ that is compatible with $R$. Such algorithms of course depend on the kind of information available to the broker about both $R$ and $P$, as well as on the organization of $\mathcal{P}$.
- *Adaption*: For a given provider service $P$, the composition $P \oplus R$ may only be "almost reasonable". The broker may (automatically) construct a service $A$ ("adapter") such that $R$ is a strategy for $P \oplus A$. In technical terms we are behind a solution $X$ of the problem

$$R \in Strat(P \oplus X).$$

This is equivalent to the problem

$$(R \oplus X) \in Strat(P).$$

- *Composed adaption*: As a special case of the general adaption problem, an adapter may be just some other service in the depository. Even more, the broker may compose two or more services $P_1, \ldots, P_n$ such that $P_1 \oplus \ldots \oplus P_n$ is compatible to $R$. Formulated differently, the repository $\mathcal{R}$ may be virtually extended by the n-fold composition of all its services.

A concrete modeling technique for services should provide efficient algorithms to answer the above questions and to construct corresponding services.

## 4    Service Nets

Above we compiled a number of requirements at a proper framework for the notion of services. Here we strive for a more concrete, operational model that would meet those requirements. To this end we suggest *open workflow nets* (*oWFN*) as a staring point to model services. Before launching into details, we justify and motivate this approach.

### 4.1    The Motivation for Open Workflow Nets

As outlined in Sect. 2.2 already, the essential components of a service are its interface and its internal control. Here we stick to those two aspects:

*Modelling interfaces with oWFN*: Open workflow nets represent asynchronous communication, along message ports, with the order of sent messages not necessarily preserved upon their arrival: A message port contains an unordered set of messages (just as your home letter box). Even more, two different messages may have identical content, i.e., cannot be distinguished in any respect. The messages in a port thus constitute a *bag* (i.e. a finite multiset). This is the most liberal and general form of asynchronous communication, and the most common form in the world of business processes.

*Modeling internal control with oWFN*: An open workflow net is not confined to sequential control, but may very well exhibit *concurrent* control flow. This is most useful: Firstly, composition of two oWFNs results in an oWFN again, with the previous components' two flows of control merged into internal concurrent control of flow of the composed system.

Secondly, languages such as WS-BPEL anyway exhibit concurrent control flow. This can adequately be modeled in the framework of oWFN.

## 4.2   The Formal Framework of Open Workflow Nets

Technically, an open workflow net $N$ is a conventional Petri net with distinguished input and output places to store input and output messages during computation. Consequently, an input place has no ingoing arcs in $N$, and an output place no outgoing arcs. Furthermore, an oWFN has an initial marking $m_0$ and a set $\Omega$ of final markings. Summing up, an oWFN can be written as

$$N = (P, T, F, in, out, m_0, \Omega),$$

with $in, out \subseteq P$ , $^\bullet in = out^\bullet = \emptyset$, a marking $m_0$ and a set $\Omega$ of markings.[1]

Graphically we extend the classical Petri net representation by an encompassing dotted line. The input and output places are located on the line's surface. The initial marking is explicitly represented. The final markings have to be described elsewhere. Figure 2 shows an example.

According to the usual notions of Petri nets, a step

$$m \xrightarrow{t} m'$$

of an oWFN $N$ transforms a marking $m$ into a marking $m'$, following the well-known occurrence rule for transitions $t$. A *run* of $N$ is a sequence

$$m_0 \xrightarrow{t_1} m_1 \xrightarrow{t_2} \ldots \xrightarrow{t_k} m_k$$

with $m_0$ the initial marking, $m_k$ a final marking, and $m_{i-1} \xrightarrow{t_i} m_i$ a step of $N$ $(i = 1, \ldots, k)$.

---

[1] We assume the reader's familiarity with elementary notions of Petri nets. The appendix provides formal details.

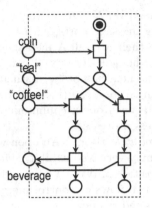

**Fig. 2.** Example of an oWFN: A beverage service $A$

The pragmatic idea of oWFNs is obvious: An oWFN $N$ describes a set of runs, starting at the initial marking.

According to the above described pragmatic idea of oWFNs, *termination* is a crucial issue. An isolated oWFN rarely terminates; usually a partner is required, such that the composed system would terminate. We consider the weakest version of termination in the sequel: An oWFN $N$ is *weakly terminating* if each sequence $m_0 \xrightarrow{t_1} m_1 \xrightarrow{t_2} \ldots \xrightarrow{t_k} m_k$ of steps $m_{i-1} \xrightarrow{t_i} m_i$ $(i = 1, \ldots, k)$ is a prefix of a run of $N$ (i.e. can be extended to eventually reach a final state).

A sequence of steps may fail to be extensible to a run due to a wrong number of tokens at input or output places.

We occasionally want to abstract from input and output and concentrate on the *inner subnet*:

For an oWFN $N$, the set

$$I =_{def} in \cup out$$

is the *interface of $N$*, and

$$J =_{def} P \setminus I$$

is the set of *inner places of $N$*. Furthermore,

$$inner(N) = (J, T, F', m'_0, \Omega')$$

is the *inner subnet of $N$*, generated by the restriction to the inner places of $N$, the transitions of $N$, and the corresponding restriction of $F, m_0$ and $\Omega$ to $J$ and $T$. As an example, Fig. 3 shows the inner subnet of the oWFN in Fig. 2.

$N$ is apparently ill designed in case $inner(N)$ is not weakly terminating.

Historically, the term "open Workflow Nets" has been derived from workflow nets [15]. A workflow net is a formal model of the process logic of a workflow. Conceptually, a service extends workflows with an explicit interface to enable

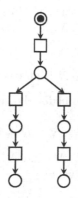

**Fig. 3.** *inner(A)*

communication with other services. Technically, the inner subnet *inner(N)* can be conceived as a representation of workflows. A workflow net $N$ additionally requires special properties of initial and final markings.

### 4.3 Composition of Open Workflow Nets

As outlined in the introduction, composition of services is a major concern of SOC. Consequently, composition of service models should be as general and as simple as possible.

We can always assume that two oWFNs $M$ and $N$ don't share inner elements, but only interface places. Then the composition $M \oplus N$ of two oWFNs $M$ and $N$ is just the (sorted) union of their elements. Figure 4 shows an example. Appendix A2 provides formal details.

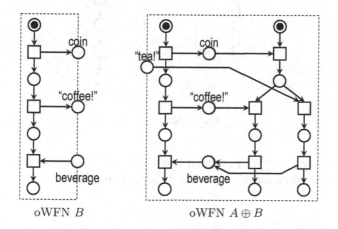

oWFN $B$                    oWFN $A \oplus B$

**Fig. 4.** Composition of services

In particular, if $p$ is an output place of $M$ as well as an input place of $N$, then $p$ turns into an inner place of $M \oplus N$. It is important to observe for two oWFNs $M$ and $N$:

$$M \oplus N \text{ is an oWFN.}$$

The above definition of oWFN immediately implies for two oWFNs $M$ and $N$

$$M \oplus N = N \oplus M.$$

Furthermore, for three oWFNs $L$, $M$, and $N$ that all three have no element in common, composition is associative, viz.

$$L \oplus (M \oplus N) = (L \oplus M) \oplus N.$$

## 4.4   Partners and Fellows

In real applications, two oWFNs $M$ and $N$ to be composed are mostly *partners*, i.e. they communicate along interface places, but do not share input or output places:

$$in_M \cap in_N = out_M \cap out_N = \emptyset.$$

The left oWFN $B$ of Fig. 4 shows a partner, to the oWFN $A$ of Fig. 2. The two oWFNs depicted in Fig. 5 are no partners.

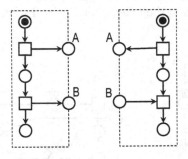

Fig. 5. No partners

Likewise interesting is the special case of $M$ and $N$ joining input or output places, and not communicating at all: $M$ and $N$ are *fellows* iff

$$in_M \cap out_N = out_M \cap in_N = \emptyset.$$

The interface of the composition $M \oplus N$ of two fellows $M$ and $N$ is the union of the interfaces of $M$ and $N$. Figure 6 shows an example. The two oWFNs of Fig. 5 are neither partners nor fellows.

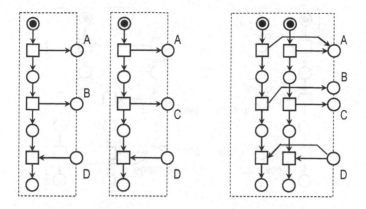

**Fig. 6.** Two fellows and their composition

If $L$, $M$ and $N$ are pairwise partners, then $L \oplus M$ is a partner of $N$ and $\oplus$ is associative i.e. $(L \oplus M) \oplus N = L \oplus (M \oplus N)$.

Likewise, if $L$, $M$ and $N$ are pairwise fellows, then $L \oplus M$ is a fellow of $N$, and $\oplus$ is associative, as described above.

### 4.5  Open Workflow Nets with Ports

Experience shows that the composition of services requires more flexibility than offered by oWFN as defined above.

As an example, the composition $A \oplus B$ of the beverage service A and its strategy B of Fig. 4 remains with a fairly unintuitive input place, *tea!*. Intuitively, $A$ and $B$ fit perfectly and consequently their composition $A \oplus B$ should be a "closed" net, i.e. a net with empty interface. More flexibility is also required when the issue of *refinement* and *abstraction* is taken into account in the sequel.

A fairly simple idea suffices to provide oWFNs with the required degree of flexible composition: The interface places are grouped into *ports* such that each interface place belongs to exactly one port. The ports are decorated with (pairwise different) *names*. As an example, Fig. 7 equips the beverage service $A$ of Fig. 2 with three ports. One of them, "select", contains two input places "coffee" and "tea". The other two, "pay" and "offer", contain one element each. The graphical representation is obvious. Correspondingly, Fig. 7 identifies three ports for the strategy $B$ of Fig. 4 one for each place.

Composition of two oWFNs with ports, $M$ and $N$, say, then follows a simple rule: Just glue ports of $M$ and $N$ with identical names. Gluing the ports of $M$ and $N$ with name $\alpha$ then means to identify a place $p$ of the $\alpha$-port of $M$ with a place $q$ of the $\alpha$-port of $N$ if and only if $p = q$, described in Sect. 4.3. As an example, Fig. 8 shows the composition of the port equipped oWFN of Fig. 7.

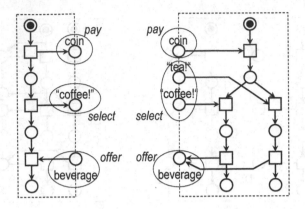

**Fig. 7.** Beverage service and a strategy, equipped with ports

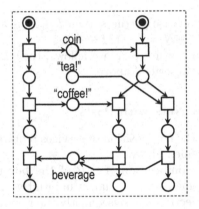

**Fig. 8.** Composition of the port equipped oWFNs of Fig. 7

## 4.6   Hierarchical Open Workflow Nets

Abstraction and refinement are fundamental construction principles for complex systems: Only a hierarchical design process makes complexity tractable. oWFN allow for a simple, canonical notion of refinement. The basic idea is the replacement in $N$ of a transition $t$ by an other oWFN $M$, written (as usual for replacement operators)

$$N[M \setminus t]$$

("in $N$, replace $M$ for $t$"). This is possible whenever the interface of $M$ coincides with the environment $^\bullet t \cup t^\bullet$ of $t$.

As an additional technicality, the addition $m + m'$ of markings $m$ and $m'$ of oWFN $N$ and $N'$, respectively, is defined for each $p \in P_N \cup P_{N'}$, by

$$(m + m')(p) = m(p) + m'(p),$$

with $m(p) = m'(p') = 0$ if $p \in P' \setminus P$ and $p' \in P \setminus P'$. Furthermore, for two sets $\Omega$ and $\Omega'$ of markings, let

$$(\Omega + \Omega') = \{m + m' \mid m \in \Omega \text{ and } m' \in \Omega'\}.$$

With this in mind, we define refinements of two oWFNs $N = (P, T, F, in, out, m_0, \Omega)$ and $N' = (P', T', F', in', out', m'_0, \Omega')$ as follows:

i   A transition $t \in T$ *coincides with the interface of* $N'$ iff $^\bullet t = in'$ and $t^\bullet = out'$.

ii  Let $arcs(t) =_{\text{def}} (^\bullet t \times \{t\}) \cup (\{t\} \times t^\bullet)$ ("the *arcs of* $t$").

iii Let $t$ coincide with the interface of $N$. Then $N[N' \setminus t] =_{\text{def}}$
   $(P \cup P', (T \setminus \{t\} \cup T', (F \setminus arcs(t)) \cup F', in, out, m_0 + m'_0, \Omega + \Omega')$
   is the *refinement of* $t$ *in* $N$ *by* $N'$.

Refinement in fact meets all properties one would expect. Firstly, refinement of $t$ by $N'$ in $N$ is independent of the context of $N$:

$$(N \oplus M)[N' \setminus t] = N[N' \setminus t] \oplus M.$$

Secondly, the order of refining $t$ by $N$ and $t'$ by $N'$ in $M$ is irrelevant:

$$(M[N \setminus t])[N' \setminus t'] = (M[N' \setminus t'])[N \setminus t].$$

Finally, weak termination is preserved: If $N$ and $N'$ weakly terminate, then $N[N' \setminus t]$ weakly terminates, too.

### 4.7  Analysis Techniques for Open Workflow Nets

Open workflow nets are generell enough to capture decisive properties of services, and are simple enough to allow for formal analysis techniques. Due to the structure of oWFN it should come without surprise that most analysis techniques are based on variants of automata.

The most important kind of automata to analyze an oWFN $N$ is its operating guideline, $OG(N)$. This automaton describes $Strat(N)$, viz. the set of all strategies of $N$. $OG(N)$ is essentially a finite state automaton, inscribed by Boolean expressions, built from the interface of $N$. Details are given in [16]. Most of the questions discussed in Sect. 3.4 can efficiently be answered for any oWFN $N$ by help of $OG(N)$. Corresponding algorithms have been implemented in the Petri net analysis tool Fiona, and successfully been used to analyze Petri net models of realistic BPEL processes. Details can be found in [17].

## 5   Conclusion

Models of interactive computation have been constructed since the early days of computing. In recent years, started as a smart combination of existing middleware techniques, *services* achieved prominence as a general, albeit variable software architecture model. We suggest to establish this model as a standard model of asynchronous interactive computation, complementing process algebras as a standard model for synchronous computation. Open workflow nets are a most useful starting point as a representation technique for asynchronous interactive computation, as they provide a lot of techniques to effectively analyze the most important properties of asynchronous interactive systems. In their given form, open workflow nets stick to control flow of services. Data and data dependent behavior can easily be incorporated, extending the formalism as usual in high level Petri nets.

# References

1. Gandy, R.: Church's thesis and principles for mechanisms. In: The Kleene Symposium, pp. 123–148. North-Holland, Amsterdam (1980)
2. Petri, C.A.: Kommunikation mit Automaten. PhD thesis, Bonn: Institut für Instrumentelle Mathematik, Schriften des IIM Nr. 2 (1962) also: Griffiss Air Force Base, Technical Report RADC-TR-65-377, vol.1(1), English translation (1966)
3. Thomas, W.: Automata on Infinite Objects. In: Handbook of Theoretical Computer Science, Volume B: Formal Models and Sematics (B), pp. 133–192 (1990)
4. Kahn, G.: The semantics of simple language for parallel programming. In: IFIP Congress, pp. 471–475 (1974)
5. Broy, M., Stoelen, K.: Specification and Development of Interactive Systems: Focus on Streams, Interfaces, and Refinement. Springer, Heidelberg (2001)
6. Milner, R.: A Calculus of Communication Systems. LNCS, vol. 92. Springer, Heidelberg (1980)
7. Lamport, L.: Specifying Systems, The TLA+ Language and Tools for Hardware and Software Engineers. Addison-Wesley, Reading (2002)
8. Gurevich, Y.: Interactive Algorithms 2005. In: Jedrzejowicz, J., Szepietowski, A. (eds.) MFCS 2005. LNCS, vol. 3618, pp. 26–38. Springer, Heidelberg (2005)
9. Misra, J., Cook, W.R.: Computation Orchestration: A Basis for Wide-Area Computing. Journal of Software and Systems Modeling, 83–110 (May 2006)
10. Wegner, P.: Why Interaction Is More Powerful Than Algorithms. Commun. ACM 40(5), 80–91 (1997)
11. Wegner, P.: Interactive Foundations of Computing. Theor. Comput. Sci. 192(2), 315–351 (1998)
12. Goldin, D., Smolka, S.A., Wegner, P.: Interactive Computation - The New Paradigm. Springer, Heidelberg (2006)
13. Goldin, D.Q.: Persistent Turing Machines as a Model of Interactive Computation. In: Schewe, K.-D., Thalheim, B. (eds.) FoIKS 2000. LNCS, vol. 1762, pp. 116–135. Springer, Heidelberg (2000)
14. van Leeuwen, J., Wiedermann, J.: On Algorithms and Interaction. In: Nielsen, M., Rovan, B. (eds.) MFCS 2000. LNCS, vol. 1893, pp. 99–113. Springer, Heidelberg (2000)
15. van der Aalst, W.M.P.: The Application of Petri Nets to Workflow Management. The Journal of Circuits, Systems and Computers 8(1), 21–66 (1998)
16. Lohmann, N., Massuthe, P., Wolf, K.: Operating Guidelines for Finite-State Services. In: Kleijn, J., Yakovlev, A. (eds.) International Conference on Applications and Theory of Petri Nets and Other Models of Concurrency, ICATPN 2007. LNCS, vol. 4546, Springer, Heidelberg (2007)

17. Lohmann, N., Massuthe, P., Stahl, C., Weinberg, D.: Analyzing Interacting WS-BPEL Processes Using Flexible Model Generation. In: Dustdar, S., Fiadeiro, J.L., Sheth, A. (eds.) BPM 2006. LNCS, vol. 4102, Springer, Heidelberg (2006)

# A    General Notions and Notations

### Definition 1 (Net)
*Let $P$ and $T$ be finite, disjoint sets.*
*Let $F \subseteq (P \times T) \cup (T \times P)$.*
*Then $N = (P, T, F)$ is a net.*

The elements of $P$, $T$ and $F$ are *places*, *transitions* and *arcs*, graphically depicted as circles, boxes and arrows, respectively.

In the rest of this Appendix A we assume a net $N = (P, T, F)$.

### Definition 2 (Pre-set, Post-set)
*For $x \in P \cup T$, let*
$^\bullet x =_{def} \{y \mid (y, x) \in F\}$ *is the* pre-set *of $x$*
$x^\bullet =_{def} \{y \mid (x, y) \in F\}$ *is the* post-set *of $x$.*

### Definition 3 (Marking)
*A marking of $N$ is a mapping $m : P \to \mathbb{N}$.*

Graphically, a marking $m$ is depicted by $m(p)$ black dots (*"tokens"*) at each place $p \in P$.

For two markings $m_1$ and $m_2$ of $N$, let $m_1 + m_2$ be the marking of $N$, defined for each $p \in P$ by $(m_1 + m_2)(p) =_{def} m_1(p) + m_2(p)$.

For a marking $m$ of $N$ and a set $Q \supseteq P$, extend $m$ canonically to $m : Q \to \mathbb{N}$ for each $q \in Q \setminus P$ by $m(q) = 0$

### Definition 4 (Enabling, Step)
*Let $t \in T$,*
*and let $m$ be a marking of $N$.*

1. *$m$ enables $t$ if for each $p \in {}^\bullet t$ holds: $m(p) \geq 1$.*
2. *Let $m$ enable $t$ and let the marking $n$ be defined by*
   $n(p) =_{def} m(p) - 1$ *if $p \in {}^\bullet t \setminus t^\bullet$*
   $n(p) =_{def} m(p) + 1$ *if $p \in t^\bullet \setminus {}^\bullet t$*
   $n(p) =_{def} m(p)$, *otherwise.*
   *Then $(m, t, n)$ is a step of $N$, frequently written $m \xrightarrow{t} n$.*

### Definition 5 (Run)
*A finite or infinite sequence $m_0 t_1 m_1 t_2 \ldots$ is a run of $N$ if $(m_{i-1}, t_i, m_i)$ is a step of $N$ for $i = 1, 2, \ldots$.*

# B    Open Workflow Nets

**Definition 6 (Open Workflow Net, oWFN)**
*Let $(P, T, F)$ be a net,*
*let $in, out \subseteq P$ with $^{\bullet}in = out^{\bullet} = \emptyset$,*
*let $m_0$ be a marking of $N$,*
*let $\Omega$ be a set of markings of $N$.*
*Then $N = (P, T, F, in, out, m_0, \Omega)$ is an open workflow net (oWFN for short).*

$in$ and $out$ contain the *input* and *output places*, $I =_{def} in \cup out$ is the *interface*, $J =_{def} P \setminus I$ contains the *inner places* of $N$ respectively. Whenever $N$ is not obvious from the context, we affix the index $N$, as in $P_N, T_N, F_N, m_{0_N}, \Omega_N, in_N, out_N, I_N, J_N$.

**Definition 7 (Inner(N))**
*Let $N$ be an oWFN. Then*
$inner(N) =_{def} (J_N, T_N, F_N \cap ((J_N \times T_N) \cup (T_N \times J_N)))$,
*is the* inner subnet *of $N$.*

**Definition 8 (Internally disjoint oWFNs)**
*Two oWFNs $M$ and $N$ are* internally disjoint *iff $(P_M \cup T_M) \cap (P_N \cup T_N) \subseteq (I_M \cap I_N)$.*

*Remark 1.* Two oWFNs can canonically be made internally disjoint: Each shared internal element is replicated.

General assumption: Two oWFNs $M$ and $N$ will always be assumed as internally disjoint.

**Definition 9 (Composition of oWFNs)**
*The* composition $M \oplus N$ *of two (internally disjoint) oWFNs $M$ and $N$ is the oWFN*
$$M \oplus N =_{def} (P_M \cup P_N, T_M \cup T_N, F_M \cup F_N), \text{ with}$$
$in_{M \oplus N} =_{def} (in_m \setminus out_N) \cup (in_N \setminus out_M)$,
$out_{M \oplus N} =_{def} (out_m \setminus in_N) \cup (out_N \setminus in_M)$,
$m_{0_{M \oplus N}} =_{def} m_{0_M} + m_{0_N}$,
$\Omega_{M \oplus N} =_{def} \{m + n \mid m \in \Omega_M \text{ and } n \in \Omega_N\}$.

**Definition 10 (Partners)**
*Two oWFNs $M$ and $N$ are* partners *iff $out_M \cap out_N = in_M \cap in_N = \emptyset$.*

**Definition 11 (Fellows)**
*Two oWFNs $M$ and $N$ are* fellows *iff $out_M \cap in_N = out_N \cap in_M = \emptyset$.*

# Author Index

Aguirre, Nazareno   435

Bjørner, Nikolaj   1
Brekling, Aske Wiid   300
Bretschneider, Jan   521
Broy, Manfred   24
Butterfield, Andrew   45

Chen, Yinghua   67
Chen, Zhenbang   83

Damm, Werner   115
Dang, Van Hung   170

Eir, Asger   188
Estevez, Elsa   217

Fahland, Dirk   521
Fitzgerald, John   237
Freitas, Leo   255

George, Chris   280

Hansen, Michael R.   300
Haxthausen, Anne E.   320
Hayes, Ian J.   364
He, Jifeng   349

Jackson, Michael A.   364
Janowski, Tomasz   217
Jones, Cliff B.   364
Joseph, Mathai   391

Knudsen, John   399
Krishnan, Padmanabhan   280

Langmaack, Hans   414
Larsen, Peter Gorm   237
Li, Xiaoshan   83
Lin, Huimin   467

Ling, Xiang   435
Liu, Daguang   467
Liu, Xinxin   472
Liu, Zhiming   83
Lohmann, Niels   521

Madsen, Jan   300
Maibaum, Tom   435
Massuthe, Peter   521
Mikschl, Alfred   115
Mosses, Peter D.   483

Oehlerking, Jens   115
Olderog, Ernst-Rüdiger   115

Pang, Jun   115
Peleska, Jan   320
Pěnička, Martin   504
Platzer, André   115

Ravn, Anders P.   399
Reisig, Wolfgang   521

Salas, P.A.P.   280
Sanders, J.W.   280
Segelken, Marc   115
Skou, Arne   399
Stahl, Christian   521
Stolz, Volker   83

Wirtz, Boris   115
Woodcock, Jim   255
Wu, Peng   467

Xia, Bican   67

Yang, Lu   67
Yang, Lu   83

Zhan, Naijun   67

# Lecture Notes in Computer Science

Sublibrary 1: Theoretical Computer Science and General Issues

For information about Vols. 1– 4445
please contact your bookseller or Springer

Vol. 4770: V.G. Ganzha, E.W. Mayr, E.V. Vorozhtsov (Eds.), Computer Algebra in Scientific Computing. XIII, 460 pages. 2007.

Vol. 4743: P. Thulasiraman, X. He, T.L. Xu, M.K. Denko, R.K. Thulasiram, L.T. Yang (Eds.), Frontiers of High Performance Computing and Networking ISPA 2007 Workshops. XXIX, 536 pages. 2007.

Vol. 4742: I. Stojmenovic, R.K. Thulasiram, L.T. Yang, W. Jia, M. Guo, R.F. de Mello (Eds.), Parallel and Distributed Processing and Applications. XX, 995 pages. 2007.

Vol. 4736: S. Winter, M. Duckham, L. Kulik, B. Kuipers (Eds.), Spatial Information Theory. XV, 455 pages. 2007.

Vol. 4732: K. Schneider, J. Brandt (Eds.), Theorem Proving in Higher Order Logics. IX, 401 pages. 2007.

Vol. 4731: A. Pelc (Ed.), Distributed Computing. XVI, 510 pages. 2007.

Vol. 4710: C.W. George, Z. Liu, J. Woodcock (Eds.), Domain Modeling and the Duration Calculus. XI, 237 pages. 2007.

Vol. 4708: L. Kučera, A. Kučera (Eds.), Mathematical Foundations of Computer Science 2007. XVIII, 764 pages. 2007.

Vol. 4707: O. Gervasi, M.L. Gavrilova (Eds.), Computational Science and Its Applications – ICCSA 2007, Part III. XXIV, 1205 pages. 2007.

Vol. 4706: O. Gervasi, M.L. Gavrilova (Eds.), Computational Science and Its Applications – ICCSA 2007, Part II. XXIII, 1129 pages. 2007.

Vol. 4705: O. Gervasi, M.L. Gavrilova (Eds.), Computational Science and Its Applications – ICCSA 2007, Part I. XLIV, 1169 pages. 2007.

Vol. 4703: L. Caires, V.T. Vasconcelos (Eds.), CONCUR 2007 – Concurrency Theory. XIII, 507 pages. 2007.

Vol. 4700: C.B. Jones, Z. Liu, J. Woodcock (Eds.), Formal Methods and Hybrid Real-Time Systems. XVI, 539 pages. 2007.

Vol. 4697: L. Choi, Y. Paek, S. Cho (Eds.), Advances in Computer Systems Architecture. XIII, 400 pages. 2007.

Vol. 4688: K. Li, M. Fei, G.W. Irwin, S. Ma (Eds.), Bio-Inspired Computational Intelligence and Applications. XIX, 805 pages. 2007.

Vol. 4684: L. Kang, Y. Liu, S. Zeng (Eds.), Evolvable Systems: From Biology to Hardware. XIV, 446 pages. 2007.

Vol. 4683: L. Kang, Y. Liu, S. Zeng (Eds.), Intelligence Computation and Applications. XVII, 663 pages. 2007.

Vol. 4681: D.-S. Huang, L. Heutte, M. Loog (Eds.), Advanced Intelligent Computing Theories and Applications. XXVI, 1379 pages. 2007.

Vol. 4672: K. Li, C. Jesshope, H. Jin, J.-L. Gaudiot (Eds.), Network and Parallel Computing. XVIII, 558 pages. 2007.

Vol. 4671: V. Malyshkin (Ed.), Parallel Computing Technologies. XIV, 635 pages. 2007.

Vol. 4669: J.M. de Sá, L.A. Alexandre, W. Duch, D. Mandic (Eds.), Artificial Neural Networks – ICANN 2007, Part II. XXXI, 990 pages. 2007.

Vol. 4668: J.M. de Sá, L.A. Alexandre, W. Duch, D. Mandic (Eds.), Artificial Neural Networks – ICANN 2007, Part I. XXXI, 978 pages. 2007.

Vol. 4666: M.E. Davies, C.J. James, S.A. Abdallah, M.D Plumbley (Eds.), Independent Component Analysis and Blind Signal Separation. XIX, 847 pages. 2007.

Vol. 4665: J. Hromkovič, R. Královič, M. Nunkesser, P. Widmayer (Eds.), Stochastic Algorithms: Foundations and Applications. X, 167 pages. 2007.

Vol. 4664: J. Durand-Lose, M. Margenstern (Eds.), Machines, Computations, and Universality. X, 325 pages. 2007.

Vol. 4649: V. Diekert, M.V. Volkov, A. Voronkov (Eds.), Computer Science – Theory and Applications. XIII, 420 pages. 2007.

Vol. 4647: R. Martin, M. Sabin, J. Winkler (Eds.), Mathematics of Surfaces XII. IX, 509 pages. 2007.

Vol. 4646: J. Duparc, T.A. Henzinger (Eds.), Computer Science Logic. XIV, 600 pages. 2007.

Vol. 4644: N. Azémard, L. Svensson (Eds.), Integrated Circuit and System Design. XIV, 583 pages. 2007.

Vol. 4641: A.-M. Kermarrec, L. Bougé, T. Priol (Eds.), Euro-Par 2007 Parallel Processing. XXVII, 974 pages. 2007.

Vol. 4639: E. Csuhaj-Varjú, Z. Ésik (Eds.), Fundamentals of Computation Theory. XIV, 508 pages. 2007.

Vol. 4638: T. Stützle, M. Birattari, H. H. Hoos (Eds.), Engineering Stochastic Local Search Algorithms. X, 223 pages. 2007.

Vol. 4628: L.N. de Castro, F.J. Von Zuben, H. Knidel (Eds.), Artificial Immune Systems. XII, 438 pages. 2007.

Vol. 4627: M. Charikar, K. Jansen, O. Reingold, J.D.P. Rolim (Eds.), Approximation, Randomization, and Combinatorial Optimization. XII, 626 pages. 2007.

Vol. 4624: T. Mossakowski, U. Montanari, M. Haveraaen (Eds.), Algebra and Coalgebra in Computer Science. XI, 463 pages. 2007.

Vol. 4619: F. Dehne, J.-R. Sack, N. Zeh (Eds.), Algorithms and Data Structures. XVI, 662 pages. 2007.

Vol. 4618: S.G. Akl, C.S. Calude, M.J. Dinneen, G. Rozenberg, H.T. Wareham (Eds.), Unconventional Computation. X, 243 pages. 2007.

Vol. 4616: A. Dress, Y. Xu, B. Zhu (Eds.), Combinatorial Optimization and Applications. XI, 390 pages. 2007.

Vol. 4613: F.P. Preparata, Q. Fang (Eds.), Frontiers in Algorithmics. XI, 348 pages. 2007.

Vol. 4600: H. Comon-Lundh, C. Kirchner, H. Kirchner (Eds.), Rewriting, Computation and Proof. XVI, 273 pages. 2007.

Vol. 4599: S. Vassiliadis, M. Berekovic, T.D. Hämäläinen (Eds.), Embedded Computer Systems: Architectures, Modeling, and Simulation. XVIII, 466 pages. 2007.

Vol. 4598: G. Lin (Ed.), Computing and Combinatorics. XII, 570 pages. 2007.

Vol. 4596: L. Arge, C. Cachin, T. Jurdziński, A. Tarlecki (Eds.), Automata, Languages and Programming. XVII, 953 pages. 2007.

Vol. 4595: D. Bošnački, S. Edelkamp (Eds.), Model Checking Software. X, 285 pages. 2007.

Vol. 4590: W. Damm, H. Hermanns (Eds.), Computer Aided Verification. XV, 562 pages. 2007.

Vol. 4588: T. Harju, J. Karhumäki, A. Lepistö (Eds.), Developments in Language Theory. XI, 423 pages. 2007.

Vol. 4583: S.R. Della Rocca (Ed.), Typed Lambda Calculi and Applications. X, 397 pages. 2007.

Vol. 4580: B. Ma, K. Zhang (Eds.), Combinatorial Pattern Matching. XII, 366 pages. 2007.

Vol. 4576: D. Leivant, R. de Queiroz (Eds.), Logic, Language, Information and Computation. X, 363 pages. 2007.

Vol. 4547: C. Carlet, B. Sunar (Eds.), Arithmetic of Finite Fields. XI, 355 pages. 2007.

Vol. 4546: J. Kleijn, A. Yakovlev (Eds.), Petri Nets and Other Models of Concurrency – ICATPN 2007. XI, 515 pages. 2007.

Vol. 4545: H. Anai, K. Horimoto, T. Kutsia (Eds.), Algebraic Biology. XIII, 379 pages. 2007.

Vol. 4533: F. Baader (Ed.), Term Rewriting and Applications. XII, 419 pages. 2007.

Vol. 4528: J. Mira, J.R. Álvarez (Eds.), Nature Inspired Problem-Solving Methods in Knowledge Engineering, Part II. XXII, 650 pages. 2007.

Vol. 4527: J. Mira, J.R. Álvarez (Eds.), Bio-inspired Modeling of Cognitive Tasks, Part I. XXII, 630 pages. 2007.

Vol. 4525: C. Demetrescu (Ed.), Experimental Algorithms. XIII, 448 pages. 2007.

Vol. 4514: S.N. Artemov, A. Nerode (Eds.), Logical Foundations of Computer Science. XI, 513 pages. 2007.

Vol. 4513: M. Fischetti, D.P. Williamson (Eds.), Integer Programming and Combinatorial Optimization. IX, 500 pages. 2007.

Vol. 4510: P. Van Hentenryck, L.A. Wolsey (Eds.), Integration of AI and OR Techniques in Constraint Programming for Combinatorial Optimization Problems. X, 391 pages. 2007.

Vol. 4507: F. Sandoval, A.G. Prieto, J. Cabestany, M. Graña (Eds.), Computational and Ambient Intelligence. XXVI, 1167 pages. 2007.

Vol. 4501: J. Marques-Silva, K.A. Sakallah (Eds.), Theory and Applications of Satisfiability Testing – SAT 2007. XI, 384 pages. 2007.

Vol. 4497: S.B. Cooper, B. Löwe, A. Sorbi (Eds.), Computation and Logic in the Real World. XVIII, 826 pages. 2007.

Vol. 4494: H. Jin, O.F. Rana, Y. Pan, V.K. Prasanna (Eds.), Algorithms and Architectures for Parallel Processing. XIV, 508 pages. 2007.

Vol. 4493: D. Liu, S. Fei, Z. Hou, H. Zhang, C. Sun (Eds.), Advances in Neural Networks – ISNN 2007, Part III. XXVI, 1215 pages. 2007.

Vol. 4492: D. Liu, S. Fei, Z. Hou, H. Zhang, C. Sun (Eds.), Advances in Neural Networks – ISNN 2007, Part II. XXVII, 1321 pages. 2007.

Vol. 4491: D. Liu, S. Fei, Z.-G. Hou, H. Zhang, C. Sun (Eds.), Advances in Neural Networks – ISNN 2007, Part I. LIV, 1365 pages. 2007.

Vol. 4490: Y. Shi, G.D. van Albada, J.J. Dongarra, P.M.A. Sloot (Eds.), Computational Science – ICCS 2007, Part IV. XXXVII, 1211 pages. 2007.

Vol. 4489: Y. Shi, G.D. van Albada, J.J. Dongarra, P.M.A. Sloot (Eds.), Computational Science – ICCS 2007, Part III. XXXVII, 1257 pages. 2007.

Vol. 4488: Y. Shi, G.D. van Albada, J.J. Dongarra, P.M.A. Sloot (Eds.), Computational Science – ICCS 2007, Part II. XXXV, 1251 pages. 2007.

Vol. 4487: Y. Shi, G.D. van Albada, J.J. Dongarra, P.M.A. Sloot (Eds.), Computational Science – ICCS 2007, Part I. LXXXI, 1275 pages. 2007.

Vol. 4484: J.-Y. Cai, S.B. Cooper, H. Zhu (Eds.), Theory and Applications of Models of Computation. XIII, 772 pages. 2007.

Vol. 4475: P. Crescenzi, G. Prencipe, G. Pucci (Eds.), Fun with Algorithms. X, 273 pages. 2007.

Vol. 4474: G. Prencipe, S. Zaks (Eds.), Structural Information and Communication Complexity. XI, 342 pages. 2007.

Vol. 4459: C. Cérin, K.-C. Li (Eds.), Advances in Grid and Pervasive Computing. XVI, 759 pages. 2007.

Vol. 4449: Z. Horváth, V. Zsók, A. Butterfield (Eds.), Implementation and Application of Functional Languages. X, 271 pages. 2007.

Vol. 4448: M. Giacobini (Ed.), Applications of Evolutionary Computing. XXIII, 755 pages. 2007.

Vol. 4447: E. Marchiori, J.H. Moore, J.C. Rajapakse (Eds.), Evolutionary Computation, Machine Learning and Data Mining in Bioinformatics. XI, 302 pages. 2007.

Vol. 4446: C. Cotta, J.I. van Hemert (Eds.), Evolutionary Computation in Combinatorial Optimization. XII, 241 pages. 2007.